'GATHERED UNDER APOSTLES'

'Gathered Under Apostles'

A Study of the Catholic Apostolic Church

COLUMBA GRAHAM FLEGG

CLARENDON PRESS · OXFORD
1992

Oxford University Press, Walton Street, Oxford OX2 6DP
Oxford New York Toronto
Delhi Bombay Calcutta Madras Karachi
Petaling Jaya Singapore Hong Kong Tokyo
Nairobi Dar es Salaam Cape Town
Melbourne Auckland
and associated companies in
Berlin Ibadan

Oxford is a trade mark of Oxford University Press

Published in the United States
by Oxford University Press, New York

British Library Cataloguing in Publication Data
Data available
ISBN 0–19–826335–X

Library of Congress Cataloging in Publication Data
Flegg, Columba Graham.
Gathered under apostles · a study of the Catholic Apostolic Church
/ Columba Graham Flegg.
Revision of the author's thesis (doctoral)—Open University.
Includes bibligraphical references and index.
1. Catholic Apostolic Church.   I. Title.
BX6571.2.F54   1992   289.9—dc20
ISBN 0–19826335–X

Typeset by Hope Services (Abingdon) Ltd.

Printed in Great Britain by
Biddles Ltd, Guildford and King's Lynn

Behold the Bridegroom cometh in the middle of the night: and blessed is the servant whom He shall find watching, . . . Beware, then, O my soul, and be not overcome by sleep, lest thou be given over to death and be shut out from the Kingdom, But return to soberness and cry aloud: Holy, holy, holy art Thou, O God: . . .

(From a *Mattins* hymn of the Orthodox 'Service of the Bridegroom', Great and Holy Week).

Preface

MOST existing accounts of the Catholic Apostolic Church contain serious errors and distortions, often due either to brevity or selectivity. This work (which derives from an Open University doctoral thesis) is designed to provide an extensive account of this unique body based upon authoritative primary sources. It is hoped that it will fill a gap in the current literature: most other recent works on the Catholic Apostolics deal with individual aspects of the body, and hence cannot adequately indicate either its overall nature or the way in which its various features are interrelated and underpinned. Because the relevant sources are extremely difficult to access (and becoming increasingly so), and because it is necessary to show the precise terms in which Catholic Apostolic theology and practice were expressed, it has been deemed essential that primary source extracts be a significant feature of this present work. The 'history' of the body has been presented by others: it is included here for completeness and in order that a number of errors of fact and certain misunderstandings can be corrected. The chapter on 'ecclesiology' deals, for the first time in depth, with the Catholic Apostolic understanding of the nature of man and the ministries deemed necessary for his spiritual welfare, and distinguishes between the different types of prophetic witness. The chapter on 'liturgy' considerably extends existing scholarship by providing fresh insights into the typological background of Catholic Apostolic worship on a wider basis than the Eucharist alone. The chapter on 'eschatology' provides a new analysis of the sources of Catholic Apostolic eschatology (for the first time including an examination of the work of Lacunza) and of the eschatological understanding of the body's rites. In the final chapter, the underlying common themes are brought together to expose the strengths and weaknesses of the body, the question of its debt to Eastern Orthodoxy is examined, and its current significance is considered. A classified bibliography (not otherwise generally available) has been provided, and an appendix gives the contents of the Catholic Apostolic service book.

Cambridge   C. G. F.
1991

Acknowledgements

THE Author wishes to express his gratitude to the following: Dr
Francis Clark and Dr Esther de Waal for their encouragement and
helpful suggestions throughout the period of research which
preceded the preparation of this work; Mr Donald Nye (formerly
Secretary to the Catholic Apostolic Trustees) and the late Mr
Norman Priddle (formerly Librarian at the Catholic Apostolic
Central Church, Gordon Square, London) for supplying copies of
documents, otherwise impossible to obtain; the late Revd Geoffrey
Mather for bequeathing to the author his small library of Catholic
Apostolic books; Catholic Apostolic Church members, and others,
for giving or lending works in their possession; the Revd Eero
Sepponen (of the Finnish Lutheran Church) for providing copies of
two rare relevant works; the staff of the Open University Library for
their persistence in obtaining copies of scarce articles and books; His
Grace the Duke of Northumberland for granting permission to
consult the private papers in the Drummond Collection at Alnwick
Castle, and Dr Colin Shrimpton (Archivist) for so efficiently setting
out the papers for examination; members (now sadly deceased) of
the author's family circle for passing on many Catholic Apostolic
documents and for responding to frequent requests for information
about their understanding of these works and their past experiences
as members of the body; and lastly the Oxford University Press for
the excellent work of production which has enabled this book to be
published in its present form.

Contents

xiiContents

V Eschatology

1. Preliminary General Remarks   292

Jewish Apocalyptic—The Patristic Period—The Middle
Ages and the Reformation—The Eighteenth Century

2. The Immediate Background I: Faber and Frere   298

Faber's *Dissertation on the Prophecies*—The Principles of
Frere's *Combined View*

3. The Immediate Background II: Lacunza and Irving   304

Lacunza's New System—On the Millenarian Difficulty—
On Augustine, Origen, and St Basil—On Apocalypse
19 and 20—On the *simul et semel* Difficulty—On Two
Further Difficulties—On the Antichrist—On the Jews—
On the New Jerusalem—On the Final Release of Satan—
On the Ultimate State of Man and Creation—On the 'One
Prime and Principal Subject'—The Nature and Importance
of Lacunza's Work—Irving's Criticism of Lacunza's
Work—Support for Lacunza's Main Thesis—Irving's
Apocalyptic Beliefs

4. The Immediate Background III: The Albury Conferences
   and *The Morning Watch*   331

The Conclusion of the Conferences—Some Details from
the *Dialogues on Prophecy*—The Signs of the Times and the
State of the Church—The Response to the Attacks by the
Evangelicals

5. Catholic Apostolic Eschatology I: *The Great Testimony*   342

The Dangers of Liberalism—The Implications of
Nebuchadnezzar's Vision—The Errors of Rome and
Protestantism and the Apostasy of the Church—The
Restoration of Apostles for the Preparation of the Bride—
Some Important Aspects of *The Great Testimony*

6. Catholic Apostolic Eschatology II: Other Apostolic Writings   352

On the 'Letters to the Seven Churches'—On the Visions of
the Apocalypse—Sitwell's Eschatological Work—On the
Six Epochs—On Interpretations of the Apocalypse—On
the Jews—On the Millennium—On Certain Problems of
Scripture—The Significance of Sitwell's Work—

List of Illustrations

Abbreviations

AV	Authorized Version of the Bible
C/*RL*	J. B. Cardale, *Readings on the Liturgy and Other Divine Offices of the Church*
D/*DP*	H. Drummond, *Dialogues on Prophecy*
D/*FD*	H. Dalton, *Four Discourses on the First and Second Advents*
D/*TLD*	H. Drummond, *Tracts for the Last Days*
GT	*The Great Testimony*
L/*CM*	M. Lacunza (J. J. Ben-Ezra), tr. Irving, *The Coming of the Messiah in Glory and Majesty*
L/*CM: PDT*	Translator's *Preliminary Discourse* to L/*CM*
LXX	Septuagint
MW	*The Morning Watch*
M/*HDI*	E. Miller, *The History and Doctrines of Irvingism*
S/*PG*	F. Sitwell, *The Purpose of God in Creation and Redemption*

The above abbreviations are to be found especially in the notes. The full titles of works are often shortened in the main text, however: e.g. C/*RL* (see above) may be given as 'Cardale, *Readings*'.

I

Introduction

1. THE BACKGROUND, PURPOSE, AND LIMITATIONS OF THIS WORK

THERE is considerable justification for the claim that, of all the nineteenth-century phenomena within the Christian Churches in Britain, less is known today about the body variously called the 'Catholic Apostolic Church' or the 'Irvingites'—after the Revd Edward Irving (1792–1834)—than about any other group or movement. This is due largely to two principal factors. First, for all practical purposes this body has ceased for some years to exist in any meaningful way as an organized Church. Secondly, records normally available to researchers in other circumstances have been, for the most part, carefully withheld from general public access or even, in some cases, deliberately destroyed.

It is largely fortuitous (or, some might say, providential) that the present writer has been able to build up a substantial private library of relevant documents through personal inheritance, extensive contact over many years with Catholic Apostolic Church members in Britain and on the Continent, a friend's bequest (see Acknowledgements), and the occasional purchase of books and collections of pamphlets through the second-hand market. This has made possible a detailed study of many primary sources not available to those outside the Catholic Apostolic community itself.

Some Theses and Books on the Catholic Apostolic Church

Despite the great difficulties of access to primary source material, there has been over the past few decades a small number of theses and books devoted (in whole or in part) to the Catholic Apostolic Church, written mainly by Anglican writers and, in some cases, arising from researches initially directed towards the history of the Oxford Movement. Of the theses, the most important are those of Orchard (1968), Stevenson (1975), Lively (1977), and Lancaster

(1978).[1] Of the books, those of Shaw (1946), Davenport (1970), Cousland (1983), and Standring (1983)[2] can be singled out for their integrity and general accuracy. A number of other works are also of interest.[3] These comparatively recent works contrast with the standard nineteenth-century Anglican work by Miller (1878)[4] in that they are written from largely unbiased or even (in a number of cases) sympathetic viewpoints.

Miller's work was (by its author's own admission) written primarily for polemical purposes, though it would be unfair to suggest that it is grossly inaccurate in matters of history. However, Miller's presentation of the theology and ecclesiology of the so-called 'Irvingites' suffered from an outsider's lack of understanding in depth, and his commentary was manifestly hostile. Thus, in the preface to his book, he wrote:

'I was anxious, if I could, to make it for ever impossible that well-informed Clergymen,—or indeed well-informed laymen,—should be thus led away from the teaching of the true Branch of the Church in this country.'[5]

There had been considerable alarm at the defections to the Catholic Apostolic Church from Anglicanism. Miller was prepared to accept

[1] S. C. Orchard, 'English Evangelical Eschatology 1790–1850', thesis (Cambridge University, 1968); K. W. Stevenson, 'The Catholic Apostolic Eucharist', thesis (Southampton University, 1975); R. J. Lively, Jun., 'The Catholic Apostolic Church and the Church of Jesus Christ of Latter-Day Saints: a Comparative Study of the Two Minority Millenarian Groups in Nineteenth-Century England', thesis (Oxford University, 1977); J. Lancaster, 'John Bate Cardale, Pillar of Apostles: A Quest for Catholicity', thesis (St Andrews University, 1978).

[2] P. E. Shaw, *The Catholic Apostolic Church* (New York: Kings Crown, 1946); R. A. Davenport, *Albury Apostles* (United Writers, 1970; rev. edn. London: Neillgo, 1973); A. O. Cousland, *How Hidden it Was* (Bognor Regis: New Horizon, 1983); G. L. Standring, *Albury and the Catholic Apostolic Church* (published by the author, 1985). This descriptive work is arranged alphabetically in the form of a dictionary or encyclopaedia.

[3] For example: C. F. Andrews, *What I Owe to Christ* (London: Hodder and Stoughton, 1932); L. Christenson, *A Message to the Charismatic Movement* (Minneapolis: Dimension Books, 1972); S. Newman-Norton, *The Hamburg Schism* and *The Time of Silence* (London: Albury Society, 1974 and 1975 respectively); J. Pinnington and S. Newman-Norton, *Apostolic and Conciliar Witness* (London: Albury Society, 1978). It should be noted that the Albury Society has no formal connection with the Catholic Apostolic Church.

[4] E. Miller, *The History and Doctrines of Irvingism*, 2 vols. (London: Kegan Paul, 1878). Miller was a Tractarian, Vicar of Butler's Marston, and formerly Fellow and Tutor of New College, Oxford.

[5] Miller, *History and Doctrines of Irvingism*, i, p. vii.

something of the motives behind such defections despite his concern about them, for a little later he wrote:

I have wished also, if I should be enabled by the Grace of God, to become a means of bringing back from error some of those who, moved by a revulsion from narrow modes of apprehending the Truth, and actuated by the tendencies which have marked the present century towards Catholic unity, and towards the length and breadth and depth and height of the Catholic Faith in the love of God, have wandered from the true fold.[6]

He was prepared to recognize some good in the Catholic Apostolic body, not least the sanctity of life of its members, but he saw them as latter-day Montanists[7] to be saved only by a return to the Church of their baptism. Miller's work is important, however, because it influenced the attitude adopted by many Anglicans, including the bishops at home and abroad, towards the Catholic Apostolic Church.

Like the present writer, Stevenson, Davenport, and Cousland had family connections with the Catholic Apostolics and hence greater ease of access to source material than other writers. The books of Cousland and Shaw both arose from research theses, and are primarily historical works; Shaw's has an emphasis upon American developments not to be found elsewhere in 'external' writings. Orchard's thesis includes reference to the formative period of the Catholic Apostolic body within the context of the contemporary eschatological debates. Lancaster's thesis is a study of the life and work of the Catholic Apostolic 'apostle',[8] John Bate Cardale (1802–77)—the 'Pillar of Apostles' and *primus inter pares* of the body. Lively's thesis is a comparative study of the millenarian teachings of the Catholic Apostolics and the Mormons, whilst Stevenson's is an historical study of the evolution of the Catholic Apostolic Eucharist. All these works have considerable merit, though by their very nature none claims to be comprehensive.

---

[6] Ibid., pp. vii–viii.

[7] The Montanists (after Montanus) formed an apocalyptic movement within the 2nd-cent. Christian Church in Phrygia. They looked for a further special outpouring of the Holy Spirit upon the Church, and believed this to be the experience of their own leaders.

[8] Quotation marks indicate that it has a special meaning—the Catholic Apostolic Church was governed by an apostolic college of twelve 'apostles' (see Chs. II and III). Hereafter 'apostle' will be used to denote an apostle of the Catholic Apostolic Church and 'Apostle' to denote one of the twelve Apostles of the Gospel. No other interpretation fo this distinguishing convention should be inferred.

Lively's work is particularly specialized in purpose and, by approaching the Catholic Apostolic Church merely as a millenarian sect, fails to do justice even to those aspects which Miller felt reluctantly bound to commend. But it is Davenport's book which is generally recognized by Catholic Apostolic members to be the best and fairest account written by a non-member—though one with a considerable degree of sympathy and understanding for the subject. Its main weakness lies in its very brief summaries of the body's theology, together with limited references and inadequate quotations (many unidentified) from the primary sources. It may be described as 'a good outline sketch, but little more'.

In addition to the major works devoted exclusively, or specifically in part, to the Catholic Apostolic Church, there are many short references to the body in dictionaries and encyclopaedias. A majority of these appear to be based upon the entry in the *Encyclopaedia Britannica* (1929). They suffer from their brevity and are not infrequently marred by inaccuracies. There are also references to the Catholic Apostolics in works primarily devoted to the Oxford Movement,[9] though Geoffrey Faber's *Oxford Apostles* (1933; Harmondsworth, 1954) surprisingly makes no mention of them. They have their place in R. A. Knox's *Enthusiasm* (Oxford, 1950), though their presentation here is somewhat one-sided, and they appear in a few other works by Roman Catholic writers.[10] Certain aspects of their history and beliefs are briefly treated in Einar Molland's *Christendom* (London, 1959), in Horton Davies' *Worship and Theology in England: 1850–1900* (Oxford, 1962), in E. T. Sandeen's *The Roots of Fundamentalism* (Chicago, 1970), in J. E. Worsfold's *A History of the Charismatic Movements in New Zealand* (n.p., 1974), in *The Church in Victorian Scotland: 1843–1874* by A. L. Drummond and J. Bulloch (Edinburgh, 1975), and in a number of other more general works. A few less scholarly publications have also appeared in the course of millenarian debates in the United States, of which one of the most widely known is D. MacPherson's *The Incredible Cover-up* (Plainfield, NJ, 1975), a journalistic account of what is claimed to be the 'true story' of belief

---

[9] For example, D. Morse-Boycott, *The Secret Story of the Oxford Movement* (London: Skeffington, 1933) and *They Shine like Stars* (London: Skeffington, 1947).
[10] For example, K. Algermissen, *The Christian Sects* (London: Burns and Oates, 1962).

in the pre-tribulation 'rapture'.[11] The conclusions reached in this work and the rationale behind them are hardly convincing.

Problems Raised by Existing 'External' Works

Unfortunately, in most of these writings—even the best—there are various errors and distortions which quite commonly appear. Small errors of fact are easily corrected, but serious errors of emphasis give rise to general misconceptions about the body which only an in-depth study can correct. Thus, there is often a tendency to exaggerate either the charismatic and millennial elements within the Catholic Apostolic Church, or the role played within it by Irving, who (it should be noted) did not himself 'speak in tongues'. This role was much slighter than is generally supposed despite the name 'Irvingism' being popularly applied to its witness (see Ch. II), and certainly does not justify his being called its 'founder'. Sometimes, too much concentration on what some have perceived as the 'extravagances' of the early years has distorted the history of the body and its theology—how would, for example, Quakerism or Methodism appear if treated in this way?

It is unfortunate, though understandable, that few (if indeed any) 'external' writers have penetrated fully into the complex nature of the Catholic Apostolic ministry, the details of the eschatology, or the extent of the typological interpretation of Scripture underlying both its theology and its worship. The relation of the Catholic Apostolic Church to the 'mainstream' Christian Churches is seldom understood, and the present situation of surviving members seems largely to be misjudged, because it has been deduced from premises which they would not themselves accept. Perhaps the most serious problem has been created by researchers' concentration upon single aspects of Catholic Apostolic witness. Such concentration, whilst it has its value for scholarship, does not reveal either the coherence which undoubtedly existed over the whole spectrum of the theology and practice of the body or the interrelation between the different aspects of that theology.

---

[11] The pre-tribulation 'rapture' refers to the belief that an elect number of living Christians will be caught up from the earth before the days of Antichrist. It was especially associated with the Plymouth Brother J. N. Darby (1800–82), but has been revived amongst certain American evangelicals in recent decades.

Works on Irving

Works devoted to Irving himself are comparatively plentiful, some
of the more recently published books being those of Drummond
(1937), Whitley (1955), Strachan (1973), and Dallimore (1983),[12]
and there remain readily available the standard nineteenth-century
biography by Mrs Oliphant, *The Life of Edward Irving* (London,
1862, revised edition 1864—upon which so many other writings on
Irving are heavily dependent), and the long chapter devoted to Irving
in Thomas Carlyle's *Reminiscences* (ed. Froude, London, 1881).
Much rarer and hence little-known are: William Jones' *A Biographical
Sketch of the Revd. Edward Irving, with Extracts from and Remarks on
his Principal Publications* (n.p., 1835); Washington Wilks' *Edward
Irving: an Ecclesiastical and Literary Biography* (London, 1854);
W. W. Andrews' 'Edward Irving' (1863—originally two extensive
articles published in *The New Englander*); and J. C. Root's *Edward
Irving: Man, Preacher, Prophet* (Boston, Mass., 1912).

It is clear from these works on Irving—as well as from reliable
accounts of the Catholic Apostolic Church—just how misleading the
term 'Irvingism' is when applied to the developed theology of the
body. Irving died on 8 December 1834, having been for only a short
period 'angel' of the Newman Street Church—an episcopal office to
which he had been consecrated by Cardale. This was only during the
initial embryonic years of the Catholic Apostolic body, whose formal
'birth' is usually dated from the event known as 'the separation of
the apostles', which took place in London on 14 July 1835—more
than six months after Irving's death (see Ch. II).

[12] A. L. Drummond, *Edward Irving and his Circle* (London: Clarke, 1934);
H. C. Whitley, *Blinded Eagle* (London: SCM Press, 1955); see also the same author's
Edward Irving: An Interpretation of His Life and Theological Teaching, thesis
(Edinburgh University, 1953); G. Strachan, *The Pentecostal Theology of Edward Irving*
(London: Darton, Longman and Todd, 1973); A. Dallimore, *The Life of Edward
Irving* (Edinburgh: Banner of Truth, 1983). Material on Irving can also be found in
two recent books: I. Murray's *The Puritan Hope* (Edinburgh: Banner of Truth, 1971),
and G. C. Cameron's *The Scots Church in London* (Oxford: Becket, 1979). An
extensive list of works dealing with Irving and his ministry is provided by
H. B. Copinger: *A Bibliography of Works related to the Catholic Apostolic Church*,
privately published, pp. 40–1. This covers material on Irving published up to 1925.

The Scope of this Book

This present work is primarily devoted to a detailed examination of major aspects of the theology and practice of the developed Catholic Apostolic Church, though it has been thought necessary also to include a chapter on its history. This last is included because the history is not generally known in any detail (even by many nineteenth-century Church historians) and, where it is presented, there are usually distortions and inaccuracies.

This is the first investigation of the Catholic Apostolics to be undertaken by a member of one of the Eastern Orthodox Churches. Its major objective is to present Catholic Apostolic teaching with the support of extensive selected extracts from primary sources, thus making available to scholars material which is otherwise largely inaccessible. However, the background of the author in both the Catholic Apostolic community and the Eastern Church has facilitated an approach which is sensitive to those aspects of Catholic Apostolic theology and practice which appear to be particularly in accord with Eastern Orthodoxy (see esp. Ch. VI, § 4). This is believed to be especially apposite for several reasons, amongst which are the obvious liturgical borrowings from Eastern liturgies, the many references in the source material to the writings of the Eastern Fathers, remarks by commentators on the Eastern ethos of Catholic Apostolic worship, and the physical link created by the present use of a number of former Catholic Apostolic buildings for Orthodox worship both in Britain and abroad.

Inevitably, much Catholic Apostolic theology was entirely consistent with that to be found in all the 'mainstream' Christian Churches. Although it would have been useful to consider this assertion in detail and to support it with appropriate primary source extracts, time and space have not permitted this. There is hence only limited presentation of the orthodox teaching of the body, concentration necessarily being directed towards those aspects which distinguish the Catholic Apostolic witness from that of other Christians—either because they were peculiar to that body or were given particular emphasis by it (see esp. Chs. III and V)—and towards particular areas of convergence with the special witness of the Eastern Churches. This latter point has necessitated considerable discussion of Catholic Apostolic liturgical material (see Ch. IV), but the emphasis is on the underlying theology rather than on the liturgical texts themselves.

The precise content and development of the Catholic Apostolic Eucharist have been discussed by Stevenson (op. cit., n. 1), and the Service Book is not particularly difficult to obtain.[13] Stevenson has also set this Eucharist within the overall context of eucharistic development in a recent work, *Eucharist and Offering*.[14] The particular interpretation of the word 'liturgy' in Catholic Apostolic writings is important, and is discussed in Chapter IV, Section 1. For reasons already apparent, there will be reference to Irving's theology only where his particular views can be seen to have had a significant effect on Catholic Apostolic theological development or practice.

The Catholic Apostolic Church and the Oxford Movement

Much Catholic Apostolic teaching reflects the revival of catholic tradition within the Anglican Church, largely initiated by the parallel Oxford Movement, though it is difficult to determine the precise extent of direct influence of one upon the other—it will be suggested that this was slighter than often supposed. Both were seeking a return to the theology and worship of the Undivided Church as understood from a study of early liturgies and the writings of the Fathers. That they followed different, rival, and largely independent paths was due to two principal factors. One of these was the effect of the legal establishment militating against reforms and innovations within the Church of England—the Catholic Apostolics were entirely free of such legal restrictions and hence were able to move much more quickly to 'advanced' ceremonial. The other was the particular and peculiar emphases within the Catholic Apostolic body, especially upon the apostolic and prophetic ministries. The claim that a new apostolic succession had been initiated by the Holy Spirit (see Chs. II and III) ran entirely counter to the emphasis upon the traditional succession by the Oxford Movement and, indeed, by the Roman Catholic and Eastern Orthodox Churches also. A further point of divergence was the insistence, particularly in the early days of the Catholic Apostolics, upon the imminent return of Christ in

---

[13] *The Liturgy and other Divine Offices of the Church* (various publishers for the different reprints); for the content of this service book, see App. I.

[14] K. W. Stevenson, *Eucharist and Offering* (New York: Pueblo, 1986).

glory, together with unacceptable chiliastic overtones in some of their writings.

The Use of Primary Source Material

As has already been noted, it is clearly impossible within the scope of one work of this nature to present, still less to discuss, all the theology and practice of the Catholic Apostolic Church. It is equally impossible to provide more than a small sample of the totality of Catholic Apostolic writings. Nevertheless, the selection of topics covered here, the inclusion of a chapter on the history of the body, and the provision of many primary source extracts prompt the hope that there has been sufficiently wide coverage to provide a reasonable overall view of Catholic Apostolic witness not available elsewhere. In particular, the inclusion of the primary source material will, it is believed, allow the Catholic Apostolics to 'speak for themselves', thus providing an authoritative account of their theology in a way which secondary accounts alone cannot achieve. There is often a peculiar importance to be found in their precise words, though care must be exercised in interpreting these, since terms are not always used with their present conventional meanings. The primary sources noted in the body of this book do not, however, represent more than a small proportion of those consulted during its preparation; the extracts have been selected because (in the opinion of the writer) their inclusion is essential or because they express the theology under consideration in a particularly clear manner.

Because of the homogeneity of Catholic Apostolic writings, it has been possible to include extracts from works by a wide variety of authors, thus providing an opportunity of access to some otherwise largely inaccessible material covering the unique aspects of the body. It was the ecclesiology and eschatology of the body, in particular, which were largely unique, and its liturgy has been singled out by a number of writers of different traditions for the highest praise. It is these three aspects, therefore, which have been selected for detailed treatment, though it has been possible also to introduce a number of other theological topics at appropriate places.

2. CATHOLIC APOSTOLIC PRIMARY SOURCES

The primary source material essential for a study of the Catholic Apostolic Church exists in many forms. Many of its church buildings are still standing and can be visited, though almost all have undergone some changes to accommodate worship by other Christian bodies. Most of the written sources are in English or German, though a few works are in other languages; English translations exist of most of the major works first appearing in German. These written sources take the form of books, pamphlets, sermons, homilies, pastoral letters, articles in journals, private reports, newsletters, manuscript correspondence, diaries and notes, and there is one liturgical audio recording. The recording, which is in German, comprises extracts from a Eucharist, recorded in 1951 in the Catholic Apostolic Church in Zurich (from which it may still be available). Catholic Apostolic writers contributed extensively to various ecclesiastical and secular journals, and articles about the body received wide publicity. Important sources can be found, for example, in issues of *Blackwood's Magazine*, *The Church of England Quarterly*, *The Ecclesiologist*, *The Evangelical Magazine*, *Fraser's Magazine*, *The Old Church Porch*, *The Preacher*, *The Pulpit*, and in a number of local publications, both British and American. The most important early articles are those in the volumes of *The Morning Watch*, a quarterly journal of prophecy edited by John Tudor (later an apostle of the Catholic Apostolic Church, Ch. II).[15] In addition there are printed service books in English and in eleven other European languages,[16] and manuscripts of services in a few more. The language distribution gives some indication of countries and communities in which Catholic Apostolic witness had its greatest success. Rubrics for the conduct of services were published separately under the title of *General Rubrics* (1878), often bound together with the *Book of Regulations* (1878), the latter providing

---

[15] Published quarterly by James Nisbet of Berners Street, London, until the June issue of 1833. The title was inspired by Isaiah 21: 11–12, which was quoted on its title page.

[16] Danish, Dutch, Esthonian, Flemish, French, German, Italian, Lettish, Polish, Swedish, and Wendish.

detailed instructions for the clergy on pastoral and administrative matters.

The only extensive, though not entirely complete, bibliography of Catholic Apostolic works is that by Copinger (see n. 12). Limited bibliographies are provided in or can be compiled from the secondary sources, but it is not possible to obtain an adequate let alone a comprehensive list in this way. A great deal of manuscript material must still be in existence, but it is widely scattered in different hands, and extremely difficult to locate. A number of the more important manuscript letters can be found in the Northumberland Collection at Alnwick Castle. This Collection includes, especially, some of Drummond's correspondence with Irving and with several of his fellow apostles. The sixth duke of Northumberland and his wife Louisa (Drummond's daughter) were both members of the Catholic Apostolic Church. The correspondence, along with other Drummond papers, has passed down to the present duke and has been transferred from Albury to Alnwick Castle.[17]

It is still possible to draw upon oral tradition, though the opportunity to meet with members of this body who have experienced even a limited liturgical life within it is rapidly diminishing. It must be doubted if more than a handful remain alive of those who can recall details of the full services which ceased in 1901. Much of the oral tradition is now at least second-hand and is becoming increasingly distorted with the passage of time. Fortunately, the present writer has had considerable access to this oral tradition in the course of his life, and can himself recall Eucharistic worship from his early days. In addition to a large library of printed sources, he also has manuscript sources dating well back into the last century, including letters, lecture notes taken at Albury (the apostolic centre of the body), and two histories.

Apostolic Writings

Although works by each of the apostles exist, only three of them can be said to have written extensively: Cardale, Thomas Carlyle (1803–55: not to be confused with the author of *Reminiscences*), and Henry Drummond (1786–1860: not to be confused with the Scottish

---

[17] A catalogue is now available; J. Agnew and R. Palmer, *Report on the papers of Henry Drummond of Albury (1786–1860) and members of his family (1670–1865)* (Royal Commission on Historical Manuscripts, 1977).

philosopher–scientist and author of *Natural Law in the Spiritual World* (1883), *The Ascent of Man* (1894), and other works).

Cardale is noted particularly for his comprehensive study of liturgical theology, *Readings upon the Liturgy and Other Divine Offices of the Church*. Although focused on the liturgical worship of the Catholic Apostolic Church, this monumental work ranges over many of the main areas of Christian theology. Its importance is reflected by the many quotations from it to be found in other Catholic Apostolic writings. It appeared in two volumes, each with several parts, over the years 1848 to 1878. The content of this work—a most significant work on liturgical theology—is as follows:

Volume I
1: *On the Eucharist* (London: Barclay, 1848) 1–204
2: *A Dissertation upon the Types of the Law* (London: Barclay, 1849) 205–363
3: *The Office of Morning and Evening Prayer* (London: Barclay, 1851) 365–554
Contents (London: Barclay, 1851) i–xl

Volume II
1: *The Forenoon and Afternoon Services and Other Subordinate Offices of Prayer* (London: Barclay, 1852) 1–19
2: *On the Proper Services for Holy Days and Seasons* (London: Barclay, 1852/4) 20–234
3: *The Order for the Administration of Holy Baptism* (London: Bosworth, 1874) 235–374
4: *The Order for the Laying On of Apostles' Hands* (London: Bosworth, 1876) 375–466
5: *Ordination* (London: Bosworth, 1878) 467–592
Index of Texts (London: Bosworth, 1878) i–v
Index of Subjects (London: Bosworth, 1878) i–xxiv

The work was not completed, nor was the fifth part finally edited by Cardale. A note on p. 592 reads:

At the death of Mr. Cardale, this treatise on Ordination was found in MS, in its present state. He had no doubt the intention of adding to and completing it. However, this he did not do, and the Editors consider its advisable to print it in the form in which it was left by him.

The *Readings* was translated into German and published in Breslau in 1873.[18] Although over thirty of Cardale's other writings exist in

---

[18] The German translation of 1873 (by Bolko von Richthofen) was published by Mar and Co. with the title *Vorlesungen über die Liturgie*.

print, a number of which are of considerable significance, none is as
extensive or as comprehensive as the *Readings*. For the most part
they cover specific topics, such as the events at Port Glasgow (see
Ch. II), Eucharistic doctrine and the Real Presence (see Ch. IV),
miracles, marriage, tithing, the Judgement, prophecy, and the
fourfold ministry (see esp. Ch. III), the Incarnation, and so on.[19]

Carlyle wrote in both English and German, though mainly in the
former. His works appeared over the period 1827 to 1854 and
covered such topics as the Incarnation, eschatology (see Ch. V), the
ordering of worship, baptism, the work of the Paraclete, the role of
apostles (see Ch. III), the Epistles to the Seven Churches (see Ch.
V), errors in the Church of Scotland, the Mosaic Tabernacle, the use
of symbols in worship (see Ch. IV), and so on. He also wrote a short
history of the apostolic work, and provided the Preface to Thiersch's
History of the Christian Church (London, 1852), which he had
translated from the German. His work on the Mosaic Tabernacle is
of special interest, appearing first in German in 1847 as *Die
Mosaische Stiftshutte* and later in an English translation by Jackler
(New York, 1857). Twenty-three years after Carlyle's death (1855),
his *Collected Writings* appeared, but this volume contains only some
one quarter of his total published output.

Drummond was the most prolific of all the apostolic writers, not
least because he wrote on a wide spectrum of political topics arising
from his interests as a Member of Parliament. His published output
runs to over 140 works. Theological writings cover liturgy (see Ch.
IV), critiques of Roman Catholicism, eschatology (see Ch. V),
Christology, the nature of the Church, and so on. Of special
importance are: *Dialogues on Prophecy* (3 vols., London, 1828–9),
Abstract Principles of Revealed Religion (Murray, 1845, with a
postscript in 1846), and *Discourse on the True Definition of the Church*
(London, 1858). Drummond also wrote two short historical works
on the early period of the Catholic Apostolic Church: *Narrative of
Circumstances which led to the Setting up of the Church at Albury*
(privately published, 1834) and *A Brief Account of the Commencement
of the Lord's Work* (n.p., Whittingham, 1851).

---

[19] Important works by Cardale include: *A Manual or Summary of Special Objects of
Faith and Hope* (London: Barclay, 1843); *Discourse on the Doctrine of the Eucharist as
Revealed by St. Paul* (London: Bosworth, 1856); *The Character of our Present
Testimony and Work* (London: Strangeways, 1865); *A Discourse on the Real Presence*
(London: Bosworth, 1867); *The Fourfold Ministry* (London: Strangeways, 1871); and
The Doctrine of the Incarnation (London: Strangeways, 1875).

The published works of the remaining apostles comprise mainly sermons and homilies, some of which appear in collections, lectures and speeches. For example, two volumes of 40 sermons each by Armstrong were published in 1854 and 1879 respectively by Bosworth, and a volume of 87 homilies was published, also by Bosworth, in 1870. A volume of 17 discourses by William Dow was published by Grant in 1850, and two volumes of sermons and homilies by the same apostle were published, also by Grant, in 1856. Other sermons, homilies, and addresses by various apostles are to be found in privately bound collections of Catholic Apostolic writings, and an important set of apostolic homilies is to be found in *Homilies Preached at Albury*, published by Norton in 1888. There are three notable exceptions, however. The first is a general work covering many aspects of Catholic Apostolic teaching: Sitwell's *The Purpose of God in Creation and Redemption* (Edinburgh, 1865), which subsequently ran to seven editions and appeared in a Danish translation in 1875 and in German in 1880; the second is primarily historical: Woodhouse's *A Narrative of Events affecting the Position and Prospects of the Whole Church* (London, 1847); and the third is Dalton's *Four Lectures on the First and Second Advents* (London, 1846), an eschatological work which ran to four editions and was later translated into Danish. Sitwell wrote also on the dangers of mesmerism (see Ch. III), on baptism (see Ch. III), and on the Bishop Colenso dispute.[20] Woodhouse wrote also on the apostolic and prophetic offices (see Ch. III), on prayer, on eschatology (see Ch. V), and on socialism and temperance societies (see Ch. II). Dalton wrote also on the Eucharist, and on various aspects of ecclesiology.

Finally, it must be remembered that Tudor, as editor of *The Morning Watch*, wrote many articles in this journal. He also wrote papers, mainly on prophecy and the interpretation of the Apocalypse (see Ch. V), published elsewhere.[21] Articles, sermons, and homilies

[20] John William Colenso (1814–83), Bishop of Natal, aroused storms of protest by challenging the authorship and accuracy of a number of Old Testament writings, and also by questioning the idea of eternal punishment (in a commentary on Romans). He was deposed by his ecclesiastical superior, Bishop Robert Gray of Cape Town, but appealed successfully to the Judicial Committee of the Privy Council. Gray appointed another bishop as Colenso's successor, but the latter was able to retain the Cathedral and the endowments of the see. This created a schism not healed until 1911.

[21] In addition to his many contributions to *The Morning Watch*, Tudor contributed articles to *The Church of England Quarterly*, *Proceedings of the Society for the Investigation of Prophecy*, and Tupper's *Survey of the County of Surrey*.

by these and all the other apostles are to be found in various collections and a great many exist as individual pamphlets.

Works (in English) by Other Catholic Apostolic Writers

It is not practicable to attempt to give more than a brief indication of some of the more significant Catholic Apostolic writers other than the apostles. Copinger's *Bibliography* (see above, n. 12) lists over 550 names in all. Many of those named there wrote but few works; others were prolific writers with fifty or more works attributed to them. Of course, the number of works attributed to any particular author is not necessarily an indication of the significance of his or her[22] writings. Certain writers and certain works should, however, be indicated as being of special importance; they are included here in the main text because much can be learned from a study of the titles and authors of a reasonable sample of Catholic Apostolic writings relative to the status and geographical distribution of important authors, the nature and frequency of the subjects treated, and the particular publishers who produced the works. It should be remembered that the majority of Catholic Apostolic works (including those listed below and elsewhere) were published anonymously: the importance of any work was to be judged from its content rather than from its author, and its status as 'official' derived from its having been issued and distributed through Church channels. Other writers and their works can be noted from the quotations selected for inclusion in the course of Chapters II to V below.

Some important writers and works (in English) are as follows:

William Watson Andrews (1810–97), angel-evangelist, New York:
The True Constitution of the Church and its Restoration (New York: Moffet, 1854)
Woman: Her True Place and Standing (various editions, 1872–1900)
more than 40 other works.

Charles William Boase (1804–72), angel-evangelist in Scotland:
The Elijah Ministry (Edinburgh: Grant, 1868, and unfinished supplement)
some 15 other works.

---

[22] Copinger lists 46 female Catholic Apostolic writers in his *Bibliography*.

William Rennie Caird (1823–94), apostles' coadjutor, Germany, Switzerland, and America:
On Worship in Spirit and in Truth (London: Boswell, 1877, and later editions)
7 other works (see also Lutz, below).

Isaac Capadose (1834–1920), apostles' coadjutor, Denmark:
Various sermons and homilies preached at Albury (see Note 20): some 30 works in all.

Walter Arthur Copinger (1847–1910), angel, Manchester; later angel-evangelist:
Various addresses and articles, including a translation of the *Imitatio Christi* of Thomas à Kempis (Glasgow: Hobbs, 1900), and legal and other secular works: 40 or more works in all.

John Sidney Davenport (1809–1900), angel-evangelist, United States:
The Permanence of the Apostolic Office (New York: Wiley, 1853)
Edward Irving and the Catholic Apostolic Church (New York: Moffet, 1863)
Christian Unity and its Recovery (New York: Appleton, 1866)
'Sacramental Christianity and the Incarnation', *The Family Churchman* (1891)
other works, especially on eschatology: some 30 in all.

John George Francis (d. 1889), angel-evangelist, later angel, Brighton:
Discourses and lectures on a wide variety of subjects: some 20 works in all.

Thomas Groser (d. 1898), angel, Wells:
The Four Ministries of the Church (London: Boswell, 1857)
The Functions and Credentials of Apostles (London: Bosworth, 1872)
some 60 other works, mainly sermons.

Edward Heath (1845–1929), apostles' coadjutor, Australia and New Zealand:
Sermons and homilies on many subjects, a number published posthumously: some 60 works in all.

Herbert Heath (1849–1932), angel, Bishopsgate (London):
Addresses, sermons and homilies on many subjects: some 80 works in all.

Samuel Mee Hollick (d. 1940s), angel, Manchester:
Sermons, homilies, and pastoral letters on many subjects: some 80 works in all.

Richard Hughes (1836–1902), archangel, latterly in charge at Albury:
The Liturgy of the Holy Eucharist (London: Boswell, 1865)
Eucharist and Daily Sacrifice (London: Boswell, 1866)

Apostles' Doctrine and Fellowship (London: Boswell, 1871)
some 10 other works, including volumes of 'Readings' for Sundays
and feast days, and a major work on homeopathy of which he was a
noted pioneer).

Henry Strange Hume (1840–1928), angel, Central Church (London):
Pamphlets, sermons, homilies, and pastoral letters on many subjects:
some 80 works in all.

William Joseph Bramley Moore (1831–1918), elder, Central Church
(London):
A Tabular View of the Holy Eucharist (London: Pitman, 1891)
The Sacrament of Christian Baptism (Pitman, 1894)
The Church's Forgotten Hope (Glasgow: Hobbs, 1902)
Baptism Didache: Scriptural Studies on Baptism (London: Bemrose,
1907)
some 30 other works.

Robert Norton (d. 1890?), formerly minister at Holbeach:
*Reasons for Believing that the Lord has Restored to the Church Apostles
and Prophets* (London: Boswell, 1852)
*The Restoration of Apostles and Prophets in the Catholic Apostolic
Church* (London: Boswell, 1861)
The True Position and Hope of the Catholic Apostolic Church (London:
Boswell, 1866)
some 15 other works.

Henry John Owen (1795–1872), angel, Chelsea:
Discourse on the Sacrament of the Lord's Supper (London: Tilling, 1830)
some 10 other works, including especially comments on the Papacy.

William Fettes Pitcairn (d. 1891), angel, Edinburgh:
Warnings and Exhortations (Edinburgh: Wilson, 1858, and many later
editions)
The Passion and Resurrection of the Lord (Edinburgh: Laurie, 1867)
many homilies, teachings, pastoral letters, etc.: some 50 works in all.

William Henry Baptist Proby (1832–1915), angel, Islington:
Discourses upon Old Testament Types (Glasgow: Hobbs, 1904)
Notes on the Revelation of St. John (Nisbet, 1910)
some 30 other works.

Thomas Edward Rawson (1859–1942?), angel, Bristol and Southwark:
Teaching on the Removal of the Last Apostle and the Last Coadjutor
(London: Southwark Church, 1929)
The Covering of the Altar (London: Southwark Church, 1941)
sermons, homilies, pastoral teachings, etc.: some 60 works in all.

Charles Edward William Stuart (d. 1925), angel's coadjutor, Central
     Church (London):
     Teachings on the Liturgy (London: Central Church, 1907)
     6 other works.

Edward Oliver Taplin (1800–62), pillar of prophets:
     The Chronology of the Scriptures (London: Goodall, 1854)
     some 20 other works, mainly on eschatology.

William Tarbet (d. early 1900s), angel, Liverpool:
     Shadows of the Law: the Realities of the Body of Christ (London:
     Boswell, 1855)
     pamphlets, sermons, and addresses on a wide variety of subjects,
     including apostleship, ecumenism, dangers of spiritualism, typo-
     logy, etc.: more than 80 works in all.

James Thonger (1838–1918), angel, Leeds; later archangel:
     Eight Sermons on the Seventy (n.p., 1897)[23]
     The Catechism with Aids to Parents (London: Chiswick, 1908)
     ministries, pastoral letters, etc.: some 20 works in all.

Of Taplin's works, Copinger lists only *The Chronology of the
Scriptures*. The omission of other works is something of a mystery,
since they were certainly available to him in the library of the Central
Church in Gordon Square. An easy conclusion to draw would be that
Copinger did not find them personally edifying, but this is hardly
likely since similar works by other writers appear in his *Bibliography*.
As late as the 1970s, a number of works by Taplin could be obtained
from the librarian at Gordon Square, so there seems to be no
question of them having been 'disowned' in any way.

   The basis of the choice of these non-apostolic authors and their
particular works as being of special note has been: the importance of
the content of the works quoted; the extent of references to them in
other writings; their being widely in the possession of members of
the body; and information received during private conversations
with members. It is not claimed that they constitute a 'scientifically
based' sample, though comparison with much larger lists does
suggest that they are reasonably representative of Catholic Apostolic
writings as a whole.

   From the details of their authors, it can be noted that (as might be
expected) the majority of the works quoted were written by senior
ministers with appointments in England, though Scotland, the

---

[23] Not in Copinger's *Bibliography*.

Continent of Europe, the United States, and even Australia with New Zealand are represented. These last three countries reflect those areas of the English-speaking world outside Great Britain where the Catholic Apostolics were most widely established. All the authors were ministers of the body, only two being below episcopal rank; and, perhaps surprisingly in view of the emphasis upon prophecy in the Catholic Apostolic Church, only one was a prophet. The two principal areas of theology covered in the works were 'ecclesiology' and 'liturgy and the sacraments', with 'eschatology' next in importance—the three principal headings under which Catholic Apostolic theology is considered in this work (see § 5 below). It is important, however, not to associate the works mentioned too rigorously with individual theological topics; many of them were wide-ranging despite the seemingly specific nature of their titles. Eschatology was never far from the writers' thoughts, and (as will be seen) a strongly typological interpretation of Scripture was fundamental to all aspects of Catholic Apostolic witness.

Writings Originally in Languages Other than English

Mention has already been made of works written initially in German. Amongst the Catholic Apostolic writers whose German works can be consulted in English translations, the most important are:

Ludwig Albrech (d. 1931), archangel, Bremen:
   The Work by Apostles at the end of the Dispensation (Ger. 1924; Eng. edn. 1931, for private circulation)
   also works originally written in English, Spanish, and French: some 20 works in all.

Charles John Thomas Böhm (d. 1880), apostle's coadjutor, North Germany:
   Lights and Shadows in the Present Condition of the Church (Ger. 1855; Eng. edn. London: Bosworth, 1860)
   also other German works, and works originally in English and French: some 28 works in all.

Johann Evangelist Georg Lutz (1801–82), angel, Berne; later angel-evangelist:
   God's Purpose with Mankind and the Earth (Ger. undated, written with W. R. Caird, see above; Sidney: Cook, 1893)
   7 further works in Germany only (one with Caird).

Ernst Adolf Rossteuscher (d. 1892), angel, Kassel then Leipzig:
>*The Rebuilding of the Church of Christ* (Ger. 1871; published in part, London: Boswell 1875, full manuscript translations 1850 and 1928)
>4 other works in German only.

Heinrich Wilhelm Josias Thiersch (1817–85), apostles' pastor, Basle:
>*History of the Christian Church* (undated Ger; trans. T. Carlyle, see above, London: Boswell, 1852)
>*Christian Family Life* (London: Boswell, 1856)
>*The Parables of Christ* (London: Boswell, 1869)
>*Summary of Christian Doctrine* (Glasgow: Hobbs, 1888)
>some 40 further works in English, German, and French.

Hermann Thiersch (dates not known):
>*Our Russian Brethren* (Ger. 1932, trans. Lady Percy (typescript) 1933)
>6 other works in German only.

Anton Valentin (1865–1951), evangelist, Austria:
>*The Present Time of Silence* (Ger. n.d.; Eng. 1938)
>7 other works in English, French, and German.

Significant untranslated German writers include: Viktor von Dittmann (6 works); Emil Geering, coadjutor (4 works plus one in French, and a German translation from F. Sitwell, above); Karl von Mickwitz (9 works); Max von Pochhammer (4 works, but a translation by Evelyn Everett Green exists of stories narrated by him which was published in 1900 by Ambrose Dudley); Gotthard Freiherr von Richthofen (5 works); Carl Rothe (7 works); and Louis Alphonse Woringer (5 works plus 1 in French). Of those writing in French, the following should be noted: Gollnigs Manger Carré, angel, Paris (7 works); William de Caux; angel Bristol, then Liverpool, Paris, and London (17 works in French and English); and Pierre Mejanel, angel-evangelist, France (2 works, 1 translated into English).

The predominance of German fairly reflects the relatively considerable adherence to the Catholic Apostolic Church from amongst German-speaking Lutherans. Again, the majority of the writers quoted were of episcopal rank, but there appears to be greater emphasis upon the history of the body than in the English writings, though the historical works were, in the main, written as apologetics.

The apostolic and non-apostolic English and other writings noted above, though representative, are necessarily selective—the basis of selection having already been indicated. They are regarded as important supporting sources for the present study, though only a very small fraction of the works in the possession of the present writer or which have been consulted by him, and an even smaller fraction of the total published output of Catholic Apostolic writers— Copinger's *Bibliography* runs to 74 A4 pages.

'Internal' Histories of the Catholic Apostolic Church

For the details of the history of the Catholic Apostolic Church it is possible to refer to a considerable number of 'internal' works, of which some have already been mentioned (see L. Albrecht, C. W. Boase, J. S. Davenport, H. Drummond, R. Norton, E. A. Rossteuscher, and F. V. Woodhouse above). Not all of these works appear to have been available to 'external' historians of the body. In addition to those already noted, there are a score or so further works which can be regarded as significant, including especially:

J. Aarsbo: *Komme dit Rige*, 5 vols. (Copenhagen: publisher unknown, 1930–6)

W. W. Andrews, *The History and Claims of the Body of Christians known as the Catholic Apostolic Church* (printed from the *Bibliotheca Sacra* for January and April 1866), various editions (1866–1945)

K. Born, *Das Werk des Herrn unter Aposteln* (Bremen: publisher unknown, 1974)

T. Carlyle, *A Short History of the Apostolic Work*, from the German (London: Barclay, 1851)

W. de Caux, *Early Days of the Lord's Work in France*, privately published (1899)

H. B. Copinger (ed.), 'Annals: The Lord's Work in the Nineteenth and Twentieth Centuries', MSS Gordon Square (London)

T. Dowglasse, *A Chronicle of Certain Events which have taken place in the Church of Christ, principally in England between the Years 1826 and 1852* (London: Goodall, 1852)

R. M. Hamilton, *A Short History of the Remarkable Spiritual Occurrences in 1827–8 among Peasants in Bavaria, and the Sequel in 1842, 1870* (London: Goodwin, 1893)

C. C. Schwartz, 'The Chronical of the Setting Up of the Church in Berlin', from the German, MSS (1952)

E. Trimen, *The Rise and Progress of the·Lord's Work*, 13 lectures, privately published (1904)

K. von Mickwitz, *Ein Beitbild in Michtigen Beugnissen uber die Gegenwartige Lage der Christenhelt* (Berlin: Hoffman, 1902)

Anon., *The History of the Lord's Work in These Last Days*, undated MSS of the 19th century

Works by Catholic Apostolic 'Defectors'

A few early defectors from the Church wrote works which are a mixture of polemic and fact. These are of considerable interest, especially in what they reveal of its internal affairs, but because of their nature they have to be treated with special caution by the historian. Four such persons are of particular note: R. Baxter, W. Grant, J. Harrison, and H. M. Prior.[24]

The case of Baxter is quite remarkable. A lawyer from Doncaster, he attended one of Irving's meetings in London in 1831 and in the following year became one of the most respected of the prophetic speakers in Irving's group, prophesying in particular the restoration of the apostolate and the importance of 14 July 1835—the date which was to see the event known as the 'separation of the apostles', the formal 'birth' of the Catholic Apostolic Church. However, later he became convinced that his prophesyings were of the Devil and not of the Holy Spirit, and so severed his connection with the embryonic Catholic Apostolic Church, though that body continued to accept his witness and respect his person. Baxter's writings do not add to our knowledge of the history of the Church, but they are of particular value in that they include the only detailed self-analysis of the spiritual and psychological state experienced during ecstatic prophetic utterances.

Grant was at one time a minister of the Catholic Apostolic Church. He became dissatisfied with the rigid hierarchical structure which eventually developed along with, as he perceived it, an extreme tendency towards secrecy militating against the possibility of frank discussion of theological issues between clergy in priests' orders and their superiors the angels.

Harrison was also a one-time minister of the body, and for a much longer period than Grant. Like Grant he complained of the tendency to secrecy, but he also saw the claims of the apostles as an attempt to

<hr>

[24] R. Baxter, *Narrative of Facts Characterizing the Supernatural Manifestations in Members of Mr. Irving's Congregation and Other Individuals, in England and Scotland, and Formerly in the Writer Himself* (London: Nisbet, 1833); and *Irvingism in its Rise, Progress, and Present State* (London: Nisbet, 1836); W. Grant, *Apostolic Lordship and the Interior Life: a Narrative of Five Years' Communion with Catholic Apostolic Angels* (n.p., 1873); J. Harrison, *The Catholic Apostolic Church: its Pretensions and Claims* (London: Stevenson, 1872); H. M. Prior, *My Experience in the Catholic Apostolic Church* (Stratford: Wilson and Whitworth, 1880).

restore medieval Roman principles and practices, and the Eucharistic Liturgy with its emphasis on the Real Presence and its sacrificial interpretation (see Ch. IV) as betraying the English Reformation inheritance.

Prior was a minister in one of the London congregations for over twenty years, but was eventually deposed and excommunicated for heresy by Cardale in 1873. He had circulated a tract attacking any divine inspiration of Scripture, the doctrine of the Trinity, and the possibility of the miraculous, along with the historical truth of much that is to be found in the Gospels. His Christian Faith had degenerated to, at best, deism. In particular, he extolled 'reason' as the 'surest guide', quoting Mahomet as his authority for so doing. It is also of interest that he refers favourably to Bishop Colenso (see above, n. 20). It is thus not surprising that Cardale considered him unfit to continue ministering to an apostolic congregation or to remain in communion with those whose beliefs were diametrically opposed to his free-thinking.

The writings of all four of these defectors, though almost certainly full of exaggerations, do provide illumination on certain aspects of Catholic Apostolic theology and practice, but each has its own particular bias and each relates to the personal experience of its individual author. Such experience was not necessarily typical of the Catholic Apostolic body as a whole. In studying these works, it is not always easy to disentangle the truth from the deliberate fabrications. However, what does seem to emerge (especially from Grant and Harrison) is that there was sometimes a reluctance on the part of certain of the angels to engage in theological discussion, particularly with those of their subordinates previously trained for the ministry of other Churches, and that this reluctance did reflect to some extent a lack of general theological training within the body.

The Homogeneity of Catholic Apostolic Writings

One of the most striking aspects of Catholic Apostolic writings, taken overall, is their homogeneity, a homogeneity which is found no matter what theological or pastoral area is under discussion. This is largely due to the derivative nature of much of the writing—to which the frequent references to works by the apostles testify—and to the fact that the (mainly anonymous) writings which were published and circulated to members were distributed through the

Church authorities. From this it can be assumed that their content had formal approval and thus fairly reflects the official teaching of the body.

The theology of the apostolic writings, and particularly that of Cardale's *Readings*, was thoroughly disseminated throughout the whole ministry of the Catholic Apostolic Church: indeed, the bulk of the laity were almost equally as well instructed as the clergy. Even the comparatively unlearned studied the circulated sermons and homilies, and they could often quote verbatim from them when challenged on points of doctrine or practice, though they might well be unable to enter into any detailed discussion of these. This unanimity amongst the writings militates against any inherent dangers usually resulting from enforced selection of source material. Where extracts from works of non-apostolic origin are used critically in the following chapters, they have been carefully compared with those by other 'internal' writers to ensure the authenticity of the views represented. It was precisely in the course of making such comparisons that the homogeneity referred to above became so strikingly apparent.

3. PROBLEMS ASSOCIATED WITH CATHOLIC APOSTOLIC SOURCES

Anonymity of Authors

One of the problems presented by Catholic Apostolic source material, in addition to its current scarcity, is the difficulty of identifying individual authors. As already noted above, the bulk of the writings were presented without identification of author, though occasionally pseudonyms would be used or simply initials (often reversed). Examples of pseudonyms include 'Basileutos', 'Christianus', 'Clericus', 'Evangelus', 'Filea', 'Philalethes', 'Presbyteros', and titles such as 'a presbyter', 'a prophet', 'a working man'. Often identification is made easier by headings such as 'a sermon preached at . . .' together with the date, and sometimes concluding with 'by the Angel in charge', or 'by the Deacon-Evangelist', etc. It then becomes a matter of recourse to historical sources to determine the name of the writer. In the case of initials, even when reversed, identification is, of course, easier.[25] Apart from recourse to Copinger's *Bibliography* (which is extensive but not complete), identifying authors is largely a matter of comparison of texts, assistance from quotations and references, identification by external writers, and even oral tradition. Even Cardale's *Readings* was published with no indication of its author. Quite often, however, Cardale's works can be identified because they are stated to be 'by the Author of *Readings upon the Liturgy*'. In other cases there is a reference to an anonymous work whose authorship has first to be established. A typical example can be taken from Cardale's responses to attacks published in *The Old Church Porch* by the Revd W. E. J. Bennett and, later and anonymously, by the Revd E. B. Pusey. Cardale's first response appeared in the form of an anonymous letter, but a second was identified as being 'by the Author of a letter . . .'. This kind of semi-anonymity was quite frequently made use of. Unfortunately no classified bibliography has been in existence: Copinger's work is arranged alphabetically by author.

Ambiguity of Titles

Another serious difficulty is that titles of works are often not sufficiently comprehensive to indicate the nature of the subject being covered. In the case of sermons, homilies, and addresses (which form a considerable amount of the extant material), the heading is usually no more than a text of Scripture or a note of the particular Sunday or feast day on which the material was first delivered. Furthermore, such titles as do exist may actually mislead as to content because their interpretation by Catholic Apostolic writers can often be unconventional. A typical example is a work entitled *The Procession of the Holy Ghost*, which makes no reference to the 'filioque'. This work, a sermon delivered by J. B. Heath (Archangel) at the Bishopsgate Church in 1903, deals only with the activity of the Holy Spirit in the world.

---

[25] In the present work, actual authors have been given wherever it has been possible to identify them: it has not been thought necessary or desirable to indicate those instances where the author's name is printed.

Absence of Indexes

Yet another problem arises from the near universal lack of indexes in Catholic Apostolic works, though in a few cases a generous list of contents helps to mitigate this situation.[26] On occasion some idea of the detailed content of a specific work can be gleaned from its introduction, though such introductions are provided only in the case of the longer works and they are not infrequently dissertations in their own right, ranging widely and not necessarily reflecting specifically the content of the main text to follow. Hence it is not unusual to find such introductions published as separate works.[27] Identification of the particular places in a work where a given topic is treated is more often than not impossible apart from a complete reading of it.

Scarcity of Primary Sources

Attention has already been drawn to the scarcity of Catholic Apostolic material. Although a number of the printed works and some manuscript material are available for consultation in the British Library (London) and the Bodleian Library (Oxford), and there are a few works in specialist libraries such as that of Dr Williams in Gordon Square (London), most of the relevant documents remain in private hands. This is especially true of relevant correspondence, though much of Drummond's correspondence is available for consultation by arrangement at Alnwick Castle (to which reference has already been made). An extensive library is held by the Catholic Apostolic Church trustees, but access to this is very severely restricted and, with very few exceptions, is confined to members of the body. A significant number of documents has been withdrawn even from this limited access. The practice of selling typed copies of non-restricted material, which had assisted earlier research, seems to have ceased several years ago with the death of the former librarian and a much stricter policy being adopted by the trustees.

---

[26] Cardale's *Readings* is one of the works where a very extensive and helpful list of contents is provided. Thus, the full 'Contents' of Volume I alone runs to 40 pages.

[27] One of the most significant examples is Irving's *Preliminary Discourse to the Work of Ben Ezra* (London: Seeley, 1827), published separately from the main work and running to 203 pages.

Discouragement of Research

The effect of these difficulties is to make both historical and theological research extremely difficult for any 'external' scholar. Indeed, it is the express policy of the trustees to discourage research on the grounds that Catholic Apostolic witness has been withdrawn from the world by divine act—the present 'time of silence' is regarded as precisely that. Surviving members are encouraged to ensure that on their deaths material in their possession is returned to the trustees. As individual churches have been closed down, it has not been uncommon for the bulk of their libraries to be destroyed. The total quality of works destroyed, in order to prevent their getting into outside hands, cannot be estimated but must be very considerable.

Requests to Catholic Apostolic Church members or descendants of members for access to works in their possession receive an unhelpful response in the majority of cases; it is only where people are unaware of the present official policy that the response is positive, though in one or two rare cases there can be a positive response because that policy, though known, is not accepted. This general hostility towards research can take the form of a strongly worded though courteously expressed warning concerning the spiritual dangers of attempting to reopen a curtain closed by divine will. The following extracts received by the present writer, one from England and the other from abroad, will suffice to indicate the general attitude:

As a brother in Christ and a colleague in science I feel that I have to warn you especially against writing a thesis on the theology of the Catholic Apostolic congregations. . . . The Apostles' doctrine and fellowship (how much more an appropriate term than 'theology') belong in the Church, not in the University.

Such sacred and spiritual things as have been committed to us are not suitable or proper matter for use in academic exercises. They cannot carry spiritual conviction and can therefore only be misleading to those who subject them to mere intellectual examination. . . . Let me beg you . . . to turn to some other and more suitable field of research, and not to jeopardize the salvation of others by putting them in the position of being required to pass judgement upon what in general will be beyond their spiritual apprehension. It is in mercy that the Lord hides His work until such time as He becomes able to reveal it in glory and perfection, and our task at this time is to humble ourselves . . .

These two extracts, one of which is from an underdeacon and the other from a layman of some stature in the body, reveal that part at least of the reluctance to have the Catholic Apostolic witness examined by present-day scholars is a serious concern to set what are regarded as spiritual matters outside the realm of academic research. Other researchers have reported similar responses. The present writer understands such concerns, but considers that any genuine research which enriches the intellectual or spiritual understanding of any part of our religious heritage is worthy of being pursued. It is part of the task of the researcher to ensure that his results are presented fairly and that misunderstandings are avoided, so that a genuine contribution is made to our awareness and comprehension of 'the truth'. It seems that the Catholic Apostolic trustees have become concerned because of past unscholarly approaches on the part of some of those who have sought access to sources under their control, especially where the reasons given have been frivolous or the outcome has been polemical or a caricature of the truth. This is fully understandable, but ought not to result in a total opposition to all research. The 'spiritual' reasons given presuppose an attitude which is not necessarily that of every enquirer, and certainly not that of the present writer.

4. SOURCES USED BY CATHOLIC APOSTOLIC WRITERS

The apostles and other Catholic Apostolic writers were concerned almost exclusively with the specific message which they regarded themselves as called by the Holy Spirit to convey. They were not intentionally writing works of scholarship, though much of their writing has considerable scholarly merit. In the main their works were directed towards the education and edifying of their faithful, though in the early days many were addressed to the Christian community in general. This is especially true of collections of lectures originally given at public meetings, of which there are several,[28] and of pamphlets and articles written to refute accusations

---

[28] e.g. Hughes' *Apostles Doctrine and Fellowship* and Sitwell's *The Purpose of God in Creation and Redemption*.

of creating schism. Some works, such as the Testimonies (see Chs. II and V), had specific external addresses.

The accusation of creating a schism was often made by critics of the body and was invariably answered by the statement that the apostles' doctrine and fellowship were a work of the Lord *within* the Universal Church. Potential clergy 'converts' were often surprised to be instructed to continue their ministry where they already were, even though they had received the apostles' sealing (see Ch. II). On the Continent of Europe, and especially in the case of Lutherans, dual church membership was a commonplace. Even in England, it is a fact that one of its apostles held an Anglican living after his acceptance of the call to the apostolate.

Scriptural, Patristic, and Other References

In general, though scriptural references were very faithfully presented, sources were noted only very occasionally. It is quite clear from the content of Catholic Apostolic writings (and especially of works by the apostles) that considerable effort had been made to augment the study of Scripture by reference to the Fathers and the early liturgies of the Christian Church. Further, most direct references to early Christian works were to the original Greek or Latin texts.[29] References to the Psalms occasionally quote the Hebrew.[30]

It is clear, therefore, that, though the majority of the apostles and other writers had had a secular training rather than a theological one, they were not only well versed in the Classical languages (which might be expected of educated persons of the time) but also widely read in the historical documents of the early centuries of the Christian era. The apostles made themselves familiar with contemporary theology and literature not only by reading but also by undertaking journeys to the different Churches of Christendom (see Ch. II) in order that by observation and, where possible, discussion they might discover and comprehend all that was best in the various traditions.

Such references as were included provide some insight into what works, in addition to Holy Scripture and the Creeds, were accepted as having a recognized degree of authority. The ultimate authority

---

[29] At the Albury Conferences (see Ch. II), the Scriptures were available throughout in their original languages.

[30] See e.g. E. Baker's *The Christ of the Psalms*, 2 vols. (London: Bickers, 1872).

was, however, always that of Scripture (often as interpreted by the prophetic ministry). Of the texts quoted, it is clear that some were held in especial esteem. Amongst these can be included patristic writings, both Greek and Latin, early Christian documents such as the *Apostolic Constitutions*, early liturgies such as those ascribed to St James and St Mark, Greek and Latin liturgies of later periods (particularly that ascribed to St John Chrysostom) and commentaries upon them,[31] the dogmatic statements of the Ecumenical Councils, and some works of Reformation writers, though in the last case restricted to points where such writers were considered to be returning to earlier truths forgotten or distorted in the medieval West. The writings of the Fathers were accepted as authoritative wherever they were deemed to reflect a consensus view in accord with Holy Scripture. It was, however, clearly stated that individual Fathers could and did err on some critical matters of doctrine.

The Nature of Catholic Apostolic Teaching

Despite the Protestant background of its founders, the whole ethos of the Catholic Apostolic Church was rapidly to become both Catholic and Orthodox in most of its teaching, though it always retained its own special emphasis upon the apostolic and prophetic ministries and eschatology (see Chs. III and V). It must be remembered in this context that the Catholic Apostolics accepted the words spoken ecstatically by their prophets and authenticated by their apostles to be directly inspired by the Holy Spirit. Two particular forms of ecstatic speaking were a regular feature of the Catholic Apostolics in their early days: speaking in unknown tongues, and interpretation of tongues and of passages of Scripture; both were regarded as an activity of the Holy Spirit. The term generally adopted was 'speaking in prophecy' or 'speaking in the power'. The prophetic ministry was a special feature of Catholic Apostolic ministry as a whole (see Ch. III), though, as the Church developed, it was found necessary to regulate prophetic utterances and to ensure that the prophets remained under apostolic control (see Ch. II). Records were kept of all words spoken ecstatically, but

[31] Cardale, in particular, makes many references to ancient liturgies and to commentaries upon them—specifically those of St Germanos (8th cent.) and St Nicholas Cabasilas (14th cent.). See Ch. IV.

they were not made generally accessible—they were not circulated to ministers below the order of angel.

Since authentication and interpretation of prophecies were in the last resort a matter for the apostles (and, later, their coadjutors), it is largely from their writings, and the writings of those who followed their teaching directly, that the authoritative doctrines of the Catholic Apostolic Church must be extracted. It is mainly in the apostolic works that the majority of the references to patristic and other early Christian sources are to be found. Other writers can, however, be quoted with considerable confidence on account of the general homogeneity already noted and because their works were, for the most part, circulated officially through Church channels. With certain exceptions, the non-apostolic writers quoted the apostles, where appropriate, as their authoritative sources, thus giving to the whole body of Catholic Apostolic writings an authority which is seldom found in the writings of members of other Churches.

The often heavy reliance upon the writings of Cardale and his apostolic colleagues does give some support to the idea of a lack of general theological training of the local clergy of the body, though there are exceptions to this. The more important point is that such clergy were well prepared for a task of ensuring that there was uniformity of doctrine throughout the Catholic Apostolic body, and such unanimity was a requirement of the apostolic college. This made the existence of dissidents, particularly after the full development of the Church, a rare phenomenon.

5. THE STRUCTURE OF THIS BOOK

In the light of the availability of primary sources and in the context of the objectives of this work, Catholic Apostolic theology and practice will be presented and analysed in three main chapters (III–V) with the titles: 'Ecclesiology', 'Liturgy',[32] and 'Eschatology'. These chapters follow 'A Short History of the Catholic Apostolic Church' (Ch. II). The various other theological topics considered here appear under one of these general headings. Within each

---

[32] The Liturgy had a wider though restricted meaning for Catholic Apostolics than its familiar use as a way of denoting the Eucharist (see Ch. IV).

32   *Introduction*

chapter there are numbered subsections with additional headings. The procedure adopted is to present Catholic Apostolic teaching with the support of quotations from appropriate primary sources included within the main text, and a final section of each of the three main chapters is devoted to 'Survey and Comment'. This has been thought preferable to a continual interspersion of both quotation and comment throughout the main text, though some comment has been included wherever appropriate. It has not been thought necessary to include such a final section in Chapter II, since this work is primarily concerned with the theology of the Catholic Apostolic Church.

Since the theological teachings of the Catholic Apostolic Church present great difficulties of access for scholars, their collection and presentation from a wide variety of primary sources is regarded as one of the major contributions of this work. Further subsidiary contributions are the identification of authors, the provision of a classified bibliography, and the noting of the extent to which aspects of Catholic Apostolic liturgy and theology derive from Eastern as well as Western Christian traditions.

In addition to the 'Survey and Comment' at the end of Chapters III, IV, and V, there is a final chapter devoted to a more general assessment of the Catholic Apostolic body and its witness, to the charge of sectarianism, to a discussion of the question as to the extent to which it can be regarded as reflecting an ethos and tradition which is that of Eastern Orthodoxy as well as the obvious reflection of its base and origins in the West, and to a consideration of its ecumenical implications for today.

A collected bibliography is provided following the conclusion of the main text. The major part of this is devoted to Catholic Apostolic works classified by subject matter, since no such extensive bibliography has previously been generally available. Appendices give the contents of the Catholic Apostolic service book, and of Drummond's *Dialogues on Prophecy*—a work which provides details of the topics discussed at the Albury Conferences from which much of Catholic Apostolic eschatology developed.

II

A Short History of the
Catholic Apostolic Church

1. PRELUDE TO A CHURCH

THE roots of the Catholic Apostolic Church have a number of
distinct strands which, though separately identifiable, are nevertheless
closely linked together. These can be roughly identified as being
adventist, charismatic, apostolic, and ecumenical. The Church came
into being within an historical period which was especially marked
by the aftermath of the French Revolution of 1789, the general
reaction to which in Britain—greatly influenced by Edmund Burke's
1790 pamphlet *Reflections on the French Revolution*—was one of
horror and fear. It is significant that Burke was not a Tory but a
Whig and an Irishman. This reaction was heightened within the
Tory party because of the potential unrest arising from poverty
amongst agricultural labourers and the effects of the early stages of
the Industrial Revolution.

The French cataclysm had also brought religious doubt in its
wake, a doubt which could easily be aroused in the British lower
classes. Such doubt was seen as being all too often the parent of
disorder. Those who fervently desired the maintenance of the
existing social order turned with evangelical fervour to the Scriptures,
seeking confirmation of the view that this order was in full
conformity with the will of God. Movements towards electoral
reform were interpreted as evidence of growing secularization based
upon the principle that 'power belongs to the people', a direct
contradiction of the concept of a Christian state within which
authority was derived from above. Catholic emancipation appeared
to strike at the Protestant roots of the Established Church and
society as a whole. Liberalism seemed to imply a usurpation by the
State of one of the traditional roles of the better-off—for the old-
fashioned Tory the lot of the poor was to be ameliorated by works of
charity not by social legislation.

The Adventist Root and the Albury Conferences

The adventist root of the Catholic Apostolic Church owes much to the Albury Conférences, held in the private home of Henry Drummond (1786–1860). Drummond was a wealthy landed aristocrat, a banker like his father, and an independently minded Tory 'of the old school'. He was raised in the house of his grandfather, Henry Dundas, Viscount Melville, and educated at Harrow, being a contemporary there of Byron and Peel, and subsequently attended Christ Church College, Oxford, leaving after two years without taking a degree. He then became a partner in the family banking business at Charing Cross, a business which he was later to be accused of neglecting because of his preoccupation with the Catholic Apostolic Church. His wife Henrietta, who was also his cousin, was the daughter of the tenth earl of Kinnoul.

In 1810 Drummond became Tory Member of Parliament for Plympton Earls; later he was to represent West Surrey. He had a special interest in land reform, and was to found (in 1825) the Chair of Political Economy at Oxford. At the age of 31, he tired of the fashionable world and devoted his energies and much of his wealth to religious matters, initially becoming interested in Swiss Calvinism. He was a founder-member of the Continental Society—formed with the objective of spreading evangelical principles in France, Switzerland, and Germany—but soon became chiefly interested in eschatology. He also took an active part in the Jews Society, being considerably influenced by its benefactor Lewis Way.

Much of the same evangelical fervour that was being devoted to missionary activity at the time was also brought to bear on the whole question of the restoration of the Jews. Way, a trained barrister of considerable personal wealth and an ordained Anglican, had become especially interested in prophecies of the return of the Jews to Palestine. He rescued the London Society for Promoting Christianity among the Jews (founded in 1809 by a converted Jew, Joseph Frey) from a bankruptcy which was largely the result of quarrels between Anglican and Dissenting members, subsequently changing its objective to the training of Jewish converts for work in Eastern Europe and the Middle East.[1] In 1817 he made a journey through

[1] E. R. Sandeen, *The Roots of Fundamentalism* (Chicago: Chicago University Press, 1970), 9–12.

Europe in order to appeal to the heads of states on behalf of the Jews—a journey which took him as far afield as Moscow, where he attempted unsuccessfully to persuade Tsar Alexander I to set up a Jewish colony in the Crimea.

In 1819, Drummond bought Albury House, which was to be his 'country seat' for the rest of his life, and which became the spiritual and administrative centre of the Catholic Apostolic Church of which he was to be an apostle. He has been variously described as being learned, witty, restless, inconsistent, and proud. Something of his complex character can be learned from Thomas Carlyle (1795–1881).

Carlyle, who must not be confused with the Catholic Apostolic apostle of the same name, was born in Ecclefechan, Scotland, and educated at Edinburgh University. In 1826 he married Jane Welsh, and in 1834 moved to London where he became known as 'the sage of Chelsea'. Originally intended for the ministry, he turned to writing and established a reputation with works such as *Sartor Resartus*, *Critical and Miscellaneous Essays*, and *The French Revolution*. He was unpopular with liberal thinkers because of his views on slavery and the social evils of the time. After the death of his wife in 1866, he devoted his time to writing his major published work, *Reminiscences*, which was edited from manuscripts after his death by James Anthony Froude. The publication of this edition of *Reminiscences* in 1881 created a storm of protest, and a more accurate (and now standard) edition was produced by Charles Eliot Norton in 1887.

Carlyle described Drummond as follows:

A man of elastic pungent decisive nature; full of fine qualities and capabilities,—but well nigh cracked with an enormous conceit of himself, which, both as pride and vanity (in strange partnership, mutually agreeable), seemed to pervade every fibre of him, and render his life a restless inconsistency: that was the feeling he left in me; nor did it alter afterwards, when I saw a great deal more of him,—without sensible increase or diminution of the little love he first inspired in me.[2]

Irving (see below) warned him of his 'recklessness of language' and his propensity for scoring 'brilliant and striking points of interpretation', accusing him of being more interested in intellectual truth than

---

[2] T. Carlyle, *Reminiscences* (London: Dent edn., 1972), 294.

edification.[3] After attending a meeting of Evangelicals chaired by Drummond in November 1825, Irving wrote:

Henry Drummond was in the chair; he is in all chairs—I fear for him; his words are more witty than spiritual; his manner is *spirituel*, not grave . . .[4]

Such was the man who was to host the Albury Conferences.

The Albury Conferences were called for the purposes of examining the Scriptures—and especially the prophetic writings—with a view to interpreting the political and social events of the day, and also of determining the extent to which biblical prophecies had already been fulfilled in the life of Christ and the history of the Christian Church, thus making it possible to identify those still awaiting fulfilment in the future. The political and social ferments of the age suggested the possibility that they could be interpreted as signs of entering into the 'last times'.

Edward Irving (1792–1834) was one of those attending the Conferences, and it is to him that the record of the proceedings of the first of them is owed.[5] These proceedings set the pattern for the remainder of the Conferences. Each day followed an agreed pattern: an address on the topic of the day before breakfast, examination of the Scriptures after breakfast until mid-morning, group discussion until mid-afternoon, and an attempt to reach an agreed synthesis after dinner. The membership included Anglicans, Independents, Presbyterians, Methodists, and Moravians, and came from widely differing professions. The maximum number of persons attending at any one time seems to have varied from forty to forty-four. Clergy outnumbered laity by roughly two to one, and Anglicans formed about two-thirds of those attending. Those who attended were:[6]

---

[3] Letter, Irving to Drummond, 4 May 1833 (Northumberland collection).
[4] Letter, Irving to his wife, quoted in Oliphant, Mrs, *The Life of Edward Irving* (London: Hurst and Blackett, 1864). References to Mrs Oliphant's *Life*, as above, are to the 3rd and revised single-volume edition. Earlier editions were in 2 vols.
[5] E. Irving, *Preliminary Discourse to the Work of Ben Ezra* (London: Seeley and Son, 1827), clxxxviii–cxciv.
[6] The list given cannot be taken as finally authoritative, since the sources disagree slightly. The internal sources are Drummond's *Narrative of Circumstances which led to the setting up of the Church of Albury* (n.p., 1834), and C. W. Boase's *Supplementary Narrative to the Elijah Ministry* (Edinburgh: Grant, 1868). There are also external sources, including especially J. H. Bransby's *Evans's Sketch of the various Denominations of the Christian World* (London: 1841).

Clergy: Revd G. Beckett (Anglican)
Revd W. Bryan (Anglican)
Revd H. F. Burder (Independent, Hackney)
Revd T. W. Cole (Anglican, Vicar of Wanersh, Surrey)
Revd W. Dodsworth (Margaret Chapel, London)
Revd W. Dow (Presbyterian, Minister of Tongland)
Revd C. Hawtrey
Revd J. Hawtrey (Methodist)
Revd J. Hooper
Revd E. Irving (Presbyterian, Minister of the Caledonian
    Chapel, Hatton Garden, London)
Revd H. B. Maclean (Presbyterian, Minister of London Wall
    Church)
Revd H. McNeile (Anglican, Rector of Albury)
Revd W. Marsh (Anglican, Vicar of St Peter's, Colchester)
Revd Dr Okeley (Moravian, Shoe Lane Chapel, London)
Revd H. J. Owen (Anglican, Minister of Park Chapel, Chelsea,
    London)
Revd G. W. Phillips (from the United States)
Revd W. Probyn (Anglican, Archdeacon of Landaff)
Revd J. Simons (Anglican, Rector of St Paul's Cray)
Revd R. Story (Presbyterian, Minister of Rosneath, Scotland)
Revd J. H. Stewart (Anglican, Minister of Percy Chapel,
    London)
Revd J. Stratton (Independent, Paddington, London)
Revd E. T. Vaughan (Anglican, Vicar of St Mary's, Leicester)
Revd J. White (Baker Street Chapel, London)
Revd Dr Wilson (Anglican, later Bishop of Calcutta)
Revd R. Wolfe (Anglican, Rector of Crawley)
Revd R. Wolfe, Jun. (Anglican, Curate at Albury)
Revd J. Wolff (Anglican, Missionary to the Jews)

Laity: Mr J. Bayford (Anglican, Proctor in Doctors' Commons)
Mr T. Borthwick (later Member of Parliament)
Mr T. W. Chevalier (London surgeon)
Mr W. Cunninghame (Presbyterian)
Mr H. Drummond (Anglican, landowner, Member of
    Parliament)
Mr J. H. Frere (Anglican, civil servant in the Army Office)
Capt. G. Gambier (Anglican, later Admiral)
Mr A. Haldane (Editor of *The Record*)
Mr W. Leach (member of the Board of Control)
Lieut. Malden (Anglican, son of the Revd T. W. Cole)
Lord Mandeville (Anglican, later Duke of Manchester)

Mr S. Perceval (Anglican, son of former Prime Minister)
Mr E. Simon (Anglican, Director of the Jews' Asylum, London)
Mr Staples
The Hon. J. J. Strutt (Anglican, later Member of Parliament,
    subsequently Lord Rayleigh)

The 'syllabus' for the first Conference included investigations of
Scriptual doctrine on 'the times of the Gentiles', on the present and
future condition of the Jews, on the future advent of Christ, and the
system of prophetic numbers in Daniel and the Apocalypse. In each
of these matters an important issue was the determination of the
duties of Christian clergy and laity in the light of Scriptural
examination. Throughout the deliberations appeal could be made
only to the Scriptures, which were available to the company in their
original languages, Hebrew and Greek.

   After the fourth of the meetings at Albury, certain conclusions
were published in Drummond's *Dialogues on Prophecy* of which
Irving was a co-editor. The *Dialogues* appeared in three volumes
(1828–9); they indicate the general content of the Albury debates,
but are written in the form of dialogues between participants to
whom Drummond gives pseudonyms: Anastasius, Aristo, Basilicus,
Crito, Evander, Isocrates, Josephus, Justus, Philalethes, Philemon,
Polydorus, Sophron, Thales, Theodorus, Theophilus, Thraso, and
Valerius. Attempts have been made from other sources to identify
these pseudonyms with known persons attending the conferences,
but with limited success. It would seem clear, however, in view of
the discrepancy between the number of those known to have
participated in the conferences and the number of pseudonyms, that
no direct identification is possible. Indeed, Drummond himself
declared that the content of the *Dialogues* did not represent the
actual debates which took place:

A publication in the form of dialogues was suggested, that being the
shape in which discussions had been most successfully conducted upon
all subjects, from the days of Plato, Tully, and Lucian, down to those of
Bunyan, Littleton, and Horne Tooke. The conversations which had just
been held seemed to point out a convenient basis: but the published
Dialogues have borne little or no resemblance to these real conversations:
much that was spoken was not printed; and much that was printed was
never spoken. Fictitious names were assumed, and sentiments put into

the mouths of the supposed collocutors, without any reference to the real opinions of anyone who was actually present.[7]

However, from the other accounts, it can be taken that the statement of conclusions reached does have the status of an agreed document. These conclusions were stated to be as follows:

1. That the present Christian dispensation is not to pass insensibly into the millennial state by gradual increase of the preaching of the Gospel; but that it is to be terminated by judgements, ending in the destruction of this visible Church and polity, in the same manner as the Jewish dispensation had been terminated.

2. That during the time that these judgements are falling upon Christendom, the Jews will be restored to their own land.

3. That the judgements will fall principally, if not exclusively, upon Christendom, and begin with that part of the Church of God which has been most highly favoured, and is therefore most deeply responsible.

4. That the termination of these judgements is to be succeeded by that period of universal blessedness to all mankind, and even to the beasts, which is commonly called the Millennium.

5. That the second Advent of Messiah precedes or takes place at the commencement of the Millennium.

6. That a great period of 1260 years commenced in the reign of Justinian, and terminated at the French Revolution; and that the vials of the Apocalypse began then to be poured out; that our blessed Lord will shortly appear, and that therefore it is the duty of all, who so believe, to press these considerations on the attention of all men.[8]

Comparison of these conclusions with the original syllabus indicates the extent of the ground covered during the first four Conferences. Views expressed at the Conferences and ideas developed from them were published in *The Morning Watch*, edited by John Tudor (1784–1861), from March 1829.[9] Tudor was a Welsh artist and writer who was one of the Conference participants and, later, an apostle.

The pre-millennial Adventist elements in the conclusions (above) were a striking contrast with much of the evangelical eschatology of the day. In essence, the 'pre-millennial' position was that the Second Coming of Christ would occur *before* the inauguration of a universal kingdom of peace on earth which should last for 1000 years. In the

[7] H. Drummond, *Dialogues on Prophecy* (London: Nisbet, 1828), i, p. iii.

[8] Ibid., pp. ii–iii.

[9] Published quarterly by James Nisbet of Berners Street, London, until the June issue of 1833. The title was inspired by Isaiah 21: 11–12, which was quoted on its title page.

eighteenth century, the 'post-millennial' view had come into prominence amongst evangelicals:

In harmony with the Lockean tradition of rationalism and optimism, a new eschatology, most influentially stated by the Salisbury rector Daniel Whitby, emphasized the continued success of the church, the steady improvement of man and society, and the eventual culmination of Christian history in the coming of a literal millennium. Only at the end of that blessed age was Christ's coming expected.[10]

The French Revolution had made pre-millennial Adventism much less tenable, and was largely responsible for the rapid growth of the prophetic and apocalyptic Adventism of the nineteenth century.

The conclusions reached at Albury were considerably influenced by Irving, whose developing interest in eschatology was greatly enhanced through undertaking the translation into English of *Venida del Mesias en Gloria y Megestad* (*The Coming of the Messiah in Glory and Majesty*) by the Jesuit priest, Manuel Lacunza (1731–1801), writing under the pseudonym of 'Juan Josafat Ben-Ezra, a converted Jew'. Lacunza was born in Chile in 1731 and admitted to the Society of Jesus in 1747. He was forced out of his country in 1767 when the Society was suppressed by the Spanish Crown, and spent the remainder of his life as a recluse in Italy, where he died in 1801. This one major work by him was entered in the *Index Librorum Prohibitorum*. It was not published during the author's lifetime, though manuscript copies were circulating in Latin America and Spain from about 1812. An abridged version was published at the Isle of Leon, followed in 1816 by a complete version in four volumes published by the Diplomatic Agent of the Argentine Republic in London. Irving's translation, which runs to 766 pages and for which he taught himself Spanish in a remarkably short time, was published in London by Seeley and Son in 1827.[11] He prefaced it with a translator's *Preliminary Discourse* in which he expanded his eschatological beliefs to the extent of 194 pages. In addition, there was also included a short critique by a certain Father Paul of the Conception of the Order of the Barefooted Carmelites, dated 17 December 1812.

In the Summer of 1826, Irving, together with Way and James Hatley Frere, had founded the Society for the Investigation of Prophecy. Frere was a pre-millennialist and author of several books

---

[10] Sandeen, *Roots of Fundamentalism*, 5.
[11] Lacunza's work is discussed in some detail in Ch. V.

and many articles on prophetic interpretation, of which he was a leading scholar.[12] However, at the invitation of Drummond, its meetings were subsumed within those taking place at Albury, which then became for a time the principal centre in England for prophetic studies.

The Charismatic Root: Events in Scotland

The charismatic root of the Catholic Apostolics had its beginnings in what were to be interpreted as divine responses to fervent prayer for an outpouring of the Holy Spirit to revive the low condition of religion in Britain. In 1826 (the year of the first Albury Conference) the Revd James Haldane Stewart, Anglican Priest at Percy Chapel, London—formerly curate at Basildon to the Revd William Marsh, a noted millenarian and staunch supporter of mission to the Jews— published a pamphlet which had a very wide circulation stressing that only an outpouring of the Holy Spirit could provide a solution to the many problems and difficulties facing the world.[13] This had become essential, he claimed, because of the disquieting portents of ominous times, the total inadequacy of human means to ameliorate the state of mankind, the supineness of many professing Christians, and the manifest increase of the activity of Satan. He referred to Scriptural promises of an abundant giving of the Holy Spirit, which were only partly fulfilled at Pentecost, and whose complete fulfilment was yet to come. It was only with this fulfilment that the kingdom of the Lord Jesus Christ could be established. Prayer for this outpouring was needed from the whole Church and could be a means of uniting the divisions within it. The suggested form of prayer included the following words:

Lord, fill the earth with Thy glory. Pour Thy Spirit upon all flesh. Convert the Jews. Convert the Gentiles. Destroy the power of Satan, and reign Thyself for ever and ever.[14]

The pamphlet had been composed whilst its author was staying in Nice on account of ill health, but, following its appearance, he

---

[12] His most important work was *A Combined View of the Prophecies of Daniel, Esdras, and S. John Shewing That All Prophetic Writings Are Formed upon One Plan . . .* (London: Hatchard, 1815).

[13] J. H. Stewart, *Importance of Special Prayer for the General Outpouring of the Holy Spirit* (London: Religious Tract Society, 1826).

[14] Ibid. 27–8.

travelled extensively in England and Scotland, preaching in both churches and chapels and exhorting their ministers and heads of families to join together in using the prayer. He was successful, and a large number of people responded to his wishes. He also participated in the Albury Conferences.

The fifth and last of the Conferences met in 1830 in response to an emergency summons to consider reports that there was indeed a divine response to this prayer manifestly taking place in Scotland. These reports included accounts of the life and death of a remarkable 'saint', of ecstatic utterances, of cases of miraculous healing, of inspired interpretations of Scripture, and of remarkable public preaching from within the Scottish Church against its narrow Calvinistic doctrine of election—preaching which declared that salvation was offered to all. All these reports related to events taking place in the country districts bordering on the Clyde.

Details of the life of Isabella Campbell of the parish of Rosneath were published as a memoir by the parish minister, the Revd Robert Story.[15] So great was the impression made by the memoir, of which more than 6000 copies were sold within a few weeks of its publication, that there was a continuous stream of pilgrims from both sides of the border to see the place where one now widely regarded as a saint had lived, and to converse with her surviving sister. It was not long before the sister, Mary, began to utter words in an incomprehensible tongue.

At about the same time, at Port Glasgow, a certain Margaret Macdonald and her two brothers, James and George, had ecstatic experiences, details of which were later recorded by the Revd Robert Norton, MD, of Greenock.[16] The most remarkable of these occurred whilst Margaret was seemingly on her deathbed. Her doctor had confirmed that she was beyond medical help. Norton's account was as follows:

the power of the Spirit came upon her. She said 'there will be a mighty baptism of the spirit this day', and then broke forth in a most marvellous setting forth of the wonderful works of God, and . . . continued with little or no intermission for two or three hours, in mingled praise, prayer, and exhortation. At dinner-time James and George came home as usual, whom she addressed at great length, concluding with a solemn prayer for James that he might *at that time* be endowed with the power of

---

[15] R. Story, *Peace in Believing* (n.p., Lusk, 1829).
[16] R. Norton, *Memoirs of James and George Macdonald* (Dundee: Shaw, 1840).

the Holy Ghost. Almost immediately James calmly said, 'I have got it'. He walked to the window and stood silent for a minute or two. I looked at him and almost trembled, there was such a change upon his whole countenance. He then with a step and manner of the most indescribable majesty walked up to Margaret's bed-side, and addressed her in these words of the twentieth psalm, 'arise and stand upright'. He repeated the words, took her by the hand, and she arose.[17]

Although Norton's account was not published until 1840, news of what had passed spread rapidly, and within days the house was scarcely ever empty of visitors.

There was an equally remarkable sequel. By 1830 Mary Campbell, following the death of her betrothed (a young missionary), had become seriously ill—consumptive like her sister Isabella and also suffering from an incurable heart condition. James Macdonald wrote to her, commanding her to rise up and walk as his sister had done. The following were her own words:

I had scarcely read the first page when I became quite overpowered, and laid it aside for a few minutes; but I had no rest in my mind until I took it up again and began to read. As I read every word came home with power, and when I came to the command to rise, it came home with a power which no words can describe; it was felt to be indeed the voice of Christ; it was such a Voice as could not be resisted; a mighty power was instantaneously exerted upon me: I felt as if I had been lifted from off the earth, and all my diseases taken off me at the Voice of Christ. I was verily made in a moment to stand upon my feet, leap and walk, sing and rejoice.[18]

Shortly after this event, both the Macdonald brothers began to speak in tongues, and within weeks a total of nine persons followed suit during prayer meetings. By no means were all the utterances incomprehensible, however; in many cases there were ecstatic interpretations of Scripture and ecstatic extempore prayers.

All the participants in these remarkable and well-recorded events had been greatly influenced by the preaching of the Revd John McLeod Campbell, Minister of Row, and others associated with him, to the effect that Christ's atonement was available for all. As this was in sharp contradiction to the strict Calvinistic view of election which dominated the Presbyterian Church at that time, Campbell's preaching was condemned by the General Assembly of his Church,

---

[17] Ibid. 107–8.   [18] Ibid. 110.

and in 1831 he was deprived of his parish. However, by this time his preaching had become widely known and had resulted in the formation of many house groups, a number of which experienced what came to be called 'Baptism of the Spirit'. As well as being influenced by Campbell, the Macdonald brothers had also accepted the doctrine of the permanence of the miraculous gifts of the Spirit being preached by an associate of Irving, the Revd Alexander Scott, who had preached on the charismata of the Spirit for Campbell at Row in 1829, an occasion which had led to manifestations of tongues and prophesying. Scott's visit had been arranged following a meeting between Campbell and Irving in London at which the two had reached agreement on a number of issues.

Scott was a graduate of the University of Glasgow and had been licensed by the Presbytery of Paisley. He first met Irving in 1828, agreeing to be his assistant in London. In 1830 he was appointed to the Scottish Church at Woolwich. However, his licence was withdrawn by the General Assembly in 1831 because he accepted Irving's doctrine of Christ's humanity—though he did not accept the tongues in Irving's church as supernatural gifts. In 1848 he became Professor of Language and Literature at University College, London, and in 1851 Principal of Owens College (later Manchester University).

The events which took place in an otherwise unremarkable part of Scotland have been presented in some detail because of their influence upon members of the Albury Conferences. The final Conference had decided that they should be formally investigated. In fact, it was an independent group who visited Scotland to make the investigation, though with the knowledge of Irving and others attending the Conference of 1830. Accounts as to the number of persons conducting the investigation differ, but within the limits of six and eight. All were Anglicans, though one—a Dr J. Thompson—regularly attended Irving's church. Two of the members, both of whom were to be of great significance in the history of the Catholic Apostolic Church, were a young London lawyer, John Bate Cardale (1803–55)—later to be the 'Pillar of Apostles'—and a schoolmaster, Edward Oliver Taplin (1800–62)—later to become the 'Pillar of Prophets'.

The group stayed for three weeks in the West of Scotland, attending prayer meetings and discussing the manifestations with those who had experienced or witnessed them. Cardale described one of the prayer meetings in a letter to the editor of *The Morning Watch*:

The mode of proceeding is for each person who takes a part first to read a Psalm in metre, which is sung by the meeting; then a chapter from the Bible; and he then prays. On this occasion, after two other gentlemen, J. M'D. read and prayed. His prayer was most remarkable. The sympathizing with the mind of our Saviour; interceding for a world which tramples on his blood and rejects his mercy, and for the church which grieves the Holy Ghost; the humiliation for sin, and the aspirations after holiness, were totally different from anything I had ever before heard. He then, in the course of prayer, and while engaged in intercession for others, began speaking in an unknown tongue; and after speaking for some time he sung, or rather chanted, in the same tongue. He then rose, and we all rose with him; and, in a very loud voice, and with great solemnity, he addressed us in the same tongue for a considerable time: he then, with the same loudness of voice, and manner, addressed us in English, calling on us to prepare for trial, for we had great trials to go through for the testimony of Jesus; to crucify the flesh; to lay aside every weight; to put far from us our fleshly wisdom, power, and strength; and to stay us in our God. . . . The meeting concluded with a psalm, a chapter, and prayer from another gentleman.[19]

In the same letter, Cardale described how one of the women present, 'who had received the Spirit [of prophecy], but had not received the gift of tongues', began to speak of the coming judgements. He wrote:

It is impossible to describe the solemnity and grandeur, both of words and manner, in which she gave testimony to the judgements coming on the earth; but also directed the church to the coming of the Lord as her hope of deliverance.[20]

Cardale's reaction to what the investigating group witnessed was typical of all its members. On their return from Scotland, three of them were invited to meet Drummond, Irving, and a small group of Anglican members of the Conference. It is not surprising, in view of such reaction, that the conclusion was reached that the manifestations were supernatural acts in the power of the Holy Spirit. What was found especially convincing was the simple life-style of the people visited, together with the complete absence of 'anything like

---

[19] *MW* viii, Dec. 1830, p. 870. [20] Ibid. 870–1.

fanaticism or enthusiasm'. They were deemed to be persons of simplicity of character and great common sense, living lives of obvious holiness 'in close communion with God, and in love towards Him, and towards all men'. Cardale added:

> They have no fanciful theology of their own: they make no pretensions to deep knowledge: they are the very opposite of sectarians, both in conduct and principle: they do not assume to be teachers: they are not deeply read; but they seek to be taught of God, in the perusal of, and meditation on His revealed word.[21]

News of the investigation's conclusions spread rapidly to the various groups who had gathered in response to Haldane Stewart's pamphlet, and became the subject of Irving's preaching. It was widely held that the events in Scotland were a direct divine response to the prayer for the outpouring of the Spirit. It was not long before similar manifestations made their appearance, the most notable of which (though by no means the only example) were associated with Irving's church in Regent Square, London.

The Revd Edward Irving

The details of Irving's life and ministry are too well known to be repeated here other than in outline: extensive accounts are readily available to scholars and others.[22] It is, however, unfortunate that Mrs Oliphant's hagiographic work, *The Life of Edward Irving*, was for nearly a century the only readily available biography. As a result, other works on Irving have tended to rely heavily on Mrs Oliphant, who was unsympathetic to the Catholic Apostolic apostles, regarding them (unjustly) as the destroyers of her hero.

Irving was born in Annan, Dumfries, on 4 August 1792. He went to Edinburgh University at the age of 13, graduating in 1809, and deciding to enter the Church of Scotland's ministry. He combined his theological studies with working as a schoolmaster first at Haddington (1810–12), and then at Kirkaldy (1812–18) where he began his life-long friendship with Thomas Carlyle. In 1819 he became assistant to the famous Dr Chalmers at St John's Church, Glasgow. Thomas Chalmers (1780–1847) was born in Anstruther, Fife, educated at St Andrews University, and ordained Minister of Kilmany in 1803, at the same time undertaking the teaching of

[21] *MW* viii, Dec. 1830, p. 873.   [22] See Ch. I, § 1, and n. 11.

mathematics and chemistry at St Andrews. He moved to Glasgow in 1815 and became famous for his oratory, first at the Tron parish and then at St John's. He was appointed Professor of Moral Philosophy at St Andrews in 1823, moving to the Chair of Theology at Edinburgh in 1827. On account of struggles over patronage, he left the Church of Scotland in 1843, along with 470 other ministers, and founded the Free Church, of whose College he was Principal until his death. Chalmers was a prolific writer: his works, published during his lifetime, covered scientific, economic, and ecclesiastical topics. The posthumous works, edited by William Hanna, ran to nine volumes appearing over the period 1847 to 1849.[23]

Irving worked with Chalmers for only two years, for in 1821 he received a call from the Caledonian Chapel[24] in Hatton Garden, London, which he took up in the following year. By 1823 this little-known Chapel had become a centre of attention for London's fashionable and wealthy society, initially because of a chance remark made by George Canning in the House of Commons.[25] The chapel was crowded for Irving's Sunday sermons: it has been said that, on one occasion at least, the queue of carriages waiting to return the worshippers to their homes was four miles in length. It was not merely the content of his sermons which attracted his hearers, but also his remarkable presence and personality. He was usually described as a tall, handsome man with a large head and a mass of black hair, though with an appearance slightly marred by a squint. Carlyle, his most reliable biographer, wrote of his appearance:

[He] looked very neat, self-possessed, and enviable . . . with coal-black hair, swarthy clear complexion; very straight on his feet; and, except for the glaring squint alone, decidedly handsome.[26]

Of his character, the same writer said:

He was . . . never ungenerous, never ignoble: only an enemy could have called him 'vain' . . . His pleasure in being *loved* by others was very great; and this, if you looked well, was manifest in him when the case offered; never more, or *worse* than this, in any case; and this too he had

[23] Hanna also edited Chalmers' correspondence, published in Edinburgh in 1853. See esp. N. Hanna, *Memoirs of the life and writings of T. Chalmers D.D. LL.D.*, 4 vols. (Edinburgh: 1849–52).
[24] For a history of the Scots Church in London, see J. Hair, *Regent Square* (London: Nisbet, 1899), and G. G. Cameron, *The Scots Kirk in London* (Oxford: Becket, 1979).
[25] See Oliphant, *Life*, 79. [26] Carlyle, *Reminiscences*, 180.

well in check at all times: if this was vanity, then he might by some be called a little vain; if not, not. To trample on the smallest mortal or be tyrannous . . . was never at any moment Irving's turn; no man that I have known had a sunnier type of character, or *so* little of hatred towards any man or thing. On the whole, *less* of rage in him than I ever saw combined with such a fund of courage and conviction. Noble Irving . . . generous, wise, beneficient, all his dealings and discourses with me were.[27]

Drummond was equally impressed:

a man who of all I know has the largest head, and largest, and kindest heart of any man I ever met in the course of my mortal pilgrimage . . . this great saint . . .[28]

Of his early preaching, Carlyle wrote:

From the first, Irving read his discourses, but not in a servile manner; and of attitude, gesture, elocution, there was no neglect:— his voice was very fine; melodious depth, strength, clearness its chief characteristics; I have heard more pathetic voices, going more direct to the heart, both in the way of indignation and of pity, but recollect none that better filled the ear. He affected the Miltonic and Old-English Puritan style, and strove visibly to imitate it more and more, till almost the end of his career, when indeed it had become his own . . . [His] style was sufficiently surprising to his hide-bound Presbyterian public; and this was but a slight circumstance to the novelty of the matter he set forth upon them. . . . There was doubtless something of rashness in the young Irving's way of preaching; nor perhaps quite enough of pure, complete and serious conviction (which ought to have lain *silent* a good while before it took to speaking): in general, I own to have felt that there was present a certain inflation or spiritual bombast in much of this, a trifle of unconscious playactorism (highly unconscious, but not quite absent) which had been unavoidable to the brave young prophet and reformer. But brave he was; and bearing full upon the truth, if not yet quite attaining it; and as to the offence he gave, our withers were unwrung; I . . . grinned in secret to think of the hides it was piercing! . . . In Irving's Preaching there was present or prefigured, generous opulence of ability in all kinds (except perhaps the very highest kind, not even prefigured?) but much of it was still crude: and this was the reception it had, for a

[27] Carlyle, *Reminiscences*, 230.
[28] Letter, Drummond to Charles Kirkpatrick Sharpe (1810–41) of Christ Church, Oxford, 11 May 1830 (Northumberland collection).

good few years to come; indeed, to the very end, he never carried all the world along with him, as some have done with far fewer qualities.[29]

Of his later style, Carlyle was to write:

Irving's preaching . . . did not strike me as superior to his Scotch performances of past time, or, in private fact, inspire me with any complete or pleasant feeling . . . The force and weight of what he urged was undeniable; the potent faculty at work, like that of a Samson heavily striding along with the gates of Gaza on his shoulders; but there was a want of spontaneity and simplicity, a something of strained and aggravated, of elaborately intentional, which kept gaining on the mind. One felt the bad element to be and to have been unwholesome to the honourable soul.[30]

Much less favourable comment on Irving's abilities appeared in 1823 in *The Times* of 15 July, and in a popular parody of his preaching, *The Trial of Edward Irving: A Cento of Criticism*, which ran to eleven editions in only two years. He was flattered by the appearance of Canning and other notables sitting at his feed Sunday by Sunday, but inevitably their fickle interest waned—his fashionable popularity did not last out the year.

In May 1824, Irving was invited to preach the anniversary sermon for the London Missionary Society, which had been founded in 1795 (as 'The Missionary Society') by Anglicans, Congregationalists, Presbyterians, and Wesleyans to promote Christian missions to the heathen—it was ultimately to be subsumed within the Congregational Council for World Mission. At this time, it was thought that Britain was eminently suited to sponsor missionary activity because it was held to be untainted by Rome—a view which was one of the strands in later evangelical opposition to Catholic emancipation. The treasurer of the Missionary Society was a certain Joseph Hardcastle, a keen student of prophecy who had anticipated that the 'third woe' (Apoc. 11: 14) would be fulfilled in 1797. Irving's sermon lasted for three hours, his principal thesis being an attack on the concept of any man-made organization being able to advance the Christian faith effectively.[31] Thus he attacked the very body which he had been invited to praise—an attack which caused a considerable stir.

---

[29] Carlyle, *Reminiscences*, 195–6.
[30] Ibid. 254.
[31] The sermon was published in 1825 as *For Missionaries after the Apostolic School: A Series of Orations.*

Nevertheless, in the following year he was invited to preach the anniversary sermon of the Continental Society, at which he took the opportunity to expound at great length the prophetic interpretation of history together with a pre-millennial eschatology.[32] The identification of the Roman Church with Babylon in this address, together with the contemporary agitation over Catholic emancipation, led many of his hearers to assume that it was to the latter that he was referring, though there was disagreement as to whether he supported it or opposed it. From this time onwards, he continually preached on the imminent advent of Christ, expounding his rejection of the popular evangelical 'error' that the whole world would be converted to Christ; and in 1826 his views were greatly strengthened when he translated Lacunza's book (see above, and esp. Ch. V, § 3). Later, he was to extend 'Babylon' to include the Protestant Churches because they refused to accept the charismatic phenomena which occurred in his congregation (see below) as the voice of the Holy Spirit. He also attacked evangelical societies, claiming that many of their members used them primarily to obtain the necessary patronage for obtaining powerful positions in public life.

In 1827, Irving opened the new National Scotch Church in Regent Square, London, with almost a thousand pew sittings taken—a far cry from the mere fifty members at the Caledonian Chapel at the time of his arrival in London just five years previously. Dr Chalmers, who participated in the opening service, commented in his diary:

I really fear lest his prophecies, and the excessive length and weariness of his services, may unship him altogether . . .[33]

The following year he revisited Scotland for a highly successful preaching and lecturing tour in which he drew large crowds to lectures on the Apocalypse held at 6 a.m. Much of the substance of his dissertations was published in *The Last Days: A Discourse on the Evil Character of these our Times* (London, 1828). Here he made it clear that he regarded toleration of Catholic emancipation as one of many reasons for an impending judgement on Christendom. A second Scottish tour, undertaken in 1829, also drew large crowds,

---

[32] An expanded version of the sermon, dedicated to Frere, appeared in 1826 as *Babylon and Infidelity, Foredoomed of God.*

[33] Hanna, *Chalmers*, iii. 163 (entry for 19 May 1827).

but some of these proved hostile and a number of churches were closed to him.

Irving, who had married in 1823, had lost three of his four children by 1830 either in childbirth or in infancy. In July of that year his remaining child, a son, lay desperately ill. Despite the fervent prayers of his wife and himself together with their friends, the boy died. Irving was, for a while, demoralized by the blow: it seemed to undermine his ardent belief in the efficacy of prayer and the continuing possibility of miracles, which he did not accept as limited to the period of the early Church. When the reports of the occurrences in Scotland reached London, he saw them as vindicating his shaken beliefs. Prayer meetings, seeking the outpouring of the Holy Spirit, sprang up widely in London and elsewhere. Irving made the gifts of the Spirit a major component of his sermons. Expectations were further heightened with the apparently miraculous healing of Elizabeth Fancourt, a daughter of an Anglican Clergyman in London, through the prayers of a friend.[34]

The Manifestations at Regent Square

Manifestations in London began to occur in 1831. Cardale's wife and sister both spoke with tongues on 30 April, but his parish priest, the Revd Baptist Noel, refused to accept them as of divine inspiration.[35] As a result, the Cardale family joined Irving's congregation, and attended the prayer meetings which Irving was holding both in Church, in his own home, and in the homes of a number of church members. In August, Taplin began to speak in tongues and to prophesy, but Irving remained adamant at this time that such manifestations could not be allowed in the public services.

On Sunday 16 October of the same year, immediately following the reading of the Scriptures at the morning service, a young woman (Miss Hall, a governess) rushed into the vestry and prophesied there, behind closed doors, in a loud voice which could be heard all over the building. Irving tried to reassure the startled congregation with explanations based on 1 Corinthians 14, and, when the woman returned to her seat, to calm her with soothing words. Following the

[34] For accounts, see *The Christian Observer*, 1830, p. 708, and R. Norton, *The Restoration of Apostles and Prophets* (London: Bosworth, 1861), 44–5.

[35] See B. Noel, *Remarks on the Revival of Miraculous Powers in the Church* (London: 1831).

service, in the presence of the elders and deacons, he was exhorted in utterances by the same person to follow his Master and not to shrink from the insults of others. By the time of the evening service on the same day, a large crowd had assembled, many of whom had had no previous connection with Irving's church. There was considerable disorder whilst Irving preached on the events of the morning, exhorting his hearers to receive the spiritual gifts with love. As he finished speaking, to the great consternation of the assembly, Taplin spoke in a great voice—'as though it would rend the roof'—first in a tongue and then with the words:

Why will ye flee from the voice of God? The Lord is in the midst of you. Why will ye flee from His voice? Ye cannot flee from it in the day of judgement![36]

There were screams from many of those who rushed to the doors to escape; others stood on the pews and other furnishings in order to get a better view. Irving, with outstretched arms, prayed in a loud voice: 'O Lord, still the tumult of the people!' When order was eventually obtained, he told those who remained that what they had heard was the voice of the living God.

The following Sunday (23 October) immense crowds had gathered, and the atmosphere in the church was a mixture of expectation and hostility. Irving preached on 'the Antichrist'. When the manifestations began, there were calls of 'Blasphemy!', followed by hissing, hooting, and a general disorder that threatened to disintegrate into actual violence. Irving, worried about the safety of his church members, announced at the prayer meeting which followed that all prophesying in public had to end, but by the next Sunday (30 October) he had retracted his prohibition and committed himself and his congregation to God's care, though he also sought protection from magistrates and the police. The die was cast.

The manifestations had full rein, and many of the church members became 'infected'. The church doors had to be closed hours before the advertised times of services—services which had to be conducted, not only accompanied by the interruptions of the prophets, but also (for several weeks) by the hammering on the doors on the part of the large crowds who had failed to gain admission. Outside reactions were, for the most part, unfavourable, though it was admitted that in their daily lives the prophets were

[36] Norton, *Memoirs*, 49.

usually quiet, normal, even self-effacing people who would not otherwise be suspected of exhibitionism.[37]

Similar, though less publicized occurrences were taking place at prayer meetings held by Drummond at Albury. Here, there was strong opposition from the rector, the Revd Hugh McNeile (later Dean of Ripon), who, though he had been an active participant in the Conferences, taking the chair at many of the meetings, could not accept the prophetic gifts, arguing that the wisdom of the Holy Spirit lay only with the ordained ministry. As a result, Drummond left the Parish Church, whose living was in his gift, to form his own group of persons who accepted the gifts as being of the Holy Spirit, this group soon associating itself with those centred on Irving. There were calls for Irving to ordain Drummond as pastor for the Albury group, but Drummond was not prepared to receive such ordination, for he did not accept the validity of Presbyterian ordinations.[38]

Because of the manifestations at his church, Irving was expelled from the Presbytery of London. Further, according to the trust deed of the Regent Square church, the Presbytery was the arbitrator in any dispute Irving might have with his own Kirk Session. The Session pleaded with him to abandon ways which they regarded as not in the tradition of the Scottish Church, in particular objecting to the active participation in services of those who were not duly authorized ministers. The local dispute being unresolved, appeal was made to the Presbytery on 22 March 1832, and the hearing took place on 26 April. Irving was supported at the hearing by Duncan Mackenzie (one of the elders), David Ker (a deacon), and Taplin, who interrupted the proceedings with words of prophecy. All testified to their belief in the divine inspiration of the tongues.

Irving's Expulsion and Deposition

The judgement was published on 2 May, and it required Irving's removal from his charge. Accordingly, on 4 May, the trustees of the Regent Square church locked Irving and his supporters out of the building, and he was forced to conduct his prayer service in the open air. Eventually, he and his congregation were able to use the Socialist Rotunda for worship, moving again, after some five months, to the

[37] Accounts of the manifestations appeared in *The Times*, 19 Oct.; 15, 21, and 28 Nov.; and 22 and 26 Dec. 1831.
[38] Drummond, *Narrative of Circumstances*, 7.

Exhibition Hall in Newman Street (also known as the 'West Picture Gallery' after the painter Benjamin West who had exhibited there). The Newman Street church was opened for worship on 19 October and became the principal centre of Catholic Apostolic activities in London for some twenty years.

The disciplinary action against Irving did not stop, however, with his expulsion from the London charge. Following a motion in the General Assembly of the Scottish Church, he was arraigned before the Presbytery at Annan, in the Parish Church of which town he had been ordained. This time his enemies had managed to arrange that the charge was one of Christological heresy (see below). The case was heard in the dimly lit church on 13 March 1833. Irving was found guilty after a long hearing and was sentenced to be deposed from the Church of Scotland ministry. However, immediately before the prayers which had to precede the formal pronouncement of the sentence, the Revd David Dow (Minister of Irongray and a friend of Irving) was moved to cry ecstatically:

Arise, depart! Flee ye out of her! Ye cannot pray. How can ye pray to Christ, Whom you deny? Depart, depart! Flee, flee![39]

The Christological Controversy

The important point of Christological theology, which was made the excuse for the charges at Irving's trial at Annan, related to the human nature taken by the Second Person of the Trinity at the Incarnation: was it fallen or unfallen? Irving was quite clear in his belief that it was the former, though he was equally clear that Christ did not sin. He always maintained that the Son of God inherited from His Mother a humanity existing under the conditions which had been imposed by Adam's sin—this he regarded as essential if fallen humanity was to be redeemed. Equally, he maintained that, through the indwelling presence of the Holy Spirit, the man Jesus was Himself entirely free of all sin. Those who had heard his sermons on this subject generally commended their content; thus, his elders particularly requested that they should appear in three volumes of sermons being prepared for publication.

---

[39] W. Wilks, *Edward Irving: An Ecclesiastical and Literary Biography* (London: Freeman, 1854), 250.

However, the Revd Henry Cole, an Anglican, took it upon himself to expose in a pamphlet (taking the form of a letter to Irving) what he regarded as heretical teaching. Cole was a graduate of Cambridge (Clare College) and known for his pamphlet *Popular Geology subversive of Divine Revelation*, in which he attacked from a fundamentalist viewpoint the lectures of the Revd Adam Sedgwick, Woodwardian professor of Geology at Cambridge. Cole had visited Irving's church once, and after the service had talked with him in the vestry. It is not unlikely that Irving, who was a highly volatile preacher, had from time to time used phrases which he would afterwards wish to modify. Cole describes himself as hearing words which made him 'tremble from head to foot'. His interview is said to have ended with him asking the question, 'Do you then, sir, really believe that the body of the Son of God was a mortal, corrupt, and corruptible body like that of all mankind—the same body as yours and mine?', a question to which Irving replied in the affirmative.[40]

Irving's views have to be seen, however, in the context of his overall teaching on the Incarnation, which he published in 1830.[41] The material was presented in four main sections:

I. Statement of the doctrine from Scripture.
II. Confirmation of it from the Creeds of the Primitive Church and of the Church of Scotland.
III. Objections to the true doctrine considered.
IV. The doctrines of the Faith which stand or fall with it.

To these there were added a Preface and a Conclusion. The point at issue was stated with great clarity:

Whether Christ's flesh had the grace of sinlessness and incorruption from its proper nature, or from the indwelling of the Holy Ghost. I say the latter. I assert that in its proper nature it was the flesh of his mother; but by the Holy Ghost's quickening and inhabiting of it, it was preserved sinless and incorruptible. This work of the Holy Ghost, I further assert, was done in consequence of the Son's humbling himself to be made flesh. The Son said, 'I come'; the Father said, 'I prepare thee a body to come in'; and the Holy Ghost prepared the body out of the Virgin's substance. And so, by the threefold acting of the Trinity, was the Christ constituted a Divine and human nature, joined in personal

[40] An account of Cole's encounter with Irving can be found in Hair, *Regent Square*, 89–90.
[41] E. Irving, *The Orthodox and Catholic Doctrine of Our Lord's Human Nature* (London: Baldwin and Craddock, 1830).

union for ever. This I hold to be the orthodox faith of the Christian church.[42]

Irving was inspired by a wish to counteract contemporary teaching, which he saw as having Docetist, Gnostic, Eutychian, and Monothelite tendencies, whereby the balance of the two natures of Christ was distorted. The Docetists considered the human body and sufferings of Christ as apparent rather than real. The Gnostics regarded Christ's body as being temporarily inhabited by a divine being—a kind of phantasm—come to bring 'gnosis' (secret knowledge). The Eutychians denied that Christ's human nature was consubstantial with that of mankind, and maintained that there was only one nature in Christ after the union of the human and the divine. The Monothelites believed that Christ had only one will. All these heresies were condemned by Ecumenical Councils, but Irving believed that he could detect them in much contemporary preaching and writing. In particular, he saw amongst some of his contemporaries a desire to magnify the divine nature at the expense of the human, at times exaggerated to the extent of presenting Christ as a phantasmal figure, thus undermining in particular not only incarnational theology but also the true significance of the Resurrection and its promise. In his Preface he wrote:

The great point between us, the precious truth for which we contend, is, not whether Christ's flesh was holy—for surely the man who saith we deny this blasphemeth against the manifest truth—but whether during his life it was one with us in all its infirmities and liabilities to temptation, or whether, by the miraculous generation, it underwent a change so as to make it a different body from the rest of the brethren. They argue for an identity of origin merely; we argue for an identity of life also. They argue for an inherent holiness; we argue for a holiness maintained by the Person of the Son, through the operation of the Holy Ghost. They say, that though his body was changed in the generation, he was still our fellow in all temptations and sympathies: we deny that it could be so: for change is change; and if his body was changed in the conception, it was not in its life as ours is. In one word, we present believers with a real life; a suffering, mortal flesh; a real death and a real resurrection of this flesh of ours: they present the life, death, and resurrection of a changed flesh: and so create a chasm between Him and us which no knowledge, nor even imagination, can overleap. And in so

---

[42] Irving, *Orthodox and Catholic Doctrine*, 53.

doing, they subvert all foundations: there is nothing left standing in our faith of Godhead, in our hopes of manhood.[43]

Underlying Irving's concern was the fear of any diminution of the promise of a future resurrection from the dead of which the Resurrection of Christ represented the first-fruits. In this, perhaps especially, he was to have a lasting influence on Catholic Apostolic theology.

The Apostolic Roots and the Passing of Irving

During the years 1832 to 1835 there took place a gradual process of integration into an identifiable body of Christians of the various groups associated with prayer for the outpouring of the Holy Spirit, the appearance of spiritual gifts, and the awareness of the impending second advent of Christ. The groups which found themselves experiencing this process of convergence came from within the Church of England as well as from the Scottish Church and English Dissent. The separation from their traditional places of worship was usually a matter of considerable unwillingness and regret, and followed expulsions rather than from any desire to form a sect—an idea which the Catholic Apostolic Church members were always to reject. Examples of such expulsions can be found both in Britain and abroad—for the manifestations occurred very shortly on the Continent also, particularly in Germany.

The German manifestations were associated with a religious revival in the area of the Roman Catholic parish of Karlshudd, Bavaria, which began in 1827 and culminated in ecstatic utterances prophesying the restoration of apostles, prophets, evangelists, and pastors to the Church, the nearness of the Second Advent, and the restoration of the spiritual gifts of the primitive Church. The priest of the parish, Fr Johann Evangelist Georg Lutz, was eventually suspended, disciplined, and finally excommunicated in 1857, after which he ministered within the Catholic Apostolic Church. This is the first recorded instance of a Roman Catholic group being incorporated into this body.[44]

It would not have been possible for the various scattered groups spread throughout Britain, which had come into loose association

[43] Ibid., x–xi.
[44] For an account of these events see L. W. Scholler, *A Chapter of Church History from South Germany*, tr. W. Wallis (London: Longmans, Green, 1894).

during the 1830s, to have become welded together into a single communion without some form of centralized leadership. This was provided by the gradual emergence of an apostleship. Intimations that a need for apostles was beginning to be felt can be found in a number of the ecstatic utterances. We are told:

> It was declared in utterance that the Lord would again send apostles, by the laying on of whose hands would follow the baptism of fire, which should subdue the flesh and burn out sin; and should give to the disciplines of Christ the full freedom of the Holy Ghost, and full and final victory over the world.[45]

Amongst the prayers being offered, there began to be those which explicitly called for a restoration of the apostolic office, and these were reinforced by prophecies that this would indeed be granted to the Church. On 7 November 1832 these prophecies appeared to be fulfilled for the first time. Accounts differ in detail, and it is not absolutely clear from the sources whether or not there was more than one separate occasion on which the call of the first of the new apostles took place—it seems likely, however, that it was a multiple call. What is clear is that Drummond had risen at the end of the first service held in the Newman Street church and had given an ecstatic blessing, and that Cardale had spoken in prophecy the next day.

The date of this first service at Newman Street is given as 19 October in some sources and 24 October in others. Norton, who gives the earlier date, states that Cardale's call came 'a few days after'.[46] He does not state that this call was spoken by Drummond. It is therefore possible that, as some sources suggest, Cardale was called to the apostleship on more than one occasion. It is clear, however, that the call accepted by members of the Catholic Apostolic body was that from Drummond. An account of the call of Cardale to be the first new apostle was given by his sister in a letter written nearly forty years later:

> On the evening of November 7th, 1832, I was at a prayer meeting at Mr. Irving's house amongst a great many more, and my brother engaged in prayer, and was very earnestly asking the Lord to give us the Holy Ghost, when Mr. Drummond rose from his knees and went across the

---

[45] R. Baxter, *Narrative of Facts, characterizing the Supernatural Manifestations in members of Mr. Irving's Congregation and other individuals, in England and Scotland, and formerly in the Writer himself* (London: Nisbet, 1833), 65.

[46] Norton, *Memoirs*, 64–6.

room to my brother, and said, in great power, 'Convey it, convey it, for art thou not an Apostle?'[47]

The following morning Irving narrated to his congregation what had happened, adjuring Cardale to be faithful and warning him of the awful responsibilities of the apostolic office. At the same time he warned the congregation against the undue exaltation of any one man, stressing that the apostolic nature of the Church arose from its totality and not from any individual: it was the whole Church that was the 'pillar and ground of truth'.

No apostolic acts were carried out by Cardale until 24 December of that year, when, acting upon words spoken ecstatically in prophecy during a prayer meeting held at Drummond's house at Albury, he was moved to ordain a young man as an evangelist by the laying on of hands and prayer for the gift of the Holy Spirit. The young man in question was William Rennie Caird, the husband of Mary Campbell, who had been doing great work among the poor of the district. Two days later (26 December) and also at Albury, Taplin, by this time well established as one of the chief prophets of Irving's congregation, called ecstatically for an ordination to the episcopate, and Cardale felt himself spiritually impelled to ordain Drummond as Angel (Bishop) of the Albury congregation. This ordination was a response also to anxieties about the lack of celebration of the Eucharist, widely expressed in a number of prophetic utterances.[48] Its acceptance by Drummond is significant in view of his earlier refusal to accept ordination at Irving's hands.

The removal of Irving's 'orders' by the Presbytery at Annan raised a serious problem for the Newman Street congregation. After his deposition, Irving had remained for a short time preaching to large crowds in the open air, but soon returned to London to resume his duties. However, on the first Sunday after his return (31 March), when about to administer the sacrament of baptism, he was stopped by Cardale on the grounds that he no longer had any authority to act

[47] Letter of (Deaconess) Emily Cardale dated 13 Feb. 1872 (quoted in a sermon delivered in the Central Church, Gordon Square, by the Revd William Bramley Moore, 10 July 1895). Extracts from the letter are given in P. E. Shaw, *The Catholic Apostolic Church* (New York: Kings Crown, 1946), 75 and Davenport, *Albury Apostles*, rev. edn. (London: Neillgo, 1973), 77.

[48] Details are to be found in a letter of the Revd Robert Story, dated 28 Dec. 1832, which forms Appendix IV of R. H. Story's *Memoirs of the Life of the Rev. Robert Story* (London: Macmillan, 1862), 409–12. Fuller information of the setting up of the church at Albury is in Drummond, *Narrative of Circumstances*.

as a minister, though he could be permitted to preach. With a heavy heart, Irving accepted the injunction. However, a promise had been made prophetically that his orders would be renewed by apostolic authority, and on the Thursday Cardale was called by one of the prophets to ordain him as angel of the church. On the next day, Taplin, speaking in the power at the evening service, called upon Irving to kneel, and he was ordained to the episcopate by Cardale with prayer and the laying on of hands.

The small number of days between the injunction and the ordination needs to be noted in view of the attempts by Mrs Oliphant and other writers (basing their accounts upon hers) to represent Irving as a victim of apostolic oppression. Mrs Oliphant considered that his decline in health and eventual death were in considerable measure due to the restrictions put upon his ministry by the apostles. Thus she calls him 'martyr' as well as 'saint'.[49] She wrote, with considerable exaggeration:

Those lingering March days glided on through all the oft devotions of the church: the prophets spoke and the elders ruled—but in the midst of them Irving waited, listening wistfully if perhaps a voice from Heaven might come to restore him to that office which was the vocation of his life. Few of God's servants have been so profoundly tested; and small would have been the wonder had his much-afflicted soul given way under this last unkindness, with which Heaven itself seemed brought in, to give a climax to man's ingratitude.[50]

For the remainder of his life, Irving was required to accept apostolic rule and to be guided by the words of the prophets. It says much for the humility of the man that, for the most part, he was able to do so, though there is evidence in his correspondence with Drummond that he attempted to exercise episcopal control over the prophets of his own congregation, and also that he warned against apostolic authority that was not exercised in the power of the Holy Spirit. He wrote:

Now beware lest the word in thee as a Prophet from its striking character match itself well the word of edification in thee as the Angel . . . The prophet is the eye, but the angel is the hand of the church, the prophet the watchman, the angel the Father of the house.

[49] Oliphant, *Life*, 427j, 428.   [50] Ibid. 398.

And a few months later:

There is no doubt that the Angel of the Church is set to rule in the word
. . . if false doctrine arise the Lord looketh to him as responsible.

Subsequently he was to write:

You should neither write nor speak but by the Holy Ghost. . . . the *mind*
of the apostle is no ordinance within the Lord's house.[51]

Of this period, which was to last only until his death in the following
year, W. W. Andrews wrote:

Mr. Irving's position after his reordination was in some respects less
independent than before owing to the necessary subordination in which
he and his flock were placed in the Universal Church, in which apostles
are the chief rulers. As head of a separate congregation, his authority
was augmented, and his power of administering the grace of God
enlarged; but in all that respects the Church as one great Whole, he was
now under limitations, for this had been committed to another office.
Mrs. Oliphant complains of this, but it seems to us without reason. If
the work was of God, as Mr. Irving believed as firmly as any man, such a
change was inevitable. It was simply impossible that a pastor should
have the same range of authority when in subordination to an apostle, as
when no higher authority was over him. If the apostolic ministry is
restored, it must assert itself, and reclaim powers which in its absence
have necessarily been used by others. . . . Once admit that the Holy
Ghost is reviving the ancient gifts and ministries, and we must look for a
new order of things which shall involve many changes.[52]

During 1834 Irving developed consumption, and in the autumn he
was persuaded by his friends to seek a rest from his heavy duties,
which included much public preaching as well as care of the
Newman Street congregation, and a change from the bustle of city
life. However, against the advice of his doctor and the pleas of his
ecclesiastical superiors, he chose to revisit Scotland, travelling on
horseback and making a detour into Wales. Inclement weather and
increasing weakness made him abandon his ride in Liverpool. He
travelled by boat to Greenock, and arrived in Glasgow in late
October, having summoned his wife to join him as nurse as well as

---

[51] Letters to Drummond, 28 Apr., 2 Sept., and 21 Oct. 1833 (Northumberland
collection).
[52] W. W. Andrews, *Edward Irving: A Review of Mrs. Oliphant's life* (Edinburgh:
1864) (taken from articles in *The New Englander*, July 1863), 143–4.

companion.[53] He managed some preaching, but was eventually confined to bed and, despite an apostolic laying on of hands by Woodhouse, died 'unto the Lord' (his own words to his Father-in-law) on 8 December.

Woodhouse had been sent from Albury to effect a cure by the laying on of hands. At the same time, acting on words of prophecy spoken by one of the women members of the Greenock congregation, two of its elders (Tait and Wilkinson) were sent to anoint Irving. Woodhouse would not, however, permit this as he regarded the authority for it as being insufficient.[54] He attributed the absence of any recovery on the part of Irving, following his laying on of hands, to 'a chastening of the Lord's hand upon him' on account of his having behaved in a headstrong and stubborn manner, and because of an *admitted* jealousy of the authority of the apostles.[55] All this should be taken along with the statement in Boase that Irving had expressed to Woodhouse his complete confidence in the apostolic witness.[56] The 'confidence' and the 'jealousy' are not, however, necessarily mutually incompatible.

Although Woodhouse had seen Irving's illness and death as divine judgement upon a secret jealousy of the apostles, for many, they were both unexpected and spiritually disappointing. For example, Sitwell described Irving's death as

unexpected for I had always formed the idea in my own mind that it would be the Lord's will to raise him up.[57]

Though not present at Irving's death, he saw only the passing of a great Christian:

From all that I could gather from those who witnessed the closing scene of Irving's life it manifested the same faith, the same patience, the same joy and peace in believing, the same glorious hope which had animated his breast, the same looking for and hastening the Coming of the Day of the Lord and the Coming of The Great God and our Saviour Jesus Christ which had always been the object and end of his existence. . . . It is most manifest then that in his soul his last end was the last end of the righteous which is *peace*.[58]

[53] W. W. Andrews, taken from articles in *The New Englander*, July 1863, 149–50.
[54] Letter, Woodhouse to Drummond, 20 Dec. 1834 (Northumberland collection).
[55] See var. letters from Woodhouse to Drummond written Nov.–Dec. 1834 (Northumberland collection).   [56] Boase, 'Supplementary Narrative', 812.
[57] Letter to Drummond, 24 Dec. 1834 (Northumberland collection).
[58] Sitwell to Drummond, as above, n. 57.

Irving's last request had been that his wife should read to him Psalm
18 and 1 Thessalonians 4–5, and his last intelligible words were
'Keep that day'.

In view of the frequent identification of the Catholic Apostolic
Church with Irving, three points are important to note here: first, his
authority rested upon that of Cardale, who had ordained him to the
episcopate; secondly, he was never of apostolic rank within the
body—indeed, words of prophecy had declared that the limitation
on his authority was a judgement on the Scottish Church for its
rejection of episcopacy;[59] and thirdly, his death occurred during the
early formative years before the Catholic Apostolic Church had been
fully established as an ecclesiological body. Clearly, he played an
important role as a catalyst in bringing that body into being, though
no more important a role than that of Drummond. The eventual
liturgical and ecclesiological developments of the Catholic Apostolics,
due especially to Cardale as well as Drummond, went far beyond
anything that Irving could have envisaged. The extent to which he
would have approved of these is a matter of speculation only.

Growth of a Ministry

As has been seen, by 26 December 1832, three distinct orders of
ministry had come into being: those of apostle, angel, and
evangelist. During the following year, ordinations to the priesthood
and diaconate were performed by Cardale. Words of prophecy had
declared that elders should possess the charism of priesthood, and
the first such ordinations took place at Irving's church. Further,
Taplin was formally ordained prophet. There thus was coming into
being a twofold (as it were 'vertical' and 'horizontal') structure of the
Catholic Apostolic ministry. Across the traditional threefold ministry of
bishop, priest, and deacon (to which had been added the apostleship),
there was also a ministry of function—prophet, evangelist, etc.
(This structure will be discussed in Chapter III.)

All the ordinations were carried out after prophetic words,
accepted as the voice of the Holy Spirit, had been spoken. The
situation was, however, clearly open to the charge of 'circularity', for
Drummond (as prophet) had called Cardale to the apostleship, after
which Cardale (as apostle) had ordained Drummond (and Irving) to

[59] Baxter, *Narrative of Facts*, 69.

the episcopate. This charge was frequently levelled against the Catholic Apostolic ministry in letters, articles, pamphlets, and books, mainly by Anglican writers. The response was always a frank and straightforward account of the events as they had happened. The most notable example is a letter by Cardale published in 1855[60] in response to articles which had appeared anonymously (actually by Dr Pusey) in *The Old Church Porch*—an Anglican journal—during 1854 and 1855 within a general series with the overall title *The Church's Broken Unity*. These had commenced with the first issue (2 January 1854) and continued after April 1855.[61] They were republished two years later by the Revd W. E. J. Bennett, and drew a further response from Cardale in the same year.[62]

It is difficult now to appreciate the power exercised on the participants by the charismatic phenomena of more than a century and a half ago, considerably different in character from the practice of the Pentecostals and other charismatics of today. In any assessment of the establishment of the new apostleship it has to be remembered that the persons involved were not ignorant, uneducated, emotionally unstable, or fanatically driven, but highly educated, cultured, and respected members of society: Cardale a lawyer, Drummond a landowner and Member of Parliament, Taplin a schoolmaster. It is not, however, the intention at this point to debate the 'validity' of the new apostleship—the purpose here is to record its appearance. It is clear that the ordinations performed by Cardale were occasions of great solemnity, and that there was particular concern that priestly functions should not be performed other than by those who had received a prophetic and hence divine call to perform them. The account of the ordination of Drummond to the episcopate, given by Story (see above, n. 48), should be carefully studied.

Ten and a half months after the call of Cardale to the apostleship, a similar call was made in respect of Drummond. On 24 September 1833, during the evening service at Albury, it was prophesied that a further divine act was imminent. The following morning, prayers

---

[60] J. B. Cardale, *A Letter on certain statements contained in some late articles in 'The Old Porch' entitled 'Irvingism'* (London: Goodall, 1855).

[61] The references to the articles on 'Irvingism' to which Cardale replied are: vii–xvi (1 July 1854–1 April 1855), 97–103, 113–17, 129–33, 145–9, 161–6, 177–81, 193–6, 217–24, 241–8, 265–71.

[62] J. B. Cardale, *Remarks on Republication of articles from 'The Old Church Porch'* (London: Bosworth, 1867).

were offered that further light should be given on this prophecy, and in response Drummond was called to the apostleship, that is, he was declared 'in the power' to be an apostle. The declaration was immediately followed by an outburst of praise on the part of the assembled congregation, Drummond, on his knees, protesting his unworthiness and asking for divine strength and counsel to undertake his new responsibilities.

The Completion of the Apostolic College

Two other apostles were called in 1833 and another two in the following year, and there were insistent calls for the number to be brought up to twelve. In 1835, acting on prophetic instruction, Cardale and Taplin visited various congregations which had come into existence, and six more apostles were added to make up the 'college'. One of those called, the Revd David Dow (Parish Minister of Irongray, Dumfries, who had accompanied Irving during his trial at Annan—see above), failed to respond to a summons to gather at Albury, though much later he was to become an elder in the Edinburgh congregation. He was regarded as having fallen from the apostleship, and by analogy with the case of Judas, two possible replacements were called, Dr James Thompson (one of the party which had investigated the manifestations in Scotland in 1830) and Duncan Mackenzie (the elder who had supported Irving before the London Presbytery). Of these two, Duncan Mackenzie was chosen. The apostolic college now consisted of:

John Bate Cardale (1802–77): solicitor;[63]
Henry Drummond (1786–1860): landowner and Member of Parliament;
Henry King-Church (1787–1865): formerly 'King', Clerk in the Tower of London—called 1833;
Spencer Perceval (1795–1859): Member of Parliament and eldest son of the Prime Minister assassinated by Bellingham in 1812—called 1833;
Nicolas Armstrong (1801–79): Anglican priest, formerly Rector of St Dunstan-in-the-West, London—called 1834;
Francis Valentine Woodhouse (1805–1901): barrister and eventually 'Father of the Bar', son of the Dean of Lichfield—called 1834;

---

[63] For an extensive account of Cardale's life and work, see J. Lancaster, 'John Bate Cardale, Pillar of the Apostles: A Quest for Catholicity', thesis (St Andrews University, 1978).

Henry Dalton (1805–67): Anglican Priest, formerly Church of Scotland minister, incumbent of St Leonard's, Bridgenorth, Shropshire, later Vicar of Frithelstock, Devon (whilst retaining his apostleship)—called 1835;

John Owen Tudor (1784–1861): author, artist, editor of *The Morning Watch*—called 1835;

Thomas Carlyle (1803–55): advocate at the Scottish Bar, defended Irving before the General Assembly—called 1835;

Frank Sitwell (1797–1864): of Barmoor Castle, Northumberland, brother-in-law of Archbishop Campbell Tait of Canterbury—called 1835;

William Dow (1800–55): formerly Parish Minister of Tongland, Dumfries, deposed like Irving—called 1835;

Duncan Mackenzie (1785–1855): wholesale chemist, and elder at Irving's church; later (1840) withdrew from apostolic work—called 1835.

The social status and backgrounds of the apostles are worthy of note. With one exception they came from either the lower aristocracy or the professions. Of those who had been previously ordained, two were Anglicans and one a Presbyterian. Most were in their thirties at the time of their call; Drummond (at 47) was the oldest and Woodhouse (at 29) the youngest. They had all enjoyed good educations: Cardale, Drummond, and Woodhouse had attended (respectively) Rugby, Harrow, and Eton. Two had studied at Oxford—Drummond (Christ Church) and Woodhouse (Exeter), the latter graduating; two were graduates of Trinity College, Dublin—Armstrong and Dalton; and two were graduates of Edinburgh—Carlyle and Dow. Mackenzie, as a wholesale chemist, appears to have had the lowest social status.

The Ecumenical Roots

The ecumenical roots of the Catholic Apostolic Church have two aspects. First, there is the fact that the participants in the Albury Conferences came from several different church traditions, although, as already noted, the majority were Anglicans—a majority which applied equally to those called to be apostles. This is important because of the widely held view that the Catholic Apostolics were largely of Presbyterian origin, a view probably derived from overemphasis on Irving's role and from the fact that it was from Irving's Newman Street congregation that the worshippers at the large church in Gordon Square, London, evolved. In 1853, at

Christmas, the Newman Street congregation had moved to a magnificent new church building—known as 'the Central Church'—in Gordon Square. Designed by the well-known architect, J. Rafael Brandon, it was and remains today of cathedral design and proportions, though it was never completed. (It is now leased to the Church of England by the Catholic Apostolic Trustees for use as the London University Church of Christ the King.) At the time of the establishment of the Apostolic College, there had been no Roman Catholic participation in the activities which were to give birth to the Catholic Apostolic Church, though a number of Roman Catholic clergy and laity were to join later. At no time does there seem to have been any participation by members of the various Eastern Churches, though the influence of Eastern Christianity was eventually to become significant.

The second ecumenical aspect derived from concern over the visible divisions within Christianity. Haldane Stewart's pamphlet had referred specifically to the divisions 'which now unhappily subsist in the Church of Christ',[64] and had seen their healing as one of the results which could come from the outpouring of the Spirit for which he demanded prayer. In many prayer meetings, held up and down the country, one subject of prayer increasingly being heard related to the restoration of the unity of the Church. However, although prayer for the restoration of apostles certainly did occur in a number of meetings, it does not seem that this was at that time specifically linked to the concept of Christian unity. It became, however, a major topic of discussion when the whole apostolic college retired to Albury for prayer and study following the event which is usually regarded as the 'birthday' of the Catholic Apostolic Church—the 'separation of the apostles' (14 July 1835). It was to become an important plank in the apostolic claim to be set in authority by the Holy Spirit over the whole Christian Church—together with their division of Christendom into 'tribes' (see § 2 below)—and was reflected significantly in intercessory prayers of the Catholic Apostolic Liturgy (see Ch. IV).

The four strands within the roots of the Catholic Apostolic Church presented above—adventist, charismatic, apostolic, and ecumenical—remained characteristic of the body throughout its history, though, with its development, the balance between them was to change

[64] Stewart, *Importance of Prayer*, 25.

significantly. But a new and especially noteworthy element—the liturgical and sacramental—was to emerge once it had become organized as a single ecclesiastical body with a centralized authority, a comprehensive hierarchical ministry, and an established body of belief.

2. THE BIRTH AND DEVELOPMENT OF THE CATHOLIC APOSTOLIC CHURCH

The 'Separation' of the Apostles

Early in July 1835, it was prophesied that on the fourteenth of that month the Spirit would 'separate' the apostles for their work just as Paul and Barnabas had been 'separated' (Acts 13: 2–3). A summons was sent out for all the apostles to gather at Albury, by this time designated by words of prophecy as the centre of apostolic work. (This was the summons which David Dow declined—see § 1 above.) There were by now seven principal congregations in London, each with its own angel. These were located in Newman Street (Irving's congregation), Bishopsgate (formerly the congregation of the Old French Chapel in the care of the Revd J. L. Miller), Southwark (the Salem Chapel, placed in the care of the Revd N. Armstrong), Chelsea (formerly the congregation of the Park Chapel under the Revd H. J. Owen), Islington, Paddington, and Westminster. All these congregations had been expelled from their normal place of worship because of the occurrence and acceptance of the revival of spiritual gifts.[65] Prophetically, they formed a council said to be representative of the whole Church—following the interpretation of the seven churches of Asia (Apoc. 2 and 3)—and typified by the pillars of the Mosaic Tabernacle. This council was designated as the 'Wall' or 'Council of Zion' because it typified the perfect Church, though currently imperfect and awaiting perfection 'when God's Church and kingdom shall be one'.[66]

On 14 July, the Council of the Seven Churches was called together for the formal act of 'separating' the apostles for their work as ministers of the universal Church, thus setting them apart from

[65] See Boase, 'Supplementary Narrative', 793–4, 808–9, and 814.

[66] Woodhouse, *A Narrative of Events affecting the Position and Prospects of the whole Christian Church* (London: Barclay, 1847), 45.

those ministries which belonged to the local churches. An account of what took place has been provided by Woodhouse:

The Angels of the Seven Churches in London . . . were bidden together to lay hands on the Apostles, one after the other, in the order of their seniority and call to that office; and the other Angels who were present as witnesses, and as heads and representatives of their own several flocks, were bidden to stand up together, in token of their assent to and participation in this holy act; and with words of blessing were the Apostles thus one after the other separated to the work whereunto the Lord had called them, receiving each one, through this act, the blessing of the Church their mother upon the son of her right hand.[67]

It was made clear that in no sense was this ceremony to be regarded as an ordination:

The apostolic office has this distinction from all other ministries and offices of authority in the Church—that while these were derived only mediately from the Lord, the gift and authority belonging to them being conferred by the laying on of Apostles' hands, the Apostle is commissioned and endowed immediately by the Lord Himself, without men's intervention, and must be able to say to himself, with Paul, that he is 'an Apostle not of men, neither by man, but by Jesus Christ and God the Father:' his separation and dismission from under his mother's care are by the act of man, his sending forth is of the Holy Ghost (*Acts* xiii, 4), and of the Lord Jesus Christ (*Acts* xxii, 21; xxvi, 17; *Gal.* i, 1).[68]

The new apostles remained at Albury for the rest of 1853 except for occasional visits to the various congregations and attendance at the Council of the Seven Churches in London, now held on a monthly basis. This situation continued until the Summer of 1836. A prime consideration was the setting in order of the ministries and worship of the Church, for, up to this time, each congregation had continued to worship according to the tradition from which it had emerged. The forms of the ministries and liturgical worship which eventually developed were highly dependent upon the typological interpretation of Scripture, the Mosaic Tabernacle being taken as the type of Christian worship. In all this, the apostles were guided not only by those amongst themselves who could speak ecstatically but also by a number of prophets who were designated to support their deliberations. A fourfold ministry was established, fourfold in

[67] Ibid. 48.   [68] Ibid. 49.

order and, independently, fourfold in function (see Ch. III). A start was made on developing a liturgy which would eventually replace the various traditions of worship being used in the local churches, though it was not until 1838 that the first (lithographical) form for the celebration of the Eucharist was formally circulated for general use. It was during this period at Albury that a weekly celebration of the Eucharist was introduced there, a practice subsequently extended to the London congregations in the Summer of 1836 and then gradually spreading throughout the provinces. There was as yet little intimation of the highly developed ritual of Catholic Apostolic worship (to be discussed in Ch. IV).[69]

The Tribes

In the course of the last of the 1835–6 deliberations at Albury, Drummond called prophetically for a worldwide perspective to be adopted, stating that Christendom was to be divided up amongst the apostles as princes of the tribes of Israel. In accordance with this, the Continent of Europe was divided into 'tribes'. This division was 'typical' rather than geographical or political, that is, what were declared to be the distinctive characteristics of each nation determined the tribe to which it was said to belong—following the Scriptural precedent in which Assyria, Edom, Egypt, Moab, Tyre, etc. were seen as representing varieties of character. The allocation of the tribes to the apostles varies slightly in the different sources, but the list in Table 2.1 can be taken as authoritative.[70]

The characteristics according to which the division was made included 'submission to reasonable rule' (England), 'dignified patriotism' (Scotland and Protestant Switzerland), 'civic virtues' (Italy), 'yearning after fraternity' (France and Roman Catholic Switzerland), and so on.[71] Although the formal division was

[69] A full account of the evolution of the Catholic Apostolic Eucharist is to be found in K. W. Stevenson, 'The Catholic Apostolic Eucharist', thesis (Southampton University, 1975).

[70] The list given here is taken from a manuscript compiled at Albury by a designated angel (J. J. Hewitt) during his period of training under the apostles, and has been confirmed by reference to other internal sources. Davenport, following Shaw on The Catholic Apostolic Church, gives a somewhat different list, one for which no specific authority is quoted. However, Davenport does allow for variations: see his *Albury Apostles*, 116.

[71] See Davenport, *Albury Apostles*, 110–11.

TABLE 2.1. *The Allocation of Tribes to Apostles*

Spiritual tribe	Countries	Apostle	Gem
Judah	England	Cardale	Jasper
Reuben	Scotland and Protestant Switzerland	Drummond	Sapphire
Gad	Denmark, Belgium, and Holland	Kingchurch	Chalcedony
Asher	Italy	Perceval	Emerald
Naphtali	Ireland and Greece	Armstrong	Sardonyx
Manasseh	Austria and S. Germany	Woodhouse	Sardius
Simeon	France and Catholic Switzerland	Dalton	Chrysolite
Levi	Poland	Tudor	Beryl
Issacher	N. Germany	Carlyle	Topaz
Zebulon	Spain and Portugal	Sitwell	Chrysoprase
Joseph	Russia	Dow	Jacinth
Benjamin	Norway and Sweden	Mackenzie	Amethyst

confined to Europe, other parts of the world were added as 'suburbs'. Further elucidation is provided by Woodhouse:

thus bringing out the twelvefold character of the Spiritual Israel, answering to the twelve tribes in the Revelation, from among whom the sealed ones, the twelve thousand out of each tribe, should be gathered, who should be the first-fruits to God and the Lamb. . . . Nations have characteristics of their own as much as individuals . . . And in the same way the twelve tribes, out of whom the sealed ones are gathered, who attain to the first resurrection (*Rev.* xiv, 1–5; xx, 4–6), indicate a twelvefold character in the Christian Church, to which diversity this prophetical division primarily applies. That this distinction and division are of a permanent character, and universally applicable, not to Christendom alone, but to the whole world, and not to this dispensation only, but to the future dispensation also, is clear from the description of the Church perfected and triumphant in *Rev.* xxi, 10–21; in whose light the nations of them that are saved shall walk (v, 24); with the tree of life yielding twelve manner of fruits, whose leaves are for the healing of the nations (*Rev.* xxii, 2).[72]

[72] Woodhouse, *Narrative of Events*, 58.

The allocation of precious stones to the tribes followed the garnishing of the wall of the heavenly Jerusalem (Apoc. 21: 19–20). Judah was the leading tribe within which the Council of the Seven Churches—the Council of Zion—met. It was therefore allocated to the senior (i.e. first-called) apostle.

The Testimonies

It was at one of the meetings of the Council of Zion that ecstatic words were spoken commanding that the apostles should journey throughout Christendom to ascertain the state of the Christian religion in the countries visited and to bring back details of what was especially to be commended in what they saw and experienced. They were to go as learners only 'as Joshua and the spies of old went forth to spy out the land which God had promised to give them for a possession'.[73] They were also to have in mind the preparation of a 'testimony' to be sent to all the spiritual and temporal rulers of Christendom. The preparation of this testimony occupied the apostles for much of 1837. It was to be presented in the following year to the three persons considered to be the primary heads of Christendom: the Pope, the Emperor of Austria, and the King of France. Though recognized as 'heads' they were all regarded in different senses as usurpers: the Pope was seen as the usurper of the rule of Christ, the only king and priest; the Emperor was seen as the symbol of the claim to universal sovereignty of the Roman Caesars, a sovereignty which belongs to Christ alone; the French King was seen as symbolizing, as a monarch by popular choice, the unacceptable principle that authority stems from the people rather than from God.

Drummond and Perceval delivered a copy of the testimony to Cardinal Acton for transmission via the Secretary of Memorials to the Pope. Drummond and Woodhouse delivered a copy to Prince Mitternich for the Emperor. Drummond and Dalton attempted unsuccessfully to deliver one to the French monarch because the Court was in formal mourning, though it was subsequently laid before the King. Copies were later delivered to other European heads of state. The content of this testimony included a detailed analysis of the spiritual ills of Christendom, a pointing to the consequent coming anarchy which would destroy the ordinance of

[73] Woodhouse, *Narrative of Events*, 58.

both Church and State, and a summons to repentance, calling to mind the hope of a return of the Lord in glory.[74] This testimony became known as *The Great(er) Testimony*—or sometimes 'The Catholic Testimony'—to distinguish it from other and shorter testimonies delivered to King William IV and members of the Privy Council, and to the Archbishops of Canterbury and York to other bishops of England and Ireland.[75] There was also an American testimony prepared by the angels of the congregations in the United States and Canada.[76]

The content of *The Great Testimony* has been described by W. A. Curtis as follows:

Christendom is in spiritual distress, the clergy discredited, apostasy rampant, church discipline in abeyance; revolution and godless trust in the power of the masses are supreme; a judgement of God is imminent upon the Christian Church and nations; they will suffer most whose trust and responsibility have been greatest; God has appointed fresh apostles to exhort and evangelise the twelve tribes of His people, to build up anew His fallen Church; rulers and princes in Church and State are admonished to give heed to their doctrine and accept their message and authority; that doctrine is set forth with its Scripture warrant. . . . The admonitions are couched in the prophetic manner and diction, often with much dignity and impressiveness; the survey of the state of Christendom is powerful and moving; the historical passages, which reveal a wide outlook . . . show also a profound insight into the spiritual perils of the new regime.[77]

The testimonies represent a development of the ecumenical aspects of the apostolic work, namely that they now saw themselves as a focus to which all Churches were to turn in order that the Bride might be prepared for the coming Bridegroom. This was contrasted with the work of the first Apostles:

the work of the first Apostles proceeded from a unity, which, however, after their departure, was speedily interrupted; while the work of the last Apostles, who have every form of disorder and discord, and strife, to contend with, is directed continually to the restoration of that unity;

[74] The full text can be found in E. Miller, *The History and Doctrine of Irvingism* (London: Kegan Paul, 1878), i. 347–436.

[75] The texts of these are in ibid., ii. 80.

[76] The text of this is in Shaw, *The Catholic Apostolic Church*, 244–50.

[77] W. A. Curtis, *Creeds and Confessions of Faith* (Edinburgh: 1911).

and to the bringing the Church forward to perfection, as its crowning effort (*Eph*. iv).[78]

The Title 'Catholic Apostolic Church'

It was not considered at this time to be any part of the apostles' role to pass judgement upon the existing Churches, other than in general terms in relation to widespread apostasy—though (as we shall see in Chapter III) a number of specific criticisms were later levelled at the national Churches of England and Scotland as well as at the Roman Church. According to words of prophecy, it would be the hands of the wicked that would eventually tear down everything that was hindering God's purposes. The apostles saw themselves as ministers of the Spirit to all who would accept them, and they did not envisage the setting up of separate congregations except in the case of those who were cast out of the existing Churches. Judgement upon those who rejected them and their witness would follow with the speedy return of the Lord. They vigorously denied that they had created a new sect, as did all their followers throughout the history of the body. The claim is that they represented a work of the Lord by the Holy Spirit within the Universal Church—a preferred title for their witness being 'the Lord's Work'.[79]

In 1851 the Whig government of Lord John Russell implemented a census, the first in England to enquire into attendances at services and the church property of each denomination. It is unique in that it remains the only official British census to enquire into the religious activities of the people.[80] According to the census data, approximately three-quarters of the Catholic Apostolic members then resided in the south-east of England—the region of middle-class 'respectability'—and their buildings tended to be located in urban areas of social and political conservatism. This distribution of members was roughly in accord with the membership of the Established Church, though too much should not be deducted from the available statistics because only thirty-two Catholic Apostolic congregations responded to the

[78] Woodhouse, *Narrative of Events*, 59.
[79] This was the title of a history of the body, written in 1899 by Miss L. A. Hewett for the instruction of the younger members of the congregations. It ran to eight editions, all published by Hobbs and Co. of Glasgow, the last edition appearing in 1933.
[80] The information collected is to be found at the Public Records office—*Ecclesiastical Returns 1851* (London: H.O. 129).

census. Those which did respond indicated that there were 7437 sittings (of which 6460 were free) and over 6000 recorded communicants.[81] From later internal sources, it would seem that about half the total membership of the body had formerly been Anglicans, a third Nonconformists, and less than a sixth Roman Catholics. The majority belonged to the professions or were members of the households of professional men.

The title 'Catholic Apostolic Church' was an accident of this census: it was not intended to be in any way representative of exclusive claims. A census clerk, enquiring about the Newman Street church, requested information from a member of the congregation regarding its denomination. On receiving the reply that members belonged not to a denomination but to the 'One, Holy, Catholic and Apostolic Church', the clerk registered the building as 'the Catholic Apostolic Church', and a plaque still hangs on the left wall of the Gordon Square porch of the Central Church with the wording: 'Formerly known as the Catholic Apostolic Church'. In general, members have always preferred to be referred to as 'congregations gathered under apostles'. Intercessions were always made for the whole Catholic Church of Christ, considered to be the body of the baptized, within which the apostolic congregations were gathered. Nevertheless, it was clear that all Christians were called to accept the apostles' witness and the apostolic rule arising out of what was regarded as a second Pentecost—the 'latter rain' (Hos. 6: 3).

Apostolic Journeyings

In the early part of 1838 the apostles fulfilled the prophetic demand that they should visit their respective tribes in Europe. This demand had also stipulated that they should continue the visits for 1260 days, reckoned from the date of their separation. Cardale, who had therefore remained in England, was left in sole apostolic control. Each of the apostles who travelled took one of the ordained clergy with him as a companion and fellow-witness of what was seen and experienced. They thus regathered at Albury for Christmas 1838 in order to compare notes of their experiences and seek for further prophetic guidance. This done, they continued their respective travels until recalled by Cardale in December 1839 to deal with

[81] The apostles' reaction to the census can be found in F. W. Woodhouse, *The Census and the Catholic Apostolic Church* (London: Bosworth, 1854).

urgent matters at home. Because of the difficulties of travel and communication, it was not until June 1840 that the complete college was able to reassemble at Albury.

It is difficult to assess the visits paid by the apostles to their tribes in the period 1838–40 in terms of 'success' or 'failure'. In terms of missionary success, the results were negligible in the majority of the tribes. No headway was made in Orthodox countries. Great difficulty was encountered in Roman Catholic areas, though there seems to have been small success in France and Ireland. Most promising of all for the future were the results in Protestant areas, especially North Germany. But it must be remembered that their chief task was one of 'spying out the land', and here they seemed to have been highly successful. Dowglasse summed up their achievements as follows:

By coming into contact, not only with various classes of religionists, but also with the varieties of thought and action which prevailed amongst them, the apostles acquired a more comprehensive view of the field in which they were called to labour, and were able to form a more accurate and unprejudiced judgement. As sectarianism and exclusiveness were engendered by confining our observations within a narrow, contracted sphere, so largeness of heart and catholicity of spirit are produced and fostered by extending the bounds of our acquaintance with men and things . . . It is scarcely necessary to say that they were able to testify that Christianity is not to be found in England alone; that the feelings and qualities most appreciated there are not the only feelings and qualities esteemed by God; that there are grand truths in the Greek and Roman Churches, as well as in the Anglican; and forms and ceremonial observances and devotional practices in other lands which are as acceptable to God as the simplicities, or severity, of Protestantism. Their part was to sift the wheat from the chaff . . . A practical lesson in catholicity was taught, which was more efficacious that any amount of merely theoretical knowledge. They had heard that the Church of Christ was One; now they knew it . . . Their hearts had been enlarged to embrace all the baptized, and they longed for the perfecting of that one body, of which every tribe was an essential part, and each necessary to the completeness of the whole.[82]

Today, such views would be described as 'ecumenical' rather than 'catholic'.

[82] T. Dowglasse, *A Chronicle of Certain Events which have taken place in the Church of Christ, principally in England between the years 1826 and 1852* (London: Goodall, 1852), 6–8.

A Crisis of Authority

The reason for Cardale's recall of the Apostolic College to Albury was that, in the course of the eleven's further travels abroad, a crisis of authority had arisen. This was the first of three crises which were to affect the Catholic Apostolic Church during the remainder of the nineteenth century—the second and third were crises of apathy and schism respectively.

In this first case, the precise nature of the authority vested in the Apostolic College had been questioned, and this was seen by Cardale to be a challenge to the authority itself. There were two strands in this challenge. The first arose from the anterior nature of the prophetic ministry—the charismatic activity had preceded any call of apostles. To whom, then, did the final authority for determining the interpretation of prophetic utterances belong? This question was not new—it had existed as early as Irving's short period in the episcopate. The second strand was even more serious. The apostles had been separated for their work in the universal Church by an act within the Council of Zion: was ultimate authority within the Catholic Apostolic body the prerogative of the Apostolic College alone, or did it rest with the apostles acting together with the Council? There were even those who suggested that it might rest with the Council alone, the apostles being required to act as an executive carrying out the decisions of the Council. The situation had no doubt been exacerbated by the long absences of eleven of the apostles abroad. It was also natural for those whose backgrounds were originally in the dissenting Churches to recall the role of the assemblies and conferences to which they had formerly been accustomed—autocratic rule by apostles (and by one apostle in the absence of the others) was a strange and not entirely welcome novelty for them.

There were by this time both a 'universal' and a 'local' ministry. These had been prophetically declared to be 'the mystery of the Tabernacle' and 'the mystery of the candlestick' respectively. The latter comprised the angel of the congregation together with elders, prophets, evangelists, and pastors (see Ch. III). There were also ministers appointed specifically as aids to the apostles; these, together with the apostles, formed the universal ministry, i.e. the ministry of the universal Church. When the apostles assembled to deal with this crisis, their first act was to invite all the angels and also the various ministers attached directly to themselves, to state in writing their views both on the place and standing of apostles within the Church and on any other matters which they wished raised. In a statement calling for this response, they expressed themselves willing either to be set aside or to rule the Church as directed by the Lord. They also suspended the right of their subordinates to interpret or apply any further words spoken in prophecy. Their views on this last matter were plainly set out by Woodhouse, who appealed to the experience of the early Church:

Almost all the disorders in the churches, and certainly the greatest difficulties which the Apostles had to encounter, arose from words of prophecy, which were taken up and acted upon without the proper ordinance for the discernment of the same. The words of prophecy are as light, which is useless to those who are blind; the gift of prophecy is a gift of knowledge, which will mislead without the control of wisdom; the utterances of the Holy Ghost through Prophets, without the discernment of Apostles, are like a parable in a fool's mouth . . . The Prophet is no interpreter of his own word, and with all the light of prophecy which the Church has received during the last fifteen years, nothing but disorder and error would have been produced, had not the Apostolic ministry been raised up to discern and arrange, according to the mind of Christ, the light thus given.[83]

Although prophetic utterances had been responsible for the calling of the apostles and, certainly in the early period, for the selection of those called to the ministries of angel and priest, there had been increasing potential difficulties associated with the prophetic utterances, which clearly needed some measure of control, as the following account indicates:

All being at first alike ignorant of the nature and management of spiritual gifts, of the responsibility of each individual for the control and proper exercise of his own, as well as the limits within which they should be retained, there was at the public assemblies, and especially at the private meetings for prayer and reading the Scriptures, an unbounded stream of supernatural utterances. . . . While such things were taking place, Satan sought to gain an entrance, and by imitating the spiritual utterance, and by provoking evil passions, to cast discredit and doubt upon the work of the Lord: nor is it surprising that he should, to a certain extent, have succeeded. The excitement was great, and many

[83] Woodhouse, *Census*, 56.

foolish things were done and said by those who were carried away by the novelty of the movement; hasty conclusions were arrived at, and erroneous interpretations given of the meaning of the word spoken by the prophetic persons. Some, emulous of distinction, either deliberately feigned the tone and manner of those under spiritual power, or were tempted, in a moment of excitement, to give expression to their own thoughts in a loud voice, believing themselves to be exercising a spiritual gift. Others, no doubt, through unholy living, or the cherishing of some secret sin, laid themselves open to Satan, who, taking possession of them, came amongst God's people as an angel of light. . . . In some cases, those who had imitated confessed their sin, and some were delivered from the evil spirits which troubled them.[84]

This clearly highlights the problem which inevitably arises with charismatic phenomena not subject to the ordinances and hence the discipline of the Church.

The offer made by the apostles to be set aside if they could not rule was, in effect, an ultimatum. It is perhaps, therefore, not surprising that the fear of anarchy within the body lent support to the acceptance of apostolic rule. Once they had considered the various submissions made to them, the apostles acted swiftly. They asserted their right to absolute rule and disbanded the Council which they saw as a potential challenge to it. They also reserved to themselves absolutely the final right of interpretation of words spoken prophetically. In this they were supported by prophetic words spoken within their own number, showing 'the analogy between Aaron's sin in making a calf when Moses was away, and the sin of setting up a subordinate ministry in place of the apostleship'.[85] At the same time, however, they were themselves warned prophetically against the sin of Moses, being cautioned against being provoked into judging the people as rebels. As a further protection of their authority, they dispensed with the services of the ministers who had travelled with them during their visitations of the tribes, some of whom had reported critically on their lack of missionary success.

The great majority of the ministers and people accepted the conclusions and decisions of the apostles, though a few groups and individuals left the body on the grounds that the charismatic aspects of the Church were superior to the institutional ministry. There was also some protest at the suspension of the Council of Zion. For

---

[84] Dowglasse, *Chronicle of Certain Events*, 6–8.
[85] Woodhouse, *Census*, 85.

example, in October 1842, David George Foster (an elder of the Islington congregation) published a formal protest against the closing down of the Council of Zion and the introduction of what he saw as excessive ceremonial in worship. Amongst those who left was one of the apostles. Mackenzie (the 'Matthias' of the Apostolic College), having consented to the outcome of the deliberations in order to preserve unanimity, withdrew from association with his colleagues stating that he could no longer act as an apostle without a further endowment of supernatural manifestations confirming the rights being claimed by the apostolic body. Dr Albrecht wrote:

Although in full agreement with the apostles as to the truth, Mr. Mackenzie's faith was not sufficient for this exercise of apostolic authority by insisting upon it over and even in opposition to other ministries. . . . But . . . he never doubted that he was really an apostle.[86]

In deference to his attitude, the final statement issued to the angels and the Church at large was published expressing the 'sentiments' of the apostles. Nevertheless, it was almost entirely effective, and represents a turning point in the history of the Catholic Apostolic Church in that it was now clear that the prophetic elements within it were thereafter to have a role subordinate to that of the apostles. They had provided an initial impetus which had led to a break with the tradition of the Established Church, but, having provided that impetus, they became, unless suitably brought under control, a danger to the very authority which they had brought into being.

With the final determination of the superior authority of the apostleship, the way was opened for the full development of the body into an institutional church with a clearly defined hierarchical ministry and a universally ordered system of worship under a ruling apostolic college. The prophets were still a recognized and often important element within the ordained ministry—particularly in times of special difficulty—but the place for prophetic utterances during public worship was now regulated, acceptance of the words spoken was dependent in the first instance upon the local angel, and any final interpretation rested with the apostles. The first of the crises had been resolved, in no small measure due to the prompt manner in which the apostles acted. The full-time ministry was placed on a sound financial footing by the introduction of tithes. All

---

[86] L. Albrecht, *The Work by Apostles at the End of the Dispensation*, privately published from the German of 1924 (1931), 23.

members were required to pay one tenth of their earnings (and inheritances) as a gift owed to God to be used for the maintenance of the ministry. Free-will offerings at the services were used for other purposes, and alms were collected for distribution to the poor. (Catholic Apostolic teaching on tithes is discussed in Chapter III.)

Liturgical Evolution

The apostles were now to turn especially to liturgical development. It was clear to them that liturgy and doctrine were 'two sides of the same coin', and therefore that, if the Church which they ruled was to have a single body of doctrine, it should have forms of liturgical worship which were uniform throughout. By this time many congregations had sprung up, not only in Britain, but on the Continent also, and congregations were to come into being in America, Canada, and eventually in Australia and New Zealand.[87] There is clear evidence that many of these congregations were dissatisfied with the Protestant forms of worship which most had inherited and had begun to conduct experiments in liturgy in order to express more fully the typological and eschatological aspects of their beliefs and to satisfy a deep feeling of need for this ceremonial enrichment of their worship. Here again was a potential source of anarchy, requiring apostolic action, though not with the urgency which would justify describing the situation in any sense as a crisis.

Within the Apostolic College the driving force behind the liturgical development was Cardale, who, as well as responding to prophetic utterances, sought the advice not only of his apostolic colleagues but also of the senior angels of the particular churches. As time passed, it would appear that the College met less frequently—often with only a partial attendance—and that much of the apostolic consultation on liturgical matters had therefore to be carried out by correspondence. Cardale wrote, deploring

circumstances which deprive individual Apostles and the Church of a 12 fold Apostleship—'God's Ordinance for rule'. . . . I dread the evil effects which may follow from the *necessary isolation* in which individual Apostles must now remain, and from the lack of that general direction

[87] See W. W. Andrews, *The Work of the Catholic Apostolic Church in America* (New York: Moffet, 1856); J. E. Worsfold, *A History of the Charismatic Movements in New Zealand* (n.p., Julian Literature Trust, 1974).

and guidance which individual Apostles ought to receive from the
Corporate Body.[88]

As a result, to a considerable extent the final decision on liturgical
matters had to be taken by Cardale himself, after he had weighed up
the advice received from the various quarters.

Two main sources lay behind the liturgical evolution which took
place during the 1840s: the details of the worship of the Mosaic
tabernacle, and the experiences of the apostles whilst attending
Eastern Orthodox and Roman Catholic services on the Continent
during their visitations to the tribes. The former, regarded as having
been set in order by Divine will, had been declared by words of
prophecy to be the type of the worship of the Christian Church to
which the antitype must conform. The latter was a matter of
experience and the principle that all that was best in the worship of
the various Christian traditions should be reflected in that of the
body which had been raised up to restore perfection to the Bride in
preparation for the coming of the Bridegroom. Of his written
sources and the way in which they were used Cardale wrote:

> Only this I will say—that the more persons will study in an impartial
> spirit the Offices of the Church, Eastern or Western, the more readily
> will they recognize the ground and reason for the things contained in the
> services. . . . they were composed with a view to the requirements, as
> shown in the light of prophecy—and were not copied nor initiated from
> services in use. Still, wherever those requirements and the light of
> prophecy could be fully answered by the words of existing forms I had
> always sought to use those forms, rather than to originate new ones; but
> . . . existing forms, brought into existence in an Apostate condition of
> the Church, could never satisfy the exigencies of the Church renewed
> and restored and therefore new forms or the enlargement of old forms
> and the development of ideas contained in them could not be avoided.[89]

Subsequent to a lithographed Eucharist—issued in 1838 for
temporary use—and instructions for the conduct of the Forenoon
Service on Sundays (1839), an order for the daily services and the
administration of the sacraments was printed for experimental use at
Albury in 1842, and this was made available to the congregations in
the following year. Further editions appeared in 1843 and 1847, and
these were followed by some fifteen more up to 1880, including

---

[88] Letter, Cardale to Drummond, 29 Oct. 1846 (Northumberland collection).
[89] Letter, Cardale to Drummond, 17 Dec. 1847 (Northumberland collection).

editions published in Canada (1850) and the United States (1851). Published translations into languages other than English followed from 1850 onwards. Throughout the period up to 1880, liturgical development continued, though there were few changes in the later editions.

For the most part, the apostles were happy with Cardale's liturgical development—which was all in a 'catholic' direction—though there is some evidence that, at times, he wished to pursue a faster pace than his colleagues desired, as, for example, with the use of oil in Confirmation. He even encountered attempted vetoes of his proposals on the part of individual apostles, especially Drummond, and was then forced to exercise his authority as 'pillar of apostles' and proceed alone, following consultation with the angels in order to 'exclude the individual and to substitute the Church'.[90] He did, however, accept a need for caution in all such situations, and had earlier expressed concern when Drummond introduced his own version of services in Scotland without consultation with the angels.[91] In pressing for the use of oil in Confirmation, Cardale claimed that

there is as much evidence in primitive practice as for any single thing not enjoined in Scripture.[92]

Nevertheless, despite the support of Carlyle, a majority of the apostles voted against the proposal—though in this instance Drummond did not vote. He did not, however, necessarily expect unanimous support, though he would not normally act against the majority:

Those things which the Apostles have approved of . . . I can introduce without difficulty. Those approved by a majority but disapproved by individual apostles . . . I should be slow to introduce but am prepared to do so if necessary. Those which they have positively negatived by a majority I altogether deny your right or mine to introduce . . .[93]

It was due to the caution which his colleagues insisted upon, that the newly developing services were not rigorously imposed upon the congregations, but were 'offered' to them for use as each angel

---

[90] Ibid.
[91] See letter, Cardale to Drummond, n. 88 above.
[92] Letter, Cardale to Drummond, 29 March 1847 (Northumberland collection).
[93] Letter, Cardale to Drummond, 31 March 1847 (Northumberland collection).

should determine was appropriate for the current state of a particular flock.

As a result of this tactful approach, there was but little opposition—though there is evidence that some of the congregations of Presbyterian origin expressed concern at the rate at which ritual was being introduced, and a few had to be dissolved because of their intransigent attitudes. The liturgical innovations were thus the cause of a small number of churches closing down because of the fading away of support. This had severe financial implications for the local ministers, some of whom had to seek regular work outside the Church.[94] It is clear, also, that the ritualistic innovations resulted in the loss of some members from those congregations which had accepted them, but it is not possible now to estimate the numbers involved. The history of this liturgical development will not be considered here: a full account of the evolution of the Catholic Apostolic Eucharist is to be found in Stevenson's 1975 thesis (see above, n. 69), and a description and discussion of the developed liturgical worship of the body appears in Chapter IV, below.

Development of Catholic Apostolic Writings

At the same period as the liturgical development was taking place, there began to appear that stream of apostolic and other writings by means of which the clergy and laity of the body were instructed and edified. For the most part, these were published anonymously and 'for private circulation only'.[95] Because of their basic assumptions, such works for 'internal' consumption need to be considered separately from the more public (and sometimes signed) works, which were published either to inform other Christians about the principles of the apostolic work or to refute the attacks upon the body—of which there were a considerable number—in various ecclesiastical and secular publications (as has been noted earlier). This stream of publications, most of which are noted in Copinger's *Bibliography*, was to continue well into the twentieth century, beyond the time of the passing of the last of the Catholic Apostolic apostles (1901). It came virtually to an end in the 1960s as the last priest of the body approached the end of his earthly life (1971: see § 3 below).

---

[94] See *Apostles Reports*, July 1853, p. 5.   [95] See Ch. I, § 3.

A Second Crisis and the 'Sealing'

At the end of the first part of his *Narrative of Events*, Woodhouse provided a postscript describing the general state of the Catholic Apostolic body at Easter 1847. It is clear from this, and the opening paragraphs of the second part of the work proper, that there was at that time a serious diminution in the expectancy of the imminence of the Second Coming. There was also sadness and even dismay at the passing of many of the ministers, and at the departure from the body of individuals who had lost confidence in the apostolic witness, and even the apostles themselves were feeling weakened by trials and disappointments. Woodhouse wrote of them:

And they, with all the Ministers, and all the churches, are in the position of the Apostle John, when, beholding in vision the history and the end, the dangers and the triumph of the Church, the apostasy and the glory, he found comfort and consolation in these words—'He which testifieth these things saith, Surely I come quickly; Amen. Even so, come, Lord Jesus.'[96]

There seem to have been two strands which led the apostles to accept that a (second) situation of crisis existed. One was a general apathy amongst the congregations, coupled with a lack of confidence in the universal mission of the body—parochial attitudes had begun to become dominant. The other was the admitted failure in respect of the tribes abroad to gather together the prophetic number of 12,000 in each tribe (Apoc. 7: 4–8). Drummond, in particular, complained at the inactivity of some members of the Apostolic College in regard to the tribes allocated to them.

Once again, following deliberations at Albury, the apostles took decisive action. By instituting a special rite of anointing and laying on of apostles' hands, they determined to convey to each member of the Church the assurance of the gift of the Holy Spirit, even though that assurance should on this occasion be something inward not accompanied by outward spiritual manifestations. The view held was that the crisis was a spiritual one, and thus only a spiritual response would suffice. Baptism had indeed conveyed the 'Spirit of Life'; what was now lacking was a special gift of the 'Spirit of Power', which alone could re-energize the spiritual life of the people.

---

[96] Woodhouse, *Narrative of Events*, 114–15.

The rite introduced was known as the 'sealing'. It was to be administered to all adult (20 or older) members of the apostolic congregations, and to be offered also to members of other Christian Churches. However, as with the liturgical reforms, it was introduced with tact. Cardale administered it first at Albury (31 May 1847) to the other three 'pillars'—'of prophets', 'of evangelists', and 'of pastors'. On 8 June, it was administered in the Newman Street church to the angels serving in England. Later that month, some 130 priests were sealed, to be followed by over 1000 deacons and laity in England. True to their stipulation that the effects were inward only, any manifestations which occurred during the ceremonies of sealing were immediately stopped as being inappropriate interruptions of the rite. Woodhouse wrote thus:

Still the apostles felt the solemnity and responsibility of the step they were taking, and they endeavoured to guard against any exaggerated notion, or any unjustifiable expectation concerning it. They sought to disabuse the people of the idea that because, at the beginning, the laying on of hands was, in most cases, followed by tongues and prophesying, therefore that some immediate outward manifestation, or inward consciousness of spiritual grace or power, was to be expected or looked for. They endeavoured in their teachings to disabuse the minds of the people as to any such supposition or expectation, by showing them how much higher and greater the gift of the Holy Ghost was than any mere spiritual manifestation. . . . And yet there is no one who has been a partaker of this holy rite, who would for a moment think of questioning or denying that he had indeed received the gift, because at the time of receiving it, or afterwards, he was not conscious of any sensibly miraculous power resting on him. 'By their fruits ye shall know them,' is the only evidence of that divine operation peculiar to and characteristic of the Christian dispensation, by which the members of Christ are brought into the unity of the Spirit, and by which, through the gift and operation of the Holy Ghost, that prayer of Our Lord to the Father, on behalf of all those whom the Father had given him, is answered. 'That they may be one as We are one, I in them and Thou in me, that they may be made perfect in one' (John 17).[97]

This indicates how far the Catholic Apostolics had travelled from the heady days of their charismatic roots.

The sealing also had specific apostolic and eschatological implica-

---

[97] Woodhouse, *Narrative of Events*, 130–1.

tions. Acceptance of the sealing was regarded as a confirmation of acceptance of the apostolic authority within the Church. Cardale wrote:

My firm persuasion is, not only that the seal of the Lord hath been affixed upon these His children, but that thereby they have been brought into their true relation to the Apostles as children to their fathers, to those through whom God would reveal Himself as the Father of the whole family in heaven and earth.[98]

Here again is a specific reference to the ecumenical aspect of the apostleship. The eschatological significance of the sealing related to the belief that, once the 144,000 from the tribes had been sealed, the Second Coming of Christ would take place. No such number of persons was ever sealed by the apostles.

The sealing was universally administered within the body to all those eligible so long as the Apostolic College survived, and its effects were remarkable: the apathy largely disappeared, and there was a renewed sense of urgency in the local witness of ministers and congregations. The apathy was indeed not to return, despite the severe trauma of the eventual passing of all the apostles—the last of whom (Woodhouse) died in 1901. Once again the prompt action of the apostles had overcome a crisis within the apostolic community. The sealing was one of the most precious spiritual experiences treasured by members. The extent to which it was sought and accepted by members of other Churches is difficult to ascertain, but it is known that a number of Anglican laity and clergy, including bishops, were sealed by the apostles. In Copinger's *Bibliography* works by a number of non-members sealed by the apostles are listed. Official lists of those sealed are in the Church archives, but are kept strictly from any outside examination. Their content, if made available, would throw considerable light on the extent to which the apostles had been accepted by those who nevertheless remained within their own Churches. In view of, especially, the apostolic implications (mentioned above), this is a matter of no small interest.

A Third Crisis and Schism

The third crisis which the apostles had to face was the only one leading to a definite schism in the Catholic Apostolic Church. The

---

[98] *Apostles Reports*, July 1853, p. 4.

question before them was one which related to the heart of their authority and witness. In 1855 death struck the Apostolic College for the first time. Three apostles died in that year: Mackenzie (still regarded as an apostle) on 26 January, Carlyle on 28 of the same month, and Dow on 3 November. Two days after Carlyle's death, Cardale, speaking at a meeting of the seven churches in London (by new revived, but as a council of the tribe of Judah only), declared his disappointment that one of his apostolic colleagues had passed away and thus shattered the hope that the apostles, if remaining faithful, would be alive at the Lord's coming to lead His people into the heavenly inheritance. It is significant that Cardale considers here only the death of Carlyle and does not mention Mackenzie's death of which he was nevertheless aware. Clearly, by this time the latter had ceased to all intents and purposes to be regarded as an apostle, whatever his own view of the matter.

During the Summer, the remaining apostles debated the question whether or not those who had passed away could be replaced so that the college could retain its full complement. The conclusion reached through an examination of Scripture was that no authority existed for such replacement:

The Apostles considered that in the Scriptures no warrant is given for taking such a step, that the example of Judas, who fell by transgression, did not apply to this; that therefore they could not consent . . . That they therefore must submit this matter wholly to the Lord and must content themselves with labouring with so much the greater zeal, in order that they might be acknowledged as faithful servants before Him in the day of His Appearing.[99]

This decision was eventually to bring the body to an end as a visible institution. Other members of the Apostolic College were soon to pass away: Perceval in 1859, Drummond in 1860, Tudor in 1861, Sitwell in 1864, and Kingchurch in 1865.[100] With Dalton's death on 6 November 1869, only three apostles were left: Cardale, Armstrong, and Woodhouse.

In 1860, Heinrich Geyer (angel-prophet in Berlin) prophetically called two angels to the apostleship during a meeting at Albury

[99] In an Apostles' circular letter to the angels, June 1855.
[100] There are slight variations amongst the various sources in the dates of the deaths of some of the apostles. The dates given here conform to those in Albrecht, *The Work by Apostles*, are confirmed in *Neue Apostelgeschichte: New Acts of the Apostles* (German and English) (n.p., New Apostolic Church, 1982), and may be taken as correct.

which he had been summoned to attend. However, the apostles rejected this and instead decided to appoint the two angels called by Geyer as 'apostolic coadjutors'. It appears that Geyer was not clear as to the precise nature of the apostleship to which he was calling the two angels. Woodhouse wrote:

The views expressed by the prophet H.G. are so variable that it is scarcely possible to know what he really means. Three years ago he expressed to me his opinion that, as the apostles from time to time were taken away by death, they should be replaced by others. Later on he took up another position and spoke of another Apostleship, which after the removal of the present Apostles should be raised up. To the priest B. he seems to have said that his call had to do with the filling again of the places of those who had fallen asleep, but finally uttered a word which he spoke in power, away in Hamburg, that this new Apostle might be the first of a new series of Twelve Apostles and that these might be represented by the Twelve Pearly Gates of the New Jerusalem.[101]

In the following year Geyer, whilst on a visit with Woodhouse to Königsberg, called Rudolf Rosochacki—an elder in whose house he was lodging—to be an apostle. This call, made without Woodhouse's knowledge, was then recognized by Friedrich Schwartz, angel at Hamburg. Like Geyer's earlier call of two angels to the apostleship, this also was rejected by the Apostolic College when knowledge of it reached them. Geyer, Schwartz (together with his Hamburg congregation, which had supported him), and Rosochacki were suspended from office and subsequently excommunicated (1863) in a ceremony conducted by Woodhouse in the Berlin church. Thus the 'Hamburg schism' had begun,[102] a schism which was never to be healed.

Further apostles were called by the German group at Hamburg, which now called itself 'the German Christian Apostolic Mission'. It was later to develop into what it still is today—the 'New Apostolic Church', an organization within which more than 270 apostles have been called, some fifty or more of whom are currently working. It has congregations in many countries, and claims continuity with the

[101] F. W. Woodhouse, 'On the possible call of New Apostles and the special hope of the First fruits, with particular reference to Herr H. Geyer and his New Apostolic Church', apostolic teaching 19 Feb. 1863 (tr. from the German), p. 3. The full text of this teaching is in S. Newman-Norton. *The Hamburg Schism* (London: Albury Society, 1974).
[102] For an account of the details of the schism see Newman-Norton, *The Hamburg Schism*.

restored apostolate led by Cardale despite its clear break by excommunication from that tradition in 1863. In general, it has shown a tendency to revert to Protestantism, much of the ceremonial and the attendant sacramental teaching of the Catholic Apostolic Church having been abandoned. In 1982 the New Apostolic Church issued its most significant work, *New Acts of the Apostles*, in celebration of the 150 years that had passed since the call of Cardale to the restored apostolate. It includes a history of the apostolic work of the Catholic Apostolic Church up to the schism, followed by a continuing history of the New Apostolic Church. Lists of the Apostles of the Early Church and 'of the end time' are appended: 24 of the former and 285 of the latter (including the Catholic apostolic apostles).

The Last Surviving Apostle

With the death of Cardale, the 'Pillar of Apostles', on 18 July 1877, the Apostolic College was effectively reduced to one, since Armstrong had become paralysed and hence unable to fulfil any apostolic duties. Armstrong died on 9 October 1879, leaving only Woodhouse, who was to survive for a further 22 years as the sole member of the College. Upon the removal of Cardale by death, a prophetic voice had declared that the work of the apostles had reached its full measure. This was reinforced on a number of occasions during the period when Woodhouse alone represented the apostolic ministry, though, with the assistance of his coadjutors, he managed to continue the sealing and to maintain apostolic oversight of the congregations. Up until 1891 he continued celebrating the Eucharist at the Apostles' Chapel at Albury, but from that year onwards until his death the celebration was undertaken by the coadjutors with an apostolic benediction given whenever the apostle's health permitted it. Woodhouse passed away on 3 February 1901 at Albury at the age of 96. It was said of him that his face shone with an inward beauty and that, even in death, he appeared worthy to be called an apostle.

3. THE CATHOLIC APOSTOLIC
CHURCH WITHOUT A VISIBLE
APOSTOLATE

The Church under Coadjutors

Following the death of Woodhouse (declared prophetically to be the 'covering of the ark'), great changes in the Catholic Apostolic Church were to take place, reflecting the spiritual significance of the withdrawal of the living apostolate.[103] Although two apostles' coadjutors were still living (Edward Heath and Isaac Capadose), no apostolic functions could continue, since coadjutors could act only for living apostles. Capadose expressed this as follows:

When the right hand of the Lord [the apostleship] is withdrawn for a time, then also the stars [the angels] held in that right hand are affected. . . . They cannot shine as stars in the firmament in the same way as before, so long as the right hand which upheld them in their heavenly standing is hidden in the bosom of the Lord. All ministers, not one excepted, continue to exist, but as it were veiled in a cloud; they can act only in a modified and limited manner. There would be great danger in ignoring this. We may not smooth over our present condition, lest we give way to the temptation to which the Church succumbed after the departure of the first Apostles—the temptation to help ourselves and devise makeshifts.[104]

However, for some further years, the two coadjutors were able to offer general spiritual guidance to the ministers and congregations. Of this period it was said later:

The sun of the day of apostolic salvation had indeed set, but a clear twilight remained, in the light of which the congregations were still to find their way.[105]

The sealing ceased, as did the full services at the Apostle's Chapel at Albury. Acting upon prophetic instruction, celebration of the Eucharist in the local congregations was resumed after cessation for

[103] An account of the spiritual significance of the withdrawal of the apostolic ministry is to be found in A. Valentin, *The Present Time of Silence* (from the German), published for private circulation 1938.
[104] Dr I. Capadose, Sermon delivered at the meeting of the Seven Churches at the Central Church, Gordon Square, 26 Feb. 1901.
[105] Valentin, *The Present Time of Silence*, 3.

three weeks, but the level of ceremonial was reduced. The rites of Morning and Evening Prayer were also curtailed.[106] Thus, the solemn intercessions in the Sunday Eucharists and in the Offices (see Ch. IV), together with the offering of incense, ceased, since worship was no longer being conducted under living apostles—prophetically, the 'covering of the golden altar'. Most significant of all for the body's future, no ordinations to the episcopate, priesthood, or diaconate could take place, since ordination had been reserved to the apostles or to coadjutors acting with express apostolic authority.

No further witness to Christendom was now permitted, the time following the death of the last apostle having been declared in prophecy (during his lifetime) to be the 'silence in heaven for the space of half an hour' (Apoc. 8: 1). The period following Woodhouse's death has thus come to be known generally within the body as 'the time of silence'. During this period new members have been admitted to the body only through birth or marriage. Words of prophecy were heard, not only about the covering of the altar of incense, but also about the 'covering of the table of shewbread'—that is, the cessation altogether of the offering of the Eucharist, inevitable in view of the cessation of ordinations. The central administration of the body eventually passed from Albury to Gordon Square, London, where the office of the trustees and the library are to be found today.

On 29 November 1908, the first death from amongst the angels of the seven churches in London occurred with the passing of John William Ackery (angel at Southwark since 1873). Pastoral oversight of his congregation was given to one of the other angels. However, this death brought to an end the possibility of the angels of the seven churches meeting, and the meetings were therefore suspended. This was declared prophetically to be the 'covering of the candlestick'. On 13 October 1920 at the age of 86, apostles' coadjutor Capadose died after a long illness—he had been confined to a wheelchair since 1906. The surviving coadjutor, Heath, followed him on 29 August 1929, aged 84. The period under the coadjutors was to come to be seen as the period of the 'two witnesses' (Apoc. 11: 3). On 1 March 1931, the archangel Ludwig Albrecht,[107] the last of the ministers

[106] See quotations from a sermon (delivered by W. A. Copinger in the Central Church, Gordon Square) in Davenport, *Albury Apostles*, 174–5.

[107] Author of *The Work by Apostles*. This small work is the only internal Catholic Apostolic publication outlining the history of the body from its beginnings to times as recent as the 1930s.

who had been appointed to serve with the apostles, died also; no ministers of the universal Church therefore remained.

The Church under Angels

With the death of Albrecht, the Catholic Apostolic body became in effect a collection of local congregations under their respective angels, assisted by a rapidly diminishing number of ministers in the priesthood and diaconate. The angels were able to continue to bless men for service as underdeacons (subdeacons), but, with the passing of the last angel (Karl Schrey) in Germany on 3 November 1960, such blessings ceased also. The Eucharist and the Offices continued to be celebrated by a rapidly ageing ministry, often required to travel long distances so that members of the scattered congregations could have the joy of receiving the Sacrament. However, when more and more churches were closed down due to the declining number of clergy and the inability of those who survived to undertake travel, it was the laity who soon came to have to make the journeys to attend worship. As the surviving priests grew feeble with age, the services tended to lengthen and to become less audible. Few printed accounts exist of the atmosphere of worship at this time. One such account (of services in Scotland) describes

sitting wearily through the age-long sermons and services held by tottering old men who had no power to ordain successors. . . . the tired trembling old voices—voices belonging, each one, to personalities of patently unusual saintliness—that read the prayers seemed to be reciting dirges of dreary defeat, and the adult choirs sang at a tempo so slow that all music seemed to be lament.[108]

By contrast with the above, an existing recording of extracts from a Eucharist in Switzerland in the 1950s suggests remarkable fervour on the part of the congregation and an atmosphere of considerable spiritual uplift.[109] The present writer's regular experience of the Eucharist and Offices from the 1920s to the 1940s suggests that the atmosphere varied considerably from congregation to congregation, and was much influenced by the age and enthusiasm of the choir and

---

[108] G. Maxwell, *The House of Elrig* (London: Longmans, 1965), 23. The author, a member of the Northumberland family, was a great-great-grandson of Drummond. He is best known for his stories of the lives of otters: *Ring of Bright Water* and *The Otters' Tale.*

[109] See Ch. I, § 2.

organist. The heightened atmosphere and expectation caused when words were spoken prophetically was, however, by then becoming a comparatively rare experience.

4. THE CHURCH WITHOUT AN ORDAINED MINISTRY

The last surviving priest, Dr Wilfred Maynard Davson (of the church in Paddington, London),[110] died at the age of 95 on 16 February 1971, just 70 years and 13 days after the death of Woodhouse, and the celebration of the Eucharist in the Catholic Apostolic Church ceased for ever—the table of shewbread was finally covered. The last deacon, Charles William Leacock of Sydney, Australia, died (at the age of 95 also) on 25 July 1972.

The surviving members of the apostolic congregations still meet in a number of countries (including England) for services conducted by underdeacons. These services consist of the Litany,[111] lessons from Scripture, hymns, and the reading of homilies and sermons dating from before 1971. The present writer's occasional experience of these services both in England and abroad confirms that the faith and loyalty of the members remain unshaken, together with their fervent hope for the Lord's coming again. Except in the Paddington church, which has continued such worship despite the death of its last underdeacon, only prayer meetings are held where no underdeacon is available. These surviving underdeacons are elderly men, except in Germany (where Schrey had blessed a number of young men for the office before his death). The congregations in Germany are still active today, and there are regular services in a number of places. The present writer recalls that, when taken ill during a conference in Karlsruhe in the mid-1970s, he was visited by a number of members of the local congregation, and that these were by no means confined

---

[110] Much light is thrown upon the significance of the removal of the last angel and the 'time of silence' by W. M. Davson's *Sermons and Homilies on the Third Stage of the Lord's Work*, delivered in the Paddington church 12 Feb. 1961–1 Nov. 1965 (pub. 1966 for private circulation only).

[111] *The Litany*, which follows closely Cranmer's form in the *Book of Common Prayer*, is printed as a distinct Office in the Catholic Apostolic service book (see App. I) with instructions that it is to be said or sung on Wednesdays and Fridays during the Forenoon Service and, as appointed, on other occasions also.

to the older generations. There are also a few active congregations in Scandinavia, including one in Finland where there is a weekly Litany taken by an elderly underdeacon and attended by a small ecumenical group—the spiritual atmosphere of this service is quite remarkable. However, the time when only prayer meetings are permissible outside Germany cannot be long distant.

The congregations have retained such identity as has been possible, though many members rely on Anglican, Lutheran, and other episcopal Churches for their sacraments. They continue to look for the coming of the Lord, and are content to wait until either that event takes place or there is a new prophetic manifestation of the Holy Spirit to instruct and guide them. A number of members witness to their hope of the Lord's coming through membership of societies with a special interest in the prophetic Scriptures, the most notable of which is an Anglican guild, the Guild of Prayer for the Return of Our Lord, which publishes a regular newsletter, intercession sheets, and the occasional booklet. The Guild was formed in 1920 with the twofold objective: witness to the Second Coming of Christ, both 'as a fact' and 'as a hope', and prayer for the return of the Lord. Originally largely an 'Anglo-Catholic' body, it is now ecumenical and there have been recent problems of unacceptable influence from American Adventism. The Guild has its own particular litany, *The Litany of the Second Advent*, compiled by Canon W. H. Connor, a (sealed) Anglican priest.[112]

Thus, to all intents and purposes the Catholic Apostolic Church and its witness appear to any outsider to have been brought to an end through the failure to make provision for the continuation of its ministry, though this is not the view taken by members of the body—the members regard the 'Lord's Work' as having been withdrawn by divine act because of the rejection of the apostolic witness by the Christian Church as a whole. It is because of this view that there is a strong objection to the carrying out of research into the history and theology of the body.[113] However, the Catholic Apostolic Church now provides a remarkable opportunity to study the history and doctrine of a comparatively recent Christian body, having extensive ministerial, liturgical, and geographical development, from its 'birth' to its 'death'. Here, the presentation of the history

---

[112] Its present (1991) episcopal patron is the Rt Revd Maurice A. P. Wood, DSC, formerly Bishop of Norwich.

[113] See Ch. I, § 3.

has been restricted to a broad outline, with concentration upon the earlier period of the body's life since, in the presentation and discussion of its developed theology and practice which is to follow, it is important to keep in mind the roots from which they sprang.

III

Ecclesiology

1. THE NATURE OF THE CHURCH

IN THE NAME OF THE FATHER, AND OF THE SON, AND OF THE HOLY GHOST, ONE GOD. AMEN. The Church of Christ is the company of all who are baptized in the name of the Father, and of the Son, and of the Holy Ghost, without distinction of age or country, and separated by their baptism from all other men. One body (Ephes. IV, 4); the pillar and ground of the truth (1 Tim. III, 15); the dwelling-place of God; the Temple of the Holy Ghost (2 Cor. VI, 16); the declarer unto all men of God's will (Ephes. III, 10); the teacher unto all men of God's ways; the depository of God's word and ordinances;—wherein is offered up all true worship, which God receives from his creatures of Mankind;—through whom have been conveyed all those blessings, in civil and domestic life, which have distinguished Christendom; wherein are contained the only hope for man and the only means of accomplishing that purpose, for which God waits, and which all creation earnestly expects (Rom. VIII, 19).

So began *The Great Testimony* of 1838 (see Ch. II, § 2). Membership of the Church was thus drawn very broadly, being conferred by baptism, which was seen as

the *act of God*, whereby man is taken out of a state of nature, and brought into a state of grace. All who are baptized are 'baptized into Christ,' and all who are 'baptized into Christ have put on Christ.' They are 'baptized into one body,' the mystical body of Christ, the Church.[1]

---

[1] H. Dalton, *What is the Church?* (London: Bosworth, 1863), 9. The most extensive and complete account of the Christian doctrine of baptism by a Catholic Apostolic writer is in W. J. Bramley-Moore (Philalethes), *Baptismon Didache or Scriptural Studies on Baptisms, especially Christian Baptism* (London: Bemrose, 1907). Of this comprehensive work, reviewers wrote: 'the most comprehensive treatment of the doctrine of Christian Baptism that has ever appeared in English' (*Glasgow Herald*), and 'there has never before been written so full an account of what Baptism is and what it leads to' (*The Expository Times*).

Baptism and Church Membership

Baptism was thus seen primarily as an act of God rather than as an act of an individual. The incorporation into Christ at baptism was regarded as indelible, even if an individual should later become apostate. Membership of the Church was thus in principle public and visible. The Church had its unsound and unhealthy members as well as its sound and healthy ones, just as a vine had fruitful and unfruitful branches or a family its obedient and disobedient children. The unsound and unhealthy members could only become separated from the Church by a judicial act. The Protestant concept of an 'invisible' Church, made up of all those who were inwardly converted, was explicitly rejected. Conversion was considered to be, like baptism, an act of God which was

not the cause or origin of regenerate life (in the baptized), but the restoration or revival of regenerate life already received.[2]

The visible part of the Church was that part which is on earth; the invisible Church comprised all those departed members with whom the living have a continuing fellowship in Christ. It was said to be a confusion of terms to apply both 'visible' and 'invisible' to that part of the Church which was on earth, unless, perhaps, it was intended solely to indicate that those on earth should not make any final judgement as to who were true and who were false members of Christ.

Any concept which separated baptism by a ministerial act with water and in the name of the Trinity from baptism by the grace of God through the Holy Spirit was considered a serious error

which sets aside the truth concerning baptism, nullifies the unity of the body, and which tends, in no small degree, either to puff up with pride, or depress with holy fear, those who maintain it. The Scripture knows but of *one* Church, speaks to but *one* Church, exhorts, rebukes, encourages, and commends but *one* Church—the Church of Christ— the baptized.[3]

---

[2] Dalton, *What is the Church?*, 10.   [3] Ibid. 11.

Pneumatology: The Holy Spirit in the Church

It was taught that within the Church—the company of the baptized—God dwelt: the Church was said to be by definition 'the dwelling-place of God' and 'the Temple of the Holy Ghost'. It was the kingdom of heaven set forth in a mystery, the glory of the kingdom being hidden until it shall be made visible at the Second Advent. It was the divinely created organism within which Christ remained incarnate through and in the Holy Spirit. The Holy Spirit sustained the Communion of Saints, living and departed. The faithful departed remained *of the Church*, in peace, yet not unconscious but sustained by the same Spirit:

If when separated from the body the spirit be then devoid of consciousness, this would be not merely death of the body but death of the spirit also; whereas, they that depart in Christ do all live to God, live in Christ, sustained in their life by the continual supply of His Spirit, who is about again to unite both body and spirit. Concerning the extent and manner of that consciousness . . . we do not venture to speculate, nor do we profess to understand; but that the departed do truly continue to live in spirit we unfeignedly believe; and without spiritual consciousness there is no life of spirit. 'God is not a God of the dead, but of the living: for we all live to Him' (Luke xx. 38). And in using these words our Lord hath deduced the certainty of the resurrection from the fact, that they who die in the body yet do live in the spirit . . .

We cannot, therefore, doubt that our communion with the saints departed does not merely consist in our being objects of the same providential care . . . nor merely in our having in common a future hope . . . but that the like spiritual apprehensions of faith, and the like joyful anticipations of hope, and the like affections of love and holy desire, are inspired and shed abroad, and consciously entertained, in the spirits of the living disciples and of the departed saints. Our communion with our brethren in Christ, even when the body is dead, is a communion with them that live in Christ unto God by the power of the Holy Ghost—'for whether we live, we live unto the Lord; and whether we die, we die unto the Lord; whether we live, therefore, or die, we are the Lord's' (Rom. xiv. 8.)[4]

Thus, the Holy Spirit was clearly seen as the sustainer of the whole Church, visible and invisible. Within the Church, the Holy Spirit

---

[4] J. B. Cardale, *Readings upon the Liturgy and Other Divine Offices of the Church*, ii (London: Barclay, 1852), 211–12 (henceforth C/*RL*).

bore witness to the Son even as He had borne witness to the Father in the Jewish dispensation. It was the Holy Spirit who, in a fulfilment of Christ's promise (John 16: 13), had revealed to the Church from Scripture the truth of the Holy Trinity. The Holy Spirit sustained all life within the divine economy:

All the processes that go on in creation are manifestations of the power of the Holy Ghost—all the forces of nature, gravitation, electricity . . . they are the manifestations of the putting forth of the power of the sustaining Spirit in the outward creation. . . . Where there is any life . . . it is the action of the creating Spirit. And . . . to come to the question of what are called moral agents . . . if they have any knowledge of right or wrong, then indeed, it is by the enlightenment of the Holy Ghost, the Spirit of God. Jesus Christ lighteth every man that cometh into the world, and the way He gives them light is by His Spirit.[5]

All this shows that the Catholic Apostolics had a vision of the Church which cannot be separated from their pneumatology. All actions of God within history were seen as actions *through* the Holy Spirit:

The Father sent the Son, and the Son came; but there was the action of all the three Persons of the blessed Trinity. It was by the power of the Holy Ghost that there was separated off from the nature of the Virgin Mary a human body, and a human soul and spirit, and after He was born into the world, the Lord Jesus was continually sustained by the Holy Spirit . . . Again . . . at the time of His baptism in Jordan, the Holy Ghost came down upon Him and gave Him power for the work of His Ministry. . . . and, at last, when He ascended into heaven, was He to receive the infinite endowment of the Holy Ghost. He had prayed, 'Glorify Thou me with Thine own self with the glory which I had with Thee before the world was.' (John XVII, 5). The glory was the Holy Ghost, the uncreated glory. . . . And, therefore, as on this day [Pentecost], the Lord Jesus sent down the Holy Ghost upon His disciples. Before that time the Holy Ghost had been working in the natural, or in the moral world; now He came as the Spirit of Christ to work in the Church.[6]

Of the Baptism of Christ in Jordan, Carlyle wrote:

Previous to that time the Holy Ghost had acted in His incarnation and sanctification. But then the Spirit of God, the Spirit of the Father and

[5] J. B. Heath, *The Procession of the Holy Ghost* (n.p., Everett, 1903), 2.
[6] Ibid. 2–3.

the Son, became the spirit of the Son in a new manner, as the Spirit of the Man Jesus Christ. In other words, the change wrought on the relations of the Son by His adoption of a created subsistence into His divine person, induced an analogous change in the Holy Spirit when He took His abode in the Son as man. The Holy Spirit neither did nor could become incarnate; and He did not, by dwelling in the Son, assume the place of the human spirit in man. But the Son, in becoming man, became capable of being His dwelling-place. In descending on the Son, the Holy Spirit found a dwelling-place in one who had become man, and thenceforward He was not only the Spirit of God, but also the Spirit of the Man Jesus Christ.[7]

Carlyle went on to argue (quoting Tertullian: *adv. Prax.*) that the Spirit suffered 'as the Spirit of Him who died' in a way 'akin to' and 'resulting from' the humiliation and suffering of Christ. This, and other similar passages in a number of Catholic Apostolic writers, must be understood in the context of their Christology, in which they followed Irving's teaching on the human nature of Christ: that the human nature assumed from the Virgin at the Incarnation was subject to all the consequences of the Fall, though Christ was at all times Himself sinless (see Ch. II, § 1). For this reason, in particular, they regarded the Roman doctrine of the Immaculate Conception as a serious heresy.

The Holy Spirit was seen as the revealer of God's will to the Church. The Spirit guided the Church in its ordinances, inspired all true worship, and effected the grace of the sacraments. Hence the importance of the double epiclesis in the Eucharist (see Ch. IV, § 3). Of this, Carlyle wrote:

The Invocation of the Holy Ghost, omitted in the Roman but retained in the Greek Liturgy, is not a mere prayer that the Holy Spirit would do something in or for us, by assisting us to consecrate aright; nor is it a mere prayer that He would put forth His power in making bread and wine to be Christ's body and blood; nor is it a mere prayer that Christ would, by the Holy Ghost, perform the consecration . . . but, in addition to all this, it is a prayer that, after the priest, abiding in Christ . . . has done his part, his very best—he in Christ, and Christ in him—the Holy Ghost Himself would, as a Divine person . . . descend and impart to the offering the virtue of His Divinity, that what the work of faith has produced may be perfected . . . as an offering crowned with the Divine

---

[7] 'On the Office of the Paraclete in the Prayers of the Church', in T. Carlyle, *Collected Works* (London: Bosworth, 1878), 331—originally published separately by Goodall, 1853.

presence—a sacrifice at once acceptable and accepted by the fire of
God—an earthly offering converted by one Divine Person into a
heavenly one, to be presented by another Divine Person, not upon the
altar on earth, but upon the altar in Heaven.[8]

In particular, the Holy Spirit conferred the nine gifts, which are
properly His (prophecy, tongues, wisdom, etc.), as He willed upon
the members of the Church—it was considered that such gifts
should be part of the 'normal' life of the Church. But, just as our
Lord was to be 'despised and rejected of men' (Isa. 53: 3), so also
within the Church the Holy Spirit had been largely rejected. The
command of St Paul (Eph. 4: 30) had often gone unheeded, and as a
result the spirit of prophecy had been rendered dumb. It was only in
recent years that the Holy Spirit had been able to resume the
building up of the Church—the work begun at Pentecost, but
hindered for so many centuries. The Spirit was seen as having been
hindered by continuing apostasy within the Church, evident from
Scripture even in apostolic times.[9] Nevertheless, throughout the
Church's history, the Spirit had been the inspirer and sanctifier of
the prayers of the faithful, perfecting the Church's offering of prayer
and praise to God. This work of the Holy Spirit was seen as
supplementing but not replacing the work of Christ as mediator
between God and man:

In the mediation of Christ we see that none but He who is God can
present our offerings to God; in the office of the Holy Spirit we see that
none but God can perfect our offerings, and so make them fit to be
presented. . . . the Holy Spirit neither speaketh, nor acteth, nor showeth
of Himself. The perfection with which He crowns our offerings is,
though wrought by Him, still the perfection of Christ. His office bears
the same relation to that of Christ, that His presence with us does to
Christ's presence with us.[10]

During the period of the rebuilding of the Church, a period in which
the Pentecostal gifts had been restored, one of the particular roles of
the Holy Spirit was seen to be the preparation of all those who were
'in Christ' to receive the fruits of the Resurrection at the Parousia,
together with the effecting of the 'translation' (as the agent of Christ)
in those who would remain alive at the Second Advent (see Ch. V, § 6).

[8] Carlyle, *Collected Works*, 333–4.
[9] This is a reference to the charismatic basis of the Catholic Apostolic Church (see
Ch. 2, § 1). The Holy Spirit was seen as having been hindered by continuing apostasy
within the Church, evident from Scripture even in apostolic times.
[10] Carlyle, *Collected Works*, 332.

The whole life of the Church was said to be rooted in the Incarnation and Resurrection of Christ, and her strength in any age to depend upon the faithfulness of her witness to what she proclaimed in her Creeds. The basis of the sacraments lay in the Incarnation, and it was through the visible agency of the sacraments, and especially baptism and communion, that the Holy Spirit enabled the fruits of Christ's resurrection to be conveyed to those who partake in faith, fear, and love. Indeed, by His sending of the Holy Spirit, Christ had provided the means whereby all faithful Christians could become

one with Him in all the fruits of His resurrection and entrance into heaven. . . . For as it was a new and more glorious condition into which manhood was brought, when He rose from the dead, and entered into the presence of God for us; so it is the peculiar office of the Spirit since His Ascension, to effect the same transformation in them that believe— not in its completeness, indeed (which cannot be till the resurrection), but in its essence and true beginnings.

This is the express teaching of St. Paul, who, in writing to the Ephesians, says that the greatness of God's power toward us who believe, is 'according to the working of His mighty power, which He wrought in Christ, when He raised Him from the dead, and set Him at His own right hand in the heavenly places.' (i. 19,20.) And He then completes the parallel by saying, that 'He hath quickened us together with Christ, and hath raised us up together, and made us to sit together in heavenly places in Christ Jesus.' (ii. 5,6.) The work done in us is the counterpart of that done in Him. The life given to us by the Holy Ghost, is the very life wherewith He was quickened in the tomb, when He was 'declared to be the Son of God with power, according to the Spirit of holiness, by the resurrection from the dead.' (Rom. i. 4.) . . . Though we have the heavenly treasure in earthen vessels, in bodies of sin and death, we are none the less . . . the very members of Christ; 'members of His body, of His flesh, and of His bones.' (Eph. v. 30.)

The Church is, therefore . . . the BODY OF CHRIST. There is no other definition so exact and so comprehensive as this . . . It is a new creation, as truly as the life of the resurrection is a new life. . . . The characteristic mystery and blessing of this dispensation is, that we are verily made one with Jesus in the heavens, and so constitute that body by which He can ever work in executing the will of God towards the whole creation.[11]

---

[11] W. W. Andrews, *The True Constitution of the Church and its Restoration* (New York: Moffet, 1854), 8–9.

The Church was thus regarded as a divine creation, infused by the Holy Spirit with the resurrection life. She was also seen as the mystical Bride of Christ, being prepared by the Holy Spirit for the coming of her Bridegroom at the Parousia, when the full union of Christ and the Church, of which Christian marriage was the type, would be consummated. This last—eschatological—viewpoint lay at the heart of the Catholic Apostolic vision of the Church.

The Church as 'the New Creation'—a Divine Election

Holding this extremely 'exalted' ecclesiology, it is not surprising that strong condemnation was expressed of the view of 'the Men of the world' that the Church was 'merely a worldly human establishment, an appendage to the State . . . a needful machinery for the preservation of religion and public morals'. Such a view led inevitably to a situation in which 'her sacred offices and functions' were 'regulated and distributed by the temporal power; her services and forms subjected to the sanction and authority of the civil ruler'. It was 'dishonouring to the great Head of the Church' and it brought 'sore injury and loss to the members of His body'. The Anglican 'High Church Party' view of the Church was also criticized. It was accepted that this view held the Church to be 'a Divine institution, founded by Christ, endued with spiritual life, and enabled by His grace to fulfil its vocation'. However, the problem was that this view, though correct as far as it went, was severely defective—indeed, 'so defective as to omit altogether the *real distinctive* feature of the Church'. It was seen as making no more claim for the Church than could be made 'for the Jewish polity', which was also 'in the strictest sense a Divine institution'. It failed to make the point that the Church was an entirely new creation, having a heavenly and not an earthly constitution. All this was very clearly brought out by Dalton,[12] who also attacked the Roman Catholic definition of the Church which labels as 'schismatics' all those not in communion with the Bishop of Rome. His chief ground here was that it nullified the truth of the doctrine respecting baptism.

To the question, 'What is the Church?', the Catholic Apostolic answer was:

[12] Dalton, *What is the Church?*, 3–8.

The Church is the election out of mankind, who, by the Holy Ghost given at baptism, are partakers (first in their spirits, hereafter in their bodies) of the life of the incarnate Son of God risen from death.[13]

The Interpretation of 'Election'

The Catholic Apostolics did not use the word 'election' in a Calvinistic sense, however. For them, God had always used election as the means of revelation of Himself and His will to the world. Individuals had been so chosen by Him (as, for example, with the Patriarchs); a whole nation had been so chosen (as with the Jews)—a separation which was the type of the Church, the spiritual Israel. The outward sign of the Jewish election was circumcision; similarly, the outward sign of the Christian election was baptism, the antitype of circumcision. In each election, those chosen were to be the witnesses to others for their benefit and blessing. There was no sense of a consequential exclusion of those not chosen as the elect—only those who remained impenitent and who resisted God's will to the end would be finally cast away. Thus, the family of Abraham had been chosen that 'in them all the families of the earth might be blessed'. From among the Jews, the family of Levi had been chosen 'for sanctifying and imparting blessing unto all'. The Church was the new election with a universal ministry of witness and prayer:

And now, from among all peoples and nations and languages . . . He separated His Church, His ἐκκλησία . . . in order that they may gather unto Him the fulness of the Gentiles; may offer supplications and prayers, intercessions and thanksgivings, for all men; and, in the fulfilment of God's purpose, may finally lead the way for the introduction of that future age, when, the Church of the first-born having entered into the glory of the resurrection, Israel after the flesh shall be graffed once more into their own olive-tree, and the receiving of them again shall be to the world life from the dead (Rom. xi. 15.)[14]

However, even this new election could fail; it was not immune from falling away from its high calling, though, because of the indwelling of the Holy Spirit, it could never become totally apostate—against the Church the gates of Hell could never entirely prevail (Matt. 16: 18). Further, just as there was salvation outside the Jewish election, so there was salvation outside the Church. The Church, as an

---

[13] Ibid. 17. [14] *C/RL*, ii. 37.

election, was not the whole kingdom of Christ. She existed in the world to prepare those who would participate in the revelation of the eternal kingdom of Christ—a kingdom which would include all the saved. Thus the Church had to be typical of the form and order of the eternal kingdom, just as the Tabernacle had been typical of the form and order of the Church. The Church was also, but in a spiritual sense only, an anticipation of the kingdom in that, through her worship and sacraments, the faithful received spiritually and inwardly a foretaste of the blessings which would be manifest to all in the eternal kingdom. This divine election participated in the life of the risen Christ. Although a spiritual election, it was none the less real and substantial:

It is the body of Christ, spiritually yet substantially existing. He rose out of death, and thence became a 'quickening spirit,' and being ascended to the right hand of God, He received and gave from the Father the Holy Ghost, to form, organize, and vivify that body, which is thus united to Him in real spiritual membership. The Church is a reality, an existence, not an ideal thing. It is the body of Christ, existing after a spiritual manner, yet substantially existing. It partakes of that life of which He, quickened from death, is the fountain and source.

Hence the Church is said to be 'the fulness ($\pi\lambda\dot{\eta}\rho\omega\mu\alpha$) of Him that filleth all in all' (Eph. i. 22); to be raised up with Christ and to sit in 'heavenly places' (Eph. ii. 6); to have her 'life hid with Christ in God' (Col. iii. 3). Hence it is called to have His mind (Phil. ii. 5); to do His works (John xiv. 12); to follow His example (1 Peter ii. 21); to be conformed to His image (Rom. viii. 29, 1 Cor. xv. 49, Col. iii. 10); to share His kingdom (Rev. iii. 21, v. 10); to make known to the ages to come His grace and manifold wisdom (Eph. ii. 6,7, iii. 9,10); to judge creation (1 Cor. vi. 2,3, Ps. cxlix. 9, Jude 14,15).

Such is the Church—such her calling. She is heavenly, the new creation of God.[15]

Christendom

The Catholic Apostolics made a clear distinction between the Church and Christendom. The latter was not a community of *persons*, but a community of *nations* formally professing the faith of the Church, whose rulers accepted that all power was given by God, and who had therefore submitted to anointing by the Church in token that they occupied their seats of authority only until Christ

[15] Dalton, *What is the Church?*, 15–16.

should return to claim all His people. Thus Christendom was separated from the remainder of the nations by its recognition of the Gospel as the basis of both national and international law. It was

the nations in covenant with God, through *their* respective anointed heads, their Kings and all their chief governors, whose acknowledged duty is to rule by God's laws, and to hear His Word from His Church . . .[16]

The rulers of Christendom should have no power over the Church, except in so far as their legislation for public order and the public good was binding upon the consciences of Church members. The position in England was unacceptable, however benign the ruler. It was a continuation at the Reformation of the situation in which the Church had been placed 'in the captivity of the mystical Babylon' when first she admitted an Emperor 'to sit in her Council as ἰσαπόστολος'. It was a 'seeking to perfect by the flesh that which had begun in the spirit', of which St Paul had written to the Galatians. By this act the Church was a consenting adulteress with the world. For this, it was the Church herself and not the State which should be blamed. God had permitted it as a consequence of apostasy, even as he had permitted the captivity of the Jewish people. Until this great sin was recognized and confessed, the Church could not regain her freedom in the Holy Spirit. As long as 'she will loiter in some of the lanes and alleys of Babylon' she could never play her full part in 'the building up of the Spiritual Jerusalem'.[17] (The question of the apostasy of the Church in the light of the prophetic scriptures is taken up in Chapter V.)

The rulers of Christendom had a duty to make civil laws in accordance with the Gospel, but, as individuals, they had to submit to Christ as members of His Church. Neither the anointed monarchs nor the anointed ministers of religion should consent to civil or religious licentiousness either by deferring to popular opinion or for the sake of worldly popularity. Departure from the moral law as revealed by God would inevitably lead to their destruction:

if the rulers in the state will veil the authority which God hath committed to them before the the usurped majesty of the people, and will govern, not according to God's laws, which are eternal, but according to a supposed expediency, ever varying, because dependent on the fitful movements of the people;—if any have fallen into this fatal

---

[16] *The Great Testimony* (1838) (henceforth *GT*).
[17] W. H. Place, 'Church and State' (litho MS, 1846), 1, 4, 6–7.

snare, and will not repent of their wickedness, and will not . . . correct the error of their way, and will not look to God to deliver them in as far as they have involved themselves in bondage to those over whom they should bear rule;—then indeed hath the disease reached the very centre of life—God is not merely rejected but betrayed—and He hath no further dealing in store, but the out-pouring of the vials of consuming judgement.

Nor are these principles affected by the diversities in the forms of government, whether the supreme power is distributed among many, or vested in the power of one. It matters not who are the organs for exercising that supreme power.[18]

It was as a warning against the impending judgement of God upon Christendom that the apostles had issued their testimonies, and *The Great Testimony* in particular. Many of the rulers within Christendom were seen as having failed in their duty as God's ministers to administer justice and to preserve order, and, as a result, their subjects had 'done ill' and forgotten their duty of obedience to the powers ordained of God:

They do ill when, through envy, through lust of power, through covetousness, through discontent and ill regulated activity, through rebelliousness and refusal of those social arrangements under which alone the common welfare can be secured; they thrust themselves into places where they are not lawfully called to act, or lay violent hands upon that which does not belong to them. . . . They who do ill, or who willingly would do ill if they could, they fear the power, hate it, speak evil of dignities, are already in spirit disobedient to it; and sooner or later they show themselves, bring in wars and fightings; promising liberty— or embracing a promise of liberty, [they] are themselves the servants of corruption . . .

And what incalculable amount of power lurks in the multitude of human minds and bodies, imagination cannot conceive. . . . By humility, patience, contentment, submission to God, submission to the existing powers, as ordained of God; by believing in the wisdom and goodness of God, by consenting to the checks and limitations with which men are surrounded: thus only can men live. In any other way, they must either waste themselves in strivings and contentions, or else crush their own consciousness of what God had hidden in them.[19]

[18] *GT*, xiii–xiv.
[19] W. Dow, 'The Organization of the Church of Christ' in *Discourses on Practical and Doctrinal Subjects*, 1st ser. (Glasgow: Hobbs, 1900), 106–8. (Originally published 1847, and published separately by Glaisher, 1924.)

It was precisely through such rebelliousness that the judgement of God upon Christendom could be seen as having already begun, a judgement of which the French Revolution was but a prelude.

The Church had not always been faithful to her own divinely appointed role within Christendom, which was a spiritual one. She had forgotten that she had 'nothing to do with the setting up or the pulling down of earthly governments'. She had in many places been too closely associated with exaggerated nationalism, forgetting that her goal was not on earth but in heaven. This was firmly brought home to Catholic Apostolic members:

If, as God's children, we are to rise up into our heavenly standing, it is very necessary that we should realize that those social or national distinctions, which have their proper places in the grouping of men in their earthly relationships, have no place in the Church of Christ which is the congregation of the baptized gathered from among all nations. As members of Christ our citizenship is in heaven. Such an expression as 'a national church' would surely never have found currency if the baptized had not forgotten their heavenly standing.

. . . .

The only thing which concerns the baptized is the accomplishment of God's purpose in Christ, and the setting up of His kingdom which is not of this world.[20]

Since the Church had involved itself with the nations in an earthly rather than a spiritual way, the judgement soon to descend upon Christendom would descend also upon the national Churches. A warning of this was also included in the testimonies.

The Four Traditional 'Marks' of the Church

The Nicene Creed proclaims the Church to be 'one, holy, catholic, and apostolic'—these traditional four 'marks' of the Church played a significant role in Catholic Apostolic teaching. Because the Church was seen as a divinely constituted body—the Body of Christ—it was seen also as being essentially *one*, united by a single source of life, by holding one Faith, by being nourished by one and the same holy food, by having one apostolically constituted administration, and by the indwelling of the one Spirit of glory within her. The Church was

---

[20] S. M. Hollick, *The Church and the Nations* (privately published, 1938), 2–3.

One inwardly and *one* outwardly; *one* in mind, *one* in heart, *one* in spirit, *one* in word, *one* in ordinances, *one* in faith, *one* in worship, *one* in administrations;—*one* as a vine is one tree, and not another;—*one* as a temple is one, and not another;—*one* as a human body is one, and not another;—*one* as the only individual of its kind; yea, *one*, as no other body in existence is one; even *one*, as God the Father and the Lord Jesus Christ are *one*: as it is written, 'That they all may be one; as Thou, Father, art in me, and I in Thee, that they also may be one in Us: that the world may believe that Thou hast sent Me' (John XVII, 21–23).[21]

The Church had always been *one* internally, because it had been uniquely brought into existence by the descent of the Holy Spirit at Pentecost and uniquely sustained by the same Spirit Who imparted the mind and will of Christ to all her members, though many had resisted the Spirit by unbelief, hardheartedness, and wilfulness.

The Church was also *one* externally, because its government and discipline proceeded from Christ and were effected through divinely given ordinances:

The Church is one polity, with fixed institutions and offices, which are ordained by God, are perfectly adapted to their end, and are incapable of being changed. The means by which the Lord began to work, are those by which He will complete and perfect His work: for the Church is one and the same, united and bound together under the same offices for government and discipline, for guidance, for pastoral care, for dispensation of the grace and blessing of God. . . . If . . . the organization be disordered, and its action imperfect, we may be sure that there will be a failure in the visible unity of the body, that the purpose of God will be delayed, and that the special ministry of the Church in the midst of the world will be impeded; until the complete organization is restored, and the Church is seen to be one united body, the same in manifestation through her proper organs, as at the beginning. However, at any given time, the unity of the Church may appear to be infringed upon, and its ordinances curtailed, it follows, from our belief in the Church as the body of Christ, that sooner or later that perfect unity, which ever subsists, must be brought again into manifestation before the eyes of men; and those ordinances and gifts which are ever in Christ, as the head of His Church, must be put forth again, be restored to their perfect exercise, and attain with the Church itself their full growth and development.[22]

The Catholic Apostolic Church did not (by its own definitions) claim to be 'the Church'. It saw itself as being no more than a work of the

---

[21] *GT*, xcvi.   [22] *C/RL*, i. 113–14.

Lord within the Church, providing order amidst chaos—it had been established by an outpouring of the Holy Spirit (the 'latter rain') to recall the Church, the company of all the baptized, to its primeval divinely established order. Indeed, no one part of the company of the baptized could claim to be 'the Church', whose completeness would not be revealed until after the Second Advent. In the meanwhile, the work of preparation of the Bride for that Day of the Lord would continue.

The Church was said to be *holy*

as becometh the bride of Him who is the Holy One of God;—*holy*, as the living sacrifice, holy and acceptable, presented continually unto God the Father by the true High Priest who is at His right hand;—*holy*, as the dwelling-place of the High and Holy One, who dwelleth in the Church, as it is written, 'I will dwell in them, and walk in them; and I will be their God, and they shall be my people' (2 Cor. 6: 16).[23]

The Church's holiness also derived from regeneration of her members by the indwelling Spirit, and was revealed by the bearing of the fruits of the Spirit (Gal. 5: 22–3) and the manifestation of His gifts (1 Cor. 12: 8–10). She was holy, also

because the Church is a royal priesthood, and a holy nation, consecrated, sanctified, and set apart in Christ, for the fulfilling of the eternal purpose and will of God throughout all ages.[24]

No justification was perceived for the omission of the word 'holy' in versions of the Nicene Creed in use in the West; indeed, it was expressly stated to be a serious corruption of the text.

A detailed historical account of the omission of 'holy' from the Creed is provided by Cardale.[25] In this, he placed the blame on Joseph Bingham (1668–1723) or his printers—Bingham was the translator of the two Creeds of Epiphanius into English, and it was clear that the edition of Epiphanius used by Bingham (Paris, 1662) had included the word 'holy'. There had, however, been earlier omissions of the word—for example, in the Acts of the Lateran Council of 649, which other local councils in the West had followed, though it reappeared in the Acts of the Council of Friuli of 791. The Roman Missal, like the liturgies of the Eastern Churches, rightly included it. Cardale's conclusion was that the omission in the

---

[23] *GT*, xlvii.   [24] *C/RL*, i. 115.
[25] See 'Additional Notes on the Eucharist' in *C/RL*, i. 201–4.

English Book of Common Prayer was probably an unintentional error, since no reason for it had ever been put forward.

The Church was said to be *catholic*—she was the gift of God to all never to be withdrawn, catholic in her diffusion of blessings to all nations, in her preaching of the Gospel to every creature, in the universality of the truths and their interpretations entrusted to her, in her intercedings for all men, and in her going forth to claim all men for her Lord. The Church comprehended all particular Churches and congregations of the faithful, and because she was catholic she was necessarily *one*. She was also catholic because she imparted the fulness of God to all creation:

pardon to the guilty, sanctification to the unholy, knowledge to the ignorant, health to the diseased, strength to the infirm, consolation to the poor and sorrowful, ability and sufficiency to all who have duties to fulfil, and the treasures of goodness, love, comfort, and blessing, from God Himself the Comforter, to all who wait upon God, and look to Him to be satisfied.[26]

The Church was said to be *apostolic* because apostles were the foundation upon which she was first built, and it was through building upon this foundation that the unity, sanctity, and catholicity of the Church were manifest. The Church was apostolic both in form and in office: 'God has appointed in the Church first apostles' (1 Cor. 12: 28), sent forth 'not from men nor through man, but through Jesus Christ and God the Father' (Gal. 1: 1). The Apostles, upon whom the Holy Spirit fell at Pentecost, formed

the link between Him [Christ] in the heavens and the Church on earth; they are the gift of God, the instrument and ordinance, through means of which, at the beginning, 'the multitude of them that believed were of one heart and of one soul;' and 'the disciples were filled with joy and with the Holy Ghost.' (Acts iv. 32, xiii. 52.). By the imposition of their hands, those that believed were 'sealed with the Holy Spirit of promise.' (Eph. i. 13.). By their word the Church was governed and directed. . . . The Church is essentially Apostolic: it is essential to her perfect manifestation as the Church, to her own complete development and perfection, and to the fulfilment of her mission, that she should be under the ministry of men sent forth by Christ immediately, and not through the intervention of others.[27]

---

[26] See 'Additional Notes on the Eucharist' in *C/RL*, i. 115.   [27] Ibid. 116.

The significance of apostolic rule in the Church was heightened for the Catholic Apostolics because of their insistence that the New Testament account (Acts 2: 1–4) indicates that the tongues of fire were distributed only upon the Apostles, amongst whom was now numbered Matthias. The crucial exegesis depends upon the meaning of 'all' in Verse 1—it was argued that it was used specifically to indicate that Matthias was present along with the Eleven.

For the Catholic Apostolics the decline in the true apostolicity of the Church had begun in early times with the acceptance of apostolic rule as temporary. This was one of the acts of apostasy for which apostles had been withdrawn by God. It had led eventually and inevitably to schism (the episcopate being a 'local' not a 'universal' ministry—see below), to the extinction of the voice of prophecy, and to the loss of the Church's true hope—the hope of the Second Advent.

The Church had, however, retained the outward traces of her apostolic character through the derived apostolic succession of her episcopate, which was the token of an apostleship which had once existed. She had thus, over the centuries, failed to remain truly and visibly apostolic—her history had become one of mutual exclusions and anathemas, and contentions for rule and power, instead of a continuing history of the 'Acts of Apostles'. The restoration of apostles, called directly by God, was therefore an essential ingredient of the eventual perfecting of the Bride in preparation for the coming of the Bridegroom.

The Universal Church and Particular Churches

The Catholic Apostolics made a clear distinction between the *universal* Church and *particular* (i.e. local) Churches. The role of apostles was to rule in the universal Church in Christ's name. This rule naturally extended also to particular Churches in as much as the universal Church is the fellowship of all particular Churches. Christ was seen as the 'angel' (bishop) of the universal Church: no bishop on earth could therefore claim this role. Particular Churches should each have their own angel, ordained by an apostle.

The 'golden candlestick' of Exodus 25: 31–7 was declared to typify the particular Church in its completeness, with the angel-in-charge (typified by the central lamp), assisted by six elders (typified by the six lamps on the branches). The angel was responsible for ensuring the effective undertaking of the three ministries of rule, prophecy, and teaching and feeding (typified by the three bowls), and for the oversight of the manifestation of the gifts of the Spirit— wisdom, knowledge, faith, healing and miracles (typified by the knops). The rejoicing of the particular Church (typified by the flowers) should branch out into the fruits of the Spirit. Christ Himself would minister through His Spirit within the Church through apostolic exhortation and encouragement (typified by the tongs raising the wick and thus increasing the light) and through prophetic rebuke (typified by the snuffers). The people should overflow with love without constraint (typified by the oil), expressed both within and without the Church by the deacons as their representatives (typified by the keeping of the bowls of oil continually filled).[28]

The Eucharist, whenever and wherever it was celebrated, was deemed to be an offering of the universal Church, and hence the intercessions were always presented in the sanctuary. The Offices were always offerings of a particular Church, and hence the intercessions were always presented in the upper choir (see Ch. IV, §§ 1–3). The prayers and intercessions of the universal Church were presented spiritually through apostles (as its elders) into the hands of Christ, its angel; the prayers and intercessions of a particular Church were presented visibly by its elders into the hands of its angel for offering to the Lord.

The particular Church was said to be the image and representation of the Church Catholic in its own locality. It could consist of more than one congregation (each typified by a horn—Ps. 118: 27), gathered under the rule of one angel. Within such individual 'horn' congregations, the Eucharist might be celebrated by a priest alone, but this would show forth only an image of the unity of the Church and could not manifest her completeness:

Wherever there is a congregation of faithful men under the care of a priest, duly ordained to his charge, and subject to the episcopacy of his Angel, the Holy Eucharist may be duly celebrated . . . But it is only at the Angel's seat, where he is present with the proper ministers in the priesthood under him—elders (ruling with him and under him), prophets, evangelists, and pastors—that the perfect and complete

---

[28] J. B. Cardale, 'The Mystery of the Candlestick', letter 1833. The text of this can be found as an appendix in E. Miller's *The History and Doctrines of Irvingism or of the so-called Catholic and Apostolic Church*, ii. (London: Kegan Paul, 1878), 381–2.

service of God's worship can be offered up. The reason for this distinction is obvious. The true forms of Christian worship . . . are the very image of the heavenly things, that is to say, of the way wherein the Holy Ghost acts in His temple, the Church of Christ—in the heavenly places where Christ now abides. Of this Church, a congregation committed to the care of a single priest is a representation and image only in respect of its unity, not of its completeness as one body with many members. But the Lord, in consigning each particular church, with the priests of the fourfold ministry, the deacons, and the other subordinate officers and ministers, to the care and headship of one Angel, doth thereby give a figure and representation of His one Church, embracing all His saints, as they shall be hereafter gathered into one under Hinself; and in a body, thus complete in itself, and comprising under the Angel a fourfold ministry, and other members analogous to those of the true mystical Body of Christ, the worship of God in its exact order and complete forms becomes possible, while in any other body or congregation it is impossible.[29]

Thus, whilst apostles had universal rule in the Church, that rule was committed to and represented by angels in the particular Churches —it could not be represented by a priest ministering alone. (For a discussion of the 'fourfold ministry', see below, § 2.)

The Tabernacle as the Type of the Church

From what has been presented above, it is clear how important it was for the Catholic Apostolics that the Old Testament types should be fully reflected in their antitypes within the Church. The principal type of the constitution of the Church on earth was understood to be the structure of the Tabernacle in the wilderness, and the various services of the Tabernacle were types of the worship of the Church (see Ch. IV). (The Temple was the type of the Church after the resurrection of the dead.) A typological understanding of the Church was essential because the types themselves had been given by God:

It had been the object of the ordinances under the Old Testament to foreshadow and typify Christ in all His offices, characters, actions, and operations. The New Testament ordinances were to be the very living image of these; to embody them; to represent them visibly; to symbolise

[29] *C/RL*, i. 24–5.

them to the senses; and to convey the life and power of them to the souls of men.[30]

The three main divisions of the Tabernacle—the Outer Court, the Holy Place, and the Most Holy Place—were said to reflect the threefold nature of man: animal, intellectual, and spiritual (body, soul, and spirit). They also typified respectively the Jewish dispensation (Israel after the flesh), the Church on earth (the new spiritual Israel), and the Church in heaven. This typology was extensively developed: the Outer Court with the brazen altar and brazen laver typified confession of sin and the ministry of the word within the Church; the Holy Place with the golden altar of incense, golden candlestick, and table of shewbread typified the Church's intercessions, spiritual illumination, and the Eucharistic oblation. In the Most Holy Place, the mercy seat typified the Church's communion with God in Christ, the two cherubim typified the apostolic and prophetic ministries, the ark typified the spiritual centre in man and Christ in the Church, the tables of stone the spiritual strength of Scripture, the pot of manna the hidden spiritual reality of the Eucharist, the almond rod the grace conferred by those entrusted with spiritual authority, and the golden censer the offering of the Eucharist—the highest act of intercession.

The materials of which the Tabernacle and its furnishings were made were seen as typifying the abstract spiritual materials or characteristics out of which the Church is formed and built up:

Gold, the most enduring of all metals, is the symbol of truth formed in the understanding, and embraced in the heart, through the operation of the Holy Ghost. Silver is the symbol of love,—that love which is shed abroad in the heart by the Holy Ghost . . . Brass is the symbol of that spiritual corroboration and endurance which enables regenerate man, in the strength of the Holy Ghost, firmly to resolve, and faithfully to execute, all that God enjoins as His will.

Purple, and blue, and scarlet, and white . . . represent abstract qualities. Purple is the emblem of dignity, decision, and command; blue, of heavenly-mindedness or spirituality; scarlet, of that cleanness of conscience, that unconsciousness of imputed guilt or of evil, which can only be wrought in the intelligent Christian through faith in the blood of Christ . . . white is the symbol of the pure and spotless righteousness

---

[30] F. Sitwell, *The Purpose of God in Creation and Redemption and the Successive Steps for Manifesting the Same in and by the Church* (Edinburgh: Laurie, 1865), 28.

which is in Christ, and is imputed unto the believer, and imparted unto the regenerate.[31]

On the assumption, following the Rabbinical writers, that the materials displaying the various colours were of wool and linen, the former was said to typify actions taken with ecclesiastical authority, and the latter acts of men in society and in the world generally. The outer coverings of the Tabernacle were made from the skins of three animals: goats, rams, and badgers. These typified respectively the ministries of prophets, deacons, and evangelists within the Church. Shittim-wood typified human nature, which was weak and unstable in itself, but which had been assumed by Christ at the Incarnation and thus made the basis of His spiritual Tabernacle—the universal Church—composed of men endowed by His Spirit with the powers of the world to come. These materials had been applied in the building of the Tabernacle in various ways, thus indicating that the universal Church would be built up through many combinations of the spiritual characteristics typified. The rites, offices, and ministries of the Church were all typified by the Tabernacle, its construction and its services.

Since each particular Church was modelled upon the universal Church as far as was possible, its features were also similarly typified by the Tabernacle—in this case by the arrangements of the Holy Place and the Outer Court. The golden altar typified priestly mediation, properly fulfilled in the particular Church by the Angel, its four horns (symbols of power) indicating his rule over the four priestly ministries under him. These ministries were typified by the Table of Prothesis fitted with its four rings. In the Outer Court, the four horns of the brazen altar typified similar kinds of ministry— whether exercised by a priest or a deacon.

The five pillars at the entrance of the Tabernacle (overlaid with gold and of the same height as the four leading to the most holy place, but with sockets of brass), together with the sixty brass pillars around the Outer Court (four of which formed the means of access), were said to typify the ministries under the apostles in the universal Church:

The five Pillars typify a Ministry committed to men, whose duty it is to prepare the way, and to give access, to the several rites symbolized by

---

[31] C/RL, i. 240.

those in the Holy Place. The four Pillars . . . typify an office committed to men, and ordained for preparation and access to the rites symbolized by those of the Brazen Altar and the Court.

Upon each of these—upon the five Pillars, and upon the four—hung a veil of the same four colours as those of the Veil which separated the Most Holy from the Holy Place, manifesting that we can make no progress unto the perfection of the Christian man except through the operation of the fourfold Ministry exercised towards us in every stage of our approach.[32]

This typological approach to the structure of the Church, its ministries, and its worship was a predominant feature of Catholic Apostolic ecclesiology. (It was applied also to the teaching on the nature of man—see § 3 below.) So important was it as a foundation-stone for Catholic Apostolic teaching, that it is difficult to appreciate the full meaning of many of the works by Catholic Apostolic writers without first undertaking an in-depth study of their interpretation of the Mosaic Tabernacle. For them, the structure of the Christian Church and its worship (other than the Eucharist itself—see Ch. IV, § 3) had already been given by God in the Jewish dispensation, and it was therefore not subject to any change by man. It was not to be found directly in the New Testament.

The absence from the New Testament of details concerning the structure of the Church was not because the Apostles were left free to build the Church upon foundations of their own devising, but because they were given the authority by the risen Christ and the spiritual insight through the Holy Spirit to build the Church upon foundations *whose details were already laid down*. What was abundantly clear from the New Testament was the apostolic basis of the Church. The New Testament, most notably through the Epistle to the Hebrews, did nevertheless clearly indicate the typological *principle* upon which the Christian Church was to be built. The Church had often lost sight of this, and men had attempted to introduce changes contrary to divine revelation. This was another result of the loss of apostolic rule. The restoration of apostles was thus essential for the rebuilding of the Church in its divinely appointed form.

---

[32] C/RL, i. 260–1.

2. THE FOURFOLD 'ORDER' OF MINISTRY

In the Catholic Apostolic Church the apostles were set, as ministers of the universal Church, over the traditional threefold catholic ministry of angel (bishop), priest, and deacon. There was thus a fourfold *order* (or *degree*) of ministry, outwardly similar to that which has existed in the Church Catholic from early times, except for the superimposition of the apostolic office. However, a more restricted view of the role of the episcopate was held—angels being seen as ministers of particular Churches only (as has been noted earlier)—and the diaconate was restored as a permanent office with duties more nearly approximating those indicated in the New Testament writings. Superimposed upon this fourfold order was a fourfold *character* (or *function*) of ministry—representing the fourfold ministry of Christ as apostle, prophet, evangelist, and pastor—derived partly from Scripture, partly from the nature of man, and (inevitably) partly from typology. This latter fourfold division of the ministry was peculiar to the Catholic Apostolic Church: it will be considered in Section 3.

The Restoration of Apostles

In the course of the justification of the need for a visible apostolic office in the Church, reference was often made to past 'prophecies' that apostles would one day be restored by the action of the Holy Spirit. The concept of the restoration of apostles to the Church did not begin with the Catholic Apostolics, nor did they claim that it did. They were keen to point out that there had been a number of occasions in the Church's history when prophetic voices had claimed that apostles would be restored in association with a special work of the Spirit within the Church before the Parousia.

Particular reference was made by Catholic Apostolic writers to the following works:

the *Commentary on Ephesians* of St Jerome (*c*.342–420);
the *Institutes* of John Calvin (1509–64);
several of the writings of Jane Leade (1623–1704);
the interpretation of the Apocalypse by Isaac Newton (1642–1727);

a study of the Apocalypse by Johann Albrecht Bengel (1687–1752);
records of debates in De Maistre's *Soirées de St. Petersburg* (1809);
works by Philip Matthew Hahn (b. 1790);
La Venida del Mesias en Gloria y Majestad by the Jesuit, Fr Emanuelo
  Lacunza (1731–1801), subsequently translated by Irving (see Ch. V,
  § 3);
a pseudonymous Roman Catholic work, Père Lambert's *Exposition des
  predictions et promesses, faites à l'êglise pour les derniers temps de la
  gentilité* (1806);
a sermon included in the works of the Russian Orthodox Bishop
  Innokenti of Cherson (preached in his Cathedral at Pentecost 1857).[33]

In all these writings there was reference to a special work of the
Spirit to be done in the last days, and most included specific mention
of restored apostles. It should be noted that Bishop Innokenti's
sermon (one of the works in which 'new apostles' were mentioned)
postdates the inauguration of the Catholic Apostolic apostolate.
However, it would appear unlikely that the Russian bishop would
have had prior knowledge of the restored apostles in England—*The
Great Testimony* (1838) was not presented to the tsar, and Dow's visit
to Russia during the apostolic visitations to the 'tribes' (1838–9) was
of such brief duration that it is most unlikely that any content of this
witness would have become known to the bishop.[34] Indeed, the text
of the sermon clearly indicates that the bishop was speaking of future
possibilities not of contemporary events. It is therefore not
unreasonable for this sermon to have been included as a (possible)
prophecy of the Catholic Apostolic witness.

In addition to the writings quoted above, there had been frequent
references to the restoration of apostles during the charismatic
phenomena which occurred in Scotland, England, and (later)
Bavaria in the 1820s and 1830s (see Ch. II, § 1).

---

[33] Full references to most of these works, with appropriate quotations, can be
found in K. von Mickwitz, *Ein Zeitbild in wichtigen Zeugnissen* (Berlin: Hoffman,
1902), 7–46, 159–72. See also K. Born, *Das Werk des herrn unter Aposteln* (Bremen:
1974), 7–8. Von Mickwitz's work is also especially notable for including an account of
how the strong impression made by the Catholic Apostolic witness on King Friedrich
Wilhelm IV of Prussia led to consideration of the possibility of the Lutheran Church
in that country being placed under the rule of the restored apostles.

[34] On presenting himself to the Tsar, Dow was given 48 hours to complete
preparations for leaving the country.

Apostolic Authority and Other Successions

The Catholic Apostolics did not argue that apostles were essential for the Church in the sense that valid orders could not be conveyed nor valid sacraments administered without the existence of a living apostolate. It was expressly stated that the restoration of the apostolate was not intended as a replacement for the existing episcopate of the Church Catholic:

> A restoration of the Apostolic office is in no respect an interference with the legitimate authority of Bishops; for Episcopacy and Apostleship are not the same, and each has its separate sphere. Their *co-existence* in the primitive Church proves this; and that the right place of Bishops is along with and under Apostles: not in becoming their successors and substitutes. . . . Bishops in the absence of Apostles partially supplied their place.[35]

Apostles were considered essential, however, for the *perfecting* of the Church and for the conveying of *plenary* charism.

Episcopal succession was recognized as having validity, but of a diminished spiritual content. Episcopal ordination did provide a guarantee that priests so ordained were acting within the communion of the universal Church. Such priests could administer valid sacraments, but these were considered to be of a lower spiritual order than those administered by priests ordained by apostles. Presbyteral succession was also regarded as having a validity, though of a further diminished spiritual order, and related primarily to pastorship, preaching and teaching. The distinction here was made plain in that Presbyterian ministers were considered as requiring apostolic *ordination* to the priesthood, whereas Anglican (and Roman Catholic) priests needed only to have their orders *confirmed* by an apostle. The underlying principle was based upon the idea that all ministry in the Church is *derived* from Christ, indeed *is* Christ's. Only those called directly by Christ through the Holy Spirit had the authority to convey the full charism of holy orders. It was therefore wrong in principle that bishops should consecrate other bishops, or presbyters ordain other presbyters—authority must be derived *from above*. God had not, however, left His people entirely without means of grace since the

---

[35] R. Norton, *Reasons for Believing That the Lord has Restored to the Church Apostles and Prophets* (London: Bosworth, 1852), v–vi.

time when the episcopate had usurped apostolic authority. The charism received through the episcopate alone had, however, not been sufficient to prevent the rending apart of the Body of Christ by heresy and schism or the contamination of the Church through 'fornication' with the world. Only the restoration of apostles, with the consequent fullness of charism guaranteed by the apostolic ministry, could rebuild the Church, make her once again complete, and perfect her as a Bride for the coming Bridegroom.

The unity of the Church manifested at its beginning, had been realized so long as her members 'continued steadfastly in the apostles' doctrine and fellowship' (Acts 2: 42). It was the Apostles who were the focus of unity, something which neither bishops alone nor the Roman Pontiff could ever be:

Apostles were ordained by Christ heads over the universal Church, to rule in doctrine, in discipline, and in ministry, the centre of unity. Bishops were constituted, under apostles, heads to their respective churches; and being necessarily independent of each other, they can never be the head of the universal Church. Without a centre of unity, they themselves, as the fact has proved, become divided, if not antagonistic. For unity without headship, is an impossibility. (It is to no purpose to assert, as some do . . . that Christ in the heavens is our Head. . . . Christ acts towards, and in His Church through ordinances, and the simple question is, what is the right ordinance for the rule and government of the Universal Church? Will anyone say there should be none?)

It was the feeling of this necessity, this want, which, in great measure, gave rise to the assumed headship of the Bishop of Rome. The gradual rise of the Pope of Rome was the putting forth of a spiritual instinct—the effort of man to supply the absent ordinance of God.[36]

All man's efforts to replace apostolic headship had, however, proved to be in vain. Rather than building up the Church, they had served only to distort and fragment her.

The restored apostles claimed that their authority derived from their direct call by Christ through the Holy Spirit speaking through prophets, and that their understanding of the responsibilities of that call was conveyed to them by the same Spirit. This was seen as being in accord with the call of the first Apostles—they had been chosen by Christ, instructed in their apostolic responsibilities by Him in the period between His Resurrection and Ascension, and confirmed in

[36] Dalton, *What is the Church?*, 29–30.

their call by the descent of the Holy Spirit at Pentecost. Thus, it was claimed that the authority of the restored apostolate was implied by that of the Apostles of the New Testament. The Church was a theocracy—those with the responsibility of exercising rule within her were chosen by God and not by men. Apostles could not receive their appointment through the working of any democratic principle. When challenged with the case of Matthias (Acts 1: 23–6), the response was to point out: first, that Barsabbas and Matthias were nominated by the Apostles alone; secondly, that the Apostles asked the Lord to indicate which of the two *He* had chosen; and thirdly and most particularly, that the completion of the Twelve in this way occurred *before* their sealing as Apostles at Pentecost. The Gentile apostleship of Paul was also quoted: Paul had had a spiritual encounter with Christ followed by a confirmation by the Holy Spirit through Ananias—an inward intimation of calling followed by an outward validation. It was claimed that, in a similar way, the restored apostles—also called to a Gentile apostleship—had had an inward intimation of apostleship followed by an outward validation by the Holy Spirit speaking through prophetic utterances.

The Gentile Apostolate

The apostolate of the Catholic Apostolic Church was seen as being, particularly, a restoration of the *Gentile* apostolate. Reference was made to the special revelation—the 'mystery of Christ'—of which St Paul wrote (1 Cor. 15: 51; Eph. 3: 4–5; Col. 1: 26). This mystery concerned the Church and its future hope and was a revelation for the Gentile mission, a revelation which the Holy Spirit had restored to its proper prominence in the Church in the last days:

And the Gospel, as declared by St. Paul, was the 'Ministration of Righteousness' *and* 'the Ministration of the Spirit' (2 Cor. iii. 8,9): and its hope (the hope of the Gentile Apostleship, *so* ministering the Spirit in Paul's day,) was the 'forming Christ in his people the hope of glory,' and the presenting them perfect in Christ Jesus. It was something *additional* to what the Jewish Apostleship had preached; something revealed . . . outside of the College of Apostles to the Circumcision, which they had not had revealed to them, and which St. Paul had to communicate, in private conversation, 'unto such of them as seemed to be pillars' (Gal. ii. 2–9): a supplementary, not a contradictory, truth; for God's apostleship is one Apostleship . . . and cannot . . . be contradictory. It was a supplementary and additional revelation, *consequent on the refusal of the Jews to accept the Gospel as a nation* (Acts xiii. 41–6, 47, 48, xxviii. 28). The Gospel preached by Paul was a Gospel of special grace unto God's election, the Church (Acts xv. 14). . . . The Jewish Apostles 'preached Jesus and the Resurrection,' the forgiveness of sins, the fulfilment of the promise made unto the fathers, and the sending of Jesus, whom God had raised up, first of all unto the Jews, 'to bless them by turning them away from their iniquities.' (Acts ii. 38, 39, iii. 15, 26.) Paul alone taught the mystery of the Church . . . the predestined Bride of the Lamb, His Body and Fulness, the sharer of His throne, the partaker of His glory. . . . The hope of St. Paul, the Gentile Apostle's hope, remaineth. It survives even unto us. To a Gentile Apostleship was it revealed and committed; and by a Gentile Apostleship must it be fulfilled.[37]

It had not been a requirement for the Gentile apostolate of St Paul and St Barnabas that they satisfy St Peter's criterion imposed on candidates for the completion of the Twelve, namely that they 'should have accompanied us during all the time that the Lord Jesus went in and out among us . . . a witness to his resurrection' (Acts 1: 21–2). This was not, in any case, the sole function of apostles, of which there were several indicated in Scripture, amongst which were: witnessing *to* the resurrection, guiding and governing the Churches, conferring the Holy Ghost by the laying on of hands, and the presentation of the Church to Christ at His coming. It was noted that the Gospel message preached by the Apostles was 'Jesus Christ and the resurrection of the dead' (e.g. Acts 4: 2; 17: 18; etc.). This was a message which St Paul had *received*, and it related not merely to Christ's Resurrection but to the promise of resurrection for all. It clearly did not require that everyone accepted as an apostle should have been a witness *of* as well as a witness *to* the Resurrection of Christ. The need for apostles for the conveying of the Holy Spirit by the laying on of hands was clearly indicated by a number of quoted instances in Acts (e.g. 8: 17; 19: 6; etc.)—it was quite clear from 8: 12–17 that Philip, a deacon, could not convey the Holy Spirit, but that apostles were specifically required for this.[38] All the functions of

[37] W. Flewker, *The Restoration of the Gentile Apostleship* (London: Bosworth, 1874), 5–7.
[38] For an extended and detailed argument, see T. Groser, *The Functions and Credentials of Apostles* (London: Bosworth, 1882). A defence of the apostolate of the Catholic Apostolic Church with reference exclusively to the Gentile apostolate of St Paul can be found in id., *The Call of St. Paul to the Apostleship* (London: Bosworth, 1854).

apostleship were undertaken by St Paul and St Barnabas, though in the last case the work of preparation was only begun, its later continuation having been frustrated by the 'mystery of lawlessness' working within the Church (1 Thess. 2: 7). To deny the apostolate of the restored apostles on the grounds of Acts 1: 21–2 (as many had tried to do) was to deny the Gentile apostolate of the New Testament.

St Paul's Epistles were considered as revealing the purposes of God to be accomplished specifically through a Gentile apostolate. This apostolate's prime role was the gathering of the Church as an election *out of* the Gentiles—there was no suggestion that all or even the majority of the Gentiles would be converted. It was clear from the New Testament that, even in this, St Paul had had to experience and recognize failure. God's purposes had to await a restored Gentile apostleship in the last days for their fulfilment, though it was again probable that the apostolate would be rejected by many.

Nowhere is there a fuller summary of how the restored apostles saw their role than the following, written in the early days of the Catholic Apostolic Church before there was any real experience of the practical working of that office:

Looking at Paul's Epistles to discover the purpose of God by an Apostleship in the Gentile Church, we find that they are the wise master-builders to build the tabernacle, Christ's house. They are labourers together with God in the Church, which is God's husbandry, God's building. They are the channels for blessing and filling the Church with the Holy Ghost, the witnesses to the Man Jesus at the right hand of God, who baptizes with the Holy Ghost . . . They are the ministers of the Spirit to the Church, shewing her forth, the Epistle of God written in their hearts, known and read of all. They are the ministers of Christ and stewards of the mysteries of God, of whom it is required that they be found faithful; but no man may judge them. They are the preparers of the Bride of the Lamb for her marriage. They are the espousers of the Church to one husband, to present her a chaste virgin to Christ, preparing the New Jerusalem, as a bride adorned for her husband. They are the fathers of the Church . . . They are the heads of the Twelve Tribes, the Israel of God. They are nurses to the infant, cherishing the children, labouring day and night, feeding them as babes and carnal with the milk, and ministering to them the strong meat when they can bear it . . . They are the foundations of the city, the New Jerusalem, the Church perfected, and the crown of the twelve stars on her head. They have the twofold office of Moses bringing out of Egypt, and of Joshua, the captain of the hosts of the Lord, by the twelve men, one out of each tribe, bringing into the land of promise Israel, the Son, the first-born. They have the full ministry of Jesus raised from the dead, and fulfilling the office of the Prophet like unto Moses. All offices of authority in the Church are carved out of the Apostleship, and are contained in it, and whosoever rejects their authority, put forth in the ministries, shall be cut off from Israel. They are instead of God to Aaron, the priesthood of the Church; and to Israel, the Church to bless; and in the place of God to Pharoah, the world, for judgement. Theirs is not the word of God coming in vision or in dream, as it comes to the Prophets, but it is the word of the Son of Man, the Man of God's image, having the mind of Christ, and speaking God's word. . . . They have the care of all the Churches, and are to the whole Church what Angels and Elders, Deacons and Governments are to each—the servants of all. They shall lead the Church now into the glory of the Only Begotten of the Father, the fulness of grace and truth, and shall also prepare the saints for the visible glory, to be revealed when the Son of Man cometh.[39]

In accordance with the teaching on the call of apostles, no rite of ordination to the apostolate was provided:

Apostles are neither of men nor by men. They alone are set over the whole Church. They cannot appoint one another. And, if so, how can inferior ministers appoint them; or the whole Church create them? How can the Church set them over herself?[40]

The only rite permissible was a solemn act of 'separation' for their work, said to parallel the separation of St Paul and St Barnabas. This rite, performed in 1835, was regarded as a formal *act of recognition* by the Church of their apostolate (see Ch. II, § 2)—it could be no more than that.

In the Catholic Apostolic Church all ordinations to the three major orders of angel, priest, and deacon were reserved to the apostolate, as these were seen as ministries of the Church Catholic requiring a special endowment of the Holy Spirit. Also reserved to the apostolate were: the laying on of hands and sealing with chrism (see below); confirming the orders of episcopally ordained priests; the

---

[39] F. W. Woodhouse, *The Substance of a Ministry on the Office of the Apostle in the Gentile Church* (London: Bosworth, 1882), 37–8. This work was compiled from lectures delivered in Edinburgh in December 1834, and first published by Graham, 1835.

[40] T. Carlyle, *Apostles Given, Lost, and Restored* (London: Goodall, 1853), 33. This work is included in Carlyle's *Collected Works* (London: Bosworth, 1878), 271–325.

presentation of priests before the Lord as candidates for the
episcopate—to be confirmed in their candidature by the voice of
prophecy; the induction of angels into their particular charges and
the blessing of angels for special missions; the consecration of
churches and altars, fonts, etc. The blessing of priests and deacons
for special missions, together with the dedication of church
furniture, vessels, and vestments, though properly an apostolic
prerogative, was often delegated to an angel. The apostles also made
the final determination concerning words spoken in prophecy—
whether or not they were of the Holy Spirit.

The Rite of Sealing

The apostolic rite of sealing was introduced in the Catholic Apostolic
Church in 1847 (see Ch. II, § 2). Its formal title was 'The Order for
the Laying on of Apostles' Hands'.[41] It was preceded (on one of the
ten previous days) by a formal renewal of baptismal vows and a
personal rededication to God's service, made before the angel of the
congregation to which the candidates belonged. This was seen as a
completion of

that work of ministry in which he [the Angel] and the priests and
deacons have been engaged, in the spiritual education and preparation
of the candidates in order to the due reception by them of the gift of
God.[42]

The limit of *ten* days for the prior rite was in order that

the spiritual attention and thoughts of the candidates may be directed to
this great crisis of their life; and that they may be, as it were, sanctified
and set apart as vessels to be made meet for the Master's use.[43]

Sealing was administered (during the Eucharist, immediately
before the administration of Communion) to members of the Church
on their reaching the age of 20. This particular age was chosen
because it was said to be typified in the Law of Moses

wherein every circumcised man, at twenty years old and upward, should
present his half shekel of silver for the service of the Sanctuary, as a
ransom for his soul—that is to say, as the outward sign of his own

---

[41] *The Liturgy and other Divine Offices of the Church* (London: Bosworth, 1880),
401–9.
[42] C/RL, ii. 452.   [43] Ibid.

personal faith in Jehovah, the God of Israel, who dwelt in that
Sanctuary, and could alone provide, and would provide, for his
redemption. . . . So in the Church of Christ, it is the duty of every
baptized person . . . to present himself as a free-will offering to the
Lord, that he may receive the heavenly gift which Christ would bestow
upon him, and through the inspiration of the Holy Ghost may exercise
those powers of the world to come which in that Gift would be conferred
in fulfilling his part in the spiritual temple, to the glory of God.[44]

The age of 20 was seen to be appropriate for this rite not only in
terms of spiritual development but also in terms of maturity of
general abilities. These ought to be put to the service of the Church
as well as being used for progress in secular life. All Church
members should offer their capabilities to God—only in this way
could they play their part as *members* of a corporate body:

In the affairs of this life, when a man comes of age, he develops qualities
and capabilities which were before only latent. He takes part with his
fellow men in the duties of their common life. He becomes a Statesman,
a Soldier, a professional man, or even if he be only 'one of the many' still
he has his place and duties in the Community. All this is important. But
it is only the shadow of the higher reality—a reflection of the action of
the One great Body of Christ—a feeble illustration of the great truth
that 'ye are all members one of another . . .'. And thus, not only because
the interests of all are the same (for that is true of any corporate body)
but because the organization, and the *very life* of the One Body of Christ,
are as the organization and life of every member—in short, an
organization and life of which each individual member is a constituent
part.

> .   .   .   .

But suppose that in the State for example, its Citizens did not come
forward to take up the duties proper to them, and suitable to their
capabilities, but were all minding only their own private affairs, or living
in ease, regardless of public duty, why then we say that, the State is
going to decay.

The same thing is true for the Church, in a far higher degree. If its
members become engrossed in their own private affairs and in selfish
aims and ends, and forget the work of God and their duties as members
of a corporate body; then rapid declension must follow. And the people
in the Old Dispensation who produced a Moses, and a David, and a
Solomon, end with 'Scribes, and Pharisees, and Lawyers'. And the
Church in this dispensation, which began with Apostles and Prophets,

---

[44] C/RL, ii. 455–6.

Evangelists and Pastors and Deacons—ends in its most favourable aspect, with Pastors only—in its lowests aspects, with Infidels, Socialists, and Anarchists—for these come out of the Church, and not from the Heathen—ends, as the Apostle Paul says expressly, in a *great apostasy*, or falling away. And this, we grieve to say, is what is now visible in the Church of Christ.[45]

Thus, sealing—which included not only the laying on of apostles' hands but also the signing of the forehead with chrism—was seen as the conveying of a special gift of the Holy Spirit for the exercise of 'ministry' in its widest sense within the Church, according to the gifts given by God to each individual member.

The words spoken by the apostle upon laying his hands upon each member were:

Receive the Holy Ghost, In the Name of the Father, and of the Son, and of the Holy Ghost.

God the Father Almighty confirm and perfect thee; seal thee [chrismation] with the seal and signet of the Lord; and anoint thee with the ointment of salvation, unto eternal life.[46]

Then, stretching out his hands from the altar over the candidates as a whole, he added:

Ye are washed, ye are sanctified, ye are anointed with the unction from the Holy One. In the Name of the Father, and of the Son, and of the Holy Ghost.[47]

By these words the Sealing was linked to the renewal of baptismal vows, and, by an individually conferred rite followed by a communal blessing, the responsibilities of each member to exercise his personal God-given gifts for the good of a corporate body was visibly signified.

The Catholic Apostolic rite of sealing must not be confused with the blessing of persons to receive regular Holy Communion—an office performed by angels. Neither was it considered to be the same as chrismation in the Eastern Churches or confirmation administered in the Churches of the West. It was the gift of the *Spirit of power* in all its sevenfold fullness, which Christ received when He was exalted to the right hand of God (Isaiah 11: 1; Heb. 6: 5–6, etc.), and which *the Apostles* had conferred by their laying on of hands (Acts 8: 17

---

[45] W. W. Wright, *The Holy Sealing* (n.p., Huxley, 1892), 5.
[46] *The Liturgy*, 407.   [47] Ibid.

etc.): it could not be episcopally conferred since there was no scriptural warrant for this. Sealing, as understood by the Catholic Apostolics, required living apostles, whose restoration of the rite they saw as having been foretold in Scripture (Apoc. 7: 3–8).

In relation to baptism (of which the type was circumcision) it was not a matter of an initial gift for generation and a later gift for continued growth. It was a *new* and different gift of the Spirit from that conveyed by baptism:

These two gifts are distinct, and as different each from the other, as was the work of the Holy Ghost in the conception of the Lord and the grace bestowed upon Him . . . from that descent of the Holy Ghost upon Him, when He came up from the waters of Jordan, and was sent forth, the Christ, the Anointed One, on the work of His Ministry. Or again, they are as distinct and different as was the work of the Holy Ghost, when the Lord took again His body in the grave and was raised from the dead by the Spirit of holiness, from that fulness of the Spirit of Glory and of God, which He received when he was exalted to the right hand of the Father, and made in the fullest and highest sense both Lord and Christ.[48]

The gift of the Spirit conveyed by sealing had a 'higher purpose' than the gift at baptism because it related specifically to the functioning of the individual *within the Body* so that

each in his place in the Body may minister the gift divided to him to the edifying and profit of the rest, and may fulfil his part in the general mission on which Christ has sent the Church into the world, and for which He endowed her at Pentecost with supernatural and heavenly powers of the Holy Ghost.[49]

The charism conferred in the East by chrismation and in the West by confirmation could not have the same fullness as that conferred by apostles. East and West were divided on the outward form of the Sacrament; many in the West did not hold it to be a sacrament. In particular, in the West the rite was primarily or even exclusively one of admission to Holy Communion—the gift of the Spirit being understood as being merely for the confirming or strengthening of the gift received at baptism. The understanding of the much deeper significance of the true rite had been forgotten:

They do not hold that the proper object and effect of the sacrament of Chrism is that every baptized person, duly receiving it, is therein made

---

[48] C/*RL*, ii. 421–2.   [49] Ibid. 426.

partaker of the powers of the world to come, and of the inspiration and supernatural gifts of the Holy Ghost. And they are so far right. They could not claim for any rite administered by them, more than in truth they claim, and in the absence of ministers immediately sent forth from Christ . . . it is not to be anticipated that they should discern the universal need of those heavenly powers, which are, as it were, the jewels and ornaments of the bride, the Church, but which they suppose to be the jewels and ornaments appropriated exceptively to individuals . . .[50]

Apostles' Coadjutors and Delegates

Although sealing and other apostolic acts were, strictly, reserved to the apostles, with the passage of time it became impossible for the diminishing Apostolic College to fulfil the duties demanded of its members. During the 1860s apostles' coadjutors were appointed from the senior ranks of the episcopate. These coadjutors were in no sense apostles, nor was there any question of an expectation of succession. Each was individually appointed to a specific apostle, during whose lifetime he could perform such apostolic functions as were delegated to him as a matter of practical necessity. With the death of an apostle, the corresponding coadjutorship immediately lapsed.

A similar situation existed with apostolic delegates (authorized during the last decade of Woodhouse's life only). A 'delegation' consisted of two angels commissioned by the apostle to perform specific apostolic acts, though their authority could not extend to the consecration of other angels. The coadjutors and delegates were thus, for a strictly limited time, angels authorized to act on behalf of individual apostles for specific purposes as a kind of 'extension of their arms'. Neither formed in any sense a distinct order of ministry.

Angels: The Catholic Apostolic Episcopate

The Catholic Apostolic episcopate combined the New Testament office of bishop (i.e. overseer) with the apocalyptic office of angel. Thus, in the Order for the Ordination or Consecration of an Angel—

[50] Ibid. 447–8.

an ordination which took place during the Eucharist after the Nicene Creed—the consecrating apostle prayed to God the Father:

Send down, we beseech Thee, the Holy Ghost upon this Thy servant, whom Thou hast called to serve Thee as an angel and a bishop in Thy Church. Grant unto him, O most merciful Father, such fulness of Thy grace, that he may be a faithful and wise steward over Thy household . . . that he may be a faithful leader of the blind and of them that are out of the way; a light unto those who are in darkness; a watchful guardian over Thy fold, and a follower of the True Shepherd, giving his life for the sheep . . .[51]

Then, after a further prayer, the apostle laid his hands upon the angel-elect, saying:

Receive the Holy Ghost for the office of Angel and Bishop in the Church of God. In the Name of the Father, and of the Son, and of the Holy Ghost. Amen.[52]

It should be noted that on both occasions the phrase 'angel *and* [a] bishop' was used. The words 'angel' and 'bishop' were thus not regarded as synonymous—the two offices were not identical though united in the same individuals and conveyed by the Holy Spirit through the same laying on of hands:

The name bishop or overseer directs our thoughts to one who superintends the doings of others; in this case one who superintends the doings of priests, deacons and laymen. But as all such, though engaged in spiritual things, yet set on earth, this all refers to those earthly things which Our Lord, in His discourse with Nicodemus, contrasted with heavenly things (John III, 12).

But the name of angel at once draws all our thoughts away from the earth; it lifts us up in spirit towards the throne of God Almighty, where cherubim and seraphim, angels and archangels, and all the host of heaven . . . join in the one hymn of adoration, 'Holy, holy, holy . . .'[53]

In the 'Office for Presentation of Priests for the Episcopate', after special prayers by the apostle, the rubrics state:

Then there shall be a sufficient pause, during which all shall remain kneeling, and shall lift up their hearts to Almighty God; and shall wait, if He be pleased to make known His will concerning any who have been presented.[54]

[51] *The Liturgy*, 520.	[52] Ibid. 521.
[53] I. Capadose, 'On the Office of Angel in the Church of Christ' (MS, 1889), 2.
[54] *The Liturgy*, 500.

Those, chosen by the Lord in this way through the voice of prophecy for the episcopate, were required to be like angels, free from earthly cares—heavenly. The words, 'who makest . . . fire and flame thy ministers' (Ps. 104: 4), were taken as applying as much to angels in the Church on earth as to angel-messengers in heaven. The angel was to be 'robed in heavenly conversation' in conformity with Aaron's garments (Exod. 28) and Ezekiel's vision (Ezek. 1: 26): the robe of blue and the sapphire stone, representing heavenly-mindedness and its fruits—calmness, meekness, gentleness, purveying of peace, faithfulness to God's purposes, unseeking of the favours of men, oneness with the mind of Christ. The angel's office was also said to be one of the stars held in the Lord's right hand (Apoc. 1: 16).

It was expressly stated that no bishop could also be an angel unless within the fellowship of living apostles. Thus, over most of the long history of the Church, the office of angel had been in abeyance, not revived until the first ordination of an angel by an apostle at Albury in 1832 (see Ch. II, § 1):

Bishops, unless upheld by the immediate ambassadors of the Lord, and abiding in the fellowship of apostles, cannot be stars; they miss that constant influx of Divine light and life, which is indispensable to the angelic heavenly-mindedness. Let the history of the Church in all its parts and divisions bear witness to this. Bishops, no longer ruled, guided, shielded by apostles, have lost their heavenly standing of angel, dwindling down to earthly lords, claiming territorial jurisdiction and social distinction. How could then the congregations entrusted to their charge abide in the heavenlies? The very hope and expectation of the coming of the Bridegroom to make His Church partaker of His celestial throne and glory died away, and with it vanished the bride's love, the bride's chastity, the bride's purity.[55]

The Catholic Apostolic angel was primarily the head of the particular Church entrusted to his charge, and he was the 'normal' celebrant of the Eucharist in particular Churches. His powers of 'ordination' were restricted to the *blessing* of those serving in the minor offices of deaconess, underdeacon, acolyte, organist, singer, doorkeeper, etc. This was because these related to lay ministries which were seen as restricted to particular Churches and hence not considered to require a special gift of the Holy Spirit for the ordained catholic ministry.

Other functions reserved to angels were: the dedication of

---

[55] I. Capadose, 'On the Office of Angel', 6.

catechumens; the receiving of persons into regular communion; the renewal of vows and dedication, prior to apostolic laying on of hands (see above); the blessing of laypersons offering themselves for special works of charity and piety; the presentation and dedication of candidates for the priesthood—to be confirmed in their candidature by the voice of prophecy; the receiving of priests and deacons already ordained; the laying of the foundation stone of a church; the blessing of holy oil; and such blessings as might, from time to time, be delegated by an apostle (e.g. of clergy setting out on special missions, and of church furniture, vessels, vestments, etc.). Also entrusted to the angels was the 'discernment of spirits', that is, the *initial* acceptance or rejection of ecstatic words spoken within particular congregations. Also, to the angel in particular belonged the ministry of offering the Intercession during liturgical worship. The office of angel was said to be typified by the seraphim—the symbol of the presence of Jehovah—and the angel in his particular Church represented both the presence and the unity of God.

The case made by the mainstream episcopal Churches that bishops were successors of apostles *in function* was expressly refuted by reference both to Scripture and to patristic writings. The facts were said expressly to deny that

Timothy, Silvanus, Andronicus, Junia, the angels of the Seven Churches, Epaphroditus, etc. were of the same rank with Paul and John. . . .

After the appointment of Matthias to fill the vacancy in the Twelve . . . no mention is made of any to whom the Apostolic office is pretended to be ascribed, till we come to Barnabas and Saul, who were called by the Holy Ghost, and separated for their work, without the agency, or even knowledge, of the Apostles of the Circumcision. . . . Judas and Silas were prophets (Acts xv. 32) . . . but they were of no higher rank. When the dispute arose between Paul and Barnabas as to Mark . . . Paul chose Silas . . . and they went through Syria and Cilicia, strengthening the churches. Here was an Apostle accompanied by a Prophet as a subordinate minister; not two Apostles, each officially independent of each other. At Derbe, or Lystra, they find Timothy, already a believer, and, not improbably, one of the elders ordained on the former visit, as mentioned in Chap. xiv. 23. If so, as he had proved faithful in the lesser thing, the Apostle may have now received him to the higher calling of a minister in the Church Universal, guided therein by prophetic words spoken through Silas by the Holy Ghost, and consecrating him to the office by the laying-on of his hands, with the concurrence of the elders.

(This would have been an ordination to the episcopate, the essence of which lies in the authority vested in it over presbyters . . .)[56]

No evidence existed in the New Testament to suggest that Silas or Timothy performed any apostolic acts—they neither ordained bishops, nor laid on hands for the conveying of the Holy Spirit. The same applied to Epaphroditus and Tychicus. All these clearly had episcopal authority but not apostolic authority, nor did they have any authority over each other. If they had also been apostles, they would have been called so.

Early patristic writings[57] were quoted to show that the name 'apostle' was never *rightly* given to those who were ordained as chief pastors, i.e. bishops, and that a distinction between the two offices was constantly implied in them. Thus, Theodoret wrote of a 'promiscuous' confusion of names, adding that

shortly after, the name of apostle was appropriated to such only as were apostles indeed (ἀληθῶς); and then the name bishop was given to those who before were [promiscuously] called apostles.[58]

Similarly, St Ambrose had written:

the holy apostles being dead, they who were ordained after them to govern the [local] churches, could not arrive at the excellency of those first [the Apostles]; nor had they the testimony of miracles, but were in many other respects inferior to them; therefore they thought it not decent to assume to themselves the name of apostles; but, dividing the names, they left to presbyters the name of the presbytery, and they themselves were called bishops.[59]

It therefore appeared clear from early writings that even if bishops were misnamed apostles on occasion, the Church soon discovered the difference

and the name was, by common consent, appropriated . . . to those who were Apostles indeed; that is, whose Apostleship was not through 'human ordainers' but immediately from the Lord.[60]

---

[56] Andrews, *The True Constitution*, 121–2.

[57] Patristic writers referred to included Clement, Ignatius, Justin Martyr, Polycarp, Tertullian, Theodoret, and Ambrose.

[58] Andrews, *The True Constitution*, 126 (quoting from Bingham, *Antiquities of the Christian Church*, 10 vols., 1708–22).

[59] Ibid.

[60] Ibid.

The fact of the deaths of the Apostles was seen to compel a special meaning to be given to the Lord's promise to be with them until the end (Matt. 20: 20), which seemed to imply that the apostleship would not cease until the final consummation. It was to be interpreted as a promise that the ministry which had begun in them should not fail and that a measure of charism would always remain to be conveyed through the Church's ministry, but not that the fullness of apostolic authority and charism would necessarily continue irrespective of the faithfulness of the Church. The promise had been fulfilled through the episcopal office, but the fullness of the distinct and higher apostolic authority and charism had had to await the raising up of new apostles in the last times.

In defending the principle of episcopacy against Presbyterianism, it was admitted that the purely scriptural evidence was initially unclear, in that the terms 'bishops' and 'elders' (or 'presbyters')—ἐπισκόποι and πρεσβύτεροι—were at times applied interchangeably to the same persons. Both elders and presbyters were 'overseers'—ἐπισκόποι—over individual congregations, and the use of the word 'bishops' in the English translation could therefore be confusing. It was not until overseers were appointed with authority over elders, presbyters, and deacons that the episcopal office could be clearly distinguished, for example, in the cases of Timothy and Titus. Such overseers (bishops)

were set [by Apostles] at the head of the presbyters, deacons, and people, as might enable them not only during the lifetime of the Apostles, but afterwards, to defend and guard each their separate charge, waiting for the coming of the Lord; enjoining upon them that what they had thus learned they should commit to others—a charge, however, [in] which [it] is in no way whatever implied that they (bishops) should or could transmit their own order or office to others.[61]

When only one Apostle survived, he wrote Epistles to Churches in Asia, in which he addressed one, and only one—called the 'Angel'—who was head of each particular Church addressed. The conclusion to be drawn from Scripture seemed clear:

Hence, then, we arrive at this obvious conclusion, that as at first the Apostles set and appointed deacons who were chosen by the people, and as they afterwards appointed presbyters, elders, overseers, priests, who

---

[61] H. Dalton, *The Office of Bishop under Apostles and the Office of Bishop without Apostles* (London: Bosworth, 1866), 4.

are interchangeably called *presbuteroi* and *episcopoi*, so did they finally appoint one of them in each particular Church or congregation to be the head over the other presbyters and deacons, as well as over the flock, who, under the title of Angel of the Church, was recognised and established as the ruler, responsible in doctrine and discipline within the border and limits of that church. These were, to use the words of Hooker, 'bishops with restraint', as apostles were bishops or overseers without restraint, being elders or *episcopoi* of the Universal Church.[62]

The Catholic Apostolics admitted that, without the headship of living apostles, the bishops had had to attempt to meet the various evils which arose in the Church by acting in a corporate capacity, even though they had not been constituted by the Apostles as a corporate body. This was, however, a poor substitute for ruling apostles. Nevertheless, through the promised continuing divine charism, they were able to discern revealed truth and to formulate the Creeds as bulwarks against heresy. But the strifes and divisions in the Church witnessed to her departure from the ways of God. Her condition under an episcopate without apostles differed greatly from her condition when having an episcopate under apostles. This could be seen in a number of ways: her incessant desire for a visible headship as a centre of unity; the subjection of her episcopate to secular rulers; her loss of prophetic and other spiritual gifts, together with the loss of the angels' ministry of interpretation; the association of the episcopate with territorial claims; and the general episcopal anarchy of mutual excommunications and anathemas:

In a word, there was none to rule as Elders in the Church Universal in the name of Christ; and evil came in and abounds. . . . But God changeth not. Jesus is the Head of His Body. In Him all fulness dwells. Therefore, He has been with, and He has kept that Body, weak and feeble, and denuded though it is, until this day; and now He would bless and help it by the same ordinances and means given at the first. . . . the prayers of the Body, the cry of the Body, that has gone up from age to age, and from the ends of the earth, for help and deliverance, shall be heard, are heard, and shall be answered.[63]

The answer was the restoration of the apostolate and the renewal of the angelic ministry of the episcopate—an episcopate set over *congregations* and their ministers as at the first (not associated with territorial jurisdiction), and one in which the fullness of episcopal

[62] Ibid. 6.   [63] Ibid. 16.

charism (including especially the intercessory office and the interpretation of prophecy) had been restored.

Archangels

Certain Catholic Apostolic angels were designated 'archangels',
namely those associated with the apostles in the universal ministry of
jurisdiction over all the Churches, angels specifically appointed as
evangelists to the 'tribes' (five to each tribe), the angels of the seven
churches in London (see Ch. II, § 2), five angel-evangelists in
London (typified by the five pillars of entrance into the Holy Place of
the Tabernacle), and angels appointed in charge of metropolitan
particular Churches (of which there were intended to be six of each
tribe). Those appointed with the apostles had the special duty to

hearken to the voice of the Lord declared by His Apostles and then
go forth to do His commandments and bear the message to their
brethren.[64]

They were essentially apostles' messengers, having no independent
standing, and thus their role was not at all comparable to that of
archbishops in the Churches.

After the death of the last apostle in 1901, the visiting archangels
acted as representatives of the surviving apostles' coadjutors, being
sent out to

act as their eyes and ears, and to report to them whatever they have seen
and heard while visiting the Churches.

The Archangels have no authority to correct or to set in order. They
act as elder brethren. They give brotherly counsel, advice and
sympathy. They carry out their instructions; they do no more. They
return to him that sends them, and to him they say, as it were 'It is done
as thou hast commanded'.

. . . The visiting Archangels do not deal with matters of administration.
They do not require reports . . . nor do they examine the work of the
ministers. They do not take any official part in the services of worship.
The character of their ministry is that of enquiry. The expression *enquiry*
is intentionally used, in order to prevent misunderstanding and to guard
against the idea that anything like former Apostolic visitations can now
be held.

.   .   .   .

[64] H. Stewart, 'The Ministry of Archangels' (MS Glasgow, 1907), 1.

The single aim of the ministry of Archangels will be that, by the Holy Ghost, there may be wrought in all our hearts that sacrifice of a broken spirit which God will not despise, and by which the way may be prepared that he may do good in His good pleasure unto Zion, and build up the walls of Jerusalem.[65]

The formal visitations of apostles (or their coadjutors) to their tribes or to individual congregations were of an entirely different character to the (later) visitations by archangels. They were formal occasions of great solemnity. Special propers were provided for the Eucharist for invoking God's blessing at the beginning of an apostolic visitation.[66] (It is interesting that these included petitions specifically for the local diocesan bishop.) The apostles came as the rulers of the Church, the archangels merely as enquirers on behalf of others.

It was especially required that the archangels' ministry should in no way be interpreted as the 'mission of the Seventy', a mission concerning which many prophetic words had been spoken since the loss of the apostleship—at most, their mission could be seen as an earnest of a future mission of the Seventy, a mission still awaited by Catholic Apostolic members today. Their special work after the passing of the apostles had been foretold in prophetic words spoken in one of the Berlin congregations, in which it had been declared that 'they shall see the fulness of the glory and power of that office, when the Lord shall work in another manner'.[67] That 'fulness' had, however, remained visible only to the eyes of the spirit; at that time, outwardly, it was accepted that they 'like all other ministers of Christ must partake of the weakness of the whole body. They must be scant in proportions. They must be weak and small in her stature.'[68]

The Priesthood

All priestly ministry was accepted by the Catholic Apostolics as belonging to Christ. The office of priesthood—an office shared by both the angels and those ordained to the priesthood only—was seen as a testimony on earth to the High Priesthood of Christ in heaven, Christ Himself being its Head. Christian ministry should have the altar as its centre, for this was the place from which all men were blessed. This was true of all ministry in the Church, including the ministry of preaching. Those Churches which had instituted a

---

[65] Ibid. 2–3.   [66] See *The Liturgy*, 335–6.
[67] Quoted in Stewart, 'The Ministry of Archangels', 1.   [68] Ibid.

ministry of preaching divorced from an ordained priesthood and the offering of the Eucharistic sacrifice could not sanctify their members nor prepare them for the coming of Christ (see § 5 below).

Objections to the sacerdotal priesthood, on the grounds that nowhere in the New Testament are Christian ministers called ἱερίς (sacrificing priests), were said to be based on a misunderstanding of the role of the ordained priest:

> The Apostle [St Paul] says that we, who have an altar, and have right to eat of it, are bound to offer up sacrifices of praise to God continually. In like manner St. Peter speaks of the church as an holy priesthood, using the very word twice over which signifies a sacrificing priesthood— ἱεράτευμα. Now observe, that the name so used is applied to the whole Church; which may help us to understand how it is that individual ministers do not happen to be named Priests. Doubtless this arises from the fact, that in the highest sense there is only one Priesthood, even that which includes all the faithful alike. As Priests, in holy worship, the ministers are regarded as Representatives of the flock—not so much as being over them, as being one with them. . . . Again, it is the voice of the whole Church that is uttered by the officiating Priest; and they are the spiritual sacrifices of the whole Church that he offers up unto God. Our holy worship is the united action of the one holy Priesthood, of which Christ is the Head in the heavens. And we may well add that it is the inseparable oneness of Christ with His Church, as the High Priest of our profession, which gives us the name and the character, and entitles us to have part in the worship, of the One holy Priesthood. The consecrating Oil poured upon His head flows down still to the skirts of His garments here below.[69]

The Eucharist was thus always the offering of the universal Church, whether celebrated by an angel or a priest acting on behalf of an angel. The celebrating minister acted as the representative of the people—the Church. At the same time

> Men, in the ministries, symbolise Christ ministering to us in His various offices. He is the great Apostle, Prophet, Evangelist, Pastor, and Teacher; He is our Bishop, Priest and Deacon. He ordains divers men to represent Him in these characters, and to symbolise Him in action towards us in them, and to convey to the members of the Church the grace and blessing which are in Him, and given to us from Him in each of these offices. And only by these men so appointed can we receive the

---

[69] W. Tarbet, *An Holy Priesthood and Spiritual Sacrifices* (London: Bosworth, 1870), 4–5.

blessing of each office. A deacon cannot represent, symbolise, Christ to us as a Priest; nor minister and convey to us the grace which, as a Priest, He dispenses. Why? Because he is not the ordinance, the appointed symbol of Him, in that office. . . . If the visible, present symbol is wanting, if the ministry is wanting, the grace is wanting.[70]

The priesthood was thus regarded as essential for the conveying of the grace of Christ's High Priesthood to the people. However, in so far as an ordained priest was the visible symbol of the Great High Priest, he could stand only for Christ's glorified humanity. Hence, both as the representative of the people and as the sign of the glorified Son of Man, he must stand before the altar on earth (i.e. East-facing) in his offering of the Eucharist, never behind it.

The duties of a priest in the Catholic Apostolic Church were: celebration of the Eucharist when no angel was available; assisting the angel in his ministerial acts whether in church or amongst the people generally; baptizing (though this might be delegated to a deacon); receiving into the Church those who had been privately baptized in emergency; absolving penitents; blessing marriages; receiving catechumens; receiving persons into regular Communion (if delegated by the angel); offering prayers on behalf of a woman after childbirth and dedicating the new-born infant(s); visiting the sick, giving them Holy Communion, and (if requested) anointing them; the commendation of departing souls (which could also be performed by a deacon or layperson in emergency); and the blessing of houses and ships. In the exercise of his ministry to the people generally, the specific role of any individual priest depended upon the particular 'character' of the ministry to which he was commissioned (see § 3 below).

The anointing of the sick, which was greatly valued in the Catholic Apostolic Church, was not seen in the light of that recorded in Mark 6: 12, whereby miraculous healing was conveyed, but of that of James 5: 14–15. It was for the strengthening of faith, the forgiveness of sins, and a confirmation of the promise of spiritual health for the faithful. In respect of physical healing, it was regarded as an indefinite seal: evidence of God's loving care for the bodies of his faithful people rather than any infallible guarantee of restoration to health. In no sense was it a 'last rite'.

---

[70] Sitwell, The Purpose of God, 30–1.

After presentation for the priesthood and acceptance by word of prophecy, candidates were duly ordained by an apostle during the celebration of the Eucharist after the reading of the Gospel and its associated homily. At the laying on of hands, the apostle said to each candidate:

Receive the Holy Ghost for the office of Priest. Whosesoever sins thou shalt remit, they are remitted unto them; and whosesoever sins thou shalt retain, they are retained. In the Name of the Father, and of the Son, and of the Holy Ghost.

After the singing of the 'Venite, Creator Spiritus', the apostle signed each candidate twice with chrism, saying:

Vouchsafe, we beseech Thee, O Lord, to consecrate ✠ and sanctify ✠ these Thy servants unto the priest's office, to which we have now admitted them, with the anointing of the Holy Ghost and the fulness of Thy heavenly benediction.
R. Amen.
That whatsoever they shall bless in Thy Name may be blessed; and whatsoever they shall consecrate in Thy Name may be consecrated and hallowed.
R. Amen.

He then delivered to each the paten (into the right hand) and the chalice (into the left hand)—with unconsecrated elements in them— saying:

Take thou authority to offer the sacrifice which Christ hath instituted in His Church, and to present the prayers and offerings of the people, as thou shalt be appointed.

Then the Bible was given to each with the words:

Take thou authority to minister the word of God, and to teach His flock according to thy border [character] and ministry.

Each candidate was then blessed by the angel present, together with two elders (priests).

Confirmation of Existing Orders

The rite for 'Confirming the Orders of such as have been ordained Priests by the Laying on of hands of the Bishop', like the ordination of priests, took place during a Eucharist after the Gospel. The apostle laid his hands upon the candidate, saying:

The Holy Ghost rest upon thee, and the power of the Highest keep thee, in the Name of the Lord.
R. Amen.
The Lord confirm thee in thy priestly office, clothe thee with the garments of salvation, and cover thee with the robe of righteousness.
R. Amen.
God the Father bless thee, God the Son be thy salvation, God the Holy Ghost be thy light and thy sanctification. The Lord God Almighty seal and confirm thee to be His faithful priest and servant, even to the end.
R. Amen.

Then, at the altar, the apostle offered a prayer for the increasing and multiplying of the gifts bestowed at the candidate's ordination by a bishop.

This rite of confirming orders should be carefully compared with the rite of ordination itself, and the missing elements noted.[71] It can be seen that if a priest had received Anglican orders followed by the apostle's confirmation of these, certain elements of the ritual would be missing. This would not apply, however, to priests received from the Roman Communion. Clearly, the important element in both rites was the laying on of the apostle's hands, signifying the receiving of a special charism conveyed through the Holy Spirit.

The rite of 'Confirming the Orders of Priests' was not an *ordination* to the priesthood. Nevertheless, it was regarded as essential for the priestly ministry of the Catholic Apostolic Church, and it was intended to convey a special gift of the Holy Spirit mediated through an apostle. This was entirely in accord with the view that episcopal ordination lacked the plenary charism conveyed only under living apostles. No Anglican or Roman Catholic priest was permitted to celebrate the Catholic Apostolic Eucharist or minister its sacraments without an apostolic laying on of hands. Offers to celebrate this Eucharist, which have occasionally been made since the death of the last Catholic Apostolic priest in 1971 (see Ch. II, § 3), have always been firmly refused by the congregations concerned. It has, however, been celebrated since that date on one or two occasions both in the United States and in continental Europe, much to the dismay of surviving underdeacons and other faithful laity. For the

[71] The full rites are to be found in *The Liturgy*, 458–85.

most part, members of the body have attended worship and many
have accepted the sacraments of their local episcopal Churches,
though regarding the grace received as of a lower order than that
received before.

The Diaconate

The diaconate of the Catholic Apostolic Church—symbolized by the
sixty pillars of the court of the Tabernacle—was a permanent office
with clearly defined duties, largely modelled on New Testament
records. In no sense was it regarded as a period of probation, long or
short, for the priesthood. Each congregation was intended to have a
complement of deacons—seven chosen by the people (following
Acts 6: 3), and others (as required) chosen by the angel with the
agreement of the clergy and the people. Deacons (who should be
married men) were *admitted* by the angel, to be *blessed* subsequently
by an apostle, during the Eucharist immediately after the reading of
the epistle. The angel laid his right hand on each candidate, saying:

Take thou authority to execute the office of Deacon in the Church of
God, which office I do now commit unto thee. In the Name of the
Father, and of the Son, and of the Holy Ghost.

Then, after a prayer for the descent of the Holy Spirit upon the
candidates, he placed a stole over the left shoulder of each, saying:

Take thou upon thee the yoke of Christ, and learn of Him, for He hath
said, 'Whosoever among you will be chief, let him be the servant of all'.

Each candidate then received a New Testament with the words:

Take thou authority to read the gospel in the Church of God, and to
preach the same, as thou shalt be sent. In the Name of the Lord.

It should be noted that, whilst the angel prayed for the charism of
the Holy Spirit, he did not himself convey it. This was reserved to an
apostle, who also laid his right hand on the head of each newly
admitted deacon, with the words:

The Holy Ghost rest upon thee, and the power of the Highest keep thee.
In the name of the Lord.
R. Amen.

God the Father bless thee, God the son be thy salvation, God the Holy
Ghost be thy light and thy sanctification. The Lord God Almighty seal

and confirm thee to be His faithful servant and minister even unto the end.

R. Amen.

Then, extending his hands over all the candidates, the apostle added:

God Almighty, the Father, the Son, and the Holy Ghost, be with you.

R. Amen.

By adopting this procedure in the case of deacons, it was emphasized that a deacon was, peculiarly, the representative of the people, having been chosen (or approved) by them. Thus, deacons were admitted to the office by an angel, as head of the particular Church, before receiving the necessary charism through specific blessing. This had a scriptural basis in the apostolic command recorded in Acts 6: 3: 'Therefore, brethren, *pick out from among you . . . whom we may appoint . . .*'. Following ordination, deacons were formally 'received' as deacons into the particular Churches in which they were to function by the angels-in-charge and the elders, the receiving of a 'deacon of the seven' being specifically noted in the wording of the rite.

The duties of all deacons, whether 'of the seven' or not, included: baptizing (if no priest was available); visiting all the people in their homes, and especially the sick; ministering gifts (*not* loans) to the poor and preaching the Gospel to them; giving advice, when asked, on personal and family affairs; religious education, and especially reminding the people of apostolic teaching and instructions received through his angel; initially receiving those brought into the Church by evangelists' witness; reading the Gospel and administering the chalice at the Eucharist (though it was admitted that there was precedent in the Fathers for deacons administering in 'both kinds'); reading the minor Offices, including the Litany (if no priest was present); presiding at officially sanctioned prayer meetings; offering prayers for women after childbirth and dedicating the newly-born infant(s) (if no priest was available); preaching; and generally offering assistance to the higher clergy as required. Special roles also pertained to them in accordance with their 'character' (see § 3 below). Their participation in the Eucharist, celebrated by an angel together with all his clergy, was seen as a visible sign of the work of the Holy Spirit throughout the Church's ministry. In addition to fulfilling their general and liturgical duties, the 'deacons of the seven' had specific responsibility for the administrative and financial affairs of a congregation.

The deacons were considered to have special importance, not only because of their distinctive role, but also because they were the first ordained ministry in the Church to be appointed by the apostles. They were ordained to exercise towards the apostles a similar ministry as that exercised by the Apostles during Christ's ministry on earth.

The deacons' role as preachers was especially noted, because (according to Scripture) in exercising this they were acting specifically as apostles' helpers—the preaching of the Gospel was essentially an apostolic act. Ordination was regarded as essential for public preaching in Church:

We have no example from Scripture of the employment by the Apostles of unordained persons in the public preaching of the Gospel even to unbelievers; and previously to the ordination of the Seven the Apostles only . . . are expressly mentioned as preaching the Lord Jesus, or as fulfilling any public ministry directed either to the Church or to their countrymen. (In Acts viii. 4, and xi. 19, it is said that those who were scattered abroad upon the persecution about Stephen went preaching the word—but there is no *proof* that those who preached were not ordained. The only names given are those of Philip, who was one of the Seven, and Barnabas . . . Apollos . . . taught in the synagogue—but in so doing exercised his privilege as a Jew, nor was he at the time referred to as acting under the Apostles . . .)[72]

The diaconate was considered to be essential for the well-being of the Church—without it the diaconal ministry of Christ towards the world (symbolized by His washing of the Disciples' feet) could not be represented. It was through the diaconate that that ministry was effected:

After a spiritual manner He [Christ] fulfils towards us that which He did for the Disciples both literally and spiritually, in washing their feet. This He effects through the Deacons. By their word He purifies His children in regard to their walk, and keeps them from pollution through contact with the world. The Deacons are shown by the figure of the washing of the feet what is their duty towards the flock. The washing of the feet is a duty, but one requiring humility, and patience, and love.[73]

---

[72] C/RL, ii. 509–10.
[73] H. W. J. Thiersch, *The Order of the Deaconship in the Christian Church: its Place and Duties* (from the German) (London: Bosworth, 1875), 27.

Such diaconal ministry was a symbol of the calling of the elect to reign with Christ in the coming Kingdom:

It is as a Deacon and servant that Christ will reign for God the Father; for He will sit as a Priest upon His Throne, yet His reign will be Diaconal; He will reign to minister for the blessing of God on the work of His Hands: this will be seen when, having put down all authority and power, He shall deliver up the Kingdom to God the Father, that the Son Himself may be subject to Him that did put all things under Him. . . . True rule, subordinate to the Father, is for the ministration of blessing . . . God's true King reigns for Him Who hath sent Him, and for the creatures that He hath made.[74]

The emergence of deacons from amidst the congregations was considered to be, like the budding of Aaron's rod, the sign of true life in the Church. Deacons—the 'rams'—were seen as being the binding link between the people—the 'sheep'—and the priests—the 'shepherds'. Deacons' work should not be done by others: neither by priests (who should work *with* the deacons, not *instead of* them), nor by the civil power, which had often attempted to usurp the deacon's role towards the people. Deacons were the 'door' into the Church for those outside her, and the means of protecting those who came in from straying back into the world:

without Deaconship, priesthood is but priestcraft—a machinery for acquiring power over the bodies and souls of men. . . . for the office of Deacon lies at the threshold of the Church; Deaconship is as the floor of the garner where the harvest is trodden out—while it is lacking, the Evangelist cannot bring in *sheaves*: there is no garner prepared to receive them—no floor to cast them upon . . . while Deaconship is lacking, there is nothing to sustain those who are gathered . . . Take away the *floor* of the garner, and the feet of the oxen tread the grain back again into the *earth*, from which it had been separated and gathered.[75]

The deacon had also a special responsibility of reminding the faithful of the Lord's coming, remembering that it was to the first deacon, Stephen, that the Lord gave the vision upon which he called out: 'I see the heavens opened, and the Son of man standing at the right hand of God' (Acts 7: 56). This was further emphasized in 1 Cor. 11:

[74] J. Leslie, 'The Deaconship' (MS, 1860), 2. (There appears to be some doubt as to the authorship of this work: Copinger inserts '?' before the author's name.)

[75] W. H. Place, *Notes of a Ministry to the Deacons of the Churches* (London: Barclay, 1854), 5, 7.

26, where the ministry of both priest and deacon were seen as being expressed: 'proclaiming the Lord's death' denoted the testimony of the priesthood, but the phrase 'until he comes' denoted the substance of true deaconship.

Deaconesses

Note has already been made above of the existence, in the Catholic Apostolic Church, of the minor (lay) ministries of deaconess, underdeacon, acolyte, organist, singer, doorkeeper, etc., for whom forms of blessing by an angel were provided. The work of deaconesses was confined to assisting priests and deacons with their ministries to women, particularly those living on their own and those whose husbands or fathers objected to male visitations. Church rules demanded that candidates for this office should be

of mature age, and whose circumstances permit them to dedicate their services to the church without hindrance from family duties.[76]

They were thus modelled to a considerable extent upon the office of 'widow' in the early Church, from which the order of deaconess probably derived. They were not and could not be clergy, and hence could not be ordained, neither did their blessing for office take place in the context of a Eucharist. However, they did not receive second or subsequent blessings on moving from one congregation to another: they were merely 'received' by the angels concerned. It is thus clear that, although they were not *ordained*, the blessing which they had received was regarded as having an indelible quality.

Deaconesses had no liturgical or preaching role. Whilst they could give instruction in private to children, it was expressly forbidden for women to preach (in accordance with 1 Cor. 14: 33–5 and 1 Tim. 2: 12), though, subject to stringent regulations, women might prophesy in church. They were, however, encouraged as singers and expected to participate in communal prayers in the services. The strictures of St Paul were not regarded as absolute:

I think it is impossible to construe this injunction absolutely . . . for it has never been laid down in the Christian Church that the voices of women are never to be heard. On the contrary, it has always been permitted to them to join in the Confession and Responses, and to sing

---

[76] *Book of Regulations* (London: Strangeways, 1878), 66.

the praises of God. I understand the injunction only to forbid such speaking as would be indicative of non-subjection. This is the speaking which is forbidden; therefore they must not teach (I Tim. ii, 12), nor even show their independence by asking questions for their own satisfaction, independently of their husbands.[77]

Women were enjoined to model themselves upon Mary, Mother of the Lord, who had pondered the heavenly mysteries *in her heart*, and was content to abide under Joseph's headship and later to remain within the protection of St John. Mary was the true type of the Church abiding under Christ's headship, and in this an example for all women to follow. This was visibly symbolized by the requirement that women in church should at all times have their heads covered, as had been the tradition from earliest times.

Deaconesses were not entitled to use their office as an excuse to stray beyond the boundaries of what was permitted for women to do. The Catholic Apostolic teaching on the nature of male and female was strict and firmly scriptural:

The great principles underlying the whole subject began to be set forth even at the creation. Read I Tim. ii, 12, I Cor. xi, 3 and verses 7–9, also Romans v, 14. From these passages we learn that:
Man is the type of
Christ, whom God has made **Head** and Ruler. Source of Wisdom and Fountain of Blessing to all.
Woman is the type of
The Company of those who have been given by God to His Son; lifted up into mysterious unity with Him, and called to be sharers of His dominion; but who must ever be **subject and subordinate to Him**, the Head—**receivers from Him.**
Therefore in the Church of God, not only all **rule**, but also the ministry of the **Word** and of the **Sacraments** and **Benediction**, are committed by Christ to **men only**, for the Son ever carries out the perfect will of the Father. There is here no question of arrogance on the part of man—but of great responsibility to God; there is no 'degradation' suffered by woman; for her holy subjection is her 'glory'. Christ being the Head of the Church, man is the head of the woman. It is an abiding truth; as binding now as when the Lord's Apostle wrote, or as when Eve was formed.
But the passages referred to show that the holy subordination of woman is not only a witness to the **Purpose of God in Christ**, but also—

[77] J. B. Cardale, *Directions on the Subject of Women Prophesying in Church*, privately issued (1866), 1.

like the cross itself—a perpetual acknowledgement of the **Fall**. (I Tim. ii, 11. See Gen. iii, 16). No wonder the enemy labours to get rid of it.

Maybe the great rebellion of mankind—even of God's own children against Him—will not be completed until the appointed subordination of women, that humbling reminder of human failure—that bulwark of godliness—has been abandoned; rejected by both sexes as an old-world custom and delusion, unsuited to these 'enlightened days.' Remember the words of Jesus in the Gospel:—'Beware of false prophets.' (Matt. vii, 15).[78]

The abiding tradition on the place of women in the Church was seen as something determined by God in His wisdom and love, pointing to eternal truths. Opposition to that tradition was the work of Satan, who desired to remove the one great witness to man's fragility and dependence upon God, and to usher in the ultimate blasphemy whereby man claimed to be divine:

It stands directly in his way. He cannot bring forth the Antichrist—he cannot transform man into a God till it is removed. It reminds men of what he would have them forget . . . it is the prophecy of a coming deliverance and glory through Christ Jesus, to which he would blind them by every artifice of hell. He must sweep it away in order to deceive man with the lie that . . . he needs no redemption which he cannot work our for himself.[79]

When, in later years, Catholic Apostolic members necessarily attended services in Anglican and other Churches, they were instructed not to remain present if any woman officiated, instructed, or preached. They were also told that

they should make no secret of their reason for absenting themselves on occasions when women are appointed.[80]

Underdeacons

Catholic Apostolic underdeacons, who were male only and preferably married, had the prime task of supervising the congregation during

---

[78] *Ministries on the subject of Woman, a type of figure of the Church, the Bride of Christ,* various authors, privately reissued (1974), 11–12.

[79] W. W. Andrews: *Woman: Her True Place and Standing* (Edinburgh: Laurie, 1872), 14.

[80] *Ministries on the subject of Woman,* 2. The present writer has frequently seen televised religious services immediately switched off by Catholic Apostolic members if a woman offers a prayer or reads a lesson.

worship. It was intended that there should be one for every sixty communicants. They were nominated for office by the angels and confirmed by the congregations. They marshalled the communicants at the time of Holy Communion, ensuring that everything took place with due reverence and order. They also gave general assistance to deacons as required, including assisting them in their task of visiting parish members in their homes. In particular, they were instructed to enquire as to reasons for members absenting themselves from worship, and to report instances where a visitation was desirable to the deacons.

Unlike subdeacons in the various Eastern and Western Churches, underdeacons had no liturgical role: they were not permitted to read the Scriptures publicly. They were considered to be typified by the 48 containing boards of the Tabernacle, and hence their ministry was part of the constitution of the Church. As such, it was no menial task that was entrusted to them—members should respect their office and welcome their enquiries, appreciating that they were acting under apostolic instructions, as the following 'teaching' indicates:

Observe . . . they are *bound to enquire*. It is no inquisitiveness on their part, but the fulfilment of a bounden duty, when they make such enquiries. Let them find in you a corresponding readiness to meet the enquiry frankly, and in the spirit of charity. . . . do not resent the enquiry, but accept the reminder which comes to you, not through one having the authority to rebuke or correct, but by the gentle word of an elder brother, one of yourselves calling your attention to a neglected duty, that so you may *correct yourself*. . . . It will be given and received aright only as each recognizes in the other his brother in Christ, and both are abiding in the spirit of charity, which enables us to submit ourselves one to another in the fear of God.[81]

It is clear that the underdeacons needed great gentleness and tact in enquiring as to absences from worship, and that their enquiries were not always welcomed by members of the congregations.

Like deaconesses, underdeacons did not require a second or subsequent blessing for their office on moving from one congregation to another, being just 'received' by their new angel.

---

[81] H. S. Hume, *On the Office of Underdeacon* (London: Central Church, 1926), 5.

Other Minor Offices

The remaining minor offices require no discussion, as their titles
clearly indicate their respective functions. The only point to note is
that all those who performed offices in the Church, however slight,
were deemed to require formal blessing for which appropriate rites
were provided. The various minor offices were said to be typified by
the different utensils of sacrifice used at the brazen altar: ash-pans,
shovels, basins, flesh-hooks, and fire-pans.

3. THE FOURFOLD 'CHARACTER' OF MINISTRY

In addition to its fourfold *degree* (discussed above), the Catholic
Apostolic ministry also had a fourfold *character*, corresponding to
what was seen to be a fourfold constitution within man, and typified
by the four-sided brazen altar of the Tabernacle with its horns at the
corners. The essential form of this fourfold ministry had been
declared prophetically by Cardale (as early as 1833) in his revelation,
'The Mystery of the Candlestick'.[82] This revealed what was
considered to be the divinely instituted nature of the Church's
ministry, a nature not to be altered by any decision of man. Thus, as
well as being composed of a hierarchy of apostles, angels, priests, and
deacons, the true ministry of the Church was also characterized by
apostles, prophets, evangelists, and pastors and teachers (the last
two taken together as one 'character'), soon to be restored to the
Church throughout the world:

Thou wilt again manifest Thyself in Thy Church. Thou art giving, and
wilt give, Apostles, Prophets, Evangelists, Pastors and Teachers. In this
land shall be a company of Apostles, Prophets, Evangelists, Pastors and
Teachers. And in other lands Thou wilt have Prophets, Evangelists,

---

[82] One version of the text in the present writer's possession is in manuscript form,
written at Albury but undated. It can be found printed (with very slight and entirely
unimportant differences) in C. W. Boase, *Supplementary Narrative to the Elijah
Ministry* (Edinburgh: Grant, 1868), 797–800; P. E. Shaw, *The Catholic Apostolic
Church* (New York: King's Crown, 1946), 85–6 (taken from Boase). An abridged
version is in Miller, *History and Doctrines of Irvingism*, n. 28 above.

Pastors and Teachers. And in all lands, in all the Churches, Thou wilt
manifest Thyself in all gifts of the spirit [in all holy fruits of the Spirit].[83]

This fourfold ministry was the 'Elias ministry' foretold in Malachi 4:
5, to be realized not in a single person but in a restoration (in the last
days) of the ministries referred to by St Paul (Eph. 4: 11 and 1 Cor.
11: 28), reflecting the fourfold nature of that ministry which was,
however, found in its perfection only in Christ. It was typified in a
number of places in the Old Testament, but most notably by the
'four living creatures' of Ezekiel 1: 5–14: the lion symbolized rule by
apostles (and elders), the eagle the heavenly visions of prophets, the
man the evangelists' preaching of the Gospel, and the ox the
shepherding and guiding of the flock by the pastors.[84] Their mention
by the seer St John (Apoc. 4: 6–7) was taken as confirmation that
this ministerial structure belonged to the eternal Church. The
fourfold ministry of rule, prophecy, evangelizing, and pastorship
corresponded to the division of man's 'soul' into the will, the
imagination, the understanding, and the affections. The basis of this
fourfold ministry cannot be understood without a consideration of
the Catholic Apostolic doctrine of man.

The Doctrine of Man's Threefold Nature

The Catholic Apostolics saw man, having been made in the image
and likeness of God (Gen. 1: 26–7), as possessing a threefold
nature—body, soul, and spirit—reflecting as a shadow the trinitarian
nature of God. The body was material, created from the dust of the
earth, yet fearfully and wonderfully made (Ps. 139: 14)—one should
never cease to wonder at the body's beauty and intricacy of
structure, a structure whose totality surpassed man's understanding.
It was into the nostrils of this material body that God had breathed
the breath of life, making man a living being (Gen. 2: 7). As a gift of
God, it should never be wantonly defaced or destroyed—hence
cremation was forbidden for Christians.

Cremation was regarded as pagan, linked at best with the idea of
the existence of the soul after death. Whilst the 'resurrection of the

[83] MS (see n. 82). The phrase in square brackets is in the printed versions only.
[84] Other typological 'fours' included the river divided into four rivers (Gen. 2:
10), the four standards of the host of Israel (Num. 2), the four jars of water (1 Kings
18: 33), the four youths (Dan. 17), the four winds of heaven (Dan. 7: 2), the four
smiths (Zech. 1: 20), the four chariots (Zech. 6: 1), etc.

body' did not depend upon the way in which the physical body had ended its earthly existence, cremation was nevertheless a public denial of any manner of continuity of the resurrection body with the earthly flesh. This was, in effect, a denial of the doctrine of Christ's Resurrection. Burial, and burial alone, was in accordance with Scripture—it was the divinely appointed custom of the Jews and had been commended by Our Lord, who

accepted and everlastingly commended (Matt. xxvi. 13) the good deed done to Him in the anointing of His sacred head and feet by the woman who brake the box of precious ointment, assigning it, as a reason, that it had reference to His burial; as if a special sanctity was given to the act by this connection with His burial.[85]

It was pointed out that 'cemetery' was derived from a Greek word signifying 'a dormitory—a place in which to sleep', and that it witnessed to the Christian belief that the dead were only sleeping until they should be awakened by Christ, a belief to which all nature testified. To commit a body after death to the flames was to do dishonour to its Maker—this was expressly stated by many of the Fathers. Cremation was also said to have serious social dangers—no system of death certificates was infallible, and cremation excluded the possibility of exhumation.

The soul was created as the seat of man's intelligence, understanding, and emotions. Thus, animals could be said to have souls—less developed than the soul of man, and with less potential because they were not open to spiritual influence. Man's soul was something of which he was as aware as of his body:

we know that we are possessed of bodies capable of actions, subject to wants, and exposed to death. Of the second part of our being, viz. the *soul*, we are likewise intuitively conscious. There is that within us that thinks, that feels, that loves or hates, that joys or sorrows, that desires or dislikes; to all that is contained under the words reason, judgement, affection, hatred, desire, and such like; to all these we are alive, and we are able readily to admit and appreciate the distinction between soul and body. We know also, that the heathen themselves acknowledged and discerned this distinction, always regarding the body as the grosser, and the soul as the more elevated and purer part of man.[86]

[85] C. J. Rutter, *Cremation versus Christian Burial: A Word of Warning* (Glasgow: Hobbs, 1901), 6–7.
[86] H. Dalton, *Body, Soul, and Spirit* (London: Cleaver, 1847), 3.

Yet soul and body, though distinct, were closely related—for example, sickness in one could result in sickness in the other, and health in one could promote health in the other. Thus, in ministrations to the body, the need for ministrations to the soul should not be overlooked.

The spirit was the gift of God which was unique to man. It was that part of man's nature which placed him above the animal creation, for the spirit existed on a higher plane than the soul. Man as a material creature was subject to time, and hence death; man as a spiritual creature transcended time and was therefore immortal. Through being body and soul as well as spirit, he had been created 'for a little while lower than the angels' (Heb. 2: 7), but was capable of achieving a higher perfection than they. The spirit of man was the source of his knowledge of and communication with God through its indwelling by the Holy Spirit—'the Spirit himself bearing witness with our spirit' (Rom. 8: 16). On its own, the soul (being 'unspiritual') could not apprehend God's revelation (1 Cor. 2: 14 and Jude 19). True wisdom lay in being alive and open in spirit to receive God's revelation, and alive and open in soul to consent to that revelation—only in this way could knowledge of eternal truths be obtained. The intellect, left to its own devices, quickly became earthly, sensual, and devilish—this is why in Scripture the 'psychic' man was contrasted with the spiritual man. The 'science' of psychology was considered dangerous precisely because it reduced everything to the level of the soul: it was considered a modern example of the 'godless contradictions' against which St Paul had warned Timothy—1 Tim. 6: 20.

The distinctive roles of the soul and the spirit were taught in Holy Scripture, the Greek text revealing the explanation more clearly than the English:

These . . . operations of the soul and of the spirit in man are, among many other passages of Scripture, very clearly indicated in the second chapter of the First Epistle to the Corinthians, where it is written: 'The natural man receiveth not the things of the Spirit of God: for they are foolishness unto him: neither can he know them, because they are spiritually discerned.' Again, in the Epistle of Jude, we read concerning certain 'ungodly' men who in the last days (at the end of this dispensation) shall mock and scoff and deny the truth—and they are declared to be men who are 'sensual, having not the spirit'. . . . the words respectively translated, in the one place 'sensual', and in the other 'natural', are translations of the same Greek word *psuchikos*, which has the same root meaning as the Greek word *psuche*, which is translated 'soul'. And he goes on to explain that in the 'natural', that is 'soulish' or 'psychic' man, as distinguished from the 'spiritual' man—the workings of his spirit are so overborne by the workings of his soul, that his spirit is so much in abeyance that he may be said not to have it.[87]

The soul and spirit in man, despite their being separate and distinct God-given faculties, ought to be closely knit together so that the soul (as far as it is able) can apprehend those things of God which can only first be revealed to the spirit.

In his response to God, and especially in worship, whether public or private, man had to be involved in his threefold totality. Only in this way could he have *personal* communion with God in Christ through the Spirit. The words heard in public worship spoke primarily to the soul, and preaching almost exclusively to the intellect and (on occasion) emotions. But the reading of the Scriptures had a double function: as a *lesson* read for the instruction of the mind, and as a spiritual *portion* offered before the Lord. Ceremonial was essential, for this spoke beyond the mind to the spiritual consciousness. Spiritual realities required material means: hence the essentiality of the sacraments.

Man had been born to achieve the likeness of God, but he had lost that potential at the Fall—though God's likeness was later to be assumed by Christ, the Son of Man. Man had been created priest, prophet, and king of creation, but had been seduced by Satan, the angel who had exalted himself against God. Of Satan it was said:

There are many passages of Holy Scripture . . . in which we learn that before the Creation of this world GOD had already created a countless host of happy spirits, known to us under the name of angels (Job xxxviii. 4–7.) Although the disclosures given to us concerning these unseen beings are few and do not go much into particulars; yet we learn this, at least, that they also had a probation to undergo. One of the most prominent of these Angels, however, with a great attendant company, exalted himself against GOD. These sinned as we read (Jude 6) to such a measure that they kept not their first estate, but were compelled to leave their habitation, and are appointed to be instruments of the righteous judgement of GOD upon the wicked in the great day of judgement. (Compare 2 Peter ii. 4; Rev. xii. 7; John viii. 44.) Their leader is called Satan, i.e. enemy and adversary of GOD. Out of hatred

[87] A. E. Capadose, *Body, Soul, and Spirit* (London: Central Church, 1942), 3.

towards GOD and envy towards our first parents, he seduced them to disobedience of the Most High, and a transgression of His command. Probably he supposed that he would thereby bring the plan of GOD with the human race altogether to nought. (Gen. iii. 1; 2 Cor. xi. 3; Rev. xii. 9.)[88]

Following his seduction by Satan, man had used God's gift of freedom of the will to gratify his own desires instead of remaining in voluntary dependence upon God and in implicit obedience to Him. With this sin, he had brought all creation down with himself.

His position in relation to the rest of Creation, moreover, makes it easy to understand that when the head of the Creation fell, all that was under him, and which stood in such intimate connection with him, would also fall and be drawn down with him into the same ruin. . . . The exalted Prophet who was just before endowed with the knowledge of God and with an insight into the purpose and properties of every created thing, is now debased from his lofty position to such an extent that he fancies he can conceal himself from the All-seeing eye of God . . . and can put off the blame of his sin upon his wife and by that means upon God Himself.

. . . Instead of a prophet, priest and king furnished with wisdom, holiness and might, we see man now in folly, sin and weakness, subject to all kinds of infirmities of body and spirit . . . And it is not only in the first pair of the human race that we behold this mournful transformation: we can, alas! see its reality every day and every hour in our own selves and others.[89]

Yet shadows of man's former roles remained. Scientific enquiry— the search into nature—was goaded by his spirit's attempt to recover long-lost knowledge and to exercise his prophetic faculty within the circumscribed area of Creation. His striving for the peace of a good conscience, his systems of acceptable behaviour, and even the superstition and idolatry of the heathen, were pointers to his original priesthood. His desire for power and possessions pointed to a lost kingship. But all these inevitably became Satanic without the indwelling of the Spirit of God:

There is the Spirit of God, and there is the Spirit of Satan, and of one or the other must our spirits be the habitation. The one, our privilege, by

[88] W. R. Caird and J. E. T. Lutz (tr. from the German by J. C. Corlette), *God's Purpose with Mankind and the Earth: An Introduction to the Right Understanding of the Holy Scriptures of the Old and New Testament* (Sidney: Cook, 1873), 33.
[89] Ibid. 34–5.

the free grace of God, given to us at Baptism; the other, our
condemnation and chastisement for sin unrepented of.

. . . .

. . . we have to do with a *personal* God, for God the Holy Ghost is a
Person; and with a *personal* Devil; and to one or other of these persons
we yield ourselves obedient. Yea, and by one or other we are indwelt in
our spirit.[90]

God's revelation of Himself after the Fall had been a progressive
revelation: through the senses (in the patriarchal period), the reason
(the Law and the prophets), and finally the spirit (the sacraments
and spiritual gifts of the Christian dispensation). The truths of
Christianity were a spiritual revelation, and hence directed 'above'
the body and mind to the spirit.

All these human aspects were typified in the Tabernacle's brazen
altar (Exod. 27: 1–2) by its four sides, its three cubits of height, and
its five-by-five cubits (length by breadth). The four sides typified the
four aspects of man's soul. The three cubits typified man's threefold
nature of body, soul, and spirit: the lowest level (the level on earth)
the body; the intermediate level the soul; and the upper level the
spirit, which received 'fire' (the Holy Spirit) from God. The five-by-
five cubits typified man's five senses. The shittim (or acacia) wood
of which the altar was made typified the common humanity of
mankind, weak and unstable, and unable to offer itself to God
without the indwelling of the Spirit:

In itself this nature is, like the shittim wood, weak, unstable and
corruptible. Its utter emptiness being further set forth by the altar being
made hollow. Such a material would never have been used alone for an
altar of burnt offering. It was overlain with strong brass, and so made fit
for its purpose.

Brass, then, represents something needed in order that man may
become a burnt offering. What is it that is needed? We read even
concerning Jesus that it was 'through the Eternal Spirit' that He offered
Himself. Brass stands for spiritual power and here it reminds us that our
continual offering of ourselves can only be effected in the power of the
Holy Ghost. . . . You *will* find the shittim wood frail but remember the
shield of brass, ye are not in the flesh but in the Spirit '*strengthened with
might*' by *His* Spirit. Following your Lord, offer your burnt offering
'through the Eternal Spirit'.[91]

[90] Dalton, *Body, Soul, and Spirit*, 8–9, 13.
[91] W. de Caux [?], *The Brazen Altar* (London: Central Church, 1926), 3.

The threefold nature of man (especially in regard to worship) was also typified by the threefold division of the Tabernacle: the Outer Court typifying the body, the Holy Place the soul, and the Most Holy Place the spirit:

As in the Jewish tabernacle there were *the outward court, the holy place*, and *the most holy*; and within this latter dwelt the *Schecinah* or manifestation of the presence of God; so in man, there is the body, with its services in varied actions and in busy life and in bodily worship—*the outward court*. There is also the soul, with its complex affections, and thoughts and meditations, where higher service is given—*the holy place*. And beyond all this there is the *innermost sanctuary*; even the spirit of man, into which the Holy Spirit entereth, and wherein communion with God is held, such as even the thoughts of the heart may not intrude upon; and where rapt with the vision of God, such as Stephen had, we may worship, unheard, unseen, unknown, save by Him Who is invisible.[92]

Man must not allow the body and soul to predominate over the spirit. St Paul prayed that man's 'spirit, soul, and body be kept sound and blameless at the coming of our Lord Jesus Christ' (1 Thess. 5: 23). Until that day there would be conflict within man's nature—evil, through 'the desires of the flesh' (here including the soul in its relationship to the flesh) striving against good (the indwelling Spirit) and good against evil, as St Paul had taught (Gal. 5: 17).

Death and Resurrection

Death, the penalty of sin, was the separation of man's soul and spirit from the body; resurrection was their reuniting—God would not leave them for ever separated, for death was abhorrent to man's created nature. Man was not created for death, but for life; hence, death was a violation of God's creation, though there was a sense in which death was a 'mercy' of God, namely in that it brought release from temptation and the fear of apostasy.

The true hope of Christians was not the happiness of a departed 'soul' after the death of the body, but the resurrection and beatification of the whole person—body, soul, and spirit—in the Kingdom. This had been often either forgotten or denied by

[92] Dalton, *Body, Soul, and Spirit*, 7–8.

Christians in the interest of a spurious spirituality, which ignored the Scriptures (pandering to the ephemeral fashions of modern criticism) and attempted to confine the spiritual mysteries of faith within man's limited understanding. With such people:

The Scriptures are accepted only in a modified way. If their statements conflict with men's intellectual conclusions, the latter must be regarded as the more trustworthy; hence, divine truth, to be acceptable, must be arguable; dogmatic assertion, however well avouched, goes a very little way; so-called 'revelation' must now be tried at the bar of reason.[93]

Not only the promise of the resurrection of the body but the very Resurrection of Christ Himself had been called into question in this way. This was human pride in its most dangerous form, elevating man's soul over his spirit and setting it against the witness of the Holy Spirit within him, forgetting that 'the Spirit is the witness, because the Spirit is the truth' (1 John 5: 7). It was not only apostasy but also idolatry, in that, for such persons, the worship of man's intellect had replaced the true worship of God 'in spirit and truth' (John 4: 24). They were unable to grasp the great spiritual truth of the Resurrection as the foundation of a new creation, whose hidden life was not mediated through the sacraments, but which would be fully manifest in the Kingdom yet to come.

The Fourfold Constitution of the Psyche

The threefold constitution of man (just considered) was seen as hierarchical, but the fourfold constitution of the soul was not. Thus the will, the imagination, the understanding, and the affections were of equal importance in the dedication of man's life to God. *All* that was within man should be used to His honour (Ps. 103: 1); it was for this purpose that he had been endowed with his faculties by the Creator:

All man's faculties and emotions are comprised under, or immediately connected with, one or other of these four; and each . . . is more or less brought into action in all that we say or do. By a truly dedicated people all their faculties should be employed in doing the will of God. As it is expressed in the Liturgy, God has ordained the faculties of man to be the eternal instruments of rendering to Him glory and praise.[94]

---

[93] R. Duke, *The Resurrection of the Body* (Glasgow: Hobbs, 1904), 2–3.
[94] S. M. Hollick, *The Dedication of our Faculties to God*, privately published (1946),

Of all man's faculties, it was the *will* that was most difficult to dedicate to God. This was because of the gift of freedom: God had required of man that he should obey His will, not under compulsion, nor from a strict sense of duty, but because, as a response to His love, man would *desire* to come to know His will and to do it. Such desire could arise only out of the working of the Holy Spirit within. Thus the will was the most spiritual of the faculties in that *its exercise* was a spiritual action beyond man's understanding:

When we speak of the Will, we include the faculty of deliberate judgement. For, whether we exercise our personal liberty in choosing that which is right and true, or otherwise, our exercise of will proceeds upon some motive, good or bad, upon some assumed principles derived from reason or affection; and upon these principles, thus derived, there must be deliberation, in order to the exercise of the will. And yet, considered in itself, the will is a spiritual faculty,—an endowment, by the possession of which God has made man most to resemble Himself . . . The exercise of the will supposes choice, and choice supposes deliberation, more or less attentive and complete; but, beyond the mental operations concerned in the act of deliberation, there is, in the exercise of the will itself, in originating action, a spiritual action, of which we may become conscious, but which it surpasses our power to intellectualize or explain.[95]

There were three spheres of activity within which the human will had to be directed in fulfilment of its voluntary submission to God's will: response to God, response within the person, and response to the world, and particularly to others. In respect of the second, *self-control* was critical:

sensual desires need to be kept in check; unholy or uncharitable thoughts need to be subdued; the tongue, the most unruly of our members, needs to be governed; and our actions need constant restraint.[96]

People with strong wills need to be constantly on guard against imposing their wills wrongfully upon those of others. This was a danger in all matters of rule, and especially within the family:

It is, perhaps, within the family that failure most frequently occurs. The husband and father is the true ruler in the home, but he must be ever

2. The reference to 'the Liturgy' is to the Blessing of God on Singers and Players on Instruments—*The Liturgy*, 436.
[95] *C/RL*, i. 263.   [96] Hollick, *The Dedication of our Faculties to God*, 4.

watchful that his rule be not overbearing nor oppressive. . . . St Paul not only bids children to be obedient to their parents, but also bids fathers to provoke not their children to wrath. (Eph. vi. 4)

Now it happens that in some cases the wife is endowed with a stronger will than her husband, and when this is so she has to be watchful that she does not exercise it in opposition to him. Her true part is to uphold and strengthen him.[97]

Strength of will was not to be confused with strength of character. Strength of will should be exercised in self-restraint rather than self-expression. Those with true strength of character were not those who succeeded in imposing their wills upon others, but those who, following the example of Christ, exercised their wills according to the will of God.

Imagination was described as 'the great laboratory of ideas' external to man:

It is the faculty by which we take cognizance of external objects, and apprehend those suggested by our inward consciousness, so as to make them the subject of thought; and thus it is the organ of knowledge. Thus far it has to do with the images of things present to our minds, and is strictly an intellectual faculty: but we are also endowed with a capacity of receiving light and knowledge in the spirit, as well as by mental apprehension. And, except this were so, man could not be the subject of inspiration; and neither future events nor hidden truth could be revealed by God to men through the agency of their fellow-men inspired by Him.[98]

Thus, like the will, the imagination was seen as having a spiritual dimension. Like the will also, it had to be dedicated to God, because it could be employed for evil purposes as well as good as it was subject to the promptings of Satan as well as those of the Holy Spirit. The imagination acted for good or evil within man's thoughts, and he therefore had a constant duty to guard and control his thoughts:

It is the fostering of evil thoughts, the imagining of evil, that . . . not only alienates people from one another, but finally alienates them from God. In the prophecy of Zechariah, chapter vii, verse 10, the prophet gives this solemn warning: 'Let none of you imagine evil against his brother in your heart'; and later (viii. 6) he emphasizes it by repeating it in nearly the same words . . .[99]

[97] Hollick, *The Dedication of our Faculties to God*, 4.
[98] C/RL, i. 263–4.   [99] Hollick, *The Dedication of our Faculties to God*, 6.

St Paul had laid down the lines along which the imagination should be exercised, namely in respect of things which were true, honourable, just, etc. (Phil. 4: 8). The imagination should be used to interpret experience gained in the world in terms of heavenly things, following the pattern of Christ, Who had brought home heavenly things to men's hearts by the imagery of natural things (see e.g. John 15: 1–5). The dedication of the imagination to God required that man must first receive from Him the revelation of heavenly mysteries.

The *understanding* was the reasoning faculty, a faculty which was purely intellectual and, to some extent, mechanical. By it man considered propositions, assenting to or dissenting from them, and drew conclusions from propositions already accepted. It had a spiritual dimension in as much as conscience was permitted to influence or override its arguments and conclusions. The highest exercise of the understanding was its use in enabling man to grasp the truths which God had revealed through the Spirit. Initially there was the act of faith, the act of reason then followed:

It is not by our reasoning faculties that we are enabled to *believe* these things. That can only be done by faith, which is God's gift to all who seek it. Nor is it within our reasoning powers to explain these mysteries. Through faith we are enabled to believe things which go beyond the reach of reason; but none of the things which we are bound to believe is contrary or opposed to reason. It is as God's reasonable creatures that we are capable of receiving and appreciating them. . . .

. . . The worst use of men's mental and intellectual powers is when, ignoring all revelation from God, or the need of it, they attempt to explain the nature of God, and speculate about the destiny of man, according to their own ideas. This men call philosophy. Is there not in it more of the pride of man than any true love of wisdom?[100]

Man should remember the commandment: 'Trust in the Lord with all your heart, and do not rely on your own insight' (Prov. 3: 5). Intellectual powers were a help to those who set their minds on God and believed; they were a snare to those who thought only of worldly things. Man, as a 'reasonable' being, should dedicate his understanding to God and turn away from the intellectual temptations of the world. In order to dedicate himself in this way, man must first receive the light of divine truth.

[100] Ibid. 9–10.

The *affections* (and emotions), often spoken of as being located 'in the heart', exercised their influence upon the will, the imagination, and the understanding, but God's grace was required in order that this influence should be for good. The affections could be the agent of order or disorder. It was *love*, in the true sense of the word, which could bring order within man's soul. All men were constituted with the ability to love, but, for the right exercise of that ability, it was necessary that the love of God should first be kindled in their hearts. God required of man that He should be given the first place in his heart, otherwise man could not be 'worthy' of Him (Matt. 10: 37).

The greatest snare for man's affections was self-love, a snare which would become especially dangerous in the last days (2 Tim. 3: 1–4) and which could be avoided only by setting the heart on 'things above'. It was self-love which lay behind love of the things of the world, against which the Apostle had issued this warning. In the influence of the affections upon the understanding, it was important that love of truth and not love of disputation should be the motivating force. Such love of 'things that are above' would strengthen love for others:

The word of the Lord to us through the prophet Zechariah is '*Love* the truth and peace' (Zech. viii. 19). St. Paul, in the 2nd Epistle to the Thessalonians, shows how the followers of Antichrist become deceived and condemned because they receive not the *love* of the truth (2 Thess. ii. 10). . . . If our hearts are truly set upon heavenly things we shall be strengthened, not weakened, in love to our brethren.[101]

It was not sufficient to respond to the poor and needy by alleviating their temporal needs only. Those who truly *loved* their neighbour should not be satisfied to engage merely in schemes of social welfare: such 'charitable' works could often be undertaken for selfish reasons and in a spirit of condescension. It was necessary to have a loving concern *for the whole person*, as Christ had been moved by more than the purely physical needs of those to whom He ministered. Meditation on the compassion of Christ led inevitably to the great mystery of the Incarnation. Christ manifested a sympathy for others which was inspired by the divine love within Him—a divine love of which the Incarnation was the mysterious expression. It is from the indwelling of that love within men that man became able to dedicate

---

[101] Hollick, *The Dedication of our Faculties to God*, 15.

his affections to God and so able to manifest that love in acts of compassion towards others.

The general character of a man was determined by the relative strengths of the four faculties of his soul, as was the part which he could most appropriately play both in Church and in society. This would not cease to be true in the world to come:

Although both we ourselves, and the circumstances surrounding us, will have undergone important changes; nevertheless we can have no doubt that in the Kingdom of Heaven, as now, God will appoint to every man a specific place to which he will be perfectly adapted.[102]

However, although the relative strengths of the four faculties might vary acceptably from person to person, no one of them should be allowed to achieve undue sway. Where this occurred in people, their essential 'moral symmetry' would be impaired, and, until this situation was remedied, they could not move forward towards perfection—indeed, serious evil would result. A similar situation arose if one of the faculties was excessively weak:

The undue prominence of the will becomes manifested in overbearing wilfulness and obstinacy. The unrestrained and excessive action of the imagination leads to frivolity, extravagance, and madness. The exercise of the mere reasoning powers, without the control of wisdom, or the softening influence of the heart, leads to intellectual pride and scepticism. The affections, left without the guidance of judgement and reason, betray men into sensual indulgence, or lead to mysticism, which is but a subtle form of spiritual licentiousness.

And so again, the absence of the due influence of judgement and determination renders a man the victim of his own propensities, whether imaginative, or intellectual, or sensual; the deficiency of imagination leaves him dark and barren; without the due intervention and influence of the understanding, he is devoid of just and right principles; and if destitute of feeling, he is cold and indifferent to others. And thus deficiency in any one of these parts of man's being stamps imperfection upon the whole, and renders him unfit for the due exercise of any of them.[103]

The Ministries in Relation to Man's Constitution and Needs

The fourfold ministry was God's response to the needs of His people for spiritual help and guidance in all four of their 'psychical'

---

[102] C/RL, i. 265.   [103] Ibid. 265–6.

faculties. Each of these ministries was divinely given for a special work in relation to the constitution of man which could not properly be fulfilled by the others. Thus the apostolic ministry of rule was directed towards man's will; the prophetic ministry was directed towards his imagination; the ministry of the evangelist was directed towards his understanding; and the pastorship was directed towards his affections.

This fourfold ministry belonged both in the universal Church and in particular Churches. In the universal Church, of which the sole ruler was Christ, the apostles fulfilled their ministry (as elders) together with prophets, evangelists, and pastors (of episcopal rank), the senior member of each of the universal ministries being known as its 'pillar'.[104] In each particular Church, the rule of Christ was represented by its angel. He was supported by a fourfold priestly ministry of elders, prophets, evangelists, and pastors. This was visibly proclaimed in each particular Church when the procession of ministers entered for the celebration of the Sunday Offices. First came the deacons as the representatives of the people. They were followed by the priests with the colour of their stoles indicating their 'character'—white (the symbol of purity) for pastors, red (the symbol of blood) for the evangelists, blue (the symbol of the heavens) for the prophets, and gold (the symbol of truth) for the elders. Finally, the angel appeared with stole and cope of purple (the symbol of rule). (In the absence of an angel, one of the ruling elders would wear a purple stole, thus ensuring that the rule of Christ was visibly represented.) Deacons could also be appointed to exercise a particular character of ministry, and each wore a stole of the colour appropriate to his appointment. All stoles were lined with red, signifying that the message of redemption through the Blood of Christ was the foundation of the Gospel of salvation entrusted to the whole Church. As rule in the universal Church belonged to Christ alone (as angel), the apostles did not wear purple (the symbol of rule) during services at the Albury headquarters, but reserved the colour for apostolic visitations to the tribes and to particular Churches.

A very large establishment of ordained clergy was implied by this whole system. It required that in each tribe there should be an apostle, assisted by a prophet, an evangelist, and a pastor—each

[104] The 'Pillar of Apostles' was J. B. Cardale, the 'Pillar of Prophets' E. O. Taplin (later C. Hammond), the 'Pillar of Evangelists' W. H. Place, and the 'Pillar of Pastors' J. Thompson.

denoted as being 'with the apostle'. In addition there should be five angel-evangelists, each set over twelve evangelists, answering to the 'sixty mighty men . . . expert in war, each with his sword at his thigh' (S. of S. 3: 7–8). Their evangelistic duty was

to carry on the war against the powers of darkness with the Sword of the Spirit. . . . further (the five [angel-evangelists] in each tribe corresponding to the Five Pillars at the entrance to the Tabernacle) to give full and final teaching to those whose hearts, through the preaching of the Deacon Evangelists, have been opened for the truth, and who desire to be admitted to the full blessings of the Church. The Angel-Evangelist should give instruction to those who believe concerning the mysteries of the Kingdom of Heaven, and concerning the order of God in His Church. He should prove them . . . he should bring them to the measure of knowledge fitting them to be presented for and to receive the laying on of hands of the Apostles . . .[105]

However, the message of the evangelists was intended to be a warning of the approaching judgements and a testimony to the availability of the fullness of God's grace for all. They were not expected to proselytize deliberately from the Churches. Indeed, all were charged

to put away the thought, that the object in view is to break up the existing ties between pastors and their flocks; or between the heads of the different Churches, whatever be their existing organization, and those under their episcopal rule or oversight. The first thought in their hearts should be that they are sent, not to destroy, but to build up and strengthen the things which remain, and are ready to die.[106]

There were also various ministers who had been set apart for financial and administrative duties in the universal Church. The maintenance of the link between the apostle and the angels of particular churches within the tribe (each of whom had the status of angel-pastor in the universal Church) was the duty of the pastor-with-the-apostle.

In each particular Church, it was required that there should be a ruling angel, together with a 'help' (also of episcopal rank). 'Helps' were of the same order as the one to whom they were appointed.

[105] Thiersch, *The Order of the Deaconship*, 36–7.
[106] G. C. Boase, *The Restoration of Apostles and the True Position of those who acknowledge them in relation to the Rest of the Church*, 3rd. edn. (London: Pitman, 1893), 34, quoting 'From an Official Address'. (Originally published Shaw, 1867.)

Ideally, every angel, priest, and deacon appointed to the formal establishment should have a help. The functions of helps had been declared prophetically by Cardale to be to assist those to whose ministry they were attached. Their ordination was stated to be in accordance with 1 Corinthians 12: 28.[107] Immediately below the angel, there should be six ruling elders, six evangelists, and six pastors, each with his help (making twelve of each ministry)—all in priestly orders. There should be the seven deacons, each with his help. Also, there were additional clergy, both priests and deacons, as required, and various unordained assistants: underdeacons, deaconesses, doorkeepers, acolytes, organists, and singers. The total complement of ordained clergy in a particular Church was thus a minimum of fifty-two. Each ruling elder was supposed to be responsible for 500 full communicants, of whom it was thus implied there should be 3000. It is clear that in practice all this was an ideal towards which to strive, rather than a state actually achieved, though the full complement of clergy was reached in a few very large congregations. Not all the clergy were 'separated', that is, relieved of the need to engage in secular work through being paid a stipend by the Church. Many, including in particular all the additional clergy (see above), served in a non-stipendiary capacity. Nevertheless, the maintenance of the ministry presented the Church with a financial need which demanded generous giving on the part of its communicants. The problem was solved by the adoption of the principle of tithing in addition to the normal offerings of the people at services (see § 4 below).

Within the worship and public ministries of the Church, it was the apostle who spoke to the whole man—body, soul, and spirit:

the word of the apostle, or ruler in word and doctrine, is addressed to man, especially as an individual person, and as a rational and moral agent; it is addressed to and embraces the whole man, spirit, soul, and body; and acts upon the will and conscience in the fullest sense and extent of the word, as conscience is the supreme inward judge and determiner of what ought to be done, and what ought not to be done . . .[108]

Further, the apostles claimed to minister 'the Spirit of Life *immediately* from the Lord Jesus Christ' and hence to be 'the source

---

[107] See Boase, *The Restoration of Apostles*, 808.

[108] J. B. Cardale, *A Manual or Summary of the Special Objects of Faith and Hope in the Present Times* (London: Strangeways, 1893), 18. This work (orig. pub. Barclay, 1843) is mainly an abridged version of *The Great Testimony* with notes.

and strength of every other ministry.[109] They alone were the dispensers of the Holy Spirit, and, in exercising their apostolic ministry within their respective tribes, each had the authority of the whole college. But, if acting as an agent of the college on some particular mission, they could be exercising any one or more of the four distinct ministries:

But as a minister acting under the direction of the College of Apostles, each apostle, in some respects, stands on a like footing with the prophet alone, in other cases with the prophet, evangelist, and pastor, as one of a fourfold ministry by whom the Lord edifies His Church, and the Church serves the Lord. This fourfold ministry is a fourfold distribution of the stream of life in the unity of Christ and of the Holy Ghost, whatever be the rank of the ministry through which it is exercised or the sphere of its operation. . . . in the Universal Church the Lord's rule . . . is exercised through Apostles, who in addition to their special office have also a function in common with others, both in worship and in teaching. For the rest, the part taken by the fourfold ministry in the service of the House of God is the same, whether that service be fulfilled by ministers of the Universal or of the particular Church.[110]

Within the particular Churches, the apostolic ministry was represented by the angels, but as those who could exercise a ministry of life only (not of the Spirit Himself), since their authority was not immediately from Christ but mediated through apostles. In each particular Church the angel was the representative of Christ's rule over the whole Church and of the apostle's rule in the tribe to which that Church belonged; he could not, however, exercise the fullness of an apostolic ministry within it—he was restricted to the functions appropriate to his rank.

The role of the elder—indicated by gold (truth)—was to remind the people of the truth 'as it is in Christ Jesus'. This truth should sit both outwardly and inwardly in a man:

This truth is both outward and inward, as suggested in the type of the Ark, covered within and without with gold, and as fulfilled in Jesus, the Perfect Antitype. Truth outwardly in word and doctrine, holding fast the form of sound words, declaring the truth of the Christian faith. Truth inwardly—as it is said, 'Behold, Thou desirest truth in the

---

[109] C. E. L. Heath, *The Four Colours* (London: Paddington Church, 1928), 2.
[110] T. Carlyle, *Concerning the Right Order of Worship in the Christian Church* (tr. of the 'Preface' to the German edition of *The Liturgy*, 1850) (n.p., Crerar and Smith, 1905), 38.

inward parts, and in the hidden part Thou shalt make me to know wisdom' (Ps. LI, 6). This is the Ministry of the Elder, and the man in whom the shittim wood of weak humanity is covered within and without with gold need fear no assaults without, or doubts within, for he is established in the truth.[111]

Having been reminded of this by the elders' ministry, men's wills should be strengthened to do good and to resist evil. In liturgical worship (see Ch. IV), it was normally an elder who pronounced on the truths contained in readings from Scripture and in the Creeds, unless this was undertaken by an angel or visiting apostle.

The role of the prophet—indicated by blue (the heavens)—was to direct men's imaginations to the heavenly truths revealed by God through the Spirit, upon which they should reflect in depth and with calmness, for the colour of the heavens presented 'the idea of secure untroubled calm and profound depths'. The voice of prophecy was also a reminder of the holiness to which all were called to show forth in their lives, for God had commanded every Israelite to 'make tassels on the corners of their garments throughout their generations, and to put upon the tassel of each corner a cord of blue' (Num. 15: 38) in order that he might remember to do His commandments and 'be holy' to Him (Num. 15: 40). Such holiness should be seen by God and be an inspiration to others:

It is a colour that others may see, for it should be conspicuous in all your garments; but it is a reminder to each individual that he is holy to the Lord; even as Aaron wore upon his forehead a lace of blue and a golden plate thereon with the inscription, 'HOLINESS TO THE LORD' (Exod. xxviii, 36–38). Brethren, the ribband of blue reminds you at all times and places, you are holy unto the Lord, and that therefore the daily round becomes a thing dedicated and a song of praise, for it is done as unto the Lord . . . Moreover . . . in the heavenlies, all is calm and serene, and with unclouded vision you survey great distances and obtain wondrous views, while the troubled clouds of earth pass unheeded beneath you. Take care then that the ribband of blue is in every garment, that both God and man may see it.[112]

In liturgical worship, it was normally a prophet who read passages of Holy Scripture.

The role of the evangelist—indicated by red (blood)—was to remind men's understanding of the foundation of the Gospel:

[111] *GT*, xlii.   [112] Heath, *The Four Colours*, 1.

salvation in Christ. Christians should read the Bible daily, but their understanding needed the instruction of the evangelist, expounding the 'opening up' of the Scriptures by the prophet. In this way, their faith would be deepened and confirmed, enabling them to stand against the assaults of unbelievers and the apostasy within the Churches:

This Gospel of Redemption is not only the faith we hold; it is also our covering and protection, for there are the winds of false doctrine abroad, icy and chilling blasts, causing men even to deny the Lord Who bought them, and to think lightly of the price that was paid. But the children of the Virtuous Woman are protected from these wintry blasts of infidelity. 'She is not afraid of the snow for her household, for all her household are clothed with scarlet' (Prov. XXXI, 21). This is the work of the Evangelist, and men who see your warm clothing envy the security of your faith.[113]

In liturgical worship, it was normally an evangelist who solemnly recounted before God the sins subsequently to be confessed by the people.

The role of the pastor—indicated by white (purity)—spoke to men's hearts, reminding them of their baptism, when they were clothed with the 'garment of salvation' and the 'robe of righteousness'. Christians should continue to walk in these white robes. This was possible only if they set their hearts on the things of God, keeping themselves 'unstained from the world' (Jas. 1: 27):

It is the Pastor who reminds us that we must walk with care along the muddy roads of this life, that we must keep ourselves unspotted from the world. If it should chance that our white robes become soiled, then it is [from] this ministry we seek the cleansing and absolution. It is the raiment of the Bride that we wear, and in the moment of transfiguration it shall be seen that our garments are not only white but clean and shining, glistening, radiant, as no fuller on earth can white them.[114]

Thus one specific duty of the pastor (or, in his absence, the elder) was to hear confessions, and later, if appropriate, to pronounce absolution, for which a special rite was provided.[115] A penitent could apply to his angel for permission for his confession to be heard by a priest other than a pastor or elder. Priests were warned that, before using the order for 'Solemn Absolution', they should ensure that the penitent was 'in a fit state of mind' and that, where appropriate, due

[113] Ibid.   [114] Ibid.   [115] See *The Liturgy*, 590–6.

'remedy or compensation' had been effected or was intended to be effected. Preparation for absolution involved fasting. The rite included a number of prayers together with Psalm 51. The words of absolution (with a laying on of hands) were:

The almighty and most merciful Lord God grant unto thee, through the ministry of me, His unworthy servant, full absolution and remission of all thy sins, iniquities, and transgressions, and blot them out for ever. In the Name of the Father . . .

The same rite, but without the pronouncing of absolution, was directed to be used for persons 'distressed and troubled in mind'. A further duty normally undertaken by the pastor was the offering of supplications (during liturgical worship) on behalf of the people.

The four ministries of apostles (including rule when represented by angels or ruling elders), prophets, evangelists, and pastors kept constantly before the people the ministries exercised by Christ but not able to be so exercised in the Church by any one person:

the Lord Jesus Christ, the revealer of the Father (for every one who saw Him had seen the Father) (John XIV, 9, 10), did bear in Himself all these offices when upon earth. He was the Apostle of our profession (Heb. III, 1), the Sent of God (John III, 34), filled with the wisdom of God, in words of wisdom and holy doctrine, in wisdom of conduct and rule; He was the Prophet mighty in word and deed (Acts III, 22), the revealer of the mysteries of God, the interpreter of His word; He was the Evangelist, the preacher of the Gospel to the poor, the anointed healer of the sick (Isaiah LXI, 1; Matt. XI, 3, 5), the wounded, and the maimed; He was the good Shepherd who laid down His life for the sheep, the teacher sent from God (John X, 11).

In like manner God is still to be revealed by Jesus Christ in His body the Church. . . . all the four offices, whereby God should be made known and which were centred in Jesus Christ, must still be exercised in His Church . . . until the consummation of the age . . . yet not through the agency of any *one* man, for that would be to make that man the container of the incommunicable fulness, which the Lord Jesus Christ Himself alone can be; but by distributing unto the several members, and exercising through them, those several offices, each fulfilling his own functions, and no one usurping the functions of another; otherwise the proprieties of the several parts of the body would be violated, and one member would be enabled to say to another, 'I have no need for thee' (I Cor. XII, 21).[116]

[116] GT, xxxiii–xxxiv.

TABLE 3.1. *The Fourfold Ministry of Character*

JESUS			
The Apostle,	The Prophet,	The Evangelist,	The Pastor
		ministers to His people by	
Apostles,	Prophets,	Evangelists,	Pastors;
		addressing Himself to	
The Will,	The Imagination,	The Understanding,	The Affections,
		by the word of	
Doctrine,	Reproof,	Correction and	Instruction in Righteousness
		that we may grow in	
Wisdom,	Heavenly mindedness,	Uprighteousness,	Holiness,
		as being	
Sons of God,	Begotten to a lively Hope,	Dead to Sin,	Alive to Righteousness,
		that when He appears we may be like Him	

The fourfold ministry of character may be summarized as in Table 3.[117] Catholic Apostolic members were regularly exhorted to yield their will, imagination, understanding, and affections to their elders, prophets, evangelists, and pastors, as the ministers divinely set in place in the Church. It was believed that, only in this way, could they be wholly prepared for Christ's imminent coming. These ministries were heavenly and witnessed to heavenly things; they were ministries of the ascended Christ, and as such above all earthly limitations, and would have their place in the eternal Kingdom:

They do not belong to, and they do not tie us to, an earthly state or condition. On the contrary, they are the evidence of our being set free from that condition. If they are exercised here, whilst the Church is on the earth, that is, so to speak, but an accident. Their true condition, and true exercise, do not belong to that, nor are they limited to it. They . . .

[117] Taken from G. C. Boase, *Three Discourses on Certain Symbols Used in Worship* (London: Bosworth, 1874) (orig. pub. Dundee, 1855), 38. Also (taken from Boase) in W. R. Brownlee, *The Gifts of the Spirit and the Ministry of the Lord* (Glasgow: Hobbs, 1877), 37 (orig. edn. London: Bosworth, 1874).

are in Christ *ascended*; and He can put them forth and exercise them
without any necessary limitation or restriction to the continuation of any
earthly state or existence on earth. How He may or will so put them
forth and exercise them we know not. But this we do know that four and
twenty Elders surround the throne, when the Church is seen in the
vision of glory. We know that the City that cometh down from Heaven
lieth four-square. And we know that the wall of the city hath twelve
foundations.[118]

Prophets and Prophesying

Before leaving discussion of the ministries of the Catholic Apostolic
Church, it is necessary to emphasize the difference between the
ordained ministry of prophets and the extempore prophetic utterances
which were spoken at prayer meetings and (in the appropriate place)
in liturgical services. The prophetic gift of the Spirit might be
manifested in any member of the Church:

We may all prophesy: but all are not prophets. The Holy Ghost may
divide and impart the gift of prophecy to any individual . . . but his
having the gift of prophecy does not make him to be a Prophet. The
ministry of Prophecy is one of the four ministries of the Church—one of
the four principal organs of the Body of Christ. . . .

The gift of prophecy, then, may be exercised in the Church by any of
its members. It is (as St. Paul tells us) 'for edification, exhortation, and
comfort'. It should be exercised, as it were, by equals among equals, in
brotherly love, lifting up the hearts of all into the fellowship of the Holy
Ghost. The functions of the Prophet require a higher endowment. . . . it
is his especial duty to acquaint himself with the prophetic interpretations of
Scripture; so that ministering and speaking in the Holy Ghost according
to the analogy of the one faith and of the revelation which God may from
time to time give, through the Angels and Prophets, of His will and
purpose, he may be an ordinance for light to the Angel, and through the
Angel to the ministers and people.[119]

---

[118] H. Dalton, *The Fourfold Ministry a Permanent Gift unto the Church, its
Restoration a Sign of the Nearness of the Second Advent, with Answers to Objections*
(London: Bosworth, 1866), 16.

[119] J. B. Cardale, *A Short Discourse on Prophesying and the Ministry of the Prophet in
the Christian Church* (London: Strangeways, 1868), 5–6. This work was published six
years after the death of Taplin—the 'pillar of prophets'. It is an interesting
speculation to consider how its content (and the regulations on prophesying) might
have been ultimately determined had Taplin lived to continue exercising his influence
over the apostles.

The ministry of prophecy was itself hierarchical, and members of each order of the ministry were confined to their 'border', that is, the limits within which they had apostolic authority to act. Thus, in the universal Church, the apostles were seen as the ultimate source of revelation, having the highest gift of the Spirit, though sharing the prophetic ministry with their angel-prophets. The latter were to communicate to the Church at large only those things revealed to both apostles and prophets,[120] and, when speaking within an apostolic council, they were to

remember that God does not reveal His mind through Prophets only, but to Apostles and Prophets; so that by the authority of the Apostles the things revealed may be taught and ministered to the Church by all the ministers, according to their respective borders.[121]

The relation of the prophet to the apostle was said to be like the relation of the Old Testament prophecies relating to God's purposes to the fulfilment of those prophecies in the person of Christ. The prophet should in no way attempt to take to himself any function rightly belonging to the apostle. As early as 1834 Irving, having warned against 'undervaluing the office of the prophet' on account of the difficulties which some of the utterances had caused, had written:

the order of the Lord is through the Prophet to bring the word of the Lord of what he will do, but the ordering of it to be done, and the setting of it into fact, he will perform by his Apostle.

. . . .

If the prophet occupy himself in his heart with the setting in order and the obedience, he layeth a snare for his own self and for all the Church because he is breaking into the house of another . . .[122]

Within the ordained ministry of a particular Church, the angel was the chief source of revelation:

Prophets set in the particular Church receive from the Angel the things revealed; they feed upon them in their hearts, and bring them forth in such form as to give light thereon to the Angel and ministers, and to all the people. Their office is to give light, not to teach or to correct—not to

---

[120] Validated prophecies were distributed under the title 'Apostles' Determinations' and were circulated to the angels, who had instructions to keep them locked up as confidential documents.

[121] Cardale, *A Short Discourse*, 7.

[122] Letter to Drummond, 1 May 1834 (Northumberland collection).

fulfil the duty of Elder, Evangelist, or Pastor. . . . but it is plain that they will not fulfil them, if they suppose themselves to be set for giving light to the Apostles and to the Church Universal, or if they imagine that their ministry is to be employed for the correction, or even the setting forth, of doctrine, which is the office of the Elder; or for the correction of life and conduct, or for the persuasion of the heart and conscience, which are the specific functions of the Evangelist and the Pastor.[123]

Thus, the ordained prophet, be he of the universal Church or of a particular Church, was strictly subject to authority and exercised his ministry within clearly defined borders. He was not forbidden to exercise the *charismatic* gift of prophecy—for who could forbid the Holy Spirit?—but in this he was in precisely the same situation as any other member of the Church, ordained or lay.

Those who exercised the charismatic prophetic gift of the Spirit were warned against pride—against imagining that this elevated them above their fellows or gave them a status equal to that of the ordained prophets. They were reminded also that the words of the Holy Spirit were not 'a matter of one's own interpretation' (2 Pet. 1: 20). It was for those with apostolic authority to exercise rule (i.e. the angels)—or ultimately the apostles themselves—to determine what was and what was not the voice of the Holy Spirit. There were false prophecies as well as true ones, and false prophecies might be spoken by true prophets. The Holy Spirit spoke through prophetic utterances into the ear of the ruler; thus it was for those exercising rule to determine what was true and what was false through the spiritual authority given to them, and to declare the voice of the Lord—'If anyone thinks that he is a prophet, or spiritual, he should acknowledge that what I am writing to you is a command of the Lord. If anyone does not recognize this, he is not recognized' (1 Cor. 14: 37–8).

The exercise of spiritual gifts was more freely permitted in prayer meetings than in public worship. In the former, anyone might prophesy at any time—there was no restriction other than the practicalities of the situation. During worship, the angels were responsible for exercising judgement so as to ensure not only that prophetic utterances were (as far as possible) confined to the allotted place but also that they were for edification and not confusion:

[123] Cardale, *A Short Discourse*, 8.

No one should be permitted to speak in the Service for worship without the express leave and sanction of the Angel. In giving this leave and sanction, the Angel should consider himself acting judicially. He must not withhold it from any whose prophesying would be for comfort and edification. He must withhold it from all such as, in his judgement, from the imperfection of the gift, from peculiarity of voice and manner, from the general character of the words, would not edify and comfort the people. In arriving at his decision, he must purge himself from all prejudices and personal peculiarities of taste; and seek to act as head of his church, embodying their feelings, and acting in the interest of all.[124]

The two distinct prophetic witnesses to Christ—of the Spirit, and of men having their minds illuminated by the Spirit—were seen as fulfilling the Lord's promise: 'But when the Counsellor comes . . . he will bear witness to me; and you also are witnesses . . .' (John 15: 26–7). The witness of men enlightened by the Spirit was seen as taking place whenever the Gospel was faithfully preached or its truths faithfully proclaimed. The witness of the Spirit Himself occurred whenever the charismatic gifts of the Spirit were manifested:

For example, the Spirit bore His witness, when, on the Day of Pentecost, the Apostles 'were filled with the Holy Ghost, and began to speak with other tongues as *the Spirit* gave them utterance;'—the Apostle Peter bore his witness, the witness of a man having his mind enlightened by the Spirit, when he stood up, and explained to the assembled multitude what had taken place. Another example is found in the narrative recorded in Acts iii. The Holy Ghost bore His witness to Christ, by inspiring Peter and John to heal the cripple lying at the beautiful gate of the Temple; Peter bore his witness, the witness of a man having his mind enlightened by the Spirit, when he explained to the crowd of people . . . by what power the man had been healed, and preached Christ to them.[125]

There was seen to be a further important distinction between these two witnesses which singled out the special nature of the witness of the Spirit—unlike the witness of enlightened men, it was not exercised by the will of man, but through men acting and speaking solely in the power of the Spirit. This did not, however, imply that

---

[124] J. B. Cardale, *Directions on the Subject of Women Prophesying in Church*, privately issued (1866), 2. This work contains general directions on prophesying as well as remarks applicable specifically to women.

[125] R. G. Flegg, *The Nature, Character, and Place of Prophecy in the Christian Church* (London: Goodwin Norton, 1888), 4.

the responsibility of the person by whom the Spirit may manifest His gifts is destroyed, or even overridden for the time being; but, that the motion, the impulse, to do the act, or speak the word, does not originate in the will of the person by whom the act is done, or the word spoken. Neither does the power . . . proceed from the person used by the Holy Ghost. Both the motion to act or speak, and the power by which the act is done, or the word spoken, are of the Spirit.[126]

It was clear from John 16: 13–14 that the chief (though not the only) means used by the Holy Spirit to bear witness to Christ would be intelligible language. It was also clear from St Paul that the gift of speaking in a tongue *understood by the hearers* was more edifying, and hence of a higher order, than speaking in an unknown tongue (1 Cor. 14: 1–19), since the latter was a matter of comfort to the speaker only. However, words spoken in prophecy needed interpretation, and it was this interpretation, mediated through apostolic authority, which should take the highest place in men's regard. This could be seen, for example, from the account of St Paul's decision to return to Jerusalem (Acts 21: 11–14). The words of the Spirit spoken by Agabus seemed to all except St Paul to be a warning, if not a command, that he should not proceed to Jerusalem. However he put a different interpretation on them, regarding them, not as a warning or command to stay away from the city, but as a 'light' upon what should befall him there. This demonstrated that words spoken in the Spirit became the property of the Apostles, who were the only ones who could discern their true meaning or decide on what action they implied. 1 Cor. 10–16 showed that this applied equally to spiritual mysteries: for St Paul spoke first of their revelation by the Spirit and then of those, the Apostles, who, having the mind of Christ, had the authority to impart and interpret the revelation to the Church. This was taken as indicating that the place of prophecy in the Church was intended to be secondary. Words spoken in the Spirit were always addressed to apostles for their interpretation. They were not to be taken by the hearers as authoritative commands or declarations of doctrine, but as words of light addressed to those to whom Christ had committed the Church for her rule and guidance until His appearing.

---

[126] Flegg, *The Nature, Character, and Place of Prophecy*, 4–5.

4. THE MAINTENANCE OF THE MINISTRY: TITHES

The Catholic Apostolic ministry was maintained by the payment of *tithes*. It was taught that there was a perpetual obligation of conscience, laid upon all members, to pay their tithe to God. Tithe was formally defined as

the tenth part, or the equivalent of the tenth part, of increase, whether such increase be derived from property of any kind, or from the labour and skill of man.[127]

Such payment was voluntary—it was left entirely to members' consciences, no record being kept of those who paid and those who did not. Indeed, unless payment was made through some form of identifiable cheque or draft, this would not have been possible in view of the method of payment adopted. Thus, the compulsion was one of the spirit not of the law:

The contributions of the faithful in the Christian Church are all voluntary, in the sense that if withheld they are not to be enforced by penalties. It is contrary to the spiritual character of the Church, and to its proper relation to the kingdoms of this world, to enforce money payments, or other transactions touching this world's goods, either by appeal to the laws of the State, or even by spiritual penalties. The kingdom of Christ in this dispensation is 'not of this world'.[128]

The Authority for the Obligation of Tithing

The obligation of tithing was of divine origin, being God's provision for those called to the priesthood of Melchizedec. It antedated the Law, and stood on a footing with the Sabbath, whose origin was not the Law but God's act of creation. The Sabbath had been blessed and sanctified by God from the beginning (Gen. 2: 3), and its keeping recognized God as Creator of all things. Similarly, the payment of tithe recognized Him as the possessor of heaven and earth:

Through the sanctifying of the Sabbath, we testify that we are God's creatures, and that to him we owe not the seventh day only, but all the

---

[127] *Book of Regulations*, 132.
[128] J. B. Cardale, *A Discourse upon the Obligation of Tithe* (London: Pitman, 1892) (orig. pub. London: Boswell, 1858), 3.

days of our lives; through the separating and sanctifying of the tenth part of our earthly substance, we testify that not only this part, but all our earthly possessions are God's property.[129]

It was also suggested—on patristic authority and by reference to Hebrews 11: 4—that Cain's sacrifice had been rejected by God (Gen. 4: 3–5) not because of its nature but because of its deficiency in quantity. Abel had brought the separated tithe of his flock, but his brother had withheld the due amount; its rejection was not because it was not an animal sacrifice but because of its insufficient proportion:

There is certainly nothing in the Hebrew text to show that Cain was rejected because he did not bring an animal. . . . fruits have always been recognised as proper and suitable oblations: Cain brought of such fruits as he had, of the increase which God had bestowed upon *him*. . . . In the original Hebrew, the meaning of the 7th verse (of Gen. iv), in which the sin of Cain is adverted to, is confessedly obscure; but this obscurity would be to some extent cleared, if we could rely upon the Septuagint, in which the Lord, in expostulating with Cain, is represented as saying, 'If thou hast rightly offered, but hast not rightly *divided*, hast thou not sinned?' The text is thus quoted, both by Clement of Rome . . . (ad Cor. 4); by Irenaeus . . . (adv. Haeres. iv. 34); by Tertullian, and others. Tertullian expressly says (adv. Jud. ii.) that 'Cain's sacrifice was rejected because he had not rightly divided;' and at a later period, at the Council of Seville (A.D. 590), it was declared that whosoever did not pay tithes of all, 'would be liable as a thief and a robber to the plagues inflicted upon Cain, who divided not aright'.[130]

The patriarchs had paid tithes: Abraham had paid them to Melchizedec when, as 'priest of God Most High', he had 'brought out bread and wine' (Gen. 14: 18–20), and, at Bethel, Jacob had promised to God 'the tenth part of all that thou givest me' (Gen. 28: 22). The recognition of Melchizedec by Abraham showed that the Levitical priesthood was neither the original nor the enduring ministry, and that the right to receive tithes belonged not to Levi but to Melchizedec. Since he was the type of Christ, who was declared in Scripture to be 'after the order of Melchizedec' (Heb. 5: 6, 10; 6: 20), the right had passed to those who exercised Christ's ministry in

[129] C. J. T. Bohm, *Lights and Shadows in the Present Condition of the Christian Church* (from the German) (London: Bosworth and Harrison, 1860), 282.
[130] Cardale, *A Short Discourse*, 5.

the Church, since they were chosen, not by men but by the Holy Spirit:

If we view this last institution [the Christian priesthood and ministry] as one blessed, indeed, to our benefit by God, but proceeding from some movement or choice on the part of the flock, separating of their own will certain of the brethren to minister to them in holy things; then we can conceive that the question of the subsistence of the ministers, both as to amount and mode of provision, also depends upon the discretion and judgement of those who appoint them. If that were true, the Church would be founded on the voluntary principle, and reason is that the sustenance of her ministers should depend upon the like principle. But if we believe that *God* chooses and sends forth whom He will have to serve Him in holy things, and that their choice and their number are subjects of rule and government, and do not depend upon the will of the people—then we shall also be prepared to admit, that it is equally impossible that the provision for them should be dependent upon the mere voluntary gifts of the people. It must be a matter for Divine regulation, by precept.

It is very true that the Dispensation of the Law is passed away, and that we are under a spiritual dispensation—that our offerings are to be brought up, not from a sense of penal compulsion, but out of a ready and willing heart—from love, and not by necessity. But this has respect to the motive for our conduct, and not the duty itself. We cannot suppose that, because we obey the law of love, therefore we are under less stringent obligations than were the faithful followers of God in former and inferior dispensations.[131]

It was said to be clear from the last chapter of Leviticus that the obligation under the Law in respect of tithes was no innovation (though it had probably largely fallen into disuse during the period spent in Egypt):

After treating of things voluntarily devoted to the Lord, with the rules of redemption of them, and adverting to the first-born of beasts (which would not be voluntarily devoted, they being already the Lord's), we are told not by way of injunction, but of declaration, that all the tithe of the land 'is the Lord's: it is holy unto the Lord'; and redeemable only by adding to the value an additional fifth part: and then it is declared that the tenth of the herd and of the flock is the Lord's, and absolutely irredeemable. There is here, therefore, no enactment of a new law, imposing that they were to pay tithes. The Lord claimed them to be His,

---

[131] *C/RL*, i. 126–7.

placing them upon the same footing as the first-born, and as things devoted. . . .

The method, therefore, in which the separation of tithes was renewed under the Law, gives further testimony and confirmation that the payment of tithes is an aboriginal institution, of perpetual obligation upon the faithful.[132]

Christians were regarded as being under an even stronger obligation to pay tithes than their Jewish predecessors had been—the argument in Hebrews 7 clearly stated this. The early Church had accepted that argument:

Origen, Jerome, and Augustine give their testimony to the same truth; and the testimony of Augustine extends to the practice of the early Church. He explains in one passage (Homil. 48) that his own contemporaries failed in this duty, which had been faithfully fulfilled by those who had gone before them. . . . at the second Council of Macon (A.D. 585), not only were tithes enjoined, but now was introduced . . . the unjustifiable practice of punishing the non-payment of tithes by the spiritual penalty of excommunication. The fifth canon of this Council grounds the obligation of tithes on the Divine laws, 'which laws' (the canon states) 'the whole multitude of Christian people, for a great length of time, preserved inviolate.'[133]

Tithing—Spiritual not Legal

Involving the State in punishments for failure to pay tithes, as had subsequently happened in a number of countries in Europe, was totally condemned. The payment of tithe was primarily a spiritual matter; so, therefore, was its non-payment. To fail to pay it was to rob God of His due (Mal. 3: 8–10); it was also a denial of God's right to all that man possesses. If the obligation was not met, God would withdraw His blessings, both material and spiritual:

If we obey it not, the penalty which we must expect is the forfeiture of His blessing upon our worldly substance (except He leave us altogether to ourselves), and the drying up of the streams of life and grace which flow to us from His altar.[134]

This was on an entirely different basis compared with taxes due to the state; these were imposed by law and the penalties were enforced

---

[132] Cardale, *A Discourse on the Obligation of Tithe*, 7–8.
[133] Ibid. 11–12.   [134] C/RL, i. 129.

by the law. Christians had an obligation to meet the demands of the state—to render Caesar's things to Caesar—but they also had the higher obligation to render God's things to God (Matt. 22: 21). God had never relinquished His right to possess the earth. As its possessor

> He requires always to be acknowledged, not only in word but in deed. . . . And as God has given to Christ, the king of righteousness and peace (Hebrews vii, 2), the eternal High-Priest, all power in heaven and earth, when we keep back our tithes, we deny Christ as priest of the most high God, and must lose the blessing with which He blesses the true children of Abraham.[135]

First-fruits

There was also a similar obligation upon Catholic Apostolic members to offer *first-fruits*, defined formally as

> the value of the first year's return from all property accruing to the offerer through the bounty of others, and not being the result of his own industry, nor devolving upon him by course of municipal law, nor by the gift or bequest of near relatives, nor property coming to him by any bequest or gift when the same property, without such bequest or gift, would have devolved upon him by course of law.[136]

Such first year's return on new capital or property was due to God as an offering of praise and thanksgiving, since it was not the reward of a person's own exertions.

Free-Will Offerings

First-fruits and tithes (which were themselves also a form of first-fruits) were considered to be the absolute minimum of financial offering which should be given to the Church. Over and above them were the *free-will offerings* given as an overflowing of love and gratitude towards God. These could be *general* offerings, whose disposition was at the discretion of the clergy, or *special* offerings for the relief of the poor, to support clergy travel, for the work of evangelism, for clergy widows and orphans, or in response to some particular appeal. The general offerings could be used for any of the following purposes: the maintenance of worship—provision of

---

[135] *Book of Regulations*, 133. [136] Bohm, *Lights and Shadows*, 284.

bread, wine, oil, incense, vestments, etc.; *local* evangelistic work; the payment of rent, rates, taxes, insurance, and repairs; heating and lighting; payment of Church caretakers, cleaners, etc.; and relief of the poor, in augmentation of earmarked offerings for this purpose. These were used at the local level, whilst the majority of the special offerings were passed on to the seven deacons of the universal Church.

Certain days were appointed for certain special offerings: Christmas Day, Easter Day, and Pentecost for the support of particular Churches in financial difficulties and clergy of the universal Church in need of special help; 14 July (when the 'separation' of the apostles was commemorated) for the universal Church travelling fund; and All Saints' Day for the widows and orphans of deceased clergy. A long box with separate named compartments (or separate boxes) had to be provided in each church for the offerings of the people, which were brought up during the Eucharist to be placed on the table of prothesis, it being noted that the apostolic canons of the Church Catholic forbade their being placed upon the altar.

No 'Right' to Clergy Salaries

Though God had the right to tithes, the clergy had no right to receive salaries obtained through them. Even those clergy who had relinquished secular work, and hence their means of livelihood, had no *right* to any income from the Church. They were paid on a regular basis, but each payment was to be regarded as a gift from God through His Church, and not as an instalment of an annual stipend paid by the people. This was emphatically laid down:

All ministers who receive portions from tithes or offerings receive the same as gifts or benefices from God to facilitate their labours, not as stipends to which they are in any way entitled, nor as payments from the people. Such portions are paid in advance, and do not entitle the ministers receiving them to make a claim for the continuance of these payments. The service which ministers render is not given in return for any such benefice: ministerial service is a duty binding upon them independently of any payment.[137]

All clergy were required to sign a paper agreeing that they accepted and would be bound by this principle. In view of this fact,

[137] *Book of Regulations*, 133.

it is remarkable that there should have been a number of Anglican clergy willing to give up their livings in order to accept a ministry whose remuneration must have seemed entirely insecure. In fact, the situation was regarded as providing an opportunity for trust in God's continuing bounty towards His servants. The same situation applied to pensions paid to clergy widows: these were generous and regular, but with precisely the same lack of any guarantee of continuity.

Tithing: A Continuing Obligation

With the decline of the number of Catholic Apostolic clergy during the present century, the amounts received through tithes came gradually to exceed greatly the amount required to maintain the 'separated' clergy who remained. With the closing down of churches, the question arose as to where and how the tithe should be paid, and even the question of whether it remained an obligation. A further problem arose because in the Anglican churches, which many members now attended, the principle was not taught and there was therefore no way of distinguishing tithes from other offerings.

The promulgated decision reaffirmed the obligation of tithing as being universally applicable to Christians and indicated ways in which it could continue to be directed for its proper purpose—the maintenance of the ministry:

It would be a great mistake to suppose that because Tithe cannot now be received and dealt with by Apostles personally, therefore it need not be rendered; it is a universal obligation resting upon all Christian people, and where the duty is fulfilled we can be sure that the promised blessing will follow.

. . . Since the death of the last of the Seven Deacons the administration of the Universal Church Funds has devolved upon others who have recently pointed out that owing to the greatly reduced number of ministers serving under apostles there is no longer the necessity to make the same provision as formerly. In view of this they have considered the question as to whether the time has now come when Tithe can be better employed in the service of the Anglican or other branch of the Church. Whenever Tithes and Offerings are presented in the Eucharistic Service we pray that they may be used for God's glory and for the welfare of His Church and people; and if the needs of the other branches of the Church are greater than ours, then it would seem to be more to God's glory and the welfare of the Church that they should be used where they are most needed.

.   .   .   .

It is therefore advised that those who are deprived of the restored ordinances should feel at liberty to render their Tithe (perhaps monthly or quarterly) in the local churches which they attend, and that to ensure a proper use of it they should place it in an envelope marked 'Clergy Sustentation Fund' or 'Maintenance of the Ministry', or whatever the local equivalent may be.[138]

Where the tithe involved small amounts, it was recommended to be placed in the normal alms-dish, together with any offering, in the confidence that God would distinguish between the two, use them and give His blessing accordingly. All such payments were to be made discreetly, and preferably not by cheque, so as to avoid comment by others and the dangers of consequent pride or self-satisfaction. The gradually increasing surplus in the universal Church funds has been disbursed at intervals, equally discreetly, to the Anglican authorities for maintenance of the Anglican ministry. Because of the deliberate and highly laudable policy of secrecy, it is impossible to determine the amounts involved, though it has been suggested that they are very substantial.[139] Grants for special purposes have also been made to other Churches.

5. SECTS AND SOCIETIES

The Catholic Apostolic view of the Church as consisting of all the baptized did not extend to an equal recognition of the validity of the structures of the various Churches. As has been noted, they regarded the divinely given structure of the Church, which included the fourfold ministries of order and character, as immutable. Episcopal Churches were seen as having preserved the greater part of the ministry of order, but their lack of apostles had seriously reduced the spiritual level at which they were able to function. Presbyterian order necessarily functioned at a still lower spiritual level, since the lack of a priesthood implied a lack of valid sacraments other than baptism. Nevertheless, both episcopal and presbyterian national Churches were accorded the title 'Church'; this was not seen as

---

[138] Private circular, 1949.
[139] According to the late Dr D. Tierney (London University), lecture at Dr Williams' Library, 1981.

conflicting with the Catholic Apostolic belief in the *one* Church—the company of the baptized.

Beyond those bodies given the title 'Church' were the various sects and religious societies, some of whose members might also, through baptism, be members of the one Church. However, their organizations and many of their beliefs came in for severe criticism, and their members were regarded as having seriously departed from fundamental ecclesiological principles. Sectarianism was seen as involving the serious sin of schism: it was also associated in the minds of Catholic Apostolics with radicalism and socialism, indications of the coming judgements on Christendom. In as much as even the episcopal Churches contained sectarian seeds, their ultimate destruction was ensured unless they accepted the restoration of apostolic rule. This did not imply that their members should join the apostolic congregations, but that, as organized bodies, they should accept the ultimate authority under Christ of the restored apostles.

The Anglican Church was seen as having sectarian seeds within it:

The Reformed Church of England, however, contained within itself the seeds of certain destruction. Instead of being the result of Catholic Reformation, or an effort to restore the whole Catholic Church to its pristine purity, it was an attempt merely to repair that section of the Church which was under the sway of the King of England. Thus its very principle was sectarian . . .[140]

The same was true of the Church of Scotland, and, indeed, of any purely national Church even though it might claim to be part of the Church Catholic. Nationalism almost inevitably involved intolerance, the want of Christian tolerance being the result of the loss of true Church government.

The appearance of sectarianism early in the Church's life was seen as being coincident with the first disappearance of the obedience of faith:

It sprang out of a failure to appreciate, or a disposition to deny, the true grace of Christ's Apostleship in living men. Paul observed the evil on its first manifestation, and severely rebuked it . . . (1 Cor. i, 11–13).

. . . the Apostle declares that those who were influenced by Sectarianism were *fleshly* in opposition to their spiritual standing in Christ the Head of the Body, the Church. . . . Whatever ministry the Lord gave to man, He expected His people to recognize and submit to in

[140] H. Drummond, *Tracts for the Last Days* (London: Painter, 1844), 261.

man. But the Lord gave not to Apollos the ministry and standing which He gave to Paul; and therefore Apollos was not to be followed as Paul was: . . . and the faith of Christian men was not to stand 'in the wisdom of men, but in the power of God' (1 Cor. ii. 5) bestowed upon men. This sectarianism was the denial of the very foundation of the Church; for Christ built the Church upon the foundation of Apostles and prophets, Himself being the chief cornerstone . . . (Eph. ii. 2). To build, therefore upon mere men, i.e. men *unattached* to Christ, was to build upon a wrong foundation, even one of sand (Matt. vii. 24–28).[141]

The grounds of St Paul's condemnation were its carnality and its essential opposition to inner spiritual growth—it kept men in a state of spiritual infancy. These characteristics had always been apparent in sectarian movements, which were the product of the unsound Christian mind. They were to be seen as fundamental to the Reformation, which, though rightly involving protest against spiritual evils in the Roman Church, was

instrumental in opening the floodgates of individual pride and presumption, by which Christendom became more intensely and wickedly Sectarian than in any preceding age. . . . The Reformation, so called, taught men, to a previously unheard of extent, to see reasons why they should choose to become one man's followers rather than another's; but the preference proceeded from reasons apart from any supremacy of the man *in Christ*: it must, therefore, have been carnal: it was a following of men after the flesh.[142]

Wesleyanism and other similar sects were regarded in the same way—men followed Wesley, not because he had apostolic grace conferred upon him by Christ, but because they preferred him as a superior example of piety, shrewdness, and zeal, when compared with the largely apathetic clergy of the Established Church. It was recognized that such zeal was often supported by a superior individual knowledge of the Scriptures. However, the Scriptures were not given to the Church for private interpretation, and, apart from authoritative apostolic authority and teaching, they could easily be abused by men and turned to evil ends.

---

[141] T. Fowkes, *Sectarianism* (London: Bosworth, 1874), 10.
[142] Ibid. 19–20.

The Salvation Army

The Salvation Army—whose title was described as 'presumptuous'
—was seen as a grotesque distortion of Christian mission, because it
displayed great eagerness to destroy what it judged to be the Devil's
works, but had little thought of 'making men sons of God and heirs
of eternal life'. Its concentration was excessively on the things of this
world, avoiding anything which savoured of Church ordinances. Its
military organization and its aggressive mode of operation were
unchristian, and its prominent use of women unacceptable:

The organization of this body is entirely on a *military* model. Titles,
uniforms, terms, are all military. This is grotesque; and . . . it invites
attack needlessly and to no good purpose. It is impossible to approve the
deliberate and systematic provocation of opposition which is effected by
aggressive ostentation, upon the strength of which this body assumes an
air of being persecuted. The reproach of the Cross comes unsought, and
will invariably attend all faithful witness to Christ; but it is a reproach to
be *suffered* for Christ's sake, not to be *courted* and invited for the sake of
gaining notoriety or calling forth sympathy. The employment of *women*
in prominent places, particularly in preaching, and the authority
exercised by them, are unscriptural, and opposed to the teaching and
practice of the Church.[143]

No one should consider themselves competent or authorized to set
about preaching the Gospel without Divine authority: men cannot
preach unless they are 'sent' (Rom. 10: 14).

The Salvation Army's attitude towards sacraments and ordinances
was seen as the inevitable outcome of Protestant evangelicalism and
radicalism, culminating in will-worship and infidelity—it was the
apostasy of the last days. The doctrine of 'sudden conversion' was
contrary to the Christian principle of growing in sanctification; it led
to self-glorification and the conviction that an awareness of
forgiveness of sin elevated a man to the rank of a saint and martyr:

It is presumptuous in those who have come to the knowledge of their
sinful state of life and have been brought to repentance to assume that
this is all they need, that they *are saved*.[144]

---

[143] H. S. Hume, *The 'Temperance Movement' and the 'Salvation Army'* (London:
Strangeways, 1882), 13.

[144] F. V. Woodhouse, *Socialism and Temperance Societies—with Some Additional
Remarks on the So-called 'Salvation Army'* (London: Bosworth, 1883), 13.

The practice of the Army in the matter of the public acknowledgement of conversion was totally lacking in humility:

Indeed, a great danger is indicated in the Leader's boast: 'We compel all our soldiers to live under the blazing light of public service' . . . 'The moment any man, woman, or child, professes to have received the remission of sins through faith in Christ, we require them to stand up and tell the audience' [at a crowded meeting] 'what the Lord has done for them.' Can it be supposed that such a course is anything other than injurious? In the first place, everyone is made a judge of his own state; and secondly, the instant and public profession *must* be destructive of that humility which accompanies true repentance.[145]

Salvationists totally ignored the warning, 'let anyone who thinks that he stands take heed lest he fall' (1 Cor. 10: 12). The thrusting forward of children was considered to be especially dangerous, since they were expected to express their sorrowful conviction of the unconverted state of their parents and teachers—it was a system leading to pride, vainglory, and hypocrisy. Salvationist preaching and literature were considered to be full of profanities; such profanities were anything but the things which were 'honourable, just, pure, lovely . . .' (Phil. 4: 8); they led to the treatment of sacred things with contempt by others, since their newspapers were widely and thoughtlessly bought, like comic papers, for purposes of deriving amusement from their content. Nevertheless, it was admitted that there was a vast field for rescuing men and women from degradation; it was the Established Church's lack of interest in such matters that had given the Army its *raison d'être*. In this sense they were a judgement on the Anglican Church.

Religious Societies

Equally strong condemnation was applied to what the Catholic Apostolics called 'societism'—the formation of supposedly self-governing religious societies, either functioning allegedly within the Churches or completely outside them. The condemnation included missionary societies, temperance societies, and especially societies devoted to any form of spiritualism or occultism. The criticism of missionary societies—in which the Catholic Apostolics followed the lead given by Irving—was based largely upon the emphasis on fund-raising (see Ch. VI, § 4).

[145] Hume, *The 'Temperance Movement'*, 14–15.

Temperance societies were criticized because the pledge demanded by them was considered to be a denial of the pledge involved in baptism:

Every baptized person is pledged by the vows taken at Baptism to keep his body in sobriety, temperance, and chastity; and to those who were baptized, and who feel the force of the vows taken by them, any pledges, such as those imposed by these societies, are useless and indeed inconsistent with those vows, because they imply that the baptismal vows are insufficient, and that a pledge given to men is of greater weight and of higher obligation than vows taken before God.[146]

Total abstinence pledges were considered to be opposed to Christian liberty and entirely unscriptural—they were a following of doctrines of men inconsistent with the rules laid down by St Paul (Col. 2: 16). They were also a rejection of Our Lord's teaching and example, ignoring His express sanction of wine for the enjoyment of men at the marriage feast at Cana. It was clear from the New Testament that the drinking of wine was not forbidden—it was drinking in excess that was to be deprecated. Many Christians had been attracted to the temperance movement as a result of seeing the results of intemperance around them, and these had blinded them to its denial of Scripture: it was based upon an old heresy which had first appeared in the early years of the Church:

The Scripture says, 'Every creature of God is good, and nothing to be refused, if it be received with thanksgiving; for it is sanctified by the word of God and prayer' (1 Timothy iv, 4). . . . We give God thanks not only for barns filled with home-grown corn, but also for stores replenished with 'wine and oil and all good fruits' . . . (The Liturgy of the Apostles).

Among the heresies which sprang up as tares sown by the enemy at a very early period in the history of the Church, was one which consisted in regarding all 'matter' as being *inherently evil*, though God, Who created all things, pronounced everything that he had made 'very good'.

If it were necessary to point out to you the monstrous character of this error, it would be sufficient to say that its logical consequences would be to make the Incarnation of God the Son inconceivable, and Sacraments impossible.

.   .   .   .

It is therefore an error to make a crusade against some material thing, as though it were a personified evil. It is to the *hearts of men* that the

---

[146] Woodhouse, *Socialism and Temperance Societies*, 7–8.

appeal must be made; *there* the evil must be sought, and *thence* it must be cast out.[147]

For Catholic Apostolics, the fundamental error of temperance societies was that they attributed evil to a thing rather than to persons. By their concentration on one thing, they shut their eyes to other evils constantly springing up in men's hearts. Further, they themselves exhibited evil: spiritual pride, vainglory, hypocrisy, and disparagements of the sacraments of the Church.

Spiritualism, Occultism, and Hypnosis

Spiritualism and occultism had grown into prominence in Europe and America in the early part of the nineteenth century, though such subcultures had always existed throughout the world, even in Christendom. They included mesmerism, clairvoyance, table-tapping, psychical research, theosophy, mind-reading, and all other forms of necromancy. These were regarded by the Catholic Apostolics as yet another sign of the coming of the Antichrist.

One commonly experienced phenomenon was automatic hand-writing. This was described as an evil parody of the writing seen upon the wall at Belshazzar's feast (Dan. 5), and those who went in for it should beware lest they too see a hand from God declaring that their days were numbered, that they had been found wanting, and that their possessions would be given to others (Dan. 5: 25–8).

Even more evil were the attempts to get into communication with the spirits of the departed. Those who imagined that they could do so were deluded:

Now we cannot believe them to be the spirits of departed men. It is far more likely that they are evil spirits, personating the departed the better to accomplish their insidious designs. . . . In all . . . parts of Holy Scripture, where sorcery and soothsaying, and such like curious arts, are spoken of, they are attributed directly to the agency of evil spirits—the spirits of devils working miracles, and teaching doctrines subversive of the faith (1 Timothy iv, 1).

. . . .

. . . the prevalence of satanic power in these startling forms of wickedness is one of the most appalling things on earth in the present day. Such powers, so manifestly of the unseen world, and so crafty and

[147] Hume, *The 'Temperance Movement'*, 6–8.

successful in snaring unstable souls, are indeed the spiritual wickednesses in high places against which we are warned by St. Paul. They shew also the power and signs and lying wonders which are to deceive, if it were possible, the very elect; and which are eventually to come to a head in the last Antichrist, now near to be revealed. For he must be near, seeing that the powers he is to use are being put forth even now.[148]

Thus, the phenomena of spiritualism were accepted as being actual 'signs and wonders', not mere sleight-of-hand deceptions. Christians who found themselves inadvertently faced with such signs and wonders should act in accordance with the teaching of St John: 'Beloved, do not believe every spirit, but test the spirits to see whether they are of God . . . every spirit which does not confess Jesus is not of God. This is the spirit of Antichrist . . .' (1 John 4: 1–3):

Here then is the infallible test, a test which does not apply to men, but to **spirits** who may manifest themselves to men. A man may say 'yes' or 'no' in answer to this test question, but those spirits who are evil and opposed to God will **not** confess that 'Jesus Christ is come in the flesh' because they hate Him.[149]

Of mesmerism (hypnotism), it was stated that the Scripture forbade all forms of divination and enquiry into 'things secret and hidden from the natural and waking understanding' and all attempts to cause any spirit to answer such questions; and further . . .

That it is a wicked thing, both in the person doing it, and in the person permitting it to be done upon them, to suspend, and *pro temporare* annihilate, a man's will and conscience, and yet give him power to act . . .[150]

It was noted that hypnotism had been introduced by a number of doctors with the object of relieving or removing pain, and that it was contended that this was acceptable because no honourable physician would use it other than for the patient's good—this could not, however, be guaranteed, and, even if it could be, it would be contrary to God's order:

But even if it could be guaranteed that such a physician would never be tempted to misuse his power, the practice cannot be justified. It is not

---

[148] W. Tarbet, *Spiritualism—a Sign and Prelude of the Coming Judgements* (London: Boswell, 1862), 2–4.

[149] A. G——, *A Letter on Spiritualism* (Glasgow: Hobbs, 1902), 3.

[150] F. Sitwell, *What is Mesmerism? and what its Concomitants—Clairvoyance and Necromancy* (London: Bosworth and Harrison, 1862) (orig. pub. 1853), 30.

right to do evil that good may come of it. Just as peace in itself is good, but peace at the sacrifice of honour no self-respecting man would accept, so bodily health is in itself a good thing, but health obtained by means which are contrary to God's order and involve disloyalty to Him, no faithful Christian man will desire.[151]

Everyone fearing God should pause at the thought of tampering with forbidden things, and should refuse

to be brought . . . into a condition where he sleeps and yet is awake; a helpless child, and yet a man to do or submit to evil; not a dead man, nor yet a living one; not a soul without a body, nor yet a body without a soul; but a strange unnatural condition of both, in which the door is open to every evil, while every power of conscience, affection, reason, memory, and will, which God has given to guard this door, is suspended and locked up in deep and deadly slumber.[152]

It was too easy for Christians to be led merely to smile at warnings against such things as mind-reading, but they were not radically different from the witchcraft of the days of heathenism so bitterly and terribly denounced in the Bible: 'Among the last words to be found in the book of Revelation are these: "Without are dogs and sorcerers . . . and whosoever loveth and maketh a lie." "Sorcerers . . . shall have their part in the lake of fire." Touch not the unclean thing!'[153]

Christian Science

Amongst the cults singled out for special condemnation was Christian Science, described as a 'deadly error'. It was condemned for many reasons: denying the existence of created matter; claiming that sickness, disease, and death were delusions; denying the personality of the Holy Spirit and the doctrine of the Trinity; repudiating fundamental Christian truths, such as the Incarnation, the Atonement, and the Resurrection; ridiculing the efficacy of prayer; and worshipping the human mind as God. Of the last, it was said:

---

[151] S. M. Hollick, *The Substance of Addresses on Spiritualism and Hypnotism* (Manchester Church, 1968) (orig. edn. 1920), 5.

[152] Sitwell, *What is Mesmerism?*, 31.

[153] J. B. Davenport, *The Spiritual Danger of Occultism and Sorcery* (Glasgow: Hobbs, 1902), 14.

The unchristian nature of Christian Science is seen in this: they say that Jesus worked miracles and healed sickness by the power of the human mind, as they pretend to, not by the power of God, the Creator—His Father. They call their cult 'Divine healing', not because they claim to do it by faith in God, but because they say their own minds are actually God. To represent this as Christian is to convict themselves of deceit in open day.[154]

Like the sects, Christian Science was seen as associated, not with divinely given ordinances, but with an individual claiming the right to usurp them—it should be called 'Eddyism' for it was neither Christian nor scientific. Any supposed healing received in this way was diabolic, achieved only by means of spiritual poison. Satan was always eager to deceive; hence, the love of truth, as it is in Christ, was the only antidote for such wicked deceptions (2 Thess. 2: 9–10).

Christians had to turn away from all these various evidences of the coming power of Antichrist in the same way as they had to turn away from the unclean and impure in books and newspapers. If they did not, then they would inevitably be defiled or even possessed by evil. Heads of households had the responsibility to guard all in their charge against the ever-increasing incursions of evil in the world. Light could have no fellowship with darkness or 'Christ with Belial' (2 Cor. 6: 14). Christians were called to 'cast off the works of darkness and put on the armour of light' (Rom. 13: 12).

6. SURVEY AND COMMENT

Catholic Apostolic ecclesiology was based upon certain basic premises of which the most important were: that its apostolic constitution and ministry were divinely given and heavenly; that its structure was revealed in Scripture: that it was indwelt and prophetically directed by the Holy Spirit; that it was a Eucharistic and sacramentally based election (though not in the Calvinistic sense); and that, as the Bride of Christ, it was to be perfected under apostolic rule for the imminent appearance of the Bridegroom. However, it is clear that this ecclesiology was also influenced by certain other factors, of which the two most important were the

---

[154] J. B. Davenport, *The Deadly Error of Christian Science* (Philadelphia: Library Publishing Company, 1901), 27.

separation of the Church from the world and the principle of 'hierarchy', the latter no doubt reflecting to some extent the political and social views and the status of the body's founders.

In their definition of the Church, the Catholic Apostolics combined an extremely 'high' doctrine of its nature with a 'broad' interpretation of its membership. By adopting baptism as the criterion of the latter, they avoided 'unchurching' individual Christians, whilst at the same time being able to point to the deficiencies in the structures and ministries of other Churches. Their concept of 'unity' was also 'broad'. They regarded the Church's unity as a spiritual matter, and not as a matter of ecclesiological uniformity. Indeed, they saw the diversity within mankind, with regard to endowments both of character and of spiritual gifts, as pointing to the Church's unity as necessarily being a 'unity of diversity'. They did not demand that all members of other Churches should join the Catholic Apostolic body, but that apostolic rule should be recognized by their leaders. What was crucial was that unity should be made visible in all other Churches by the manifestation of the fullness of divine ordinances.

However, according to the Catholic Apostolics' assessment of their own position, it is strictly incorrect to refer to 'other' Churches—they did not claim to be *the* Church, nor even to be *a* Church, and they emphatically rejected any charge that they were a sect. Their claim that they were a work of the Holy Spirit *within* the universal Church—congregations of the 'One Holy Catholic and Apostolic Church' *gathered under apostles*—gave them a freedom of outlook towards other Churches which enabled them to attend worship elsewhere and not infrequently to enjoy joint membership of their local Catholic Apostolic congregation and another Church (more usually Anglican or Lutheran). This became of increasing importance in the later years when their own ministry declined in number and eventually disappeared—the transition to worshipping exclusively elsewhere was not a traumatic experience, since for most it was a gradual change.

Their attitude towards the Churches as a whole was therefore one of fellowship, despite many of them having been expelled from their original congregations, and this was reflected in their Liturgy by the ecumenical nature of the intercessions. This attitude must be contrasted with the contemporary one of the Roman Church towards other Churches, of the Anglican Church towards both Rome and

Dissent, and of the Dissenting bodies towards everyone else. However, it may well have had a disadvantage in the period of the body's greatest numerical strength in that the focus of ecclesiastical loyalty was less clearly defined than, for example, in the Roman Church, in Dissenting bodies, or in 'national' Churches; this may have contributed to the admitted creeping apathy, for the cure of which the Sealing was introduced and remained a strong sacramental focus so long as sealed persons were living, emphasizing the priesthood of all believers and thus giving the laity a feeling of a share in the witness of an otherwise extremely hierarchical body.

The lack of any protest on the part of the laity when the crucial decision was taken that no ordinations could proceed after 1901, with its implication for the consequent gradual disappearance of the ministry, may well have been in part the result of their 'broad' attitude to other Churches, though a major factor was the strong tradition within the body of *rule from above*. The early reliance on prophecy once again came to the fore immediately following the death of Woodhouse, the last surviving apostle—to this day the members await further prophetic revelation and perhaps the appearance of a 'seventy'. Meanwhile they accepted the inevitable demise of their Church as they once knew it.

The Catholic Apostolic insistence on the absolute indissolubility of baptism sprang from their view that it was an act of God rather than an act of the individual. Thus there was no problem with the baptism of infants. Their strong emphasis upon the sacraments as *the* means of conveying the Holy Spirit also contributed to their rejection of any need for a second (adult) 'baptism of the Spirit'—in this they were in sharp contrast to many modern charismatic bodies. Nevertheless, they did claim that sealing conveyed a higher charism than that of baptism, being a gift of the 'Spirit of Power' for lay 'ministerial' service and thus related spiritually to ordination.

Ordination, like baptismal entry into the Body of Christ, was seen as having an indelible quality. However, this emphasis on indelibility did not appear to have allowed for individual apostatizing, though they had much to say about the apostasy of the Church. It seems that they did not envisage the possibility of a baptized person ceasing to be a member of the Church, despite New Testament indications that this could and indeed did happen.

The hierarchical principle, so manifest in the Catholic Apostolic Church, greatly influenced its structure, ministry, and doctrine. It was supported by belief in the immutable God-given nature of apostleship and in all the ordinances as being typologically prefigured in the Old Testament. This principle was of God and not of man, and hence could not be varied by man. Support for the primacy and intended permanence of apostles in the Church was said to be based upon Scripture, but the argument becomes weaker when expressed in historical terms. Apostles, in their original form, did *not* remain in the Church (though 'apostolic men' did), and the explanation of their 'withdrawal' as God's response to the onset of apostasy raises difficulties which were not confronted. It is clear from the New Testament, and admitted by Catholic Apostolics, that signs of apostasy existed virtually from the beginning—Apostolic rule had not prevented this. Indeed it is clear that the 'wheat and tares' would grow together until the 'harvest'—why then should the disappearance of apostles (in the New Testament sense) be interpreted as a specific act of divine judgement? No scriptural support is offered for this. Also, how could schism be described as the inevitable consequence of *episcopal* government? Having admitted that the Church under the Apostles was not perfect—how then can the Church under restored apostles be guaranteed to be made perfect?

Careful scrutiny of the documents which were stated to prophesy a restoration of apostles in the last days—which for the main speak in very general terms—does not suggest that there was prophetic support for the specific form of apostolate developed in the Catholic Apostolic Church. Indeed, it is doubtful if there was any prophetic witness to this before the call for ruling apostles which was an occasional feature of the charismatic phenomena in Scotland, England, and Germany which preceded the setting up of the body.

Rule in name of Christ had to be collegiate, hence the claims of Rome were rejected, but rule by councils of bishops was also rejected because of the restricted definition of the role of the episcopal office. It was and had to be admitted that, without a college of apostles, recourse to such councils was the only possible choice for the Church: the charge of deliberate usurpation of apostolic rule by the episcopate seems therefore unsubstantiated. The confidently presented account of the appearance of the separate episcopate and priesthood in the early Church, whilst plausible, does not take account of the fact that the matter has never been a matter of agreement amongst scholars—even those belonging to episcopal Churches. This suggests a tendency to present as fact what was at best a reasonable hypothesis, possibly because all the ecclesiological aspects of the body were felt to require watertight justification. Thus, whilst the principle of episcopacy did not need to be defended in an Anglican or Roman Catholic context, the Presbyterian element in the body, which included most of Irving's personal followers and sympathizers, needed to be convinced that the structure being built was based on sound biblical principles.

The general need to defend the concept of a restored apostolate against attack seems to have led to an over-emphasis upon one of the four 'marks' of the Church—its apostolic nature—interpreted in a particular way. The principle, that for the Church to be truly apostolic it had to be ruled by *living* apostles, required an exceptionally strong argument in its support, since it called into question the fullness of the charism within the Church Catholic for almost all of its existence. Anglican attacks upon the credentials of the restored apostles, and hence against the orders of all those ordained by them, were not deflected by the usual response—a narrative account of the charismatic beginnings of the body. An argument supporting the essentiality of apostles was therefore needed.

Despite the negative view taken of the democratic principle by the Catholic Apostolics—for them it was the heresy of deriving power from the people—it would be unfair to suggest that there was no form of democratic participation in the affairs of the Church. The restoration of the diaconate in a form similar to that which it had had in the early Church meant that the lowest of the major orders of ministry was an elected body with significant responsibilities. The fact of a deacon's election by the people was visibly represented, and hence emphasized, in the form for ordination to the diaconate. Although deacons did have a liturgical role, similar to that in the various episcopal Churches, they were primarily responsible for the local administration and financial affairs together with pastoral work (especially amongst the poor), and were the clergy in immediate contact with the laity. Even the financial affairs of the universal Church organization were in the hands of deacons.

The large numbers of clergy required to complete the ministry of particular Churches meant that there were greater chances for serving in that ministry than might be expected in most other Christian bodies, though, as a result of the numbers involved and absence of any theological school, the quality of the clergy could be and sometimes was questioned from within as well as without the body. Although many senior clergy had been required to attend short courses at Albury, the content of such courses was highly specialized and, hence, seriously limited in scope. Nevertheless, there were opportunities for gaining a certain status inside the Church which must have been for many members greater than the opportunities for obtaining a comparable one outside it. The comparative isolation of the body from other Churches meant that the lack of external recognition of such status was of less importance than it would be today.

Since the conveying of the Holy Spirit was seen as *the* function of the apostles, all final decisions on matters of doctrine and interpretation of prophecy—both considered to be revelations of the Spirit—were necessarily reserved to them. This was also the basis for denying the episcopate the authority to ordain to the major orders, though an 'equals should not create equals' argument was also used in the case of the consecration of bishops in episcopal Churches and the ordination of presbyters in Churches with a presbyterian structure. The tradition of episcopal consecration whereby the collegiate nature of rule in the Church was represented by having a minimum of three episcopal consecrators was not accepted as guaranteeing the transmission of apostolic authority.

The existence of underdeacons (with their important role of enquiry), deaconesses (though limited to 'mature' women as in the early Church), and other minor offices meant that the exercise of 'ministry' was widely diffused in the body. However, the overall balance between the democratic principle and hierarchical oversight was very much in favour of the latter, as indeed the Catholic Apostolics (and perhaps others) would regard as only right in a body in which all ministry belonged to its Divine Head and was merely exercised in His Name.

The prophetic ministry was also diffused throughout the body from the apostles to lay men and women. However, here again the hierarchical principle was to come to predominate. In the period of the formation of the Catholic Apostolic Church, and especially in the calling of the apostles, the free exercise of prophecy had been paramount, being regarded as the voice of the Holy Spirit—the 'latter rain'. Once the apostles had been called and the principles of apostolic rule determined, it had become necessary to incorporate prophetic activity within the hierarchical structure of the Church if the apostolic rule was not to be put under intermittent threat. Scriptural support (from St Paul) was therefore put forward for declaring that the functions of an ordained prophet—a man illuminated by the spirit—required a higher endowment of the Holy Spirit than that required for the exercise of the charismatic gift by lay men and women (for clergy).

Since the apostles were the ordainers, all ordained prophets received their charism through them; the source of illumination through the Spirit therefore depended upon the apostolic ministry. Further, scriptural arguments were put forward to show that God's revelations were made to apostles and prophets, hence *all* charismatic utterances were subject to apostolic validation. Thus, although prophecy was diffused in the body—being also involved in the validation of candidates for orders—its interpretation was in the last resort in the hands of an élite and decreasing few. Thus, a prophetic validation of an ordination candidate, though essential, did not remove from the ordaining apostle an ultimate right to refuse ordination. The hierarchical order of the ministry was imposed within the ordained ministry of prophets—thus a deacon-prophet with the charismatic gift was considered to exercise it at a lower level than a priest-prophet, and so on. Similarly, a deacon-prophet exercising the illumination of the Spirit in the interpretation of Scripture did so at a lower level than his superiors.

The control of prophecy was inevitable for good order in the Church, so long as its exercise was to remain diffused. (Other bodies, such as the Mormons, reserved prophecy entirely to an élite.) Good order was considered paramount, since the Church was always seen as contrasted with the contemporary world, where anarchy and revolution were taken as signs of the imminent judgement of God falling upon an unfaithful Christendom and an apostatizing Church. Nevertheless, the continuing exercise of prophecy within the body was seen as a guarantee of the diffusion of the Spirit throughout. The Catholic Apostolic Church always saw itself as being inspired and sanctified by the Holy Spirit. One effect of the strict controls placed upon prophesying, and the relegation of the charismatic gift to a lower status than it had held in the early days, was the reduction of the importance of any role played by women in prophesying. Great care was taken that women should not be seen to exercise 'headship' in any way—evidenced by the requirement to have their heads covered in Church. It may be that the reduced role of women played a small part in the apathy which developed and for which the rite of sealing became the antidote.

The role of the Holy Spirit was recognized as having always been paramount in the world: in Creation; in the witness of the Prophets; in the Incarnation and Resurrection; as the indwelling sustainer of the Church since Pentecost—though often resisted; and as the conveyer of a further special charism through the ministry of the restored apostles. This very 'strong' Catholic Apostolic pneumatology was not in any way weakened by the Trinitarian theology, which included acceptance of the 'filioque'—though interpreted in a way specifically intended not to deny the Father as the sole source of the Godhead. Thus the argument that the 'filioque' necessarily implies a diminishing status for the Holy Spirit did not apply in their case. This heightened importance of the role of the Spirit arose, not primarily from the charismatic origins of the body, but from its Christology, which, because of the teaching on Christ's human nature (inherited largely from Irving—see Ch. II, § 1), gave far greater prominence to the Holy Spirit's sanctifying activity within *the man Jesus* than more conventional Christologies require.

There are a number of further points of note in the Catholic Apostolic concept of ministerial order. Thus, whilst the angels were declared to be of episcopal rank, the office of angel—in its eschatological aspect, which included the offering of intercession with incense—could not be properly exercised by bishops not under apostles. The idea of the angel or bishop as the head of the local Church and hence the normal celebrant of the Eucharist was in conformity with the practice of the early Church, but the extent and form of the separation of the structures of the local and universal Churches was not. It is of interest that any celebrant of the Eucharist (whether angel or priest) was seen as acting as the representative of the people and hence should adopt an East-facing position visibly demonstrating this. This was in accord also with the belief that, in as much as he represented the High Priesthood of Christ, it was the ascended *humanity* of Christ that was set before the people.

Although it was clearly stated that in Churches without apostles the grace of ordination and other sacraments was of a reduced order, the precise meaning of this was not made clear. No scriptural evidence was presented for the theory of a hierarchy of divine charism in the sense suggested, though it was applied to the Churches. The Catholic Apostolics objected strongly to territorial episcopal jurisdiction. This was based on several principles: bishops were set by the Apostles to be the heads of *congregations of people*, not rulers of geographical areas; claims to rule on a geographical basis led to contamination with the world through the seeking of worldly authority; theological disputes could rapidly take on a national and political dimension; and geographically denoted and (especially) national Churches led to a sectarian outlook. The argument was that, through such worldly contamination, the greater part of the Church had sunk into apostasy and become the Babylon spoken of in the Apocalypse. Thus there was continual emphasis on the unworldly nature of the Church and its separation from the world (including its clear distinction from Christendom).

This horror of worldly contamination (and especially of anything that was associated with 'socialism') may have been to some extent behind the apparent lack of Catholic Apostolic concern for social welfare and their opposition to reform movements (equated by Drummond as, like cholera, a 'horrid infliction').[155] It is more likely, however, that the major reason was the predominant emphasis upon the imminence of the Second Advent and the urgent need for the Bride—the Church *not* the world—to be prepared for the coming Bridegroom.

The most unique aspect of the Catholic Apostolic ministry was its fourfold 'character' linked to what were seen as fourfold faculties within man. The concept of the trinitarian constitution of man—body, soul, and spirit—was in conformity with mainstream Christian teaching, though not with the 'popular' idea of a twofold nature of body and soul only. The latter was seen as dangerous—tending to lead to the idea of the permanent destruction of the body at death and the immortality of the soul alone. Catholic Apostolic belief in the resurrection of the dead emphasized the restoration of the *whole* person—though the resurrected flesh would be transformed in accordance with St Paul's teaching. It also emphasized the transfiguration of the created matter—not its destruction. The idea of the eventual destruction of the physical creation was seen as stemming from the heresy that matter was intrinsically evil, which was a denial

---

[155] Letter to Charles Kirkpatrick Sharpe, 10 Apr. 1832 (Northumberland Collection). Drummond wrote: 'We can think of nothing but Reform and cholera: both are horrid inflictions: the latter may pop away, but the former never can; thanks to the Whigs; lampoon them, and that will drive away your headaches; send it up to me and that will drive away mine.'

of the clear statement in Genesis that the Creator had made all things 'good'.

It is important to note that the definition of the soul was precisely in accord with the Greek and patristic use of ψυχή, and that the concept of the Fall was patristic and Eastern rather than of the form which became accepted in the West from the time of Augustine and which was further emphasized in Protestantism. Within this was to be found the distinction between 'image' and 'likeness' which appears in Patristic writings, but which became particularly emphasized in modern times in certain Eastern Orthodox theological works.[156]

The division of the psyche into the four faculties—the will, the imagination, the understanding, and the affections—and its consequent association with the ministries of elders, prophets, evangelists, and pastors (respectively) seems to have had an exclusively typological basis. It provided an opportunity for ministry to the whole psyche, whilst at the same time protecting the uniqueness of Christ by separating the four ministries exercised in His Name. This great care for setting forth the uniqueness of Christ's Headship had also formed an important element in the rejection of papal claims, and was visibly reflected in the role taken by the apostles in worship at Albury, the centre of the universal Church.

The ministry of the body thus had a highly commendable comprehensiveness, reflected not only in the four priestly ministries to the soul, but also in the threefold local ministry by means of which, in addition, bodily needs were attended to by the deacons and spiritual ones by the angel. Whilst stressing that the predominance of the different aspects of the psyche were the basis of the uniqueness of each human person, there was nevertheless an equal stress on the need for 'balance' within certain limits. Variations in the faculties between different people was the basis of the different roles which they were called to play both in the Church and in life generally; here again balance between limits was important. Despite the charismatic element in the Church, excesses and 'enthusiasms' of any form were universally disparaged—no doubt further evidence of the requirement for good order.

The Catholic Apostolics believed that worship should involve the whole person. They were concerned at the over-importance given to

[156] See esp. V. Lossky, *In the Image and Likeness of God* (from the French, London: Mowbray, 1975).

preaching in Protestant Churches. It was necessary to involve man's body—other senses than the ear alone—as well as his mind and spirit. Hence there was a need for beauty of colour and ceremonial, which had the triple role of involving the senses, reminding the understanding of spiritual truths, and appealing above the psyche directly to the spirit. They also believed that the acquisition of true knowledge involved the whole person. The quest for knowledge, including scientific research, was seen as dangerous unless it involved spiritual as well as intellectual awareness. Curiously, this reflected to a considerable extent the way of thought of the contemporary Russian religious philosophers with their idea of 'integral knowledge',[157] though it is highly unlikely that there could have been any awareness of it in England at this time.

The requirement for adequate finances to meet the large body of clergy, rather than theological considerations, must have been primarily responsible for the introduction of tithing and the care which was taken to justify its introduction from Scripture. There is surely no way in which congregations of the sizes involved could have maintained such numbers of clergy from free-will offerings alone. Although many members of the hierarchy, including the apostles, were men of considerable private means, there is no way in which the Church structure could have functioned as designed without a guarantee of the availability of substantial funds, for many of the 'separated' lower clergy were entirely dependent upon their Church stipends. The apparently uncertain nature of these stipends is a testimony to the sincerity of the men involved and their faith in apostolic rule. Today, it seems extraordinary that such a system should have existed. It must be remembered, however, that tithing was not by any means a new principle in the Church, but a restoration of an ancient one, as they were at pains to point out; nor were the Catholic Apostolics the only body to introduce it in their day. Perhaps even more to be commended was the faith displayed by the authorities in the ordinary church member, whose payment of the tithe due was entirely a matter of trust. That the tithes were actually paid faithfully, and continued to be so paid even when the ministry was declining and such extensive funding was unnecessary,

---

[157] See esp. the works of I. V. Kireevsky (1806–56), A. S. Khomyakov (1804–60), and V. S. Soloviev (1853–1900). The idea of 'integral knowledge' was further developed by Pavel Florensky (1882–1943?).

is a tribute to the comprehensive teaching with which their introduction was accompanied.

The scriptural justification for tithing and the general arguments in its support are extremely convincing, and deserve serious study. The reference to spiritual reward only contrasts with the literature of some modern American evangelists, who obtain large gifts from the public by promising that God will grant bountiful material rewards proportional to committed financial support for their organizations.

Catholic Apostolics were not infrequently charged by other Christians with having created a sect, a charge which they vehemently denied (see Ch. VI, § 3 where this is further discussed). Such a charge must have been deeply hurtful, for some of their strongest language was reserved for the condemnation of sects. There were various reasons for this: sectarianism was, of course, viewed as a grave breach of Church order; it was associated with liberal and socialist philosophy; it evidenced a number of what seemed to be highly offensive traits; it tended to distort the role of women; and, in the worst examples, it traded with the Devil. Objections to the Salvation Army involved all but the last of these, and were further fuelled by the Army's adoption of military titles— taken as evidence of worldly contamination. Public preaching by unordained persons (especially women) and the repudiation of sacraments were regarded as serious departures for Church order. They did not object to the concept of the Church itself as a Christian army at war with evil, nor does there seem to have been any condemnation of the Jesuits for their 'military' approach to mission. But the Salvation Army openly displayed a number of symptoms of precisely those things which always invited Catholic Apostolic indignation and hence condemnation.

The Catholic Apostolic teaching on the state of the departed accepted that their spirits were 'not devoid of consciousness' but forbade absolutely any attempts to communicate with them. Spiritualism was taken seriously. Angels were seen as playing an important spiritual role in God's purposes, and evil spirits were accepted as playing a role in direct opposition to His will. This was inevitably linked to eschatological belief: the increasing popularity of various types of spiritualism was interpreted as increasing Satanic activity—a sign of the nearness of Antichrist. The opposition to hypnotism, even when used for medical purposes, was based upon an objection to the suspension of conscience, together with a general dislike of all psychological study (because it was considered to isolate one part of the human person, the psyche, from the rest). Underlying all this must have been the suspicion that it was an area which was the prerogative of God alone—part of the knowledge from which man had been commanded to fast (Gen. 2: 17).

Finally, there was the permeation of all Catholic Apostolic ecclesiology with typology, and especially that associated with the Mosaic Tabernacle. Typology is an ancient and respected method of biblical interpretation to be found in Scripture itself and extensively in patristic works, though in some Christian writers, such as Origen, it was largely abandoned for the allegorical approach. It was developed by the restored apostles and other Catholic Apostolic writers to a degree to be found nowhere else either before or after them. It underpinned not only their ecclesiology and their doctrine of man, but also their liturgy, their interpretation of history (both ecclesiastical and secular), and their eschatology, as will become apparent later, in Chapter V.

The emphasis on the typological justification of their theology and liturgy required not only an extensive knowledge of the Bible (and especially the Old Testament) but also many hours of research, including patristic reading, and mutual discussion. It is difficult to assess how much of their typology was the result of prophetic utterances: some certainly was, and was admitted to be so, such as the opening of the 'mystery of the candlestick'. It is clear, however, that much of the groundwork was laid during the Albury Conferences where there must have been contributions on the subject from those who did not eventually join the apostolic body.

For many outside the body, the reliance upon the typological approach to the Church and its ministry must have seemed exaggerated, and its extension to the nature of man somewhat laboured. For members of the body, however, it was to become a common 'language'. All were as well versed in its principles as they were in the Scriptures themselves, which were faithfully read and studied daily—typological 'light' on them being provided by the many pamphlets which were widely and frequently circulated by the Church authorities. It is, perhaps, not unfair to suggest that typology played something of the role in the body which codes and signs play in secret societies, that is, providing a sense of the possession of something 'special' and hidden to others—a psychological 'cement' binding members together in fellowship and strengthening their sense of belonging to a unique community. This would have been very much contrary to the body's principles in its earlier years, but it would seem that in its period of decline members did become increasingly inward-looking, even secretive. In those later years, typological language could well have assumed precisely the role just suggested.

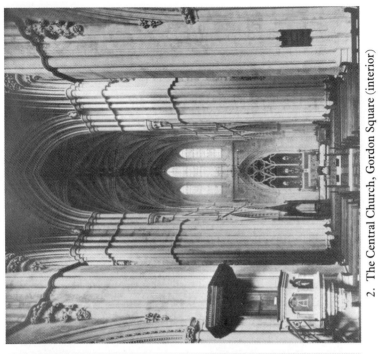

1. The Central Church, Gordon Square (exterior)

2. The Central Church, Gordon Square (interior)

3. The Apostles' Chapel, Albury (exterior)

4. The Apostles' Chapel, Albury (interior)

5. The Catholic Apostolic Apostles

7. Henry Drummond (apostle)

6. The Revd Edward Irving (angel)

9. Francis Valentine Woodhouse (apostle)

8. John Bate Cardale (apostle)

10. The English Chapel of the Central Church, Gordon Square, with a
temporary iconostasis for Orthodox worship

IV

Liturgy

1. THE NATURE OF LITURGICAL WORSHIP

Before considering the form of the liturgical worship of the Catholic Apostolic Church, and the Eucharist in particular, it will be helpful first to indicate in general terms the view held about the central role of the sacraments in the life and worship of the Church.

The Sacramental Principle

Catholic Apostolic writers, all of whom followed closely the principles earlier enunciated by Cardale, emphasized that the sacramental concept of Christianity derived from the early Church:

That the Christianity of the post-apostolic age, from which later the constitution of the Catholic Church was derived, was distinctly sacramental, no one who has the smallest acquaintance with early Church teaching will deny or question.[1]

This sacramental tradition, though found in the New Testament, was said to derive its authority not from the written word but from the living tradition, a tradition which the Church received from the risen Lord through the Apostles and their immediate successors. It was of divine origin, for it could not have been conceived or arranged by human thought alone.

The precise details for the conduct of Christian worship and the administration of sacraments did not appear in the Scriptures, for they grew out of the life of the Church. This was seen as being in contrast with the written code of the covenant made through Moses:

All such minuteness of rule and distinction would have been foreign to the spirit of the dispensation of the Church. God purposed that the

---

[1] J. S. Davenport, *Sacramental Christianity and the Incarnation* (London, 1891) (repr. from *The Family Churchman*), 3.

Christian community . . . should be a living body, continually connected with the living Head in the heavens, through living apostles on earth, sent forth from Himself, by means of whom, on the one hand, the Holy Ghost should be administered, and, on the other hand, the commandments of the Lord should be delivered, and the government of the Church should be conducted.[2]

The sacraments, whose basis was declared to be the Incarnation, were material signs of the invisible divine presence within the Church, the presence of the Holy Spirit the comforter. Material things were therefore no longer types; they represented spiritual blessings already present:

the difference between the ordinances of the Law and the sacraments of the Gospel is precisely the difference between shadow and substance, between prophecy and fulfilment, between the testimony to Christ which was to come, and that to Christ already come, seated at the right hand of power, and present by the Holy Ghost to effect all that is signified in the words and acts of His servants.[3]

Sacramental Christianity thus brought in a new and supernatural order of life, uniting the spiritual and the material. The Church was a continuation of Pentecost, and the powers granted at Pentecost were received by her members through ordinances divinely appointed for conveying them.

Although special prominence was accorded to baptism and the Eucharist, the title 'sacrament' was also accorded to confirmation with chrism, absolution, marriage, unction for the sick, and ordination, and a sacramental character was given not only to the bread and wine of the Eucharist but also to water, oil, imposition of hands, incense, vestments, lights, and colours, all of which were seen as 'means of conveying truth to the spirit through the senses'.[4] Indeed, it was stressed that there was a sacramental element in every ordinance connected with worship. Worship and sacrament are thus inextricably linked. The whole life and worship of the Church had grown out of the sacramental principle, and it was through the sacraments that the effects of the redemption in Christ were imparted to her members.

---

[2] J. B. Cardale, *Readings upon the Liturgy and other Divine Offices of the Church*, i (London: Barclay, 1848), 15 (henceforth C/RL).

[3] *C/RL* i. 161.

[4] Davenport, *Sacramental Christianity*, 6.

Catholic Apostolic writers were especially critical of the lack of an adequate sacramental doctrine amongst the Churches of the Reformation. Such a lack was considered to undermine the very nature of the Church because the strength of the Church lay in her sacraments:

The non-sacramental theory of Christianity assumes that the blessings of salvation are secured to the souls of men by the mental act of faith; that the intelligence is the faculty and organ by which God works in the soul mainly by the means of preaching and instruction: consequently what are specifically named Sacraments are simply subsidiary to those means for intensifying faith and devotion and for bringing men into a more receptive condition for spiritual blessing—in fact another form of preaching. The logical consequence of such a view is, that no particular constitution of the Church has any special claim to acceptance, but that Church order is simply a matter of expediency.[5]

In the view of the very high doctrine of the Church and the emphasis upon her 'true constitution' (see Ch. III), any neglect or distortion of her sacramental basis was regarded as a fundamental departure from Catholic truth. The Protestant reduction of the status of sacraments to symbols or signs was condemned, and Anglican teaching was dismissed as being so ambiguous as to admit differing and conflicting interpretations. Part of what was considered to be the contemporary rejection of the efficacy of the sacraments was ascribed to a general spirit of anarchy, for

sacraments imply order and authority, and the religious tendency is not that of submission to order and authority.[6]

This 'religious tendency' was seen as a reflection of the general social and political unrest, as evidenced most particularly on the Continent but which was infecting also the religious and social 'spirit of the age' in Britain.

If the sacraments were rooted in the Incarnation, they were equally rooted in the Resurrection:

In the risen Christ there is seen a new revolution of humanity, and the effect of the sacraments is to impart to men the seeds of this evolution, to be hereafter manifested in the resurrection of the body.[7]

Thus, for a proper understanding of the sacramental principle a right doctrine of both the Incarnation and the Resurrection was

[5] Ibid. 8.   [6] Ibid. 28.   [7] Ibid. 13.

essential. The concept of sacraments as an extension of the
Incarnation related also to the resurrected and glorified physical body
of Christ, and to the ultimate Christian hope—the Parousia and the
resurrection of the dead. Sacraments thus had an essential eschatological dimension.

The Meaning of 'Liturgy'

In Catholic Apostolic writings the term 'liturgy' referred not only to
the Eucharist, but also to the daily Offices of Morning and Evening
Prayer which were specifically associated with it. It was the
Eucharistic extension to these two Offices which brought them
within the liturgy proper; without such Eucharistic extension they
would not be 'liturgy':

We may hold it as certain, therefore, that the word [liturgy] is
improperly applied to Offices of Common Prayer unconnected with the
holy Eucharist.[8]

Although it was recognized that in the Old Testament the word
referred to any service of the Jewish priesthood in the Tabernacle or
in the Temple, appeal was made to the LXX version of Joel 1: 9[9]
and, in the New Testament, particularly to Luke 1: 23 and Hebrews
7: 2 to claim that 'liturgy' was most appropriately reserved for those
services where the ministry was performed at the altar. Roman
Catholic Hours and Anglican Morning and Evening Prayer (a fusion
of the Hours) were seen as having no sacrificial content; they
corresponded to Synagogue services and not to those of the
Tabernacle or Temple, and were hence not 'liturgy'.

The principal link between the Eucharist and the Offices of
Morning and Evening Prayer of the Catholic Apostolic Church was
the continuance of intercession. This link was made actual by the
'proposition' of the Holy Gifts upon the altar at these Offices. As the
intercession at the Eucharist was made before the Holy Gifts,
consecrated and resting upon the altar, so the intercession at the two
Offices was made before the same Gifts 'proposed' upon the altar
(see § 2 below). The Offices thus extended the Eucharistic participation
of the Church in the intercession of the Great High Priest at the right
hand of God (Romans 9: 34).

[8] C/RL i. 2.
[9] 'The priests, οἱ λειτουργοῦντες θυσιαστηρίῳ, who liturgize at the altar.'

For Catholic Apostolics the liturgical worship of the Church was intended to make present and thus reveal both what Christ achieved on earth and what He now continually performs in Heaven:

Although His [Christ's] priestly office is exercised in heaven . . . He yet exercises it as Head of His Church. As High Priest, He is 'a minister of the sanctuary, and of the true tabernacle, which the Lord pitched, and not man' (Hebrews viii, 2). This tabernacle is His Church . . . one with Him as He is one with the Father (Ephesians v, 30; John xvii, 21). In the Church His acts are manifested; in His Church must be revealed not only what He did when on earth, but what He is now doing as High Priest in Heaven.[10]

That it is Christ Himself Who is the true minister of the ordinances of the Church was fundamental:

His Church on earth is His hand. He hath left with His Church His ordinances. His Church in faith administers His ordinances. In her hand, they are external things. But she is His hand, and in His hand they are spiritual. . . . For she is His hand, and she looks to Him, and she beholds Him making an inward use of spiritual things. She beholds Him by faith. She *believes* that He does that. She does not doubt that He does it. She does not merely suppose that He does it. She does not persuade herself that He does it, She does not anxiously and uncertainly hope that He does it. . . . She has really done in His ordinance that which He commanded her, and she believes that He really has done that which He promised, in that ordinance.[11]

Christian worship was thus not the independent homage of man, but a faithful expression of that which is offered to the Father by Christ, the very image of His intercession before the Father.

Liturgical worship was seen as having a further function also, for it was through the liturgy that the participants could offer themselves within the company of all believers. For, wherever a congregation of the faithful was gathered together, there the whole company of believers was represented, and hence all were spiritually present. Along with themselves, the whole of creation could be offered to God through the representative materials of Christian

[10] C. J. T. Böhm, *Lights and Shadows in the Present Condition of the Church*, tr. from the German (London: Bosworth and Harrison, 1860), 263. (Also separate printing of ch. VIII, *Sacrifice and Priesthood* (Glasgow: Hobbs, 1902), 259.)

[11] W. Dow, *God's Ordinances are Evermore Realities* (repr. from *Discourses*, 1847 and 1850) (London: Glaisher, 1924), 10. Dow is here writing especially of Baptism, but it is clear from the context that the remarks apply to sacraments generally.

worship: bread, wine, oil, water, incense, and so on. Moreover, the company of all believers extended beyond the living to the departed saints and the hosts of heaven:

Therefore, in declaring that we join our voices to those of angels and archangels, and cherubim and seraphim, and all the host of heaven, we refer to the whole Church of Christ; to apostles, and prophets, and evangelists, and pastors, to angels or bishops of all classes and degrees, and to all others the saints of God, both living and departed; for all are spiritually present through the presence of Christ and in the Holy Ghost.[12]

Intercession in the presence of all therefore had to be for all, that is, for the departed as well as the living, even as Christ's heavenly intercession was and is for all.

The Hallowing of Time

The liturgical worship of the Church had yet a further purpose which can best be called 'the hallowing of time'. God had appointed lights in the heavens for signs and seasons, days and years. Man in his physical nature was a creature of time, thus 'coexistence, succession, and duration must for ever be ideas in his mind, resulting from his communications with sensible things'.[13] Time, as a God-given gift, must like material things be offered by man to God. Such offering was achieved by the liturgical year, week, and day. The century was not regarded as liturgical because it exceeded the life of the individual except in a few cases.

The week was the most important division of time in the Law of Moses, hence it was the most important also in the spiritual life of the Christian. Of special importance spiritually was the concept of the 'eighth day', the day to which every octave pointed, for it pointed from the Resurrection of Christ—an event in time—to the Parousia, the event which shall end time:

The ecclesiastical week appointed for observance by Israel terminated with the Sabbath of rest, upon the seventh day; it pointed backwards to that week in which the heavens and earth were finished . . . when 'God ended all His work which He had made', and rested from it (Genesis ii, 2). . . . the Jewish Ecclesiastical week, and its Sabbath on the seventh day, are in this aspect a memorial of hope, looking forward to that kingdom

---

[12] *C/RL* i. 151.   [13] *C/RL* i. 21.

of peace which shall be established on the earth. But the resurrection of
the Lord, on the first day of the week, gives new significancy to the
symbolic use of this portion of time. It is the memorial of the present
period of the world's history, and points to that work of the spiritual
creation which is now proceeding—a period which commenced with the
resurrection of the Lord . . . and which will terminate with the
destruction of the Man of Sin, and with the in-gathering of the full
number of God's elect. It also points forward to that new day, that
eighth day—the day of the regeneration, the day of redemption—when
the period of suffering shall be terminated, and the earnest expectation
of the creature, waiting for the manifestation of the sons of God, shall be
satisfied; and the new series of the future ages of glory and blessedness,
of rest and peace, in the world to come, shall commence their ceaseless
course.[14]

The Law of Moses required a perpetual remembrance of the week.
This was thus the type of which the liturgical celebration of the week
by the Church was the antitype. The Jewish rites of perfection on
the eighth day were the types of that perfection revealed by the
Resurrection in time and the perfecting of the saints at the
Parousia.[15] The octave was always a reminder that God had his
appointed time for bringing all things to perfection.

The Typological Basis of Liturgy

The divisions of time, as well as having their liturgical application,
were also regarded as having a prophetic and symbolic value. Any
one of them could be a type of a longer period. In Morning and
Evening Prayer there was the antitype of the morning and evening
sacrifices under the Law by means of which the day of twelve hours
was sanctified. The fulfilment of these could, however, be seen in the
life and ministry of Christ also. The day, according to the Law, must
begin with the morning sacrifice, a sacrifice fulfilled by Christ when
He offered Himself as a lamb without blemish, wholly dedicated to
the will of the Father:

> Thou wast the Morning Lamb, Lord Jesus Christ!
> Who for Thine own hast once been sacrificed.[16]

---

[14] *C/RL* i. 22.
[15] The Jewish rites specifically referred to are: (1) circumcision (Lev. 12: 2–3); (2)
the use of young beasts for sacrifice (Lev. 12: 27); and (3) rules of uncleanness
through illness (Lev. 14: 8–10, 15: 13–14; Num. 6: 9–10).
[16] E. W. Eddis, from *Hymns for use in the Churches*, no. 80 (London: Pitman,

The Confession was the type of Christ's baptism, the Absolution the voice from Heaven saying 'This is my beloved Son in Whom I am well pleased' (Matt. 3: 17). The meat and drink offerings were the type of the continual offering of the word of God, through the indwelling of the Holy Spirit, throughout Our Lord's ministry. The work of the Outer Court having been completed, Christ had ascended to the throne of His Father to offer His intercession, thus fulfilling the offering of incense and the trimming and setting in order of the lamps. All this was represented in detail liturgically by the separate parts of the Office of Morning Prayer. (The structure of the Offices is discussed in § 2 below.)

When the evening sacrifice was considered, however, there was an important difference. It was not possible to see in Christ Himself the antitype of the evening lamb. His offering of Himself could not be repeated; He was now exalted above the earth. The antitype of the evening lamb was therefore the Church, which should be presented before God 'not having spot, or wrinkle . . . but . . . holy and without blemish' (Eph. 5: 27). Christ had indeed a part to play in the evening sacrifice as the High Priest and Intercessor, but He could not be the Sacrifice. Again in the Office of Evening Prayer, there was a detailed liturgical representation of the type under the law. There was also, as will be seen in the discussion of the sacrificial aspects of the Eucharist (§ 5 below), another important set of types fulfilled by Christ and liturgically represented in the Church's worship.

The Catholic Apostolic insistence upon the details of liturgical worship being antitypical of the worship offered under the Law was derived from the principle that all true forms of worship had been revealed by God, hence even those services which were not specifically 'liturgy' were termed 'Divine Offices'. The words suggested not only that such worship was addressed to God:

It conveys more to us than this. It conveys that God alone can prescribe the way in which He ought to be worshipped; that all true knowledge of God proceeds from God, so the way of approach unto Him must also be revealed by Him.[17]

1900). Eddis was a prophet at Westminster, London, and wrote the words of a number of hymns. (This particular hymn was numbered differently in earlier editions of the Catholic Apostolic Hymn Book.)

[17] *C/RL* i. 3.

The priests of the Old Covenant had received detailed instructions through the God-given Law as to the ordinances which God required of men. These therefore were the types of Christian worship, whose ordinances were revealed to the Apostles by Christ before His Ascension and by the Holy Spirit after Pentecost. The only guarantee of the validity of Christian rites therefore lay with the apostolic authority within the Church.

Liturgy: God's Ordinance

Just as the priests of the Old Covenant had received divine ordinances through the Law, so the priests of the New Covenant received their instructions from the Holy Spirit:

We conclude, therefore, that the Offices of Christian worship are perfect, just so far as they embody and carry forth that order, which is according to the eternal purpose and mind of God. They are Divine, not merely because they are the prescribed worship of God, but because in all their essential parts they follow that order which God Himself prescribes for His worship . . . because in their essential forms they are the expression of that Divine order and mode in which the Holy Ghost acts in His Temple, the Church, in fulfilment of the will of God, and according to the mind of Christ . . .[18]

The form of all Christian worship, and the sacraments in particular, should be such as to fix the mind of man on the ordinances of God rather than on his own subjective experiences, however deeply felt. God, and not man, was the author of all forms of worship; all the things pertaining to God were revealed to man by the Holy Spirit. Thus, although there was a prescribed place in liturgical worship for the exercise of the gift of prophecy, this was certainly not in order to hear the voice of man, but rather the voice of the Holy Spirit speaking through a man or woman. This was the voice of God revealing His truth and His will through those whom He had chosen.

The Catholic Apostolic authorities strongly condemned worship of 'mingled congregations of converted and unconverted persons' gathered to hear 'no more than a discourse on the first principles of

[18] C/RL i. 18.

Christianity'. The solemn celebration of the liturgy was neglected at great spiritual risk:

If this be neglected, and anything else put in its room; and if Christians allow themselves to get accustomed to such a mutilation of the solemn services of the Church of Christ, then we may rest assured that the Divine life in the members of the one body will gradually dry up. We can scarcely conceive to what a degree Christendom is spiritually famished. The present disquiet among Christians; their running, and seeking, and catching after the dangerous excitement of religious oratory; their anxious acceptance of every newly-invented means of defence against the undeniable danger of increasing infidelity: this all testifies of weakness rather than of true Divine strength.[19]

The only source of divine life and the only focus of unity for members of the Body of Christ was participation in the divinely revealed sacramental worship of the Church, the worship typified by that of the Tabernacle and contrasted with worship constructed according to the whimsies of the human will and imagination.

God was seen as having led man throughout history towards the true spiritual worship. Man was created in the image and likeness of God. The trinitarian nature of God was reflected in the tripartite nature of man: body, soul, and spirit. After the Fall, God first approached man through his bodily senses:

and the Divine rites consisted of the offering to God of animals, to the exclusion even of the fruits of the earth, which under the Law were brought into use in the service of God.[20]

This sentient period of worship related to the patriarchal period of Israel.

The second period, the period of the Law, was the time when man approached God through his reason. It coincided in time with the wisdom of Egypt, terminating in the wonderful intellectual attainments of Greece. Throughout this period there had been an increasing appeal to man's rational soul together with a gradual revelation of the spiritual nature of God's dealings with man. Finally, in the Christian dispensation, worship was revealed in all its spiritual aspects:

At length, the fulness of time arrived when the Son of God became incarnate; and, through His death and resurrection, and the outpouring

[19] Böhm, *Lights and Shadows*, 249–50. (Also separate printing of Ch. VII, 'The Lord's Supper' (Glasgow: Hobbs, 1902), 246.)
[20] C/RL i. 6.

of the Holy Ghost, it became possible that the Father and the Son should dwell by the Holy Ghost in the regenerated spirit of man, and that the Church, the mystical Body of Christ, should become the Temple of the Holy Ghost, to the intent that, in the Church, all things should be fulfilled according to the will of God.[21]

This did not mean that the senses or the reason of man were omitted from the ordinances of Christian worship, but their use had now become subservient to the spiritual part of man. Material things now became the vessels of spiritual gifts, and the written New Testament was given 'not, indeed, as a law in the letter', but so that through the Holy Spirit its true meaning might be comprehended

that our service and sacrifice may be reasonable in order that it may be acceptable.[22]

The gradual revelation of the spiritual nature of worship had been given through the Prophets to those who worshipped faithfully in the Tabernacle (the type of the present condition of the Church) and the Temple (the type of the future condition of the Church made perfect in the coming Kingdom). Faithful worship meant worship precisely according to divine prescription both as to form and to place. The type must be realized equally precisely in the antitype. This necessitated a particular typological interpretation of the various parts of a church building. Thus the lower choir was the antitype of the Outer Court of the Tabernacle; the upper choir was the antitype of the Holy Place, and the sanctuary with its altar of the Most Holy Place. The location of the celebrating angel and the other clergy during the services was therefore dictated by the typological interpretation of the various prayers and actions. All these liturgical considerations had to be taken into account when Catholic Apostolic places of worship were being designed. The design of churches should be in conformity with the requirements of divine ordinances —their design should never dictate the liturgical forms of the Church.

[21] C/RL i. 7.　　　　[22] C/RL i. 7–8.

2. THE OFFICES OF MORNING AND EVENING PRAYER

Morning and Evening Prayer were, as has been noted above, the antitypes of the daily morning and evening sacrifices in the worship of the Tabernacle. The structures of these two Offices were identical, having the following form (reading by columns):

Entrance	Psalm(s)
Invocation	Proposition of the Sacrament
Exhortation	Salutation
Confession	Prayers (Litany etc.)
Absolution	Intercessions and Lord's Prayer
The Peace	Thanksgivings
Dedication Prayer	Incense Anthem
Versicles and Responses	The Great Intercession
Scripture reading	Ministry
Creed	Benedictus/Magnificat (Morning/Evening)
Anthem after the Creed	Benediction

The Typology of the Offices

The typological interpretation of the Offices divided each into two parts, the first part being the antitype of the service at the brazen altar and the second the antitype of that at the golden altar, the singing of the appointed psalm or psalms marking the point of division.

The Exhortation and Confession with which the Offices began (after the entrance of the clergy and the Invocation) were the antitypes of the laying of the priest's hand on the head of the lamb and the slaying of the victim—the pouring out of its life:

Both form one act of faith—an act of faith by which we lay hold upon the Lamb of God Who died for us, upon Whom was laid the iniquity of us all, Who shed His precious blood that we might be cleansed from all sin: an act of faith by which, as it were, we pour out the natural life, renouncing again all sinful affections and desires, confessing our sins, trusting in the mercy of God through Jesus Christ our Lord.[23]

[23] C. E. W. Stuart, *Teachings on the Liturgy* (London: Central Church, 1907) (TS from orig. edn.), 13.

The pronouncement of the Absolution by the angel together with the Peace was the antitype of the sprinkling of the blood of the lamb, reminding the faithful that Christ had made peace through the blood of His Cross. The Dedication Prayer which followed, read by the elder, represented the self-offering of the people:

Thus we lay ourselves upon the altar, a living sacrifice to be consumed by the fire of God's love working in us by the Holy Ghost.[24]

The reading of the appointed portion of Holy Scripture by the prophet and the response, the recital of the Creed, were the antitype of the meat-offering of fine flour mingled with oil. The Anthem sung after the Creed answered to the drink-offering of wine:

Herein we dedicate to God our intellectual and spiritual faculties. Fine flour mingled with oil symbolizes reasonable thought and word sanctified and illumined by the Holy Ghost; wine symbolises the operation of the Holy Spirit making glad the heart of man with the joy of God's salvation, and leading him to express this joy in songs of praise and thanksgiving to God.[25]

This concluded the part of the Offices corresponding to the service of the brazen altar and conducted in the lower choir.

During the singing of the appointed psalm or psalms, a deacon lit the seven lamps from the flame of the sanctuary lamp in preparation for the following part of the Office to be held in the upper choir, the part representing the service in the Holy Place—the ministry of the High Priest at the golden altar of incense. The seven lamps

symbolise the presence in the Church, the Body of Christ, of God the Holy Ghost in his sevenfold fulness . . . enabling the Church by His indwelling to worship God in spirit and in truth.[26]

It was at this point that the proposition of the Holy Gifts upon the altar took place. The Gifts had remained in the tabernacle on the altar since their consecration at the Sunday Eucharist. The seven days of the reserved sacrament were considered antitypical of the seven days of Passover, reminding the faithful that Christ is our Passover, sacrificed for us. It was in the Holy Place that there was the promise of being admitted within the veil. Thus the ascent of the clergy from the lower choir to the upper choir symbolized God drawing man to Himself. The celebrating angel then removed the

---

[24] Ibid.   [25] Ibid.   [26] Ibid.

Holy Gifts from the tabernacle and placed them upon the altar, covering them with a transparent veil, whilst saying secretly the following prayer:

Lord God Almighty, we come before the throne of Thy glorious Majesty, presenting the emblems of the passion of Thy Son, the bread of everlasting life, and the cup of eternal salvation. Have respect, O Lord, unto His sacrifice; remember Thou His offering; and let His intercession on behalf of Thy Church, and of all Thy creatures, ascend up before Thee; to the glory of Thy holy Name. Amen.[27]

The veil, which remained upon the Holy Gifts, was the reminder that Christ had gone within the veil to offer intercession and that at the Parousia He shall appear unveiled in glory.

The angel was then directed to go 'to the place of Intercession',[28] for the offering of prayers, intercession (including the Lord's Prayer) and thanksgivings, thus extending to the Offices the Eucharistic participation of the Church in the intercession of the Great High Priest at the right hand of God (Rom. 9: 34). The proposition of the Holy Gifts was regarded as essential to remind the worshippers, through their visible presence upon the altar, of the only acceptable approach to God.

After the Holy Gifts had been proposed upon the altar, the angel gave the usual salutation, and there then followed the prayers (commencing with a supplicatory litany), intercessions and thanksgivings. These were symbolized by the different ingredients of the incense brought up to the angel at the altar together with the censer containing live coals. Stacte (myrrh-tree gum) symbolized supplications, also denoting Christ's sorrow for His people. Onycha (shell of shell-fish) symbolized prayers, and, particularly, persistence in prayer. Galbanum (gum of the fennel plant) symbolized thanksgiving, and hence the gratitude owed to God. Frankincense symbolized intercession and the near approach to God.

Immediately before the intercession, the angel placed two spoons of incense upon the live coals and offered the censer before the Lord whilst the following anthem was sung:

> Upon the golden altar before Thy throne:
> Let the sweet incense from the Angel's hand continually ascend.

---

[27] *The Liturgy and Other Divine Offices of the Church* (London: Bosworth, 1880), 61–2, 82–3.

[28] *General Rubrics* (London: Strangeways, 1878), 25.

So shall the words of our mouth and the meditations of our heart:
Be acceptable in Thy sight, O Lord, our Strength and our
   Redeemer.'[29]

(It should be noted that incense was invariably offered to God as a
'sweet-smelling savour', its rising smoke representing the winging of
Christian prayer to the heavenly places.[30] Neither objects nor people
were censed.)

   The angel now offered the following intercession for the living and
departed, the earlier prayers and thanksgivings having been said by
the representatives of the four ministries of pastor, evangelist, elder,
and prophet (see Ch. III, § 4):

Almighty and everliving God, we draw near in the Name of Thy Son
Jesus Christ, our High Priest and Mediator, who hath passed into the
heavens, where He abideth before Thee, and ever liveth to make
intercession for us. We bring unto Thee the supplications of Thy
people, and the prayers, intercessions, and thanksgivings of Thy
Church, and we beseech Thee that they may come up with acceptance as
incense upon Thine altar, and that Thou wilt be favourable unto us, and
answer us in peace. We bring into Thy presence all for whom we have
besought Thee, that they may receive the dew of Thy blessing, and the
outpouring of Thy Holy Spirit. Revive us, O God; revive Thy Church,
we beseech Thee; have mercy upon all men; gather all who shall be
saved into Thy fold; bring in the fulness of the Gentiles; accomplish the
number of Thine elect; vouchsafe unto Thy Church the ministry of
Thine apostles, prophets, evangelists, pastors and teachers; and unite
and carry onward to perfection all Thy saints. Grant unto Thy servants
departed in the faith rest and joy and peace, in the hope of a blessed
resurrection; and hasten the appearing and kingdom of our Lord and
Saviour Jesus Christ. These things we ask, O heavenly Father, in
patient confidence and joyful hope, being assured that we ask them
according to Thy will; that the voice of Thy Church is heard by Thee;
that the intercessions of the Holy Ghost are known unto Thee; and that
the mediation of Thy well-beloved Son, our Lord and Saviour, doth
prevail with Thee. Wherefore we glorify Thy Name; we fall down, we
worship, we adore Thy glorious Majesty; we praise and magnify Thee,
heavenly Father, with Thine eternal Son, and with the Holy Ghost, One
God, world without end. Amen.

---

[29] *The Liturgy*, 72, 91.
[30] 'Let my prayer be set forth before thee as incense; and the lifting up of my hands
as the evening sacrifice' (Ps. 141—LXX 140, v.2).

The form included in the evening Office differed to some extent from the above,[31] though it was permitted to repeat the morning form at Evening Prayer with a short insertion referring to all the prayers offered during the day. The intent and general content of both intercessions were similar, however. By each of them the angel was held as having gathered up

into one holy and complete offering the supplications, prayers, intercessions and thanksgivings which have been uttered; together with those unuttered yearnings of the living and departed saints, which the Spirit, helping our infirmities, brings to the ears of the Lord God of Sabaoth; and he presents them as one holy sacrifice of Intercession before God; putting, as it were, into the hand of the Angel of the Covenant, our High Priest in the heavens, the Incense representing the needs, desires, pleadings and thanksgivings of all His Church and people, and pleading with God in patient confidence and joyful hope for the fulfilment of all His promises, and especially for the revelation of the presence and kingdom of His Son.[32]

There then followed a ministry of the word, known as the 'candlestick ministry' because it answered to the trimming of the lamps of the golden candlestick in the morning and the lighting of them in the evening. In the morning this ministry was delivered by the angel alone. In the evening it was delivered by the angel in association with the elders, the latter being required to reflect upon the spiritual light given to them upon the subject of the angel's morning discourse. This ministry of the word testified that the Joy of the Church in the indwelling of the Holy Spirit and in the sacramental presence of her Lord will not be made complete until the personal appearing of Christ in glory at the Parousia. The Holy Gifts were then replaced in the tabernacle by the angel whilst a hymn of praise was sung—in the morning the Song of Zacharias (the Benedictus) and in the evening the Song of the Mother of God (the Magnificat)—after which the angel pronounced a benediction, thus bringing to a close that part of the Office answering to the service at the Golden Altar.

The Offices and the Eucharist

If the two Offices of Morning and Evening Prayer were supplementary to the Eucharist, they were also complementary to it. The Eucharist

[31] See *The Liturgy*, 91–2.   [32] Stuart, *Teachings on the Liturgy*, 14.

(see §§ 3–5 below) was considered to be always the act of the universal Church, and to represent the activity of the Holy Spirit within the universal Church. The Offices were seen, on the other hand, to be acts of each particular Church and to represent the activity of the Holy Spirit within the world. This distinction was indicated by the place from which the intercession was offered: the sanctuary in the case of the Eucharist, and the upper choir in the Offices.

The unity of the particular Churches within the universal Church was represented by the fact that the chief celebrant was always the angel-in-charge, assisted in the Offices by his priests:

The unity of the particular Church, and the unity of the Liturgical Offices ministered therein, and forming one whole, are ensured by the existence of the office of Angel as head of that particular body. And therefore the sacrament of the Eucharist celebrated on the Lord's Day . . . ought to be celebrated by the Angel, and by no other. The intercession offered upon this occasion is offered during the celebration of a Sacrament or Mystery, and immediately consequent upon the consecration and oblation of the holy gifts by which the memorial of Christ's sacrifice is made. [See the structure of the Eucharist, § 3 below.] This act of intercession, therefore, ought to be offered at the altar within the sanctuary; for the sanctuary symbolizes the heavenly place where the Lord is now present in His own person, presenting the Memorial of the same His sacrifice.

The Office of Morning and Evening Prayer, on the other hand, is, in its introductory parts, the commemoration of that work of the Holy Ghost which is now doing upon the earth; and therefore it is not conducted by the Angel alone, but in the greater part by priests of the four ministries under him. Moreover, the intercession offered in this Office, not being offered in the celebration of a sacrament or ordinance peculiar to the Universal Church, but, on the contrary, forming part of a service peculiar to the particular Church, and offered by the Angel in the distinct capacity of the head of that particular body, ought to be presented, not at the altar, but without the sanctuary; thus testifying to the office and place of the Angel as ministering in the midst of one of those separate gatherings, into which the Universal Church is necessarily divided during its present militant state upon earth in this dispensation.[33]

The essential link between the Offices and the Eucharist provided by the intercession and the presence of the angel as chief celebrant was

[33] *C/RL* 388–9.

further indicated by the vestments worn and by the offering of the incense. By all these means Morning and Evening Prayer were visibly proclaimed to be 'liturgy'.

The Shorter Offices and Other Services

The cessation of the full Offices on the death of the last of the Catholic Apostolic apostles in 1901 (see Ch. II, § 3) was regarded as the antitype of the covering up of the vessels and furniture of the Tabernacle and its being taken to pieces when the Children of Israel left the wilderness to move forward. Although the Holy Gifts were then no more to be proposed upon the altar and the intercession of the angel was silenced, the faithful were nevertheless bidden to study the full Offices and to give thanks that, although this ministry of intercession was in abeyance on earth, the intercession of the Great High Priest is unceasingly offered in heaven. It was taught that even the very deprivation of the intercession at the Offices should be regarded as a ground of hope and comfort, because the Tabernacle was no more than a temporary tent and its covering should indicate a moving forward towards the eventual heavenly inheritance. The present 'time of silence', as it is called, is the 'silence in heaven about the space of half an hour' (Apoc. 8: 1) after which the seven trumpets shall be sounded by the seven angels (see Ch. VI, § 1).

Linked with the Offices of Morning and Evening Prayer, but distinct from them, were special services to be used on the forenoon and afternoon of the Lord's Day. The order followed that of the Offices up to and including the psalm(s), after which came versicles and responses, prayers, the 'Gloria Patri', and a concluding benediction. The structures of the forenoon and afternoon forms were identical, though there were differences in the prayers offered. (The corresponding forms to be used on weekdays had a somewhat different structure.) It is not necessary to go further into details of their content here, since these services were not 'liturgy'—there was no proposition of the Holy Gifts, nor were they necessarily conducted by the angel. They were included within the category of 'other divine Offices'. It is sufficient to point out that they were the antitypes of the offering of the two additional lambs as whole burnt offerings, with their respective meat and drink offerings, on the Sabbath in addition to the morning and evening sacrifices.

3. THE CATHOLIC APOSTOLIC EUCHARIST

For Catholic Apostolics the Eucharist was the central act of Christian worship from which all other services drew their spiritual meaning; thus, all other acts of worship were said to be

meaningless, disconnected and confused, so long as the Eucharistic sacrifice is lacking.[34]

Before detailing its structure, it is useful to consider the understanding of its typological background.

The Sacrifices of the Tabernacle and the Eucharist

The Eucharist differed from the daily Offices in that it was not the antitype of any of the daily sacrifices of the Tabernacle. Indeed, the type of the Eucharist was not to be found in any of the ordinances of the Law: its order having been determined at the institution of the Last Supper by Our Lord Himself. Nevertheless, all the sacrifices under the Law were said to prefigure Our Lord's death 'in some peculiar and partial point of view',[35] and therefore to have their fulfilment in the Christian Eucharist.

According to Catholic Apostolic teaching the sin-offering typified Christ's sacrifice as the atonement for sin, and it represented the possibility of prayer and worship offered by sinners being acceptable through the propitiation of the Blood of Christ. The burnt-offering pointed to death as a consequence of sin, and the consumption by fire was the type of the introduction of man, through death and resurrection, to a new and heavenly life, though its destruction by fire failed to show the grace flowing from the Resurrection of Christ. The peace-offering pointed to the willingness of Christ to die for all mankind: 'it is the type of the Saviour's sacrifice of Eucharist.'[36] The eating of this sacrifice by the offerer pointed to the indwelling of Christ within those who believed in Him and were faithful members of His Church, 'whereof the Holy Communion is the symbol and sacrament'.[37]

---

[34] T. Carlyle, *Concerning the Right Order of Worship* (1850) (tr. 1905 from the Preface to the German edition of *The Liturgy*), 3.
[35] *C/RL* 26.   [36] Ibid.   [37] Ibid.

The Passover embraced both the sacrifice and the eating of it, but it separated the oblation from the act of communion. It was therefore a type of the Christian Passover of Holy Thursday and Good Friday:

It points to the blood of Christ, not so much as constituting the atonement for sin, but as it is the sign of salvation from impending judgements, which is the consequence of atonement; and it sets forth our communion with Christ . . . as it is the Viaticum and provision of grace and strength for our passage through the wilderness of this world. And the Feast of the seven days of unleavened bread . . . is equally imperfect in these particulars; while yet it sets forth the solemn consecration of the Sacrament on the Lord's Day as the basis of worship and communion throughout the week. And, (considering the week as one whole period) it represents the truth, that the sacrifice of Christ was once for all, but the memorial of it was to be perpetual.[38]

The sacrifice of the shew-bread, continually set before God with the frankincense, pointed to Christ's abiding presence with the Father, of which the sign in the Church was the presence of the Holy Gifts upon the altar. Atonement, however, was not considered to be typified here: it was assumed, Christ being prefigured as the representative of all his people rather than as the slain lamb. Finally, there were the rites of the Day of Atonement itself. These pointed expressly to atonement:

They signify the utter abolishing of the old man through the death of Christ, as the bullock was wholly burnt without the camp. . . . They prefigure the way in which Christ, our High Priest, hath entered into the holiest of all, into the presence of the Father, through the rent veil of His flesh, and with His own blood pleading the merits of His sacrifice upon the cross, and making intercession for us. In these respects they furnish types of the Eucharist, inasmuch as in that sacrament we 'show forth the Lord's death till He come' (1 Corinthians xi, 26).[39]

The ceremonial of the Great Day of Atonement also looked forward to the Parousia, but it failed to represent the grace of the Lord received through the gift of the Holy Spirit.

These various types, each seen as incomplete in itself, were embraced in Christ's death, Resurrection, and Ascension, the coming of the Holy Spirit at Pentecost, and the Parousia. They were also embraced, therefore, in the Eucharist, in which the whole work of Christ was made manifest. They all found their antitypes in the

---

[38] C/RL i. 27.   [39] Ibid.

Liturgy, that is, either within the Eucharist itself or in one of the Offices deriving from it, but no one of them could be of itself the type of which the Eucharist is the antitype, since the form of the Eucharist had been first revealed by Christ Himself to the Apostles.

The Structure of the Eucharist

The structure of the Catholic Apostolic Eucharist was as follows (reading by columns):

Invocation	The Thrice-Holy
Confession	The Lord's Prayer
Absolution	Consecration (with double epiclesis)
The Peace	Prayer of Oblation after Consecration
Versicles and Responses	Incense Anthem
Prayer of Access	The Great Intercession
Kyrie	Concluding Prayer before Communion
Gloria	The Reservation
Salutation	Invitation to Communion
Collect	Prayer to the Father
Epistle	Agnus Dei
Anthem after the Epistle	Invocation of the Son
Gospel	Invocation of the Holy Spirit
Homily	'Holy Things . . .'
Creed	Special Benediction (if appropriate)
Offertory	Special Peace
Introit	Communion
Invitatory	Exercise of Prophecy and Tongues
Response	Communion Anthem
Prayer of Oblation before Consecration	Post-Communion Prayers
	Te Deum
Salutation	Final Benediction
Preface	

The service had two basic parts: the Preparation (Invocation to Offertory) and the Eucharist proper (Introit to Final Benediction). Within these two parts a number of sections were recognized. Thus, the Preparation had a first section (Invocation to Kyrie) taking place at the access to the sanctuary, Godward, and priestly in character, and a second section (Gloria to Offertory) taking place in the sanctuary, mainly manward, diaconal, and characterized by a plurality of action.

The various components of the first section of the Preparation were penitential, leading to the Gloria as the opening anthem of the second section. In response to an objection to the change from the familiar Anglican pattern of 1662—which had penitential material later as well as the Gloria at the end—Cardale wrote:

> They are all a preliminary act of humiliation and confession of unworthiness and form no real part of the Service. . . . The real Service commences after the humiliation with a Song of Introit. And in my opinion, nothing can be better suited than the Gloria in excelsis. It is quite out of place at the end of the Service, for it is not wholly triumphal—quite the contrary—I think it a great error to close the Service with it as in the English and Scotch services.[40]

The Eucharist proper had four recognized sections. First, there was the Sacrifice (Introit to Prayer of Oblation after Consecration), taking place at the altar, Godward, priestly, and characterized by the concept of unity. Secondly, there was the Intercession (Incense Anthem to Concluding Prayer before Communion), at the heart of which was the Great Intercession for the living and departed, offered at the altar before the consecrated Gifts, Godward, episcopal, and hence always offered by the presiding angel. Thirdly, there was the Preparation for Communion (The Reservation to the Special Peace), at the altar, partly Godward and partly manward, the Reservation of the Gifts being for proposition during the octave immediately following as well as for daily Communion after the morning Office and for administration to the sick, the Special Peace corresponding to the Kiss of Peace of early Liturgies. (The Special Benediction before the Special Peace was pronounced by the apostles on the occasion of an apostolic visitation.) Finally, there was the Administration of Communion (Communion to Final Benediction), mainly at the access to the sanctuary though concluding at the altar, manward and Godward, including an opportunity for ecstatic utterances, and characterized by God's blessing upon His people.

The Great Intercession here was much more comprehensive than the angel's intercessions at the Offices. It comprised some sixteen distinct prayers in all. These were offered for:

> the restored apostles and the ministers serving with them;
> the angels of the various congregations;
> the rest of the Catholic Apostolic ministry;

[40] Letter, Cardale to Drummond, 2 Dec. 1846 (Northumberland collection).

the bishops and all holding office in the Church Catholic;
the low estate of the whole Church;
those 'in bitterness because of their transgressions';
those possessed by evil spirits;
all Christian rulers and others set in authority (with special reference
   to the British Royal Family and all subjects of the British Crown);
peace;
parents;
the propagation of the Gospel;
seasonable weather and protection from famine and pestilence;
the sick and suffering (with mention of the ministry of anointing);
the dying;
all faithful departed;

with finally, a special calling to remembrance of the patriarchs and prophets, of John the Forerunner, of the Mother of God, of the Apostles, of all the saints, and of

those who, in these last times, have rejoiced in Thy returning grace unto Thy Church, in the reviving of the ordinances which Thou gavest at the beginning, and in the manifestations of the Holy Ghost.[41]

The congregational response to the commemoration of the departed was:

May they rest in peace and awake to a joyful resurrection.

At each appropriate place during the Great Intercession there was the opportunity to mention individuals by name.

The Typology of the Eucharist

Although it was recognized by the Catholic Apostolics that there was no direct Old Testament foreshadowing of the *form* of the Eucharist, its individual parts were nevertheless given their respective typological interpretations, particularly those associated with the Passover and the rites of the Day of Atonement. These were as follows:[42]

Answering to ceremonies in the Court:
   Confession: The great sin offering (for the priests a bullock and for the

---

[41] *The Liturgy*, 20–1.
[42] Compiled by reference to *C/RL* and W. J. Bramley-Moore, *A Tabular View of the Holy Eucharist* (London: Pitman, 1891).

people a goat on the Day of Atonement) and the lesser sin offering together with the trespass offering for individual sins. (Lev. 16; Heb. 13: 11–13)

Absolution and the Peace: The sprinkling of the blood of victims. (Lev. 16: 14–16)

Prayer of Access and Kyrie: The blood brought within the veil and sprinkled on the Mercy Seat. (Lev. 16: 11–20; Heb. 10: 19–22)

Answering to ceremonies in the Court and the Holy Place:

Gloria, Salutation, and Collect: The approach to the brazen laver.

From the Epistle to the Homily: The use of the laver. (The Gospel, revealing the Word of Life, was typified by the golden candlestick. Replacing the Book of the Gospels upon the altar answered to the placing of the tables of the Law in the Ark of the Covenant, which in turn signified that the Gospel of Christ must be hidden in the heart. The Homily answered to the golden crown of the table of shewbread.)

Creed: Salt, with all its sacrifices, signifying faith. (Lev. 2: 13)

Offertory: Alms, answering to the tithe, the Feast of First-fruits, the wave offering and the heave offering. (Lev. 27: 30–2)

Answering to ceremonies in the Most Holy Place:

Introit, Invitatory, and Response: The burnt offerings. (Ps. 66: 13–15)

Prayer of Oblation before the Consecration: The burnt offering of two rams upon the brazen altar. (Lev. 9 and 16)

Salutation: The peace offering, not on the Day of Atonement. (Lev. 7; John 10)

Preface: The meat offering accompanying the burnt offering. (1 Cor. 14; Heb. 13)

The Thrice-Holy: The drink offering accompanying the burnt offering. (1 Cor. 14)

Lord's Prayer: The golden spoon of incense. (Num. 7: 20)

Consecration: The Passover—slaying of the Paschal lamb. (Lev. 16; Apoc. 5 and 6: 6)

Prayer of Oblation after the Consecration: The sprinkling of the blood within the veil. (Lev. 16; Heb. 10: 19–22)

Incense Anthem and the Great Intercession: The ministry of the golden censer with its cloud of fourfold incense. (Lev. 16; Heb. 9: 4)

Concluding Prayer before Communion: The waving of the sheaf of first-fruits. (Lev. 16 and 23)

The Reservation: The golden pot of manna in the Most Holy Place, the seven days of reservation answering to the seven days of the Feast of Unleavened Bread. (Lev. 23; 10–11; Apoc. 2)

From the Invitation to Communion to the Special Peace: Preparation for the Passover and the peace offering.

Answering to ceremonies mainly in the court:

Communion and Communion Anthem: The Passover feast, with the consumption of the Holy Gifts reserved the previous week answering to the consumption of the shewbread. That a part of the Holy Gifts must be consumed by the chief celebrant answers to the peace offering, which was part burnt and part eaten.

Post-Communion Prayers and Te Deum: Praise and thanksgiving to God. In the Te Deum, reference to the Cherubim and later to Apostles and Prophets had a typological significance, since the Cherubim of Glory typified apostleship and prophecy, the twofold manward ministry. (Eph. 3: 5; 2 Pet. 3: 2)

Final Benediction: The High-Priest's reappearance in the evening of the Day of Atonement. (Lev. 16: 24)

Although this typological interpretation of the different parts of the Eucharist was extremely detailed, Catholic Apostolics (both clergy and laity) were thoroughly grounded in it, as they were also equally aware of the more direct and complete typological interpretations of the Offices.

In addition to their typological interpretations, the various parts of the Eucharist were also given significance in terms of the ministry of the Incarnate Son of God and human response to God's love and bounty towards mankind. Thus, in the course of the Preparation, the Confession pointed to the baptism of repentance undergone by Our Lord, though Himself sinless, as our representative, and the Absolution to the voice of the Father saying 'Thou art my beloved Son, in Thee I am well pleased' (Mark 1: 11). The Confession was expressly an admission of sinfulness in general terms—any confession of sins by enumeration was deemed inappropriate in a public preparation for the Eucharist. In singing the Kyrie, the faithful were said to be identifying themselves with the publican, smiting his breast and saying 'God be merciful to me a sinner' (Luke 18: 13).

It was required that the Epistle and Gospel be read by different ministers, thus making the distinction between the word of God given through man (the Epistle) and the words of God Incarnate Himself (the Gospel). The Gospel was seen as pointing to the preparation for the Cross in the life of Our Lord; it was therefore never to be read from the altar.

The Creed and the Offertory were seen as the manifestation of the Christian faith in word and deed respectively, but the former was 'more than the dry assent of the natural understanding to certain propositions':[43] because its recitation was in the context of 'liturgy', it was primarily an act of worship directed Godward, its repetition invoking a divine response—the strengthening of faith through the Holy Spirit. The term 'Offertory' denoted the presenting of the alms of the people. This was made clear by the Offertory sentences, which referred to the offering of firstfruits of increase and of tithes. The Offertory was kept entirely separate from any act of Oblation; this was made clear by a rubric forbidding presentation of alms at the altar (which would have been contrary to the apostolic canons—a point specifically noted). Alms were directed to be placed on the table of prothesis only.

At the beginning of the Eucharist proper, the entry of the ministers into the sanctuary was seen as pointing to Our Lord's Ascension into the heavens. The overall structure from this point onwards, having been dictated at the Last Supper, followed traditional lines, though with various insertions (as can be seen by reference to the structure table given earlier). This structure was seen to have five essential parts:[44]

1. Oblation of bread and wine already set apart for holy use.
2. Solemn thanksgiving.
3. Consecration of the blessed bread and wine to be the Body and Blood of Christ.
4. Oblation of the consecrated elements before God.
5. Consumption of the consecrated elements by the faithful.

The bread and wine taken from the table of prothesis to the altar during the Introit were said to represent 'every human being yet within the reach of salvation'.[45] Here, all were equally represented in contrast to the situation at the Offertory, where each person was represented in accordance with his ability to give alms. The double Epiclesis, separating the blessing and consecrating of the bread from that of the wine, was said the show forth the Incarnation. Whilst the angel blessed the elements separately, invoking the name of the Trinity and making the sign of the cross on each occasion, the consecration was seen as the divine responses to each of two invocations of the Holy Spirit, first upon the bread and then upon the wine (previously mixed with a little water). The separation of each blessing from each invocation of the Holy Spirit signified the awareness that no operation of man's faith could effect the

---

[43] C/RL i. 123.   [44] C/RL i. 34.   [45] C/RL i. 141.

consecration of the elements: only the Holy Spirit could make bread and wine the Body and Blood of Christ.

The requirement that the angel should break the consecrated bread was to point to the willingness of Christ's sacrifice, not to denote that His Body was broken—which it was not (John 19: 33–6). (The teaching on the sacrificial nature of the Eucharist and the Real Presence are presented in §§ 4 and 5 below.) The consumption of the elements by both clergy and laity was considered to be essential to the completion of the sacrament:

The entire consumption [except for the part reserved] is necessary to the perfect ordinance of the Lord; it is the seal and consummation of the service and sacrifice offered unto God in the Sacrament of the Eucharist. . . . It is essential to the idea of sacrifice that the sacrifice be consumed. . . . And the whole service . . . would fail of its true symbolical character as manifesting, not only the death of Christ, but also the entire acceptance of his sacrifice—the entire abolition of sin—the entire and perfect gift of the Holy Ghost, by which we become partakers, through the death of the old man, of the regenerate life—the entire and perfect glory of the future kingdom, which at the resurrection awaits the saints of God,—except there were an entire and total consumption . . . of the sacred elements.[46]

The consumption of the Holy Gifts thus pointed to all the benefits made possible for the faithful through the life, death, Resurrection, and Ascension of Christ and the sending forth of the Holy Spirit, benefits shared by the faithful through participation in the sacrament. The Final Benediction pointed to the reappearance of Christ at the Parousia, whose presence would no longer be veiled under the forms of bread and wine but would be revealed to all mankind in glory.

The Full and Shorter Forms

The Eucharist was essentially the service of the Lord's Day, Sunday. It was only in places where there were many members and a comparatively large number of priests that a daily Eucharist was celebrated. Indeed, the idea of a daily celebration was considered a spiritual luxury, and the form used on weekdays differed from that used by the angel on Sundays. This weekday order of the Eucharist was used on Sundays when the angel was not available to celebrate,

---

[46] C/RL i. 200–1.

in smaller dependent congregations where there was no angel's seat, and universally after the general curtailment of services which followed the death of the last apostle (see Ch. II, § 3). Both orders for the Eucharist were claimed to be purged of accretions of centuries and to be 'replenished with Godly customs'.[47] Although their precise forms had been shaped in the light of ecstatic utterances of the prophets with the apostles, the principal architect of all Catholic Apostolic liturgical worship was undoubtedly Cardale himself (as has been noted in Ch. II, § 2).

The curtailment of the services after Woodhouse's death in 1901, and especially the cessation of the solemn forms of intercession offered by the angel on the Lord's Day, became a continuing reminder to the faithful that apostolic headship had been withdrawn. Without such headship, it was no longer thought appropriate to celebrate the Eucharist in its full form nor to offer incense: Catholic Apostolic worship could no longer be offered 'on the same spiritual plane as before'.[48] In fact, many apostolic functions had either ceased or been gradually restricted during the last two decades of the century due to Woodhouse's failing health; most of those which continued during this period had eventually to be carried out by the two living apostles' coadjutors acting under apostolic warrant. The basic teaching on the sacramental nature of Christianity, the typological interpretations of the liturgy, and the Eucharistic doctrine of sacrifice and real presence (see §§ 4 and 5 below), of course, remained unchanged.

Note on Sources

The details of the Office and of the Eucharist, described and discussed above, have been taken from their finally published forms. These services were developed in the period up to the 1850s, after which only minor changes were made, though there were some variations, in the forms used outside England which persisted beyond that decade—for example, there were variations in the version of *The Liturgy* for use in Scotland (originally compiled by Drummond) until 1870, when the book was withdrawn at the

[47] H. S. Hume, *Ministry on the Morning and Evening Sacrifice* (London: publisher unknown, 1923) (TS from orig. edn.), 1.

[48] A. Valentin, *The Present Time of Silence* (Vienna: 1938) (tr. from the German), 8.

request of the Apostolic College. After Cardale's death in 1877 no further changes were made in any of the texts of the service book, the final edition being published in 1880. Any additional prayers subsequently authorized for use were issued on individual sheets.

4. THE EUCHARIST AS SACRIFICE

That the Catholic Apostolics acknowledged the sacrificial character of the Eucharist is clear not only from the content of the service itself but also from the typological interpretation given to its various parts. That the Eucharist is both sacrament and sacrifice is explicitly stated in numerous works by Catholic Apostolic writers. It was not regarded, however, as merely a celebration of Christ's death, but, like all sacraments, it was a means of conveying to the faithful the benefits of His Resurrection. The Cross and the Resurrection were not to be regarded as separated events; the Cross without the Resurrection could not bring salvation to mankind. Indeed, the Eucharist was seen as a celebration of the whole economy of salvation, of which the Resurrection was the crucial event: 'We do not celebrate only Christ Who died, but Christ Who rose from the dead.'[49]

Sacrifice: A Divine and Continuing Ordinance

The sinfulness of fallen man was contrasted with the holiness of God by reference to the need of man to offer sacrifice as the only way of approaching Him. This was no human invention, but a divine ordinance appointed by God and revealed to man. God had accepted Abel's sacrifice 'of the firstlings of his flock' (Gen. 4: 4), a sacrifice which had involved the shedding of blood and had thus pointed to the future death of Christ on the Cross:

Only by looking upon the future death of the righteous One could God endure the sight of sinful man, and could fallen man dare to appear before the most holy God. After the fall no acceptable worship could be offered to God by man except such as bare witness to the future sacrificial death of Christ.[50]

[49] Stuart, *Teachings on the Liturgy*, 9.
[50] Böhm, *Lights and Shadows*, 256.

With the death and Resurrection of Christ and the establishment of His Church, the merely symbolic sacrifices of the Law were brought to an end, because He, as the all-sufficient Sacrifice, became 'the source and foundation of a more perfect way of glorifying God on earth'.[51] The need to follow the divine ordinance to offer sacrifice remained, however, and so, in the Eucharist, the Church had offered the all-sufficient Sacrifice with Christ as the victim. This sacrificial aspect was considered essential to the nature of the Eucharist. The Eucharist could not be deprived of its sacrificial content and at the same time remain the obedient act of the Church to the command of Christ to 'do this' (1 Cor. 11: 24–5):

> He gave thanks, and hallowed, and brake. . . . The action and the words were enough. If '*do this* in remembrance of me' did not mean, besides other things, 'offer this sacrifice', then the acts of our Lord were not calculated to convey their intended meaning.[52]

Reference to the New Testament (both Our Lord's own words and St Paul's interpretation of them) and to the Fathers of the second and third centuries convinced the Catholic Apostolics that from the beginning the Eucharist had been regarded as a sacrifice; not to accept its sacrificial nature was to suggest that Christianity had been corrupt from its foundations.

The Two Oblations

In the Catholic Apostolic rite of Eucharist (described in the previous section) the bread and wine were brought at the Introit from the table of prothesis to the altar, on which they were 'laid in order for the sacrifice'.[53] According to the principle that every sacrifice presupposes a previous oblation, there then occurred the first Prayer of Oblation, recited over the gifts before their consecration, in which 'we offer and present unto Thee this bread and this cup, in token that we are Thine'.[54] The sacrifice itself was seen as taking place through the operation of the Holy Spirit at the consecration of the elements, following the double epiclesis, after which there was offered the second Prayer of Oblation in which the Holy Gifts,

---

[51] Böhm, *Lights and Shadows*, 258.
[52] R. Hughes, *Eucharistic and Daily Sacrifice* (London: Bosworth, 1866), 7.
[53] C/RL i. 145.   [54] *The Liturgy*, 8.

'containing in them the presence of the sacrifice of Christ',[55] were presented to God:

Almighty God, we Thy servants, calling to mind the most blessed Sacrifice of Thy Son, showing forth His death, rejoicing in His resurrection and glorious presence at Thy right hand, and waiting for the blessed hope of His appearing and coming again, do present unto Thee this reasonable and unbloody sacrifice which Thou hast instituted in Thy Church . . .[56]

The Invitation to Communion comprised the words of St Paul: 'Christ, our Passover, is sacrificed for us . . .' (1 Cor. 4: 7–8); the faithful were thus invited to communion, 'the sacrifice having been slain'.[57] The consumption of the Holy Gifts was not a setting forth of Christ's death but a proclamation of the benefits available through the whole economy of salvation.

No Repetition of Calvary

Catholic Apostolic writers were careful to state explicitly that the Eucharistic rite did not and could not include any repetition of Calvary: it was a showing forth of Christ's death, in accordance with His command, until He should reappear at the Parousia. This was supported by appeals to typology, the Scriptures, and the Fathers. The seven days of the Feast of Unleavened bread were said to typify the sacrifice of Christ being once and for all, but with its memorial being repeated. As the High Priest went into the Holiest Place to sprinkle the blood (typifying intercession) and not to repeat the sacrifice, so Christ, our great High Priest in Heaven, intercedes with the Father, pleading but not repeating His sacrifice on the Cross.

In the Apocalypse, the Lamb was to be seen, not *being* slain but standing 'as though it *had been* slain' (Apoc. 5: 6). The sacrifices under the Law had to be repeated with each victim and could not make atonement for sin; Christ's death on the Cross, the righteous dying for the unrighteous, was a unique and hence unrepeatable event in the history of man 'that He might bring us to God' (1 Pet. 3: 18):

On the Cross His blood was shed; there He died as an atoning sacrifice. He suffered once for all. 'He died unto sin once' saith the Scripture; but,

[55] Böhm, *Lights and Shadows*, 269.
[56] *The Liturgy*, 14. [57] *C/RL* i. 193.

'being raised from the dead, He dieth no more' (Romans vi, 9–10). The death of Christ was accomplished once for all, at an appointed place, and at an appointed time. What took place on Golgotha, when, having exclaimed 'It is finished', He bowed His sacred head and died (John xix, 30), can never be either continued or repeated. Under the law fresh victims were continually offered up, because it was impossible that the blood of beasts could make reconciliation for sin. But after Christ appeared and His blood was shed, no further atoning sacrifice could take place (Hebrews x, 1–18), and any worship in which the sufferings and atoning death of Christ are professedly continued or repeated, is an actual denial of that perfect atonement which was accomplished on the cross.[58]

The consecration in the Eucharist did indeed represent Christ's death, but in the sense that the consecrated elements were 'the representation and figures of the sacrifice of Christ'[59] laid before God.

The Eucharist as a Heavenly Image

The sacrifice of the Eucharist was seen as an act performed by Christ on earth through the Holy Spirit, which was at the same time an image of what He performs in heaven:

Christ's offering of Himself is the great central and all-determining act in heaven. Nothing that is done in the Church can be this act itself, because the Church, though she be the Body of Christ, yet be not Christ Himself. But just for this reason, because she is His Body, should she manifest on earth the reflection of that heavenly act. But this reflection (image) is not a mere shadow, like the acts of worship of the Old Testament, neither is it a sort of dramatic representation, but it is a living action, wrought by Christ Himself through the Holy Ghost. The relation of this reflected act to its archetype in heaven is the same as the relation in which the Church herself stands to her Head, the Lord Jesus. As she is not the Lord Himself and yet is one with Him and filled with His life, even so is her celebration of His offering not that offering itself, yet is one with it and filled with its energy (Hebrews x, 1). The offering in heaven is the personal act of Christ, which no creature, however filled by God, can fulfil, continue, or repeat. The celebration or memorial of the same on earth is the same act, but, as it were, separated from the

[58] *C/RL* i. 171.   [59] Böhm, *Lights and Shadows*, 259.

character imparted to it by Christ's Person, and fulfilled, as a creature can fulfil it, by the Church in whom the Holy Ghost dwells and Christ works.[60]

Catholic Apostolic writers emphasized that there was but one High Priest and one sacrifice, and that in heaven God rejoices in the offering of it in its heavenly reality. The Church on earth shared in that rejoicing, but *in a mystery*. The Church, as Christ's tabernacle on earth, performed what the one High Priest performed in heaven, and in so doing revealed in this mystery both His present heavenly action and what He did for our sakes when on earth. Thus, in the second Prayer of Oblation, when the Holy Gifts were presented before God

we pray God to accept them upon His altar in heaven, where Christ abides, the Angel of the Covenant, the High Priest of our profession. For that which by His minister He doeth on earth, He is engaged in fulfilling in heaven: and His Body and His Blood, which after the manner of material substances are in the presence of God, where He Himself pleads His sacrifice on the cross, and offers His intercession, are also here after a spiritual manner, where we, in His Name, plead the same sacrifice, and seek acceptance only through His intercession.[61]

The presence of the Holy Gifts upon the altar, the antitype of the Most Holy Place, revealed the presence of the risen and ascended Christ, who had entered into the holiest place in heaven, and pointed forward to His revelation of Himself in glory at the Parousia. At the Communion, whilst the consumption of the Holy Gifts conveyed the blessings of the Cross, confirming the partakers in the assurance that by it Christ had blotted out all their sins, essentially they were partaking in His glorified humanity. Thus the spiritual sight was directed towards present events in heaven and the future Parousia rather than towards past events on earth, the Eucharist being the image of that which now takes place before the Father's throne. The whole emphasis of Catholic Apostolic teaching on the Eucharist was heavenly and eschatological rather than earthly in respect of both the offering and the consumption of the sacrifice.

[60] Carlyle, *Concerning the Right Order of Worship*, 2–3.
[61] C/RL i. 173.

Sacrifice and Sacrament

The essential sacramental character of the Eucharist was seen as complementary to its equally essential sacrificial character. For a proper understanding of both, the key was an appreciation of the spiritual nature of the Eucharistic rite, and especially that of the act of consecration of the elements:

But the quality of this sacrifice, and its acceptableness with God, must depend upon the way in which we look upon the effects of consecration. If we deny any real effect to the act of consecration, we deprive our service of the character of a *Christian* rite, and reduce it to the level of a sacrifice under the Law; it becomes a mere type of an absent thing. On the other hand, if we deprive it of its sacramental character, that is to say, if . . . we suppose the bread and wine no longer exist . . . our sacrifice assumes to be a positive repetition of the One Sacrifice for sins once offered; nor can that be called an 'unbloody sacrifice', of which the material substance of blood substituted for the wine forms a part. The material substances which our eyes behold are bread and wine: but the spiritual substances which our faith discerns (for we believe them to be truly present) are the Body and Blood of Christ, present, not after the manner of material substances, but after a spiritual manner, and by the operation of the Holy Ghost. And therefore our sacrifice is not a Jewish rite, a mere figure of the truth; nor does it violate the character of a sacrament . . . It is a 'reasonable sacrifice'; for it is worthy of the Church filled with the Holy Ghost to offer, being no less than the Body and Blood of Christ present by the self-same Spirit. It is an 'unbloody sacrifice'; for the Body and Blood of Christ are present spiritually, and not after the material flesh and blood. But being really present, the oblation which we offer is 'the holy bread of everlasting life, and the cup of eternal salvation'.[62]

It was through the consecratory act that it became possible for the sacrifice to be presented. This act was seen as essential for the Eucharistic thank-offering, because it was considered insufficient for the people merely to offer themselves: the Eucharist was much more than an offering of the Church by the Church. As a sacrament it was a means of grace, an ordinance for

communicating or sustaining the life of God. But the Christian should remember that the Eucharist is much more than this. It is a great act of

[62] C/RL i. 172–3.

worship; and in all its parts, including the communion itself, it is a service instituted in the Church for the offering of glory and praise, and for paying our vows, to Almighty God, where it is called the Eucharist. It is a sacrifice of thanksgiving, wherein bread and wine, set apart to the service of God, and placed upon His altar, are consecrated by the Holy Ghost, in answer to prayer, to be . . . the body and blood of Jesus Christ; and with these, memorial is made unto God of the great sacrifice offered upon the Cross, for the sake of which sacrifice, thus memorialized and presented before Him, His mercy and grace, that is to say . . . 'remission of sins and eternal life', are besought and without doubt obtained, for all the faithful.[63]

Sacrifice and Priesthood

Sacrifice and priesthood were seen as inseparable, each implying the other and each being of divine appointment. Every ordained priest was appointed to offer sacrifice (Heb. 5: 1). At the same time, the only true priesthood was acknowledged to be that of Christ, our High Priest after the order of Melchizedek (Heb. 5: 6), Who is present in every true Eucharist, both as the offered victim and as the offerer, by the power of the Holy Spirit:

In His double character of victim and priest the Lord is personally present in the invisible before God. . . . In this double character, as sacrifice and priest, is He present in His Church by the Holy Ghost. . . . When the Church assembles for a right and worthy celebration of the holy Eucharist, the eye of faith sees the glory of heaven in the midst of her. Christ, as the Lamb of God who died upon the cross, appears on the altar in the consecrated elements of the glorious sacrament. . . . Christ, as invested with the eternal priesthood, is present in those clothed with His authority, who worship God, and bestow benediction on men in His name.[64]

Thus, every duly authorized celebrant of the Eucharist on earth was seen as sharing in the priesthood of Christ, and it was only through this sharing that he was vested with the authority to exercise the ministry of sacrifice. Our own faith could create nothing, for 'it is not the province of faith to create, but to accept what God creates'.[65]

[63] J. B. Cardale, *A Manual or Summary of the Special Objects of Faith and Hope in the Present Times* (London: Barclay, 1843), 11.

[64] Böhm, *Lights and Shadows*, 265.

[65] J. B. Cardale, *A Discourse on the Doctrine of the Eucharist as Revealed to the Apostle Paul* (London: Boswell, 1856), 10.

Whenever man decided to act according to his own reason, whether in matters of doctrine or ordinance, the result was heresy and schism. This was especially true of the doctrine and ordinance of the Eucharist, as evidenced by St Paul's rebuking of the Christians at Corinth (I Cor. II: 17–30):

The Lord's Supper . . . is not a supper to which we can help ourselves; it is not by our taking bread and wine, and calling them by venerable and grand names; it is not by our appropriating this Supper for ourselves, grasping at it for ourselves, presuming that, by some act of ours, mental or otherwise, we can make it profitable for ourselves,—it is not thus that we shall receive benefit from it. This is not to eat the Lord's Supper; it is the very sin denounced by the Apostle,—whether in the carnal form in which it was manifested among the Corinthians, or under the veil of a more spiritual and therefore a more dangerous form. . . . This is to set aside the Lord in His ministering servants, to pass by the showing forth of the Lord's death, and to fail to discern the Lord's body.

For the Apostle proceeds to show from the history of the institution of the Holy Eucharist by the Lord Himself, that it is He who gives us His body to eat and His blood to drink. We cannot give to ourselves this heavenly food—we cannot by any act of ourselves procure it; it is for us humbly to receive what the Lord Himself gives us.[66]

It was thus the Lord Who offered His Body and Blood to the Father at the Church's altars through His duly appointed priests. It was His sacrifice, offered by Himself; yet at the same time it was the sacrifice of the whole Church, both priesthood and laity. This was made clear in the Catholic Apostolic Eucharist by the Invitatory before the first Prayer of Oblation:

Brethren, pray that *our* sacrifice may be acceptable to God the Father Almighty, through our Lord Jesus Christ.

The whole Church, as represented in the local congregation, shared in the offering of the sacrifice by virtue of participation in Christ through the Holy Spirit.

The Eucharist was also the sacrifice which revealed that the Church was one. The unity of God and hence also the unity of the Church (which reflects that of God) was symbolized by the presence of the angel, as the normal celebrant of the Eucharist. The participation of the other ordained ministers with the angel, symbolized the activity of the Holy Spirit in the Church, making the

---

[66] Cardale, *A Discourse on the Eucharist*, 5.

sacrifice of the Eucharist a reality. The entrance into the sanctuary by the angel symbolized the entrance of Christ, after His Ascension, into the Holiest Place as the only One worthy to plead His sacrifice before the Father. By these visible means, the faithful were reminded that all priestly ministry in the Church is the ministry of Christ through the Holy Spirit.

The offering of the Eucharistic sacrifice by a 'duly authorized' priesthood was considered essential for the well-being of the Church. The absence of these divinely instituted ordinances would inevitably lead to a general decay in worship and hence also to the withering away of the spiritual life of any Christian body which neglected them. Thus the Greek and Roman 'portions of the Catholic Church' were commended for having continued to recognize the sacrificial character of the Eucharist, though the latter was criticized for converting the great service of the Lord's Day into a daily sacrifice. The 'Protestant divisions', on the other hand, by rejecting both sacrifice and priesthood, were seen as having departed from 'the belief of the Church from the days of the Apostles':[67]

One seeks in vain for Christian Churches, in the apostolic sense of the word, amongst those confessions into which the one Church is divided. . . .

When the eucharistic sacrifice disappears from the altar, a blank is left which nothing can fill up, and the worship of the Church sinks down to a service not essentially different from that of a missionary preaching the Gospel, or from private meetings held for edification.[68]

The Church of England was included amongst those bodies which were said to have rejected the doctrine of Eucharistic sacrifice:

Even the Church of England, although following in her Communion Service the general order of ancient Liturgies, unlike these gives no word or sign to intimate a sacrifice in what she is doing. . . . she has deliberately committed herself to the Protestant negation. . . . The English Communion Office has never recovered from the death-blow inflicted upon it at this time [1552] by the influences of foreign Protestantism. . . . Mutilated of some of its most important elements, and full of infelicities and malarrangements, it resists alike the endeavours made by partizans for its glorification, and the attempts by another party to revive by its means the Eucharistic worship of the Church.[69]

[67] Hughes, *Eucharistic and Daily Sacrifice*, 3.
[68] Böhm, *Lights and Shadows*, 249, 275.
[69] Hughes, *Eucharistic and Daily Sacrifice*, 3, 39.

Indeed, it was claimed that *by law* the Church of England was denied altar, sacrifice, and priesthood.

5. THE DOCTRINE OF THE REAL PRESENCE

The Catholic Apostolic doctrine of the Eucharist made it abundantly clear that the Consecration effected a real change in the offerings of bread and wine, a change brought about by the operation of the Holy Spirit. This was much more than merely devoting the offerings to God or setting them apart for the worship of God—acts already performed earlier in the rite:

The holy gifts have already been hallowed by prayer and dedicated to Him, when they were first brought up to the table of prothesis . . . and by a further act, when presented upon the altar [at the first Prayer of Oblation], they were separated from all common use, and consecrated and devoted to holy purposes. Our desire is now, through God's blessing, to effect that further end, which the Lord effected when He instituted the sacrament.[70]

That blessing was not on the people but specifically on the bread and wine so that they might become 'most really and truly'[71] the Body and Blood of Christ:

Our answer, therefore, to the question, What is the meaning of the words of the Lord—'This is my body'—'This is my blood'? is this—We unfeignedly believe these words in the plain grammatical meaning of the words—simply and unequivocally, and without questioning. We believe that, in answer to the Prayer of the Church and Invocation of the Holy Ghost, through the instrumentality of His ministering servant . . . God is pleased to make the bread and wine to be to the Church the body and blood of Christ.[72]

This change in the Eucharist elements was regarded as a divine act brought about 'by the instrumentality of the celebrant';[73] it was in no way dependent upon the faith of the communicants present at the

---

[70] C/RL i. 157.
[71] J. B. Cardale, *A Discourse on the Real Presence of the Lord* (London: Boswell, 1867), 13.
[72] Cardale, *A Discourse on the Eucharist*, 15.   [73] C/RL i. 162.

service. The gifts, which before were bread and wine, had become the Body and Blood of Christ, both His divine and human natures being then present upon the altar. Thus, in receiving the Holy Gifts, the faithful became partakers of His humanity, crucified, risen and glorified, and were therefore

pledged to show forth the very life of Christ in mortal flesh, as it is written,—'He which saith he abideth in Him, ought himself also so to walk even as He walked' (1 John ii, 6).[74]

The Mystery of the Presence

Although both the bodies and the souls of the faithful were nourished in Holy Communion, the sacrament being both physical and spiritual, this reality of the presence of Christ was spiritual and not carnal, that is to say, it was effected neither by a change of place from Heaven to earth nor by a change of the matter of bread and wine, but 'by a spiritual operation of the Holy Ghost'—it was a divine 'mystery'.[75] This mystery transcended human explanation or investigation; it could not be penetrated by man's reason:

Of this change, then, and of the presence of the Body and Blood of Christ upon the altar, we can give no sensible proof. We believe it on the word of Christ. . . . we dare not explain away His words, or give them a merely figurative explanation. . . . in simplicity of faith, heartedly and unfeignedly, we receive His words, believing that He is able to effect that which He says, without violence to the physical qualities of matter, or to the human understanding . . .[76]

It was precisely because this presence, though real, was spiritual and invisible that belief in it did not contradict either man's reason or the evidence of his senses.

This doctrine was also beyond man's invention: man could not have known Christ's sacramental presence upon the altar unless it had been declared by Christ Himself. Yet Christ gave no explanation of His command to His disciples to eat His Flesh and to drink His Blood (John 6: 51–6). It was 'not His concern to meet the objections of the understanding, but rather to awaken faith in the hearts of the humble'.[77] There was to be no explanation in words. 'The explanation was to take place through an act . . . (Matt. 26: 26–8).'[78] The

[74] Cardale, *A Manual*, 11.   [75] Cardale, *A Discourse on the Eucharist*, 15.
[76] C/RL i. 167.   [77] Böhm, *Lights and Shadows*, 228.   [78] Ibid. 230.

meaning of the sacrament of the Eucharist was to be one of the things of God revealed to us by the Spirit of God, transcending our intellects but not our faith:

With what assurance of faith should we listen to the words of Christ spoken in His Name, 'This is My Body'—'This is the New Testament in My Blood'! With what humble and devout adoration should we give our response, and our seal, to all that is transacting, by uttering from our hearts, 'Amen'; 'So be it'![79]

It was pointed out that for centuries the Fathers, Doctors, and faithful had been content to believe without questioning, and to adore in silence. Yet, at the same time, such adoration must be offered by the heart of man with longing as well as with thanksgiving. Thus, the fact that Christ's presence is today hidden under a veil, should fill the faithful with longing for the time when, at the Parousia, sacraments shall cease, that veil shall be removed, and He shall be revealed in His true glory. This eschatological aspect of the Real Presence is expressly declared in the Concluding Prayer before Communion, a prayer addressed to the Father:

Hasten O God, the time when Thou shalt send from Thy right hand Him who Thou wilt send; at whose appearing the saints departed shall be raised, and we which are alive shall be caught up to meet Him, and so shall ever be with Him. Under the veil of earthly things we have now communion with Him; but with unveiled face we shall then behold Him, rejoicing in His glory, made like unto Him in His glory; and by Him we, with all Thy Church, holy and unspotted, shall be presented with exceeding joy before the presence of Thy glory . . .[80]

Worthy and Unworthy Partaking of the Sacrament

Contemporary with the setting down of the Catholic Apostolic Eucharistic doctrine was the debate in the Church of England as to whether or not the wicked, on consuming the Sacrament, also receive the 'inward sign'. The Catholic Apostolic writers made it clear that only those alive in Christ ought to receive the Holy Gifts, because food was for the sustenance of a life already in existence. The unworthy should not approach the Lord's table, though those who might approach were deemed worthy only inasmuch as they were living in Christ. Nevertheless, the unworthy who participated

---

[79] C/RL i. 170.   [80] *The Liturgy*, 21.

received, along with those deemed worthy, not only the bread and wine but also the Body and Blood. But, as with the physically sick food can nourish disease, so the unworthy ate and drank damnation (1 Cor. 11: 29):

> And if it be asked, whether the wicked eat the flesh of Christ, and drink His blood, in this holy supper, we answer, that they *do* eat the Sacrament of those holy things. Their teeth press the consecrated bread, they drink of the holy cup,—and Christ gives unto them, as He gave to Judas, the apostate traitor, His flesh to eat and His blood to drink. But these heavenly mysteries can only be partaken spiritually, through faith; and the wicked have not faith. They partake of the Sacrament, but they partake not spiritually of His flesh and of His blood; and receiving those holy gifts carnally and sacramentally, and not spiritually, they receive them to their own damnation, and are guilty of the body and blood of Christ, of which they could not be guilty, if those mysteries were not given to them, and if the presence of those mysteries depended only upon their own faith.[81]

The debate in the Church of England was seen to touch crucially on the nature of sacraments:

> The present discussion, indeed, in the Church of England is apparently limited to the point, whether that which the wicked receive in the Lord's Supper is merely the outward sign of bread and wine, or whether they . . . to their own condemnation and judgement receive the Sacrament of the body and blood of Christ in the full meaning of the word 'Sacrament', comprising not merely the outward sign, but also the inward part or thing signified. The question, except as regards the fearful consequences to the unfaithful, is of no more importance than the speculations as to what becomes of the Sacrament, when particles of holy bread are accidentally dropped on the ground and trodden under foot, or consumed by animals. But the real question which agitates the opposed parties in the Established Church is one of far higher consequence—it extends to the efficacy of the consecration, and to the nature of the sacrament.[82]

The kernel of the debate was considered by the Catholic Apostolics to be the question of the Real Presence. The feeding on the Body and Blood of Christ was, for the faithful, both a sacramental and a spiritual reality. In making this distinction between sacramental and spiritual participation in Christ, it was always emphasized that the wicked, in receiving the Holy Gifts, were

[81] C/RL i. 198–9.   [82] Cardale, *A Discourse on the Eucharist*, 2–3.

incapable of the latter and therefore dishonoured the Body and Blood of Christ:

The *manner* in which it is received in the two cases is different. The faithful, in receiving the Sacrament, spiritually eat His flesh and drink His blood: they receive both sacramentally and spiritually. The wicked, in receiving the Sacrament, reject the spiritual and most precious food conveyed thereby: they receive sacramentally and not spiritually.[83]

It was, however, considered that for the faithful to receive 'worthily' due preparation was essential—a preparation in which both confession of sin and fasting had a role to play. Although there was a general confession of sinfulness in the preparatory rite, provision had also been made for solemn absolution in private. Such solemn absolution was needed for those whose consciences did not allow them to approach the Lord's Table. Fasting was considered a personal discipline to be relaxed in cases of illness, old age, or other bodily weakness, and on those occasions when the Sacrament was to be received later in the day than was usual. It was also relaxed for children, who, it was considered, should receive the Holy Gifts as well as adults, it being said both that evidence from the first four centuries of the Christian Church supported this and that Holy Scripture demanded it (Matt. 19: 14). Children did not, however, receive Holy Communion as frequently as adults might do: it was the normal practice to admit children (but not babies) to monthly Communion—the text of Scripture was thus taken absolutely literally.

Explanations of the Real Presence

At the same time as emphasizing that the presence of Christ in the Eucharist was a mystery beyond human understanding, Catholic Apostolic writers were severely critical of what they saw as false explanations in the various Christian Churches, from the extreme of transubstantiation on the one hand to the mere eating of a memorial meal on the other. Their objections included criticism of the use, in this context, of the traditional Aristotelian concept of 'substance', which, it was said, should not be applied to spiritual things. Further, it was said that there was no warrant for belief in the separate

---

[83] Cardale, *A Discourse on the Eucharist*, 18.

existence of substance without sensible qualities or, for that matter,
in sensible qualities without substance:

The idea of substance, apart from all the sensible qualities belonging to
it, is a metaphysical idea, very useful for the purposes of mental
abstractions and metaphysical reasoning . . . Such a state of things,
however, has no existence anywhere in nature: neither is it alleged to
have any existence, except in this particular instance, for the purpose of
supporting a theory, and giving an explanation how, in the Sacrament,
the presence of the Body and Blood of Christ is compatible with what
our senses tell us concerning the outward species. But this theory and
this explanation are so repugnant to the fundamental principle of faith,
understanding, knowledge, and reason, and so utterly unnecessary to a
right belief in our Saviour's words and in the truth of the Sacrament,
that we cannot but reject them.[84]

It was said to be manifest that, after their consecration, the
elements not only continued to appear as bread and wine, but were
resolvable into the physical elements of which bread and wine are
composed. Transubstantiation, which demands belief in the visible
presence of Christ, was thus contradictory to the evidence of our
God-given senses. Further, it led to a situation of idolatry:

This erroneous persuasion leads to the most serious consequences. . . .
We give loose to our imagination as to the nature and manner of the
spiritual change, which has most certainly been effected in consecrating
the Sacrament. Being thus under the persuasion that the natural
substances visible to the eye have, after consecration, become the
natural Body and Blood of the Lord, the object of our worship is no
longer the One who is invisible to our senses, seated in His visible Body
at the right hand of the Father and invisibly present in the holy
Sacrament. He is visible, and His Body and Blood are visible; for,
according to this hypothesis, what we see are verily the Body and Blood
of the Lord. Thus, under the influence of this error, it becomes
impossible to distinguish between the Lord and the bread and wine
upon the altar. To these visible objects, which are supposed to be in
reality His Body and His Blood, our worship is to be directed; and the
Sacrament itself, and not simply the Lord present in the Sacrament, is
worshipped. This, brethren, I fear, cannot be distinguished from the
sin, or exempted from the guilt, of idolatry.[85]

If the bread and wine were to be regarded as no longer existing in
the Sacrament, this would inevitably lead to a doctrine of the

[84] *C/RL* i. 164.   [85] Cardale, *A Discourse on the Real Presence*, 8.

repetition of Christ's sacrifice. However, objections to blessing the faithful with the Holy Gifts 'as practised in the last two or three centuries by the Roman Catholics' were said not to be directed against the practice as such so much as against the motives behind it and 'the superstitious opinions, feelings, and habits, to which it is rendered subservient'.[86] It was also pointed out that the Roman Church had distorted the order of ancient liturgies by transferring the elevation of the consecrated elements from immediately before the Communion to the words of institution in order to support the false doctrine of transubstantiation.

The Protestant denial of the Real Presence, consubstantiation, and impanation were rejected along with transubstantiation. If it was considered false to deny the continuing presence of bread and wine, it was equally false to deny the presence of the Body and Blood of Christ, to admit the presence of both, subsisting side by side, or to suggest that Christ's glorified humanity was converted into bread and wine. Merely to eat a memorial meal was to reject the revelation given to St Paul as to the nature of the Lord's Supper, and was hence a denial of the truth of Holy Scripture. Equally, to regard the bread and wine as mere figures of Christ's Body and Blood, effecting subsequent spiritual action in individuals, was to deny the reality of the sacrament and tread the downward path of serious unbelief:

Therefore, explaining the Lord's words in a purely figurative manner, it follows that the feeding upon His flesh and blood is also purely figurative; and we are driven to the conclusion (I need not say how false) that the Body and Blood of the Lord have no part in the matter at all. The mention of them is a figure expressing that, as our bodies live and are nourished by bread, so, spiritually, we live by Christ. God, through Christ, imparts to us the grace of the Holy Spirit; and so we arrive at the conclusion that the only peculiarity in the Sacrament is, that this grace which God gives to His people at all times, He gives at this time specially in answer to special prayers, devout and pious meditations, and faith in receiving, and obedience in fulfilling a prescribed duty. . . . we warn you against this unbelief.[87]

Denial of the presence of Christ was said to reduce the sacrament to a Jewish ceremony, a mere type of that which was yet to come and thus could not be present. The Catholic Apostolic position was

---

[86] C/RL i. 412.   [87] Cardale, *A Discourse on the Real Presence*, 12.

always affirmed to be belief in the Real (though not carnal) Presence of Christ, and that

> as Christ continually supplies to those that are living members of His mystical and spiritual body . . . the life and sustaining power of His own risen and glorified Humanity, which is quickened and instinct with the Holy Ghost, the Spirit of Life; so in the Holy Eucharist, the Sacrament of His Body and Blood, He doth specially give His flesh and His blood, present under the symbols of bread and wine, to be the spiritual food of those who feed thereon in faith.[88]

It can thus be seen that the essence of this theology of the Eucharist was that the reality of the Presence was spiritual, and that only terms and concepts appropriate to a spiritual reality were appropriate. The adoration offered before the Holy Gifts displayed upon the altar was the spiritual worship offered to One who was invisibly yet really present. It was precisely because the Presence was a spiritual one that it was also a real one.

When the Catholic Apostolic authorities, acting upon prophetic instruction, determined to introduce a special form of prayer to be said upon the removal of the Sacrament from the altar after the Forenoon Service on the Lord's Day (previously carried out in silence), it was noted that no appropriate form of prayer existed for this purpose in any of the Christian Churches. The form finally agreed upon, after consultation with the Angels in charge of congregations, was as follows:

> Lord, we draw near to Thy presence to remove from Thine altar these holy symbols, the Sacrament of Thy Body and Blood, the memorial of Thy one Sacrifice for sin. Thou hast vouchsafed to us herein Thy presence, and nourished us with spiritual food. Under the veil of these earthly elements we worship Thee alone. We worship not the things we see; but Thee, Who art invisible; and through Thee we glorify the blessed Name of Father, Son, and Holy Ghost, One God.
>
> **R.** Amen. Lord, we worship Thee, we praise Thee for Thy mercies, and in Thy presence we rejoice. Hasten the time when our joy shall be fulfilled, and we shall see Thee as Thou art.

This, togther with the form for the benediction of Holy Water, was added to the services in July 1868, and they were to be the last significant additions made to be printed service book. This prayer,

---

[88] Ibid.

together with the response, gathered up the various strands of Catholic Apostolic Eucharistic theology. Thus, the prayer bore witness to the Real Presence and the adoration due to Christ for making that Presence known to and available to the faithful. At the same time

Testimony was made against idolatry, the worship of the creature, the things that we see, and we were lifted up in adoration to Him Who is invisibly present under the veil of earthly things, and through Him to Father, Son and Holy Ghost, One God.[89]

The response bore witness in its final petition to the eschatological hope that was always present either explicitly or implicitly in Catholic Apostolic liturgical worship.

Baptism and the Real Presence

The mystery of the Real Presence was linked with the mystery of Baptism (see Ch. III, § 1). Any adequate discussion of one was said to require reference to the other, and any diminished theology of the one struck at the roots of right belief in the other. If the faithful are truly engrafted into Christ at baptism, thus becoming members of His Body and partakers of His Spirit, they require continuing nourishment—for this He instituted the sacrament of the Eucharist, in which His Body and Blood are given as the food which sustains that new life in Him:

Let us remember, therefore, that in baptism we are engrafted into Christ, and made very members of His mystical body. By one Spirit, the Holy Ghost, we are all baptized into one body—that is Christ. In speaking, then, of the subject of the Eucharist, we are not speaking of it in reference to so many men descended from Adam merely—rational animals. But we speak of it in reference to the Church, a living organized body, composed of many living individuals—each of them individual persons—but all of them members of this body—the body of Christ—'of His flesh and of His bones'. We speak of it as the ordained means of nourishing this body—a body which has been quickened and which continues in existence by the life of Christ. In the members of this body He lives. To the members of this body alone He gives His flesh and His blood. . . .

---

[89] Anon., *Upon the use of Holy Water and the Reservation of the Holy Sacrament, Central Church* (London: Central Church, Sermon no. 1077, between 1920 and 1924), 6.

Believing, then, that He hath incorporated in Himself all those whom the Father hath given Him—imparted to them His own life—made them partakers of His own Spirit—is it at all incredible that the means by which He sustains this special, divine, spiritual life, and nourishes the members of His own body, should be His own flesh and His own blood? No one who stands in the faith of His baptism can doubt, that for the nourishment of the life received in baptism Christ hath ordained this blessed sacrament; wherein, present in His Church by the Holy Ghost, He saith to every one that draweth near,—'Take, eat; this is my body . . .'.[90]

6. SYMBOLS USED IN THE LITURGICAL WORSHIP

For the Catholic Apostolics symbols were essential for the true worship of God offered on earth. Man is surrounded by symbols. All creation was seen as a symbol, pointing to God. Man himself was a symbol; his body was a symbol of his total being, and all his postures, words, and deeds were symbols of his thoughts and innermost life. Thus, in approaching God, man by his very nature must have recourse to symbols:

To require the exclusion of symbols from all religious exercises, is to require that man shall become not merely a new but a different creature, and live in a different world, before he can worship God.[91]

Our Lord, in instituting the Eucharist, witnessed to the spiritual need for symbols. The use of sacraments by the Church points to the centrality of symbols in the life of Christians.

Objections to symbols were usually based upon fears of superstition, idolatry, ostentation, or Judaizing. But such fears related to symbols wrongly used or misunderstood, and the way to avoid such dangers was 'not to abolish the means, but to use them in faith'.[92] Since the use of symbols was natural to man as part of God's creation, man had

---

[90] Cardale, *A Discourse on the Eucharist*, 14–15.
[91] Carlyle, *On Symbols used in Worship* (London: Goodall, 1853) (in *Collected Writings*, London: Bosworth, 1878), 341.
[92] Ibid. 343.

always used them in his institutions. The Church was no exception; Christians had used symbols from the beginning:

We may say, then, that the works of the Creator, the institutions of our Lord, and the instincts of our being, justify the use of symbols; and, if we examine, we shall find that, unconsciously, in obedience to an inward law of nature, men have always endeavoured to arrange their institutions so as to exhibit some appropriate significance . . .

By going into the house of God we do not cease to be men; that which is ingrafted into our being remains ingrafted still. And, seeing that our eyes must rest on something, it is surely good that the objects presented should be expressive of the truth of those services in which we are engaged. The primitive Christians early introduced symbolic rites, beginning perhaps with the sign of the cross; and three-fourths of Christendom not only sanction symbols, but find the greatest aid to faith in their use. Symbolism is, in fact, the science of exhibiting invisible truth by visible and appropriate signs, in order that our senses may be made the helps and handmaids of our spirit, and we may be the better able to worship God.[93]

Symbols and Types

Symbols were clearly distinguished from types, yet what had once been a type could become a symbol:

A type points to a thing absent and future, a symbol to a thing present. When the antitype appears, the type is abolished. The shadow is banished by the substance. But the symbol cannot appear till the substance is there; and its continuance depends on that of the substances. Where the type ends the symbol begins; and, therefore, symbolism can never be a return to types and shadows; nor does the previous use of a creature as a type exclude its present use as a symbol. . . . When the substance comes, the *typical use*, indeed, ceases for ever; but the *use* does not. . . . That former employment does not debar it from being afterwards employed by God. Were we to strike out from use in Christian worship every creature once used under the shadows of the law, we should mutilate the very sacraments.[94]

Thus, whilst it was not permissible to repeat the use of the types of the worship of the Tabernacle (the brazen altar, the laver, the pot of manna, etc.), it was not only permissible but necessary, because of

[93] G. C. Boase, *Three Discourses on Symbols used in Worship* (Dundee: 1855), 11–12. Boase was Angel at Brighton.

[94] Carlyle, *On Symbols used in Worship*, 342.

the nature of man, to use *as symbols* oil, water, lights, precious metals, jewels, incense, vestments, and colours, provided that they were used in ways appropriate to their particular properties, and provided that both clergy and people were aware of their spiritual meaning. Such symbols could reveal those spiritual and perfect things to which no human words could give adequate expression.

The Principles of Christian Symbolism

In order that the symbols used should deliver the faithful from the barren worship of Protestantism and the excesses of Rome, it was required that they conform to certain principles:

The conditions of true symbolism are:
  1. That symbols be used, as before God, to represent things presently existing or transacted in the Church.
  2. That they be used consistently with the qualities of the creature and the dictates of nature.
  3. That they be used according to the express directions or plain analogy of Scripture.
  4. That they be used in conformity to the best and widest practice of the Church, controlled by the natural properties and the scriptural use of the creatures.
  5. That they be used intelligently, as part of a reasonable service, in which we know what we do, what we express, and why we so express it, and believe in the thing expressed.
  6. That [outside the sacraments] they be used as accessories, and not as essentials—as aids to devotion, not as objects; and although on fixed principles, yet only in that degree and manner which wisdom and charity dictate at the time.
  7. That they be used in accordance with the present light of prophecy, by which the forgotten meaning of ancient rites is revived, and their distorted or imperfect form restored.[95]

There were four principal kinds of symbolism used in Catholic Apostolic liturgical worship: the nature and arrangement of the church buildings, the vestments worn by those officiating at services, the postures and actions of clergy and people, and the various objects and substances employed.

***

[95] Ibid. 345.

Buildings, Vestments, and Postures

Church buildings were regarded as necessary for Christian worship. God had created the world as a temple for man in which he should worship his Creator. Man was himself created as a temple—a dwelling place for God (Eph. 2: 22). Yet, although God was everywhere present, He nevertheless vouchsafed a special presence in those places which had been dedicated to Him:

In his prayer at the dedication of the Temple, Solomon said, 'heaven and the heaven of heavens cannot contain Thee, how much less this house which I have built?' (2 Chron. 6. 18). And God answered, 'Mine eyes shall be open, and Mine ears attent unto the prayer that is made in *this* place, for now have I chosen and sanctified *this* house that My name may be there for ever' (2 Chron. 7. 15). And it is written, 'where two or three are gathered together in My name there am I in the midst of them.' (Matt. 18.20.).

And wherever men dwell, they should provide a suitable building, where they may gather together in His name, and He may be in the midst of them; and whatever the style of the building may be, it should at least be so expressive of reverence and devotion that on entering we may instinctively say, 'This is none other but the house of God' (Gen. 28.17).[96]

It was therefore required that church buildings should be designed in such a way that they could readily be distinguished from buildings used for purposes other than worship. They were to be lofty, thus symbolically pointing to the heavenly places and reminding the faithful that all blessings of the Spirit were poured on man from on high (Isa. 32: 15). The most appropriate form of plan was that of the Cross, reminding the faithful of the economy of salvation. A church building should lie West to East, with the sanctuary at the East end, symbolizing spiritual progress from darkness to light, and requiring the faithful to turn spiritually towards the Sun of Righteousness, looking for His reappearing in glory. Within the sanctuary, the focal point must be the altar, upon which the Holy Gifts must be reserved and not elsewhere. There must thus be only one chief centre of honour, symbolizing that salvation is of Christ alone.

The various acts performed in the Church should have their appropriate place and furnishings. The font should be placed near

---

[96] A. Willis, *The Spirit of Church Architecture* (Shrewsbury: Wilding, 1915), 2–3.

the entrance to the building, thus symbolizing that baptism was the entrance into the life of Christ. Holy water should also be placed near the entrance to remind the faithful of their baptismal washing, and that they should approach God's ordinances with cleansed consciences. For the same reason the place appointed for spiritual counsel and absolution should also be near the entrance. Booths were, however, considered inappropriate for this last purpose—though the words spoken were personal and private, a matter only for the penitent and the priest before God, the sacrament should not be conducted in a secret or clandestine manner.

Ornamentation and decoration should increase as the sanctuary was approached, thus symbolizing the greater glory which was about the throne of God, of which the altar is the symbol. Similarly, each distinct area of the church, from West to East, should be raised by a step or steps, thus ensuring that the altar appeared at the most elevated place, reminding the faithful that the Eucharist was the highest form of worship. Paintings, sculptures, and other representations of things that had passed—such as the fall, the flood, the old covenant, and the past history of the Church—should be at the West end. Such ornamentation should not be for the purpose of gratifying contemporary artistic taste, nor should it be a matter of display: it should point to the spiritual thing symbolized and should be in accordance with the tradition of Christ's Church.

The cross, not the crucifix, should rest on or behind the altar, thus symbolizing Christ's resurrection and the presence of His glorified humanity on high; any representation of Christ's passion should therefore be placed to the West of the altar—a crucifix on or behind the altar was regarded as an anachronism. Ornamentation in the nave should symbolize the life of grace. Wherever possible, the place for the singers should be elevated, thus symbolizing that the worship of the Church was not merely worship on earth, but was one with the worship of the heavenly places. However, it was not permitted for the singers to be positioned between the deacons (whose stalls were in the lower choir) and the people; the singers, as part of the worshipping congregation, were always located in the nave. Of the actual music, it was said that the organ should be no more than a guide to the use of the human voice, and that it should be silent if it became otherwise.

Vestments were regarded as garments in which man appeared before God. Without vestments, Christ's ministers on earth would stand naked and spiritually uncivilized before Him. The form and texture of the vestments worn should be such as to symbolize the position and the particular duties and acts of service of the wearers. They should be catholic, that is, they should not reflect any local party or place, nor should they be expressive of secular tastes or fancies.

The first vestment put on was the cassock. Its primary object was to cover all the secular clothing of the wearer, a reminder that all are equal before God:

It obliterates any distinction which the poverty or the richness of work-a-day clothes might display.[97]

The black colour was to remind men of the necessary death unto sin, though the angels wore cassocks of purple to indicate their position of rule and authority. However, at the Apostles' Chapel at Albury, all ministers, including the apostles themselves, wore cassocks of black, because

there they appear merely as Ministers of the Universal Church, of which the Apostles are the Elders and the Lord Jesus Christ Himself is the Angel.[98]

The white alb symbolized the purity of the priesthood, which was Christ's alone. The girdle symbolized the strength from on high required for the exercise of ministry. The stole symbolized obedience in bearing the burden of ministry. The cope symbolized rule, headship, and mediation, the normal colour being purple. The chasuble, which was required to be in one piece, symbolized the unity of the body when covered by the glory of Christ.

The colours and ornamentations of the vestments also had their signification: gold symbolized truth; silver symbolized love; jewels symbolized the glory and beauty of ministry; colours could indicate the nature of the particular ministry being exercised (see Ch. III, § 4) or the different seasons of the Church's year. Vestments worn for the celebration of the Eucharist on the Lord's Day were always white, thus symbolizing joy and thanksgiving. Black or violet vestments were worn on Good Friday, and on the Eve of Pentecost, a day set specially apart as an occasion of humiliation for sin. The distinctive

---

[97] R. M. Heath, 'Vestments as Ordered by Apostles', lecture (MS 1942), 1. Heath was an underdeacon at the Central Church, London.

[98] Ibid.

colours of the fourfold ministry (see Ch. III, § 3) were never used for
the chasuble, since the chief celebrant, being one person, symbolized
that One alone, Jesus Christ, was the true celebrant of the mysteries.
The celebrant's vestments were to be as rich and costly as
circumstances permitted in honour of Him Who was invisibly
present in His Church. The cross on vestments symbolized the pre-
eminence in following the Lamb; a ring symbolized the marriage of
the Church with the Lamb; the mitre, if worn, symbolized the
dignity of spiritual headship.

The positions taken up by the various ministers durig the services,
their movements and their postures, were not the arbitrary choices
of individuals but were ordered for the edification and instruction of
the faithful. Thus the stretching out of the hand was an act of power;
the raising of the hand signified blessing; sitting symbolized
lordship; standing symbolized attendance and readiness to do God's
will, or triumph and praise; kneeling symbolized supplication;
prostration symbolized penitence and humiliation before God;
bowing of the head or body symbolized reverence and worship, and
especially at the name of Jesus (Phil. 2: 10); the sign of the cross
symbolized dedication to Christ and the banishment of evil through
the power of His Cross. The last of these was regarded as a private
act, other than when ordered for priestly blessings. Whilst not
demanded of the faithful, being personal and voluntary, it was
nevertheless commended on account of its patristic authority:

Tertullian and the other earliest Fathers show us how universal was the
use of this sacred sign, both in the domestic affairs of the saints, and in
the defence against, and deliverance from, calamity and evil spirits . . .
the sign of the cross is most appropriate, claiming all things for Christ,
and His protection for us.[99]

The Seven 'Creatures' used in Worship

There were seven 'creatures' used in the worship of the Tabernacle
which were regarded as having a permanent application to the seven
offices of Christ. These were

bread to the life, wine to the joy and hope, oil to the unction, water to
the cleansing, incense to the intercession, light to the guidance, salt to
the covenant standing, of the Church in Him.[100]

---

[99] Carlyle, *On Symbols used in Worship*, 352.   [100] Ibid. 353.

Bread and wine were the Eucharistic offerings of the Church, which, by the operation of the Holy Spirit in response to the prayers of Christ's appointed ministers and of the faithful, became His Body and Blood, the symbols of His presence and the spiritual food of the faithful.

For Catholic Apostolics, oil symbolized health and joy. It was the substance traditionally used for the anointing of kings and priests. It was therefore to be used in the Church:

And if we are kings and priests unto God, we should have not only the anointing, but the symbol of it . . . the work done on the body being the correlative of the work done on the soul . . . If the gift of the Holy Ghost, by the laying on of Apostles' hands, is the anointing of Christ, oil should be used at the services for sealing the faithful and for ordaining the called. And we have a full sanction for the principle of its use under the Christian dispensation, in the express command of Scripture to anoint the sick.[101]

On seeing the oil lamps burning, the faithful were

reminded of their duty and privilege to come . . . with the hearty offering of a first love. The deacons, also, remembering that it is by their hands the offerings of the people are collected, and the oil provided for the lamps, may well reflect on the necessity there is that they should know the hearts of the people, and have them in their keeping; so that the eye of God may see the faith, hope, and charity of all the flock embraced in their hearts, as oil in a vessel ready for use.[102]

For all Christians, the use of water in the sacrament of baptism symbolized death and resurrection in Christ. For Catholic Apostolics, the use of holy water, generally, was a reminder of baptism, and also symbolized the continuing need for cleansing by Christ and the presence of the Holy Spirit:

The meaning of our use of holy water is set forth in the prayer offered when the water is renewed and blessed. God has appointed his creature water to be a symbol of the presence and power of His life-giving Spirit. We beseech Him to sanctify the water presented before Him, that it may be for a sign and symbol of the washing of regeneration and renewing of the Holy Ghost. We pray Him to grant that all who come up into His courts may be reminded of the holy water of the baptismal grace wherein they stand, and may be sanctified and cleansed in the inner

[101] Carlyle, *On Symbols used in Worship*, 356.
[102] Boase, *Three Discourses*, 8.

man, and may be kept unto the day of Christ's appearing, and finally be presented holy and without blemish before the throne of God's glory.[103]

The faithful were, however, warned particularly against using holy water as a charm.

Incense symbolized prayer—a sweet odour before God—both in the self-dedication of the faithful and in the expression of their desires. It set forth Christ's ministry as the way to the Father, and thus, in particular, it signified the intercession of Christ:

To the eye, a cloud of sweet Incense rising up tells of One in the midst of us, unseen, who helpeth our infirmities; by whose intercessions, unutterable, our imperfect petitions and feeble aspirations ascend up acceptable from the Angel's hand.[104]

Light symbolized the presence of Christ—as the Light of truth— in the Church:

The kindling of light, therefore, in the Church is to symbolize the presence of Christ, not as He is in Heaven, but as He is on earth—not as He is in the world, but as He is in the Church. How is He, then, present in the Church? In four forms:

1st. By the Sacrament of His Body and Blood. . . . His presence here is indicated by one lamp burning before the Holy Sacrament . . .

2nd. By His Word, and especially by the word of the Gospels . . . His presence in this form is indicated by the one light burned at the reading of the Gospel . . .

3rd. By His ministers in the universal Church. Of these, the two chief are apostles and prophets . . . The lighting of two lights, one at each side of the altar, is our acknowledgement that Christ, the one light of the body is present in His catholic ministries . . .

4th. By His people, and the ministries of the particular Church. We who are baptized, and abide in Christ are . . . the enlightened. This truth is shown forth . . . when, on certain occasions, every person who comes to church carries a small taper in his hand, confessing thus to his standing as an individual in Christ.[105]

Of especial importance were the seven lamps hanging in the chancel. These denoted the completeness of the Church, as witnessed also by the seven lampstands in the vision of St John (Apoc. 1: 20). They symbolized that the worship of the Church proceeds from one body.

---

[103] Anon., *Upon the use of Holy Water*, 4.
[104] Boase, *Three Discourses*, 16.
[105] Carlyle, *On Symbols used in Worship*, 353–4.

All the lights burnt pure vegetable oil, symbolizing anointing with the Spirit of life and blessing, necessary for the right exercise of all worship and ministry in the Church, including the right understanding of Holy Scripture. The conversion of oil into Light by combustion symbolized that the faithful were

the oil, which, by the fire of God's presence, is converted into light, and rendered ethereal and heavenly.[106]

Moses had directed that salt was to be used with every offering as a sign of acceptance through the covenant of God. However, Christ had commanded, 'Have salt in yourselves' (Mark 9: 50), thus legitimizing the continuing symbolic use of salt. It was thought appropriate for dissolving in the holy water placed at the entrance to churches, thus symbolizing the need to receive the grace and blessing deriving from the new covenant in Christ's Blood.

Although the seven 'creatures' discussed above had a significant place in Catholic Apostolic worship, they by no means exhausted all forms of symbolism which were considered appropriate in association with liturgical worship. Symbolism was seen to lie at the heart of man's spiritual understanding, though symbols by themselves were not 'to convince us of any truth, but to remind us'.[107] From the sacramental viewpoint, as evidenced particularly in the Eucharist, Catholic Apostolics believed that it was through created material things that man received spiritual blessings by the operation of the Holy Spirit, and that it was through the appreciation of the spiritual significance of material things that man could be led to deeper understanding of and participation in the things of God:

Such, then, is the operation of the law of Symbolism. It is seen in the works of God. It pervades the institutions of men. It embraces all our words, and all our actions; demanding that we should glorify God, not only with our spirits, but with our bodies, which are God's. Its voice is the voice of Wisdom, pleading ever more for whatsoever things are lovely, whatsoever things are pure, whatsoever things are decent, whatsoever things are seemly: in a word for what is TRUE.[108]

[106] Carlyle, *On Symbols used in Worship*, 355.
[107] Boase, *Three Discourses*, 5.   [108] Ibid. 45.

7. SURVEY AND COMMENT

It is clear from the various sections above that the Catholic Apostolics, unencumbered by the legal restrictions which bound the Established Church, developed comparatively early on a 'high' sacramental doctrine and an 'advanced' ritual. This was eventually to include the acceptance of the seven catholic sacraments or 'mysteries' of Rome and the East (though this precise number has never been formally finalized in Eastern Orthodoxy). Their sacramental theology and practices anticipated the corresponding developments which were to take place in certain sections of the Church of England as a result of the Tractarian Movement. This sacramental emphasis, proclaiming the material world as the vehicle of spiritual blessings, was reflected throughout Catholic Apostolic theology and liturgical worship, and was in accord with both Roman Catholic and Eastern Churches' teaching, though not with that of the contemporary Established Churches of England and Scotland, and still less with that of the dissenting bodies. Its prominence is surprising in view of the clearly Protestant origins from which the body had sprung.

Cardale himself, the main driving force behind the liturgical and corresponding theological developments, had come into prominence as one of the investigators of the charismatic phenomena in Presbyterian Scotland and through his association with Irving's evangelical prayer and Bible-study meetings (see Ch. II, § 1). There was no suggestion at this time of any particular leaning towards or interest in 'catholic' theology or ceremonial on the part of any of those who were to become apostles, indeed quite the reverse. The remarkable liturgical knowledge, which Cardale and some of his associates clearly acquired and disseminated through their writings, arose from the need to provide rites for a body whose members had come from a variety of different Christian traditions, and which was consequently seen as needing the unifying momentum which only a centralized authority and authorized forms of worship could provide. The centralized authority was provided by the College of Apostles, completed in 1835; the authorized forms of worship were provided, first by the issue of a lithographed form for the celebration of the Eucharist and a suggested baptismal rite in 1838, and eventually by the various editions of *The Liturgy and Other Divine*

Offices of the Church, published over the period 1843 to 1880. The complicated ceremonial, designed to give visible expression to the many aspects of Catholic Apostolic liturgy and life, was developed almost half a century before the corresponding ceremonial developments of the Tractarians in the Anglican Church.

The introduction of these rites and their accompanying ceremonial meant, for many of the Catholic Apostolic congregations, a very significant change in ethos and a marked departure from existing practices: already, from 1836, it had been required that the Eucharist should be celebrated weekly rather than monthly—a highly significant change. As has been suggested earlier (see Ch. II, § 2) it is an indication of the extent to which the centralized authority of the apostles had been accepted that there was little opposition from the faithful, despite the Protestant background of the great majority and the fact that in the rites all earlier Presbyterian and dissenting elements, with which many of them would have been familiar, had been removed, altars gradually taking the place of prominence in churches previously taken by pulpits and reading desks. Indeed, in the main, the various liturgical forms were welcomed as providing the body with a distinct identity and bringing to an end the early period of liturgical disorder which had created problems for the effective presentation of any consistent sacramental theology.

The various liturgical rites which were introduced—and the Eucharist in particular—were intended to be in accord with Holy Scripture and to reflect all that was best in the various traditions explored by the apostles in their journeyings throughout Christendom (begun in 1838) and in their subsequent study of ancient liturgies and patristic sources, though they also had to give full expression to all the different aspects of the life and doctrine of the Catholic Apostolic body. The resulting Eucharistic rite was Roman in shape, Anglican in language, and Eastern in ethos—including a number of direct borrowings from Eastern Liturgies—whilst at the same time finding room for expression of the particular prophetic and eschatological emphases of Catholic Apostolic teaching. Despite the blending of these various strands, the result can fairly be described as cohesive: both experience and study of the rite reveal that it had a remarkable unity.

The teaching on sacrifice and on the Real Presence, which was essentially in accord with Eastern eucharistic theology, avoided the major historical Western controversies which had followed the

Reformation and which were to come into prominence within the Established Church following the publication of the *Tracts for the Times* (appearing over the period 1833 to 1841 and culminating in the notorious Tract xc: *Remarks on Certain Passages in the Thirty-Nine Articles*). This teaching was thoroughly biblical and patristic, yet the Catholic Apostolic Eucharist itself was notable for its comprehensiveness, the intercessions encompassing all the Christian Churches, their ministries and their faithful—a remarkable ecumenical achievement for its day.

The Eucharistic developments within the Catholic Apostolic body took place against a background stirring of social and political unrest, evidenced in many parts of Europe, which had the French Revolution as its starting point and which had stimulated the holding of the Albury Conferences. Yet at the same time, the age of romanticism was blossoming with its quest for beauty and its nostalgic yearnings after the past, and Victorian England was retaining a comparatively rigid structure of society with emphasis upon family life, a Christian (i.e. Protestant) upbringing, and filial and social loyalty and obedience. All this was reflected in the newly composed rites. Examination of them reveals that the contemporary social structure was reflected not only in the prayers but also in the strictly hierarchical nature of the ceremonial. Other aspects of Victorian culture and thought, such as the concept of the 'righteous war', can also be detected. If the length of the Liturgy was an Eastern characteristic, the lengthy phraseology of many of the prayers was typical of English nineteenth-century literary composition.

Although in the building of their places of worship the Catholic Apostolics employed a number of the same architects who were designing Anglican Victorian churches in the neo-Gothic style, such as Branden, Pearson, and Pugin, the interiors of their church buildings were designed to meet previously determined liturgical requirements (which for the larger congregations included space for a large muster of clergy) and to conform to their particular theological principles, which, for example, demanded stone altars and comparatively large tabernacles. This was in contrast to those Anglicans who, inspired by the 'ecclesiology' of the Cambridge Camden Society (founded in 1839 to promote neo-medievalism in church building),[109] started from a preconceived notion of what

[109] For an account of the Cambridge Camden Society see J. F. White, *The Cambridge Movement* (Cambridge: Cambridge University Press, 1962).

constituted a 'correct' church and adapted their arrangements for worship accordingly, one result being the increasing separation of the laity from the ceremonial taking place at the altar. Such a separation was not permitted in Catholic Apostolic churches, for which it was specifically required that there should be nothing 'which would in any way imply that the laity are spiritually excluded from the sacred precincts'.[110] It was to meet this requirement that the singers were not positioned in choir stalls between the sanctuary and the people, but were located in the nave.

However, in the matter of vestments and general church furnishings the Catholic Apostolics very largely conformed to the principles of the 'Gothic revival'. Cardale had disliked the cut-away Roman style of chasuble, stating that it was an appropriate symbol of the way in which the Roman Church had 'cut away Greeks on the right hand and Protestants on the left'.[111]

Although Cranmer had used some prayers from the Liturgy of St John Chrysostom and the Nonjurors had also looked Eastwards— though preferring the Clementine Liturgy (the Liturgy of the Eighth Book of *The Apostolic Constitutions*) and the Liturgy of St James (translated by Thomas Rattray in 1743)—there was little interest in Eastern rites in England until the period of the composition of the Catholic Apostolic Eucharist, though there had been Roman Catholic scholars on the Continent who had made compilations of Greek liturgical texts (for example Jacques Goar's *Euchologion* of 1647).

One aspect of liturgical research which developed during the nineteenth century was the quest for an 'Apostolic Liturgy', which in turn stimulated interest in the liturgies of the East, though this was a somewhat later phenomenon within the Tractarian Movement whose members were initially more interested in promoting the importance of the Eucharist *per se* and in the theory question of the apostolic succession and the validity of orders. Opinions were divided on whether or not such an Apostolic Liturgy could be discovered or constructed from surviving evidence. The construction of the new and unique Eucharistic rite of the Catholic Apostolic Church suggests that Cardale clearly belonged to those who thought that it could not. Nevertheless, it is clear that both he and other Catholic Apostolic writers on liturgical matters were seriously

---

[110] *Book of Regulations* (London: Strangeways, 1878), no. 796, p. 124.
[111] Letter, Cardale to Drummond, 19 Dec. 1846 (Northumberland collection).

concerned with patristic authority and that they looked liturgically Eastwards to a considerable extent at a time when this was the exception rather than the rule in Western theological circles, including those of the Anglican and Roman Catholic Churches. This Eastwards orientation is evidenced by both general and specific references to the Greek Fathers and to Eastern liturgies, and to the many direct borrowings from Eastern sources which can be found in the Catholic Apostolic rites, including their Eucharist.

In Cardale's *Readings* and in the other Catholic Apostolic writings from which extracts have been quoted above in this chapter, there were specific appeals to a number of Fathers as representing the authoritative Apostolic tradition of the Early Church. Thus, there were appeals to the writings of

St John Chrysostom (Cardale and Böhm),
St Cyril (Cardale and Böhm),
St Clement (Hughes and Böhm),
St Justin Martyr (Böhm),
St Augustine (Cardale),
St Gregory (Cardale),
St Epiphanios (Cardale),

as well as general appeals—for example, 'to the Fathers of the second and third centuries' (Böhm). There were also specific appeals to canons of both ecumenical and local councils (Cardale), to ancient Liturgies such as that of St James (Cardale and Böhm), and to contemporary Orthodox and Oriental Liturgies (Cardale and Hughes). Cardale compared in great detail the contemporary Roman Eucharistic rite with that of the Greek Church (almost invariably to the detriment of the former) in an analysis that was both historical and theological. The references to Eastern liturgies pre-date all the collections and translations which were to appear in England during the nineteenth century with the exception of William Palmer's *Origines Liturgicae* (in which discussion of Eastern liturgies was included), a copy of which existed at Albury and to which there was a specific reference by Cardale. Other collections and translations, such as those of Hammond, Swainson, Shann, Lady Lechmere, and Brightman, all date from the last quarter of the century, when the Tractarians' interest in Eastern liturgies began to develop, stimulated largely by the efforts of the Revd J. M. Neale in the 1860s. Cardale referred also to the eighteenth-century work by the Roman Catholic writer Renaudot, *Liturgiarum Orientalium Collectio*. It is clear, however, that he attempted, wherever possible, to turn to original sources. Thus, in his discussion of the text of the Creed (and specifically on the question of the omission, in the English Prayer Book, of the word 'Holy' from the attributes of the Church), he corrected the seventeenth-century translation by Bingham of the two Creeds of St Epiphanios by reference to the Greek text. Indeed, a significant number of references to Eastern liturgical texts in Catholic Apostolic writings quoted such texts in Greek, as indeed Roman liturgical texts were almost invariably quoted in Latin.

One of the most noteworthy aspects of Catholic Apostolic liturgical commentary is the highly developed typological interpretation of the Offices of Morning and Evening Prayer and of individual aspects of the Eucharist (presented in some detail in §§ 2 and 3 above). Although such interpretation was Biblical (e.g. it is to be found in the Epistle to the Hebrews), and the idea of Christian worship being antitypical of that of the Tabernacle is frequently to be found in writings of both East and West—in the East being especially initially associated with St Isidore of Pelusa, St John Chrysostom, and St Theodore of Mopsuestia—in no other Christian body has this kind of interpretation been so extensively developed.

The question therefore arises as to the extent to which such development originated from within the body—perhaps with Cardale himself. A clue is provided by references in his *Readings* to commentaries on the liturgy of St John Chrysostom by St Germanos (eighth century) and Nicholas Cabasilas (fourteenth century). In the latter, the idea is little more than touched on, though we do find the specific statement that 'The Old Testament . . . fulfilled in symbol what Christ has now ordained in actual fact',[112] together with the interpretation of the shedding of the blood of beasts as typical of the shedding of the blood of Christ on Calvary and an explanation of the typological significance of the Passover. It is in the former that we find a much more developed typological presentation. Thus, for example, St Germanos saw the table of manna as a type of the Holy Table upon which the unbloody and mystical sacrifice is offered; the evening lamb as a type of Christ's offering of his own body; the Holy of Holies as a type of the sanctuary; the whole burnt offering as a type of Christ's offering of Himself to the Father; Abraham's

---

[112] Nicholas Cabasilas, tr. J. M. Hussey and P. A. McNulty, *A Commentary on the Divine Liturgy* (London: SPCK, 1960), 38.

offering of a ram as a type of that part of the preparation performed at the Table of Prothesis which represents the slaying of the Lamb; and the taking of a live coal from the altar by one of the seraphim (Isa. 6: 6) as a type of the Christian priest taking the consecrated Lamb into his hands.[113] In the same work there is an interpretation of the censer, which though not typological in the same sense, nevertheless relates the various parts of the censer to Christ's human and divine natures, to baptism, and to the operation of the Holy Spirit.[114] Thus, there is to be found in St Germanos both the biblical concept of typology, relating persons and events of the Old Testament to the sacrifice of Christ, and direct typological relationships from the Old Testament to details of Eastern liturgy.

Both these aspects were to be extensively developed by Cardale in applying the typological principle to the construction of the Offices and to the interpretation of the various sections of the Eucharist. His justification for so doing was the claim that all worship is of divine origin and hence the Christian Offices must necessarily follow in detail the worship ordained under the Law, and the Eucharist (whose overall form was ordained by Christ Himself) must necessarily comprehend all the types though not being itself the antitype of any one particular type. Thus, whilst it may be suggested that the germ of Catholic Apostolic typology can be found in Holy Scripture, the Antiochene tradition, and the commentaries of Nicholas Cabasilas and (especially) St Germanos, the working out of much of the detail and the specific design of Offices to meet typological demands is a peculiar Catholic Apostolic phenomenon owing much to the efforts of Cardale himself, whose principles were subsequently followed by the various other members of that body who wrote on the interpretation of their liturgical worship. Further, Cardale was prepared to change the Eastern typological interpretation when he thought it necessary—compare, for example, his denial that the evening lamb can be the type of Christ with the typological interpretation of St Germanos (above).

Although the shape of the Catholic Apostolic Eucharist was (as already noted) Roman overall, and there were numerous direct borrowings from both Roman and Anglican liturgies, Anglican

---

[113] St Germanos of Constantinople, Greek text trans. P. Meyendorff, *On the Divine Liturgy* (New York, St Vladimir's Press, 1984), 59, 61, 63, 71, 85, 95–6.
[114] Ibid. 79, 81.

borrowings being especially prominent in the Collects, the inclusion of material taken from Eastern sources, together with ceremonial corresponding to that of the Liturgy of St John Chrysostom and the many references to Eastern liturgies in Cardale's *Readings*, are of considerable significance and help to give credence to the claim that the Catholic Apostolic rite had an Eastern rather than a Western ethos. The direct borrowings from Eastern sources were not confined to the Eucharist, though it is here that they are most noticeable. (In considering the Eucharist, it is reasonable to exclude items common to East and West, together with the numerous direct quotations from Scripture which coincide with similar quotations in Eastern rites—of which there are a number.) In the Eucharist, such borrowings were to be found in the penitential material, in the Prayers of Oblation before and after the Consecration, in the Great Intercession, in the Invocation of the Holy Spirit, in the declaration 'Holy things for holy persons' and the congregational response, and in a number of the anthems prescribed for particular Sundays or feasts and Eucharistic hymns translated from ancient sources.

Of particular importance, when considering Eastern influences, is the insistence of the Catholic Apostolics on the necessity for the inclusion of the Epiclesis for effecting the consecration of the elements. Without it, it was claimed that the sacrifice offered would be bread and wine only. All this was in accord with their emphasis upon the Holy Spirit as the source of all revelation, spiritual gifts and blessings, an emphasis which was also seen in Eastern Christianity and for which it was specifically commended. The fact that the Epiclesis was said twice would appear to result from an attempt to effect a compromise between East and West, since each Epiclesis was placed before the corresponding 'words of institution'. Both the positioning and the repetition of the Epiclesis were variations from common Eastern practice and also from the Western precedents of Laud's Liturgy for Scotland (*The Booke of Common Prayer*, 1637) and the Nonjurors' Liturgy of 1718, where, as in the East, the Epiclesis was placed after the words of institution. However, care was taken to avoid the possibility of the peculiarly Western argument as to precisely *when* the consecration of the elements took place; indeed, the force of the consecratory action was not regarded as completed until all those, living and departed, for whom the Sacrifice was being offered had been commemorated—that is, until the end of the prayers of the Great Intercession—though the second

Prayer of Oblation was entitled 'Prayer of Oblation *after* the Consecration' (italics not in the original).

Amongst the many other Eastern aspects of the Catholic Apostolic Eucharist and its associated theology, the following deserve mention here either because Cardale or other writers expressly drew attention to them as following Eastern practice, or because the theology itself is clearly Eastern rather than Western.

The two 'entrances'—at the Gloria in Excelsis and at the Introit—directly corresponded to the lesser and great entrances of the Liturgy of St John Chrysostom, as Cardale pointed out: at the former the Gospels were placed on the altar and at the latter the elements were taken from the table of prothesis to the altar as in the Greek rite.

The clear distinction between alms and oblations, together with the rubric forbidding the alms to be placed on the altar, were a departure from contemporary Western Protestant practice and understanding and in conformity with the East.

The inclusiveness of the anaphora was markedly Eastern with its lengthy recital in the Preface of God's mighty acts from Creation to Pentecost, its direct reference to the Parousia in the Prayer of Oblation after the Consecration, and the comprehensiveness of the Great Intercession. (It should also be noted that the justification given for prayers for the dead in the Commemoration of the Departed—which follows an Eastern pattern—was by reference to the Communion of Saints and not to 2 Macc. 12: 44.)

The whole orientation of the service was heavenward—a looking to a sharing on earth in the heavenly offering of His Sacrifice to the Father by our Great High Priest, rather than a looking back to past events on earth, though these past events were indeed recalled in the Preface.

In the teaching about the effect of the Consecration and on the Real Presence, the emphasis of the theology reflected the East and not, certainly, the contemporary West, either Roman or Protestant.

The positioning of the Lord's Prayer immediately between the Thrice-Holy and the Consecration, though not corresponding to its position in the Greek rite, was intended to emphasize that references to the 'kingdom' and to 'daily bread' could have a eucharistic interpretation—a concept to be found in Eastern commentaries.

Cardale and other Catholic Apostolic writers emphasized the necessity for the Holy Gifts to be received by the faithful, including children, quoting St John Chrysostom and early Church practice as the authority for the latter, and the Eastern Orthodox were particularly commended for having maintained this ancient and important tradition, largely abandoned in the West from medieval times (though persisting in the Gallican Church until the thirteenth century).

The Western Roman practice of withholding the chalice from the laity was specifically condemned, the Holy Gifts being invariably administered and reserved in both kinds.

The concept of 'low' celebrations was rejected; these were said to imply the mistaken idea of the Eucharist as the antitype of the daily sacrifices under the Law.

In any one church, there was only the one Eucharist on the Lord's Day—multiple celebrations being condemned as undermining the unity of the faithful. (Those who, for good reason, could not attend the Eucharist could receive Holy Communion from the reserved sacrament at one of the later services in the day.) Again, there was to be only one chief celebrant, normally the Angel-in-charge, signifying Christ as the *one* High Priest. The modern idea of concelebration where the consecration prayer is said by a number of clergy would have been as foreign to the Catholic Apostolic understanding of the Eucharist as it is to that of the Eastern Churches.

There was the insistence that, for all Godward actions, the celebrant must face East—in this case a departure from the contemporary Protestant practice.

The use of the Presanctified Liturgy on Good Friday and the theme of 'the Burial of Christ' for a Eucharist on Easter Eve are highly suggestive of Eastern influence, though they were to be found also in contemporary Roman Catholic practice.

A further and specific example of Eastern borrowing is provided by the Anthem and one of the Collects for Easter Eve. These emphasized Christ's descent into hell in order to 'preach to the spirits in prison', an aspect of the events of the Passion and Resurrection which receives considerable emphasis in the corresponding Greek rite. It had been the subject of some controversy: Cardale had been accused of introducing new and strange doctrine, and in response he made specific appeal to Greek sources:

The Anthem says 'When Thou hadst humbled Thyself to death: Jesu, Thou Life immortal, With the glory of Thy Godhead; Thou didst shine

into the obscure. Thou didst preach unto the spirits in prison'—so the
Collect. . . . I can say that while the Body of Christ was in the Tomb,
while His Spirit was in Hades, He was yet present in the unsearchable
mystery of His Godhead both with His Body in the tomb and with His
Spirit in Hades and also with the Father and the Holy Ghost upon the
throne, filling all things and uncircumscribed by any—The passage is an
exact and literal translation from the Greek.[115]

Overall, despite its Roman form and Anglican language, including
direct borrowings from both these traditions, it is fair to claim that
both in theology and in ethos the Catholic Apostolic Eucharist
reflects at least as much of Eastern as of Western Christianity.

It is, however, of special importance to consider also those aspects
of the Catholic Apostolic liturgy, together with its underlying
theology, which can be regarded as being peculiar to that body. The
highly developed typological understanding of the Eucharist, the
typological design of the Offices of Morning and Evening Prayer,
and the proposition of the Holy Gifts at those Offices together with
the linking role of the intercessions (all of which have been discussed
earlier) were clearly peculiarities of the Catholic Apostolic Church.
Since one of the intentions behind the composition of the various
rites was the need to reflect the whole life and witness of the body, it
is not surprising that throughout their liturgy there were frequent
eschatological references, including the use of apocalyptic symbolism,
though there was nowhere any attempt to suggest an apocalyptic
'timetable'. There was an awareness of the contemporary age as
being a part of the 'last times', since this expression occurs in a
number of places; there was also a considerable number of direct
references to the Parousia and the general resurrection, as might be
expected in a body who saw one of its chief roles to have been the
stimulation, within the Church Catholic, of a revival of the ancient
Christian hope for the Second Coming of Christ. (The eschatological
aspects of the liturgy will be further considered in Ch. V, § 7).

References to eschatology and to the restoration of the ministry
of apostles, together with the prophets, evangelists, pastors, and
teachers labouring with them, occurred in prayers of thanksgiving
and in intercessions for the living and departed, yet their inclusion
was entirely natural—they did not interrupt the natural liturgical
flow, nor were they so frequent as to suggest imbalance in the

[115] Letter, Cardale to Drummond, 23 Mar. 1847 (Northumberland collection).

liturgical rites. The special role given to a visiting apostle at the Eucharist (presiding in the sanctuary and pronouncing the absolution, blessing of the homilist, and the benediction before communion) was, of course, peculiar to the body.

The 'ecumenical' comprehensiveness of the commemoration of the living was, for its day, a remarkable aspect of the Great Intercession at the Eucharist, reflecting the Catholic Apostolic acceptance of all the baptized as members of the universal Church, and of all bishops of the Church Catholic (i.e. the Eastern and Oriental Orthodox, Roman Catholic, Anglican, and Lutheran episcopates) as chief pastors of their faithful, together with the ministry of priests and deacons in the various Churches. Prayer for 'unity' and references to 'one body' also reflected a remarkable ecumenism. At the same time there was a solemn awareness of the 'low estate' of the Church Catholic, of schism, heresy, superstition and will-worship, which was reflected in the intercessions offered during both the Eucharist and the Offices.

Quite unique, though entirely in accordance with the origins of the body, was the place allocated at the time of Communion for exercise of the gift of prophecy, though the strict regulation of this exercise reflected the ascendancy which the apostles and angels had gained over the charismatics in the Church. Nevertheless, the prophets had clearly been active in the decisions which led to the compilation of the rites, since, in commentaries upon them, though more particularly in connection with the Offices, the phrase 'the Lord having directed' is encountered from time to time.

The restriction of the offering of incense to the representation of ascending prayer at the intercessions (i.e. the refusal to permit the censing of people or objects) does not accord with either Eastern or Western usage, and the detailed interpretation of the constituent parts of the incense appears to be peculiar to the body. The reason for such restriction can be inferred to have been that prayer is a Godward activity and that it is therefore inappropriate to direct the censing manwards, though this is not explicitly stated by Cardale.

The particular use of colours for vestments was again peculiar to the body, being reserved for indication of the fourfold ministry, apart from the requirement that white should be used for the Eucharist (symbolizing the Resurrection) and that the angels should wear purple copes (symbolizing authority).

A final peculiarity which should be noted is the arrangement of the ecclesiastical year. This has not been discussed in the earlier sections of this chapter, but deserves mention here because it encompassed further reflections of particular Catholic Apostolic insights. In effect, the Catholic Apostolic liturgical year was a simplification of the traditional years observed in the East and in the Roman Catholic and Anglican Churches, together with some additions required by the history and special witness of that body. Its overall pattern was designed around the four principal periods of Easter, Pentecost, Advent, and Christmas, typified respectively by the Jewish Feasts of Pentecost, Weeks, Trumpets, and Ingatherings.

In the Paschal cycle, Lent was given the old title of 'Quadragesima' and ferial Sundays were reckoned 'after Pentecost'. In addition to Easter Day itself, special provision was made for Thursday, Friday, and Saturday of Holy Week, for Easter Monday, Ascension Day, and the Monday and Tuesday following Pentecost. The Holy Week services specifically avoided any dramatic re-enactments of the events of the Passion, reflecting what was considered to be the impropriety of directing the attention primarily to past historical events during worship in the sanctuary. The Monday and Tuesday after Pentecost commemorated respectively the consecration of chrism by the apostles and the division of Christendom into twelve tribes. The particular provision for the Pentecostal period reflected the Catholic Apostolic emphasis on the work of the Holy Spirit.

In the monthly cycle (corresponding to the Greek *Menaia*), special provision was made for Christmas Eve and Christmas Day, Circumcision, Presentation in the Temple, the anniversary of the 'separation' of the apostles (14 July), All Angels, and All Saints, though there were occasional and temporary variations outside England. Sundays were reckoned after Circumcision and not after Epiphany, as the latter was not included as a feast—the Wise Men being regarded (as in the Eastern Churches) as belonging to Christmas. Thus, most of the chief feasts of Our Lord were retained, whilst the commemoration of individual Saints on special days was rejected—the collective feast of All Saints being regarded as sufficient. This, together with the refusal to permit representations of past events in the history of the Christian Church except at the West end of churches, again reflected the desire to ensure that all that took place in the sanctuary was directed heavenwards and towards the kingdom which was to be brought in at the Parousia, not to past events on earth.

A further special provision allowed for intercession for vocations to the ministry during the 'Three Seasons' before Christmas, Easter, and Pentecost respectively. The provision for festivals included collects, anthems after the Epistle and Communion anthems, additions to the Preface and the Prayer of Oblation after the Consecration, special apostolic benedictions, and post-Communion prayers. The special anthems made extensive use of Scriptural quotations, though also drawing from Eastern Christian sources. The majority of the collects were taken from the *Book of Common Prayer*, though some were slightly modified. (General collects were not provided for each Sunday but were seasonal, except for a period of time in Scotland, North Germany, and Switzerland.) It is amongst the provision for special occasions that some of the most beautiful liturgical compositions were to be found.

In its final form, the whole arrangement for worship was a remarkably consistent one, combining traditional Church commemorations with Catholic Apostolic priorities. It had a remarkable coherence which indicates the very considerable liturgical skill of its chief architect.

If the Catholic Apostolics were willing to adopt and adapt liturgical material from Roman Catholic and Anglican sources, they were at the same time anxious to guard against importing ceremonies or doctrines which they considered not to have the clear support of Scripture and ancient tradition. They were adamant that no ceremony should be introduced for its own sake or merely to satisfy the whims or vanities of individuals, but equally critical of the absence of traditional symbolism where its presence was considered appropriate—for example, the failure of contemporary Anglicans to mix water with the wine in the chalice. Although their liturgical ceremonial was highly developed, every action and every object used had its particular meaning, which was required to be thoroughly understood by all the faithful. They were as critical of what they perceived as unnecessary or unscriptural symbolism in the Roman Catholic Church as of the almost complete lack of symbolism in Protestantism.

The interiors of their church buildings tended to have a somewhat austere appearance even when compared with many contemporary Anglican churches, despite the tabernacle on the altar, the two standing oil lamps in the sanctuary, the seven lamps hanging in the upper choir, and the many special stalls for the angel and clergy.

This austerity was in part due to their opposition to memorials and other comparable wall ornamentation; they were critical of their presence in many Anglican churches, and also of the fairly common practice of displaying the Ten Commandments and the Lord's Prayer on East walls at either side of the altar. They also singled out as inappropriate the Anglican clergy choir dress, condemning the use of the surplice with scarf and hood—academic hoods, in particular, were considered as introducing an unacceptable secular element which contradicted the principle of covering all secular clothing with the cassock. Here again, there was a consistency of principle and practice.

In regard to preaching, a clear distinction was made between homilies or ministries, which were an integral part of liturgical worship, and sermons or addresses which were appended to Sunday evening services though kept distinct from the service itself. As has already been noted, the homily at the Eucharist was restricted to a ten-minute exposition of the Epistle or Gospel for the day; the choice of subject for the (candlestick) ministries at the Offices was reserved to the angel in the morning, and this choice held in the evening when other ministers were required to reflect on the morning ministry previously delivered. There was thus a very tight control on preaching within liturgical worship, which reflected a strong reaction against the emphasis on preaching in the Protestant Churches (though the sermons, often given by evangelists, outside the confines of liturgy could be long—sometimes lasting for an hour or more). Such a control on preaching represented a significant change from the 'embryonic' days of Irving.

There was no comparable restriction on liturgical worship; indeed, there was specific condemnation of both the Roman Catholic and Anglican Churches for what were regarded as their highly abbreviated Eucharistic rites from which much of the liturgical wealth of the past had been removed. Thus, particularly censured was the Anglican practice of administering the Communion immediately following the Consecration of the Holy Gifts with the consequent omission of intercessions for the living and departed. It was, no doubt, because of the view that both Roman Catholic and Anglican Eucharists represented significant curtailments of ancient liturgical practice that specific interest was directed by Cardale towards the liturgies of the East.

The Catholic Apostolic understanding of the Real Presence,

Liturgy

together with the detailed explanation of the reasons for the repudiation of the Roman Catholic doctrine of transubstantiation, as developed by the Schoolmen and defined as *de fide* at the Fourth Lateran Council (1215), was yet a further example of the extent to which Cardale and his colleagues had studied the Eucharistic doctrines of both East and West. The underlying reasoning included, as has been seen, the view that the Aristotelian concept of substance was inappropriate for application in spiritual matters, though useful for abstract secular argument—no philosophy of man could encompass the mysteries of God. In the teaching on the Real Presence, Aristotelian 'substance' and 'accidents' were replaced respectively by 'spiritual reality' and 'sensible qualities'; it was precisely the *spiritual* nature of the Presence that made it *real*. Such a viewpoint was Platonic rather than Aristotelian, and was entirely in accord with the Patristic teaching from which the Schoolmen had departed; it also reflected and still reflects the eucharistic theology of the Eastern Churches. Many of the Tractarians were to adopt a similar understanding of the Real Presence, though, later, the Anglican 'Anglo-Catholics' tended more and more to accept the doctrines of Rome.

The extent to which there was cross-fertilization between the Tractarians and the Catholic Apostolics naturally presents itself here, but the answer must be that it was minimal. A number of Anglican Tractarians joined the Catholic Apostolic ministry (and a few accepted 'sealing' by the apostles), but the reason seems often to have been centred around a desire for freedom from the legal restrictions which bound the Established Church, and, by the time they came to this decision, Catholic Apostolic liturgical worship and Eucharistic theology had been formulated. A study of the correspondence between the Tractarians and the Catholic Apostolics, largely carried out through the medium of *The Old Church Porch* and the published replies to the allegations made there, reveals that it was devoted almost exclusively to two topics: the validity of the orders of the Catholic Apostolic ministry and, in particular, the credentials of the apostles upon whom the succession of that ministry depended, together with their claim to universal jurisdiction; and the question of whether the charismatic phenomena, experienced in the early days and continued (though in a controlled manner) through the ministry of the ordained prophets, was or could be the activity of the Holy Spirit—two topics not entirely unrelated. It would appear that concentration on these two topics effectively prevented theological dialogue on eucharistic and other doctrine. The possible contribution of the Catholic Apostolics in the early days of the Tractarian Movement to a deeper appreciation in the West of the Eucharist as being primarily a presentation on earth of Christ's perpetual offering at the Heavenly altar, rather than a re-enactment or commemoration of historical events, was thus to be lost.

Another aspect of the Catholic Apostolic liturgy deserving of notice was the importance which had been attached to achieving a balance between theological expression and the corresponding devotional response of the faithful. This balance was to be found both in the Offices and in the Eucharist, and was exemplified by the choice of opening words (at the entrance of the clergy) for the Offices:

O come let us worship and bow down: let us kneel before the Lord our Maker. For He is the Lord our God . . .

Again, in the Prayer of Dedication, the faithful are called to present themselves as 'a living sacrifice' and to dedicate themselves wholly to God's service precisely because of the very nature of God as the One to Whom praise, exaltation, and thanksgiving are due, and Who is good and merciful. The Proposition of the Sacrament was in itself an objective act, considered necessary before the prayers and supplications of the people could be offered. Then, later, in the Great Intercession, there was a particularly noticeable alternation of objective statement and subjective response.

The same kind of balance (sometimes even a tension) occurred in the Eucharist both in its distinct parts and in the rite overall. Cardale made it clear that expression of doctrine was an important objective, yet, at the same time, he was particularly attentive to the need for the worshippers to feel 'included' throughout. This was made clear in many ways, amongst which were the reminders of the spiritual unity of the laity with the clergy, of which there was a first example as soon as the faithful entered the church—the application of holy water at the door being linked with the priestly washing of hands in preparation for the Eucharistic celebration. After the Confession and Absolution, the Prayer of Access specifically included the faithful as offerers of sacrifice, an inclusion which was cemented by the Invitatory and Response. In the first Prayer of Oblation, both objective statement and subjective response were present: first, there

was reference to the particular reasons for the offering of bread and
wine, then this was followed by the self-offering of the people as 'a
living sacrifice'. The second Prayer of Oblation began with the
subjective reference, 'we Thy servants'; it then referred objectively
to the 'Sacrifice' of Christ (note the capital 'S'), next to the 'sacrifice'
presented by the faithful (note the lower-case 's', and that this was
'presented' rather than 'offered'), continuing with the petition that
they should be accepted on the Heavenly altar, and concluding with
a request that the benefits of the Passion should be granted to all
God's people—the same kind of alternation which was to be found
in the Intercession at the Offices and, indeed, in many places
elsewhere.

The double Epiclesis emphasized the objective Real Presence, yet,
at the same time, the inclusion on each occasion of the phrase 'make
it *unto us*' (italics not in the original) is distinctly subjective—an
example of the tension between the two aspects referred to above.
Nevertheless the latter was clearly not intended to imply that only
believers could receive the Body and Blood of Christ, as was made
clear by the view taken in the debate on what was received by the
wicked (though carnally and not spiritually)—which certainly
implies an objective view of the Real Presence. The idea that the
consecratory action was not complete until the commemorations had
been concluded is a further example, in this case one which sought to
catch up into the activity of the Holy Spirit all those for whom prayer
was offered. These, and other examples which could be quoted,
indicate the deliberate care which had been taken by Cardale in the
compilation of the Catholic Apostolic liturgy to steer a middle course
between purely objective and purely subjective aspects of worship—
remarkable for a man with neither liturgical nor psychological
training.

For the historian, though not necessarily for the theologian, the
importance of any particular liturgy must necessarily be associated
with its subsequent influence. Unfortunately, despite its many
remarkable qualities, the Catholic Apostolic liturgy was to have very
little influence on liturgical development and none within the
'mainstream' Churches apart from some general influence within
German Lutheranism. Its greatest influences were to be upon the
'Mercersburg Liturgy' of the American German Reformed Church,[116]

[116] See J. M. Maxwell, *Worship and Reformed Theology* (Pittsburgh: Pickwick
Press, 1976), esp. App. IV, pp. 435–7.

and the 'Euchologion' (*sic*) of the small body at present calling itself 'the Orthodox Church of the British Isles',[117] in both of which the Catholic Apostolic Eucharistic structure and actual borrowings are to be found. Nevertheless, some distinct influences from the Catholic Apostolic rite and the accompanying Eucharistic theology can be detected elsewhere.

The work of the Church Service Society of the Church of Scotland, which was formed in 1865 (with a later parallel in the United States), reveals significant Catholic Apostolic influence. A number of its members are known to have been 'sealed', most notably the influential Dr John McLeod (known as 'the high priest of Govan'), who was the author of a private Scottish Eucharistic rite. The Society's *Euchologion, a Book of Common Order* (1867) included some distinct Catholic Apostolic features, traceable through subsequent editions to the Scottish *Book of Common Order* of 1940. *Euchologion* was a remarkable work for its time—particularly the first edition, for later editions were considerably amended. It provoked widespread hostility amongst the Scottish Presbyterian laity, since it involved a considerable departure from established custom by providing forms for the various offices and sacraments of the Church of Scotland together with a lectionary.[118] In the last half-century, Irving has gone through a process of rehabilitation within the Church which once tried him for heresy, and it is possible to see in a renewed awareness of the Communion of Saints within the Church of Scotland the influence not only of Irving but also of the Church in which he was for a very short time in episcopal orders.[119]

---

[117] The 'Orthodox Church of the British Isles' has no canonical relations with the Eastern Orthodox Churches, but is a so-called 'vagantes' body, at various times known as 'The Catholicate of the West', 'The United Orthodox Catholic Rite', 'The Celtic Catholic Church', 'The Metropolis of Glastonbury' and (to the annoyance of the Catholic Apostolic Church Trustees) 'The Catholic Apostolic Church'. Its *Euchologion* was published in 1970 and is largely the work of Hugh George de Willmott Newman (who styled himself as 'Mar Georgius, Patriarch of Glastonbury'), a former acolyte in the Catholic Apostolic Church at Paddington, London. He is said to have claimed to have 'Catholic Apostolic orders' (amongst many other 'lines of apostolic succession') —a manifest impossibility since these could not have been conveyed after 1901. See H. R. T. Brandreth, *Episcopi Vagantes and the Anglican Church* (London: SPCK, 1947) (corrected edn. 1961); P. Anson, *Bishops at Large* (London: Faber, 1964).

[118] For an account of the Church Service society, see A. L. Drummond and J. Bulloch, *The Church in Victorian Scotland 1843–1874* (Edinburgh: St Andrew Press, 1975), 197–200.

[119] See *Report of the Edinburgh Conference* (1937), 16 (quoted in P. E. Shaw, *The Catholic Apostolic Church* (New York: King's Crown Press, 1946), 242).

On the Continent of Europe, the Catholic Apostolics had for some time during the nineteenth century a considerable influence within German Lutheranism, due to the membership of the Lutheran Church which many of them were able and, indeed, chose to retain and to the interest of Lutheran liturgical students in the works of Heinrich Thiersch in particular.[120] Influence on the Continent can also be found within the French Reformed Church, notably with Eugene Bersier in the 1880s, though this was limited to his own congregation and those directly associated with him. In England, traces of the Catholic Apostolic Eucharist can be found in W. E. Orchard's *Divine Services* (1919), the *Free Church Book of Common Prayer* (1929), and the *Divine Worship* of the Methodists (1935).

Such influences as the Catholic Apostolic Eucharistic rite had, however, amounts to very little in terms of the important liturgical developments which have taken place in the West over the past century. The reason for this general lack of influence must be the almost total ignorance of the Catholic Apostolic Eucharistic rite on the part of Western liturgical scholars, despite one Anglican writer on the Oxford Movement admitting that, both doctrinally and liturgically, the Catholic Apostolics were in certain respects superior to the Tractarians.[121] It is thus, perhaps, a matter of some concern that their Eucharistic rite (of which the same writer says: 'Their Liturgy is incomparable. Its beauty and form pale the richest revision of the Book of Common Prayer into insignificance')[122] should have remained for so long in almost total obscurity outside the confines of the Catholic Apostolic body.

Cardale's *Readings* is an outstanding work of liturgical theology; indeed, one of the most comprehensive liturgical commentaries ever to have been written, and its relevance is by no means confined to the rites of which he was the chief architect. It is, however, an extremely rare publication whose circulation was intended to be confined to Catholic Apostolic Church members and which few outside the body have therefore had the opportunity to study. Whilst this diminishes the historical importance of the work and the Eucharistic rite

---

[120] See D. H. Tripp, 'The Liturgy of the Catholic Apostolic Church', *Scottish Jour. Theol.*, 22 (1969), 437–54, in which the influence on Friedrich Heiler (1892–1967) and his associates is stressed (p. 450). See also R. F. Edel, *Auf dem Weg zur Vollendung der Kirche Jesu Christi* (Marburg: Oekumenischer Verlag, 1971), in which there is extensive discussion of the work and influence on Heinrich Thiersch.

[121] D. Morse-Boycott, *They Shine Like Stars* (London: Skeffington, 1947), 27.

[122] Ibid. 307–8.

associated with it, it cannot diminish their undoubted extraordinary qualities, amongst which, as has been suggested above, is a remarkable ecumenical and psychological comprehensiveness, together with a fusion of Western form and Eastern theology, which avoided the major Western theological controversies and which might have contributed much to Western liturgical development had its context been less unusual and controversial.

V

Eschatology

1. PRELIMINARY GENERAL REMARKS

THE Catholic Apostolic Catechism ended with the following question and answer:

Q. . . . what is the ultimate end of all services, sacraments, and ministries of the Church?

A. That we and all Christian people may be made perfect in holiness, and be prepared in one Body for the appearing of our Lord Jesus Christ; when He shall be revealed from heaven in like manner as He went up, and the dead in Christ shall be raised, and we which are alive and remain to His coming shall be caught up together with them in the clouds to meet the Lord in the air; and so shall we ever be with the Lord. And in this hope I say, 'Amen. Even so, come, Lord Jesus.'[1]

Such an apocalyptic vision was the context within which the Christian Faith was initially formed and first developed:

Each major tenet of primitive Christian belief must be understood in this apocalyptic context.[2]

Eschatology—teaching concerning the last times—is scriptural, apostolic, and patristic and has always had its place in Christian belief, though the emphasis given to it has varied from one period of Christian history to another, and its precise content has frequently been a topic for ongoing debate or even open battle within the Church, at times leading to schism.

The answer required to the catechetical question above is profoundly scriptural, containing a substantial quote from 1 Thessalonians 4: 16–17, and concluding with part of Apocalypse 22: 20. Indeed, much of New Testament teaching resounds with the

---

[1] *The Catechism* (n.p., Whittingham and Griggs, n.d.), 31–2.
[2] J. Pelikan, *The Christian Tradition*, i. *The Emergence of the Catholic Tradition* (Chicago: University of Chicago Press, 1971), 123.

hope of the Second Advent of Christ and with references to the 'last times'. Eschatological material is to be found in the Gospels, both in many of the parables and in Christ's own teaching on the final judgement (Matt. 25) and on the signs of the end times (Matt. 24 and Mark 13), in the promise of His return made to the witnesses of His Ascension (Acts 1), in St Paul's Epistles (esp. 1 Cor. 15 and 1 Thess. 4), and in the bulk of the Apocalypse (chs. 4 to 22). It is, however, especially to the Apocalypse and (in the Old Testament) to the book of Daniel that Christians of many ages have turned in seeking for eschatological interpretations of contemporary crises and prophetic revelations of the future. An important aspect of both these books is that they can be seen as providing a chronology of eschatological events.

Often associated with the adventist hope has been belief in a coming reign of Christ together with his saints, which is to take place on earth for a thousand years. This concept of a 'millennium' can be found in chapter 20: 1–10 of the Apocalypse, where it is associated with two resurrections: a ressurrection of those who will reign on earth with Christ, and, after the millennium and a period of renewed activity of evil until Satan is finally destroyed, the general resurrection with the final judgement. Although this is the only reference in the New Testament to a millennium, it has often captured the imagination of Christians, especially in times of calamity and persecution.

Jewish Apocalyptic

Faith in the imminence of a Messianic age as a reaction to persecution was also a feature of Jewish apocalyptic.[3] Such material was written in times of crisis to proclaim a message of hope, though it has been claimed that it was primarily 'directed to the lower strata of the Jewish population as a form of nationalist propaganda'.[4] A notable example is to be found in Daniel 7, the earliest of such works, composed in the second century BC at the time of the Maccabean revolt against the Seleucid monarch, Antiochus IV Epiphanes, who had attempted to suppress all Jewish religious

[3] For an extensive presentation of Jewish apocalyptic, see D. S. Russell, *The Method and Message of Jewish Apocalyptic: 200 BC–AD 100* (London: SCM Press, 1964).
[4] N. Cohn, *The Pursuit of the Millennium* (London: Temple Smith, 1970), 20.

observances. Many of the concepts which were to become features of Christian apocalyptic are to be found in this passage of Daniel: the division of world history into symbolic ages, the four beasts, the ten hours, and the coming of 'one like the son of man' to establish an everlasting kingdom to be possessed by the 'saints of the Most High'.

There was, however, throughout the subsequent apocalyptic literature a tension between the traditional 'political' Jewish kingdom to be established in this world according to prophetic expectation and the other-worldly, eternal, and universal kingdom of apocalyptic visionaries. The idea of a temporary Messianic kingdom on earth, preceding the heavenly kingdom, made its appearance in an attempt to resolve this tension, though it was not invariably supposed to last for a thousand years.

Cohn summarizes the central theme of Jewish apocalyptic as follows:

> The world is dominated by an evil, tyrannous power of boundless destructiveness—a power moreover which is imagined not as simply human but as demonic. The tyranny of that power will become more and more outrageous, the sufferings of its victims more and more intolerable—until suddenly the hour will strike when the Saints of God are able to rise up and overthrow it. Then the saints themselves, the chosen, holy people who hitherto have groaned under the oppressor's heel, shall in their turn inherit dominion over the whole earth. This will be the culmination of history; the kingdom of the Saints will not only surpass in glory all previous kingdoms, it will have no successors.[5]

Much of the symbolism and content of this Jewish apocalyptic, including the millennial kingdom, was taken over by the Christian Church, though with the crucial difference that Jesus, as Messiah, was now seen as the focal point of the culmination of human history. However, in the Christian apocalyptic, there was a greater emphasis on a programmic series of events preceding the end (see, e.g., Apoc. 6–9, 16–18). This made it possible during the period of the persecutions for it to become commonplace to interpret the ten-horned beast of Daniel and the Apocalypse, the 'last' world-power, as being the Roman Empire.

---

[5] Cohn, *The Pursuit of the Millennium*, 21.

The Patristic Period

In the immediate post-apostolic period millenarianism (chiliasm) was an acceptable though never obligatory Christian belief and it can be found in the writings of a number of the early Fathers, most notably Papias, Justin Martyr, Tertullian, and Irenaeus. Its chief features were usually that the millennial kingdom would be miraculous, collective, total, and terrestrial, that it was imminent, and that it would precede the ultimate and eternal heavenly kingdom. However, such teachings, particularly in their extreme forms—sometimes including crude descriptions of eating, drinking, and lechery in the millennial kingdom—were also to become a feature of heretical groups, such as the Montanists, the Ebionites, and the followers of Apollinarius, and in 381 the Second Ecumenical Council (Constantinople I) condemned the millenarian teaching of Apollinarius together with his Christology,[6] and introduced into the Creed the words, 'and His Kingdom shall have no end'. This was not, however, intended to lessen the Christian hope or expectation of the Second Advent, but inevitably, as the years passed by without that Advent taking place, alternative and less 'urgent' interpretations of the relevant scriptural passages were found.

The acceptance of Christianity by Constantine the Great as the state religion and the setting up of Constantinople as the capital city of the Empire in 330 had, however, diverted Christian expectations and hopes away from Christ's future return and given added impetus to new ways of interpreting earlier Christian eschatological teaching, a process which was to culminate in Augustine's largely allegorical interpretations of the Apocalypse.[7] A millenarian eschatology was no longer a practical requirement.

Augustine also taught that the millennial reign of Christ was the period of the Christian Church, and that the first death and resurrection was the experience of Christian baptism. For him, the only literal resurrection was that which immediately precedes the Last Judgement.[8] This has very largely been adopted as the continuing

[6] Apollinarius, Bishop of Laodicea, taught that the human nature of Christ was incomplete. Accepting the tripartite composition of human nature—body, soul, and spirit—he affirmed that in Christ only the body and soul were human, the human spirit being replaced by the divine Logos.

[7] For an account of the transformation of the early apocalyptic vision of the Church, see Pelikan, *The Christian Tradition*, i. 123–32.

[8] Augustine, *The City of God*, 20. 7–9.

view of 'mainstream' Christianity, though there have been many occasions when such allegorical interpretations have been challenged by those who would wish to re-establish the importance of the hope of an imminent return of Christ.

The Middle Ages and the Reformation

During the Middle Ages, charismatic groups—often with millennarian beliefs—arose amongst the oppressed peasantry, especially during times of war, plagues, and famine, and other periods of a breakdown of the traditional ways of life. Mystical anarchists, with the Bible as their textbook, urged the overthrow of authority and the abolishing of private property, thus establishing what was to be a continuing relationship between certain kinds of millenarianism and social revolution. The revolts of these charismatic groups were directed against both secular and religious institutions, and the response of both Church and State was invariably harsh. The Church taught that the path towards God was one of repentance and humility, not the improvement of worldly lot—though many of those proclaiming such teaching failed to practise what they preached. Often, such groups were violently anti-Jewish—for example the revolutionary flagellants of the fourteenth century.[9]

With the Reformation came a revived interest in the Apocalypse, though Luther had originally rejected the book as being neither apostolic nor prophetic. Later he was to reverse that view and to believe that it possessed authentic prophetic content, and thus to use it for interpreting history, though he regarded the millennium as past, the future holding only an increase in evil until its final destruction at Armageddon. He was also to identify Antichrist with the Pope—a popular practice with many later Protestant millenarian groups. By contrast, Calvinistic and reformed teaching tended to the view that the Kingdom on earth was still in the future and would be effected by the efforts of the elect, Christ's Second Advent taking place only after a long period of gradual improvement.

It was Luther's teaching which had the greater influence on immediately subsequent revolutionary Protestant apocalyptic, such as that of the militant Anabaptists, though they often adopted programmes which were directed as much against the Lutheran

[9] See Cohn, *The Pursuit of the Millennium*, 136–41.

Reformation as against Roman Catholicism and which saw the millennium as a future event dependent upon imminent divine intervention. Once the first Reformers had successfully challenged the power of the Church of Rome through appeal to the Bible, the way was open for the rejection of all traditional theology and for the cultivation of individual interpretations of Scripture often claimed to be the result of direct divine inspiration. Curiously enough, along with such developments there went an increasing interest in the purely ethical teaching of the Bible, though this was often associated with ideas of communal ownership and the overthrowing of private property along with the power of both Pope and Emperor.

Four distinct views of the eschatological content of the Apocalypse, and especially the millennium, can thus be seen by this period: the allegorical interpretation of Augustine with the millennium being the period of the Christian Church, Luther's view that the millennium was past and that only evil was to come until ended by divine intervention, the view that the millennium was a future event to be brought in by divine intervention, and the view that the millennium was to be brought about by the efforts of the elect.

The Eighteenth Century

The last of the four views mentioned above was to come into special prominence amongst Protestants in the eighteenth century—to a considerable extent in Britain as a reaction against the earlier often extreme views of the radical Puritans. All forms of supernatural millenarianism tended to become suspect in prosperous societies because of their association with the often anarchistic tendencies of many of the groups which had espoused them.

The eighteenth century was an age of rationalism and optimism, and the corresponding eschatology rejected any concept of a supernaturally induced millennium and emphasized a continuing success of the Church in spreading the Gospel, thereby bringing about a steady improvement in man's lot. This was associated in Britain particularly with the name of Daniel Whitby (1638–1726). A fellow of Trinity College, Oxford, who later became a prebendary of Salisbury, Whitby expounded his post-millennial ideas in his highly influential work *A Paraphrase and Commentary on the New Testament* (London, 1703). He then turned to promoting union with Dissent, but adopted an Arminian position[10] and subsequently published Arian works. He was, however, highly influential and, as a result of his preaching and writing together with widespread adoption of his eschatological ideas, there was increasing pressure in support of missionary activity and a confidence that through such activity there would eventually be brought about a Christian Utopia on earth. This view came to be strongly held for a time by virtually all evangelicals, whether of the Established Church or within Dissent. Along with it went a decline in interest in the application of the eschatological books of the Bible to history, as the Second Advent was necessarily seen as an event of the remote future.

Such views were to receive a severe blow in 1789 with the onset of the French Revolution, an event which was to give rise to a furious division of opinion within the evangelical party, to revive the whole millenarian eschatological debate, and to stimulate the birth of assemblies, societies, and journals devoted to the study of biblical prophecy.

2. THE IMMEDIATE BACKGROUND I: FABER AND FRERE

With the French Revolution and the ensuing Napoleonic Wars (during which Britain became more and more isolated), there was a revival of interest in prophetical studies, especially amongst evangelicals, and many students of the Scriptures turned to Daniel and the Apocalypse in attempts to discover eschatological explanations of what were regarded as both frightening and threatening events. With this revival there was inevitably a new urgency with which the Second Advent of Christ and the millennium were debated. Not surprisingly, such activities involved to some extent a 'lunatic fringe'—for example, the followers of Richard Brothers and Joanna Southcott. Richard Brothers (1757–1824) was born in Newfoundland and served from 1772 until 1789 in the British Army. In 1793 he announced himself as an apostle of a new religion, claiming to be the 'Nephew of the Almighty' and the 'Prince of the Hebrews', appointed to lead them to the land of Canaan'. In 1794 he published

---

[10] This involved a rejection of the strict (deterministic) Calvinist doctrine of predestination—after Jakob Harmenson [Arminius] (1560–1609), condemned at the Synod of Dort (1618–19).

his millenarian beliefs in *A Revealed Knowledge of the Prophecies and Times*. A year later he was committed to Newgate Prison and subsequently to a London asylum for prophesying the King's death and the destruction of the monarchy. Joanna Southcott (1750–1814) was born in Devonshire. In 1792 she declared herself to be the woman of Apocalypse 12. In 1803 she published in London *A Warning* and in 1813–14 *The Book of Wonders*. She began to 'seal' the 144,000 who were to partake in the millennial kingdom, and announced that she was to give birth to a new 'Prince of Peace' on 19 October 1814. Instead, she fell into a trance and died on 27 December. Her followers, who were not extinct until the beginning of the present (twentieth) century, expected her to rise from the dead. However, for the most part the students of prophecy were well-educated and respected persons, and even included members of parliament such as Drummond and Perceval, both of whom were later to become Catholic Apostolic apostles (see Ch. II, § 1). The prophetical debate was not therefore restricted to ecclesiastical circles, but even spilled over into the 'Mother of Parliaments'.

As well as a large number of articles and pamphlets and the emergence of the new journals in which such articles could be assured of publication, several major works were generated by this revival of eschatological studies, of which three deserve special note here: George Stanley Faber's *Dissertation on the Prophecies . . .,* James Hatley Frere's *A Combined View of the Prophecies of Daniel, Esdras and S. John . . .,* and Irving's translation of Lacunza's work *The Coming of Messiah in Glory and Majesty* (see Ch. II, § 1). The first of these was a post-millenarian work, the other two pre-millenarian. However, the events on the Continent of Europe, allied with the notable failure in converting Jews to Christianity—an important aspect of contemporary ecclesiastical effort—tended to provide ammunition for the pre-millennialists rather than their rivals-in-debate. The Catholic Apostolic eschatology which, at this time, was yet to be formulated, was pre-millenarian, although both eschatologies were to be extensively covered during the Albury Conferences (see Ch. II, § 1, and also § 4 below).

Faber's Dissertation on the Prophecies

George Stanley Faber was born near Bradford, the son of a clergyman not noted for especially evangelical views. He was appointed a fellow and tutor of Lincoln College, Oxford, and Bampton Lecturer 1801. He was later Rector of Stockton-on-Tees and Master of Sherburn Hospital, County Durham. His *Dissertation on the Prophecies, That Have Been Fulfilled, Are Now Fulfilling, or Will Hereafter Be Fulfilled, Relative to the Great Period of 1260 Years* (London, 1804), was one of the early evidences of the prophetic revival. Later works include: *Remarks on the Effusion of the Fifth Apocalyptic Vial* (London, 1815), *A Sacred Calendar of Prophecy*, 3 vols. (London, 1828), *Eight Dissertations . . . on Prophetical Passages* (London, 1845), and *The Many Mansions in the House of the Father Scripturally Discussed and Practically Considered* (London, 1854).

In his *Dissertation on the Prophecies* Faber saw the French Revolution as one of the woes predicted in the Apocalypse, and concluded that the fourth vial of 16: 8–9 was being poured out upon the world from the year 1804, the seventh trumpet having sounded and the first vial (or thunder) having been poured out from August 1792. He worked out that the period of the seventh vial would commence in 1866, and that after a further period of 75 years (i.e. 1941) all the prophecies would be fulfilled and the millennium would then be ushered in, though not by the Second Advent. His interpretations made use of the eschatological period of 1260 years derived from Daniel 7: 25 and 12: 7, a period assumed to commence from the year 606, held to be especially significant on account of the claims of the Bishop of Rome and the activities of Mohammed. These passages refer to 'a time, two times, and half a time'. If a 'time' is taken to be a year, this gives three and a half years. However, when the 'prophetic day' is understood as signifying a year of 360 days, the total of 1260 years is obtained.[11]

Faber's objection to the pre-millennialist position was that he saw it as requiring three advents of Christ: the first advent in humility at Bethlehem at the beginning of the Christian dispensation on earth, and two 'end-time' advents—one to bring in the millennium, and the other the traditionally accepted one which would immediately precede the Last Judgement. There was scriptural authority only for the first and last of these. Later, he was prepared to admit a 'figurative' coming of Christ before the millennium, though continuing to insist that no 'literal' coming was possible until its end.[12] Faber's work is also noteworthy in that he prescribed three fundamental

---

[11] $3\frac{1}{2} \times 360 = 1260$.

[12] These views were expressed in his *Sacred Calendar of Prophecy*.

rules for the interpretation of prophecies: that interpretation of each symbol should remain the same throughout, that prophecies should be associated with historical events only if there was complete agreement in detail, and that no one prophecy should be seen as having been realized in more than one event.[13] These rules were widely though by no means universally adopted in contemporary prophetic studies.

The Principles of Frere's Combined View

James Hatley Frere was the son of John Frere, editor of the Paston Letters and a noted antiquary who had earned the title 'the father of pre-history'. He was the last of seven brothers, of whom the eldest, John Hookham Frere—the translator of Aristophanes—became under-secretary for foreign affairs. Due to the coincidence of initials, he was generally referred to as 'Hatley Frere'. He served in the Royal Artillery from 1795 to 1802, and subsequently went to the Army Pay Office where he eventually became Chief Clerk. The full title of Frere's work, which he was alleged to have written in a matter of weeks, was *A Combined View of the Prophecies of Daniel, Esdras, and St. John, Shewing that All the Prophetic Writings are Formed upon One Plan. Accompanied by an Explanatory Chart. Also, a Minute Explanation of the Prophecies of Daniel; Together with Critical Remarks upon the Interpretations of Preceding Commentators, and More Particularly upon the Systems of Mr. Faber and Mr. Cunninghame* (London, 1815). The Cunninghame referred to in this title was William Cunninghame of Lainshaw, a millenarian who delighted in attacking his fellow millenarians, including particularly Faber, Frere, and Irving. His first work, that referred to by Frere in the title of his book, was *A Dissertation on the Seals and the Trumpets of the Apocalypse* (London, 1813). Eventually he was to build a small non-denominational chapel close to his estate and to appoint himself its minister.

Frere, like Faber and many of their contemporaries, also saw the French Revolution as a fulfilment of biblical prophecy, but entirely rejected as unscriptural the possibility of a gradual improvement in the world leading to the millennium. The millennium could only come about through the divine intervention of the Second Advent.

[13] Faber followed principles comparable with those of Isaac Newton.

His work is more closely related to subsequent Catholic Apostolic eschatology than that of Faber, largely on account of its considerable influence on Irving and on the Albury Conferences (which Frere attended).

In the *Combined View* Frere attempted a synthesis of all the prophetic scriptures, but was primarily concerned with interpretation of the Apocalypse. He also included ground-rules for prophetic study, but these differed somewhat from those of Faber, whose work was criticized both in content and method, though it was admitted that it was a valuable public asset and that it had 'undoubtedly tended to throw considerable light on some important points'.[14] Frere's rules for prophetic investigation were as follows: that the prophecies should be set out in accordance with a single overall plan, that images should be taken to have the same meaning throughout according to a Symbolical Dictionary (which he provided) and should have no far-fetched interpretations, that visible symbols should be taken to represent visible objects, that different symbols in one and the same context should have different interpretations, and that the most limited and precise meanings of words should always be preferred.

Frere saw the first of these rules as being of special significance for the reliability of his interpretations of prophecy:

The principal novelty in this work is the introduction of the rule, that in any interpretation given of the prophetic writings, *a unity of plan* should be shown to pervade them all. By the adoption of this rule . . . Prophecy will be admitted to be, what it undoubtedly is in reality, a perfect system; and the great opprobrium of the subject, which is its uncertainty, we may hope will be in a great measure removed; for the stricter the rules are by which a Commentator is confined, the greater must be the difficulty of giving any false interpretation that shall wear the appearance of truth.[15]

Frere accepted much of Faber's general system for the interpretation of world history, but adjusted the periods assumed to correspond to the seals of Apocalypse 5–8, making his own time the period of the seventh seal whilst also predicting that the sixth vial had yet to be poured out. Again, following Faber, he saw the claims of Rome and the rise of Islam as of crucial significance.

[14] Frere, *A Combined View*, 3. He also included Cunninghame's work in this brief commendation.
[15] Ibid. v–vi.

Frere considered that there were two classes of prophecies, one related to the history of the world (Dan. 2: 31–45, 'the Great Image of Daniel', and Apoc. 6–10, 'the Sealed Book of Saint John') and the other to the history of the Church (Dan. 7, 'the Four Beasts', and Apoc. 11–21, 'the Little Opened Book of Saint John').[16] These prophetic classes, though clearly distinguished, were nevertheless interrelated:

in the history of the Empire, we find as much of the history of the Church introduced, as is inseparably connected with it: and in the history of the Church . . . the kingdoms of this world are spoken of, as far as is necessary, for the purpose of introducing and explaining the subject treated of; but still, each class of prophecy has its own peculiar and distinct object.[17]

As an example of such interrelation, he pointed to Apocalypse 7 (part of the 'Sealed Book') and 14–15 (part of the 'Little Opened Book'). In the former he claimed:

The Protestant nation is introduced here in its *national* capacity, as one of the ten kingdoms of the divided Roman empire; and is described as being preserved amidst the temporal judgements, by which the others are destroyed.[18]

In the latter:

the same people, or the Protestant nation, is again introduced, and during the same Period as before, namely, that in which the last judgements are inflicted upon the Western and Eastern branches of the Empire, and upon the enemies of the Church; and we find them described in this place in their character as members of the true Church, and as triumphing in the destruction of its enemies.[19]

The same occurred with the millennium:

the principal description given of this period, in the sealed book is, that the *throne* of God should be with men, and that he should rule his people; while in the open book, the *Church*, or the new Jerusalem, is principally spoken of, its description occupying nearly the whole of chap. xxi.[20]

---

[16] Ibid. 8.   [17] Ibid. 13.   [18] Ibid. 14.
[19] Ibid. 15.   [20] Ibid. 16.

In each of the two histories, the time subsequent to the rise of the Roman Empire was said to be divided into three approximately synchronized periods, giving the following correspondences:

Roman Empire	*The Church*
I. Time of its strength	Opposed by pagan power
II. Time of its weakness	Opposed by Papal power
III. Time of its destruction	Opposed by infidel power

The third period was also the time of the Church's infidelity. Period I was said to have commenced in 330, and period II in about 606. The 1260 years (called 'The Numbers of Daniel') were said to have ended in 1792 with the beginning of period III, this period being expected to end after 30 years in 1822–3. During the following 45 years, ending 1867, the pagan nations, and especially Islam, were to be converted. The millennium would then follow.

Frere arranged the interpretation of biblical prophecies so that all the visions (except Daniel's vision of the ram and the he-goat) concluded with the 'Period of the Progress of the Kingdom of Christ' (ending 1867) and the 'Period of the Perfection of the Kingdom of Christ' (the millennium). It is neither possible nor necessary here to present or discuss all the details of Frere's association of particular prophecies with particular events in history. Of significance for present purposes are his general principles, the fact that he was prepared to make associations with specific persons and events and to assert these with confidence, together with his willingness to allocate precise dates to future events.

3. THE IMMEDIATE BACKGROUND II:
LACUNZA AND IRVING

Irving's translation of Lacunza's work was published in 1827. Although it included much material relating scriptural prophecies to past historical events, it was primarily directed towards the Second Advent for which the author claimed he had determined 'another and a new system' which was at the same time 'much more ancient than the ordinary one'.[21]

---

[21] J. J. Ben-Ezra [M. Lacunza], tr. E. Irving, *The Coming of the Messiah in Glory and Majesty* (London: Seeley and Son, 1827), i. 57 (henceforth L/*CM*).

Lacunza's New System

Lacunza's system was even more directly related to Catholic Apostolic eschatology than that of Frere, and it will therefore be presented in some detail. The general form of Lacunza's new system was:

JESUS CHRIST will return from heaven to the earth, when his time is come, when those times and seasons are arrived, *which the Father hath put in his own power*, Acts 1: 7. He will come accompanied not only by his angels, but likewise by his saints, now raised from the dead: by those I mean, *which shall be accounted worthy to obtain that world and the resurrection from the dead*, Luke xx.35. *Behold! the Lord cometh with ten thousand of his saints*, Jude 14. His visit will not be so short, but with more leisure than is thought. He will not come to judge the dead alone; but likewise, and in the first place, the living. And consequently this judgement of the quick and dead cannot be one and the same, but two judgements, widely differing not only in substance and manner, but also in time. Whence it follows (which is the principal matter to be attended to) that there must be a very considerable space of time between the coming of the Lord which we expect, and the judgement of the dead, or the universal resurrection.[22]

Lacunza admitted immediately to two apparent difficulties: namely that there was at first sight a resemblance to the chiliasm condemned by the Second Ecumenical Council, and that there was a need to accept two resurrections instead of the usual resurrection *simul et semel*. Of the former of these, 'the heresy of Cerinthus' and 'the fable of the Rabbis', he had considerable fear:

I naturally thought that it must be a point decided, that whatever had any relation, great or small, with the Millenarians, should be looked upon as a certain peril of error and heresy.[23]

He admitted, however, that this fear was the result of his Roman upbringing and training which had for many years kept him from daring to open the Bible.

On the Millenarian Difficulty

Lacunza tackled the millenarian difficulty by a careful analysis of the different kinds of millenarian teaching which had existed in the

[22] L/CM i. 57–8.   [23] L/CM i. 59.

Church and who had taught it, by looking at what the 'doctors' had said and the reasons underlying their rejection of it, and by re-examining the meaning of Apocalypse 20. His first claim was that the basis generally used to justify condemnation of millenarianism is the fourth-century Council of St Damasius. This claim was dismissed by reference to the extant act of four such councils, and the quoting of a number of Fathers who taught the millenarian hope after that time, their existence having been admitted by St Jerome—himself an antimillenarian.

Turning to Constantinople I, Lacunza wrote:

> There still remains to be examined another council, which they pretend expressly condemned the millennial kingdom, not only as to the accidents, but as to the substance of the doctrine, and consequently all Millenarians without distinction. This is the first of Constantinople, being the second Ecumenical, that which added to the Nicene creed these words, 'Whose kingdom shall have no end'. . . . If any Millenarian had said, that the thousand years being concluded, Messiah's reign thereupon determined, the argument in that case would have been terrible and invincible; but if no one has said or dreamed so, to what amounts the argument? . . . we answer briefly, that the kingdom of the Messiah, considered in itself, without any extrinsical relation, can have no end, is eternal as the king himself; but considered as a kingdom over the living, and the sojourners who have not yet passed through death, under this single aspect it must needs have an end.[24]

In essence the argument was this: that since Christ shall come to judge the living and the dead, and before the living can be judged at the final and universal judgement they too must take their place with the dead, there will be a period of reign over the living which must come to an end before the universal resurrection and judgement, but the kingdom over all will most certainly be without end as the Creed proclaims. This millenarian teaching was then shown to be precisely what was asserted in Scripture, and what the 'orthodox' millenarians had always taught as opposed to the heresies of Cerinthus and others, who were 'given up to the belly and the palate',[25] and were thus rightly vilified by Eusebius, St Epiphanius, St Jerome, and other Christian writers.

---

[24] L/CM i. 64.   [25] L/CM i. 67.

On Augustine, Origen, and St Basil

Lacunza then considered Augustine's teaching, noting that even his condemnation of millenarian beliefs was qualified:

he speaks against the errors of Cerinthus and his followers. In the seventh chapter [of lib. de civ. dei] he recounts those errors and brings forward the places of the Apocalypse which may have given occasion to them; and immediately adds these words, 'which opinion were somewhat tolerable, if spiritual delights were believed as being about to be afforded to the saints from the presence of the Lord during that Sabbath: for we ourselves once had that notion; but when they say that those who are then risen shall lose themselves in the most immoderate carnal feasts . . . these things can in no way be received save by the carnal: and they, who are spiritual, name those who hold such dogmas, Chiliasts, from a Greek word, which being literally rendered into Latin, is Millenarians'. This is all which is to be found in St. Augustine upon the doctrine of the Millenarians.[26]

The argument was thus again that it was certain excesses of certain millenarians that had been condemned—not all millenarian teaching as such. This selective condemnation had become generalized without any justifiable basis in the councils, the Fathers, or in Scripture. Lacunza was also especially critical of Augustine's preference in places for allegorizing passages of Scripture when a literal interpretation was unpalatable. Indeed, he regarded the whole allegorizing process as a departure from early patristic practice. Whilst he accepted that passages of Scripture often required a spiritual interpretation provided by the enlightenment of faith, such interpretation should, wherever possible, be founded on an initial literal reading of the text.

Much of the blame for allegorizing distortions of the understanding of Scripture was blamed on Origen, and its worst effects were seen as affecting the hope of the Second Advent, texts concerning which had been transposed so as to relate to other comings of Christ:

And in effect it came to pass, that from henceforth they began to leave the plain understanding of those things which are written in the Prophets and the Psalms, &c. for interpretations, for the worst part spiritual, allegorical, or accommodative; trying with great pains, and not less violence, to accommodate some things to the first coming of the

[26] L/CM i. 77.

Lord, others to the primitive church, others to the church in the time of
her persecution, others to the church in the time of peace; and when no
better could be made of it, as must often have occurred, there remained
a last refuge very plain and easy, to take a mental flight to heaven, in
order to accommodate the state of things there, what would not
accommodate to them here. This they began to do in the fourth age,
it was prosecuted in the fifth, and has continued even till our time.[27]

For Lacunza, it was important that the intellect should be
disciplined by faith:

when he [God] speaks, and I am certain that he speaks, I ought to bring
my understanding and my reason into captivity to the obedience of
faith, and therefore ought to believe at once what he says to me; and
that, not after the mode in which it shadows itself forth in my mind, but
precisely after that mode, and with all those circumstances, which he
has condescended to reveal to me, whether I understand them or
whether I understand them not: because it is faith, and not intelligence
which is required at my hand.[28]

Of St Basil's complaints about 'the absurdities of Apollinarius',
Lacunza wrote:

The complaint of St. Basil, is well founded and just. And not alone St.
Basil, but likewise St. Justin, St. Irenaeus, St. Victorinus, St. Sulpicius
Severus, Tertullian, Lactantius, and the rest of the great multitude of
Catholic doctors, and saints, who were Millenarians, may complain, and
with much more reason, of Apollinarius and Nepos, and all their
followers; because the absurdities which they added, much more than
the gross indecencies of Cerinthus, were the occasion and the cause, why
in the end all was confounded together, and in their zeal to punish, and
annihilate the guilty, they did not spare the many innocents . . .[29]

According to Lacunza, it was preoccupation with the Arian heresy
which had prevented an adequate in-depth examination of millenarianism; such an examination would have resulted in a separation of 'the
precious from the vile'.[30] In particular, it would have been forced,
by the evidence of Scripture, to admit that the 'orthodox' millenarianism of the early Fathers was entirely in conformity with it and should
be believed, namely that:

*After the coming of Christ, which we look for in glory and majesty, there will
still be a great space of time; that is, a thousand years, determinate or*

[27] L/CM i. 80.   [28] L/CM i. 34.   [29] L/CM i. 78–9.
[30] L/CM i. 79.

indeterminate, before the resurrection and final judgement. . . . Wherefore, if God himself declare to me clearly and expressly in the scripture, the same which is affirmed in the above proposition, in this case, were it not very wrong to doubt it?[31]

He was adamant that neither Scripture, nor any constant universal tradition, nor any decision of the Councils condemned this 'orthodox' belief—what the Church had condemned were unscriptural deviations from and additions to it.

On Apocalypse 19 and 20

Lacunza then turned to the text of the Apocalypse, and in a careful analysis of Apocalypse 20, he detailed the various ways in which those who were opposed to all forms of millenarian teaching had introduced confusions and novel interpretations, especially by denying that the previous chapter relates to the Second Advent. The result of this was its illogical separation from chapter 20, a separation achieved by claiming that the one called 'King of Kings' and 'Lord of Lords' is not Christ but St Michael, a claim that was wholly irreconcilable with the actual text.

The allegorical interpretation of this part of the Apocalypse was also seen as incompatible with both apostolic teaching and human experience, for, if the thousand years in which the devil is to be bound referred to the period of the Christian Church, how was it that he is so patently active and is said to be so in Scripture? Those who accept the allegorical view

hold against St. Peter and St. Paul . . . The one exhorts all Christians to be sober, to live watchful and vigilant, *because your adversary the devil, like a roaring lion, goeth about seeking whom he may devour.* Why caution and vigilance against an enemy chained and buried in the abyss? The other bitterly complains against an angel of Satan who troubled him: and in another place says, that he hindered him in a matter which he had purposed to do, *but Satan hindered us.* You hold, moreover, against the whole church, which, in her public prayers begs to be preserved from the snares of the devil, and useth exorcism, and holy water, *to put demons to flight.*[32]

For Lacunza, the period of the Christian Church was one in which Christians had an argument against the devil and his wiles, not one

---

[31] L/CM i. 80–1.   [32] L/CM i. 88–9.

in which the devil was bound. The binding of the devil would not take place until the Second Advent, as was clearly stated in Apocalypse 20 and Isaiah 24. Further, the first resurrection could not be the experience of baptism, nor could it be the reward of the righteous on departing from this life, since it was clear from Scripture that it would follow the coming of the Antichrist.

On the simul et semel Difficulty

The second of the two difficulties admitted by Lacunza—the *simul et semel* problem—was examined with equal care. After consideration of various Old Testament texts and a reminder of the teaching to be found in the Apocalypse, he turned to the crucial passage of St Paul (1 Thess. 4: 13–18, and 1 Cor. 15: 20–8, 51–6) noting that the Apostle is speaking expressly of a revelation granted to him. These passages were used to support the idea of two resurrections. St Paul had expressly taught:

that when the Lord returns from heaven to earth . . . and much before his arrival . . . he will send forth his commandment as King and God omnipotent . . . At this voice of the Son of God, those who hear it, shall forthwith arise . . . But who are these? May it not be all the dead, good and bad, without distinction? It certainly and evidently appears not, otherwise St. Paul would not have taught us, upon the word of the Lord, the great novelty of two things absolutely incomprehensible, as well as contradictory, to wit, that all the individuals of the human race good and bad should rise, which could not take place unless all had died; and after that resurrection that some should live and remain until the coming of the Lord.

Besides this, it ought to be remembered that the Apostle in this place is speaking of the resurrection of the dead *who are in Christ*, or of those who sleep in Jesus, and not a single word does he speak of the other infinite multitude . . . In the same way speaketh the Lord in the Gospel, and pray consider it. . . . *and he shall send his angels . . . and they shall gather together his elect from the four winds.* Matt. xxiv. 30.[33]

After the rising of the dead in Christ, the living in Christ (implied in Scripture to be but few) would be caught up to meet the Lord together with them. Lacunza pointed to the way in which

the interpreters and theologians . . . have taken all pains to elude or soften down the force of this text.[34]

[33] L/CM i. 99–100.   [34] L/CM i. 108.

In particular they had confused priority of time with priority of honour and thus done violence to the clear meaning of Scripture. Lacunza's interpretation of the first resurrection was, he claimed, expressly taught by St Paul in a form which paralleled the evidence of the Apocalypse, and which was further confirmed by reference to St Matthew's Gospel and many prophetic writings of the Old Testament (particularly in the Psalms and Isaiah).

On Two Further Difficulties

There were, however, two New Testament passages which seemed still to offer some support to the more usual eschatological system, namely Matthew 25: 31 and 2 Peter 3: 10. The former of these appeared at first sight to exclude any space of time between the Second Advent and the universal resurrection and judgement. Lacunza provided two responses to this. The first was to regard the whole passage in which the text occurs as a parable on the grounds that the preceding passages were also parables. The second was to fix upon the word 'then', which separates the coming of the Son of Man from his sitting upon the judgement throne, and to point to scriptural texts where it was clear that 'then' must be taken as meaning 'afterwards' rather than 'at the same time', thus allowing for events, not necessarily immediately described, to take place.

In relation to the Petrine text, Lacunza pointed out that support for the conventional view was entirely dependent upon an interpretation of 'the day of the Lord' which would be contrary to its clear meaning elsewhere in Scripture. The 'day of the Lord' was not normally taken as being limited to twelve or twenty-four hours, and Scripture expressly stated that 'a thousand years in thy sight are but as yesterday'. Further:

It [Scripture] always speaks to us of the coming of the Lord, as an epoch . . . upon which there shall ensue a season of time wholly diverse from all which till then shall have passed: which season of time is frequently call[ed] in the Prophets *the day of the Lord, that day, that time, the world or age to come, &c.*[35]

St Peter, in saying that the day would come like a thief, and that 'then' the heavens would pass away, etc., did this

[35] L/CM i. 128.

without determining whether it will be at the beginning, or in the middle, or at the end of that same day. . . . St. John likewise speaks of the fire that is to be rained from heaven; but he places this event at the end of his day of a thousand years, *when the thousand years were ended*: in which thousand years (be the number determinate or undeterminate) there has been time more than sufficient for many and great things which the scriptures clearly announce to us.[36]

Lacunza then turned to other scriptural prophecies. The details of his analysis are not of concern here, it will be sufficient to note the general conclusions.

On the Antichrist

The four beasts of Daniel 7 were said to represent respectively: idolatry, Islam, false Christianity, and deism—the last being the religion of Antichrist:

what evils have not begun to proceed from the last terrible and wonderful beast, which is pure deism, apostasy, the proud and scornful spirit which dissolves the bonds of Jesus![37]

After an examination of the various historical interpretations of Antichrist and the eschatological prophecies concerning 'him', Lacunza proposed 'another system', one not relying on the identification of Antichrist with any particular individual—a false supposition, which

is the thing which has rendered many of the notices, we read in the scriptures, obscure, inaccessible, and incomprehensible . . . which has made things and notions innumerable, to be imagined, divined, and added, which do not appear from revelation . . . This, in short, has made Antichrist to be sought, yea, and found, and with the eyes of the imagination beheld, where no Antichrist was, and, at the same time, neither to be seen, nor recognised, where he actually is.[38]

There was a deadly danger in attempting to identify Antichrist with any one individual, in that, while the Church was looking for just such a one to appear and

such an Antichrist not appearing, we shall be looking for him when he is already in the house.[39]

---

[36] L/*CM* i. 127–8.   [37] L/*CM* i. 216.   [38] L/*CM* i. 195.
[39] L/*CM* i. 215.

Making much of the definition of Antichrist to be found in 1 John 4: 3, but referring also to other scriptural passages, he proposed that Antichrist be interpreted as a moral body:

According to all the signs given in the Holy Scriptures . . . the antichrist, or the contrachrist, with whom we stand threatened in the times immediate upon the coming of the Lord, is nothing but a moral body, composed of innumerable individuals, diverse in themselves, but all morally united and animated by one common spirit, *against the Lord and against his Christ*; Psalm ii. This moral body, after it is grown and feeleth itself strong, robust, and furnished with abundance of all necessary arms; after it feels in a condition no longer to fear the powers of the earth, now become its principal partisans; this body, I say, in this state is the true and only Antichrist which the scriptures announce to us. This antichristian body shall fight with the greatest fury against the mystical body of Christ, which in these times shall find itself greatly weakened; shall bring upon it the greatest and most lamentable slaughters; and if it succeed not in destroying it, this shall not be for want of will, but of time; for, according to the promise of the Lord, *those days shall be shortened . . . and unless those days should be shortened, no flesh should be saved.*[40]

Such an Antichrist was claimed to be entirely in accord with the prophetic Scriptures: for example, the seven heads in one beast (equivalent to seven beasts) represent seven religions, including false Christianity, united to make war on the true Church and supported by ten secular powers—signified by the ten crowned horns. (Daniel's four beasts were in accord with the seven of the Apocalypse because the third beast of Daniel had four heads, making seven heads in all.) Other passages of Daniel and the Apocalypse were also shown to be in close agreement.

Lacunza's interpretation of Antichrist was not, however, to be taken as implying that its evil had not appeared typified throughout history both by individuals and systems. This he fully accepted. His argument was directed against those who saw Antichrist solely in terms of an individual person of the last days—a single universal ruler. Such an interpretation was demonstrated not to be in accord with Scripture, despite it being apparently supported by certain individual texts. This support was forthcoming only when the texts concerned were taken out of their general context. He was also concerned to argue against the interpretation of the beast with two

[40] L/*CM* i. 196.

horns (Apocalypse 12: 11–18) as an individual false prophet of Antichrist:

This, far from signifying a particular bishop, or an individual and singular man, signifies and foretells, according to the clear explanation of Christ himself, a most wicked and dangerous body, composed of many seducers.—*Many false prophets shall arise, and shall do great signs and wonders* [Mark xiii, 22].[41]

The whole prophecy was to be taken as signifying a miserable state of the Church brought about by an unfaithful priesthood—the beast with two horns:

Has not the Church of God in all times groaned under the load of many heresies, schisms, and scandals, engendered among the priesthood; and by them obstinately maintained? . . . Consider the matter well, and you will not count it strange, that the beast with two horns should commit so many evils in the last times. You shall understand how the priesthood, even now, in a great degree, corrupt, may in that time corrupt and ruin all, as did the Hebrew priesthood.

How think you shall it be, when the simple sheep of Christ . . . turning their eyes to their shepherds, as to their only refuge and hope, they see them trembling with still greater fear than themselves, at the sight of the beast and his crowned horns? When consequently, they see them practically approving the whole conduct of the first beast, and counselling all to yield to the times, for the sake of peace; and when, for the good end of peace (fatal to the truth) they receive the mark of the beast, that is, publicly declare for him, feigning miracles and wonders, to attain the end of bringing them over by the appearance of religion?

Not, that there shall not therefore be in those times some good pastors. Yes, there shall be such: for less cannot be believed of the goodness of the chief shepherd. But these good pastors shall be so few, and so little regarded in comparison with the others as Elias was in respect of the prophets of his times . . .[42]

This beast, though in appearance like a lamb, would speak with the two-pronged tongue of a dragon, reminiscent of the forked tongues of the serpent who beguiled Eve (Gen. 3):

He shall speak with sweetness, with fawning, with promises, with artifice, with subtleties, with good appearances, abusing the simplicity

[41] L/CM i. 219.   [42] L/CM i. 221–3.

of the poor sheep, to entice them to the wolves, that they may be rendered up to the first beast. And if any amongst them shall be found so enlightened as to perceive the deceit, and so inspirited as to resist the temptation, (as certainly there shall be,) against these shall they proceed with the arms of the spiritual power, or with the horns of a lamb, forbidding everyone to buy or sell who hath not the mark of the beast.[43]

Lacunza agreed with those who saw attempts to identify the number of the beast, '666' (Apoc. 12: 18), with individuals as a vain and profitless exercise without solution. He accepted, however, that the principles of gematria (i.e. the substitution of numbers for letters) could be used for confirming its character. The use of letters to represent numerals was a Hebrew invention taken over and modified by the Greeks. It

allowed words to be associated with corresponding numbers whenever they also made sense in the alphabetical numeral system employed. Such an association of numbers with words, and especially with the names of people and places, came to have special significance in the interpretation of religious and other texts, an idea which has persisted with some of the stranger religious sects to this present day. It is common practice to identify this principle with gematria, though it is only a part of gematria which, in the first instance, was primarily the art of devising and reading secret codes designed by making permutations of the letters of words. There are many examples of gematria in the Bible in both the Old and New Testaments.[44]

For Lacunza, the solution of the enigma lay with the Greek word ἀρνέομαι (Latin equivalent 'abrenuntio' and Spanish equivalent 'reniego'), having the English translation 'I renounce', the renouncing of Christ being precisely the specific character of the beast and of those who will bear its mark:[45]

a public and manifest quitting of Jesus, (solvere Jesum,) a formal apostasy from the Christian religion which was heretofore professed. It is said that this mark will be carried upon the forehead, or the hands, to denote the publicity and the shamelessness with which antichristianism

---

[43] L/CM i. 225.

[44] From the present writer's *Numbers: Their History and Meaning* (Deutsch, 1983), 64.

[45] Among the many names which the various interpreters of the Apocalypse had associated with '666' was 'Primatius'. The same method of association was found by Lacunza to yield the Greek ἀρνέομαι, though he (incorrectly) gives it as 'ARNOUME or ARNOUMA' (L/CM i. 232).

will then be professed; the forehead and the hands being the most public parts of man, and at the same time, the two most appropriate symbols, the former of the manner of thinking, and the latter of the manner of acting. Being disunited from Jesus, there is no doubt that the forehead and the hands, that is, the thought and operation, shall remain in the most entire liberality; that is, the freedom, not of rational creatures, but of brutes.[46]

Not even Rome would be free from this apostasy, despite its being a spiritual centre of Christendom. Attempts to identify the woman upon the beast—the harlot—with pagan Rome were simply attempts to evade the true implications of the prophecy, a prophecy which related to the 'fornication' of Christian Rome with the world and its rulers.

Lacunza admitted to the apparent difficulty raised by St Paul's words when he wrote of Antichrist specifically in the singular, calling him 'the man of lawlessness' and 'the son of perdition', etc., saying that 'he takes his seat in the temple of God, proclaiming himself to be God' (2 Thess. 2: 3–4). His response to such texts was to point to the many scriptural passages (including passages of St Paul himself) where a term in the singular clearly denotes a community of persons rather than a singular individual, and to suggest that the singulars in 2 Thessalonians are particularly appropriate to a single moral body—perhaps even more appropriate than had St Paul written 'the *men* of lawlessness' or 'the *sons* of perdition'. The popular exegesis, interpreting Antichrist as an individual, understood 'the temple of God' to signify the Temple at Jerusalem, but this had obvious difficulties—not least that in all the other six occurrences of this phrase in St Paul's writings it is clearly intended to be taken in a figurative and spiritual sense. Following, therefore, St Paul's established usage, it should be taken here in a figurative sense as referring to the Church, within which

the man of sin, the son of iniquity shall formally sit . . . as if he were God: 'shewing himself that he is God'. And what may this mean? . . . The man of sin, and son of perdition, is no other in principle than a great number of true apostates, who having first broken the bonds of Jesus, and disunited themselves from him, and so verified in themselves what the apostle mentions first, *except there should come a falling away first*, shall then unite into a moral body, and then give their labour to

[46] L/*CM* i. 233.

increase and strengthen it in all possible ways; and, after that has succeeded, shall rebel, and declare war against the same Jesus, and against God his Father. Whence indeed to this man of sin the name of Antichrist, or Contrachrist is given.

. . . .

Then, this *man of sin*, this moral body . . . shall sit in the Church of Christ, which is the temple of the true God: *for ye are the temple of God.* And there, in that temple, shall he issue mandates and be obeyed, partly for the terror and power of his horns, and likewise for the horns of the lamb pertaining to the other beast, and for his dragon speech. Then shall he at his will, within this temple, dispose of everything most holy, and most venerable, now forbidding the perpetual sacrifice, now altering, now mingling, now changing, now confounding the sacred with the profane, the light with darkness, Christ with Belial. Then shall this monster of iniquity be seen publicly to open his mouth in *blasphemies against God, blaspheming his name and his temple and they who dwell in heaven.* Then shall he be seen *to make war with the saints and to overcome them.* Then, finally, shall he be seen to be the lord and master of the house and temple of God, *which ye are.* Shewing himself within that temple, by his conduct, by his operations, by his despotism, as if he were God. *Shewing himself that he is God.*[47]

Lacunza rejected those many descriptions of the end of Antichrist which claimed that he would be destroyed by the descent of the Archangel Michael from heaven as being without scriptural warrant, Scripture clearly indicating that it was God's revelation that such end would occur upon the Second Advent of Christ, as indeed the early Fathers proclaimed:

The holy Scriptures . . . say it so frequently, and with such clearness, that it is to be wondered how doubt should ever have come over the subject. Nevertheless the interpreters of Divine Scripture (some boldly and some timorously) say it is not. From this general opinion must be excepted those many churchmen and martyrs, that very great multitude (Jerome's expressions) of the four first centuries of the church; who for some time have been undervalued by our peripatetic doctors, as being Millenarians, or favouring in some way that raving and extravagance. It is certain that the foundation of these antients neither was nor could be their own imagination, but scripture itself, as it evidently is. The foundation of the others neither is nor can be the Holy Scripture, from which they do not produce in their favour one single passage, an evident proof that one is not to be found.[48]

[47] L/CM i. 262–3.   [48] L/CM i. 268–9.

The claims by interpreters that there would be a space of time between the destruction of Antichrist and the Second Advent were shown to give rise to insuperable difficulties.

On the Jews

Lacunza dealt in some detail with the question of the Jews, a people he regarded as inseparable from the mystery of the Second Advent. They were to be considered in three greatly differing states, corresponding to the three states of the life of Job: their state before the first coming of the Messiah as the chosen of God, their (then) contemporary state of unbelief and rejection of the Messiah in which they had been disinherited, and a third and (then) entirely future state in which they should be restored in their own land. In this future state, according to Scripture before the time of Antichrist, the Jewish people, as 'the former spouse of God', would

be called again with infinite advantages, in another state and under another everlasting covenant, to her former dignity, never to lose it more.[49]

Such a call was, however, only to follow the recognition by the Jews of their true Messiah. This, according to Lacunza, was the significance of the 'woman clothed with the sun' (Apoc. 12: 1):

Now this ancient spouse of God is represented, in the time of her future vocation, under the metaphor of a woman, no longer poor, miserable, naked, and abominable, as all the world hath seen her, and as she is now seen in this day; but clothed and adorned with the most precious and brilliant garment . . .[50]

The pregnancy represented the formation of Christ Jesus in her womb, that is, the conception of Christ in the heart which must eventually be manifested in a public proclamation of Jesus as Messiah. Thus the birth of the male child 'who is to rule all nations with a rod of iron' (Apoc. 12: 5) told of the acceptance of Christ, spiritually conceived by faith and publicly proclaimed. The 'great red dragon', waiting to 'devour her child' and whose 'tail swept down a third of the stars of heaven, and cast them to the earth' (Apoc. 12: 3–4), represented the devil, attempting to frustrate the public proclamation of Christ by inspiring the apostasy of

---

[49] L/CM i. 364.   [50] L/CM ii. 83.

those principal men in the church, not only political men, but ecclesiastical doctors, and religious persons, who, like stars in the firmament, do outshine and surpass the rest.[51]

The child was said to be 'caught up to God and to his throne' (Apoc. 12: 5) in order that he might be invested with

power, and honour, and a kingdom, that all peoples, and tribes, and tongues, might serve and obey him, as his subjects, 'that all peoples, nations, and languages should serve him'.[52]

Since the dragon was unable to prevent the woman's delivery of the male child, or to gain an entry into the tribunal of the righteous judge, or to resist the Archangel Michael, he would make war on 'the rest of her offspring, on those who should keep the commandments of God and bear testimony to Jesus' (Apoc. 12: 17), that is, on the remnants of true Christianity among the Gentiles.

On the New Jerusalem

Lacunza pointed to difficulties in the conventional eschatology over the interpretation of 'the Holy City, New Jerusalem', which he saw, not as the eternal celestial city inherited by the saints after the general resurrection and judgement, but as that which shall be established on earth in the day of the 'coming of the Lord with ten thousands of his saints'—those 'who are accounted worthy to attain to that age and to the resurrection from the dead' (Luke 20: 35), that is, those who shall have undergone the first resurrection. The conventional interpreters had to evade the clear statement in the Apocalypse that the City would descend to earth. Some did this by declaring its descent to be in imagination only, so that St John could observe its size and structure. The majority, however, claimed that it would descend to earth on the Day of Judgement for a short while only:

By which they mean, that in the day of universal judgement and resurrection, all the souls of the righteous shall come with Christ to our earth, and taking their proper bodies, will compose in the air . . . a kind of city, *after the manner of an amphitheatre*; which amphitheatre *after the manner of a city* shall return to heaven before the darkness.[53]

[51] L/CM ii. 89–90. NB: This is a quotation from Theodoret.
[52] L/CM ii. 94.   [53] L/CM ii. 254.

Such interpretations manifestly violated the scriptural texts. There was, he admitted, an apparent but minor difficulty in that, in the Apocalypse, the City was spoken of in the nineteenth chapter, after the description of the general resurrection and judgement in the twentieth. This was, however, only following the general pattern of the book:

when two or three or more mysteries concur in one and the same time, he [St. John] divides or separates the one from the other, speaking of the one as if the other were not, which he leaves until he has finished with the former; which being concluded, he steps back three or four paces, and taking up the other, carries it in like manner onward to its termination: and so of the rest. . . . This order and method of the Apocalypse from the beginning to the end, it is easy to observe; and without first adverting to this, it is not conceivable how that divine book can be rightly understood, which comprehendeth in so small a space so great, so grand mysteries, pertaining all (at least from the fourth chapter,) to the revelation of Jesus Christ, or which is the same, to his second coming in glory and majesty.[54]

Lacunza was, however, reluctant to dogmatize on the New Jerusalem, which he regarded as a mystery currently beyond man's comprehension:

Do not expect . . . that I should here tell you great and extraordinary, new and unheard of things, concerning the interior glory of that new court . . . nor as little concerning what pertains to the exterior thereof. All these things are much above my comprehension; and even the Apostle says of them, 'Eye hath not seen, nor ear heard, neither have entered into the heart of man, the things which God hath prepared for them that love him' (1 Cor. ii. 9).[55]

Nevertheless, he was prepared to propose answers to certain questions. He believed that the City would be sufficiently 'material' for it to be the abode of persons resurrected in their bodies—it would not be merely a 'spiritual' abode of souls only. The twelve gates with the twelve angels standing at them represented the judgement of Christ, exercised through the Apostles in accordance with the promises of Matthew 19: 28 and Luke 22: 30. The inhabitants of the City would be able to visit not only all the earth but the whole created universe, of which they would be joint heirs with Christ. Those 'caught up . . . in the clouds to meet the Lord in

---

[54] L/*CM* ii. 252.   [55] L/*CM* ii. 252–3.

the air' (1 Thess. 4: 17) would be joint participators in the City, having also been appointed as the Lord's messengers to the relics of the surviving nations (Isa. 18: 2)—'as it were a second apostleship'.[56] Further, the saints who come with the Lord and form His court include all who have 'crucified the flesh with its passion and desires' (Gal. 5: 24),[57] and particularly but not exclusively those martyred for the Faith (Apoc. 20: 4)—not all Christians were to participate in the first resurrection (Apoc. 20: 5).

On the Final Release of Satan

Lacunza explained that with the close of the period of the heavenly Jerusalem come down to earth, it was necessary to end recourse to the Old Testament prophecies:

Henceforward we need consult them no longer, because they all forsake us. They all close their prophesies in the kingdom of God, and of Messiah his Son, here on our earth, over the living and the sojourners. They all stop here, and no one passeth beyond. The last of the prophets only, that is the apostle St. John, follows out to its very end the thread or great chain of the mystery of God to men . . . to the universal resurrection and judgement.[58]

There was, however, to be one exception. Even in the Apocalypse some things were omitted 'because it is not yet the proper time':[59] in particular, the reasons underlying and the manner of the ending of the thousand years and the releasing of Satan from prison (Apoc. 20: 7–8). This, according to Lacunza, was

exactly the ring or link of the great chain of the mystery of God which is wanting in the text of the Apocalypse.[60]

It seemed to Lacunza incredible that the releasing of the dragon and all its effects should happen without there being general and serious faults 'worthy of the most righteous indignation of God Almighty'.[61] He found the key in Zechariah 14: 16–19. The nations would again become lukewarm, as a result of which 'there will be no rain upon them' (verse 17). When this failed to bring them to obedience

---

[56] *L/CM* ii. 264. [57] Lacunza identified this text incorrectly.
[58] *L/CM* ii. 333. [59] *L/CM* ii. 333.   [60] *L/CM* ii. 334.
[61] *L/CM* ii. 334.

the time will come for opening the abyss, and giving the dragon once more his entire liberty.[62]

This reason for the releasing of Satan completed the prophecy:

Having found in Zechariah the ring which is wanting in the text of the Apocalypse, the chain of the whole mystery is consecuting and continuous.[63]

Satan would then rouse the nations living in the four corners of the earth (Gog and Magog) to a final act of rebellion resulting in the destruction of all those who still opposed Christ, the casting of Satan 'into the lake of fire and sulphur where the beast and the false prophet were' (Apoc. 20: 10), and the universal resurrection and judgement.

On the Ultimate State of Man and Creation

On the question of the precise end of those not opposing Christ and of the world itself, Lacunza was not prepared to speculate since he could not find it made clear in Scripture. Equally, he was not prepared to speculate on the precise nature of the ultimately transformed and spiritual state of creation, though on the strength of Ecclesiastes 3: 14—'whatever God does endures for ever'—he was opposed to those who believed in its total annihilation. To questions as to the outcome of the universal judgement, he could provide only

the general answer of Jesus Christ himself, 'these shall go into everlasting punishment, and those into life everlasting'.[64]

He was no universalist.

In response to questions as to the nature of heaven, the ultimate abode of the righteous, Lacunza was equally reluctant to be specific. It was not a *place* in the ordinarily accepted meaning of the word, since this would imply the enclosure of Christ and the Saints in something having a nature accessible to human imagination. Heaven was the abode of the risen and ascended Christ:

I do only know, and this without being able to doubt it, that Jesus Christ, ever since the day of his wonderful ascension into the heavens, has been, is at present . . . and shall eternally be, 'in the glory of God the Father . . .'. And there likewise he is, and shall eternally be, with all his

---

[62] L/CM ii. 335.   [63] L/CM ii. 335.   [64] L/CM ii. 345.

court, at present part only in body and part only in spirit; and after the general resurrection, all in spirit and in body. This court . . . shall enjoy for ever . . . the most beatific vision, the chiefest good . . .[65]

On the One 'Prime and Principal Subject'

Towards the end of the work, where Lacunza was prepared to admit that there are things still hidden despite the revelations of the prophetic books of Scripture, he re-emphasized what he saw as his 'prime and principal subject'. He was content to remain ignorant of all of the eschatological mystery that was not revealed in Scripture, but he was expressly convinced above all else of one particular point—one that was contrary to the generally accepted concept of the last days—namely that the general resurrection (together with the last judgement) *would not immediately follow the Second Advent*:

Nevertheless, among these individual things pertaining to this very mystery, I find only one which I am not ignorant of, nor can fail to perceive, which is, the circumstance of the time at which the whole mystery shall come to pass. I mean . . . the resurrection of all the individuals of Adam's race, the last judgement, the ultimate sentence, and the execution of this ultimate sentence, cannot take place immediately upon and in the very natural day of the coming in glory and majesty of our Lord Jesus Christ; because that idea is visibly and evidently repugnant to the very text of St. John. . . . And very much more repugnant is it, when considered in union and combination with all the scriptures of the Old and New Testaments. All which, as is the primary and principal subject of this whole book, we have continued to set forth and demonstrate . . .[66]

The Nature and Importance of Lacunza's Work

Lacunza's pre-millennial work followed, in one sense at least, the tradition set by Roman Catholic sixteenth-century eschatological commentators who took a futurist view of the Antichrist in response to Protestant identification of 'him' with the papacy. However, the identification of the Antichrist with an apostatizing Rome of the future was, not surprisingly, sufficient to have the work placed on the *Index*.

[65] L/CM ii. 355.   [66] L/CM ii. 345.

It has been thought necessary to present *The Coming of Messiah in Glory and Majesty* in some detail here, and to include numerous extracts from it, because other writers, though mentioning its existence (chiefly in connection with Irving), appear not to have had direct access to it. Even the treatment above, though sufficient for present purposes, provides no more than a brief introduction to its content, which runs to over 750 pages of closely printed text. It remains a massive, highly individual, and largely unexplored work deserving more attention than has to date been given to it. It reveals an often surprising scholarship on the part of its author, and a familiarity with Scripture unusual in a Roman Catholic missionary priest of the time—as he readily admitted.

In some respects Lacunza's exegesis of the Apocalypse is much in accord with 'modern' scholarship, most notably in the discussion of its general arrangement, and in the contrast between the faithful and the apostatizing Church and the latter's 'fornication' with the world. Lacunza was also careful not to accept specified periods in a slavishly literal sense, and he was prepared to place the millennium outside of time *as we now experience it*. His stated caution in the matter of unscriptural speculation is praiseworthy, though there must remain some doubt as to whether he himself followed this principle rigidly throughout.

The historical and patristic examination of millenarianism, which reached the conclusion that not all millenarian beliefs had been condemned by the Church, is of particular importance for Catholic Apostolic eschatology, as is the conclusion from Scripture that the Second Advent is to be accompanied by a first resurrection of those *in Christ*, and that therefore the general resurrection is distinct from it and takes place after the establishment of the New Jerusalem on earth (the millennium) and a subsequent releasing of Satan from his bonds. However, despite the many patristic references, Lacunza seems to have been totally unaware of any patristic commentaries on the Apocalypse. Indeed, this is not altogether surprising for there are only a few extant Greek patristic commentaries on the Apocalypse, a book which was not considered canonical by many of the Fathers, including St John Chrysostom (who wrote commentaries on the remaining books of the New Testament). The earliest surviving commentary is that by Oecumenos the Rhetor (sixth century)—not edited until 1928, and hence presumably inaccessible to Lacunza. Much better known and more readily available is the later commentary by St Andrew of Caesarea. Unfortunately, Lacunza gave no indication of his means of access to patristic works cited: it is therefore not possible to determine whether or not this commentary might have been accessible to him.

Two further points deserving special note in Lacunza's work are his proposal that 'antichrist' denotes a system rather than a person (though one typified by individuals throughout history), and the interpretation of the 'woman clothed with the sun', who was 'with child' (Apoc. 12: 1–2), as indicating the eventual acceptance of Christ as Messiah by the Jews.

Irving's Criticism of Lacunza's Work

Irving, the translator of Lacunza's work, was not entirely in agreement with its content, as is shown by the criticisms contained in his *Preliminary Discourse by the Translator*, which ran to 194 pages. This had to be denoted as being that of 'the Translator' because Lacunza had himself provided a (short) 'Preliminary Discourse' from which Irving's had to be distinguished. It became much more widely read than Lacunza's massive work because it was subsequently published separately (in a slightly shortened form though with an added 'Contents') by Bosworth and Harrison with the title *Preliminary Discourse to Ben Ezra*, having achieved an exceptionally high reputation in its own right.

Despite some disagreements, Irving was not stinting in his praise of Lacunza's work, particularly on account of its pre-millenarian emphasis:

in the interpretation of the various texts and contents of the prophetic Scriptures, (and to him [Lacunza] all Scripture is prophetic), there is no Protestant writer whom I know of, to be at all compared to him. His book is the finest demonstration of the orthodoxy of the ancient system of the millennarians which can be imagined: indeed I may say perfect and irrefragable. I never expect to see an answer to it, nor do I believe an answer will ever be attempted.[67]

In fact, although many other and differing interpretations of the prophetic Scriptures have appeared since, there has been no specific and detailed refutation of Lacunza's arguments. In particular, his defence of 'orthodox' millenarianism remains unanswered. For the

[67] L/CM: *Preliminary Discourse by the Translator* (henceforth *PDT*), xxvi.

most part, despite its immediate popularity and influence, his work has been ignored by later commentators on the Apocalypse.[68]

A principal source of Irving's dissatisfaction was that Lacunza had placed entirely in the future the fulfilment of the prophecies of the Apocalypse (from the fourth chapter onwards). Whilst agreeing that the apostasy of the Roman Church was an important aspect and, indeed, extending it to cover the greater part of the contemporary Church, Roman Catholic and Protestant, Irving (following the Protestant tradition) saw that apostasy as having been largely instituted by the Constantinian settlement and subsequently increasingly evidenced by Rome, thus resulting in the necessary cleansing of the Church effected by the Reformation. Whilst agreeing, not unnaturally, with Lacunza's interpretation of the beast 'with ten horns and seven heads' (Apoc. 13: 1), he saw it as representing the past and present as well as the future:

I may add, moreover, that his interpretation of the actings of this future infidel beast of ten horns, so exactly concurs with our interpretation of the actings of the past papal beast, that I oft fancied he was describing rather than anticipating; and a friend of mine in whose sound judgement I have much reliance [? Drummond], remarked to me that it confirmed him in the protestant interpretations, more than anything which he had ever read in their own works.[69]

Although agreeing in principle with Lacunza's system for interpreting the Apocalypse, Irving was by no means convinced that the events prophesied would relate as closely to the Second Advent as it suggested. For him, the Apocalypse related to the *whole* history of the Church, and this was in the tradition of all the prophetic Scriptures, which he saw as having two interpretations:

In every prophecy of the Old Testament, and in the prophecies of the Lord recorded in the Gospel, there are two parts,—the former, of private application to a people and to a time close at hand; the latter, not of private interpretation, being spoken by the Holy Spirit for the good of the elect church in all ages, and waiting for its accomplishment till the time of the end, or of the Lord's glorious advent.

[68] See, for example, the comparatively recent excellent commentary on the Apocalypse by John Sweet (1979) in the SCM Pelican series. This provides not an exception but the rule. Of more than forty such commentaries in the writer's possession, not one mentions, let alone discusses, Lacunza's work.

[69] L/CM: PDT xxxi.

For, according to his [Lacunza's] views, all from the fourth chapter forward until the end of the book, remains unaccomplished, and will be rapidly evolved in a regular succession immediately upon the eve of the Lord's coming. In which case, it is like no other prophecy that the Spirit of God ever indited; and wants the prophetic sanction of embracing what hath already come to pass, and therefore wants the irreversible claim upon the belief of the church. Whereas, taking it as I have elsewhere done (following Mr. Frere's scheme) as successive revelations of prophecy, and correspondent acts of Providence, all bearing upon, and announcing nearer and still more near, the great and glorious consummation; every thing comes out in beautiful harmony with the other revelations of the prophetic Spirit.[70]

It is clear that, for Irving, it was necessary for a prophetic work to be validated (in part at least) by history. Lacunza had been led to place the fulfilment of the prophecies of Apocalypse 4: 22 in the future through his lack of knowledge of Protestant eschatological works (especially that of Mede[71]) and by his virtually total focus on the Second Advent, thus

not perceiving that every prophecy hath a train connecting it with the time of the prophet.[72]

Irving also dissented from Lacunza over the question of the Antichrist. Whilst agreeing that the falling away from Christ described in the Scriptures was indeed a spirit of apostasy, and that there would be a conspiracy against Christ by an apostate Church aided by secular leaders, he nevertheless believed that the advent of an individual to lead that conspiracy was clearly foretold:

That the falling away or apostasy described in the Scripture properly answers to a Spirit, and that this Spirit is in the last times to be the Spirit

---

[70] L/CM: PDT xxxiv. Irving's reference to his own previous work was to *Babylon and Infidelity Foredoomed: A Discourse on the Prophecies of Daniel and the Apocalypse which Related to These Latter Times, and until the Second Advent* (Glasgow, 1826; 2nd edn. Glasgow: Collins, 1828)—his 1825 Anniversary Sermon to the Continental Society (see Ch. II), which was much influenced by Frere's scheme.

[71] Joseph Mede (1586–1638), an English Biblical scholar, had published a commentary on the Apocalypse in 1627—though ignoring the first three chapters— with the title *Clavis Apocalyptica*, in which he proposed that its visions formed an organic chronological whole. He interpreted the 'seals' as referring to the Roman Empire and the 'little opened book' to the Church. Many subsequent works, such as Bishop Thomas Newton's *Dissertation on the Prophecies*, 3 vols. (1754), followed his style, which was characterized by hostility to Rome. Faber, Frere, and other later prophetic commentators made use of Mede's ideas, though not necessarily accepting all his findings. [72] L/CM: PDT xli.

of apostasy, or dissolving the bonds of Christ, and that it will bring about a confederacy of powers now professing Christianity against the Lord and his anointed, there can be no doubt; but who may there not be a head and leader of this conspiracy?[73]

For Irving, the Antichrist was signified by Isaiah's 'Assyrian', by Daniel's 'wilful king', and by St Paul's 'lawless one', and was typified in Pharoah and Sennacharib. These, and other scriptural references, were sufficient to convince him that the Antichrist would eventually be manifested in a person.

Support for Lacunza's Main Thesis

There were a number of less significant details where Irving did not concur with Lacunza, but the greater part of his *Preliminary Discourse* was taken up with the justification of Lacunza's main thesis that the Second Advent of Christ would precede the millennium, and that the latter would separate two resurrections—a resurrection of the Saints when Christ appears in glory, and the general resurrection and final judgement of the remainder of mankind, good and evil. He compared this main thesis with the more generally accepted eschatology, indicating that the latter not only very largely removed the Second Advent from Christian consciousness, but that it led to a depleted understanding of the threefold office of Christ—as Prophet, Priest, and King of the Church. Of the imminence of the Second Advent, he was already well convinced.

Irving was equally convinced of a special need for the prophetic gift of the Holy Spirit to be poured out upon the Church, and for a renewal of faith, not merely on the part of the Roman 'beast' but equally within the Protestant Churches—seen as having grown cold and worldly. Lacunza's work, despite its occasional flaws, brought the last days into a new and inspiring perspective, demanding a return to the largely forgotten hope which had provided the urgency with which the early Church had preached the Gospel. In particular, it removed the ground from under the feet of the evangelical post-millennialists who, as Irving saw it, were preaching a dangerous error.

[73] L/CM: *PDT* xliii.

Irving's Apocalyptic Beliefs

Though influenced greatly by his translation of Lacunza's work, Irving nevertheless continued to stand in considerable measure by his own apocalyptic views, most notably as contained in his *Babylon and Infidelity Foredoomed* (see n. 70 above). In this work he had dated the beginning of the apostasy of Rome from 533, the year in which the Emperor Justinian had given the Bishop of Rome a universal authority over the Churches.[74] This enabled him to use the prophetic period of 1260 years so as to arrive at 1793, the year of the French Revolution and, for him, the commencement of the judgement upon Babylon. The first of the six vials had been poured out over the thirty years, 1793–1823, and the seventh vial was about to be poured out. Armageddon would take place in 1868, which was to be the year of the Second Advent and the setting up of the Millennium.

Like Frere, Irving was prepared to allocate specific dates to the various prophecies, though he had not always been of this mind:

I am not ashamed to confess, that, at first, my mind fell away from the system of interpretation, which, with . . . other exact interpreters, you have followed, and inclined to the simple idea, that the Apocalypse is a narrative of events running on in regular historical order.[75]

It was Frere's interpretation of the prophecies in Daniel which had most influenced him to change his mind. The extent of this influence can be judged in that it persuaded him to reinterpret Acts 1: 7—'it is not for you to know the times or seasons . . .'—as applying primarily to those to whom it was immediately spoken and to the Church as a whole only until such time as God chose to grant further revelation. For him, the Holy Spirit had now revealed through prophetic studies the relationships of the prophecies to precise past, contemporary, and future events. This was not, however, a view ever to be formally endorsed by the Catholic Apostolic Church, though some individual members of that body, along with many other Christians, looked to certain specific years with particular expectations (as will be noted later).

[74] In this point Irving followed the scheme of William Cunninghame's *Dissertation on the Seals and Trumpets of the Apocalypse*, published in 1813, where the relevant texts of Justinian were given in full in their original form.

[75] Irving, *Babylon and Infidelity Foredoomed*, iv—part of the Dedication of the work to Frere.

In his *Preliminary Discourse*, Irving summarized what had been up to that time his highly individualistic eschatological beliefs. There were, as he saw it, three 'keys' to the understanding of the last days, all of which he claimed to have

opened and defended out of the Scriptures from Sabbath to Sabbath, with all boldness, so far as the integrity of my own conscience was concerned, yet with fear and trembling so far as the sweet harmony and communion of saints, in which I delight, was concerned; for at that time I did not know of one brother in the ministry who held with me in these matters . . .[76]

First, the apostate Gentile Church would suffer a terrible judgement which was closely approaching.

Secondly:

When the Lord shall have finished the taking of witness against the Gentiles, and summed up the present dispensation of testimony in this great verdict of judgement, and while the execution is proceeding, he will begin to prepare another ark of testimony, or rather to make the whole earth an ark of testimony; and to that end will turn his Holy Spirit unto his ancient people, the Jews, and bring unto them those days of refreshing spoken of by all the holy prophets since the world began; in the which work of conveying to them his Spirit by the preaching of the word, he may, and it is likely will use the election according to grace, who still are faithful amongst the Gentiles, though, I believe, it will chiefly be by the sending of Elias, who is promised before the dreadful and terrible day of the Lord, and by other mighty and miraculous signs. This outpouring of the Spirit is known in scripture by the 'latter rain' . . . and, like all God's gifts, it will be given to those who will receive it, both Gentiles and Jews . . .[77]

The reference here to the 'latter rain'—the first such reference to be found in Irving's writings—is of especial importance, for it was to loom large in his future thoughts and to become of great significance for Catholic Apostolic witness. This 'latter rain' would give rise to a response on the part of the 'antichristian spirit among the Gentiles' and the 'enraged infidel spirit among the Jews', who would unite under Antichrist to

produce a spurious restoration of the nations to their own land, and occasion the great warfare in the neighbourhood of Jerusalem, when

---

[76] L/CM: PDT vii.

[77] L/CM: PDT v. The expression 'the latter rain' had earlier been used by Lewis Way to refer to the 'harvest time' of the restoration of the Jews.

antichrist shall fall, and his powers be broken in the battle of Armageddon. But the faithful among the Jews, now brought to believe on him whom they have pierced, shall . . . be prepared by much sorrow and distress, and supplication, for the coming of the Lord to settle and establish them surely and for ever in their own land; and the faithful among the Gentiles shall be expecting the Lord to deliver them, according to the promises which he hath made to his elect church of being raised from the dead, or changed among the living at his coming, and all gathered to him on that day.[78]

Thirdly, the judgements upon the Gentile nations would be concluded with the personal appearance of the Judge of all

taking vengeance on those who know not God, and obey not the Gospel of our Lord Jesus Christ; raising those who sleep in Jesus, and changing those of the Gentile church who still abide in life, and preserving the mourning Jewish church, as Goshen was preserved in the plagues of Egypt, and, when the promised land shall have been cleared of all intruders, and they themselves by suffering perfected for the habitation of it, he shall lead them into it with a mighty outstretched arm; and sit upon the throne of David, judging and seeking judgement, and hasting righteousness . . . and rule among the nations, and be the Prince of universal peace—using, in this judgment and government of the earth, his risen saints . . . And . . . all the nations shall enjoy that fulness of peace and joy, that millennial reign of righteousness, for which we will hope and pray, and diligently labour.[79]

Such were Irving's eschatological views when he turned to the translation of Lacunza's work. In it he was to discover much which he could and did support, but, above all, he had found at last a 'brother in the ministry' with views to such a significant extent in accord with his own.

4. THE IMMEDIATE BACKGROUND III: THE ALBURY CONFERENCES AND *THE MORNING WATCH*

Irving sent his manuscript of Lacunza's work to the printer in January 1827. However, by this time the first Albury Conference had been held (see Ch. II, § 1), and Irving added a postscript to his

---

[78] L/CM: PDT vi. [79] L/CM: PDT vi–vii.

Preliminary Discourse describing the first of these prophetic conferences, which was devoted to

close and laborious examination of the scriptures, upon these six great
heads of doctrine: First, The doctrine of Holy Scripture concerning the
times of the Gentiles. Secondly, The duties of Christian ministers and
people, growing out thereof towards the Gentile churches. Thirdly, The
doctrine concerning the present and future condition of the Jews.
Fourthly, The duties growing out of the same towards the Jews. Fifthly,
The system of the prophetic visions and numbers of Daniel and the
Apocalypse. Sixthly, The scripture doctrine concerning the future
advent of the Lord. Lastly, The duties to the Church and the world
arising out of the same.[80]

Since participants in the Conference included Frere, Cunninghame,
and Irving himself, as well as a number of persons associated with
the Continental Society and with the London Society for promoting
Christianity among the Jews (most notably Lewis Way and Joseph
Wolff), the prophetic interpretations already put forward by
participants and the Jewish question formed a major part of the
deliberations, both in this first conference and in those which
followed.

It is clear that works by the following writers were mentioned
during the Conference (and also presumably discussed to some
extent at least—some more than others): Bayford, Bishop Chandler,
Coceius, Cooper, Cressener, Croly, Cunninghame, Davison, Dunbuz,
Erkhard, Faber, Frank, Frere, Fry, Gatacre, Gill, Gisborne, Irving,
Haldane, Bishop Horsley, Hurd, Kennedy, Lancaster, Lowth,
Maitland, Mede, Bishop Newton, Isaac Newton, Penn, Stewart,
Thurston, Tilloch, Vitringa, Way (Basilicus), Wolff, Archdeacon
Woodhouse. There are also specific references in Volume I of the
Dialogues on Prophecy to Lacunza's work. However, since Irving's
translation of this was completed after the first Albury Conference
but published before the appearance of Volume I of the *Dialogues*,
this may be a further indication of liberties taken by Drummond in
the compilation of the *Dialogues*. It must be remembered, however,
that the three volumes of the *Dialogues* were published separately in
the first instance, and that there is further internal evidence that the
Preface to Volume I may have been added in 1828 after the third
conference.

---

[80] L/CM: PDT clxxxix.

Although, by mutual agreement, no formal public account of these conferences was published, and Drummond's three-volume *Dialogues on Prophecy* was admitted by its author not to be a direct record of the debates (see Ch. II, n. 7), the close agreement between Irving's 'heads' and the chapter headings of Volume I of the *Dialogues* (see App. II) suggests that it is reasonable to use the three volumes as a survey of the programme of the first four Conferences as a whole, though care must be taken in identifying specific debates with specific conferences. The fifth Conference (1830) took place after the publication of the *Dialogues*, and it seems that there is no record of its proceedings, though the views resulting from it were propagated by means of various articles in the prophetic journal *The Morning Watch*.

The Conclusion of the Conferences

The conclusions to which the Albury deliberations led, in so far as they were published, have been given earlier (p. 39).[81] These six points were to become fundamental in the nineteenth-century revival of British millenarianism. Their foundation was the assumption of a deterioration in religion which had reached a situation of crisis to be resolved only by the Second Advent. Although some members who attended the Conferences went so far as to point specifically to 1843 or 1847 as the date of Christ's return, the general consensus was somewhat less specific, being that history was entering into its final era and that the Second Advent would occur within a matter of years or decades rather than centuries.

Some Details from the Dialogues on Prophecy

Amongst the details to be found in the first volume of Drummond's *Dialogues*, there are a few that deserve special note. First, in discussing the significance of 'the day of the Lord' and its relation to the 'first resurrection', it was suggested that, as it was referred to in Scripture in terms of 'morning and evening' rather than (as with the days of Creation) 'evening and morning', it would have its 'regular portions of morning and evening, like other days' but 'with no intervening night'. The promise that the 'morning star' (Apoc. 2: 28)

---

[81] Drummond, *Dialogues on Prophecy*, i, pp. ii–iii (henceforth D/*DP*.)

would be given to those who remained faithful was a reference to their participation in the first resurrection:

As Christ also rose 'the first-fruits of them that slept', so his people rise the first-fruits of the whole regenerated creation of God. 'As in Adam all die . . . the last enemy that shall be destroyed is death' (1 Cor. xv. 22–25). Here the resurrection of all mankind is plainly declared, and that it does not take place at the same instant of time, but in a certain order: first, Christ himself; secondly they that are Christ's, who are to rise at his coming . . . thirdly, then cometh the end, which is not until the end of Christ's reign, after he shall have put all enemies under his feet, even death itself . . . it follows, that they who are not Christ's, do not rise until the end of the millennium.[82]

Secondly, it was claimed that the figure of the woman with child, wherever it occurred in the Old Testament writings or in the Apocalypse, was a reference to the Second Advent and the uncertainty of its precise day:

we know that a pregnant woman will be delivered at the expiration of nine months, nevertheless the birth may be deferred to ten months or hastened to seven. It is, therefore, a time which is both certain and uncertain: for as a virgin being with child, was a sign of the first advent, so is the woman with child every where the figure for the second.[83]

Reference was then made to John 16: 16–21 in which the Lord uses the metaphor of a woman with child in relation to his imminent departure and future return.

Thirdly, in a discussion of the biblical use of the Greek words $\pi\alpha\rho o\nu\sigma\iota\alpha$ and $\epsilon\pi\iota\phi\alpha\nu\epsilon\iota\alpha$, it was pointed out that these terms were invariably used with reference to a personal and visible appearance, however spiritual such appearance might be also—as, for example, at the Transfiguration (see 2 Pet. 1: 16). Further, the term $\phi\alpha\nu\epsilon\rho o\theta\bar{\eta}$ (1 John 2: 28) was called as witness to Christ's appearance in the flesh at the Second Advent, for it

signifies that he shall then be the object of men's senses by means of his body, as he was at his first coming.[84]

Fourthly, in considering the state of man's body after resurrection, those believers who thought of the future state of the soul alone were taken to task, for *redemption has to do with both*—the soul must have a dwelling-place. *These* bodies are incapable of sustaining the weight of glory that awaits us; they must be changed, and on this point we have explicit promise . . . and it is this change for which we *hope*: our soul's salvation is not the proper subject of *hope*, but of *faith* . . . When he shall appear, we shall be like him . . .[85]

Fifthly, on the matter of the chronology of the Apocalypse, the 'apocalyptic axiom' that the book with seven seals was a complete prophecy requiring no supplementation was challenged on the grounds that it precluded the more obvious interpretation of parallel events, an interpretation also established by analogy with Daniel. For

the opening of the seven seals opened seven periods of time, reaching to the end of all things; the events of which periods are detailed in three parallel histories, which may, by various evidences, be shewn to form but *one* prophecy. The book sealed with seven seals, refers then indiscriminately to all these three histories, and forms a general introduction to them, because it embraces the whole of their periods; nor can any one portion of prophecy be said to *contain* any other, except in reference to its *including its time*. Thus, when it is said that the seventh seal (or the last cherubic voice of Rev. xv.7. xvi.1) contains the seven vials, and that the seventh trumpet contains the seven thunders, the meaning is, that they respectively introduce the periods of these latter, which are *subdivisions* of their period.[86]

Such an opinion was in accord with Frere's apocalyptic scheme, though it was not Frere who presented it to the assembled company. However, whilst Frere's scheme was accepted in general terms, certain details came in for strong criticism, most notably his numerical calculations based on the various numbers in the Old Testament.

Finally, there was much adverse comment on the supporters of overseas missionary activities and their publications. Such persons were described as 'Idolaters of Societies'.[87] Also condemned were the various 'Dissenting Magazines' which had heaped personal abuse on Irving while at the same time claiming to be 'the spiritual part of the periodical press'. These confirmed the low state of 'erudition and piety in the Dissenting Churches', whose members

---

[85] *D/DP* i. 184.   [86] *D/DP* i. 271–2.   [87] *D/DP* i. 356.

know so little of the subjects on which they profess to sit as judges, as to declare that *'the personal reign of Christ, and the return of the Jews to Jerusalem'* are *'crudities of mere human authority'*. . . . Let them take heed how the Lord, at whose coming they mock, find them mere money changers when He appeareth.[88]

Neither were the parties within the Established Church spared:

a High-Churchman thinks he has renounced the world, because he despises the opinions of the Evangelical party, whilst he is exceedingly anxious about his reputation amongst Bishops and Cabinet Ministers. The Evangelical Clergyman, on the other hand, can make up his mind to be lightly esteemed by infidels, or even by the Hierarchy, but is tremblingly alive to what will be thought of him at a Committee of some Bible Society in his neighbourhood.[89]

For all of them alike, whether Dissenters or Anglicans, the root of the problem lay in their neglect of the scriptural doctrine of the Second Advent of Christ.

The second and third volumes of the *Dialogues* continued the themes treated in the first, though with even greater emphasis on prophetic details of future events. In the second volume typology was discussed at considerable length: in particular, Old Testament types of the two advents of Christ (in humility and in glory), and scriptural and historical types of 'the great Day of God Almighty (Armageddon)'. Again, the practical duties incumbent on those who had learned to look for the Second Advent were stressed. The third volume dealt almost exclusively with God's purposes for mankind, so far unaccomplished, through studies of the Mosaic Law and the period before the Law was given, the history of the Jews, and New Testament prophecies, concluding with the 'Signs of the Times'. The last was a matter of great importance, to be studied

Because the signs of the times are to the study of prophecy, what the separation from the evil practices of the world is to the faith of Christ crucified. . . . that nothing is more necessary, is obvious, from Matt. xvi. 3, Luke xii. 56, and xix 42. 44., wherin the Jewish nation, and the heads of it particularly, are taxed with hypocrisy, accused of wilful blindness, and charged with blackest guilt, by our Lord, for not discerning the time of their visitation, which was then drawing nigh.[90]

---

[88] D/*DP* i. 343, 345.			[89] D/*DP* i. 362.			[90] D/*DP* iii. 417–18.

The parallel with contemporary Britain, blind to the signs of the Second Advent, seemed obvious. The language of condemnation was frequently strong:

Yet I utterly despair of making this blinded, self-conceited generation to discern truth. . . . How awful it is, to see the religious world treating the subject of the coming of the Son of Man with derision, unbelief, and hostility! surely this . . . is a clear proof that the state of things predicted is come to pass, and that these are the very days of the Son of Man.[91]

The Second Advent would occur

in a day of heedlessness and inexpectancy, and unbelief, as was the day of Noah.[92]

This was seen to be precisely the current state of the Churches. Frequent and fervent prayer, together with the daily study of the Scriptures, was the first duty of every Christian who believed that the signs of the times indicated the approaching Second Advent.

The Signs of the Times and the State of the Church

The strong language was continued in *The Morning Watch*, a noted example being Irving's article entitled 'Signs of the Times, and the Characteristics of the Church', which appeared in two parts (in the December 1829 and March 1830 issues).

Irving saw the casting out of the Jewish Church from Jerusalem as the type of the judgement on the Christian Church already begun in the French Revolution and soon to become even more calamitous. Matthew 23 enumerated precisely those sins for which God was judging His Church:

This chapter consisteth of two parts: the first being addressed to the multitude and to his disciples; the second, to the scribes and the Pharisees. To the multitude and to his disciples he spoke thus; 'The scribes and the Pharisees sit in Moses' seat; all therefore whatsoever they bid you observe, that observe and do: but do ye not after their works, for they say and do not'. These words give us the key to the whole chapter . . . The parallel, therefore to the Scribes and Pharisees, must be found in the ministers and rulers and authorities in the church; not the clergy merely, but the magistrate also, who giveth execution by his authority to the decisions of the church. Secondly, This verse shews us

[91] D/*DP* iii. 447–8.   [92] D/*DP* iii. 448.

that the parallel must be taken between them and a true church, not between them and an apostate church. . . . The parallel . . . must be between the spiritual and temporal rulers of the Jewish church and the spiritual and temporal rulers of a church of which it is set forth in Scripture as the type.[93]

There was a distinction between the Church as it now appeared and the true Church. The present Church was ruled by Scribes and Pharisees, the former denoting the Anglican hierarchs and the latter the leaders of Dissent. They combined, as self-styled 'evangelicals', to deplete the Gospel and to induce only 'the rack and torture of inward uncertainty and fear' in their bearers by preaching justification by faith alone, but requiring in practice 'works' comprising a period of 'probation of doubt and uncertainty, of difficulty, and perplexity'. These were precisely the people who opposed both the concept of freedom in Christ and the hope of the Second Advent, attacking all those who rose up to 'give the people liberty from such bondage'.[94] Verse after verse of Matthew 23 was applied to those in positions of authority in the Churches.

The Response to Attacks by the Evangelicals

Irving was stung by the continuous attacks of the evangelical party, in their various journals, on those (himself included) who preached the full Gospel of salvation and interpreted the prophetic Scriptures to the people. Of their followers, he said:

I would rather go and preach the Gospel to the most untutored of the people, to a company of wretched women in the prison, or to the sweepings of the streets, which are gathered into asylums for the night, than preach it to a congregation of men resting on their experiences and their evidences: and therefore I hold it to be well spoken by our Lord, that these proselytes 'are more the children of hell than before' . . . they are further from the kingdom of heaven: according as it is written, 'The publicans and harlots enter into the kingdom of heaven before you'. These are solemn and awful truths which I utter; but the time is uncertain, and admitteth not of delay: the judgements are near. 'Behold, he standeth at the door.'[95]

---

[93] *The Morning Watch*, i. (1829), 643 (henceforth *MW*).
[94] *MW* i. 644.   [95] *MW* i. 652–3.

Also singled out again for special attack were those who thought that man could bring about the conversion of the world, together with their financially active missionary societies:

An object the wildest, the most frantic, and the most opposite to God's word, which ever deluded the minds of men—to wit, the conversion of the whole world—hath been started within these last thirty years; and to the attainment of this object it is openly avowed that money is the chief desideratum. . . . the laws both of God and man have been frustrated, under the sense of duty to these great money-getting societies. . . . the sorrow and the marvel was, that the pious men and ministers engaged in that missionary work could not see, could not be brought to see, the evil of it, but were greatly enraged that I should call it an abomination. . . . And as the Jewish Church soon came to an end . . . so believe I that the church in this land will soon, by the progress of this very same religious avarice, be visited and judged of God. . . . If this be not forgetting the temple for the gold of the temple, I know not what can be considered so; if this is not undervaluing the altar for the gift that is upon the altar, I know not what can be considered so. For my part, I believe in my heart there is in the working of this great religious system a vanity, an ostentation, an avarice, an idolatry of gold and silver, which, if it be not as great, will soon be as great, if not checked and testified against, as I now do, as ever were the Pharisaical system in Jewry, or the Mendicant system in Papal Rome. I do testify against it, after the example of my Lord; I say, Woe unto it! I say, There shall not be one stone of it left upon another.[96]

Irving, in similar language, contrasted the cheers at missionary society meetings when subscriptions were announced with the restlessness and grumbling at the same meetings when the Gospel was preached—no doubt this was inspired, at least in part, by the reception given to his anniversary sermons preached before the London Missionary Society (1824) and the Continental Society (1825).

Irving's concerns were also social concerns. He attacked the evangelicals for their 'work ethic'—those who praised the hard-working poor were precisely those shopkeepers and factory owners who 'ground the faces' of those whom they praised, taking a dreadful toll of their health. They used their donations to charities and to missionary effort to calm their conscience. He took up the figure of

[96] *MW* i. 655–7.

the cup and plate (Matt. 23: 25), expanding on the meaning given to it by Our Lord:

By making the outside of it clean, he signifies . . . the sacrifices which we make to appearances, the accommodations which we make to public opinion, the offerings to charity. By the inside of the cup full of extortion and excess, we take him to signify the unhallowed sources, the hard and severe measures, the dishonest and dishonourable practices, the unfeeling exactions, by which the cup of a man's substance is filled, and kept full. And his instruction is . . . that God looks with as an observant eye upon the secret machinations by which wealth is made, as he does upon the outward and observable methods by which it is expended . . . Their cup is outwardly clean, no one can charge them with an actionable offence: nevertheless, within it is full of extortion and excess. . . . 'Woe unto you, Scribes and Pharisees, Hypocrites! for ye are like unto whited sepulchres, which indeed appear beautiful outwardly, but are within full of dead men's bones, and of all uncleanness' (Matt. xxiii. 27). Even so ye also outwardly appear righteous unto men, but within ye are full of hypocrisy and iniquity.[97]

Language such as this did little to commend the millenarian cause of Irving and his Albury associates to the more moderate evangelicals, and they were accused of causing dissension and division in the Church. Particular exception was taken when Irving attacked the evangelical party for its 'idolatrous' regard for the Protestant reformers.[98] *The Record*, one of a number of publications which had carried discussions of millennial views and had at one time been financially supported by Drummond, appealed for moderation, though at the same time it called for the continuation of prophetic studies.[99] Various meetings were called in London and elsewhere—most were interdenominational; some were restricted to those interested in the Jewish question. A union of clergy was proposed to arbitrate in disputes.[100] Eventually *The Record* turned against Irving and his associates, and attacked *The Morning Watch* for its propagation of Irving's theological views (his Christology and his teaching on

---

[97] *MW* i. 664–5; ii. 141. Irving's attack on the Evangelicals was continued in the March 1830 issue.

[98] A major part of the March 1830 article was devoted to this topic.

[99] See *The Record*, 24 Dec. 1830. An excellent account of the debate between *The Morning Watch* and *The Record* is to be found in Orchard, *English Evangelical Eschatology 1790–1850*, thesis (Cambridge University, 1968), iii. 8.

[100] According to *The Record*, the proposal was made by Gerard Noel.

baptismal regeneration), for its undue concentration on unfulfilled prophecy, and for what were seen to be its 'high church' tendencies.

The majority of the articles in *The Morning Watch* were unsigned, Irving's two-part 'Signs of the Times' being one of the exceptions to this. Amongst the anonymous contributors were Carlyle, Drummond, and Tudor (all subsequently to be apostles). The eschatological content can be judged from the following titles selected from the various volumes:

1. On the First resurrection.
   On the Doctrine and Manifestation and Character of the Antichristian Apostasy.
   On the Priesthood of Christ, as it shall be exercised during and after the Millennium.
   Letter to the Editor on the First and second Resurrection.
   Remarks on the Period assigned in Scripture for the restoration of Israel.
   On the Apocalypse and Millennium.
   On the Structure of the Apocalypse.
   On the gradual Unfolding of Prophecy.
   On the Interpretation of the Apocalpyse.
   On the Heads of the Apocalyptic Beast.
2. On the Second Advent of our Lord Jesus Christ.
   On the received Interpretation of the fifth and sixth Trumpets, and the 'River Euphrates'.
   On the Seventh Vial of the Apocalypse.
3. Commentary on the Epistles to the Seven Apocalyptic Churches.
   On the Restoration and Conversion of the Twelve Tribes.
   On the Number of the Beast, 666.
   On the Structure of the Apocalypse, and the Events of the Sixth and Seventh Vials.
4. There remaineth a Rest to the People of God.
   Commentary on the Epistles to the Seven Apocalyptic Churches.
   The Hour of Christ's Appearance.
5. Christ the Morning Star; and Lucifer Son of the Morning.
   Commentary on the Epistles to the Seven Apocalyptic Churches.
   On the Sacred Numbers.
   Unaccomplished Prophecies now fulfilling.
   Interpretation of the fourteenth Chapter of the Apocalypse.
   Interpretation of Daniel's Seventy Weeks.
   A Literal Translation of the Opening of the Sealed Book (a Table).
6. Interpretation of the fourteenth Chapter of the Apocalypse.
   Germinant Fulfilment of Prophecies.

Unaccomplished Prophesies now fulfilling.
Protestant Apostasy.
On the Judgement before the Great White throne.
On the Return of the Jews.
7. Unaccomplished Prophecies now fulfilling.
The Bride, the Lamb's Wife.
The Alphabet of Prophecy.
The Church of the First-born enrolled in Heaven.

There were also articles devoted to the Irving's doctrine of the humanity of Christ and (increasingly) to the manifestations of the Holy Spirit in his church and elsewhere, to schism, to the Parables of the Gospel, to the gifts of the Spirit, to Old Testament typology, and comments and article-reviews of material in other journals, together with comment on current events, etc. The stand taken was unswervingly pre-millennialist.

The public scandal over the manifestations at Irving's Church and his formal condemnation by the Scottish Church (see Ch. II) discredited him in the eyes of many, and so added to the difficulties which the pre-millenarian party encountered in the propagation of their views. Though many pre-millennialists remained within the existing Churches, the main 'mantle' of the party was now to be carried by those who were to become members of the Catholic Apostolic Church. These included particularly Drummond, Tudor (the Editor of *The Morning Watch*), Sitwell (all three to be apostles of the body), and Taplin (the 'Pillar of Prophets').

5. CATHOLIC APOSTOLIC ESCHATOLOGY I: *THE GREAT TESTIMONY*

The first major presentation of Catholic Apostolic eschatology, prepared and issued by those who had become apostles, is to be found in *The Great Testimony* of 1838 (see Ch. II, § 2). Although much of the testimony was devoted to the nature and history of the Church, the ministry, and the sacraments, and to the significance of Christendom, together with an historical analysis of Church–State relations, about a third of the work was concerned with the signs of the times, the 'apostasy', and the 'last days'.

The Dangers of Liberalism

After some early paragraphs devoted to the Church and to Christ's work of salvation and faithfulness to His people, the testimony turned to the signs of the times, to what was seen as the contemporary conspiracy by 'infidels' and 'revolutionaries', a conspiracy to which many Christian 'liberals' were giving, knowingly or unknowingly, their support. The aim was

to complete the work which the revolution of the last century left unfinished, by the disorganization of all ancient principles, moral, religious, or political, and by the destruction of all established institutions in Church and State; and to establish a new era of atheistic anarchy, under the name of liberalism, on the ruins of the Christian Faith and of the governments at present existing.[101]

This dangerous liberalism was seen as infecting all aspects of life, inspiring a lack of respect for authority, whether in the home, at work, or in Church and State. Because the Christian Faith had been, historically, the stronghold of ordered government, such rule being 'by the grace of God'—a Christian monarchy was 'a national covenant with God'—those who attacked the constitutions of the nations of Europe were also assaulting Christianity itself. The increasingly popular idea that 'all power is from the people' struck at 'the very roots of all ancient obedience' since it made 'every man the judge of whom he would obey'.[102] Yet the future glory of the faithful was assured: they would be presented without spot as the Bride of the Lamb. It was therefore the highest duty of the Church

to hold fast the hope of this glory; to seek to be prepared to meet the Lord, her Spouse: to long for His appearing, when He . . . shall come again and receive them to Himself . . . for they shall be like Him, they shall see Him as He is (I John III, 2).[103]

---

[101] *The Great Testimony* (1838), para. VII (Miller, *The History and Doctrines of Irvingism* (Kegan Paul, 1878), i. 352). (Henceforth this Testimony is designated by *GT*, and Miller by *M/HDI*.) The major part of this Testimony is included by Miller as Appendix I to his first volume, and, since this is much more readily available to scholars, references in Miller are given in brackets after the original references to the Testimony itself. A number of the latter paragraphs of the Testimony are, however, omitted by Miller—a point not generally noticed to date.
[102] *GT* X (*M/HDI* i. 352).
[103] *GT* XXI (*M/HDI* i. 363).

The image of the woman in travail prophetically depicted the state of the Church awaiting the Second Advent.

The testimony reminded those to whom it was addressed—those in position of rule in Church and state within Christendom—of the basis upon which the sovereignty of the secular ruler was established when 'God's peculiar people had provoked Him to depart from Him', namely that submission to the rule of Nebuchadnezzar, King of Babylon, became the 'test of obedience to Himself (Jeremiah XXVII; XXXVIII, 20, 21.)'.

The Implications of Nebuchadnezzar's Vision

Daniel's interpretation of Nebuchadnezzar's vision (Dan. 2: 36–45) prophesied that there would be three further universal kingdoms, the last of which would be initially strong but would later be divided into separate kingdoms (as the toes of the feet of the image were part iron and part clay). It would be in the days of this divided sovereignty that God would 'set up a kingdom which shall never be destroyed' and which would 'Break in pieces and consume' all other kingdoms and 'stand for ever'.[104]

The fourth of Daniel's predicted kingdoms was the Roman Empire: the First Advent took place during its period of strength, the Second was yet to come, but would take place during the contemporary period of its weakness and division. Yet the first-fruits of the divine kingdom which should be set up were already present in the gift of the Holy Spirit to the Church, though the kingdom itself was

not yet advanced into the administration of the affairs of this world . . . The kingdom of God is yet within us (Luke XVII, 21); it hath not yet come; we yet pray unto our Father, that it may come; it shall come 'in the regeneration, when the Son of Man shall sit on the throne of His glory', and then shall the twelve apostles, who were with Him on earth 'sit upon twelve thrones, judging the twelve tribes of Israel' (Matt. XIX, 28). And then also shall come to pass the vision of St. John in the Apocalypse: 'I saw thrones, and they sat upon them, and judgement was given unto them'. 'This is the first resurrection. Blessed and holy is he that hath part in the first resurrection, on such the second death hath no power: but they shall be Priests of God and of Christ, and shall reign with Him a thousand years' (Rev. XX, 4, 6).[105]

[104] *GT* LXIX (*M/HDI* i. 406).   [105] *GT* LXXI (*M/HDI* i. 408).

In the meantime, it was the duty of Christians to follow Christ's example, to submit to the secular rulers in all worldly matters, for the throne in a Christian land was

the sure pledge, of the Eternal Lordship of Jesus Christ, even as the altar of His priesthood is the symbol of His Eternal priesthood.[106]

The duty owed to the Christian monarch was extended to the family, where the father exercised a divinely given authority, though under the rule of the monarch by analogy with rule within the Church:

The king and the father are as necessary as the apostle and the pastor.[107]

The Errors of Rome and Protestantism and the Apostasy of the Church

The apostles declared that within the Church there was a struggle between the work of the Holy Spirit within the whole Church (Catholic and Protestant) to perfect the Body of Christ in preparation for the Second Advent and the attempts by the 'mystery of iniquity' to pervert the Holy Spirit's work

in order to prepare the Church and the world for the revelation of that Wicked one, the predicted Antichrist.[108]

Both the Roman Church and the Protestant Churches had seriously erred, the former by preserving unity at the expense of life and thus preserving a unity of death, and the latter by preserving life for individual and selfish ends at the expense of unity and in ways not ordained by God. The evils of the two systems were, respectively, the love of form together with indifference to life (putting the means before the end), and the attempt to maintain life outside the ordinances of God (seeking the end without the means). The inevitable result was almost universal infidelity, one example of which was the abandonment of St Augustine's charge to give tithes both of annual produce and daily gains, despite the great increase of riches bequeathed by God to the nations of Christendom. On such infidelity God would speedily bring judgement, as foretold by the prophet Malachi—'You are cursed with a curse, for you are robbing me; the whole nation of you' (Mal. 3: 9).

---

[106] *GT* LXXI (*M/HDI* i. 409).   [107] *GT* LXXI (*M/HDI* i. 409).
[108] *GT* LXXXIV (*M/HDI* i. 421).

This step in the 'fateful descent' of Christendom was followed (particularly in countries with Protestant majorities) by the state ceasing to be Christian, either by proclaiming a principle of atheism or by giving equal recognition to the Church and the many sects. Rulers were forgetting their anointing, abusing their God-given authority and becoming oppressors, reverting to pagan misrule. It was

the consummation of the sin of the Rulers of Christendom, that they are in secret spirit disregarding and forgetting, or even renouncing and despising it. And hence the judgements and convulsions overtaking their kingdoms; for the people (. . . forgetting the source from whence the reformation of their grievances must come, even God), are rising up with impetuous violence to seek the remedies for themselves, and, led away by vain speculations of reforming and revolutionizing men, are the ready instruments for involving all institutions in Church and State in one irremediable destruction.[109]

The evil passions aroused in the French people at the time of the Revolution included a diabolical hatred of God and of all decency and virtue—murder was their policy, and atheism their religion. This was but the type and omen of the general apostasy:

and that infidelity, which flowed darkly and silently its course beneath through the period of Papal corruptions, which gained strength and has burst forth into the light of day in Protestant apostasy, shall swell out into that third and last flood of Antichristian blasphemy, which shall carry away both Church and State, as visible ordinances publicly witnessing to God, and raise up in their room the ordinances of Hell . . . and, the bands of God being broken, none other shall bind men together; every man's hand shall be against his brother, and misrule shall be the law of the world, until all are gathered up under that Antichrist who hastens to be revealed (Micah VII, 5).[110]

All this had been precisely foretold in Holy Scripture (Luke 21: 25–6; 2 Thess. 2: 3–10; 2 Tim. 3: 2–4; Apoc. 3: 10). Unless the signs of the time were heeded and God's promises believed, nothing could prevent the false priests of God's Church from allying themselves with the false prophet (Apoc. 13: 11) and the kings of the earth (Apoc. 17: 14 and 19: 19) to make war on the Lamb.

The apostatizing contemporary Church was contrasted with the Church of Holy Scripture:

---

[109] *GT* XCV (*M/HDI* i. 429).   [110] *GT* XCVII (*M/HDI* i. 430).

The apostasy and approaching judgement . . . of God's baptized people; the utter dissimilarity of those bodies called Churches, of any one of them apart, or of the whole of them together . . . to that body described under the same name 'the Church' in Holy Scripture; their consequent inability to fulfil God's purpose in them, or their duty to Him and His creatures; and their utter unpreparedness for the coming of the Lord, we have now declared; and we cite as our witnesses the consciences of all to whom this testimony comes. . . . But it is God alone 'who revealeth the deep and secret things . . .' (Dan. II). And . . . He hath now interpreted the signs of the times, and made known the hidden cause of these evils—the fearful judgements which impend,—the fierce tyranny of that enemy of God and man, the old Serpent, who deceived man at the first, and is now gathering up the deceived to involve them in one fell catastrophe,—and the near approach of Him who shall be revealed from heaven with His mighty angels, recompensing 'rest' to those who are waiting for Him, but shame and everlasting contempt 'to those who know not God, and obey not the Gospel of our Lord Jesus Christ' (2 Thess. I, 7, 8).[111]

The Restoration of Apostles for the Preparation of the Bride

Those who could abide the Day of the Lord would be those who were filled with the Holy Spirit and who were sealed on their foreheads (Apoc. 7: 3). But it was claimed that that ministry could not be provided, and hence the Church could not be perfected, without the restoration of those ordinances—the ministry of apostles, together with prophets, evangelists, pastors and teachers, ordained by apostles—which God had given to the Church at her beginning:

But they shall be given; all the promises contained in His word of the restoration of His Zion, in the hour of her greatest peril, shall be fulfilled; and that purpose shall be accomplished according to His own counsel, and by His own instrumentality, and by no man's devices.[112]

Such a work of the Holy Spirit was now being set up within the Church to prepare her as the Bride of the Bridegroom—to prepare those who

shall stand with the Lamb on Mount Zion, the manifested firstfruits (Rev. XIV, 1-5) unto God and the Lamb, the earnest of that glorious harvest, when the Son of Man shall send forth His angels, and shall

---

[111] *GT* C (*M/HDI* i. 432-3).   [112] *GT* CI (*M/HDI* i. 434).

gather His elect from the four winds, from one end of heaven to the other (Matt. XXIV, 31).[113]

It was to proclaim this calling to all the baptized that God had restored apostles to His Church—God had not cast them out. But it would be

no earthly deliverance, nor restoration of earthly dignity or power. The last notes of the knell of this world's Dispensation are pealing—the world passes away, and the things of the world; the only hope is that which hath ever been the hope of the Church, to be caught up to meet the Lord in the air, and so to be ever with him, saved from the snare of the temptation and the great tribulation which are coming upon the earth. But will ye hear? God knoweth . . . whoever will, shall be surely saved from the destruction, and kept in the pavilion of God in the time of evil: but whosoever will not hear, will not receive God's seal, how shall he escape the judgement written, that 'because they receive not the love of the truth that they may be saved, God shall send them a strong delusion that they should believe a lie, that they all might be damned who believe not the truth but had pleasure in unrighteousness' (2 Thess. II, 11, 12).[114]

In evidence of God's faithfulness, He had responded to the prayers

which in every age of the Church, by the disposition of His Providence, have been offered in the ministrations of the separate communities of the baptized . . . He hath listened to the cry of those who mourned over the low estate of His Church, and have called on Him 'to raise up in his power and come, and with great might to succour us, that that, which our sins have hindered, His bountiful grace and mercy may accelerate' (Oratio pro Domin. 4ta Adventus. Miss. Rom.—Collect for the 4th Sunday in Advent. English Com. Prayer.)[115]

This response had taken the form of outpourings of the Holy Spirit in the West of Scotland, in various congregations in London, and elsewhere. But it could not end there, because

had the work of the Lord proceeded no further, all we had gained would have been the knowledge of *our own* sin, and the sins of *our fathers*: and the result would have been the mournful expectation of the fall of all that was dear of reverence, and sacred to piety, without a vestige of hope or the possibility of remedy. But God had not forsaken the work of His own hands. . . . The work of the Lord by His Spirit has been to prepare

---

[113] *GT* CI (*M/HDI* i. 434).   [114] *GT* CII (*M/HDI* i. 435).
[115] *GT* CV (this and subsequent paragraphs not included by Miller).

men by many trials, by many chastisements, by many revelations of their own iniquity and perverseness, and of His never-failing mercy, to receive power, the very power of God, and to use it for the building up of His Church . . . for the bringing into one all the Baptized, to recall them to the Apostolic character and constitution of the Church of Christ, to prepare them to receive the fourfold ministry of Jesus, and to instruct them to submit to the order of the Lord.[116]

The cry for a 'body', heard from the first manifestations of the Spirit in Scotland—though initially little understood—was now being answered. Apostles had been restored and separated by a special act of the Church—as represented by the seven churches in London, though 'but a shadow of what His Universal Church should be'.[117] Congregations were being set up on the foundation of apostles and prophets, each under the rule of an angel, together with elders, deacons, and underdeacons, and the Gospel was being preached by evangelists. All this was not a new sect, but God's way for imparting His blessing to the whole of Christendom:

for what so bears the impress of God, as that, in the midst of a perverse and gainsaying people, a witness should be raised up against all the forms of sin which are hurrying men into the ranks of Antichrist; and in things evident to the senses also, in multiplied instances of healing the sick, and in deliverance, manifest to the eyes of men, of those oppressed by the devil in body and spirit.[118]

Because the appeal of this new work was to Christendom, it was essentially a spiritual appeal, which by its manifest truth—truth being the chief sign of apostleship—would separate out the spiritual remnant from the mass of professing Christians. The mark of Antichrist in the last times was to deceive through the working or miracles and wonders. By the revival of the fourfold ministry of apostles, prophets, evangelists, and pastors and teachers, God had

manifested again the eternal form of the going forth of the power of His Spirit for the revelation of Himself unto men, and by these . . . shall all the saints of God be gathered, cleansed, and builded into His temple; and all His people, all His Churches, all His hierarchies, shall be seen throughout the earth to be One.

For all the faithful must be gathered into one, and, by visible separation from the faithless, be shewn to be one. . . . The preparation of the baptized to receive the Lord, when He cometh, is the fulness of the

[116] *GT* CIX–CX.   [117] *GT* CXI.   [118] *GT* CXIV.

Holy Ghost. If they abide in the flesh, when He calls on them, and brings near the means, that they should be filled with the Spirit, what can hinder that they should be filled with the spirit of strong delusion and delivered up to the man of sin? If the Lord be again sending forth Apostles and Prophets to His Church, and the baptized reject and persecute them, they thereby proclaim themselves apostate.[119]

Those in authority in the Churches should acknowledge God's hand in the work being newly done, confess their sins, cease from all idolatry, stand apart from everything evil, continue in prayer, be joyful in hope, and watch day and night for the salvation of Israel, because of the approaching deliverance offered through the power of God in the Holy Spirit. Those in places of secular authority should be faithful in their duties, reject the immoral and profane, purge their courts of vice and corruption, and, above all, shield and sustain the Church, submitting themselves in spiritual matters to those set over them:

There is no refuge in any human defences from the storm which is ready to burst upon you.—The only escape is, in being taken from the evil to come; in ascending to the Hill of God; in seeking for, and hasting unto the Coming of the Lord, for which this work of GOD is only preparation.[120]

For their part, the duty of the restored apostles was to proclaim the message given to them, whether it be accepted or not, and to

abide in continual supplication, in intercessions . . . for all the Church of God . . . all the rulers of Christendom, with all estates and conditions of men . . .[121]

Some Important Aspects of the Great Testimony

Although discussion of the prophetic content of the testimony and other works will mainly be left to the final section of this chapter, a number of points about it deserve mention here.

First and perhaps most noticeable is the extreme reserve about dating future events, though their sequence was presented in outline, including specific mention of the 'first resurrection'. The signs of the times and the apostasy of the Churches were said to indicate a nearness of the Second Advent requiring urgent attention

---

[119] *GT* CXIX–CXX. [120] *GT* CXXII. [121] *GT* CXXIII.

and action on the part of Church and State, but no attempt was made to make that 'nearness' precise.

Secondly, although all parts of the Christian Church came in for selective condemnation, there was a recognition that good had been preserved and that there were faithful remaining within them. This was entirely in accord with the principles underlying the apostolic journeyings throughout Christendom, whose express purpose was to seek to discover all that was to be commended within the Churches (see Ch. II, § 2). There was yet to be a final test of faithfulness or apostasy, namely acceptance or rejection of the new work of the Spirit being presented to them.

Thirdly, there were underlying assumptions about Christendom, namely that both the secular authority of the monarch and ecclesiastical authority were given by God, the former being a witness to God's sovereignty over all things. Despotism was a misuse of that God-given power, but could not be used to justify the outrages of revolution. There was an underlying horror of 'liberalism' and what today would be regarded as the 'democratic process', which were linked to atheism and to the destruction of social order at all levels. This was a reflection of the strong upper-middle class Toryism of the majority of the Catholic Apostolic apostles. Yet, there was an almost complete absence of social concern—almost certainly due to the apocalyptic nature of the message as a whole. There was no longer time for improvement of the lot of the poor either by social reform or by charitable works: events were moving too swiftly towards the consummation of all things.

Fourthly, the credentials of the new apostles and the credibility of their apocalyptic message were to depend upon the evident truth of their witness according to the signs of the times and not upon miracles of healing and other evidences of supernatural power, which would be a witness of Antichrist. Their role was, above all else, one of intercession for all the baptized—a role which received special emphasis in Catholic Apostolic liturgical worship (see Ch. IV).

Finally, it should be noted that *The Great Testimony* (as also the two earlier 'lesser' testimonies) was addressed only to the *heads* of Church and state, no attempt being made to address it to the people at large. This was in accord with the principle that God's ordinances, whether in Church or State, should not be bypassed. It was only when it became clear that Church and State authorities rejected or

352 Eschatology

ignored the apostolic message that public witness was commenced in accordance with Luke 14: 23.[122]

6. CATHOLIC APOSTOLIC ESCHATOLOGY II: OTHER APOSTOLIC WRITINGS

The eschatological outline in *The Great Testimony* was developed in the writings of the various apostles, most notably Carlyle, Dalton, Drummond, Sitwell, and Tudor. As was the case with the prophetic studies discussed in Sections 2–4 above, scriptural references were primarily to Daniel and the Apocalypse. The latter opened up the purposes of God concerning the Church, and was intended to be understood without a further revelation:

It is not an enigma, not a hidden mystery, not a book which requires another angel to be sent from heaven to explain the things which Christ had already sent an angel to show unto his servant John: for in that case it would not be a revelation, if it needed some one to reveal it. It is to be regarded as a declaration of the future history of the Church, both in its spiritual and in its temporal aspects; coming from Christ, as Head of the Church.[123]

On the 'Letters to the Seven Churches'

However, in the Apocalypse, prophecies relating to future events were not taken as commencing with chapter 4—the 'letters to the seven churches' were regarded as having an important relevance to the whole history of the Church, though, in view of Apocalypse 1: 19, their immediate application to the times of John was not denied:

Now we know where the things future begin. At Rev. iv. 1, we read 'After these things I looked;' . . . Therefore we know that the Epistles to the Churches refer to the things present, as distinguished from the things future.

---

[122] See C. W. Boase, *Supplementary Narrative to the Elijah Ministry* (unfinished) (Edinburgh: Grant, 1868), 822.
[123] J. O. Tudor, *Six Lectures on the Apocalypse* (London: Boswell, 1861), Lecture I, MS version, p. 7.

But what do 'present' and 'future' here mean? Where does the present end? . . . It may mean either a condition and events actually subsisting when John wrote, or a dispensation of which that condition and those events formed a part—an indivisible unity embracing things then present. Here the word has both meanings, because the Churches to which it refers occupied a twofold position—on the one hand a literal, on the other a symbolical. . . . in so far as they represented the Church Catholic—the true Sevenfold Unity in all times and places—their position was symbolical, and the words addressed to them applied, not merely to their local and temporary position, but to the whole phenomena of the Catholic Church during the whole of the Christian dispensation. . . . no man can read them, without also seeing, that their contents vastly transcend all merely local and temporary application. So is it always with the words of Him who seeth the end from the beginning, and of the Holy Ghost, who is the earnest of our inheritance, our Comforter and Monitor, till Christ shall come again. These epistles are the great catholic address of the risen Lord to the Church Catholic until the end of time. And while, as regards the seven special Churches addressed, the 'present' ends, and the 'future' commences, with the writing of John; yet, as regards the Church Catholic, the one ends, and the other begins, where, and in so far as the dispensation of judgement succeeds the dispensation of grace.[124]

These epistles, representing the first vision of the Apocalypse, were seen by both Tudor and Carlyle as dealing with 'Christ's continuous spiritual presence with the universal Church on earth'.[125] They were to be applied both chronologically and simultaneously to the Church, that is, they provided a prophecy of the future state of the Church in the various periods to come, yet at the same time pointed to characteristics present in the Church at each period of time. A rainbow provided the analogy, which was confirmed later in the Apocalypse:

This is rendered plain by the natural symbol of the rainbow, in which we have a simultaneous view of the sevenfold colours of the spectrum, and at the same time a field over which the eye can range in succession through the seven colours, each imperceptibly blended into, yet distinct from, those adjoining to it. And it is equally justified by the explicit interpretation of the seven heads, mountains, and kings, in Rev. xvii. 9.[126]

---

[124] T. Carlyle, *On the Epistles to the Seven Churches* (London: Goodall, 1854), 2–3.
[125] Tudor, *Six Lectures*, 2.
[126] Carlyle, *Epistles to the Seven Churches*, 4.

No one could doubt the universal application of the seven epistles since each ended with the words, 'He who has an ear [that is, a spiritual ear], let him hear what the Spirit says to the Churches'.

It was important for the chronological interpretation of the epistles that, of the seven churches, the second and sixth were exclusively commended whilst the fifth and seventh were exclusively blamed. The chronological sequence was as follows:

Ephesus ('desirable'): The apostolic age, from the foundation of the Church to the beginning of the Roman persecution, AD 30–66.

Smyrna ('myrrh'): The period of the ten persecutions, 66–306.

Pergamos ('exaltation'): The period from the Constantinian settlement to the fall of the Western Roman Empire, the age of state patronage, 306–395.

Thyateira ('toil of sacrifice'): The period from the fall of the Roman Empire to the Reformation, the age of 'relic worship', 395–1517.

Sardis ('that which remains'): The period from the Reformation to the French Revolution, 1517–1793.

Philadelphia ('love of brethren'): The period in which God was restoring the Church through the sending of new apostles, the preparation for the translation of the saints.

Laodicea ('popular judgement'): The time (in the future) in which those who will not accept the restoration of the Church will be rejected, the period of the great tribulation.

Alternatively, the period of Thyateira was curtailed in order that Sardis could be interpreted as the 1260 'Papal' years, culminating in the French Revolution of 1793, and Laodicea was seen as coming into being along with Philadelphia.[127] By having the time of Laodicea contemporary rather than in the future, the Bible societies and (later) the Tractarian Movement were both seen as exemplifying the Laodicean spirit,

rigid, exclusive and self-righteous. It is like the Pharisee in the parable . . . not like the publican . . . It denotes . . . a people priding themselves

[127] Compare Carlyle, *Epistles to the Seven Churches*, 4, and Tudor, *A Brief Interpretation of the Book of Revelation. Suggesting those Principles, by Adhering to which, a Sound and Satisfactory Understanding may be Attained of This Last, and to us the Most Important Book, of the Sacred Canon* (London: Painter, 1855), MS version, p. 5. However, in Tudor's *Six Lectures* the scheme presented is the same as that of Carlyle. Comparison of dates would suggest that Tudor changed his 1855 version to conform to that of Carlyle.

in the persuasion of their own righteousness—not needing a Saviour—not conscious of their sins.[128]

Although Ephesus represented the greatly revered Apostolic age, it was not exclusively commended because it was also the time in which dissentions were already beginning within the Church (as the New Testament itself witnesses), and towards the end of which the Church was tempted to fall away from her 'first love'—the apostleship—and accept the 'false coin' of episcopal rule, eventually and inevitably leading to heresy and schism. Smyrna was especially commended because the period of the Roman persecutions was the period of the great Christian martyrs, a time when the Church, though in the hands of men, was also in the 'furnace' of God. Pergamos was distinguished by a holding fast to the Faith, but at the same time by a secularization of Church government both through the assumption of worldly power on the part of the Church—descending from serving in heaven to ruling on earth—and the subjection of the Church to the civil power. Thyateira had performed commendable faithful service, but at the same time allowed 'Jezebel' to teach: that is, instead of remaining silent as the Bride (the woman) so as to allow the Bridegroom, Christ (the man), to speak through her, the Church (through the Papacy) spoke as a prophetess in her own right, thus introducing great errors of doctrine and practice. Sardis was an equal condemnation of the Reformation and its results, which had the reputation of stirring up life, whilst being in reality dead within due to the rejection of apostolic ordinances and the attempt to return to so-called fundamentals determined not by God but by the opinions of men. Philadelphia was significant for what the Lord had done for the Church—the restoration of apostolic rule—rather than for what the Church had done for Him. The promise given implied the sealing of the saints through apostolic ordinance as a foretaste of His speedy coming. Laodicea was the time when men, standing up in their own name only, usurp the rule of God. The one, great, damning sin of Laodicea, the only Church given no praise, was lukewarmness—a neutrality when the contest was for the throne of the universe and the contestants are Christ and Antichrist. This showed that all who would not be *for* Christ, would be *against* Him. The promise to those

---

[128] Tudor, *A Brief Interpretation of the Book of Revelation*, 8.

who would hear Christ's voice was the translation of the saints (Apoc. 3: 20–1).

On the Visions of the Apocalypse

The visions of the Apocalypse relating to the Church were seen as having been constructed according to the pattern of the Tabernacle, whilst the civil power was always represented by symbols taken from the prophecies of Daniel.

The first vision—represented by the seven epistles—was interpreted as being set on earth in the holy place, the Church, where

Christ, through His Angel, acts as the Jewish high priest, who trimmed the lamps of the candlestick every day at morning and evening worship in the holy place.[129]

This vision, symbolizing Christ walking in the midst of the Churches, was intended to show how far the Church had departed from faith in the continual presence of Christ with His people to the end of time.

The second vision (Apoc. 4: 1–8: 4) was seen as set in heaven, symbolized by the most holy place into which the Jewish high priest entered only on the Day of Atonement. Thus Christ Himself opens the seven-sealed book which contains the history of the Church until the Second Advent. This vision referred to the abiding call of the Church to be risen in spirit with Christ. It was intended to disclose how far the Church had fallen short of realizing her own spiritual resurrection in Christ. Yet, the first and second visions had much parallelism:

They present an analogy similar to that which subsists between the body and soul of man, or between the visible and invisible Church, which ought to be, in all respects, correspondent. In the first vision, Christ is represented as spiritually present within the Church on earth: and in the second vision the Church is represented as spiritually risen with Christ in the heavens. True faith will realise both these doctrines, and it should be the condition of the Church at all times, and the evil consequences of the various degrees of dereliction of standing or of duty, are set forth in both these visions.[130]

This parallelism was further developed so that the seven seals corresponded precisely to the seven epistles and the periods of

---

[129] Tudor, *Six Lectures on the Apocalypse*, 3.   [130] Ibid. 4.

Church history to which they were applied. With the seals, however, it had to be remembered that the scene was changed from earth to heaven, the symbols undergoing analogous changes, and Christ appearing

not as the Bishop walking in the midst of the candlesticks, but as a Lamb which had been slain in the midst of the throne.[131]

This parallelism enabled the earthquake at the opening of the sixth seal to be interpreted as marking the French Revolution with its slaughter of priests—the shaking of the foundations of Christendom. The seventh seal lay still in the future.

The third vision (Apoc. 8: 2–9: 21) returned to the holy place, but to a place nearer the veil than the first vision—the golden altar before the mercy-seat. It referred to worship, and, in particular, to the one way of approach to the mercy-seat through the one Mediator. It therefore disclosed the judgements which would ensue in punishment of false worship or idolatry—an idolatry which had begun in consequence of Christianity having become the religion of the state, so that Christians sought wordly honours and temporal gain. The angel standing at the altar with the golden censer (Apoc. 8: 3) was the symbol of the intercession of Christ the High Priest before the Father. Fire was cast down from the altar of intercession and the angels prepared to sound because misguided men had set aside the one Mediator and chosen others. The first four trumpets of this vision related to the same period as the fourth seal of the previous vision, and were sounded primarily against Rome. They thus referred to the attacks of the Goths, Vandals, and Huns. The first two 'woe' trumpets, on the other hand, were sounded against the Eastern Empire, and referred to the two periods of attacks by Islam. (This was said to be symbolized also by the two little horns of Daniel 7 and 8, which represented two oppressions of the Church—by the Papacy and by Islam.)

The fourth vision (Apocalypse 10–13) was set in the outer court at the brazen altar, the chief actor being St John—personifying the Church—eating the book and prophesying to the whole world, thus indicating the recovery of the Bible by the Church at the Reformation. Having digested its contents, he becomes qualified to take account of the extent to which those who profess Christianity

---

[131] Tudor, *A Brief Interpretation of the Book of Revelation*, 15.

have departed from divine standards in both doctrine and morals. The woman clothed with the sun (Apocalypse 12: 1) represented the true Church in its perfection of purity, faith, and spiritual endowment. This was not a vision of the final consummation, but of the birth of the Church with its endowment of hope in the Second Advent. The dragon (Apoc. 12: 3) represented Satan at work within the Church to frustrate that hope. Of the two flights of the woman (Apoc. 12: 6, 14), one had already taken place during the 1260 'papal' years, whilst the other, of 1260 days only, would take place during the translation at the beginning of the tribulation.

The fifth vision (Apoc. 14–18) was set in Mount Zion, the place to which the 'first-born'—those whose names are written in heaven— will be gathered. Thus it related to the translation of the saints and to the time of the great tribulation on earth when the seven vials of God's wrath will be poured out upon apostate Christendom. The company of Chapter 15 was to be distinguished from that of Chapter 14 (the 144,000 first-fruits), since the former was in heaven and sang the song of Moses and the Lamb, whilst the latter was on Mount Zion and learned a new song which only it could utter. The three unclean spirits like frogs coming out of the dragon, the beast and the false prophet (Apoc. 16: 13) represented the three conflicting principles of democracy, absolute monarchy, and theocracy, which the Antichrist would combine in his own person to head up one great antichristian confederacy—a world confederacy with an apostate priesthood and furnished with all the wonders of modern science— which would be destroyed at Armageddon.

In the sixth vision (Apoc. 19) heaven and earth were seen as shaken in preparation for the new heaven and new earth in which Christ and His saints will have their eternal abode. The heavens open and Christ descends with His saints and the day of vengeance is come. This vision therefore referred to the Second Advent and the destruction of Antichrist and the false prophet and their followers.

The seventh and final vision (Apoc. 20–2) was of the manifestation of the sons of God, the appearance of the new heaven and earth, the casting down of thrones, and the giving of the everlasting kingdom to the saints of the Most High. It therefore referred to the setting up of the judgement throne, the beginning of the millennium, and the new Jerusalem. The final judgement would begin at the commencement of the millennium with the departed called up 'each in his new order' (1 Cor. 15: 23), those having had the greatest Christian privileges being judged first, the unbaptized heathen not being called until the millennium was ended.

In considering the millennium, it was crucial to understand the distinction between prophecies relating to the Jews and those relating to the Christian Church:

Nearly all the mistakes concerning the millennium, which have brought so much reproach on the millenarian doctrines, have had their source in not perceiving the distinction between the Jewish and Christian mysteries, and, as a necessary consequence, either treating all the promises to Abraham, Isaac, and Jacob, as having only a spiritual fulfilment, or, which is far worse, degrading the heavenly Jerusalem to the same level with the earthly Jerusalem. . . . eight whole chapters are exclusively occupied in Ezekiel with the latter-day glory of the children of Israel, when they shall be restored to the land of their inheritance, and shall build the third temple, in which the glory of the Lord shall abide for evermore. But of the heavenly Jerusalem it is written, I saw no temple therein; for the Lord God Almighty and the Lamb are the temple of it. The *glory* of the Lord filled the temple of Ezekiel: the Lord *Himself* is present in the heavenly Jerusalem.[132]

Thus the restoration of the whole house of Israel to the promised land, brought out in the Old Testament prophecies, must be carefully distinguished from the new creation spoken of in the (exceptional) prophecies of Isaiah.

Sitwell's Eschatological Work

One of the most extensive presentations of Catholic Apostolic eschatology was that of Sitwell in his 1865 work, *The Purpose of God in Creation and Redemption*. The work was written as an apologia for the Catholic Apostolic witness because there had been

a continual series of mis-statements concerning it in every sort of publication; in reviews, magazines, newspapers, histories of sects, and lastly in biographies of individuals, whether of those connected with this work, or opposed to it.[133]

The writer felt that it was a useless and undignified task to correct such mis-statements; instead he set out to present a work answering

---

[132] Tudor, *A Brief Interpretation of the Book of Revelation*, 11.

[133] F. Sitwell, *The Purpose of God in Creation and Redemption: and the Successive Steps for Manifesting the Same in and by the Church* (Edinburgh: Laurie, 1865), viii (henceforth S/*PG*).

the question, 'What are your reasons for believing this work to be of God?' The result was a work which included a restatement and expansion of the content of the testimonies, including those parts devoted to an analysis of the history of the Church and prophecies of the nearness of the Second Advent, with the usual prophetic references to Daniel and the Apocalypse.

From the beginning the work was given both an eschatological and an historical context:

The counsel of the Lord is to set His Son as King upon His holy hill of Zion (Ps. 2: 6–8), and to give Him the nations for His inheritance, and the uttermost parts of the earth for His possession.

The work of Satan, the adversary of God, is to prevent this, if possible; and the kings of the earth also, and the rulers, and the people, set themselves against it, and take counsel how to hinder it (Ps. 2: 1–3 and 33: 10). And not only these, but the Church . . . has for many generations misunderstood, and consequently greatly withstood, the plans of God.[134]

Three of the great misunderstandings were: that the Church would by the efforts of her members convert the world, including the Jewish nation; that the time of the Second Advent was far, perhaps millions of years, in the future; and that at the Second Advent the world would be annihilated by fire—the good going to a far-off heaven and the wicked to an equally far-off hell. Thus, the Second Advent was thought of in terms of the destruction of creation rather than in terms of its redemption. All these were contrary to the teaching of Holy Scripture.

The chief duty of the Church was, in the power of the Holy Spirit, to continue in the world Christ's witness to the Kingdom. The Church had failed in this mission, though in all parts of it and in all ages of her earthly existence there was much that was to be commended. Thus the Church of Rome had stood for the principle of Christian unity, for sacraments as channels of living grace, and for the idea of the eucharistic oblation as a sacrifice despite a perversion of doctrine on this point. She had also performed many works of charity. The Eastern Orthodox Churches had, in addition, refused to accept the usurped supremacy of the Roman bishop, resisted Roman theological errors, guarded the integrity of Holy Scripture, and preserved the Faith during ages of Mohammedan persecution. The

[134] *S/PG* 1–2.

Anglican Church had preserved an episcopacy free from the hands of Rome, removed many superstitions and errors, restored congregational worship to the people in their own tongue together with the free use of Scripture under subjection to the Church. The Presbyterians had vindicated the right of presbyters to have a share in the rule of the Church and kept before the Church the election of God. The Dissenters stood for the principle that the Divine life was above all forms, and for the people having a voice in the selection of their clergy. Nevertheless, this catalogue of commendation must be followed by an equal catalogue of condemnation of the Church for grave departures from her chief duty and calling, of which the most significant symptoms were the replacement of heavenly goals by earthly ones and the subjection of spiritual rule to secular rule.

On the Six Epochs

The history of the Church's unfaithfulness could be divided into six epochs, the first of which ended with the death of the last apostle, St John. Within this period strife and dissension arose, as witnessed by the epistles written to counteract errors. The Apostles nevertheless retained the Church's unity whilst they lived, guarding and protecting the truth. Yet the last Apostle's final complaint was of being withstood and hindered, and the closing book of Scripture is thus

a melancholy delineation of forthcoming scenes of crime, and spiritual adultery, and desperate rebellion.[135]

The second epoch concluded with the Constantinian settlement. It was a period without apostolic rule, for the greater part of which outward unity was largely preserved though there were many inner intrigues, scandals, and frauds. At the close of this epoch, major heresy entered the Church with the Arian dispute, which even bishops adopted, and recourse was made to the newly Christian secular ruler in an attempt to enforce unity and truth with the sword, and with anathemas and excommunications. The hope of the coming Kingdom and the Second Advent of Christ grew cold:

The theory of the Lord's coming as a Judge, at some long distant day, and of the general resurrection, was indeed retained and taught, . . . but

[135] *S/PG* 42.

the coming of a judge is not what men *hope* for; and they said also, 'I look for the resurrection of the dead, and the life of the world to come'; but they ceased to look for 'the resurrection from the dead', and 'the life of the world to come' became to them the state and place the soul went to at its separation from the body![136]

This condition continued: even in periods where expositors of Scripture had endeavoured to interpret such works as Daniel and the Apocalypse, their interest had almost invariably been in Babylon and the Antichrist, which they looked to in *dread*, rather than in the *hope* of the coming of the Bridegroom. Significantly, the gift of speaking in tongues and prophesying was lost to the Church by the end of the fourth century.

The third epoch covered the period from Constantine to Pope Gregory VII (Hildebrand), a period for the Church of visions of earthly prosperity and grandeur under the protection of the Roman Empire—'that dread Fourth Empire, the persecutor of God's people (Dan. 7)'[137]—the Emperor becoming the usurping ruler in Zion. The Great Schism occurred in this epoch, brought about not so much by dispute of doctrine (the *filioque*, unleavened bread, etc.) as by the endeavour of Pope Leo IX to bring the Patriarchates of Alexandria and Antioch under his control. Schism, heresy, and corruption spread over Christendom because of acquiescence in the earthly sovereign having power in ecclesiastical matters and because of the coveting of earthly rule by the Roman pontiff. During this period, the year 1000 had been looked to as bringing in the end, and Apocalypse 20: 2–3 was preached to the terrified people, often with resulting riots. Even kings and lords begged at monastery doors to be received as brethren, donating their estates to charity and placing the emblems of their rank on the altars and before the images of saints. Yet this all arose from the false computation of the 1000 years from the First Advent instead of the Second, a falsehood for which Augustine had been first responsible when he departed from the true teaching on the millennium. The passing of the year 1000 without the expected events resulted in the indefinite postponement of the Second Advent in men's minds, and the idea of permanence on earth took possession of the Church, together with the supremacy of the Church over the state:

[136] *S/PG* 49.   [137] *S/PG* 53.

the Emperor had proved not to be God's ruler in Zion; now a priest upon his throne should be God's ruler in Zion, and over all the earth (*urbi et orbi*).[138]

One usurper was replaced by another, and forged documents (the decretals) were used to justify the usurpation.

The fourth epoch concluded with the Reformation. If the first thousand years had not fulfilled the Church's fears, it was now expected that the next would fulfil her hopes. But these hopes were sadly changed: she no longer waited for the inheritance which was 'imperishable, undefiled, and unfading . . . to be revealed in the last time' (1 Pet. 1: 4–5); her dreams were of establishing, against all challenge, a universal rule in the world over Church and nations. Men's hearts were deceived through the loss of all prophetical understanding of Scripture. Although the East was lost to Rome

From Norway to Calabria the theory of a Universal Church, governed by an infallible chief . . . the satisfier of all doubts, and the sole instrument of salvation, was everywhere admitted.[139]

The Bull of Dissolution of the Lateran Council of 1517 had announced the accomplishment of all that had been looked for. Councils, princes, and people had all been brought under subjection:

And this very year, when the delusion had come to the full, and almost before the echo of the voices of flattering prelates and monarchs had died away, as if in mockery of their presumption, another voice was heard: Luther had begun . . . his public preaching against the most flagrant of Rome's pretensions, and had commenced the Western Schism.[140]

The fifth epoch ran from the Reformation to the French Revolution. In the preceding centuries the belief had been that the will of one man, the Vicar of Christ, was to be obeyed in all things. Now a man, Luther, had stood up for the very opposite principle, namely that the private judgement of every individual—albeit with a Bible in his hand—was to rule and guide all. Thus 'the abuse of ordinances had issued in the rejection of all ordinances'.[141] The old contest between the civil and ecclesiastical powers revived, and attempts to use the monarch again as a focus of the unity now lost was only partially successful. Lacking apostolic ordinances, the Protestants inevitably split up into many subdivisions, often

[138] *S/PG* 60. [139] *S/PG* 68. [140] *S/PG* 74. [141] *S/PG* 75.

striving as much between themselves as against Rome. Whatever good Luther and the Reformation may have done in pointing to abuses in the Church, the result was ever-increasing breaches in Church unity:

the principles then introduced, instead of restoring unity and truth, were those that, by bringing into question all ordinances, inevitably led from division to division without end, and to every heresy and every error.[142]

The reaction brought up Loyola and the Jesuits: precisely as Luther wrote against monastic vows, Loyola wrote his *Spiritual Exercises*— 'the deadliest book which ever defiled with the serpent's slime the spirit of man'.[143] Amongst the Protestant Churches, only the Anglican was conspicuous for having preserved more of Catholic truth, order, and sacrament than all the rest, since her Reformation had been the work of her bishops and priests rather than of individuals. But the seed of discord has been sown within her also by outside Calvinistic influence. Protestantism was a ready ally of eighteenth-century rationalism and utopianism, together with the perversions of philosophy and science:

And that spirit had grown, and diffused itself throughout the baptized nations, to an extent that will only be made manifest when the torch of the last Antichrist shall be applied, and shall fill the world with its flame.[144]

The sixth epoch was ushered in by the French Revolution,

the first shock of that earthquake which will overthrow every established institution of Church and State, and bring in that intolerable reign of Antichrist, which will necessitate the coming of Jesus Christ to save the world.[145]

The understanding of the events of the sixth epoch demanded reference to Daniel and the Apocalypse. The statue of Nebuchadnezzar's vision (Dan. 2: 31–5) indicated the four great earthly powers which would exist before the coming of Christ the true King: the dynasty of Nebuchadnezzar himself, the Medo-Persian empire, the Grecian empire, and the Roman empire. The latter would exist in three successive conditions: first, in an iron unity and strength, then in a divided state of many kingdoms joined by family and matrimonial

---

[142] S/*PG* 77.   [143] S/*PG* 78.   [144] S/*PG* 80.   [145] S/*PG* 80.

connections, and finally and still in the future in ten kingdoms (as symbolized by the ten toes). It was in this final state that God would break apart all these kingdoms and set up an everlasting kingdom which could not be destroyed. In Daniel 7, the prophetic history of the same four empires was given in terms of four wild beasts which would trample upon his people, the Jews, for century after century. All the beasts would oppress the Jews, and, despite its becoming Christian in name, the fourth more than the rest.

On Interpretations of the Apocalypse

If Daniel perceived what should be done to the Jews and the earthly power which awaited them afterwards, St John revealed to the Christian Church what awaited her and the glory that should be hers afterwards, the two visions running much in parallel. Thus Daniel's eleventh horn (Dan. 7: 24) corresponded to St John's Antichrist, and both visions indicated when the Second Advent would take place:

The whole of the visions of Daniel and St. John testify the same thing, and admit of no mistake, nor of any doubt, as to *when* the kingdom of God is to come. Whenever the fourth metal of the image is smitten— whenever the fourth beast is given to the burning flame—whenever the Beast and the False Prophet are cast into the lake of fire, then, and not till then, will the kingdom of Christ and the saints come, whether to Christian or Jew; but when these events do occur, then shall the kingdom be given to them, each in its place . . .[146]

St John's prophecies were concerned with the oppression which the Church would experience at the hands of the oppressor—the captivity of the spiritual Israel in the spiritual Babylon. The fourth beast of Daniel and the beast with ten horns of the Apocalypse were identical, but it had to be remembered that the symbol of a beast can represent not only an empire or monarchy, but also its head. This was important in a number of instances, but especially in Apocalypse 13 and 17—13: 1–2 referred to an empire, but 4–8 to a head; 17: 7 referred to an empire, but 11 onwards to the individual who would eventually head up the empire. The beast had seven heads, but it was an eighth head, the 'son of perdition' (2 Thess. 2: 3), who would be wounded and revived (Apoc. 17: 8, 11), and who would realize the dream of universal domination and be witnessed to by the false

[146] *S/PG* 88.

prophet before their final capture and destruction in the lake of fire (Apoc. 16: 13; 19: 20; 20: 10). When the ten kings, represented by the horns, should eventually appear, it would be the signal that Antichrist was near, as 'the old Fathers before Constantine knew'.[147] They would surrender their power to Antichrist, destroy Babylon the harlot (the apostate Church), and make war against Christ and Hist Hosts (Apocalypse 17: 13–17). Commentators who had attempted to evade the force of this prophecy by relating it to the sack of Rome by Alaric had falsified both Scripture and history.

The great sin attributed to the harlot Babylon in Apocalypse 17 was her adulterous connection with the secular power—her fornication with the kings of the earth. The Church had been constituted a pure *theocracy*—a place 'where the voice of God is heard declaring His Will in all things through His own appointed channels'.[148] God would not suffer king or priest, or the will of man, to usurp His rule over the Church:

This was to be the Woman, chosen of the Lord, the pure, the true, . . . the body of Christ; the Anointed, and the holy . . . the City . . . the spiritual Zion and Jerusalem . . . the people, the Israel of God . . . a woman, betrothed, her heart filled with the image of her Husband, and with longings for his appearing . . .[149]

Babylon was the precise opposite of this: it represented a people

breaking their baptismal covenant with God . . . disobedient to Christ's law of love to God and man, and to His last command to be united . . . mutilating, disfiguring, corrupting, perverting His holy sacraments . . . polluting His feasts . . . robbing Him of his tithes . . . profaning His name, and given over into captivity to the powers of the world.[150]

This was precisely what the mass of the baptized had come to, though they could not see it. The Church had become a body which was torn, dislocated, and full of sores, a city of confusion and disorder, a woman who had forgotten her betrothal and admitted others to her husband's place, who stored up treasures for herself on earth, and who had arrayed herself in gold and scarlet and trodden the people underfoot. She had come to live a life of continual intrigue with worldly powers. If Rome headed up this Babylon, those who had separated from her had merely built up for

[147] S/*PG* 95.   [148] S/*PG* 103.   [149] S/*PG* 105.
[150] S/*PG* 105–6.

themselves other houses in the same 'City of Confusion',[151] equally
involving themselves in secular power, often becoming almost totally
subject to civil rulers:

Let us look, for instance, at the case of the Anglican Church, where the
king's minister names whom he will for her Episcopal chairs, and where
Church and State are so mixed together, that she is unable to meet in
council to regulate her own affairs without the consent of Parliament. . . .
And, as to 'Confusion,' there is a continual contest between the parties
in her, railing at one another; while her priests teach what they please;
and men who bring into question every doctrine of the Church . . . are
applauded by the multitude.[152]

The Dissenters had thought that they had escaped from Babylon,
but had simply fallen into a different form of captivity, their clergy
were slaves to the principle of democracy. Far from healing
confusion, they had increased it—theirs was but one more step in
the Church's degradation. Only one further step remained—submission to the Beast himself. Such was the state of the Church when the
French Revolution occurred—'the commencement of the time of
the end'.[153]

It was important to recover the early patristic tradition of
typology, whereby the writings of the Old Testament were
interpreted as typical of Christ and His Kingdom. In particular, the
six days of creation followed by the Sabbath were typical of the six
thousand years of man's labour on the earth at the end of which
Christ would come to usher in the millennium. This teaching was to
be found explicitly in the Epistle of St Barnabas, which, although
doubts about its authorship were admitted, was regarded as having its
arguments validated by its early date.[154] The principle was to be
found in other patristic works, most notably in Hippolytus, St
Cyprian, and Lactantius.[155] It might be said that the 6000 years had
still 140 years to run and that therefore there was no urgency:

But this proceeds from the preconceived and mistaken notion, that the
translation, or taking up, of the saints to meet the Lord, is the *last*
instead of the *first* of a series of transactions. It may be true that one
hundred and forty years have to run their course before the final

---

[151] *S/PG* 110.   [152] *S/PG* 110–11.   [153] *S/PG* 114.
[154] Modern scholarship continues to date it to the latter part of the 1st cent.
[155] The references given are: 'Hippol. Expos. Dan., quoted by Photius, Codex,
202', and 'Cyprian *Exhort. ad Mart.* c. 12.'; no reference is given for Lactantius.

termination of the present order of things, and the perfect establishment of a new; although we must remember that 'for the elect's sake, those days should be shortened;' but . . . there is much to do in that time. . . . The Lord Jesus is not a breaker of the antitypes of the Law, but a fulfiller of them; the work must all be finished when the Sabbath morning dawns.[156]

That work consisted of the warning of the whole Church, so that those who heeded it and prepared themselves could be taken out of the great tribulation, and the marshalling of the ranks of those who should come with Christ so that each could have his right place. The great final drama was still to be played out:

Then, there is the appearing of the ten kings and of the Beast in his last form; there is the destruction of Babylon by them; also the pouring out of the seven last vials of the wrath of God (Rev. xvi. 2);[157] and the time of The Great tribulation; for the taking of the Jews into their own land is to be accompanied by such tribulation as never was known (Dan. xii. Zech. xiii, 8, 9.). There are the taking of the Jews to their land, and the dealings of God with them there. There are the doings of Antichrist and the False Prophet, and the gatherings of the kings to the great day of battle; the seige and capture of Jerusalem by Antichrist (Zech. xiv.; Dan. xi.); and the destruction of the Beast and the False Prophet, by the coming of Jesus Christ and His saints (Zech. xiv.). Then there is the binding of the Dragon in the bottomless pit (Rev. xix. 11–21.); and, lastly, the work of the Jews, whatever that may be, among the Gentile nations, to turn them unto Christ (Isa. lxvi. 19, 20.). When all these things are accomplished, the Sabbath will begin, and the earth will be at rest; for those that trouble it will have been cast out of it (Rev. xx.). The oppressors, the devil, and *his* men, their time shall have come to an end; and Christ and *His* men shall reign. Yes, there is much to do; and not much time to do it in. And we repeat, that among the *first* of these events is the taking of all who are ready out of the way of the evils that are coming upon the earth.[158]

The Church was therefore being called to her true standing by the restoration of the ministry of apostles and the renewal of her ancient fullness

---

[156] S/*PG* 122.

[157] The following point is made in a footnote: 'How can any of them have been poured out yet, when the first of them is to be poured on those who have worshipped the Beast, and received his mark and the number of his name, whereas the last and eighth head of the Beast whom they are to worship has not yet come!' (S/*PG* 123).

[158] S/*PG* 123–4.

in form, order and government; in ministry and discipline; in doctrine, in rite, ceremony, and sacrament; and in word,—conformed to Scripture; paying tithes and bringing offerings, and walking in holiness and righteousness, upholding and obeying the powers that be, whether in Church or State; offering the daily sacrifice in its true form; and waiting on God continually in the faith and hope of the coming of Jesus Christ, and of His kingdom, and proclaiming it in every land; and the Holy Ghost witnessing to the same in the midst of them by the voice of prophecy, once more heard in the Church.[159]

The many who were writing volumes in the attempt to prove that the Pope was *the* Antichrist, and that the destruction of Babylon was the destruction of the Papal system at the Second Advent, were leading their followers into a great delusion and 'working more mischief than all the declared enemies of the truth'.[160] This was immediately seen, because Babylon was clearly stated in Scripture to be destroyed *by Antichrist*. Such people were therefore declaring Antichrist to be Christ. Antichrist and the False Prophet were still to appear, and no one living knew who they would be. Lacunza had stated that the Beast, representing the False Prophet, was the Roman priesthood; but apostasy was a feature of the whole Church, not of the Roman Church alone. No one knew the meaning of the number 666, though there was

a glimmer of light thrown upon it in Scripture, viz., that while *seven* is God's number of completeness, *six* is that of man, and his day and time. Irenaeus says (Lib. v.), '666 is the true number of chapter thirteen of the Apocalypse; and that is an essential part of its meaning, for Antichrist will sum up the sins of the 6000 years typified by the six days of the world'. And Antichrist will be the completion of man's wickedness. Nebuchadnezzar's image was 66 . . . but this is 666. If it has been an abomination for kings to make images of gold, by meddling with the sacred things of God, and making decrees in the Church; how much greater will be the abomination . . . when this fearful man shall issue his decrees, abolishing the daily sacrifice, and all worship but that of himself; and command men to bow down to that image which he and his False Prophet shall set up.[161]

The error of making the Pope the Antichrist also led to misconceptions about the days spoken of in Daniel 7: 25 and 12: 7 and Apocalypse 11: 2–3 and 12: 6 and 14. All the early Fathers had agreed in interpreting these as *literal* days. Antichrist would exercise his power

[159] *S/PG* 253.　　　[160] *S/PG* 275.　　　[161] *S/PG* 277.

for 1260 *days*; it was only in attempting to fit in with the theory of the Pope as the Antichrist that the literal interpretation had come to be denied. Nevertheless, there was truth in the application of a *symbolical* meaning of the 1260 days to the *symbolical* Babylon—the apostate Church—since the number of years from the time of Justinian's edict, setting the Bishop of Rome over all Churches and exempting bishops from the jurisdiction of civil courts (533), to the decree of the French National Convention that religion should be abolished (1793) was precisely 1260.

Many commentators had also introduced errors in the interpretation of the woman of Apocalypse 12—so different from that of Apocalypse 17. Nevertheless:

> All the Fathers had agreed that this was a vision of the Church . . . and they had a very general perception that the history of the sun-clad woman and her seed is that of the Church, just previous to, and in, the times of Antichrist.[162]

Epiphanius had suggested that the vision *may* be the Mother-of-God (3. 21. 11); others had suggested the Jewish Church either before the Incarnation or restored in the last days; others still had suggested a Christian Church of converted Jews. None of these could stand serious examination. The true spiritual Church had ever been the mother of those who were destined to rule the nations—symbolized by the man-child. But the vision had special application to the period immediately before Antichrist. The Church

> is seen with the crown of apostleship around her head and as bringing into manifestation that body which is to be caught up to God and to His throne, and whereby He will rule the nations.[163]

This was a patristic interpretation to be found in Irenaeus, Methodius, and Victorinus, and which had been taken up by Faber:[164]

> Stanley Faber says, in his 'Sacred Calendar of Prophecy' (Vol. iii. 117, 119):—'In the symbolical language of the ancient prophets, the birth of a man-child denotes the setting apart of a community from the great general mass with which it was previously commingled; whilst the gestation and labour-throes which precede it refer to the difficulties, trials, and troubles, of whatsoever description they may be, which precede the setting apart the community in question. . . . the man-child

[162] S/*PG* 285. [163] S/*PG* 287. [164] See § 2 above.

must denote Christ in some sense. But he cannot be the literal Christ; because such an application is not consistent with the language of Scripture, which invariably represents our Lord as the Husband, not as the Son, of His Church . . . it will plainly follow that the birth of the Apocalyptic man-child must denote the setting apart of a faithful Christian ecclesiastical community from the great mass of God's true worshippers . . .[165]

This ecclesiastical community was that being set up by the restored apostles.

In a similar way, errors had been introduced in connection with the 'two witnesses'. The oldest of the traditions was that they were Enoch and Elijah, but, though this might be so, it had no scriptural foundation and had been vested by Tertullian with spurious reasoning. His argument was that they must return because all men had to die; this was false, because those who would be caught up and changed at the Second Advent would not die—a point made by Marcella to Jerome which the latter evaded. Other suggestions, such as that the witnesses would be Moses and St John, were equally without support in Scripture. The truth was that they had not yet appeared, and their identity was still unknown. Nevertheless it was true that Elias would come to the Jews, as this was prophesied by Malachi and confirmed by Our Lord Himself. Other errors introduced at various times included the idea that one or more of the vials had already been poured out.

The two great closing scenes of the last times related to the two mysteries of godliness and of iniquity, both of which had been present in the Church from her beginning:

The consummation of the mystery of godliness is the resurrection of the dead, and the change of the living saints, and their translation unto Christ; after which is the marriage of the Lord and His Church; and, finally, His and their manifestation in glory. The consummation of the mystery of iniquity is open battle against the Living God and Christ personal, and the casting of the Beast and the False prophet alive into the lake of fire.

The two mysteries come to their respective heads. The Lord's work issues in resurrection-life to a certain body of men, a thousand years before it reaches the rest even of saved men, and in a glory far above the condition of the latter; and in the eternal union with Christ, of which the marriage union of man and wife is only a faint symbol. Satan's work

[165] *S/PG* 288.

issues in the lake of fire for some, a thousand years before the rest of *lost* men, and even Satan himself, for whom it was prepared, are cast into it, and in a pre-eminence of shame and torment for ever. For it is written, that when the Lord hath judged the great Harlot that corrupted the earth, then the time of the marriage of the Lamb has come, and His wife hath made herself ready (Rev. xix. 1–9).

And who is His wife? The Church; she who was long ago foretold and spoken of in the 45th Psalm, and in the Song of Solomon (Cant. vi. 9); the Queen at the Lord's right hand; the *One*, the chief above all the rest, because she alone is baptized with the Holy Ghost; in *all* things made like unto her Lord; one with Him; raised from the dead at His coming, or changed in a moment; caught up to meet Him, that she may work with Him; and glorified in spirit, soul, and body, like unto Him, and filled with the Holy Ghost and all the power of God. Then shall be seen the difference between those who, faithful to their baptism and to their Lord, shall be counted worthy to be among that blessed number who shall be congregated unto Him at the day of the First Resurrection, and those who, having broken their covenant and joined themselves to the Harlot, shall be left in their graves till the time of the general resurrection, or who, having joined themselves to the Apostasy, shall be congregated unto the Beast, and shall perish by the sword of him that sitteth upon the horse.[166]

All this teaching corrected many further false notions which had abounded in the Church: that Satan was bound at the Incarnation and the millennium terminated in the year 1000; that Satan was bound at the Ascension; that the thousand years were during the Middle Ages and that Satan was loosed when Luther arrived on the scene; that the thousand years meant the period from the Resurrection to the Second Advent; and so on. It was also important to correct the mistaken notion that the idea of the first resurrection rested solely on Apocalypse 20: 6, since it could be proved from the words of Our Lord and the Apostles:

Our Lord makes a distinction between the resurrection which some shall be counted worthy to attain to, and some not (Luke xx. 35.) St. Paul says there is a resurrection 'out from among the dead,' to attain to which he strove with all his might as the prize to be gained (Phil. iii. 11 *Orig.*). He also expressly tells us, that while as in Adam all die, so in Christ shall all be made alive; yet it shall not be all at once, but 'every man in his own order; Christ, the first-fruits; *afterwards they that are Christ's at His coming*' (1 Cor. xv. 23.). It is particularly to be remarked,

[166] S/PG 294–5.

that whenever the resurrection of Christ, or of His people, is spoken of in the Scripture, it is as a 'resurrection *from* the dead;' and whenever the general resurrection is spoken of, it is the 'resurrection *of* the dead'.[167]

This distinction was sometimes omitted in English, but was always clear in both the Greek and the Latin—see and compare Luke 20: 35; John 11: 1 and 9; Romans 10: 7; Ephesians 1: 20; 1 Corinthians 15: 12–21; Philippians 3: 11; Hebrew 13: 20; 1 Peter 1: 3 and 21. Further, in 1 Corinthians 15, St Paul

marks the time when Christ's people shall be raised from the dead, namely 'at Christ's coming,' 'every man in his own order:' *1st*, Christ; *2nd*, Christ's people; *3rd*, all the remainder, at some other period, which he terms 'the end', when the last enemy, death, is to be destroyed, put an end to (Ver. 23–26). And it follows as a matter of course, that if those who are Christ's are to be raised from the dead at His coming, and if He comes previous to the destruction of Antichrist and to the Millennium, this first resurrection must be at least a thousand years before the general resurrection.[168]

The first resurrection was established absolutely from Scripture: it would stand even if there were to be no millennial reign. It was once, and always should have been, the chief object of Christian hope and of the hope of all creation:

The hope of all creation is deliverance from the vanity to which it has been subjected by Adam's fall; the common hope of all men is resurrection from *death*; the hope of the Jew is resurrection *from* the *dead* at Messiah's coming, and the first, the highest place among the nations; the hope of the Christian is the First Resurrection and the glory of Christ, the first, the highest place among all creatures whatsoever. The Church shares in the common hope of the creature and of all men, i.e., to be freed from the bondage of corruption, with the redemption of the body; she shares with the Jew the hope of being raised *from* the dead at the coming of Messiah; but she has a hope far beyond them all, which is to be changed into the body of glory, and to share with her Lord in His exaltation and power (Ez. xxxvii.; Dan. xii. 2.), and with Him to reign over all; and yet this is the hope she has forgotten.[169]

In a footnote, the following list of references is given in order to emphasize the distinction between the resurrection *out of* the dead and the resurrection *of* the dead:

νεκρῶν *with the preposition* ἐκ—1 Cor. xv. 12, 20; Rom. x. 7–9; viii. 11; Col. i. 18; Rev. i. 5 (*is in Text. Recept.*); Col. ii. 12; Eph. i. 20; v. 14;

[167] S/*PG* 302.   [168] S/*PG* 303–4.   [169] S/*PG* 306.

Heb. v. 7; xiii. 20; 1 Pet. i. 3, 21; 2 Tim. ii. 8; Matt. xvii. 9; Luke xvi. 31; xx. 35; xxiv. 46; Phil. iii. 11, 21; Gal. i. 1; 1 Thess. i. 10; 2 Tim. ii. 8; Rom. iv. 24; vi. 4, 9, 13; vii. 4; viii. 11; x. 7, 9; xi. 15; Acts iii. 15; iv. 2, 10; xiii. 30, 34; xvii. 31; xxvi. 23; Mark ix. 10. The disciples knew what the resurrection of the dead was, but not what 'the resurrection from the dead' meant.

νεκρῶν *without the preposition* ἐκ—1 Cor. xv. 12, 13, 21; Heb. vi. 2; Matt. xxii. 31; Acts xvii. 32; xxiii. 6; xxiv. 15, 21.

On the Jews

Great injustice had been done to the Jews by interpreting the passages of the Prophets in such a way that the triumph and glory of God's people was applied to the Christian Church, whilst the reproaches for unfaithfulness and threatenings of judgement were applied to the Jews. All the prophecies were of double application: to the Jews and to the Church, of which the tribes of Israel were a type. Thus, the Jews had been individually circumcised as a sign of separation from all other flesh to be God's people; Christians were similarly individually baptized. Both had turned from God's ways to the ways of the wicked. The Jews had been baptized in the cloud and the Red Sea as one nation and one body to be free to obey Moses and be led by him into the promised land; the Christian Church was made one body in Christ, to serve Him and to be led by Him into the promised kingdom. Both had rebelled and turned to idolatry, fleshly wickedness, and self-indulgence. The Jews had been led through the wilderness, but had doubted and disobeyed God; the Church was in the wilderness of the world, but had disobeyed and grieved God in the same way. The Jews had come to the promised land, but had learned the ways of the heathen and mingled with them; the Church too had mingled with the world by admitting it, unchanged, into herself and by practising its ways. The Jews were brought into the typical kingdom of David and Solomon; the Church had been brought into the kingdom of God's Son. Both had broken God's laws and followed their own inventions, joining themselves to idols.

Because of all this, the Jews had been carried into captivity in Babylon; the Church had been carried captive into the mystical Babylon. For the Jews, there had been a partial restoration under Ezra and Nehemiah; so in the Church there was a partial restoration of the true order of worship. There had been an Elias-work to the

Jews, and would be again prior to their final restoration; there would similarly be an Elias-work in the Christian Church prior to its final establishment in the Kingdom. For rejecting Christ and crucifying Him, the Jews as a nation had been given up to be destroyed by the Romans, except for a faithful remnant which passed into another dispensation; the Church would also be destroyed, except for the faithful remnant which also would pass into another dispensation. The judgements on the Jews would be fulfilled during the present dispensation as would be the temporal judgements upon the apostate Church. The promises of glory to the Jews would be fulfilled and the faithful Church would be gathered into glory at the Second Advent. In each case, there was a type with its antitype. It was because the Church had forgotten the distinction between the promises to the Jews and to the Church that so many errors concerning the millennium had crept in.

The Church had also wrongly supposed that Rome rather than Jerusalem was destined to be the ecclesiastical centre of the earth. This had encouraged shameful persecution of the Jews to be practised:

Like Edom of old, the Christians triumphed over their brother Jacob in the day of his calamity, and shed his blood; and because they did so, their blood shall be shed. . . . If anything marks Rome as the antitypical Edom, it is the cruelty she has ever shown to the Jews . . . for which there must be a terrible retribution.[170]

The Protestants had gone to the opposite extreme, and, by admitting Jews to their legislature, had forgotten the scriptural distinction between Jew and Christian. Both were wasting their energies in attempts to convert the Jews during the present dispensation, and the setting up of a Protestant bishop in Jerusalem was worse than an abortion, merely proclaiming the Church's disunity in the very place predestined to be the true centre of unity.

In 1841 a joint Anglican–Lutheran (Protestant) bishopric was set up in Jerusalem, with the incumbent to be nominated alternately by England and Prussia. This came in for considerable criticism, not only from members of the 'High Church' party in the Church of England (on the grounds of 'apostolic succession'), but also from the Orthodox Churches, who suspected it might be used for further attempts by Western Churches to proselytize Orthodox Christians.

[170] S/*PG* 313–14.

Considerable exception had been taken by the Orthodox to Protestant proselytism, especially that undertaken by American Episcopalians who actually set up a bishopric in Constantinople. The joint venture collapsed in 1886, the see having been solely Anglican since that date. For the Catholc Apostolics, the setting up of this bishopric was doubly offensive.[171]

The restoration of the Jews to their own land was clearly foretold in Scripture, though it would take place in two stages, one before and one after the Second Advent. In the former case, the majority would remain hard of heart and impenitent, many being deceived by Antichrist (as stated by the Fathers), but others refusing to submit to him. Because of this, Antichrist would attack Jerusalem, and the majority of its inhabitants would be killed—'the time of Jacob's trouble' (Jer. 30: 7; Zech. 13: 8–9). It would be then that the Lord would appear with His saints and restore the kingdom to His people, and the Jews would finally 'look upon Him whom they have pierced' (Zech. 12: 10; John 19: 37), and accept Him as Lord, and once more be His people. High above all this would be the faithful Church, seated around the throne in the heavenly Jerusalem.

Only a very indistinct idea could be formed of the relative positions of the earthly and heavenly Jerusalems. The earthly city would be the ecclesiastical and regal centre of the earth, and *over* it would be the heavenly city. The Tabernacle and the Temple were the type of this: the heavenly Jerusalem would answer to the Most Holy Place and the earthly Jerusalem to the Holy Place, with the nations gathered in the Outer Court.

On the Millennium

It was often asked what the Church or the world had to gain by the Lord's coming and what was the millennium for, though such a question seemed extraordinary in a world full of sin, sorrow, pain, war, and death. Surely the millennium would be the answer of a loving God to the universal cry of the oppressed:

man shall be placed in the most favourable circumstances,—all oppressors in Church and in State having been removed from the earth,—Satan and his evil angels bound in the prison . . . death though not abolished, yet shall be restrained . . . Christ and His saints shall be

---

[171] For an account of the Jerusalem bishopric, see Orchard, 'English Evangelical Eschatology', ch. VI.

reigning . . . and also shall teach all people the truth, and lead them up to the true worship of God![172]

Yet there would still be those who doubted, and who only feigned submission to Christ's rule. There would again be indifference and ingratitude. Satan would therefore be loosed once more, and those who would be deceived by him would rise up in a final rebellion against the rule of Christ and His saints only to be consumed by fire from heaven (Apoc. 20: 7–9). Satan himself would be cast, not into prison, but into the lake of fire into which the Beast and the False Prophet had already been cast (Apoc. 20: 10). Then would take place the final revelation to all mankind of God in all His majesty and power—His revelation in Christ during the millennium would have been a veiled one, His glory being then revealed only to those of the heavenly Jerusalem. This final revelation was not a third advent, as some had made out, but a fuller manifestation of One who had already been manifested at the Second Advent.

On Certain Problems of Scripture

There were one or two final problems of Scripture remaining: I Corinthians 15: 24 had to be reconciled with those parts which declared that the kingdom of Christ would have no end. The explanation was simple: until the end should come, the will of God would not be done in earth as it is in heaven; He would still not be all in all; there would still be those who were not truly in heart subject to Him. Christ, therefore, would still have to exercise His intercession as High Priest until the end of the millennium; His *reign* would not end then—the millennium was only the first part of that reign. Further, until all should be in subjection to Him, Christ would not be able to render up the kingdom to the Father as an acceptable offering. It was only after the last enemy should have been subdued and when all earth and heaven were obedient to Christ, and through Him to the Father, that the kingdom would finally be offered up. The transfiguration of earth and heaven would take place only after the millennium and the final destruction of death, since 'death shall be *no more* . . . for the *former* things have passed away' (Apoc. 21: 4).

[172] S/*PG* 323–4.

Difficulties could also arise in reconciling 2 Peter 3 and Isaiah 65: 17 with the sequence of events as portrayed in the Apocalypse. It might seem from St Peter that the conflagration of the earth would occur immediately upon the Second Advent. Isaiah might seem to suggest that the new heaven and earth would be established immediately when Jerusalem is rebuilt and restored. The study of the prophetic Scriptures, however, revealed that the Lord's way was often to cause events to be stated as if they occurred immediately after each other, when in reality they would be separated by long intervals of time—for example, more than 1800 years intervened between the accomplishment of the first parts of Psalm 22 and Isaiah 53, and a similar period between the fulfilment of Our Lord's words in Matthew 24 and Luke 21. The *whole* light had not been given to any one Prophet or Apostle. Isaiah's passage was

prospective, and inclusive of the whole time from the rebuilding of Jerusalem to the constitution of the new heavens and the new earth.[173]

St Peter had written what the Spirit told him of the *general* facts of the Day of the Lord; to St John and others more of the details had been revealed.

There should be no speculation beyond what is revealed in Scripture, though it was natural to ask who should be condemned to the second death—certainly, not all of those who did not participate in the first resurrection. Those raised at the second and final resurrection would be judged according to the mercy of God. Only those whose names were not written in the Book of Life would be sentenced to the second death, and no man would be condemned for Adam's sin for Christ had provided redemption from it for all: 'for as in Adam all die, so also in Christ shall all be made alive' (1 Cor. 15: 22); Christ gave Himself 'a ransom for all' (1 Tim. 2: 6). There would be many sharing in the resurrection to life as subjects of God's kingdom rather than as sharers of His rule.

The work now under way in preparation for the Second Advent was for the strengthening, sustaining, and upholding of God's ministers in whatever part of the Church they might be. They should continue with their work, and

if the Lord should come immediately, be found . . . faithfully and manfully working at their post, struggling to meet the advancing evil, . . .

to maintain Christ's cause. . . . and preparing their people for the 'Day of the Lord'.[174]

The Significance of Sitwell's Work

Sitwell's *The Purpose of God in Creation and Redemption* was the only major and detailed *public* formal presentation of Catholic Apostolic eschatology as taught by the apostles, and, as with most publications of the body, its author was not indicated—its authority was intended to derive from the manifest truth of its content. As already noted above, it was directed towards all those who questioned why the Catholic Apostolic witness should be regarded as a work of God. The testimonies had had specific addresses, and other works (including those discussed below) were written for internal circulation to Church members only. Sitwell went far beyond the testimonies in setting out the details of the expected events to come and their scriptural justification. It is difficult to determine precisely the extent of its circulation amongst Christians of other Churches, though some idea may be gained from the fact that it ran to eight English editions with three publishers (Laurie, Grant, and Pitman) over the period of 1865–99. For this reason, it is one of the comparatively few Catholic Apostolic writings which become available —though still only very occasionally—on the second-hand book market. It was certainly read and studied by Catholic Apostolic members themselves: most families seem to have possessed at least one copy. A number of points can be identified as being of particular importance in Sitwell's work.

1. There is the significance of the 'Letters to the Seven Churches' for the understanding of the history of the Christian Church, and the division of that history into seven epochs. A discussion of these epochs was regarded as an essential prelude to any presentation of eschatology, since the 'last things' were seen to be rooted in the whole history of the Church.

2. The condemnations of Rome and Protestantism were preceded by specific commendations. Amongst the condemnations, the concentration of spiritual rule in the papacy (usurping that of Christ) and the spiritual anarchy of Protestant individualism (through rejection of ordinances) were singled out for equal adverse comment.

[174] S/PG 366–7.

3. There is the emphasis on the typological parallelism between Daniel (prophecies relating to the Jews) and the Apocalypse (prophecies relating to the Church).

4. There is the detailed setting out of the order of eschatological events (of which the first sign was taken to be the French Revolution), together with the admission that much had still to be revealed, for example, the identities of Antichrist and the two witnesses. Within this eschatological presentation, there was particular emphasis upon the distinction— in both time and quality—between the first and the second resurrections: the resurrection *out of* the dead and the resurrection *of* the dead respectively. The doctrine of the 'first resurrection' was seen as being proved from Scripture and the early Fathers *even if the idea of the millennium should fall*. The 'day of the Lord' was not to be a single event, but, like the natural day, a period of time in which many events would occur in their proper sequence.

5. There is the interpretation of '666' as representing, not a person, but a summing up of the sins of the world.

6. There is the implied 'hierarchy' (related to the two resurrections) even in the coming kingdom—there are those who will *rule* with Christ and those who will be subject to that rule, though both will enjoy the state of blessedness. Further, the prophecies relating to the Jews are of a lower order to those relating to the Church—the destiny of the Jews lies in their restoration to the earthly Jerusalem, whilst the destiny of the Church lies in the heavenly Jerusalem. The true Christian hope was seen as being translation at the first resurrection, with a consequent escape from the great tribulation, and a sharing of Christ's rule when he comes with His saints—it was the forgetting of this hope that had led to the dread of a misunderstood Second Advent.

7. Attempts at any mass conversion of the Jews before the Second Advent are regarded as fruitless exercises.

8. There is the emphasis on the restoration of apostolic rule to the Church as a work of God in preparation for the return of Christ—it was indeed precisely for the justification of this that the work was written.

Drummond's Tracts for the Last Days

After the publication of the *Dialogues on Prophecy* (see § 4 above),
Drummond wrote a number of eschatological pamplets: on the study
of the Apocalypse and on the Second Advent (1829), on 'Babylon'
(1834), and on the numbers in Daniel (1835). Two later works,
however, deserve note here: *Tracts for the Last Days*,[175] and
Discourses on the True Definition of the Church.[176] The former of these
works took the form of a collection of twenty-four tracts, and of
these Tract iii ('On the Hope of the Catholic Church'), Tract xxii
('The Restoration of the Jews'), and Tract xxiii ('The Second Advent
of the Lord Jesus Christ') were directly related to eschatological
themes, though a number of the other tracts dealt with the falling
away of the Church from apostolic teaching and practice, following
the same themes as are to be found in the Great Testimony and elsewhere (see above). One such tract, xviii, singled out 'evangelicalism'
as the principle apostasy of the last days.

In Tract iii, Drummond stressed the importance of the Tabernacle
as revealing in symbols the ultimate purposes of God. In this tract,
he first pointed to Scripture as

God's own account of what He has done: in creation, when all was very
good; in judgement upon sin when man fell; and in redemption, and
recovery from its curse; . . . and also the purpose involved in each of
them, and the one end to which all things tend, and which they shall all
attain at the completion of that time which is called the RESTITUTION
OF ALL THINGS, or the KINGDOM OF HEAVEN.[177]

The coming kingdom would be a visible manifestation of heaven in
the whole of Creation. It was for this that the Church prayed daily in
the Lord's Prayer: 'Thy kingdom come, Thy will be done *on earth*
as it is *in heaven*.' The whole purpose of Creation was God's
manifestation of Himself, making Himself known in Christ, Who
was and is God manifest in the flesh. From the first moment of
Creation, God had looked onward to the day of Christ, which
Abraham had seen afar off and of which David had sung in Psalm 8.
The fullness of this image of God was first seen at the Resurrection,

---

[175] Published by Painter, 1844.   [176] Published by Boswell, 1858.
[177] H. Drummond, *Tracts for the Last Days* (London: Painter, 1844), 37–8
(henceforth D/*TLD*).

and it would be fulfilled in mankind at the resurrection of the body at the Second Advent, at which time God's wisdom would be revealed to the heavenly powers through the Church (Eph. 3: 10). Thus, man was necessary for the revelation of God in Christ, and

Christ alone in heaven, man alone upon the earth, have been dignified with the name 'Son of God' (Luke iii, 38; 1 John iii, 2).[178]

God had given dominion over irrational creation to man—this was the meaning of Adam *naming* the animals. At Creation a chain was established: God as Father over all; man obedient to God; the rest of Creation subject to man. The Fall had broken the first link in that chain, and all Creation had suffered as a consequence (Gen. 3: 17). Man had suffered the loss of his headship over Creation, a headship which was restored in the second Adam, who had restored the broken link. God's original purpose would therefore be fulfilled in man when he had learned obedience from the example of Christ, who was 'obedient unto death' (Phil. 2: 8). All who were faithful to Christ 'unto the end' would sit with Him on His throne and rule with Him (Apoc. 2: 27), and the earth would have its curse reversed and share in universal joy—the 'former things' would not be remembered (Isa. 65: 17).

Both Creation and the new Creation in Christ were for the fulfilment of one and the same purpose of God, a purpose foreordained before the foundation of the world, but not to be manifested until the last days (1 Pet. 1: 20). This whole mystery was opened up by whatever is revealed in Scripture concerning the Church. Further, our enquiries into the nature of Creation must be made in the light of faith in the restitution of all things: the basis of sound natural philosophy must be theology—man must understand what things are, not merely by their appearance but by an understanding of their place in the purposes of God; only in this way could God be glorified both for His words and for His works.

The fullest intimation of the truths were revealed to man by means of symbols, and especially in the symbolism of the Tabernacle, in its various parts and the various sacrifices performed within it. Abraham had looked for a city with foundations built by God—the heavenly city—but the Jewish dispensation had occurred between that vision and its fulfilment:

[178] D/*TLD* 40.

Instead of all nations being immediately blessed, one nation was chosen for especial blessing . . . And instead of the heavenly sanctuary coming directly into view, a worldly sanctuary (Heb. ix. 1) was interposed, the figure and shadow of the true (v. 24); and by it the preparation of the Church, and its work in making preparation for the kingdom set forth in the various symbols.[179]

The Mosaic dispensation, given by God in condescension to fallen man's blindness, revealed the same purpose as the patriarchal. This was presented to the Church in the Epistle to the Hebrews, which taught

that the symbols of the Tabernacle . . . were types and shadows of those glorious heavenly realities, into the faith of which we enter now in the Church, and into the possession of which we shall be introduced at the coming of the Lord.[180]

In contrast with the patriarchal altars, which man's hands would make polluted and unfit for God's service, the symbols of the Tabernacle were all prepared and fashioned by man. This revealed that, whilst the patriarchal altars symbolized the purpose of God in the abstract and so the hand of man was not permitted to appear, the Tabernacle symbolized the same purpose as it would be carried out by Christ and His Church indwelt by the Holy Spirit. The beaten work showed that both Christ and the Church

should be in this world subjected to the buffettings and scourgings of men who manifest their fallen condition by continual enmity to God and His truth. It represents, in short, how Christ and the Church should be perfected through suffering . . .[181]

The ultimate sovereignty to be shared with Christ would be conferred, not upon an individual nor upon a 'promiscuous mass', but upon a body, consisting of individuals

builded together according to a certain constitution which God has appointed—not the Church of Rome, nor the Church of England, nor the Church of Geneva, but the Catholic Church; composed, indeed, of a remnant in all these, and in all other sects which recognize God's ways and rejoice in and submit to the same: and who shall be builded together and brought out as a nation of kings for ever.[182]

---

[179] D/*TLD* 50.   [180] D/*TLD* 52.   [181] D/*TLD* 52.
[182] D/*TLD* 52.

In Tract xxii, Drummond deplored the lack, on the part of Christians, of understanding concerning the significance of the promises made by God to the Jews. This lack of understanding was similar to the failure of the Jews to perceive the promises relating to Christ of which the Jewish Scriptures were full. Christians had neglected the Old Testament prophecies and had failed to take serious note of passages in the New Testament, such as Romans 11, which expressly pointed their attention to the restoration of the Jews to God's favour:

knowledge of the future destiny of the Jews ought to have been one of the standing traditions and one of the abiding points of faith in the Church; especially as the ingathering of the Jews, and the fulness of the Gentiles, are made the sign and the countersign, and the *all* Israel to be saved is clearly made up both of the literal and the spiritual seeds.

. . . .

. . . it is manifest from Scripture that the great feature which shall mark the close of this dispensation and usher in the next, or the dispensation of the kingdom, will be, that God shall return again in mercy to the Jews, and they will turn with contrite hearts to Him . . . and be restored to their land: and then they, conjointly with the Church now gathering, will become instruments in carrying on still further the purpose of God in a higher dispensation than the present, and to an ulterior display of the love of God.[183]

That God was declared by Christ to be the God of Abraham, Isaac, and Jacob proved that they also would participate in the blessings to all nations. St Paul, in his pleadings with the Jews, continually appealed to the promises made by God to the Hebrew Fathers. In Hebrews 4 there was a long argument that a rest remains for God's people beyond anything to which they had been led by Joshua or David in former times. The argument was:

A *rest* was promised, of which Canaan was *the type*; the Israelites were *a type* of the people called to enter it; all who disbelieved died in the wilderness *as types* of those who should come short of the rest; all who believed entered the land, *as types* of those who should attain it; but their entering the land was *not* the rest spoken of, for even in David's day it was *not yet come*. There remaineth, therefore, a *sabbatismos* to the people of God; and it is *the rest* set before *us* in the Gospel, as well as before *them* in the Exode. . . . Preparing for the rest, was that which was

[183] D/*TLD* 344–5.

contemplated by God in the works He wrought at the foundation of the world; gathering and preparing His people for it, is the work of all the intermediate time, and shall end in putting them in possession of *God's rest*—the climax and completion of His creation.[184]

The future condition of the Jews could not be understood from their contemporary condition nor from their own expectations, but only from Scripture. The Jews were those to whom Christ had come, though they did not receive him (John 1: 11), and, as a result, salvation came to the Gentiles. But Christianity was the crown of Judaism, and

the more we can raise the thing crowned, the more do we exalt that crown which the Lord shall give to His faithful followers in the day of His appearing.[185]

The Jews were conversant with symbolic and typical matters, but they had dreamed of earthly glory *under the present dispensation*—this had been the great impediment to their receiving the spiritual truths of Christianity and had eventually caused them to become outcasts. Their great need was to return to their Scriptures, from which they would learn that the prophecies concerning themselves in relation to a kingdom cannot be fulfilled under the present constitution of things. There was to be a higher dispensation than the Mosaic, and another Temple on a different site with worship differing from that in the temples of Solomon or Zerubbabel. The prophecies of their Scriptures all pointed to a changed condition of creation in the time of latter-day glory. The great difficulty for both Jew and Christian was to keep the faith regarding both the earthly and the heavenly Jerusalems:

The heavenly Jerusalem, and its King, must be seen as the head, and complement, and exponent, and strength of the whole mystery, as that which gives it both reality and endurance . . . but as belonging to another category; yet without which all the rest is purposeless and without meaning.[186]

The Christian dispensation would end with the resurrection of all who sleep in Jesus and the change of all those prepared for His appearing. It was clearly implied by Christ that Abraham, Isaac, and Jacob, and all the 'Saints' who lived before the Incarnation, would also be raised from the dead at that time. Christians did not reflect on

---

[184] D/*TLD* 347–8.   [185] D/*TLD* 349.   [186] D/*TLD* 352.

this. Further, in forming conceptions of heaven, they assumed that nothing 'terrestrial' should be admitted into it. But God's act of Creation, together with the Incarnation, and the Resurrection and Ascension, all pointed to the restitution of all things in Christ. The principle of the necessity of the material creation to make known the purposes of God ensured belief in that restitution, for God would never abandon the world which He had made, nor would He abandon His house of Israel.

In the kingdom of heaven there would be a threefold distinction, typified in the Temple by the most holy, the holy place, and the court of the Gentiles, and spoken of as the 'heavenly Jerusalem', the 'earthly Jerusalem', and the 'nations of the earth'—all existing at the same time in the kingdom. Into the heavenly Jerusalem, the Bride of the Lamb, would be gathered all those worthy of the highest glory of which the creature is capable, the glory of the Lord Jesus Christ:

These are all in raised and glorified bodies, and the act of thus gathering them is called the first resurrection, in which none can have a part, so far as glory and dignity are concerned, save those who are regenerate, who have received the Holy Ghost, which is the earnest of the inheritance—the first-fruits of the kingdom of heaven, in this highest sense of the term. But we are taught by St. Paul (1 Cor. 15) that there is a natural body, as well as a spiritual body; and in the glory of the natural body will the faithful be raised who belong to the dispensations which preceded the giving of the Holy Ghost; and thus manifest that God has been with His people at all times, though the Christian Church alone constitutes the body of Christ, and is called the Temple of the Holy Ghost.[187]

The Bride and the kingdom were mysteries. The word 'mystery' as used in Scripture was defined as

a thing which exists in reality, but not developed; as, for example, the kingdom of Christ is a mystery, it is enveloped, masked, and concealed in the Church, but shall be hereafter revealed or manifested. So it was a mystery in the Jewish Church that the Gentiles should be fellow-heirs with the Jews.[188]

The mystery of the Bride would be followed by the mystery of the kingdom—the day of the Lord and the time of Judgement—in which the Jews would have a part to play. The two mysteries must

[187] D/*TLD* 360–1.   [188] D/*TLD* 361–2.

not be confused. The latter was the refiner's fire of Malachi, and the baptism of fire spoken of in the New Testament, typified by the first-gathered corn, which was dried in an oven to be presented to the Lord—the Roman doctrine of Purgatory was a groping after this truth. The coming in of the glory of the kingdom would be accompanied by terrible ordeals, especially for the Jews. The faithless Jews would be cut off during this time of tribulation, but those who proved to be faithful would be prepared for the glory reserved for them. It was possible that the translated Saints, including the Old Testament Saints, might be used in ministering spiritual comfort to those still in their earthly bodies. At this time of judgement Jewish and Christian apostates, together with Mahomet, the followers of the Beast and the dragon, and the false Prophet would be cast into the lake of fire.

The figure of the potter's vessel expressed the difference between the judgement on the Jews and on the baptized. The Jews were the *clay* which, not having passed through the fire, could be moulded into another form if the first form failed (Jer. 18: 6). Those baptized with the Holy Spirit and *with fire* (Luke 3: 15) were the *vessel* whose form could not be remoulded, and which therefore could only be broken in pieces (Jer. 19: 10; Isa. 30: 14). Those who had received the Gospel and subsequently apostatized would indeed be broken in pieces—it was not possible for them to be renewed (Heb. 6: 4).

Many scriptural passages showed that the Jews would receive a new covenant and new and everlasting ordinances (testified to especially in Jeremiah 31: 30–40 and the last chapters of Ezekiel). They would receive these during the times of woe at the end of the present dispensation, the tribulation having the effect of preparing them for their reception. It would be then that the promises of the Lord to them would be fulfilled and Elias would truly come. But this would not be for the incorporation of the Jews into the glorified body of the Church: it would be inferior to that, just as the ministry of John the Baptist had been inferior to that of Christ. This was all strikingly shown in the new ordinances given in Ezekiel 40 and 48,

which would be in their deficiencies *inferior* to those of Moses, were it not that these deficiencies imply that *the reality* couched under *these symbols* is come, has been believed, and so NEEDS NOT any symbolical representation; for there is nothing superfluous ordained by God.[189]

---

[189] D/*TLD* 369.

The unity which the papacy had striven to represent could only be realized in Christ *when He comes*, and when the members of His body are gathered and united to their risen Head. When this gathering of the Church under her Head was accomplished at the first resurrection, then its counterpart would appear on earth in the gathered Jews with a visible centre of unity in Jerusalem. Christian ordinances would be removed from the earth, and the nations would who wished to 'go at once to entreat the favour of the Lord and to seek the Lord of Hosts' would have to 'take hold of the robe of a Jew' (Zech. 8: 21, 23), for there would be nothing so good on earth as the earthly Jerusalem. The difference between the earthly and heavenly Jerusalems were shown by the last chapters of Ezekiel and the Apocalypse, which ran in parallel. The strength and blessing of the earthly Jerusalem and of all renewed creation would be derived from communion with the heavenly through the Holy Spirit. The symbols for the operation of the Spirit *now* were the wind, the dew, and the rain from heaven—all implying a descent from above. The symbol of the Spirit's operation *then* was the river flowing uninterruptedly from the Temple of God. The Holy Spirit was given *now* for new life and exaltation *to a higher standing. Then*, it would be given for refreshment and strength *in the same place of standing*. The work ended with the following warning against apostasy:

If the present opportunity, which the Christian dispensation offers, be neglected and lost, it does not appear that any other opportunity will be afforded of recovering our birthright, our inheritance, our *sabbatismos*—the kingdom, the rest that remaineth for the people of God. 'Let us therefore fear, lest any of us through unbelief fall short of it' (Heb. iv. 1–11); and let us take heed that in taking upon ourselves the office of teaching to the Jews their hope, we do not show ourselves ignorant of our own.[190]

In Tract xxiii, which largely re-expressed the content of an earlier pamphlet of 1829,[191] Drummond began by commenting on the unscriptural nature of the popular notion of the Second Advent, which had resulted in fear and alarm rather than in hope and expectancy. In particular, that part of the popular notion which saw the Jews being first restored to their own land and all the heathen

---

[190] D/*TLD* 372.
[191] H. Drummond, *The Second Coming of the Lord Jesus Christ* (London: Seeley, 1829).

converted to Christianity, convinced people that the last days could not occur within their own lifetimes. Equally unfortunate was the idea that the Second Advent would be a purely mystical and spiritual event, operating only on the spirits of men. Both these views saw the world as being burnt up and destroyed, rather than as renewed and transformed. There were also those, including Faber and Frere (see § 2 above), who, whilst being somewhat more definite about the Second Advent, were nevertheless far from providing a clear and accurate account of what is revealed in Scripture. All these views were based on sets of words, taken out of their scriptural context— but almost anything could be supported in this way. The only sure way was to take a view which included all relevant Scripture.

The coming Second Advent, the 'day of the Lord', was a *period* of time (of twenty-four hours or longer) with its own morning, noon, and evening. The Prophets declared that the Sun of Righteousness would *arise* with healing on His wings, and the Apocalypse declared that God would give the faithful the bright and *morning* star. These clearly showed that the Church should receive the promised blessing in the earliest part of that day. The same was conveyed by the symbolism of harvest:

In the harvest, as carried on by them [the Jews], we find three distinct acts—first, the hasty, forced, and artificial ripening of a few ears plucked out of the field by the hand, not cut in the ordinary manner by a sickle, and ripened before the fire (Lev. xi. 14); secondly, the cutting of the crop, before the carrying in of which, however, a single sheaf is taken and carried into the Temple (Lev. xxiii. 10); and, thirdly, the whole harvest is gathered in: and accordingly we find, in the book of the Revelation, a few persons gathered (xiv.), and afterwards a larger body of much people, a great multitude, even all the armies of heaven.[192]

There was a pre-eminence of blessing to which attention was directed and on which hopes should be fixed. In the harvest, all the grain was gathered in, whole and undestroyed; after grinding it was still the same grain, though more attenuated. In the vintage, every grape was crushed on the spot; wine was the juice of the grape only after it had undergone a process which totally changed its nature and properties—strictly speaking the harvest of the vine was destroyed.

The Apostle Peter twice referred to the story of Noah—only eight persons escaping from the fearful destruction of the flood. This

[192] D/*TLD* 375.

implied that the number to escape the great tribulation would be small—only a remnant of all Christians. Another typological event was the bringing of Israel out of Egypt by Moses, and the destruction of those who opposed their exodus. The history of the Jews to the time when they took possession of the land under Joshua was a type of the Christian Church to the consummation of all things, and at the close there was putting in order before the immediate entrance—the same was now taking place within the Church. After this putting in order, there would be a destruction of Babylon. In the last days, all the typical deliverances and judgements would meet, though they would not take place simultaneously—the day of the Lord would therefore consist of many acts.

The distinction between the literal and spiritual was crucial. The Jews had a *literal* dispensation: a man became a Jew by cutting off flesh; the Jews were delivered from Egypt by the drowning of Pharaoh; they entered Palestine by the sword, and retained possession of it by warfare; breaches of their law were punished with cruel death; their worship was full of symbols which they did not understand. All this was a shadow of a substance of which they were in ignorance. When the Jews should eventually return to their land, it would again be by force, and with garments stained in blood. They would only be converted when, with their fleshly eyes, they saw Christ coming with His saints after the translation at the end of the Christian dispensation. The Christian dispensation, by contrast, was *spiritual*: it was established and maintained against brute force by principles; a man joined it by voluntary submission to its truth and by immersion in waters with spiritual and not visible effect. But the Christian Church had been spoiled by the gradual inculcation of superstitions and, apart from a faithful remnant, would be finally overthrown through its lawlessness and apostasy.

There was no doubt as to the order of the resurrection of the saints and their translation because it was explicitly stated that 'the dead in Christ will rise first; then we who are alive, who are left, shall be caught up together with them in the clouds to meet the Lord in the air, and so we shall always be with the Lord' (1 Thess. 6: 16–17). The translation, the second of the two events spoken of, was identical with the gathering of the first artificially ripened ears before the gathering in of the whole field. Just as the Lord had risen early in the morning, so would be first resurrection be early in the morning of the day of the Lord. At the Second Advent, the Bride would be made manifest—until that day, no one could determine who would make up the Bride in her completion. She would, however, be completed at the Second Advent, subsequently she could receive no addition, alteration, or change. This Bride was 'the speciality of our hope beyond that of all other men',[193] of which the Blessed Virgin was a type.

The temple and kingdom were figures differing from the Bride because they began before Pentecost and would continue after the Second Advent. The temple had been visible since the Exodus

either complete or broken down, either natural or spiritual, first in Jerusalem, and next in Christendom . . . So far as it is made of men and women, God has put forth His Spirit creating a desire for its reparation; and so far as it is made of materials of this earth, it shall be rebuilded whenever God's servants the Jews regain possession of Jerusalem, where alone it can stand . . . It is made for all the circumcised, and the Church is made for all the baptized . . .[194]

The kingdom had begun with Adam, whom God created to have dominion over the earth. Christ's kingship, His highest title, would be the last He assumes. His kingdom was still a mystery, though its constitution and organization had been revealed so that men might promote its interests. Each local Church had its own bishop with priests and deacons under him, the bishops being united within the universal Church by apostles and their delegates. To preach the kingdom of Christ

is to teach and to show men the form of the government of Christ; to preach the Gospel of the kingdom is to tell men the good news that this government has begun to be organized. . . . To enter into the kingdom of Christ is for men to yield themselves up to Him, in order to be put in their proper places, and to learn how to serve Him in the government and the bringing out of that kingdom; and the proof that they who do so yield themselves have followed no cunningly devised fable, but have been led of God to bear witness to this kingdom, will be by their translation, and by nothing else.[195]

Edom, Moab, and Ammon, which were types of the three main divisions in Western Christendom (the Roman, Anglican, and Presbyterian systems), would remain to the end unchanged—each was a defilement of God's Church. They would eventually combine with infidels to resist God's will. Whatever restoration there might

[193] D/*TLD* 383.   [194] D/*TLD* 384.   [195] D/*TLD* 386.

be within the Church would be small, and despised and rejected of men, though spiritually larger than it appeared,

> because they who desire these things in their heart . . . shall not lose their reward, but are of the number of those who are prepared to meet their Lord, and shall be caught up to meet Him at His coming, and so escape the things that are coming upon the earth.[196]

Those who talked only of a spiritual as opposed to a real advent, could not see that He had already come in Spirit. All the recent events that had been taking place—the study of prophecy, the knowledge of Christ's return, the truth of His human as well as of His divine nature, the manifestations of the Holy Spirit, the strivings towards the Christian practices of Antiquity—indicated the working of the Spirit of God in a way which had no parallel for many ages. The first great event shortly to take place so as to reassure the faithful and give them the courage to bear witness unto death would be the reappearance of all who had fallen asleep in Christ. All this was the true Gospel of the kingdom which should make the heart of every true Christian leap for joy

> when he reflects on the misery accumulating around, which no political sagacity, honesty, nor talent can alleviate; when he remembers that his existence really only begins in the age to come, for which this is but a preparation full of sadness and delusion; and when he realizes that the best which things and conditions can offer here is but the shadow of that substance which he can never taste but in the world to come, in the kingdom of Christ, in the new heaven and new earth, in a new government, with a new King, and with new subjects.[197]

Drummond's Discourses on the True Definition of the Church

Drummond discussed much the same material in his *Discourses on the True Definition of the Church . . . and Kindred Subjects* of 1858, though elaborating on certain aspects of his eschatology. In particular, there was an elaboration of the difference between the mode of the raising of the saints and the translation of those alive at the Second Advent. The work was clearly for 'internal' consumption only. He began with a reference to the pre-eminent topic about which the Holy Spirit had been speaking: namely, gross ignorance in relation to those passages of Scripture speaking of the plague of

---

[196] D/*TLD* 387–8.   [197] D/*TLD* 388.

darkness in Egypt. Such passages pointed to ignorance on the part of Christians in general of the plan and purpose of God which was to be effected by His Church both in the present age and in that to come. They pointed to Christian

incapacity to see the signs in the heavens of the coming of the Son of Man, to understand the organisation of the Church in its four ministries . . . to see the true meaning of the Tabernacle as a figure of the Christian Church, the sacrifices of the Law as the guide for the ritual of Christian worship, the ceremonies for the consecration of the High Priest as the shadows of the essential characteristics of the Christian priesthood, and many similar things.[198]

But the present charge of the Holy Spirit was that the baptized were continuing in *Egyptian* darkness, and this signified that, whilst there was intellectual knowledge of these things, spiritual knowledge was lacking. A distinction had to be drawn between knowing a thing in the Spirit and knowing it in the understanding after having been taught it by the Spirit. For example, events throughout Christendom might be interpreted as signs of the Lord's approach, but that was not necessarily seeing the spiritual signs.

When Christ called forth Lazarus from the tomb, He did it in the name and in the creative power of the Father, and not in His own name. When He shall come again, he will come in His own power which has now been given to Him by the Father (see esp. John 5: 21, 25–7). Yet all the great acts of God were acts in which the Three Persons of the Blessed Trinity combine. Failure to see this had led to many confusions. In the last day, the Lord Jesus, with the power of the Father, would call the dead from their graves, and the Holy Spirit would change the bodies of those in whom He would be dwelling on the earth. Thus the Lord's action on the dead would be external and direct, whilst His action on the living would be mediate—through the Holy Spirit and from within them. The Transfiguration should be considered in relation to this. Christ was not transfigured by the power of the Father from without, but by the power of the Holy Spirit dwelling within Him. This event was therefore a spiritual pointer to the translation of the living at the Second Advent.

[198] H. Drummond, *Discourses on the True Definition of the Church, One, Holy, Catholic, and Apostolic, and Kindred Subjects* (London: Boswell, 1858), 'The Resurrection and Translation', MS version, p. 1.

There was one duty laid upon all faithful members of the Church, collectively and individually, namely to pray to God in public and in private to send Jesus Christ again into the world, to establish His kingdom, to raise those who had fallen asleep in Christ, to change the bodies of the living so that they would not see death but be clothed with immortality and escape the judgements which would fall upon the world. For all this, the faithful should 'pray constantly' (1 Thess. 5: 17), being of one mind with Christ.

The Significance of Drummond's Works

Drummond's eschatological writings are noteworthy for a number of reasons.

1. There is his emphasis on the eschatological significance of the Tabernacle and the Temple, and the contrast with the Patriarchal altars.

2. There is his teaching on the purpose of God in creation—His manifestations of Himself in Christ, for which creation was a necessity. Thus, as can be found in patristic teaching, it was suggested that the Incarnation was not necessarily or solely a response to the fall.

3. There is the assurance of the restoration of all things, material as well as spiritual, together with the condemnation of those who would make the Second Advent a spiritual occurrence only.

4. There is the stress on the need for understanding of the vocation of the Jews, said to be sadly lacking in most Christians—the Jews would have a special role at the end of the Christian dispensation.

5. The three parts of the Temple were said to typify a future threefold distinction in the kingdom.

6. The analogy of the potter's clay was used to indicate that, whilst the Jews could be remoulded, apostate Christians could not.

7. The Second Advent was said to be a *period* of time, and the day of the Lord to have a morning, noon, and evening, each with their particular events. The analogy with the Jewish harvest and the distinction drawn between the *harvest* and the *vintage* were used to stress the distinction between the first and second resurrections.

8. There is the emphasis on all acts of God being trinitarian, with nevertheless a distinction between the mode of God's operation in the first resurrection and that in the translation, a distinction pointed

to by the Transfiguration. It is of note also, that this last point was stated particularly to be one to which contemporary prophetic words had been insistently directed.

Dalton's Discourses on the First and Second Advents

Dalton's largely eschatological work, *Four Discourses on the First and Second Advents of our Lord and Saviour Jesus Christ*,[199] was a collection of four Advent addresses originally delivered in Leeds Parish Church in 1846. In the first of these, he stressed the importance of the role of the Church in bringing

the advent of our Lord Jesus Christ under our notice in a two-fold aspect namely,—First, in reference to His **coming in humility**; and, secondly, in reference to His **coming in glory**. By the one *she reminds us what we are*; by the second *she tells us what we shall be*.[200]

The Advent of Christ thus had two distinct parts. The Old Testament spoke only of the *coming* of the Messiah and the establishment of a kingdom. The Jews had been so rapt in the visions of the glory of that kingdom and the restitution of all things that they largely passed over the coming of the Messiah in sorrow and shame, with the result that they thought of one coming only, failing to see that it was the eternal purpose of God that the Second Person of the Trinity should come into the limitation of human nature:

It was this, the eternal purpose, that gave birth unto creation. . . . Adam was (*tupos tou mellontos*) the type of Him that was to come. Rom. v. 14. And where there is a type, there is in the mind of him that maketh a type, an anti-type. Where there is a shadow, there is a *substance*. Adam was . . . the shadow thrown off from the predestined purpose of the incarnation of the Son of God. . . . The creature was made in order to be put under the Incarnate Son.[201]

Almost all the heresies, both old and recent, could be traced to errors concerning the truth of the Incarnation or forgetfulness of it, since 'INCARNATION is the substance of revelation'.[202] Man had been

---

[199] This was published by Cleaver in 1846, and republished by both Boswell and Hobbs in 1883 and 1895. A Danish edition appeared as late as 1949.
[200] H. Dalton, *Four Discourses on the First and Second Advents* (London: Boswell and Hobbs, undated earlier edition Cleaver 1846), 1–2 (henceforth D/*FD*).
[201] D/*FD* 3. [202] D/*FD* 4.

prepared for it in the four dispensations of Adam, Abraham, Moses, and David, the last of which was the dispensation of hope. In all of these dispensations, man had piled up sin upon sin, outraging the majesty of heaven, and so the Incarnation involved for the Son of God the voluntary experience of rejection, sorrow, and grief (Isa. 53: 3). This was an advent of the Messiah which the Jews, with the exception of a few (such as Simeon), could not envisage.

This First Advent was linked in the Church's witness with the Second. The revealed purpose of God was the exaltation of the Incarnate Son to the headship of the Church, and for this both Advents were the means: they were two scenes of the same drama— two parts of the same whole. Neither could stand without the other:

By the first, the way is laid to the second. By the second, the first is consolidated. Take away either, and the other fails. If Jesus comes not in glory, redemption is not sealed. If Jesus came not in humility, redemption is not obtained. If the Son of God had not come to shame, suffering, and death, sin had been neither proved nor pardoned. If He comes not in glory and triumph, righteousness is neither established nor rewarded. If He had not come, the price is not paid. If He comes not again, the purchase is not obtained.[203]

The Jews had expected the immediate setting up of a Messianic kingdom, and had neglected what their Prophets had foretold. Christians seemed to be content in believing in the First Advent and regarding the Second with apathy and indifference—this was taking up Immanuel in the form of a servant without looking at His presence as a king. Like the Jews, Christians had said 'We do not want this man to reign over us' (Luke 19: 14). They wondered at the Jews, accusing them of unbelief, whilst at the same time forgetting the promise made at the Ascension and the Lord's own prophetic warning: 'when the Son of Man comes, will He find faith on earth?' (Luke 18: 8). At the First Advent, Christ took up His office of *prophet*. At the Ascension He took up His office of *priest*. At his Second Advent He would enter into His office and be manifested as *king* in the full sense of that title. Thus the Jews had been correct in looking for the Messiah as king, but had sinned in rejecting Him as the Lamb.

The kingdom of Christ would not become manifest until the Second Advent. The Church *in a mystery* was the *spiritual* phase of that kingdom, present now within us. The distinction between 'spiritual' and 'literal' was explained as follows:

> by *spiritual* I do not mean something *unreal* and *figurative*. 'Spiritual' is not opposed to 'literal'; nay, that which is *spiritual* is most *literal*, most *real*; when, therefore, I say the kingdom of Christ is now only manifested in its spiritual phase, that is, the Church, I mean that it has not yet taken its visible and outward development.[204]

Christians now had union with their invisible Head through the Spirit—this was the significance of the sacraments. That Head, Christ, had not yet received His kingdom, which was being formed secretly. He had sat down on the throne of the Father, where no one else could ever sit. Soon, He would sit on His own throne, and those who were faithful would sit with Him on it—when Christ comes again, the kingdom is set up:

> Then the Church, the budding of that kingdom, blossoms forth into the purpose of God. Then the Incarnate Son shall stand at the head of creation, and the Church, one with Him, shall share His throne. Then He comes to judge the world. And that judgement is not the mere passing of a final sentence, but is the *administration of rule*. That judgement commences with the Church of God. The first act is separation; the faithful are separated from the unfaithful; the chaff from the wheat; the sheep from the goats, the wise from the foolish virgins. And the faithful thus and then separated, enter into the joy of their Lord.[205]

The 'day of the Lord', of whatever duration it might be, was divided into its separate parts, each having its allotted work, of which the first was the judgement of the whole Church and its gathering into a perfect unity. Because the Church's true constitution was heavenly, it was only after the first resurrection that she could receive her full and perfect organization—this was the *hope* of the Church and of all creation. Both the living and the dead awaited Christ's Second Advent:

> For even if the idea be correct which some of the fathers seem to have entertained, namely, That from time to time, some of the saints have been raised from the dead and have passed into glory, still, as a whole, the dead in Christ await His coming as the time of their resurrection. The living await His appearing—creation awaits that day; and Jesus

---

[204] D/*FD* 22–3.　　[205] D/*FD* 24.

Himself waits for that day 'which the Father hath put in His own power.' But *that day shall come.* He shall step down from the throne of the Father, and take His own throne, and receive His kingdom, and all creation shall do Him homage. And the Church His spouse shall rejoice in His glory. . . . Then, the day which Abraham saw afar off, shall be realized. Then the Prophet like Moses, and David's King, and Isaiah's Child of the Virgin, and the BRANCH of Zechariah, shall be known, and all that the Prophets foretold shall be accomplished.[206]

Why did men not long for that day, as had the early Christians? The 1800 years that had passed since the Ascension seemed to be regarded as guaranteeing the distance of the Second Advent rather than its nearness. That day had been delayed by reason of the Lord's forbearance—'not wishing that any should perish' (2 Pet. 3: 9). Because He had tarried, men had slept and His servants had come to say, 'My master is delayed' (Matt. 24: 48):

And so it has gone on, till at length 'the scoffer of the last days' arose, saying, 'Where is the promise of His coming? for since the fathers fell asleep, all things continue as they were from the beginning of the world.' And thus witness is borne that 'the night is far spent'.[207]

There were, however, many 'signs of the times' to make men look for the Second Advent: 'tumults of the people', apostasy from the Faith, seducing spirits, divisions in the Church (the Greek, the Roman, and the Anglican Churches)—the unfaithful bride who did not desire her Lord to return—and all those things spoken of in 2 Timothy 3: 1–5. Those who called themselves 'the religious world' were forming schemes of their own, despising the ordinances appointed by God; none of them truly desired His coming. Those who claimed to desire it, but would not endeavour to have His house made ready for Him, were hypocrites condemned out of their own mouths. Our Lord taught that His coming would be at a time when men would be unprepared for it—'as in the days of Noah' (Matt. 24: 37). There would soon be a day—perhaps in the lifetimes of those then living—when Christ would come to judge the living and the dead, but no man could know when that day or hour would be. But, if it were true that the hour immediately preceding the dawn was the darkest, surely there was every reason to believe the day was not far off:

[206] D/*FD* 28.   [207] D/*FD* 29.

The night groweth darker and darker. 'Evil men wax worse and worse.' The signs of the last days abound. Christendom is being unchristianized; the Church is assailed on all sides. In a word, the night is far spent, THE DAY IS AT HAND.[208]

The calling of the Church was to have Christ's mind and to show forth God's will as the body of Christ, having a unity of life and a diversity of membership. The Church, as Christ's *body*, was distinct from and immeasurably above the Jewish polity. The Jews were given the Law, but the Church was entrusted with God's will. The Spirit influenced the Jews, but dwelt in the Church. If the Church truly entered into the mind of Christ, division would cease, East and West would unite, and there would not be the jealousies which were rending the Western Church apart. Rome had not understood that *uniformity* and *union* were not the same thing as *unity*. *Unity* was 'oneness of life'; *uniformity* was the mimicry of that life, bringing in the stillness of death—Rome was 'a lovely corpse decked in the garments of a bride'.[209] *Union* was the bond of a man-made confederacy—even in the tumults of the people there was union. There could be unity only amongst those who entered into the fellowship of Christ's sufferings.

The spiritual history of the Church was prefigured prophetically in the Jewish people, who were both a pattern and a warning. The facts of Jewish history were only a covering of a substance which only the Spirit could reveal. The New Testament had been designed so as to throw man back upon the Old Testament for its interpretation. Because the substance lying beneath that history was spiritual, it should not be taken as chronological when applied to the Church. Thus

in the call of Abraham, the deliverance from Egypt, the journeyings through the wilderness, the rites and services of the tabernacle; we see the regeneration, the services and government of the Church in this dispensation portrayed. So, likewise, in the captivities of Israel and Judah, and in the dispersion, we read her judgements.[210]

The strain of continual rebuke in the prophets, and especially in Isaiah, Amos, Micah, and Malachi, was of a people in covenant with God, who had turned against Him except for a small faithful remnant. The language of the Prophets was such as to forbid us to limit such rebukes to the Jewish people. The New Testament, by its

[208] D/*FD* 31.   [209] D/*FD* 38.   [210] D/*FD* 39.

many references to the Old Testament prophecies, had shown that they received their fulfilment in the Gentile Church—Jewish sins, judgements, and deliverances were all types of the sins, judgements, and deliverances of the Church. The Church was 'the vine which God had planted' but it was also the vine which 'is trodden down'.

It had been fashionable for Protestant writers to consider Babylon as a type of Rome, but this was far from giving due and adequate meaning to it. Babylon was the confusion and captivity of the Jews 'in the letter', but 'in the Spirit' the confusion and captivity of Christendom. It represented all that gave power to the infidel, and especially 'fornication' with the world. It was this, above all, that held the saints captive, but from which they would be delivered when it was overcome by the Lamb:

If you take this key, furnished by the New Testament, and then turn to the Prophets, you find the language addressed to the Jews in Babylon is too large to be limited to that event, and that it covers that captivity of Babylon into which the Spirit foresaw the Church to come—into which the Church has come—in which she is found at the second appearing of our Lord—and from which she is then finally delivered.[211]

There were many Jewish types which had been accomplished in the Christian Church, not least that the Christian dispensation was ending in great apostasy as had the Jewish. Christian apostasy had begun in the days of the Apostles, revealing even then the 'Man of Sin'. That apostasy had grown side by side with the growth of the Church—the tares with the wheat. The signs of the last days were appearing daily. The Church had gone to 'Egypt' (the world) for help, but God's people were discovering that 'Egypt' could not save—its horses were flesh and not spirit. The night was dark, but there were signs of the dawn. The apostasy had almost reached its zenith—Psalm 74 had visibly reached its accomplishment—but the cry was being heard, 'Arise, O God, plead thy cause' (Ps. 74: 22). There was a return; God's servants were awakening and His house was being made ready; the wise had arisen to trim their lamps. Some, from unguided zeal, or ignorance and spiritual selfishness, had mistaken their way; some, instead of going up to Jerusalem, had stopped at Rome; some had mistakenly thought that by leaving one part of the Church and going to another they could escape the captivity; some had forsaken altogether the mother who had

---

[211] D/*FD* 41–2.

nurtured them. But none of this should be a discouragement—such things had to be! Faith would wax cold; many would seek things of their own imaginings; many would be weary; many would seek rest and not find it. There was a present and immediate duty:

Let us, my brethren, endure to the end. . . . Let us fight the fight of faith. Let us set our affections on heavenly things—that so, when Christ who is our life, shall appear, we may appear with Him in glory.[212]

The Significance of Dalton's Work

Dalton's material was, like Sitwell's, presented publicly, though presumably, in the first instance, to a mainly Anglican audience—the addresses were given in Leeds Parish Church! Although it included many of the ideas presented in greater detail in Sitwell's book, the eschatological emphasis was more general. Some of the peculiarly Catholic Apostolic eschatological ideas were little more than mentioned and some not mentioned at all—there was, for example, no expansion upon the first resurrection and the translation. However, the addresses do include a number of interesting points, not all of them explicitly eschatological.

1. The two Advents of Christ were seen as one single event having two parts (or scenes), both essential for the fulfilling of God's original purposes.

2. There was the emphasis on the Incarnation as being crucial to those purposes, and on its overriding theological importance—it was 'the substance of revelation'.

3. Christ was seen as taking up in stages His roles as prophet, priest, and king, the last of these not being manifested until the Second Advent.

4. There was an acceptance that some saints might already have been glorified—a position not clearly indicated elsewhere, and in fact often implicitly denied by Catholic Apostolic writers.

5. There was a reason given for the 'tarrying' of the Lord.

6. There was the distinction between 'the Church' (Greek, Roman, and Anglican) and 'the religious world'. This was unusual, in that no mention was made of the Lutherans, whom many Catholic Apostolic writers appeared to accept because they were episcopal—

[212] D/FD 43.

not taking into account the technicalities of the apostolic succession (as did the Anglican Tractarians).

7. There was the usual Catholic Apostolic emphasis on the Jewish dispensation being the type of the Christian, though 'spiritually' not 'literally'.

8. There was the (also usual) interpretation of Babylon.

It might appear that Dalton had tempered his material considerably for the sake of his audience. However, it must be remembered that the addresses were given in Advent, which was then, as now, normally regarded primarily if not exclusively as a period of preparation for Christmas. Even their somewhat tempered Catholic Apostolic eschatological content must have sounded quite extraordinary to those who heard them.

7. CATHOLIC APOSTOLIC ESCHATOLOGY III: LITURGICAL WORSHIP

The importance of eschatology as a significant factor in Catholic Apostolic liturgical worship has been noted earlier (see Ch. IV, § 7). It is an aspect of the Catholic Apostolic Eucharist to which commentators invariably draw attention. Unfortunately, without a thorough prior examination of the eschatological teaching of the apostles, many of the liturgical references to that teaching either go unnoticed or are not fully understood. It is not possible to perceive their full significance solely in terms of the eschatological tradition which has become widely accepted within the 'main-line' Churches since Augustine.

Whilst it is comparatively easy, yet important, to point out the many references to the Second Advent and the resurrection of the dead, it is absolutely crucial to understand such references in the context of apostolic teaching on the first resurrection and translation, on the role of the Holy Spirit in the latter, on the restoration of the Jews and the two Jerusalems, and on the hierarchical citizenship envisaged in the eternal kingdom. Again, that there was extensive use of symbolism—and particularly apocalyptic symbolism—in Catholic Apostolic worship is patently clear, but such symbolism must be understood in terms of the eschatological typology which was such a feature of the apostles' teaching.

Further, what may seem to the 'outsider' to be fairly conventional eschatological references in the various prayers were for the well-instructed members of the Catholic Apostolic body—and they were extremely well-instructed—pregnant with meaning that is not necessarily apparent to the modern liturgical scholar. Even the order in which familiar 'ecumenical' prayers were arranged could have its own eschatological significance, and their content thereby take on peculiarly Catholic Apostolic connotations. Indeed, the prayers taken from the liturgies of other Communions—even if taken directly and without alteration—usually had a new and heightened meaning because of the pervading atmosphere of the worship, which (especially in the earlier days of the body) was one filled with apocalyptic expectation.

Classification of Eschatological Liturgical Material

The eschatological material in Catholic Apostolic worship can be classified in various ways. However, a particular classification having been decided upon, it is often difficult to determine in any particular case to which class an individual prayer or phrase belongs—it would seem that a completely discrete classification system is well-nigh impossible to contrive. For present purposes, liturgical eschatology is considered under eight headings:

1. *General references to the Second Advent and the coming kingdom* and the use of eschatological material from Holy Scripture.
2. Prayers specifically for the *hastening* of the Lord's appearing.
3. *Historical references*: these could be largely typological references to the Jewish dispensation, references to the 'low estate' into which the Church had fallen, references to the work under the 'restored apostles', or descriptions of the contemporary times as the 'last days'.
4. References to the *preparation* of the faithful for the Second Advent, to the means of obtaining strength—especially through the Eucharist—to endure through difficult times, and to the work of the Holy Spirit in such preparation.
5. References to the Eucharist as *anticipation* of the kingdom to come.

6. References to the *first resurrection and translation*.
7. References to the *final resurrection* and the *presentation* of the Church to the Father.
8. Prayers for *the Jews*, and references to *Zion* as the centre of the coming kingdom.

Clearly, these classes are unavoidably interrelated. Thus, for example, general references in (1) could have extension to either the first or the final resurrections of (6) and (7); Old Testament typology in (3) was inevitably linked to the Jews (8); historical references to the work of the 'restored apostles' (3) was usually linked to the idea of preparation of the faithful for the coming of the Lord (4); and all were in the general context of the Second Advent (1). Despite all this, the proposed classes prove useful in presenting the different emphases which could be found in *The Liturgy and Other Divine Offices of the Church*. Further, it is crucial to make the distinction between (6) and (7)—the two resurrections—and to identify references to the work of the Holy Spirit in preparing the elect for the translation. Unfortunately, external liturgical commentators have, almost without exception, failed to make this distinction or to note this particular aspect of Catholic Apostolic pneumatology. It would seem that commentators have so concentrated on the charismatic aspects of Catholic Apostolic pneumatology that teaching on the work of Holy Spirit in the translation has not been detected.

References to the Second Advent

References in the first class include phrases such as:

'the joyful/blessed hope of everlasting life' (Common Preface in the Eucharist/Prayer before Sermon or Exposition);

'the blessed hope of His appearing' (Prayer of Oblation after Consecration);

'the glory of the resurrection' (second Post-Communion Prayer);

'looking for . . . the glorious appearing of the great God and our Saviour Jesus Christ' (Thanksgivings in Morning and Evening Prayer);

'the sure hope of the speedy appearing and kingdom of Thy Son' (Thanksgiving in Shorter Evening Service);

'the faith and hope of Thy Gospel' (Three Seasons: Prayer of Oblation after Consecration);

'until Thy coming again' (Advent: Additional Post-Communion Prayer; Thursday before Easter: Collect);

'unto/until that/the day' (Advent: Additional Post-Communion Prayer/ Laying on of Apostles' Hands: Prayer of Oblation after Consecration);

'partakers of His resurrection' (Monday and Tuesday before Easter: Collect);

'the morning light' (Good Friday: Sixth Prayer);

'abounding in hope' (Good Friday: General Prayers);

'when our Lord Jesus Christ shall come' (Presentation and Dedication for the Ministry: Prayer of Oblation after Consecration);

and many other examples. It must be remembered, however, that general though many such references may seem, the Catholic Apostolic 'hope' was *translation at the Second Advent*, and, therefore, whenever that word was used in the eschatological context—however generally—it would always tend to have this specific connotation.

General eschatological references were also provided by the extensive use of apocalyptic scripture passages for lessons and anthems, and the many references to passages in the Apocalypse in prayers, including benedictions. Such passages (from Isaiah, Daniel and other prophets, and the Apocalypse) were set for reading during Advent. Passages from the Apocalypse were set for reading on the sixth Sunday after Circumcision and the week following, for the period between the second Sunday after Easter and Pentecost, from the seventeenth to the twentieth weeks after Pentecost, and for the Sunday next before Advent. Passages from Daniel were set for reading during the ninth week after Pentecost. Worshipping congregations were thus familiar with the content of the Apocalypse to an extent that was unlikely to be found in other Churches—in the Orthodox Churches, for example, the Apocalypse is never heard during public worship.

Examples of anthems with words taken from Isaiah or the Apocalypse include the Anthem at Presentations for Ordination and at ordinations themselves, especially services associated with the episcopal office, of which the following are examples (from the Presentation of Priests for the Episcopate, and the Consecration of an Angel):

> Then flew one of the Seraphim unto me:
> With a live coal from off the altar;
> And he laid it upon my mouth and said:
> Lo, this hath touched my lips;

And thine iniquity is taken away:
And thy sin is purged.   (Isa. 6: 6–7)

And:

I heard the voice of many angels;
Round about the throne;
Their number was ten thousand times ten thousand;
And thousands of thousands;
Saying with a loud voice:
Worthy is the Lamb that was slain,
To receive power, and riches and wisdom, and strength:
And honour, and glory, and blessing.   (Apoc. 5: 11–12)

The Easter Eve Anthem after the Epistle was taken from Apocalypse 14: 13 and 1 Corinthians 15: 55–6. There were several references to Christ as 'the Angel of the Covenant', as the one 'holding the seven stars', and as the one walking 'in the midst of the seven golden candlesticks' (for example—Assembly of the Seven Churches: Apostolic Benediction; Inducting an Ordained Angel: Apostolic Prayer; Consecration of a Church; Apostolic Intercession). The Intercession at Evening Prayer included a quotation from Apocalypse 7: 10 and 12.

References to 'hastening' the Second Advent—Class (2)—were frequent. For example, the Concluding Prayer before Communion (at the Eucharist) began as follows:

Hasten, O God, the time when Thou shalt send from Thy right hand Him, whom Thou wilt send; at whose appearing the saints departed shall be raised, and we, which are alive, shall be caught up to meet Him, and so shall ever be with Him.

Here, as in so many cases, there was specific reference to the first resurrection and translation. Prayer to hasten the appearance of Christ and the setting up of His kingdom, His coming among us, or His gathering up of the elect, was included especially in the Intercessions at Morning Prayer and the Shorter Morning Service, and in many prayers said during Advent. Amongst the Additional Prayers for the Morning and Evening Offices, the Anglican Prayer, 'O Lord, raise up, we pray Thee, Thy Power, and come among us . . .', clearly falls into this class, and is a typical example of the many prayers from outside sources taking on a heightened meaning in the

Catholic Apostolic liturgical context. (The same prayer formed the Seventh Collect used at the Assembly of the Seven Churches in London.) The first of the prayers following the Collects for the Three Seasons had as its last petition:

Finally, we beseech Thee speedily to accomplish the number of Thine elect, and to hasten the appearing and kingdom of Thy dear son.

The Advent addition to the Litany, to be said at the Forenoon and Afternoon Services, had as its congregational response throughout 'Come, Lord Jesu'. The Easter Eve Collect asked that the 'whole redeemed Church' should 'speedily attain into the resurrection of the dead'. The first All Saints Day Thanksgiving repeated the first part of the Three Seasons petition above. These, and other instances of 'hastening' petitions, were, like the more general eschatological references in Class (1), related either specifically or by implication to the special Catholic Apostolic hope. Thus, the Easter Eve Collect followed its petition for a speedy attainment to resurrection with the words:

when our mortal bodies shall put on immortality and incorruption, and we shall be changed into the likeness of His glorious body.

Historical References and References to the Church

As has been noted above, the third class—the 'historical' references —can be further categorized into:

- (a) references to the Old Testament history of the Jews;
- (b) references to the shortcomings of the Church—its disobedience, low estate, or entanglement with the world;
- (c) references to the new work being done under restored apostles;
- (d) specific denotation of the contemporary age as the 'last days/ times'.

In the Eucharist, the general Preface included (a), (b), and (c), the Commemoration of the Living included (b) and (c), and the Commemoration of the Departed included (a), (c), and (d).

References to Old Testament history were particularly concentrated in the various services associated with the consecration of church buildings and furniture, though they also occurred elsewhere—for example, with the inclusion of the patriarchs and prophets in the Eucharistic Commemoration of the Departed, and, notably, in the

Consecration of an Angel. In the latter case, the special Preface included the following:

Of old Thou didst show unto Thy servant Moses, in secret counsel upon the holy mount, the pattern of heavenly things, commanding that he should make for Aaron, Thine elect high-priest, holy garments for glory and for beauty, setting forth the blessed mysteries of Thy kingdom in types and figures . . . By the mystic ornaments employed in consecrating the former priesthood, Thou didst foreshow the ordinances of the heavenly kingdom . . . All that was signified by splendid garments— the breast-plate and the mitre, enriched with gold and precious stones and wrought with cunning workmanship—Thou dost now bestow on those whom Thou admittest to the higher ministries in Thy house . . .

Reference to Old Testament worship was made in the apostolic prayers in the Order for the Consecration of a Church:

Thou didst reveal Thy glorious presence unto the patriarchs, that they might worship before Thy face, and call upon Thy Name. Thou didst appoint unto Thy people Israel a place and an altar, where they might pay their vows, present unto Thee Thine ordained sacrifices and offerings, and receive Thy blessing.

.   .   .   .

[Thou, O Lord, by the inspiration of Thy Holy Spirit, didst put it into the heart of Thy servant Jacob to set up and consecrate to Thy Name a stone in Bethel . . . By Thy commandment Thy servant Moses made unto Thee the tabernacle in the wilderness . . . Thou didst accept the gifts of Thy servant David, and the house which Solomon built unto Thee . . .]

At the consecration of the tabernacle, reference was made to Moses' command to Aaron to lay up the manna continually before God. At the blessing of lights, reference was made to the burning bush and the pillar of fire in addition to a reference to Pentecost. The typological significance was taken up in the proper Preface. The same themes were repeated in the form for consecrating an altar and tabernacle in an unconsecrated building, and for consecrating a tablet-altar, and in the blessing of the table of prothesis, and eucharistic vessels and vestments.

The Exhortation at Morning Prayer was explicit about the Church's shortcomings:

we have forgotten, and lightly esteemed, the ordinances given at the beginning for the perfecting of the saints . . . The hope of His appearing and kingdom hath failed among those who are called by His name . . . We are found entangled with the world, and overcome of evil.

The Evening Prayer Exhortation extended these to include disregard for the Church's unity, lack of purity, quenching the Holy Spirit, and preferring the institutions of man to those of God. The Eve of Pentecost was set aside 'to be observed as a day of humiliation and sorrow for sin, especially in respect of the gifts of the Holy Ghost', and the Eucharist was not celebrated. The special Confession for that day was explicit about the sins of the Church, sins with which the Catholic Apostolic faithful were asked to identify themselves:

We have not used to Thy glory the gifts which Thou didst bestow in sending down the Holy Ghost upon Thy Church. . . . We have broken Thine ordinances; We have despised Thy holy word spoken to us by Thy prophets; We have disobeyed Thy commandments delivered to us by Thine apostles. We have not fulfilled the trust which Thou didst commit unto us, That we should . . . gather Thy children scattered abroad. We have hidden Thy glory from the eyes of Thine ancient people; We have caused Thy Name to be blasphemed among the nations of the earth . . .

The Service of Penitence included four special prayers, each with an accompanying lesson and psalm. These referred to rebellion against God, despising Divine government, subjection of the Church to worldly rulers, intruding man's authority into the sanctuary, individual choice of doctrine, rejection of the ministry of the first Apostles, bringing forth the 'grapes of Sodom and clusters of Gomorrah', wandering without a shepherd, changing God's ordinances, abuse of God's gifts, forgetting confidence in God, general entanglement with the world, forsaking the hope given by God, looking for a worldly inheritance, attempting to rule without God, becoming 'unholy and unclean', and so on. One of the prayers following the All Saints Day Collects graphically expressed the Catholic Apostolic view of the contemporary state of the Church and the need for Christ's coming as deliverer:

Behold, O Lord, the ruin of Thy sanctuary; Thy Church desolate; the place in which Thou wouldest manifest Thy Holiness and Thy glory profaned. See, O God, the affliction of Thy people, and send Him whom Thou wilt send, even the Lamb who shall be the Ruler, and take off the yoke of our captivity.

The prayer immediately following, addressed directly to Christ, included the following petitions:

take Thou vengeance of the blood of Thy martyrs, which hath been split in the city of confusion. . . . Hear Thou the groaning of Thy whole creation, for Thou art a God of pity: behold the tears that are shed upon the earth, and wipe them away from all eyes.

In the forenoon form for Imploring the Blessing of Almighty God upon the Labours of Evangelists, two prayers were to be introduced into the Litany, of which the second, a prayer for Christian unity, referred to the 'wanderings and divisions' of Christians, their mutual 'hatred, variance, and animosities', their deception 'by the wiles of the enemy', their forsaking of the Church, and their having been 'carried away by the vanity of error', for all of which God was asked to have mercy, restoring them

to the unity of the faith, in the one fold of Jesus Christ, Thy holy Church . . .

Such unity was regarded as possible only under the rule of apostles.

Direct references to the new work under restored apostles abounded, as might be expected, especially in the various thanksgivings, many of which included specific thanksgiving for the restoration of full ordinances and related intercession. A typical example is to be found in the second prayer after the Three Seasons Collects:

We give Thee hearty thanks that Thou hast vouchsafed to restore the ordinances of Thy house, and hast given again apostles to Thy Church. Add unto the apostles, we humbly besech Thee, the full number of those who shall serve as fellow-labourers with them; inspiring prophets who shall speak by the Holy Ghost the hidden mysteries which by apostles and prophets Thou wouldest reveal; and bringing to their help evangelists and pastors. And in all the churches of Thy people raise up prophets . . . call forth faithful men who shall labour as evangelists, and by whom Thou mayest testify Thy coming judgements, and . . . send unto Thy flock those who shall feed them in truth and love.

The phrase 'all the churches' should be noted here—the ministry of prophets, evangelists, and pastors was not seen as necessarily restricted to the Catholic Apostolic body.

An interesting example is provided by the opening of the Christmas Eve Anthem after the Epistle (taken from Hos. 6: 3):

His going forth is prepared as the morning:
And He shall come unto us as the latter and the former rain.

The 'latter rain' was, for the Catholic Apostolics, the outpouring of
the charismatic phenomena which had preceded the call of their
apostles (see Ch. II). The Preface for the Tuesday after Pentecost
provides a typical example of the linking of the restoration of
apostles with the 'low estate' of the Church. After reference to the
descent of the Holy Spirit at Pentecost and the Spirit's role in
guiding men 'into all truth' and sanctifying the Church, it
continued:

And especially on this day we thank Thee, that Thou hast regarded the
low estate of Thy Church, giving again Thine apostles, Thy holy
ordinances for rule, by whom the twelve tribes of Thy spiritual Israel
shall be gathered and united in one, and the whole assembly and Church
of the first-born, being edified in love, shall grow up into an holy temple
of the Lord.

Of special note also is the order for the Assembly of the Seven
Churches, where there was reference to both the calling and the
separation of the apostles (see Ch. II, § 2).

The references to last days or times are so numerous that they
cannot be noted, apart from a few specific examples, chosen because
they are linked to a reference to one of the other historical aspects.
Thus, the second section of the Commemoration of the Departed in
the Eucharist linked 'these last times' to both the Jewish and
Christian revelations, and to the latter-day revival of ordinances and
charismatic manifestations in the Church:

The faithful patriarchs of old, and all the prophets, Thy servant John
the Baptist . . . we remember. The Blessed Virgin Mary . . . we
remember, and with Thy Church in all generations, we call her blessed.
The holy apostles, bishops, priests, and deacons; the blessed martyrs
and confessors; all holy men and women . . . we remember and
commend to Thee. We commend to Thee those who, in these last times,
have rejoiced in Thy returning grace unto Thy Church, in the reviving
of the ordinances which Thou gavest at the beginning, and in the
manifestation of the gifts of the Holy Ghost.

The Additional Collect for the Tuesday after Pentecost linked
'these last days' with the restoration of apostles and preparation of
the people for the Second Advent. The special clause to be inserted

in the Preface on 14 July (commemoration of the separation of the apostles) at the Assembly of the Seven Churches linked 'in this last time' with the perfection of God's children by newly called apostles. The Collect in the service for Imploring the Blessing of Almighty God upon the Labours of Evangelists (which included a quotation from Isaiah 2: 2) linked the 'last days' with the completion of the Church—an implicit reference to the Catholic Apostolic witness.

In a number of cases, the reference did not specifically mention the 'last' days or times, but the nearness of the Second Advent, on occasion using the phrase, 'Behold, He cometh'—an example being provided by the Good Friday Afternoon Service, where it was used following the account of the rejection of Christ by the Jews. The second form of the Prayer of Oblation after Consecration to be used by an apostle for the tribe committed to his charge, after praying that God would give an increase of evangelists, pour down heavenly graces upon the churches and their angels, and make the priests examples to the people, concluded with the following words:

Let Thy hands be laid upon Thy children; may they be sealed unto the day of redemption. May we all deny ourselves, be crucified unto the world, and follow the Lamb withersoever He will lead us, lifting up our heads with confidence, because we know that our redemption draweth nigh.

There were also references in services connected with evangelists to 'approaching judgements'—it was one of the specific duties of evangelists to warn Christendom of these.

References to Preparation for the Second Advent

The fourth class of liturgical eschatological references comprises those relating to 'preparation' of the faithful for the Second Advent. It is not possible to give a complete list here, but a reasonably extensive list follows. The faithful had to

be perfected (Eucharistic Commemoration of the Departed, and 14 July: Preface);

be holy and unspotted (Concluding Prayer before Communion);

be revived (Morning Prayer Intercession);

be purified (Additional Prayers for the Offices, and Easter Eve: Collect at the Eucharist);

increase in true religion (Additional Prayers for the Offices);

be grafted in the love of God's holy Name (Additional Prayers for the Offices);

be cleansed in conscience (Additional Prayers for the Offices);

be healed in soul (Additional Prayers for the Offices, and Advent: Prayers after the Prayer for the Departed);

be enlightened in heart (Additional Prayers for the Offices);

be cleansed from sin (Additional Prayers for the Offices);

eschew all things contrary to their profession (Additional Prayers for the Offices);

give thanks to God (Occasional Prayers at Morning and Evening Services);

wait for the time of gathering/wait with vigilance (Occasional Prayers at Morning and Evening Services, and Third Collect for 18 December);

be fit/ready for Christ's appearing (Advent: Prayers after the Commemoration of the Departed, and Assembly of the Seven Churches: Fifth Collect);

look forward to/be athirst for/embrace the hope of the coming of Christ (Advent: Prayer of Oblation after Consecration; Ascension: Additional Post-Communion Prayer; Form of Committing to Pastorship);

be diligent in service and just works (Advent: Prayers after the Prayer for the Departed);

have an earnest desire in their hearts to meet Christ at His coming (Advent: Prayers after the Commemoration of the Departed);

rejoice in being gathered into the unity of the Faith (Advent: Prayers after the Commemoration of the Departed);

abide steadfast in faith and in all good works (Christmas Eve: Collect);

meditate on the manifestation of God's Son under the form and true nature of man (Circumcision: Additional Post-Communion Prayer);

follow the example of Christ's humility and patience (Monday and Tuesday before Easter: Collect, and Good Friday: Introductory Collect);

be confirmed in all spiritual gifts (Good Friday: Prayers);

be increased in faith and understanding (Good Friday: Prayers);

be patient in waiting for the resurrection (Easter Eve Collect);

be ready in body and spirit (Easter Eve: Fourth (alternative) Collect);

be obedient unto the faith (Easter Eve: Fourth (alternative) Collect);

be filled with divine energy (Easter: Prayer of Oblation after Consecration);

mortify all worldly and corrupt affections and desires (Easter: Additional Post-Communion Prayer);

be anointed/sealed with the Holy Spirit (Eve of Pentecost: Concluding Prayer; Monday after Pentecost: Additional Collect; 14 July: Prayer of Oblation after Consecration; Assembly of the Seven Churches: Prayer of Oblation after Consecration);

shine brightly like lamps (Eve of Pentecost: Evening Collect);

be united in the doctrine and fellowship of the apostles (14 July: Collect);

be kept from the snares of evil spirits and the seductions of flattery (Assembly of the Seven Churches: Fourth Collect);

have the grace of watchfulness and faithfulness until the end (Assembly of the Seven Churches: Fifth Collect);

be illuminated with prophetic words (Assembly of the Seven Churches: Preface);

be filled with the joy of salvation (Assembly of the Seven Churches: Prayer of Oblation after Consecration);

be sanctified in spirit, soul, and body (Assembly of the Seven Churches: Prayer of Oblation after Consecration);

be given up to seeking after righteousness (Times of Scarcity and Apprehended Famine: Additional Post-Communion Prayer);

have faith in God's love and mercy (Times of Scarcity and Apprehended Famine: Additional Post-Communion Prayer).

Such preparation of the faithful required the pouring out of the Holy Spirit both on the people and, especially, on those who were to minister to them. At the various ordinations, therefore, God's grace was called down upon the candidates so that the faithful might be made perfect by their ministrations in anticipation of Christ's appearance. The Second Advent was always the ultimate focal point towards which the perfection of the faithful and the work of the ministry was directed. Faithful participation in the Eucharist was an essential part of all preparation for the Second Advent. This was made specific in the Second Post-Communion Prayer:

O God, who in these holy mysteries has vouchsafed to feed us with the Flesh and Blood of Thy dear Son; We beseech Thee that all who faithfully partake of the same may . . . finally attain unto the glory of the resurrection, through . . .

The Prayer after Afternoon Communion emphasized the same theme, asking God that those who had received Communion might 'be nourished unto everlasting glory in the world to come'. A number of Post-Communion prayers for particular feasts had the same emphasis. Typical examples are those for Presentation in the Temple, and Ascension. In the former, it was linked to a promise of Christ:

O Lord . . . Fulfil also unto us, we beseech Thee, Thy word of promise made unto us by Thy Son, that all we, who have partaken of this blessed communion, may have our part in the glory of the resurrection; through . . .

In the latter, receiving the sacrament was a preparation for patient waiting for as well as entering the kingdom:

O Lord Jesu Christ . . . We beseech Thee so to nourish us through this holy sacrament, that we may patiently wait for Thine appearing, and be counted worthy to enter into Thy kingdom, [Who livest . . .]

References to Anticipation of the Kingdom

The Eucharist was, however, not only preparation for the Second Advent and the kingdom; it was also a present experience of the kingdom—an 'anticipation' of it (Class (5)). As has been pointed out by Stevenson,[213] one of the unique features of the Catholic Apostolic Liturgy was the position given to the Lord's Prayer in the Eucharist—between the Preface and the Consecration. This positioning emphasized the view that the petition 'Thy kingdom come' had a Eucharistic as well as an eschatological meaning. Cardale wrote:

Having then concluded the triumphal hymn at the close of the Preface, we suffer an interval to elapse before proceeding to the actual consecration, and in this interval we devoutly kneel down, and the celebrant offers the Lord's Prayer. The terms in which it is expressed are remarkably applicable to this sacrament, and evidently calculated to prepare us for the act of consecration, rather than that of communion: they seem to point to the consecration, and the worship consequent thereon, as future; rather than to imply that the holy gifts have been already consecrated, and the worship actually offered.

---

[213] K. W. Stevenson, 'The Catholic Apostolic Eucharist', thesis (Southampton University, 1975).

. . . We are about to commemorate the death and sacrifice of Christ— that death by which the Name of God was hallowed in the highest degree; which opens up for us the kingdom of heaven . . . Our commemoration . . . is the highest worship and worthiest sanctification of the Name of God which we can offer. . . . and when that is accomplished in the Church, His kingdom shall come, and His will shall be done in all the earth. . . . and when he shall come, the true Paschal supper shall be fulfilled in the kingdom of God (Luke xxii. 16). In approaching, therefore, to the celebration of these mysteries, we pray our Heavenly Father that His Name may be hallowed, His kingdom may come, and His will be done on earth as it is in heaven; which words evidently refer, not to an act of worship already performed, but to one which is yet about to be offered.[214]

Cardale and other apostles emphasized that all anticipatory experience of the kingdom was spiritual: the coming of Christ in the Eucharist spiritually anticipated the Second Advent, and the reception of Communion by the faithful was a spiritual anticipation of the marriage of the Lamb. This was made specific in the First Post-Communion Prayer:

Grant unto us, we beseech Thee, O Lord, that we may be eternally satisfied with the fruition of Thy divine glory, which Thou hast now prefigured unto us by making us partakers of Thy precious Body and Blood, Who livest . . .

The Collect for the Thursday before Easter (addressed to Christ) asked that the communicants may receive 'the full fruition' of His redeeming love—in the Catholic Apostolic context a clear eschatological anticipatory reference. The All Saints Preface referred to Christ's sacrifice through which 'an entrance is abundantly administered . . . into the everlasting kingdom', and the Additional Post-Communion Prayer of the same feast prayed that the communicants may be 'advanced' to a participation in the heavenly feast of the kingdom.

References to the First Resurrection and Translation

The sixth class comprises references to the first resurrection and translation. As has already been stated, the great majority of

[214] J. B. Cardale, *Readings upon the Liturgy and Other Divine Offices of the Church* (London: Barclay, 1848), 154–5.

references to resurrection at the Second Advent should be taken as relating to these implicitly if not explicitly. Here, only references which were quite specific to the first resurrection will be included. It is important that their wording should be noted so that references to the first resurrection can be clearly distinguished from those to the general resurrection—though in some cases a particular wording is clearly inclusive of both.

There were a number of important words and phrases which denoted reference to the first resurrection and translation:

1. 'Partakers': to be a 'partaker with Christ' in the kingdom meant to share *in his rule*, a sharing which was restricted to those resurrected or caught up to meet Him at His Second Advent (1 Thess. 4: 16–17). An example was to be found in the third of the Prayers for the Church at Morning Prayer. On occasion 'reigning with Christ' was explicitly stated, as in the Thanksgiving at the Shorter Evening Service and the Prayer before Communion at the Blessing of Newly-Married persons.

2. 'Inheritance': to receive the inheritance reserved for the saints at the Second Advent meant to participate in the first resurrection or translation. Examples were to be found in the Thanksgiving at the Shorter Morning Service; the Benediction of Oil at the Anointing of the Sick; and during the Commemoration of a Departing Soul.

3. 'Resurrection of the just' or those 'departed in faith': as found in the Easter Eve Prayer of Oblation after Consecration (where it is linked with the 'saints'); the Collect for Commemorating a Person lately Deceased; and the Absolution at the Solemn Absolution of Penitents.

4. Phrases relating the work of the Holy Spirit to the Second Advent or to the Church's 'hope' (see § 6 above): these referred to the translation, as in the Easter Prayer of Oblation after Consecration; the Collect for the Monday after Pentecost; and the 14 July Prayer of Oblation after Consecration (where reference was also made to being saved from Antichrist and the 'storm' of God's anger—that is, from the tribulation).

5. Phrases relating Christ's appearing 'to them that love/look for Him': as found in the Ascension Day Preface.

6. References to presentation *to* Christ (as opposed to presentation *by* Christ to the Father): examples were the 14 July Collect and the Form of Committing to Pastorship.

7. The 'morning' of the resurrection: the first resurrection and translation were to occur at the 'morning' of the Day of the Lord—an example was to be found in the Fourth Collect for the Assembly of the Seven Churches.

8. 'First-born': the first-born were the participants in the first resurrection and translation, as referred to in the 14 July Preface.

9. 'Receive again thy body' when associated specifically with the 'elect': this was found in the Second Prayer at the Commendation of a Departing Soul.

In addition to the above, there were a few cases where the expression 'the first resurrection' or the phrase 'caught up to meet the Lord in the air' were used. Examples were the Concluding Prayer before Communion, the Prayers following the Collects on All Saints Day, and the Anthem after the Epistle also at All Saints (which quoted Apoc. 20: 6). The first of these has already been quoted above (in Class (2)). The All Saints Epistle (1 Thess. 4: 13–5: 10) emphasized the scriptural justification underlying the specific Catholic Apostolic eschatology so evident at this Feast.

No prayer exhibited this eschatology, however, as fully as the special prayer for the Second Advent issued on a single sheet after the passing of the apostles. It was to be used in Morning and Evening Prayer immediately before the Lord's Prayer, in the Forenoon and the Afternoon Services immediately before the Concluding Collect, and in the Shorter Morning and Evening Services immediately before the Thanksgiving. It was also appointed for Good Friday and All Saints. This prayer was especially treasured by Catholic Apostolic members, many of whom were extremely reluctant to show it to outsiders. It was extremely comprehensive, referring to the restoration of apostles and prophets, the sealing of the first-fruits, the nearness of the Second Advent, the restoration of body and soul at the first resurrection, the translation (implicitly), standing upon Mount Zion with the Lamb, and final presentation before the Father (a reference to the general resurrection). Because of this comprehensiveness and its special eschatological significance, it is given now in full:

Prayer
FOR THE COMING OF THE LORD AND THE
RESURRECTION AND CHANGE OF
THE FIRST-FRUITS

O LORD JESUS CHRIST, Who art the Resurrection and the Life, we acknowledge Thy goodness in restoring the ministry of Thine apostles, and in gathering and sealing Thy first-fruits, and in warning us through Thy prophets of the nearness of the day of Thine appearing.

Hasten that day, that we may see Thee as Thou art, and be changed into Thy likeness. Bring back those, our brethren, who have rejoiced with us in Thy returning grace unto Thy Church, and have fallen asleep. Restore to them their bodies raised in glory and immortality; and vouchsafe to us who are alive and remain to be sanctified wholly; and may our whole spirit and soul and body be preserved blameless unto Thy coming.

We pray that the time may speedily come when we, and Thy saints in all generations who have been elected to this glory, may stand with the Lamb upon Mount Zion, a holy first-fruits redeemed from among men, without fault before the throne of God: and unto Thee, with the Father and the Holy Ghost, be all honour and glory, now and for ever.

R. Amen.

The prayer included references to both the first and the general resurrections. This is to be found in a number of other prayers, often implicitly by means of expressions such as 'a full entrance into the eternal kingdom' and 'receive the full reward', where the word 'full' referred not only to resurrection or translation in the morning of the Day of the Lord, but also to the final presentation of the kingdom by Christ to the Father after the general resurrection and judgement. Examples are to be found in the Intercession at Evening Prayer and in many of the services associated with the presentation and ordination of clergy.

References to the General Resurrection and Judgement

References to the general resurrection and judgement *only* (Class (7)) were considerably less numerous than those to the first resurrection and translation, though there are some two score or more of these. Key words here are 'everlasting life/glory/kingdom', often associated with 'at length' or 'finally'. Such expressions were included in the last prayer at Afternoon Communion on the Lord's Day, the Concluding Prayer of the Litany (used also on other occasions), the Collect for the Blessing of Newly-Married Persons, a prayer at Receiving one of the Six Elders of a Church, in the Presentation of Priests for the Episcopate, the Prayer of Oblation after Consecration at the Induction of an Angel, and in the Prayer for a Woman immediately after Childbirth.

Specific references to the judgement were comparatively few: they appeared in the general Advent Collect (also used as a prayer before delivering a sermon), the Collect for Christmas Eve, and the first prayer during the Dedication of Catechumens. In the last of these, after listing the many and great benefits to be bestowed in baptism, the presiding angel continued:

These are the benefits which God on His part will surely bestow, and for these, as His gift unto you, ye shall have to give account at the day of the tremendous judgement, before the judgement seat of Christ. See, therefore, that ye be wholly resolved to walk worthy of your most holy calling . . .

It should be noted that two of the prayers just referred to had come from outside sources, namely the Anglican Advent Collect and the Prayer of St John Chrysostom. There were also a few references to Christ's final presentation of the kingdom to the Father—in the Collect for Presentation, the Pentecost Collect, and the Apostolic Benediction on the Tuesday after Pentecost. The last of these included the following words:

The Lord Jesus Christ . . . Cleanse and sanctify you, and all them that are His; and keep you spotless and blameless, that He may present you in the unity of the one Body, without fault, before the throne of God.

Very occasionally, the significance was not absolutely clear. For example, an unqualified reference to the 'Day of the Lord' might not necessarily be a reference to the *morning* of that day, though in all probability it should be taken as being so (see the Good Friday Prayers). A more interesting example is to be found in the Collect for Imploring the Blessing of Almighty God upon the Labours of Evangelists:

ALMIGHTY GOD, Who hast promised that in the last days the mountain of the Lord's house shall be exalted above the hills, and that all nations shall flow into it: We beseech thee to send forth Thy light and Thy truth unto all people, guiding them in the ways of thine ordinances, and in the paths of thy commandments: that Thy whole Church, complete in every member, instructed in all righteousness, and perfected in all holiness, may be presented without spot or wrinkle, in the day of the appearing and kingdom of Thy Son; through the same . . .

Analysing this prayer starting from its ending: the 'day of the appearing' is ambiguous, as no particular part of the day is referred to, though it would more likely refer to the first resurrection and translation. The phrase 'may be presented' is also ambiguous, since it is not stated whether this is presentation *to* Christ (first resurrection) or presentation *by* Christ (after the general resurrection and judgement). The phrase 'complete in every member' certainly seems to suggest the general resurrection, though 'the ways of Thine ordinances' has overtones of the 'elect' at the first resurrection and translation. However, the reference to the flowing of 'all nations' into the 'mountain of the Lord's house' would appear to settle the matter—the prayer related to the presentation of the kingdom to the Father by Christ *after* the final resurrection and judgement. Such an analysis is essential in any consideration of eschatological liturgical references.

Eschatological References to the Jews

The final class (8) covers eschatological (as opposed to historical references) to the Jews. There were a number of these. In some cases the reference was very oblique: for example, there was a prayer for the turning of the hearts of the Jews in the Commemoration of the Living: this had an oblique eschatological reference because it was linked with the gathering of the elect. There were many references to Zion and Jerusalem, taken from scriptural sources: for example, in the general Communion Anthem and in a number of Communion Anthems set for special feasts. The Communion Anthem for 14 July quoted from Isaiah 1: 26 with clear eschatological overtones:

> I will restore thy judges as at the first:
> And thy counsellors as at the beginning.
> I will make thy rulers peace:
> And thine overseers righteousness.
> Violence shall no more be heard in thy land:
> Wasting nor destruction within thy borders.
> Thou shalt call thy walls Salvation:
> And thy gates shall be called Praise.

The prayer for the Jews on Good Friday had clear overtones of the Second Advent, asking that:

their hearts being turned unto Thee, they may behold Thy glory in the face of Jesus Christ, and may acknowledge Him to be their Saviour . . .

The Good Friday Antiphon looked to the Second Coming in which 'they also which pierced Him' would behold Christ's glory, and 'wail'. The first prayer after the Collects at All Saints asked that David as God's anointed should 'rule in Thy holy city for ever'. The last of these prayers asked for the Jews:

we beseech Thee, turn their heart unto Thyself, and take away the veil which is thereon, and remove the blindness from their mind; that they may look on Him whom they have pierced, and mourn for their iniquities. Accomplish for them . . . all the purposes of mercy and blessing which Thou hast yet in store for them; give unto them again the land of their inheritance; build speedily the walls of Jerusalem, and make it to be the joy of the whole earth.

The choice of Psalm 122 to be sung immediately before the consecration of the foundation stone of a church by the angel is also significant, not least for the promise of verse 2 in the translation used (the AV): 'Our feet *shall* stand within thy gates, O Jerusalem.'

The Reflection of Apostolic Teaching

Points relating Catholic Apostolic liturgical eschatology to its immediate context will be taken up in the next section. Here, it is sufficient to note how precisely it reflected the apostles' teaching. Cardale, as the principal liturgical author, ensured that this was so, and he had a unique opportunity in that the teaching was already well developed when the services took their final forms—thus *The Liturgy* proclaimed what already existed and did not have any role in influencing it. Without a detailed knowledge of the underlying teaching, it is not possible to appreciate the significance of many of the prayers and anthems, the nuances of which have often to be 'teased out', though they were familiar to the instructed members. Catholic Apostolic worship thus had a richness which few outside the body could fully appreciate. Those outsiders who attended the full services were invariably impressed with their richness and often startled by the prophetic utterances—their comment is mainly restricted to these two aspects. Certainly, they could detect the general eschatological atmosphere, but most were blind to the details of the eschatology actually being proclaimed around them. *The Liturgy* was and remains a remarkable work in a great many now largely unsuspected ways.

8. SURVEY AND COMMENT

Catholic Apostolic eschatology presented a comprehensive and coherent prophetic view of the whole course of future events from the contemporary scene to the final presentation of the Kingdom by Christ to the Father. It was millenarian; but it was also pre-millennialist and pre-tribulationist, that is, it taught that the Second Advent would occur before the millennium and that there would be a first resurrection and translation before the great tribulation. It was historicist, linked with and indeed developed from a comprehensive and coherent interpretation of history as revealing prophecy already fulfilled. It was rooted in a particular form of fundamentalist Biblical exegesis, applied especially to Daniel and the Apocalypse—but in the context of Scripture as a whole—and allied with a largely typological approach to Old Testament history.

It is important to see this eschatology in the context of contemporary events. The Catholic Apostolics were by no means the only group with a special interest in the prophetic Scriptures: the French Revolution had so disturbed Christians—and particularly the evangelicals in both Church and Dissent in England—that study of the prophetic books became a widespread activity, both for individuals working alone and in the several societies for prophetic study which had come into being. These prophetic studies had blossomed before the formation of the Catholic Apostolic Church, but had involved a number of those subsequently to be its apostles as well as the influential figure of Irving. The latter had not only injected his own apocalyptic ideas into the various prophetic debates, but had also brought with him the remarkable adventist work of Lacunza, an individualistic work from outside both the contemporary European context and the Protestant tradition. An important aspect of any analysis of the eschatology of the Catholic Apostolic Church is, therefore, the determination of what was derived from the general prophetic activity in which its future apostles participated, what was inspired by Lacunza, and what was peculiar to the body itself.

It is also necessary to assess to what extent the Catholic Apostolics were inheritors of any more general Christian apocalyptic tradition, whether patristic or post-Reformation. However, before proceeding

to all this, it is useful first to provide a survey of Catholic Apostolic
eschatology and interpretation of history—the two cannot be
separated. In considering such a survey, it must be accepted that
there were inevitably minor differences of detail in the application
of the prophetic scriptures to be found in the various apostolic
writings. These were not, however, of a serious nature; any major
divergences were later corrected to ensure convergence. Greater
differences could be found amongst some of the more speculative
prophetic statements of other Catholic Apostolic writers in the early
days of the body. Such statements have not been included here, as
the present study of eschatology is restricted to the official teaching
of the Catholic Apostolic Church as evidenced by its apostolic
writings and liturgical worship.

Catholic Apostolic eschatology must be seen within the cosmic
view taken of the whole purpose of God from the creation of the
world to the final kingdom of blessedness. This purpose, the
outpouring of God's inestimable love, was the manifestation of
Himself through Creation and His ultimate union with created man
along with the glorification of all that had been created in His eternal
kingdom. Thus the Incarnation, for which the creation of man had
been necessary, was always in the mind of God—it was not merely a
response to the Fall. Because of the Fall, a long preparation of man
had become necessary, which had included the Old Covenant which
had been both a preparation for and a type of the Christian Church.
For the restoration of man's ultimate destiny, the Incarnate One had
suffered and died, and had risen as the firstfruit from the dead, and
would return as the Bridegroom to claim His Bride—the elect, the
true and faithful Church. This return was but the beginning of an
eschatological chapter of events, much of which could be determined
from the prophetic scriptures.

The Catholic Apostolic teaching, as finally developed in the
writings of the apostles and liturgical worship, was created upon the
idea of an approaching Second Advent for which there was to be
made ready an elect and perfected body, prepared by restored
apostles from within the company of the baptized. This apostolic
witness was an 'Elias ministry' to the Church, just as there had been
an Elias ministry to the Jews before the Incarnation. Its rejection
would be a sign of apostasy. The Second Advent was seen as
'approaching' because of the many 'signs of the times', of which the
French Revolution and the increasing disarray and apostasy of the

Church were major heralds. Another major herald, the restoration of the Jews to the land of Israel, still lay in the future. The apostate Church, represented in the Apocalypse by Babylon (the great whore), was being prepared by the 'mystery of iniquity' working within (rationalism, humanism, and deism) for its alliance with the secular rulers of the world under the leadership of Antichrist. Antichrist was not an institution or a system, but a *person* whose identity would soon by revealed as apostasy reached its height. He would personify all that fragments and destroys both the Church and ordered human society on earth, and would indeed eventually be responsible for the destruction of each. This period of great tribulation was inevitable, but would be escaped by an elect body (those referred to by St Paul in 1 Thess. 4: 16–17) who would be resurrected by Christ or translated (caught up in the clouds) through the operation of the Holy Spirit at the beginning (morning) of the Second Advent. This was the *first* resurrection—the gathering of the 'first-fruits', the resurrection *from/out of* the dead of which the New Testament spoke and which was indicated by the woman in travail (Apoc. 12: 1–2). The Old Testament 'saints' would participate in it, and both the resurrected and the translated would receive their resurrection bodies and remain standing with Christ upon Mount Zion. This *morning* of the Day of the Lord—Christ's revealing of Himself to those 'in Him'—was the 'Parousia' together with the 'marriage of the Lamb'.

Antichrist, the Beast, would then come into his full destructive power, assisted by the False Prophet—the head of the 'antichurch' —and armed with miracles and all the devices of modern science. Christian worship and sacraments, which would cease at the Parousia, would be replaced by the worship of the Beast. The followers of Antichrist would bear the 'mark of the beast', a parody of the sealing of the elect. Any of the baptized remaining faithful to Christ would be horribly persecuted, and many would be slaughtered. These were the 'great multitude' coming out of the tribulation, who would form part of the 'harvest'. Two witnesses to God would appear, but would be killed and their bodies left in the streets. They would be objects of mockery for the apostate Church ('Babylon'). But this, together with all ecclesiastical and secular institutions, would be destroyed by Antichrist and his forces, who would then lay siege to Jerusalem.

This would then be the signal for the 'Epiphaneia', the next stage of the Second Advent, when Christ would return with his saints in full glory and power to deliver Jerusalem at the Battle of Armageddon, to cast Antichrist and the False Prophet into the sea of fire, and to bind Satan during the thousand years of millennial rule. It is at the Epiphaneia that the Jews 'will look on Him whom they have pierced' and the majority be finally converted—all earlier attempts to convert the Jews as a nation would be fruitless. The new Jerusalem would then be set up on earth, the centre of all authority and worship, above which would lie the heavenly Jerusalem, the abode of Christ and the saints.

During the millennium the converted Jews would act as Christ's witnesses, but there would still be those capable of ingratitude, pride, and rebellion, and hence Satan would be loosed and would gather again an army against Jerusalem, only to be destroyed by the direct action of God, symbolized by 'fire', and finally cast into the sea of fire to join Antichrist and the false prophet. The ultimate revelation of God's glory (the final stage of the Second Advent) would now take place, the 'great white throne' would be set in place, the books would be opened, and the general resurrection and judgement would follow, and Christ, having subjected all things to the will of God, would then present the kingdom to the Father. In this everlasting kingdom, there would be a new (transfigured) heaven and earth, in which God's will alone would prevail, Christ and the true Church reign, the Jews have a special and intermediate place in the new Jerusalem (without a temple), and the nations participate as subjects—all enjoying everlasting blessedness.

This eschatological teaching, based upon the visions of the Apocalypse, was presented as the concluding chapter of a history of the Christian Church, of which the outline could be found in the Letters to the Seven Churches—considered to be of both contemporary and future application, and hence both chronologically and simultaneously applicable to the Church. The seven letters, which corresponded to the seven seals, thus represented seven periods of the Church's history, the sixth having begun with the French Revolution (at the close of the prophetic period of 1260 years), whilst the seventh lay still in the future. Only two of the Seven Churches had been exclusively commended—Smyrna and Philadelphia. These represented the period of the great persecutions and the blood of the martyrs, and the period of the restored apostolic witness (respectively). The apostasy had begun in the first period (the Apostolic age), as was

clear from the various warnings and exhortations in the New
Testament.

The Church's entanglement with the world had become critical
following the Constantinian settlement, after which worldly aims
were largely pursued, civil rulers became prominent in the government
of the Church, and both the desire for the Second Advent and the
manifestation of prophetic gifts very largely ceased. This period,
represented by Pergamos, was followed first by papal rule and relic
worship (Thyateira) and then by the period beginning with the
Reformation (Sardis), which, because it substituted individual
opinions for divine ordinances, inevitably led to revolution in State
as well as in Church. Even during the period of apostolic renewal
(Philadelphia) the 'Laodicean spirit' was abroad, most notably in the
missionary Bible societies, whose prime concern was the raising of
money, and the Tractarian movement, whose prime concern was
directed to outward forms. The period of Laodicea (proper) would
be the time of the tribulation.

Along with this application of the seven letters of Apocalypse 1–3
to the history of the Church, there was a parallel application of the
seven seals of the second vision (Apoc. 5: 1–8: 1) to secular history
which interpreted the French Revolution as the earthquake of the
sixth seal, the seventh seal still lying in the future. The trumpets of
Apocalypse 8–9 were similarly related to history, the first four to
attacks on the Roman Empire of the West by the Goths, Vandals,
etc., and the two woe trumpets to the Islamic attacks on the Eastern
Empire. The Book of Daniel was seen as also providing a prophetic
history of the civil power as well as of the Jews. The four prophetic
kingdoms were seen as the four great Empires of antiquity, the last
being the Roman Empire, during the period of whose strength the
first advent of Christ had taken place, the second and future advent
to be during the same Empire's period of fragmentation and
weakness—the contemporary age.

It is clear that in their general approach to the prophetic scriptures
the Catholic Apostolic apostles adopted the historicist tradition
established by Faber and Frere, though differing from both of them
in a number of the details of their application of the prophetic
scriptures to history. They were clearly influenced more by Frere
than by Faber, presumably because the former was in accord with
their pre-millennialist stand and had been able to press his case
at the Albury Conferences. They were in agreement with both over

the significance of the French Revolution as the conclusion of the prophetic period of 1260 years and as one of the signs of the impending Second Advent. They followed the general rules which these two prophetic analysts had laid down, most notably adopting Frere's principle of one single unified divine plan. Whilst accepting the need for consistency of symbols, they were more flexible in their willingness to accept purely symbolic interpretations of scriptural passages where a literalist interpretation seemed inappropriate—for example, Cardale insisted that the vision of the Last Judgement did not necessarily imply the actual existence of a white throne or the opening of actual books.[215]

Unlike either Faber or Frere, however, and unlike many of their contemporaries, they refused to suggest any precise dates for future events, confining themselves to presenting a sequence of apocalyptic happenings, of which the Parousia would be the first. Thus, they kept firmly in mind the words of the risen Christ: 'It is not for you to know times or seasons which the Father has fixed by his own authority' (Acts 1: 7)—words which they quoted on a number of occasions against those who attempted to assign dates to the Second Advent. These were words which they, unlike Irving, regarded as of universal application. They were also prepared to admit that not all details of the apocalyptic events were revealed by prophecy (for example, the frank admission of ignorance concerning the identity of the two witnesses of Apocalypse 11: 3). They took directly from Frere the interpretation of the four beasts—interpreted as kingdoms —of Daniel 7, and the three stages of the last (the Roman) Empire, though without specific reference to 2 Esdras. They also adopted similar though not identical interpretations of the Great Image of Daniel 2. Following both Faber and Frere, they saw both the claims of the papacy and the rise of Islam as of special significance in the prophetic history of the Church. Unlike Frere, they did not envisage further world conversion by missionary effort before the Second Advent.

The influence of certain aspects of Lacunza's works is very clear. Perhaps most important of all was Lacunza's defence of 'orthodox millenarianism'. There seems to be little doubt, that it was this defence which enabled the Catholic Apostolic apostles to proceed to a pre-millennialist eschatology, believing that this was in accord with

---

[215] These views were expressed in sermons on the Last Judgement, 1864–5.

the teaching of Scripture and the early Fathers, and that their presentation of it did not take a form which the universal Church had condemned or which the Creed precluded. To adopt an eschatology contrary to what was believed to have been that of the early Church would have contravened basic Catholic Apostolic principles. A number of other crucial aspects of the apostles' teaching, not in the writings of Faber or Frere, can be found in Lacunza's work with the accompanying scriptural and, sometimes, patristic support. Most notably these are:

> the two resurrections (though the apostles moved the first resurrection to a position before Antichrist);
>
> the advent of Christ with the risen and translated saints;
>
> the idea of the Day of the Lord as an extended period during which a sequence of apocalyptic events would take place before the general resurrection and judgement;
>
> the interpretation of the 'harlot' as the apostate Church entangled with the world;
>
> the destruction of Antichrist by Christ Himself rather than by St Michael;
>
> the renewal of lukewarmness during the millennium leading to the loosing of Satan upon the world and his final destruction by fire;
>
> the ultimate destination of the created world as transfiguration, not the destruction which most Protestants imagined;

and a number of less important details.

Like Lacunza, the apostles were prepared to see the time-scale of eschatological events as lying outside time as currently experienced: thus the millennium was a period of a thousand years, but the precise number 'thousand' had primarily a spiritual rather than a purely literal significance. Lacunza's idea of two judgements—a judgement of the living separated in time from a judgement of the dead—was, however, changed to an initial *implied* judgement of the living and the dead (to identify the elect), and the final judgement at the general resurrection. With his idea that there would be a mission to the world from the New Jerusalem established on earth, the apostles associated a work done by the converted Jews. In general, they were prepared to be much more explicit about the new Jerusalem, a matter upon which Lacunza had been unwilling to dogmatize. His purely futurist view of the Apocalypse (which followed the eschatology of the Roman Church after the Reformation, and especially of the Jesuits) was rejected, together with his concept of the Antichrist as a system rather than a person, his identification of the woman with child of Apocalypse 12 with the Jews, and his interpretation of the four beasts (kingdoms) of Daniel 7 as false religions. Nevertheless, in the last case the apostles did follow him in associating false Christianity—the apostasy—with deism (amongst other things). Overall, a considerable debt owed by the apostles to Lacunza must be acknowledged, though their eventual eschatological teaching tended to endorse Irving's criticisms of the Jesuit's work made in his *Preliminary Discourse*.

The apostles followed Irving in extending the apostasy of the last days beyond Rome to the contemporary Church in general and to all its history, finding in the Apocalypse a guide to the past history of the Church as well as to future events. Lacunza had attributed the apostasy to a *future* Roman priesthood, whilst the popular Protestant view had confined it to the Roman Church, seeing the Reformation as a restoration of the purity of the early Church. Irving, though accepting the necessity of the Reformation, had warned against 'worship' of the Reformers, but the apostles went further, seeing the Reformation as the substitution of one usurpation of the rule of Christ for another. In view of their evangelical Protestant background, this was somewhat remarkable. Irving's general attribution of apostasy to virtually all aspects of the contemporary Church, together with his express condemnation of Bible missionary societies (a condemnation with which the Albury Conferences were to concur), was echoed by the apostles as was his conventional view of Antichrist as a *person* who would eventually head up an alliance of the apostate Church with the secular rulers of the world. His association of the fulfilment of Christ's roles as Prophet, Priest, and King also found an echo in the apostolic writings.

It is in Irving that the interpretation of the 'former and latter rain' as two outpourings of the Holy Spirit first makes its appearance, something which was always later to feature in the apostles' claim that they headed up a new work of the Lord in preparation for the Second Advent. There were, however, significant aspects of Irving's beliefs that were clearly rejected. Irving (along with Faber and Frere) had accepted that some dating of future events was essential in order that eschatological teaching could be validated. The obvious risk attendant upon this was carefully avoided by the apostles, though not always by their followers—the failure of specific prophecies to materialize was to become one of the reasons for those who had either pronounced or accepted them to leave the Catholic Apostolic body. Thus, despite certain clear disagreements with Irving's eschatology, if the apostles owed much to Lacunza, they were also considerably influenced by Irving's introduction to Lacunza's work.

The most notorious case of those who left the Catholic Apostolic Church specifically on the issue of prophecy was that of Robert Baxter, a one-time prophet of the body, who not only left it when his own prophecies were unfulfilled but also wrote a polemical work against the prophetic ministry of the Catholic Apostolic Church arguing that it was 'of the devil' (see Ch. II, n. 47). Various individual prophecies raising expectations were made for the tenth, twentieth, thirtieth, and fortieth anniversaries of the 'separation of the apostles' (14 July 1835), and also for Christmas 1838 (1260 days after the 'separation'). Much criticism was made concerning these, but it is wrong to attribute them to the Catholic Apostolic *Church* as they had no formal sanction either from the apostles or angels of the body.

All six points to which the Albury deliberations had led (see § 4 above) were incorporated into the apostolic teaching—indeed, these points had already appeared in one or other of the writings mentioned above: the Albury meetings had merely singled them out and collated them for formal approbation. The deliberations had also produced the concept of the eschatological day of a morning and evening without night, contrasting with the liturgical day (following Genesis) of evening and morning with night between. This developed Lacunza's idea of the Day of the Lord and specified the Second Advent as occurring in the morning—a concept also adopted by the apostles. Further, they took up the debate on the words παρουσία and ἐπιφάνεια, which the conference members had seen as both referring to personal and visible appearances of Christ, using them to distinguish between the coming of Christ at the first resurrection and the extension of that coming at the beginning of the millennium. They also followed the conferences in rejecting the widely held view that eternal life referred only to men's souls, insisting that at both the first and second resurrections souls and bodies would be reunited, though the latter would be 'changed' in accordance with 1 Corinthians 15: 53. It seems probable that the apostles' emphasis on the eschatological role of the Jews and their linking of the tabernacle with the scenes of the apocalyptic visions were suggested by the debates of the later conferences as well as by articles in *The Morning Watch*, a number of which were, in any case, their own contributions.

Although the apostles did not hesitate to point out the failings of both the Anglican Church and Dissent, they never resorted to the polemic of Irving's attacks on the 'scribes and pharisees'. Neither did they take up the social concerns expressed in articles published in *The Morning Watch*—in general they were suspicious of anything which could be considered to be 'liberalism', associating it with religious apostasy and the revolutionary idea that power rightly belongs not to God but to the people. Having seen the French Revolution as the beginning of an inevitable judgement upon an apostate Church, it was natural that anything which savoured of social revolution—for example, Catholic emancipation, the Reform Bill, democracy, and industrialization—should be regarded as further evidence of the evils which were about to be loosed upon Christendom. Any attempt to undermine the hierarchical structure of society was suspect as being the work of the devil. So convinced were they of this, that they translated the hierarchical principle into the eternal kingdom, and saw the final judgement not merely in terms of the passing of a sentence but as an 'administration of rule'. All this was a far departure from the millennialism of two centuries earlier.

What then was unique about Catholic Apostolic eschatology? Certainly, there was much which could be found in earlier and contemporary prophetic studies. The importance of the Second Advent as the Christian hope was nothing new: it was part of Christian tradition from the earliest days of the Church. The Catholic Apostolics did more than attempt to restore it to the forefront of Christian thought; they gave it an urgency and a relevance to the contemporary age which it had only very occasionally achieved since the time of the Roman persecutions, and they were prepared to pray for its hastening. In this they were not alone, and did not remain alone (as will be noted shortly). They had inherited much also from the Reformation eschatological tradition, particularly the criticisms of the Constantinian settlement and the strong rejection of the claims of Rome, though without the popular

Protestant identification of the papacy with Antichrist—they saw both good and evil in all the Christian Churches. They had, however, followed neither the early Lutheran nor the Calvinistic millennial traditions, rejecting entirely the eighteenth-century optimistic post-millennialist eschatology. The uniqueness of their position lay primarily with their concept of a body being prepared under apostolic rule, with the association of their eschatology with the charismatic gifts of the Holy Spirit, and with the translation of their eschatological faith into liturgy (see § 7 above). Thus, the uniqueness lay just as much in what they *were*, taken overall, as in the details of what they proclaimed.

Many, but not all, of the apostles' eschatological beliefs could be found in sources preceding their formation as a Church, though it must be remembered that some of these sources were the product of groups which future Catholic Apostolic apostles and others, later to become members of the body, had influenced. Certainly, the apostles put together a particular eschatological compilation from earlier sources which was unique and remained unique (see below), adding to it a number of aspects which appear to be entirely new— most notably the particular overall sequence of apocalyptic events, the specific role given to the Jews in the context of their attitude to Jewish conversion, the details of the eschatological working of the Holy Spirit (especially at the translation), and the hierarchical nature of the eternal kingdom. It should be noted that their opposition to attempts to convert the Jews was in stark contrast with the earlier association of some of the apostles with societies specifically dedicated to such conversion.

There were some new details in the apostles' application of the prophetic Scriptures to secular history, but these are not of great significance, and it must be remembered that their prime interest was the application of these Scriptures to the Church. Cardale's translation of the eschatology into liturgy was of unique significance, and seems to have been understood in full only by Catholic Apostolic members—neither those Churches whose worship was influenced by Catholic Apostolic liturgy (see Ch. IV, § 7) nor modern liturgical scholars appear to have appreciated its full eschatological content. However, the apostles would not themselves have claimed to have invented any new doctrine: they remained convinced that all that they taught was to be found in the Scriptures, which the Holy Spirit was 'opening up' through prophetic studies and, later, the words of their own prophets. They saw their teaching also as being consistent with early patristic writings, and, in some circumstances, as restoring a patristic tradition lost or corrupted by later generations of Christians. How much was contributed to the apostolic teaching specifically by their prophets, it is impossible to determine, since no record exists of the details of the debates which formulated Catholic Apostolic doctrine during the periods when the apostles retired to Albury with their prophets (see Ch. II, § 2). The writings of their Pillar-of-Prophets confirm the apostolic teaching. However, in a work entitled *Translation: not an Instantaneous but a Progressive Work* (1858), Taplin suggested that the translation may not be simply a single event at the time of the first resurrection, but spread over a short period of time prior to it—in this, he was extending rather than contradicting the eschatology of the apostles.[216] One clear case of a purely 'prophetic' contribution to teaching on the translation appears to be that concerned with the work of the Holy Spirit in effecting it.

The problem of the subsequent influence of Catholic Apostolic eschatology is an elusive one. There is one clear case which can easily be identified, namely the influence within Anglicanism (to be considered last). Apart from this, attempts to identify specific Catholic Apostolic influence on comparable eschatologies appear to rest on what, in other situations, could be described as 'purely statistical' arguments—that is, they rest primarily upon the identification of similarities of belief rather than on any proved direct documentary or other historical connection. In the present context, even identity of detail should not be taken as *proof* of direct influence. It was inevitable that, with so much activity in prophetic study, identical ideas should come to fruition in differing and unconnected circumstances.

There were several prophetic societies and journals, contemporary with the principal period of growth of the Catholic Apostolic Church, which had no direct connection with that body, and which became increasingly critical of its acceptance of the tongues and other charismatic manifestations. There were also other millenarian

[216] See also the following works by E. O. Taplin: *The Epistles to the Seven Churches* (n.p., 1848); *The Construction of the Book of Revelation* (n.p., 1848); *The Seven Epistles, Seals, Trumpets and Vials, and the Interpretation of the First of Them* (n.p., 1848); *The Signs of the Coming of the Lord* I–X (n.p., 1851–2); *The Chronology of the Scriptures* (London: Goodall, 1854).

religious groups coming into being, of which the first important was the Plymouth Brethren, whose early history was dominated by disagreements over specific interpretations of the prophetic scriptures. The main dispute, which centred on the idea of a secret rapture of the saints, was between John Nelson Darby (see below) and Benjamin Wills Newton (Fellow of Exeter College, Oxford). It was embittered by personal accusations of attempted dictatorship and heresy, and led to a permanent schism in the Brethren movement, Darby becoming the leader of what was known as the 'stricter' group.[217] The Brethren had millenarian views similar to those of the Catholic Apostolics in their emphasis upon the Second Advent, but they were totally rooted in the Protestant tradition and opposed to any form of the kind of liturgical development which became so significant in the Catholic Apostolic Church.

In Ireland, at Powerscourt, there had been a number of prophetic conferences (beginning in 1831), which in many ways paralleled those held at Albury. The hostess of these meetings, which were presided over by the local Anglican Rector, was the widowed Theodosia Wingfield, Viscountess Powerscourt. She had had a tenuous connection with the Catholic Apostolics in that she had once visited Drummond at Albury and had entertained Irving during an Irish preaching tour. There is no reason to construe this in any way as evidence of Catholic Apostolic influence—indeed, she left the Anglican Church for the Brethren. The conferences had covered subjects such as the 1260 years, Antichrist, the connection between Daniel and the Apocalypse, the corrupt state of Christendom, the apostasy of the Churches, and so on. Those attending—and Darby was notable amongst them—took a hostile view of the tongues in Irving's congregation, though strongly supporting the idea of the millennium.

Darby was born in 1800 and trained in law at Trinity College, Dublin. Ordained in the Anglican Church to an Irish living in County Wicklow, he soon developed doubts about the Erastian politics of his Archbishop and became interested in prophecy and the Second Advent. While recovering from a leg injury, he turned to a study of Scripture and became convinced that the visible Church was really only a manifestation of the world, and that the true Church, united to Christ, was invisible and known only to God.

[217] See H. H. Rowden, *The Origins of the Brethren, 1825–1850* (London: Pickering and Inglis, 1967).

Following a 'conversion experience', he left the Anglican Church and joined up with others of similar opinion to his own, thus forming the embryo of what was to become the Plymouth Brethren, with centres initially in Limerick, London, and Bristol in addition to Plymouth itself. The quarrel with Newton, his chief associate at Plymouth (see above), arose following his absence on a long mission in Switzerland. He left behind, after his death in 1882, a large collection of 'Writings', subsequently edited in 34 volumes. They have been described as being uniformly unintelligible.

The later Powerscourt Conferences were dominated by the new sect. The Brethren took a futurist view of the Apocalypse, attacking particularly the interpretation of prophetic 'days' as 'years', so important for all historicists, including the Catholic Apostolics. Curiously enough, they appear to have been entirely unaware that their futurist view was precisely the view taken by the Jesuits, including Lacunza. It was the adoption of this futurist eschatology by a *body* of Christians which gave it the strength to become a serious rival to the alternative historicist eschatology of the Catholic Apostolics and others. Darby introduced the concept of a *secret* rapture to take place 'at any moment', a belief which subsequently became one of the chief hallmarks of Brethren eschatology. This rapture would precede all fulfilment of apocalyptic prophecy. He also taught that the 'true' Church was invisible and spiritual. Both these ideas were in sharp contrast to Catholic Apostolic teaching, and were eventually to lead to schism amongs the Brethren. There were thus very significant differences between the two eschatologies, and attempts to see any direct influence of one upon the other seem unlikely to succeed—they had a number of common *roots*, but are much more notable for their points of disagreement. Several writers have attempted to trace Darby's secret rapture theory to prophetic statements associated with Irving, but their arguments do not stand up to serious criticism. Such attempts began in the 1860s with an attack on Darby by S. P. Tregelles, a friend of Newton—in *The Hope of Christ's Coming* (Bagster, 1864). Others followed suit. A fairly recent attempt traces the secret rapture theory through Darby to Margaret Madonald (see Ch. II, § 1).[218] Darby himself always insisted that he confined himself to the expounding of doctrines contained in Scripture.

---

[218] See D. MacPherson, *The Incredible Cover-up* (Plainfield, NJ: Logos International, 1975).

Another millenarian eschatology which was entirely independent of Catholic Apostolic influence was that of early American Adventism, which was born partly out of the Puritan vision of the United States as a land of special destiny. Its founder was William Miller, a self-educated farmer from Low Hampton in New York State. He had read two English prophetic studies, one of which was by Faber, but it has been suggested that he relied for his adventist views solely upon a Bible and a concordance.[219] Nevertheless, they bore closer resemblance to Catholic Apostolic teaching in some respects than those of Darby and the Brethren. They were historicist and pre-millennial, but differed from Catholic Apostolic teaching in a number of ways, notably in the rejection of any application of the prophetic scriptures to the future state of the Jews and the belief that no unbelievers would survive the Second Advent. Catholic Apostolic influence can be immediately dismissed on the grounds that Adventism was developed in the United States before any nineteenth-century millenarian influence from the United Kingdom had reached that country.

A further possible candidate for Catholic Apostolic influence might be the eschatology of the Mormons, who were also pre-millennialists and practisers of charismatic gifts, though their leaders were prepared to publicize prophetic revelations widely in a way which the Catholic Apostolic apostles largely avoided. The Mormon Church—also known as 'the Church of Jesus Christ of Latter-day Saints'—was founded by Joseph Smith (1805–44) at Manchester, New York State. Smith claimed to have found *The Book of Mormon* (the 'bible' of the sect) through a special revelation. In 1847 the Mormon headquarters was moved to Salt Lake City in the State of Utah, where it remains to this day. Like the Catholic Apostolics, the Mormons believed in the gathering of Israel to 'Zion' (though locating this in the United States), in a personal return of Christ to reign on earth, and in the gathering together of an elect body in preparation for the Second Advent. However, this is again a matter of some common roots rather than of direct influence, as Lively has shown.[220]

[219] See F. D. Nichol, *The Midnight Cry* (Washington, DC: publisher unknown, 1944).

[220] Robert J. Lively, Jun., *The Catholic Apostolic Church and the Church of Jesus Christ of Latter-day Saints: a Comparative Study of two minority Millenarian groups in Nineteenth-Century England*, thesis (Oxford University, 1977).

Both Adventism and Mormonism were to survive to the present day, largely because they had an ecclesiological system which could be perpetuated. Here the decision of the Catholic Apostolics not to replace their apostles and the eventual decline of their Church is of special significance in that it led inevitably to the almost total disappearance of those aspects of their eschatology which were peculiar to themselves. Yet they managed to survive in one small corner within the Anglican Church, and it is here that the present-day influence of Catholic Apostolic eschatology lies rather than in those bodies which absorbed aspects of its liturgy.

Anglican interest in the doctrine of a millennium had been evident from the beginning of the revival of prophetic studies, in which many evangelical Anglicans had participated. The scandal of the tongues, however, together with the formation of the Catholic Apostolic Church with its claims of universal apostolic jurisdiction over the Church, alienated many Anglicans for a time from prophetic studies. There was a recovery of interest during the 1840s with the formation of the Prophecy Investigation Society, which was responsible for annual addresses on the millennium at Anglican churches in Bloomsbury and Marylebone, and which was to survive for several decades. (There was little parallel interest in the established Scottish Church, the majority of those within it who espoused millenarianism having joined the Free Church schism in 1843.)

A number of individual Anglicans espoused historicist and millenarian views, amongst whom were Edward Bickersteth and his son-in-law Thomas Rawson Birks, Horatius Bonar (editor of *The Quarterly Journal of Prophecy*), Joseph Baylee (principal of Birkenhead Theological College), Edward Bishop Elliott (author of a monumental study of the Apocalypse, *Horae Apocalypticae*), and Dr William Leask (editor of *The Rainbow* and a supporter of Darby's secret rapture theory). Although individual Catholic Apostolics certainly participated in meetings organized by Anglican millenarians, it would seem that there was no formal association of the Catholic Apostolic Church with them. Anglican involvement with the Catholic Apostolics was, by this time, largely a personal and private matter. For the most part evangelical Anglicans had been estranged by Catholic Apostolic ritual, whilst the Tractarians had always attacked the validity of Catholic Apostolic orders, and those Tractarians who were interested in eschatology leaned towards the Roman futurist viewpoint. Some

Anglicans wanted a purely private spiritual and sacramental link with the apostles, and this was obtained through the acceptance of apostolic 'sealing'.

The main impetus for Catholic Apostolic eschatology within Anglicanism came with the gradual demise of the body, following the death of the last apostle in 1901 and the gradual closing down of places of Catholic Apostolic worship. By the 1920s and 1930s the situation was beginning to become serious in that many members found it difficult to make the necessary (ever longer) journeys to their nearest place of worship, though it was not until after the 1939–45 War that the situation was to become critical. The majority of Catholic Apostolics began to worship in Anglican churches, and, on the instruction of their surviving clergy, to receive Anglican sacraments also, though regarding them as being 'on a lower spiritual plane' than those of their apostles. Inevitably, this influx into the Anglican Church led to a desire for some kind of Anglican fellowship which would reflect both the Catholic Apostolics' sense of the nearness of the Second Advent and their particular eschatological viewpoint. As a result, an Anglican Guild, the Guild of Prayer for the Return of the Lord, was founded in 1920, consisting of Catholic Apostolic members and their Anglican sympathizers.

As well as the formation of an organized fellowship, a small number of books by Anglican writers appeared, presenting Catholic Apostolic eschatological beliefs, though in less than complete detail so as to have a wider appeal. Their aim was to revitalize the hope of the Second Advent within Anglicanism.[221] The Guild of Prayer, which still exists today with an Anglican episcopal patron and holds an annual conference and local day meetings, has published regular prayer leaflets as well as a number of booklets in which Catholic Apostolic teaching can be plainly discerned, as petitions and responses from one of them which is regularly reprinted, *The Litany of the Second Advent* by 'a Parish Priest' (actually Canon W. H. Connor), clearly show:

We have not been mindful of Thy Second coming as we ought to have been. Pardon us, good Lord.

[221] Two examples are *The Gospel of the Future* (London: Griffith, Farren, 1891; repr. Sale: Pilgrim Publications, 1983) and *The Second Advent and Prayer* (London: Skeffington, 1901), both by the Revd Canon W. H. Connor (a 'sealed' Anglican priest) and still being reprinted and circulated through the Guild. The former was published in a French translation in 1899.

We have not tried to be like unto men that wait for their Lord (*Luke* xii. 36). Pardon us, good Lord.

When Thou comest, may we be found an acceptable people in Thy sight. Hear us, we beseech Thee, O Lord.

Men's hearts are failing them for fear, and for looking after those things which are coming on the earth (*Luke* xxi. 26). Arise, O Lord, and deliver us for Thy Name's sake.

Grant us a part in the Resurrection of them that are Christ's at His coming, so that over us the second death may have no power (*Rev.* xx. 6). Hear us, we beseech Thee.

High Priest of our profession, tarry no longer behind the veil (*Heb.* iii. 2; *Luke* i. 21). Make Thyself known, we beseech Thee.

Gather out from among Thy kinsmen after the flesh and prepare for Thy coming those who fear Thee and work righteousness (*Acts* x. 35).

Come down from heaven, O Lord; raise Thy dead saints, and change the living [elect] into Thine own image and likeness (1 *Thess.* iv. 16, 17). Hear us, we beseech Thee.

Thou art coming, O Lord, in Thy Royal Majesty, to seek and claim Thy Bride. May she be found waiting for Thee.

When the Bridegroom's voice is heard, may we go forth to meet Him (*Matt.* xxv. 1). With our lamps burning brightly.

When the Marriage of the Lamb is come. May we be found ready.

Come, Lord Jesus, come quickly. Even so. Amen (*Rev.* xxii. 26).

Even more explicit are some of the questions and answers in *A Catechism of the Second Advent* by the same author, also regularly distributed by the Guild. The work is divided into four parts: 118 questions and answers in all. It covers the major aspects of Catholic Apostolic eschatology, but not all the details (of some of which the author may not have been aware). It refers explicitly to the apostasy of the Church in the last days, to the first-fruits as a 'gathering from the twelve tribes of the spiritual Israel', to the first resurrection and the 'rapture of the living saints', to the 'millennium', to the 'vintage', to the distinction between the *parousia* and the *epiphaneia*, to the antichrist, and to the rebellion after the *parousia* and the great tribulation, to the ultimate defeat of Satan and his being 'cast into the Lake of Fire and Brimstone', and to the final delivering up of the perfected Kingdom by Christ to the Father. In so much as this is an *Anglican* guild, the content of its publications show remarkable Catholic Apostolic influence. Its membership is, however, quite small and its influence within Anglicanism generally must be very slight.

In the light of earlier discussions, the specific Catholic Apostolic content of both these works and others distributed by the Guild of Prayer is clear. Thus, the apostles' eschatology has not entirely died with their Church, but continues as a fragile thread within Anglicanism, leaving the more strident proclamations of pre-millenarian, post-millenarian, pre-tribulationist, and post-tribulationist eschatologies to the various Protestant sects, and especially those whose base is in the United States. As the year 2000 is approached and with the advent of satellite broadcasting, it can be 'prophesied' with confidence that these strident proclamations will become even louder. It is to be hoped that the words recorded in Acts 1: 7, so often insisted upon by the Catholic Apostolic apostles, will then be remembered.

VI

Conclusion

1. THE CATHOLIC APOSTOLIC CHURCH IN ITS HISTORICAL, SOCIAL, AND RELIGIOUS CONTEXT

IN many respects, though not in all, it must be said that the Catholic Apostolic Church was a product of the age in which it came into being—born of the changes in religious thought and the general spiritual movement of the nineteenth century. It was an age in which the settled order of society in Britain was beginning to be challenged, not merely on account of the revolutionary upheavals on the Continent but increasingly by an industrial revolution and by processes of social reform. Yet at the same time it was an age of romanticism, of Gothic revival, of turning towards things ancient and venerable, and of religious fervour—partly, no doubt, as an antidote to the 'wind of change' which was being felt throughout the land.

The last of these, the revival of interest in religion, especially amongst the (mainly Tory) upper classes, was largely stimulated by the association of social disorder with religious doubt and revolutionary change with atheism. Those who had most to lose from what they saw as the increasing instability of society, and hence wished to justify the maintenance of the existing order, turned away from the theism and rationalism of the preceding century, together with the concept of 'natural religion', directing themselves to the Bible and traditional Christian doctrines in seeking assurance for the future.

The approach to Scripture centred upon the prophetic works, since it was thought that unfulfilled prophecy was the key through which intimations about the future would be revealed. Although such studies were undertaken mainly by educated individuals rather than by the academic community, social conditions and the improved means of communication made it easier for gatherings of those with mutual interests to be organized and for societies and other bodies to be set up, and the managerial capabilities needed for organizing such groups lay with precisely the classes who had begun to feel themselves threatened by social upheaval.

In earlier periods, the prophetic Scriptures had aroused millenarian views amongst those who felt themselves threatened or oppressed; they had been espoused by the very poor and the outcast—now it was members of the landed ruling class who saw themselves threatened and were therefore seeking reassurance. They fell back also on a genuine belief that the established social order was of divine making, and on this basis opposed all, whether individuals or bodies, who promoted political or social change.

The Catholic Apostolic Church thus owed its existence in some measure to the old 'high Tory' reaction to the exigencies of the age, though it would be entirely wrong to brand those who participated in its formation as 'selfish reactionaries'. They were men of the highest principles, with a strong sense of the need to care for the poorest members of society, but, at the same time, they believed in a social structure where both privilege and poverty had their appointed and permanent place. They therefore saw reforming movements—Catholic emancipation, the 1832 Reform Bill, Chartism, and the rise of democratic ideas—as evidence of the activity of the powers of evil, and their biblical studies led them to the conclusion that these, together with the French Revolution in particular, were the signs of the near fulfilment of apocalyptic prophecy: the coming of Antichrist and the 'great tribulation' from which an elect would be saved at the Parousia.

All this must be contrasted with other nineteenth-century religious movements having their origins in Britain and elsewhere, a number of which had much greater appeal for the common people because they were clearly concerned with social issues and tended to reject the established hierarchies in religion, seeing them as part of that very social order which was in need of reform. The Mormon Mission in England, for example, had a strong appeal for the lower classes, because it preached a classless society, and had the added incentive of the possibility of emigration to the New World. Methodism had (and still has) social concern as one of its fundamental principles, and therefore had a wide appeal to the industrialized classes. Further, it preached holiness of life rather than divine intervention as the Christian solution to contemporary problems—though it would be unfair to suggest that the Catholic

Apostolics were any less insistent upon holy living. The Christadelphians likewise had a firm belief in the transformation of the social order, and had highly radical views about existing Church structures; much the same can be said of the Plymouth Brethren, the Seventh-Day Adventists, and Jehovah's Witnesses. The Salvation Army was essentially a mission to the poor and underprivileged, and rejected traditional Church order and ordinances, though it did not seek the overthrow of the British social system.

It was the movements which were primarily based in America that tended to stress the possibilities of social experimentation rather than their British counterparts. The Catholic Apostolics differed fundamentally from all these movements, millenarian or otherwise, not merely because of their lack of social concern (for which they had special reasons), but also and more especially because they were a movement solely directed towards bringing existing ecclesiastical structures to perfection. They were totally unworldly in their objectives, the millennium which they offered being, unlike that of some other bodies, an exclusively spiritual one.

It would be wrong to suggest, however, that those 'high Tories' who became involved with the Catholic Apostolic Church were unconcerned about the view of labour taken by industrial and commercial employers. They had a good record of care for those who worked for them on their estates or within their professions, and they objected to any view of the working man which saw him as a mere 'pair of hands'. For them, though men were not equal within society, they were equal before God: it was precisely on this ground that Drummond and others had objected to the high proportion of pew rents in the Established Church. Such evidence as there is indicates that pew rents in the Catholic Apostolic Church were kept to a minimum—to at most some 10 per cent of the sittings in certain well-to-do urban areas. It was the apostles' conviction of the nearness of the Second Advent which led them to the conclusion that the urgent task was the preparation of the Church—not the world— for the imminent return of the Lord. For them there was no time for social reform, which they saw as irrelevant and possibly dangerous; they believed themselves called not to be reformers of society but restorers of the Church to her ancient purity as the Bride of Christ. Equally there was no time for further missionary effort: missionary societies, along with societies having specific moral concerns, were seen as too much involved in worldly matters—as attempting to do

God's work in man's way. The societies had been created with the presumption that England was divinely chosen for Christian mission because of its freedom from Roman Catholic influence. Such an attitude had been particularly strong in the eighteenth century, and had strengthened resolve to defeat the Jacobite Rebellion of 1745—a rebellion seen as essentially papalist. The religious as well as the political future of the country was thought to be tied to its Protestantism. Such an attitude had to be abandoned later in the nineteenth century, however, by those evangelicals who saw the country as having become 'chained to Babylon' by Catholic emancipation and tractarianism, the latter being described by one prominent evangelical as one of the 'three frogs' of Apocalypse 16: 13 (that 'out of the mouth of the false prophet').

Inevitably, the question must be asked: to what extent was self-interest in maintaining their existing social status an underlying motive for those who brought the Catholic Apostolic Church into being? This is a difficult matter, since it is not possible to search into men's hearts. The evidence would appear to suggest that it played little or no direct role. Two facts in particular support this. First, the concern was for man in every station of life—Catholic Apostolics genuinely believed that the existing state of society, for so long as it was permitted by God to exist and so long as it was administered justly, was of divine ordinance for the general good of all. Secondly, they also genuinely believed that the structures of both State and Church were shortly to be cast down by the forces of Antichrist in a vast act of judgement upon an apostate Christendom. They thus had no expectation of retaining their privileged position in a society which would shortly be overturned.

The Great Testimony clearly shows that the apostles had a spiritual and cosmic concern, not a narrow or selfish worldly one. That they failed to attract the lower classes was due in considerable measure to the nature of the message: it was too unworldly, too exclusively concerned with spiritual and ecclesiastical matters, and too much directed to the upper stratum of Church and State. Those who delivered the public lectures during the early stages of the work did achieve limited success in evangelizing the wider public, but they tended to assume a level of education and religious sophistication on the part of their audiences that few members of the lower classes could have been expected to achieve.

These public lectures (which largely ceased after the period of the apostles' seclusion at Albury) were, however, given mainly in urban areas, and the urban lower classes in particular were at that time suffering from depressed wages together with a dramatically inflated price of bread. Wages had become depressed following the introduction of the dole principle in 1795, and there was extensive interference with the supply of corn from the Continent as a result of two decades of war with revolutionary and Napoleonic France, which had left Britain in increasing political and economic isolation. The protective Corn Law of 1815—not repealed until 1846—had its most serious ill-effects in urban areas. Any potential lower-class urban audience was therefore likely to have its concerns directed towards the practical problems of living in a seemingly hostile world: the poor and the poorly paid looked only for words which would indicate an imminent improvement in their condition of living—for such people, a message (based upon detailed Scriptural exegesis) to the effect that society as a whole was shortly to come to an apocalyptic end had little appeal.

The radical movements of the eighteenth century had lost their momentum in Britain as a result of the general revulsion at the atrocities of the French revolutionaries, and the war with the French had allied Protestant patriotism with anti-liberalism. Evangelicals had thus become strongly 'anti-Jacobin', and it was not until the second quarter of the nineteenth century that a number of evangelicals—principally the dissenting clergy—began increasingly again to befriend the poor, bringing them a message which combined evangelical religion with radical politics. Even the Wesleyan movement started with a political conservatism, and Irving was at one with the majority of evangelicals of his day when he declared in Edinburgh:

The one thing which I have laboured at is to resist liberalism by opening the word of God.

Socialism, Chartism, the forming of unions, Catholic emancipation (associated in many minds with Irish labourers), Reform Bill agitation (at its peak around 1830), and the anti-Corn Law league were all seen as having been inspired by an atheistic revolutionary spirit. All attempts by working-class men to associate together to promote their own welfare tended to be regarded as seditious. That the Catholic Apostolics for the most part adopted conservative politics, accepting the social conditions of the day, is not therefore surprising: in this they were largely at one during their formative years with both Church and Dissent. At the individual level, however, they showed much concern for those whom they considered to be the 'deserving poor', giving generously to the relief of individuals in distressed circumstances and expending both time and effort in organizing groups who would be prepared to visit the hungry and homeless who were brought to their notice.

The Catholic Apostolic Church was not, however, by any means solely a product of the historical and religious circumstances of its day. In a number of ways it broke from the immediate past religious scene, in some cases anticipating ideas which were to come into being later elsewhere. The religious milieu of the age in Britain at the time of the 'separation' of the apostles was still for the most part deeply evangelical, optimistic, missionary-orientated, and firm in its conviction that only significant moral decline could be the precursor of any judgement. The supporting eschatology had remained firmly post-millennialist. In general, man's faith in his own potential for the creation of utopias—the result of Renaissance, Reformation, and the Age of Enlightenment—had been stimulated by the eighteenth-century growth of belief in democracy, and the results of this stimulation remained despite the shock of the French Revolution. Initially, it was only in certain circles that it all came to be interpreted, not as promise for a better future, but as the sign of Godlessness, disintegration, and impending judgement. The founders of the Catholic Apostolic body set their faces firmly against what had been the popular evangelical tide. They totally rejected any suggestion that man could improve his future by his own efforts, and they saw divine intervention as the only possible salvation from an inevitable approaching devastation of the world.

The base upon which the apostles built their apocalyptic beliefs was biblical prophecy, the approach being primarily literalist, though this literalism was relieved by a spiritual interpretation of eschatological time, a profound typological understanding of the Old Testament, and a sense of the importance of scriptural symbolism. These provided an escape from absolute literalism without any abandoning of the principle of the infallibility of Scripture. Their approach was thus no more and indeed was sometimes less literalist than that of their contemporaries, and it must be judged according to the standards of its day. They did not develop a doctrine of the Church which could escape the biblicist dilemma as Newman and

Keble did, and the biblical methods of scholars such as Lightfoot and Westcott would have seemed too radical for them. The so-called 'higher criticism' did not come into being until the restored apostles had passed away and the ultimate disappearance of the body had become assured.

It would thus be wrong to condemn the Catholic Apostolics for a naïve approach to Scripture, and it should be remembered that typology—the fundamental principle of their exegesis—has had a long and respectable history in the Church. For them it became *the* method by which Scripture underpinned and cemented together the whole of their theology and worship. This was to give it a prominence which it had not enjoyed before, but it was not the introduction of any new or foreign principle. Even their eschatology was firmly based upon the Scriptures, and they saw themselves merely as proclaiming with a revived urgency an eschatological message which had been an essential part of the Gospel preached by the early Church. Modern research has confirmed how deep-rooted apocalyptic and millenarian views were in early Christianity.

Relationship to the Tractarians

Because of certain similar developments of theology and worship, it is tempting to seek for direct links between the Catholic Apostolics and the Tractarians. Thus, both wished to restore the fullness of the 'catholic' faith and the beauty of catholic worship, and both looked to ancient sources as providing evidence of what had been universally accepted by the undivided Church. Both were theologically conservative, and both had a tendency towards authoritarianism. For both, conferences had provided an important stimulus: Drummond's Albury Conferences might be compared with the Hadleigh Conference hosted by Hugh Rose, though the former were attended by evangelicals of several Churches whilst the latter was confined to Anglicans of the 'high church' party. A further significant difference was the considerable lay participation at Albury and the non-academic nature of the clergy participants, which contrasted with the almost exclusively clerical and academic assembly at Hadleigh.

Both movements had important individuals as prime catalysts: though Irving's apocalyptic preaching had little in common with Keble's Assize Sermon except for the general theme of 'apostasy'. There were, however, very important differences. The Tractarians were concerned with the defence of the received doctrine of 'apostolic succession' and a catholic interpretation of the Book of Common Prayer—they were a movement within one Church, the Church of England, though they were eventually to have considerably wider influence. By contrast, the Catholic Apostolics claimed to have received a divine message relevant to all the baptized—Roman Catholic, Eastern Orthodox, Anglican, and Protestant alike. They too were concerned with 'apostolic succession', but gave it a specific overriding interpretation contrary to that generally accepted in the Church Catholic throughout eighteen centuries. Though in their eyes this was restoration rather than revolution, in the eyes of their critics it was a new and unacceptable departure from traditional Christian belief and practice, undermining or debasing authority within the traditional Churches. Together with the charismatic origin of its orders, this was perhaps *the* principal feature of the Catholic Apostolic Church guaranteeing its rejection by precisely those whom it wished to convince, and leading to its eventual isolation and lack of any significant widespread influence.

Debate between the Catholic Apostolics and the Tractarians was almost exclusively concentrated upon the charismatic origins and the apostolic claims of the former. Sadly, this seems to have entirely precluded debate in other areas where there might have been wider agreement and mutual stimulation and benefit—as, for example, in the field of liturgy and sacramental theology, where Cardale's work preceded that of the Tractarians. The two movements were also widely separated in the matter of millenarian beliefs: most Tractarians regarded such beliefs with grave suspicion and those who did have an interest in eschatology shared the Roman Catholic futurist viewpoint.

By having an eschatology which would appeal only to certain evangelicals and orders which were bound to be questioned by traditionalists whilst, at the same time, developing a theology and liturgy which were perceived to be respectively 'catholic' and ritualistic, they ensured that their appeal would be limited to a relatively few like-minded persons—they thus never had the potential to become a mass movement. In their blending of evangelical eschatology, sacramental theology, and ritualistic liturgy they stand in contrast with other contemporary religious movements, which were more clearly identified with certain individual aspects of Christianity. Had they taken the decision to perpetuate their apostles, no doubt they would have survived until the present day (as has the New Apostolic Church), but there seems to be no evidence that this survival could have been other than as the comparatively small and somewhat isolated body which they remained even in their brief heyday.

The Appeal of the Catholic Apostolic Church

It is right to consider precisely what it was that attracted those who became members of the Catholic Apostolic Church or were associated with it through apostolic sealing. In the earliest days of the body it seems clear that the charismatic element had considerable influence in gaining adherents, though many so attracted were either never to join formally or soon to fall away from membership of the body. The eschatological message also had considerable appeal in that it provided answers to widely asked questions and spiritual comfort for those alarmed by threatening trends and events which seemed beyond human control.

As the body developed, for some—and especially for certain Anglican clergy—it offered an opportunity to develop and practise forms of worship free from control of the state and of the Protestant-minded Anglican hierarchy who were using the courts to restrict such freedom in the Established Church. Those clergy and others who were sealed, but remained in their respective Churches, clearly accepted the restoration of apostles and the teaching of the body on the apostolic basis of the Church. The appeal here may have been in part the unanimity of the Catholic Apostolic witness compared with the many voices which were speaking from within the Churches, though such evidence as there is—and there is very little—suggests that the two main attractions were the restoration of the Christian hope in the return of the Lord and the beauty and dignity of the liturgical worship. It is to these two things that sympathizers most commonly referred.

There seems to be no evidence that the Catholic Apostolic Church had the same kind of attraction which is a feature of charismatic movements today. Indeed, apart perhaps from the prophetic activity in the early years, they have little in common; surviving Catholic Apostolics have expressed great concern about modern charismatic activity, with which they feel no sympathy whatever, contrasting what they see as the emotional excesses of charismatic worship with the dignity of the liturgy of the restored apostles.

Christology and Pneumatology

Turning aside from the more usual aspects of the Catholic Apostolic Church to its Christology and pneumatology, it is entirely fair to suggest that there was little that was new and even less, if anything, that was heretical in the teaching. Indeed, in many respects the teaching was an attempt to restore a balance felt to have been lost in the mainstream Churches. Unfortunately, the necessary emphases on certain aspects of Christian theology intended to restore that balance were often misinterpreted as distortions of catholic truth rather than re-statements of it.

Irving's Christology, which the Catholic Apostolics inherited (though without his hyperbole of speech), was not heretical. It was misrepresented and distorted at his trial—a trial of which the outcome had manifestly been determined by his judges before it began. In restating it, the restored apostles were careful to point particularly to two things (both of which are explicitly stated in Irving's works): first, Christ was born into a humanity which was subject to the consequences of the Fall, and, secondly, no sin of any kind could be attributed to Him. The former was considered essential if fallen humanity was truly to be redeemed; the second was linked to the pneumatological teaching in that it was through the indwelling Spirit in the man Jesus that no sin could be imputed to Him.

The Roman doctrine of the Immaculate Conception of the Theotokos was rejected precisely because it undermined the concept of the redemption of man achieved *within* the circumstances of the Fall. The details of the spasmodic attacks made on Catholic Apostolic Christology reveal a failure to understand its precise content—they almost invariably refer back to Irving's preaching, taking out of context his occasional use of unwise expressions and assuming that these represent the considered teaching of the restored apostles.

The pneumatological doctrine of the Catholic Apostolics, which was closely associated with their Christology and which envisaged the Spirit as a crucial participating agent in all divine acts, was no more than a re-emphasis of a then somewhat neglected catholic doctrine. The emphasis upon the gifts of the Spirit is more difficult to assess, because it arose out of circumstances of which we have only written reports and which cannot therefore be practically investigated. In principle, these gifts are entirely Scriptural and have never been totally lost to the Church, but have manifested themselves in various ways throughout the centuries. Here, it can be argued that the Catholic Apostolics took too rigid a line in denying this undoubted fact, and also in assuming that the immediate post-Pentecostal phenomena were intended by divine will to be the norm for all time.

The manifestations in Scotland which Cardale and others investigated certainly convinced them, as trained observers, that they were genuine examples of the Spirit's gifts, but, not having the benefit of recent psychological and psychical studies (which do give credence to spiritual phenomena), they may have allowed themselves to be overinfluenced by ideas of the miraculous. When prophetic utterances appeared elsewhere, their acceptance of a new Pentecost poured out upon the Church seems to have occurred with little further serious study. As is evidenced by the charismatic movements of today, spiritual 'enthusiasm' is highly contagious and engenders an atmosphere which is not sufficiently critical.

It is not possible to pass any final judgement upon the 'latter rain' today—for the Spirit, like the wind, 'blows where it wills' (John 2: 8). The interpretation placed upon that 'rain' may well be open to challenge, because it must be measured against the experience of the Church over the centuries. That the apostles came to recognize the dangers of unbridled charismatic activity is clear from the restrictions imposed upon it within the Church which they ruled. Yet there remains a seeming contradiction in that, in so doing, they were at the same time raising questions about precisely the prophetic activity upon which they based their whole apostolic authority.

It is this question of the nature of the authority by which Cardale and his fellow apostles acted which lies at the heart of the Catholic Apostolic dilemma. It is not a matter of whether or not they were good and sincere men with a genuine belief in their divine calling: upon this judgement must be given in their favour; neither should it be a matter of comparison with the first Apostles, for there seems little reason to assume that they should necessarily act in comparable ways. It is a question of whether or not their call to apostleship was what they claimed it to be: to answer this with any confidence it is necessary to 'test the spirits' (1 John 4: 1)—now an impossible task. It is therefore better to leave final judgement on this matter to God.

Theology of the Incarnation, Atonement, and Resurrection

The Catholic Apostolics attempted to redress the balance in certain other areas of theology also. Their theology of atonement moved away from the contemporary (mainly Protestant) idea that Christ, as the voluntary inheritor of man's guilt, paid the penalty for that guilt demanded by an unbending judge. In Catholic Apostolic writings there is to be found much more emphasis upon the restoration of man's divine image and his preparation for the sharing in Christ's rule in the coming kingdom. The Incarnation was seen, not primarily as a response to the Fall, but as part of the eternal purpose of God—a continuation of His revelation of Himself in creation.

Further, the Catholic Apostolics developed the witness, revived in the West of Scotland, that salvation was available to all, not just to a predestined elect, and it seems clear that adherents to the body in Scotland were considerably influenced by this aspect of their witness, which contrasted with the Calvinism of the Established Church there. The millenarian teaching was of less significance north of the Border because the majority of Presbyterian millenarians joined the secession of 1843, when nearly one third of the ministry of the Established Church left to form the Free Church of Scotland.

The Catholic Apostolics also attempted to counteract the prevailing views of resurrection, which were heavily biased towards the doctrine of the immortality of the soul. Their writings emphasized the bodily resurrection of Christ as the key to the understanding of the resurrection of all men *as complete human persons*—body, soul, and spirit. Death was for them not 'natural' but 'unnatural'—the spirit separated from the body was seen as being in an unnatural state which would be ended by resurrection. They had a reverence for the wonder of the human body, strengthened by the significance given in their theology to the teaching that at the Ascension the resurrected human flesh of Christ had been elevated to the throne of God. It was this reverence that led them to oppose so strongly the advocates of cremation.

The Attitude to 'Mission'

On the question of mission to the Jews the Catholic Apostolics took a further line which was not in accord with contemporary views. Although Drummond and others had been associated with such missionary activity at one time, the study of the prophetic Scriptures convinced them that the conversion of the Jewish people—a people who they believed had a divinely prepared role in apocalyptic events—would take place only at the Parousia. Missions to convert the Jews as a people were therefore considered to be not only useless but contrary to divine will, though individual Christianized Jews did join the body. Indeed, the attitude to missionary activity of any kind, apart from mission *within* the Church, was one of the significant aspects distinguishing it from most contemporary Christian bodies. Even mission within the Church was largely abandoned when it became clear that the apostolic witness was rejected, not only by heads of Churches and states, but also by the mass of the people.

The reasons why this abandonment of mission should have occurred well before the decline of the Catholic Apostolic Church are difficult to ascertain. After the death of the last apostle in 1901, they become quite clear however—apostolic witness had been withdrawn from the world and hence the message which it contained should no longer be publicly proclaimed. Two reasons for the gradual cessation of active mission before 1901 do, however, suggest themselves.

First, the whole ethos had become inward-looking as the failure of the apostles to gather in the 144,000 became manifest, thus suggesting more and more that the return of Christ might be a matter of future hope rather than immediate expectation. The Second Advent was seen as having been postponed before on account of the Bride's unreadiness—was this not perhaps happening again? This not only removed something of the urgency of the earlier days, but it also suggested that new prophetic guidance was required in what were, for the members, unforeseen circumstances. The pastoral care and religious education of members of the Church would have become more of an imperative if the existence of the body was conceived to be more permanent than originally envisaged.

Secondly, there was the possibility of psychological compensation for apparent failure provided by membership of a closely knit community which was tending in practice to exclusiveness and secrecy, though without changing its formal ecumenical and catholic principles. Members saw themselves increasingly as the elect taken out of Babylon by divine providence—effort on external mission seemed increasingly inappropriate. Thus, those who approached of their own volition were welcomed with courtesy: Holy Communion was offered to non-members who attended Catholic Apostolic Eucharists as serious enquirers 'as an act of hospitality'. Occasionally members of other Churches would receive the Sealing, and (less frequently) outsiders would be received into full membership—more often than not through marriage. Successful active recruitment would have brought the danger of dilution; the members had become sole guardians of inherited truths whose preservation rather than proclamation was now paramount. There was perhaps an unconscious acceptance that the body was now a product of an age which had largely ceased to exist. Yet they remained and still remain above all else 'the people of a hope'.

2. THE STRENGTHS AND WEAKNESSES OF THE CATHOLIC APOSTOLIC CHURCH

In attempting to identify the strengths and weaknesses of the Catholic Apostolic body, it is all too easy to judge it according to standards which it would not itself accept. Clearly, there is a place for such disinterested judgement, but there must also be a place for judgement based upon their own principles. This becomes abundantly clear if the obvious superficial conclusion is reached that, since the Catholic Apostolic Church attracted comparatively few adherents when measured against the mainstream Churches and since its initial apocalyptic expectations were not fulfilled, it must simply be regarded as a somewhat eccentric failure—a small and largely irrelevant backwater outside the main stream of Church history. This is surely a far too facile judgement of a body that certainly had its eccentricities, but which attracted many sincere and well-educated Christians, which produced much writing of a high spiritual character, and which developed liturgical rites which a number of commentators have described as unsurpassed in the English language. The dismissal of the body as an irrelevant failure does not do justice to its many strengths, but concentrates only on areas of apparent weakness and on interpretations of them which Catholic Apostolics would strongly challenge. It is also most important neither to satirize nor to romanticize the Catholic Apostolic Church in any attempt to come to an assessment of it.

Strengths

Certain aspects of the Catholic Apostolic Church can be regarded as strengths in that they gave the body a singleness of purpose and a cohesiveness which ensured its continuing existence until, by its own choice, it decided that it was not able to perpetuate its ministry. Amongst these the following can be numbered:

the concentration of rule in an apostolic college;

the strictly ordered and comprehensive ministry;

the focusing upon the one specific objective of preparing the Church for the Second Advent;

the biblical basis of doctrine with a unifying method of interpretation;

the development of a liturgy attuned to the underlying theology and having a breadth of intercession;

the strong sacramental emphasis;

the ultimate balance between the charismatic witness and the formal ecclesiological structure (see comment below);

the thorough teaching of the laity by means of both the spoken and the written word;

the clear insistence upon holiness of life;

the freedom from financial worries provided by tithing;

the tailoring of the ministry to the spiritual and psychological make-up of man;

the combination of a spirit of eschatological urgency which nevertheless avoided any apocalyptic time-table;

absence of deliberate and open proselytism;

the care taken to adopt a restoring rather than a reforming or innovating stance in respect of the Churches.

The Catholic Apostolics offered to all who would listen a perfection of fullness, for the most part without the tearing down of what had already been built up over the centuries. These things contributed to a sense of purpose and of divine mission, to a close spirit of fellowship amongst the members, to a feeling of continuity with the received Christian tradition, to a sense of comprehensive pastoral care, and to identification with a body whose purpose and witness were thoroughly understood. Earlier charismatic eschatological movements had always proved to be transitory, because they had set themselves against the organized Christian Church and had lacked a structured body of their own. By having been forced to establish an ecclesiastical structure, the Catholic Apostolics gave their eschatological witness a permanence which would have continued to this day had they not taken the decision not to perpetuate their apostleship.

The typological understanding of the Scriptures, together with the belief that forms of worship had been divinely given, provided a unifying basis for their theology, liturgy, and pastoral care which was quite remarkable. This cohesion in their beliefs and practices gave the whole structure a strength which was to begin to crumble only when the last member of the Apostolic College passed away in 1901. It remained a source of spiritual strength and comfort for members even in the period when most had to turn elsewhere for their worship and sacraments.

Weaknesses

Yet there were inherent weaknesses in the Catholic Apostolic body which have been and must again be pointed out. The most obvious one relates to the precise basis of the claims of the restored apostles to universal authority (a difficulty to which reference has been made above). For the vast majority of Christians these claims remained unconvincing. Anglican critics were right to point to the 'circularity' of the situation: apostles were called by prophets who were then subsequently ordained or authenticated by those whom they had called. (Specifically, Cardale's call was by Drummond who was then himself consecrated by Cardale.) The only way out of this circularity was that taken by the Catholic Apostolics themselves, namely to break it by claiming a direct action by the Holy Spirit. In theory, this must always be a possibility, but alternative interpretations of events have first to be considered. (Specifically, Cardale's call was regarded as a call by the Holy Spirit speaking through Drummond, whose subsequent consecration by Cardale was in response to the Spirit speaking through a third party.)

The events of Irving's congregation, allied to his supposedly heretical Christology, were not such as to inspire confidence in the validity of claims that it was indeed the Spirit who was speaking—it is significant that the Catholic Apostolics did much to expunge Irving's name from their records. Baxter's defection and claim that he had been inspired by evil spirits, admissions by some individuals that they had faked prophetic utterances, and the eventual restrictions put upon the prophets by the apostles, all reinforced the natural scepticism of outside observers and ensured that the apostolic claims would be accepted by but few.

Other arguments supporting the claims of the body were seen by outside observers as weak, for example:

> the historical analysis of the early Church was seriously open to question;
>
> the idea of Church structure was seen as archaic, failing to take into account the development of tradition or the changing circumstances over eighteen centuries;
>
> the attitude to matters of social concern (already referred to) resulted in isolation from the general mass of the people;
>
> the aspects of Christianity which were combined in the body were, for the majority of contemporary Christians, uncomfortable 'bedfellows';
>
> the rigidity of the hierarchical structure and the insistence upon the acceptance of the finest points of typology appeared as a practical denial of the teaching that God was unity in diversity, and that man, made in God's image, himself reflected a diversity of spiritual and intellectual gifts.

Later on, the increasing self-chosen isolation of the body and the tendency to secrecy meant that its witness was mostly misunderstood, and the highly restricted circulation of the largely anonymous spiritual and doctrinal writings ensured that their potential contribution to the Church at large was never appreciated. It came to be through occasional witnessing of their liturgy only, that a small number of Christians of other Churches obtained some idea of the richness of their theology and worship. As the liturgy gradually ceased to be celebrated, even this witness was silenced. All that has remained is the personal witness of members within the other Churches within which they have been forced to seek a temporary spiritual home—a witness which has been widely commended for its firm faith and holiness.

The 1901 Decision to Suspend Ordinations

Conventional attitudes would suggest that the decision not to perpetuate the apostolic office with its implications for the future of the Catholic Apostolic Church was evidence of weakness, weariness, and a sense of failure. The refusal to continue ordinations to any of the three major orders after 1901, despite the continuing existence of apostolic coadjutors, would seem for some outsiders only to underline that weakness. It is interesting to note that prophetic direction was accepted here without it being possible to validate it apostolically.

For the Catholic Apostolics themselves these crucial decisions were regarded as evidence of strength: firmness in obeying the direct guidance of the spirit; absolute trust in the mercy of God; and total faithfulness to the particular tradition which they had inherited from their forebears. These they have maintained without questioning God's providence or any diminishing of their eschatological hope throughout the period of their Church's gradual disappearance from the world's sight. They are content to wait upon the Spirit. This is surely remarkable in an age of rapidly changing beliefs and allegiances; it is deserving of admiration and great respect, rather than the somewhat derisive attitude which some have adopted. In the confusions of the present century, it is easy to mistake strength for weakness and weakness for strength. This is an age of quick and superficial judgements—the Catholic Apostolics deserve better of those who choose to study them.

3. THE CATHOLIC APOSTOLIC BODY: CHURCH OR SECT?

Before attempting to determine the status of the Catholic Apostolic body, it is important to state specifically the precise meanings given to the terms 'church' and 'sect'. It is also important to disregard titles by which the body is or has been known, since these can themselves prejudice the outcome of any discussion: thus the titles, 'Catholic Apostolic *Church*' and 'Irvingites', each have their own particular implication—both were disliked by members of the body, who preferred to be known by titles such as 'apostles' fellowship', 'members gathered under apostles', or simply 'the Lord's work'. With regard to the definitions of terms, it is easier to proceed first to the definition of 'sect' as a body of Christians, united by doctrines or practices which are distinct from the traditional doctrines and practices of the Church Catholic. A member of a sect has thus specifically chosen a separate path from 'mainstream' Christianity—often one which has arisen out of the life and witness of one individual or a small group of individuals claiming a special revelation from God. By contrast, a 'church' is a community of Christians professing to uphold the ecumenical faith as found in Scripture and Holy Tradition and expressed in a 'catholic' creed, who are united through acceptance of the same ministry and sacraments.

The Catholic Apostolics' View of Themselves

The Catholic Apostolics themselves totally repudiated any suggestion of sectarianism on their part: indeed, what were generally recognized as sects were severely criticized by them. It was for this reason that they objected to the title 'Irvingite', since to associate any Christian body in such a way with the name of any individual other than Christ was regarded by them as a sure sign of sectarianism. Indeed, they avoided any title which would associate them in any way with anything other than the 'One, Holy, Catholic, and Apostolic Church', regarding even national titles, such as 'the Church of England', as having sectarian overtones and the exclusive claims of Rome as betraying a sectarian spirit. They also rejected the suggestion that they were a 'Church within the Church' or indeed a Church as such at all. Their claim was to be a work of the Lord within the Church Universal. Any estimate of that claim must consider carefully the arguments which they put forward in support of it, including their repudiation of the name by which they were for some while popularly denoted.

First, they pointed to their acceptance of Scripture, the catholic creeds and sacraments, their many references to Patristic tradition, and their comprehensiveness generally, including their acceptance of all the baptized as Christians, the breadth of their ministry, their existence in all continents, and the inclusiveness of their liturgical intercessions. If the traditional aspects of catholicity were authority, tradition, and comprehensiveness, they claimed to display all these. Further, they claimed not to be introducing new doctrine, but to be restoring the orthodox teaching of the early Church in a way which they saw as entirely within the received catholic tradition.

The Catholic Apostolics did not see themselves as reformers, but as faithful Christians inspired by the Spirit to react to unacceptable innovations and distortions, and to draw the attention of all the baptized to the imminent realization of the ancient Christian hope in the promised return of Christ. The appearance of the prophetic ministry was evidence of the nearness of that return, but it was a restoration of neglected gifts, not the introduction of strange novelties. They contrasted all this with the usual features of sectarianism: hostility to the institutional Churches; exaggerated and partial theology; untraditional forms of worship; acceptance of the theories of individuals claiming special revelations; exclusivity; disorderly enthusiasm; instability; resistance to ordered rule; a tendency towards social anarchy; and so on.

All these features of sectarianism were regarded as contrary to God's revealed purposes for mankind, and were condemned accordingly. Certainly it would appear that, on these terms, the charge of sectarianism against them was an entirely unjust one. They were certainly not sectarian *by intent*. Did they, however, adopt teachings which belonged peculiarly to Irving rather than to the catholic tradition or which were unique to themselves? Also, can they be said to have evidenced sectarian trends after the rejection of their witness by the great majority of their fellow-Christians?

The Place of Irving

Irving was not the founder of the Catholic Apostolic Church, though a number of otherwise reputable articles and books allege precisely this. As has been shown, Irving's death preceded the 'separation' of the restored apostles, the event which most closely approximates the 'birth' of an organized body. Irving had participated in events which were to lead to the restored apostolate, and was himself ordained by the first of the new apostles, but it is clear that that apostolate developed in ways which he had not envisaged and with which he was by no means sympathetic. Much of the theological and liturgical development of the body would have seemed strange to him had he lived to see it.

Irving's role was therefore at most that of a catalyst, providing an initial acceptance of the validity of the tongues—though he himself never prophesied. His brief period as an ordained angel was in a role clearly subordinated to a superior apostolic authority. Certainly, the Catholic Apostolics drew to some extent upon teachings already to be found in Irving's writings: the importance of Christ's humanity; aspects of baptismal regeneration; anti-liberalism; and pre-millenarianism in particular. But these were not unique to Irving though at that time they had become closely associated with him. Even the emphasis on Christ's humanity, particularly associated with Irving and for which he had been deprived of his Presbyterian orders, was founded upon Patristic writings. Any accusation of sectarianism based upon alleged dependence upon peculiarities of unorthodox theology taken exclusively from Irving cannot reasonably be justified.

'Peculiar' Teachings

In the matter of teachings peculiar to themselves, the question is more open. The specific teaching on apostolic authority, though based upon an interpretation of Scripture extended to contemporary charismatic experiences, was certainly not generally accepted. The millenarian teaching, though certainly found in early Christian writings, was open to challenge—Lacunza's analysis of precisely what was condemned at Constantinople I satisfied the concern of the restored apostles that they should conform to traditional teaching, but was not subjected to scrutiny by other Christian authorities. The urgency of the apocalyptic message was not confirmed by the occurrence of the events prophesied—always a problem for millenarian movements—though here the Catholic Apostolics would suggest a postponement due to the failure of the Church to accept their witness.

The fourfold structure of the Catholic Apostolic ministry was unique to the body, though its justification of it was based upon largely acceptable premisses—it could be seen as a development of traditional ministry rather than a departure from it. The liturgical developments and their typological basis again could be seen as developments rather than contradictions of catholic tradition—there was nothing fundamentally unacceptable, for example, in unique liturgical features such as the proposition of the Holy Gifts during the Intercessions at the Offices.

Taken overall, the peculiar witness of the body does provide some ammunition for those who would put forward the charge of sectarianism, but these must be taken in their overall context and balanced against many of the major features of the body which were clearly within orthodox and catholic tradition, or acceptable extensions of it. It is the opinion of the writer that, on balance, the very considerable extent of the Catholic Apostolic adherence to traditional 'mainstream' Christian theology, taken with the 'catholic' nature of their liturgical worship, outweighs their 'peculiar' beliefs and practices (which were to a considerable extent peculiarities of emphasis), and that on these grounds the Catholic Apostolic body was a Church rather than a sect.

The Later Period

Notwithstanding the above, it must be admitted that in its later stages sectarian symptoms seem to become more apparent. Although the Catholic Apostolic witness was originally delivered within existing Churches with no thought of forming any separate organization, its rejection and the expulsion from the various Churches of those who accepted it forced upon the body precisely what it wished to avoid, namely the outward appearance of separation from the traditional mainstream Christian bodies. It is important to appreciate, however, that such separation was not by their own choice. The apostles set up an organizational structure with a comprehensive system of pastoral care because they had become responsible for congregations expelled from their previous Church membership.

In the later stages of the body's existence, its unsought isolation undoubtedly turned its 'soul' inwards, and it was then that the tendency to secrecy (due to the fear of being misunderstood) and some feeling of exclusiveness inevitably manifested themselves. In more recent years, there has been great resistance to any opening of debate upon either the history or the theology of the body (though for reasons which are entirely understandable if accepted on their terms). Without apostolic rule and guidance there has grown up a congregationalism which has sometimes involved the severe criticism of one congregation's actions by another.

Not all surviving Catholic Apostolics have followed the instructions of their last clergy and joined in the worship of other (usually episcopal) Churches. A few have developed highly localized traditions, such as a total Eucharistic fast; others have strayed within the influence of modern Protestant 'prophetic' bodies. Some oppose marriages outside the dwindling company of members. It must be stressed, however, that those who have abandoned the breadth of the original ecclesiological vision number very few. Symptoms of sectarianism are certainly to be found, but they are most noticeable precisely amongst those who have departed from the catholic dimension which the body displayed in its prime. It would be unjust to condemn the many because of the few.

The Absence of Sectarian Spirit

It would be equally unjust to condemn the original formation of an organized body as evidence of any sectarian spirit: it was effectively forced upon the apostles by expulsions from other Churches over which they had no control—they did not initially intend that any distinct body should emerge. Certainly, in some cases there were groups of members who welcomed the setting up of an independent body as giving cohesion to their witness and eventually providing forms of worship more acceptable than those in the Churches to which they had formerly belonged. It remains true, however, that it was the rigidity of attitude of others which largely brought the Catholic Apostolic Church into being as a structured entity. It is doubtful if such rigidity would be so much in evidence today.

The original message of the apostles had been a universal one addressed to the whole Christian Church, and one sincerely believed to be the work of the Holy Spirit. There is no trace of any sectarian intention in their writings or in the writings of those who followed them. The withdrawal of the message was the result of its rejection by the Church at large. Any sectarian tendencies which may be perceived during the later years of the body were the result of the unsought isolation of a community of Christians who had never themselves sought separation from the Church Catholic—indeed the very opposite—and who, after the demise of the apostles, had finally been forced into a form of congregationalism which inevitably invited the growth of individual opinions and inter-congregational disagreements. It is a tribute to the teaching disseminated within the body that these have occurred so rarely.

4. ETHOS AND TRADITION: EASTERN OR WESTERN?

It may at first seem strange that the question of Eastern Orthodoxy should be raised at all in connection with a Church which was so much a product of the Western Christian milieu of the early nineteenth century. It must be remembered, however, that the Catholic Apostolic apostles claimed jurisdiction over the whole Church—Eastern as well as Western—and that they travelled throughout Christendom, observing the various Christian traditions, in order that nothing which they considered true and good should be omitted from the body which they were in the process of establishing. Having accepted the shortcomings of the Churches with which they were familiar, they were prepared to go out with open minds to learn from others. This should be contrasted with the attitude of some Anglicans of the time who believed that it was the duty of the Church of England to correct the corruptions of both Rome and Constantinople. The basic Catholic Apostolic concept of the conciliar nature of rule in the Church (though expressed in terms of a college of apostles) was in principle in accord with Eastern Orthodoxy, and the reasons given for rejecting the claims of Rome were precisely those of the Eastern Churches. Further, there were manifest Eastern borrowings in their liturgy which clearly prove that the apostles did not return from their travels to Orthodox countries empty-handed.

The aborted visit made to Russia—when attempting to present *The Great Testimony* to the Tsar—meant, however, that their experience of Eastern Orthodoxy was largely gained from the Greek Churches, and indeed the many references to the Eastern Orthodox Churches in Catholic Apostolic writings, with one notable exception, relate to the Greek and not the Slav tradition. The exception, a work of the present century—Herman Thiersch's *Unsere russischen Bruder*

(Meier, 1932)—is devoted extensively to Russian Orthodoxy and is a most interesting study, though, on account of its late date, it is not of concern here. Of special interest is the typological assessment of the three main strands of Christianity, which sees Protestantism as the type of the diaconate, Roman Catholicism as the type of the priesthood, and Eastern Orthodoxy as the type of the episcopate.

Inevitably, much that is to be found in Catholic Apostolic theology and liturgy is common to both East and West. It is not surprising, however, that the apostles' desire for a non-papal catholicism together with recourse to Patristic sources should have involved what can be interpreted as moves in an Eastward direction. What is interesting is that extensive study of Catholic Apostolic writings repeatedly prompts the feeling that, even in the presentation of teaching which would be widely accepted in the West, there are undercurrents of emphasis on mystery, of the overriding significance of Easter and the Resurrection, of the acceptance that holy things transcend intellectual understanding, of the sense of the essential spiritual content of material objects, of the ultimate transfiguration of all creation rather than its destruction, of the fundamental importance of symbols, and so on—all of which are especially characteristic of Eastern Christianity, though by no means absent in the West. To develop the argument for any significant Eastern ethos it is necessary to clothe such feeling with specifics.

Liturgy

Eastern influence within Catholic Apostolic liturgy went far beyond the borrowing of prayers, as reference to Cardale's *Readings upon the Liturgy* alone clearly shows. The theology of Eucharistic sacrifice and the real presence was precisely that of Eastern Orthodoxy, and thus avoided the controversies which had proved so divisive in the West. The insistence upon the need for the inclusion of the Epiclesis, the emphasis upon the role of the Holy Spirit, the refusal to accept the Roman doctrine of transubstantiation, the reluctance to speak of a 'moment' of consecration, the emphasis upon the spiritual ascent to the heavenly altar and upon Christ as Offerer and Offered, the understanding that it is the 'spiritual' that is truly 'real', all these things are equally emphasized in Eastern Orthodox writings. The incarnational basis of the sacramental theology in general, and the concept of the material world as essentially 'spirit-bearing', received an emphasis corresponding to that given in Eastern Orthodoxy. The 'sealing', though not administered with baptism as in the East, had an underlying Eastern theological basis.

Much further liturgical convergence can be found, for example:

the insistence upon one Eucharist, one altar, and one principal celebrant on any one day;

the focus of Eucharistic worship upon Sunday and the Resurrection;

the absence of a 'low' eucharistic rite on Western lines;

the linking of the two major Offices with the Eucharist;

the two liturgical entrances during the Eucharist;

the inclusiveness of the Anaphora;

the breadth of the Intercessions (compare the Litanies of the Eastern Churches);

the restrictions upon what may be appropriately placed upon the altar (for example, *not* alms);

the form of the Commemoration of the Departed;

the Eucharistic interpretation of the Lord's Prayer (though the location of it in the apostles' rite was unique);

the admission of children to Holy Communion;

the use of a Presanctified rite on occasions other than Good Friday;

the Easter Eve Eucharist with its commemoration of the 'hallowing of Hell';

the theological basis of an Eastward-facing celebrant;

the form of priestly absolution following private confession (though the Russian Church has adopted a Western form).

All these things, amongst others, gave the Catholic Apostolic liturgical rites an Eastern ethos.

Man and Creation

The Catholic Apostolic perspective on Creation, man, and the Fall was also reminiscent of Eastern Christianity, displaying strong reservations about aspects of Augustine's teaching, and, more particularly, about Protestant developments of it. Augustine, along with Origen, was criticized for his over-allegorizing of Scripture also. Creation was seen as the first stage of God's revelation of Himself and part of a revelationary plan of which the Incarnation was always to be a natural continuation, and of which the Parousia would be a culminating act.

The interpretation of 'image' and 'likeness' and the Trinitarian image within man (body, soul, and spirit) echoed the writings of Orthodox theologians, as did the warnings about the dangers of attempting to reach the truth through intellect alone or of ministering to the human person in only one of its threefold aspects: objections to psychology and hypnotism were examples of this. In studying Catholic Apostolic works, it is important to note that ψυχή (soul) was generally used in the Greek sense, and that 'natural' tended to mean 'spiritual', 'ideal', or 'eternal'—thus the death of the body was said to be an 'unnatural' event, man's 'natural' state not then being restored until his resurrection. Protestant emphasis upon personal salvation was rejected in favour of a cosmic viewpoint: man would be saved not merely within a community of the faithful (the Church) but as part of the totality of God's creation.

The Catholic Apostolic emphasis upon the humanity of Christ—a 'restoring of the balance' rather than any new or revived Christological distortion—led them to a reverence for the human body, which (as with the Eastern Orthodox) made cremation abhorrent to them. Their theology of sexuality, and particularly their emphasis of man as the type of Christ and woman as the type of the Church, was in accord with Eastern views and would have made any proposal for the ordination of women seem a totally unacceptable departure from both Scripture and Christian tradition. The visible participation of women in the public ministry of the Church is today a reason for members to leave some Anglican parishes in which they have become accustomed to worship.

Divergences from Eastern Orthodoxy

Contrasting with the many aspects of convergence with Eastern Christianity detailed above, there were a number of points where traditional Eastern views and those of the Catholic Apostolics conflicted, and it is only right that these should also be noted.

Cardale included the *filioque* in the Eucharistic Creed, not accepting the arguments for its omission, though with a note stating that its inclusion and its omission were not necessarily theologically incompatible. Indeed, while underwriting the original reason for its inclusion (protecting the divinity of Christ), he also gave it an interpretation which would be acceptable to most Eastern theologians by, at the same time, stressing that the Father is the unique source of the Godhead and emphasizing the role of the person of the Holy Spirit in all divine activity, thus removing some of the theological though not the historical ground of Eastern objections. Thus, it should be noted that the inclusion of the *filioque* was by no means entirely a 'divergence' from Eastern Orthodoxy.

The most significant divergence, however, is to be found in the Catholic Apostolic absolute rejection of prayer being addressed to the Saints. They saw such prayers as implying a rejection of Christ as the *one* mediator between God and man—this was only one of a number of points upon which the Catholic Apostolics exhibited great fear lest the unique role of the risen Christ as Prophet, Priest, and King should be in any way encroached upon. Nevertheless, they had a profound feeling for the Communion of Saints and a view of the state of the departed as those 'asleep in Christ' (with whom they remained spiritually united within the Church) much in accord with that of Eastern Christianity—for example, repudiating the Roman doctrine of purgatory. They accepted prayer for the departed (a matter of contention in the West), and also 'veneration' of the memory of the Theotokos and the Saints of both the Old and New dispensations (though without specific feasts dedicated to Saints other than All Saints' Day). The Theotokos was commemorated at every Eucharist as a type of the Church. However, they did not accept that there could or should be direct access to the Saints through prayer, and they repudiated any doctrine of relics.

Although murals representing the history of the divine economy were permitted in Catholic Apostolic churches (as, for example, a visit to the former Edinburgh church will illustrate), there was a tendency towards iconoclasm and austerity in the adornment of their church buildings, and the erection of any form of screen, whether or not including icons, would have been contrary to their understanding of the architectural symbolism of places of worship—it was a fundamental principle that the arrangement of church buildings should include nothing which could be interpreted as restricting the laity's access to the heavenly mysteries.

Also of significance is the Catholic Apostolic interpretation of the

Constantinian settlement as a sign of the Church's adultery with the world—not a view with which Eastern orthodoxy would agree, since it holds Constantine as 'equal to the Apostles' and a great protector of the Church from heresy and schism. However, some Orthodox are tending to admit more openly that the settlement was something of a 'mixed blessing' and did indeed cause serious problems for the Church in that a 'dilution' of the faithful inevitably took place and worldly ambitions were more readily introduced amongst the hierarchy and other clergy. It is not possible, however, that the East should ever indict the settlement as totally as did the Catholic Apostolics.

Two further points of difference deserve mention here. First, the Catholic Apostolics followed Rome in understanding the Eucharistic bread of the Last Supper to have been unleavened Passover bread— for them leaven was considered to be symbolic of evil, as in 1 Corinthians 5: 8. (Despite their frequent references to the Greek text of the New Testament in other matters, no comment was made on the relevant word ἄρτος, universally used in the Synoptic Gospels and by St Paul in connection with the Last Supper.) Secondly, they were extremely rigid in the application of their 'canons', having no concept of οἰκονομία. Thus, for example, whilst they would (albeit reluctantly) countenance formal separation after marriage, in no circumstances whatever would they countenance divorce—those who availed themselves of the laws of the state in such matters were removed from the list of communicants. Such rigidity in pastoral matters was much more an inheritance from the West than from the East.

An Overview

It is obviously ridiculous to claim that the Catholic Apostolic Church was a 'child' of the East rather than the West. It is, however, equally ridiculous to see it solely as a Western body. As with the Eucharistic rite there were a number of things that were specifically Eastern and an underlying ethos which might well have made members of the body feel at home with much of the Byzantine rite of Orthodoxy, so in the theological works there was much specifically Eastern teaching together with an underlying approach which was by no means derived from Western principles alone. What can be said is that there was a blend of East and West, which, by avoiding the Western proclivity to exhaustive definition and explanation, enabled doctrines which were often also to be found in both Roman and Anglican (especially Tractarian) traditions to be presented in a way which retained the Eastern sense of mystery and transcendence whilst avoiding the pitfalls of over-detailed formulation.

All this was in no small measure due to the considerable reference to Patristic writings and to a genuine openness to the breadth of Christian traditions. Catholic Apostolics would claim that, in seeking under divine guidance to perfect the Church, their apostles had been led by the Spirit to discern and bring together all that was good and true in the Churches of West and East—on this claim it is perhaps better not to attempt to pass final judgement. Nevertheless, study in depth of both their theology and liturgy does reveal much that is clearly derived from Eastern Orthodoxy and much more that is either specifically in accord with it or can be derived by extension from it.

5. THE SIGNIFICANCE OF THE CATHOLIC APOSTOLIC WITNESS TODAY

It would be easy simply to dismiss the whole short existence of the Catholic Apostolic Church as a temporary aberration in Church history, irrelevant now that the body has ceased to exist. This would be to accept, however, that it raised no matters of contemporary interest today and left behind no written legacy of any current spiritual or theological worth. Since neither of these last is the case, the question of its significance for Christians at the end of the twentieth century should be considered.

Apocalyptic

As the end of the second millennium since Christ is approached, it is virtually certain that eschatological and apocalyptic debate will again take on a heightened significance. There is much in the history of the Catholic Apostolic body and the development of its eschatology from which useful lessons may be drawn. The inevitable prophets of various (though mainly fundamentalist) backgrounds will now have at their disposal the power of the mass-media, and apocalyptic debate will not be limited to sincere enquiring Christians as it was in the early nineteenth century—it may well become a dangerous tool in the hands of exploiters. No doubt, much that was investigated by the earlier students of prophecy will be re-presented, and it is important that Christians generally should be aware of the significance of the debates of the past as well as being armed with the insights provided by more recent biblical scholarship.

The Charismatic Movement

There is much in the Catholic Apostolic experience from an understanding of which the present-day charismatics could benefit, not least that man is so made that he needs more than a free and emotional approach to worship, that he can be deceived by what appear to be divine spiritual manifestations, and that the permanent ordinances and ministries of the Church are as important as charismatic experiences—they are neglected only at great spiritual peril. The gifts of the Spirit should be accepted if granted, not sought. It is important to appreciate also that 'enthusiasms' alone are no sound basis for Christian witness: Christian experience must involve the whole person, and not be directed disproportionately towards one aspect rather than another—least of all the emotions. It was the clear implications of the Catholic Apostolic experience for present-day charismatics that led L. Christenson to write his book, *A Message to the Charismatic Movement* (Minneapolis: Dimension Books, 1972).

Ecumenism

There are several matters of value for the formal ecumenical movement, though much has already been learned from the dialogue between participating Churches. The Catholic Apostolics anticipated some of the current programme, whilst at the same time raising issues which do not yet seem to have been adequately aired if aired at all. Their acceptance that the Church in its widest sense comprises all the baptized remains an important starting point for ecumenical dialogue; doubters would gain much from a study of the theological and practical reasons which were given for this acceptance, since it is important that it should have a sound theological basis.

Those specifically concerned with problems associated with Eucharistic doctrine—which are largely of Western origin—should study Catholic Apostolic solutions, remembering that these were acceptable within a body of almost exclusively Protestant origins. Those concerned with liturgy should search through the riches of that of the restored apostles, noting the wide commendation which it has received from the few who have studied it; in particular, the need for an eschatological dimension and a sense of mystery should be recognized. The Catholic Apostolic Eucharist and its underlying theology represented a fusion of East and West that has not been realized in the same way elsewhere.

Those concerned with the recognition of ministries might consider abandoning the traditional somewhat negative and formal concept of 'validity' and make a study of the Catholic Apostolic rite of Confirmation of Orders and the positive theological approach underlying it. It provides a middle way between total acceptance of all ministries and the rejection of many, neither of which alternatives is ever likely to prove acceptable to the Churches—it has not been seriously considered since the time of the reception of Arian clergy into the Church.

It might well be wise to consider whether the present quest for unity is not too much based upon the efforts of man. The Catholic Apostolics were led to the conclusion that this kind of unity requires divine intervention—that it cannot be achieved this side of the Parousia. It can be argued also that too much time and effort is currently spent on ecumenical effort focused on 'this world', and therefore encouragement is needed to focus attention on man's spiritual rather than on his material needs. Man's hope needs to be directed more towards the Parousia, as an event to be truly hoped for, and as an event which must always be regarded as spiritually near. The Catholic Apostolic witness to the importance of the Parousia, and their examination of its scriptural background, should not be entirely lost to the Churches.

The Catholic Apostolic arguments in favour of comprehensiveness —of attempting to bring together what is true and good from every Christian tradition—provide a better starting principle than attempts to find a lowest common denominator of faith and practice upon which the greatest majority can agree. The apostles realized the need to *experience* the different Christian traditions of worship and to search in patristic writings for an understanding of the tradition of the early Church. They approached both with open minds, seeking to move towards perfecting the Church and, in so doing, were prepared to abandon much of their own previous personal ecclesiastical experience.

The history of the Catholic Apostolic body raises the whole question of the nature and role of the prophetic ministry within the Church—this needs extensive ecumenical debate; it is not a peripheral matter but one of fundamental importance. Its experience throws light upon many of the problems which can be raised by the presence of prophets within the Church.

The Catholic Apostolic understanding of man and the need to ensure the availability of comprehensive pastoral care should be considered. Whilst their fourfold ministry may well not be appropriate today, there is significance in the belief that no one person can or should attempt to exercise the whole ministry of Christ. The recognition of the bishop as the head of the local Church and the 'normal' celebrant of the Eucharist is also a matter which should be re-examined and its implications considered, especially by episcopal Churches, as is the question of the role and significance of deacons and how they should be selected.

The Catholic Apostolic doctrine of sexuality and their view of the role of women in the Church, though obviously likely to be most unpopular in many quarters today, was nevertheless grounded in an understanding of the importance of symbolism in the Church which should not be disregarded.

In the matter of Church economics, the question of tithing as a Christian obligation should be given serious consideration. This was extensively investigated and carefully argued by the Catholic Apostolics, and their writings on it should be studied.

The Catholic Apostolic view of the divine calling of the Jewish people and the concerns about Islam may well have a contribution to make to the current debate on inter-faith relations. In particular, Christian–Jewish dialogue is continually affected by the existence of Christian missionary activity directed specifically at Jewish conversions. The arguments put forward for regarding such activity as inappropriate—be they valid or not—at least deserve study. Should they prove acceptable, a difficult problem would be resolved.

Although much modern biblical exegesis has little in common with that of the Catholic Apostolics, it is nevertheless important that typology should not be entirely neglected, for it provides not only an important link between the Old and New Testaments but also insights into early patristic understanding of the Jewish Scriptures. Nowhere has typology been more profoundly discussed and ultimately presented than at the prophetic conferences held at Albury and in the writings of the apostles and their adherents. Much can be learned from an ecumenical study of these works.

Finally, the question of the restoration of apostles throws into prominence the nature of ultimate authority in the Church under Christ—probably the most difficult area of debate for the whole ecumenical movement. The solution presented by the Catholic Apostolic apostles is not one likely to find general favour, especially as it runs contrary to today's democratic trends. Nevertheless, the fact that such a solution was seriously initiated by educated and sincere Christians suggests that there may well be aspects of the restored apostolate of relevance today—not least that it represented the principle that those in authority in the Church need to be recognized by the Church as being inspired by the Holy Spirit. The only authority which can find universal acceptance within the Church is one which clearly reflects the authority of Christ as Head, and which at the same time does not represent any usurpation of that authority.

The Uniqueness and the Comprehensiveness of the Apostles' Witness

The various matters raised above by no means exhaust the ways in which a study of the Catholic Apostolic witness might have relevance for today, though it is not suggested that it is necessarily the only or even the principal source related to them. It is true, however, that the combination of theological ideas to be found in Catholic Apostolic writings is unique, and that their fusion into a comprehensive body of theology is in itself an achievement deserving of note.

Catholic Apostolic works cover the whole spectrum of Christian theology and worship from a viewpoint which can be described as thoroughly theocentric, anthropocentric, and geocentric. Their scholarship may be dated in many ways and the method of biblical interpretation currently out of favour, but there is a wealth of fundamental Christian teaching to be found in their works, often expressed in terms and from principles of great value which are in danger of being forgotten. Again there is a wealth of spiritual writing of great beauty and deep understanding, which, even today, can shed light upon questions with which mankind must always be faced.

There is also much material deserving of serious research—theological, historical, sociological, and perhaps psychological. It is therefore much to be regretted that Catholic Apostolic primary sources are so scarce and difficult of access, and becoming increasingly so. It is to be hoped that, while there is yet time, further work will be undertaken to open up this quite remarkable chapter of Church history, now concluded, in which there came into existence a body which claimed to be neither a Church nor a sect, but which (against its principles) became an organized Church and which, throughout its existence and its eventual decline, exhibited a faithfulness and a holiness which compels great admiration.

Appendix I
The Liturgy and Other Divine Offices of the Church

CONTENTS

FORMS FOR PROPER AND OCCASIONAL USE

For Holy Days and Seasons

The Three Seasons preceding Christmas, Easter, and Pentecost
Advent
Christmas Eve
Christmas Day and Octave
Circumcision and Octave
After the Octave of Circumcision until the Sunday before Easter
Presentation and Octave
Sunday before Easter
Monday and Tuesday before Easter
Wednesday before Easter
Thursday before Easter
Good Friday
Easter Eve or Holy Saturday
Easter Day and Octave
After the Octave of Easter until Ascension Day
Ascension Day
Sunday after Ascension
Eve of Pentecost
Day of Pentecost
Monday after Pentecost
Tuesday after Pentecost
After the Octave of Pentecost until Christmas
The Anniversary of the Separation of the Apostles
Commemoration of All Angels
All Saints Day and Octave
The Assembly of the Seven Churches

For Occasional Use

On the occasion of the Meeting of the Apostles and the Ministers with
    them in Council, or by an Apostle previously to a Solemn Council in
    the Tribe
In Particular Churches on the like occasions
By an Apostle for the Tribe
At the Commencement of an Apostolic Visitation
On behalf of a Particular Church
In a time of Declension

For imploring Blessing on the Labours of Evangelists
For beseeching the Lord to raise up Evangelists
On days of Humiliation
In times of Public Calamity
On days of Rejoicing
On behalf of a Young Person entering upon any Occupation in life
The Churching of Women
On behalf of a Woman after Child-bearing
In Commemorating a Sick Person
In Commemorating a Deceased Person

SPECIAL SERVICES AND FORMS

The Order for Receiving a Catechumen
The Dedication of Catechumens previously to their Baptism
The Order for the Administration of holy Baptism
The Order for Receiving in the Church such as have been privately baptized
The Form of Committing to Pastorship
The Benediction of Persons newly committed to Pastorship; or of Persons about to be received to Regular Communion
The Renewal of Vows, and Dedication of those about to receive the Laying on of Hands
The Order for the Laying on of Apostles' Hands
The Order for the Solemnization of Marriage
The Form of Blessing Newly-married Persons
The Form of Blessing such as offer themselves for Works of Charity and Piety
The Office for Presentation and Dedication for the Holy Ministry
Form for Blessing a Doorkeeper
Form for Blessing Singers and Players on Instruments
The Form for Admitting an Underdeacon
Form for Receiving a Deaconess
The Order for Admitting to the Office of Deacon
The Office for Blessing Deacons
The Form of Receiving one of the Seven Deacons of a Church
The Form of Receiving a Deacon not of the Seven
The Order for Ordaining Priests
The Form for Confirming the Orders of Priests
The Form of Receiving One of the Six Elders of a Church
The Form of Receiving a Priest not one of the Six Elders

The Form of Receiving a Priest for Temporary Service
The Office for the Presentation of Priests for the Episcopate
A Form of Prayer on behalf of a called Angel shortly to be Ordained
The Order for the Ordination or Consecration of an Angel
The Order and Manner of Inducting an Angel into the Charge of a
    Particular Church
The Order and Manner of Sending forth an Angel-Evangelist
Forms of Benediction on the Dismissal of Ministers on New Missions
The Manner of Laying the First Stone of a Church
The Order for the Consecration of a Church
The Form for the Consecration of an Altar, &c.
The Manner of Consecrating a Tablet-Altar
The Forms for the Benediction of Furniture, Vessels, and Vestments
A Form for the Benediction of Oil for the Anointing of the Sick

OFFICES FOR USE ON PRIVATE OCCASIONS

Prayer for a Woman after Childbirth, and Dedication of the Infant
The Order for Private Baptism
The Order for the Solemn Absolution of Penitents in private
The Order for the Administration of the Communion to the Sick
The Order for Anointing the Sick
A Litany in the Visitation of the Sick
Prayers of Commendation of a Departing Soul
The Form of Benediction of a House
The Benediction of a Chamber-lodging
Form for the Benediction of a Ship

The Catechism

Appendix II
H. Drummond:
Dialogues on Prophecy

CONTENTS

XIII. Practical duties incumbent on those who are looking for the Lord's Appearance?

Volume III

*XIII. What light is thrown upon that part of God's purpose which is yet unaccomplished, by the Revelations which were given anterior to the Law?

XIV. What light is thrown upon that part of God's purpose which is yet unaccomplished, by the Mosaic Law?

XV. What light is thrown upon that part of God's purpose which is yet unaccomplished, by the Historical Events of the Jewish Nation?

XVI. What light is thrown upon that part of God's purpose which is yet unaccomplished, by the Prophecies given, and referred to, in the Gospels and Acts?

XVII. What light is thrown upon that part of God's purpose which is yet unaccomplished, by the Prophecies given, and referred to, in the Epistles?

XVIII. The Signs of the Times.

Classified Bibliography

SECONDARY SOURCES

Theses

LANCASTER, J., 'John Bate Cardale, Pillar of Apostles: A Quest for Catholicity' (St Andrews University, 1978).

LIVELY, R. J. (Jun.), 'The Catholic Apostolic Church and the Church of Jesus Christ of Latter-Day Saints: A Comparative Study of Two Minority Millenarian Groups in Nineteenth-Century England' (Oxford University, 1977).

ORCHARD, S. C., 'English Evangelical Eschatology 1790–1850' (Cambridge University, 1968).

STEVENSON, K. W., 'The Catholic Apostolic Eucharist' (Southampton University, 1975).

WHITLEY, H. C., 'Edward Irving: An Interpretation of His Life and Theological Teaching' (Edinburgh University, 1953).

Books

ALGERMISSEN, K., *The Christian Sects* (London: Burns and Oates, 1962).

ANDREWS, C. F., *What I owe to Christ* (London: Hodder and Stoughton, 1932).

BORN, K., *Das Werk des Herrn unter Aposteln* (Bremen: 1974).

BRANSBY, J. H., *Evans's Sketch of the various Denominations of the Christian World* (London: 1841).

CAMERON, G. C., *The Scots Church in London* (Oxford: Becket, 1979).

CARLYLE, T. (ed. Froude), *Reminiscences* (1881; London: Dent, 1972).

CHRISTENSON, L., *A Message to the Charismatic Movement* (Minneapolis: Dimension Books, 1972).

COHN, N., *The Pursuit of the Millennium* (London: Temple Smith, 1970).

484   *Classified Bibliography*

COUSLAND, A. O., *How Hidden it Was* (Bognor Regis: New Horizon, 1983).

CURTIS, W. A., *Creeds and Confessions of Faith* (London: 1911).

DALLIMORE, A., *The Life of Edward Irving* (Edinburgh: Banner of Truth, 1983).

DAVENPORT, R. A., *Albury Apostles* (United Writers, 1970; rev. edn. London: Neillgo, 1973).

DAVIES, H., *Worship and Theology in England: 1850–1900* (Oxford: 1962).

DRUMMOND, A. L., *Edward Irving and his Circle* (London: Clarke, 1934).

—— and BULLOCH, J., *The Church in Victorian Scotland: 1843–1874* (Edinburgh: St Andrew Press, 1975).

EDEL, R. F., *Auf dem Weg zur Vollendung der Kirche Jesu Christi* (Marburg: Oekumenischer Verlag, 1971).

HAIR, J., *Regent Square* (London: Nisbet, 1899).

HANNA, W., *Memoirs of the life and writings of T. Chalmers D.D. LL.D.* (4 vols.) (Edinburgh: 1849–52).

JONES, W., *A Biographical Sketch of the Revd. Edward Irving, with Extracts from and Remarks on his Principal Publications* (n.p.: Bennet, 1835).

KNOX, R. A., *Enthusiasm* (Oxford: O.U.P., 1950).

MACPHERSON, D., *The Incredible Cover-up* (Plainfield, NJ: Logos International, 1975).

MAXWELL, G., *The House of Elrig* (London: Longmans, 1965).

MAXWELL, J. M., *Worship and Reformed Theology* (Pittsburgh: Pickwick Press, 1976).

MILLER, E., *The History and Doctrines of Irvingism* (2 vols.) (London: Kegan Paul, 1878).

MOLLAND, E., *Christendom* (London: Mowbray, 1959).

MORSE-BOYCOTT, D., *The Secret Story of the Oxford Movement* (London: Skeffington, 1933).

—— *They Shine Like Stars* (London: Skeffington, 1947).

MURRAY, I., *The Puritan Hope* (Edinburgh: Banner of Truth, 1971).

Neue Apostelgeschichte: New Acts of the Apostles (n.p.: New Apostolic Church, 1982).

NEWMAN-NORTON, S., *The Hamburg Schism* (London: Albury Society, 1974).

—— *The Time of Silence* (London: Albury Society, 1975).

OLIPHANT, MRS, *The Life of Edward Irving* (London: Hurst and Blackett, 1862; rev. edn. 1864).

ORCHARD, W. E., *From Faith to Faith* (New York and London: Putnam, 1933).

PELIKAN, J., *The Christian Tradition*, i. *The Emergence of the Catholic Tradition* (Chicago: University of Chicago, 1971).

PINNINGTON, J., and NEWMAN-NORTON, S., *Apostolic and Conciliar Witness* (London: Albury Society, 1978).

PUBLIC RECORDS OFFICE, *Ecclesiastical Returns 1851* (London: H.O. 129).

ROOT, J. C., *Edward Irving: Man, Preacher, Prophet* (Boston, Mass.: Sherman, 1912).

ROWDEN, H. H., *The Origins of the Brethren, 1825–1850* (London: Pickering and Inglis, 1967).

RUSSELL, D. S., *The Method and Message of Jewish Apocalyptic: 200 BC–AD 100* (London: SCM Press, 1964).

SANDEEN, E. T., *The Roots of Fundamentalism* (Chicago: University of Chicago, 1970).

SHAW, P. E., *The Catholic Apostolic Church* (New York: Kings Crown, 1946).

STANDRING, G. L., *Albury and the Catholic Apostolic Church* (n.p. (published by the author), 1985).

STEVENSON, K. W., *Eucharist and Offering* (New York: Pueblo, 1986).

STRACHAN, G., *The Pentecostal Theology of Edward Irving* (London: Darton, Longman and Todd, 1973).

WHITE, J. F., *The Cambridge Movement* (Cambridge, 1962).

WHITLEY, H. C., *Blinded Eagle* (London: SCM, 1955).

WILKS, W., *Edward Irving: an Ecclesiastical and Literary Biography* (London: Freeman, 1854).

WORSFOLD, J. E., *A History of the Charismatic Movements in New Zealand* (n.p.: Julian Literature Trust, 1974).

Note: various encyclopaedias include articles on the Catholic Apostolic Church. In general these need to be treated with caution since they tend to include inaccurate or misleading information. Other works referred to, but not directly related to the Catholic Apostolic Church (including patristic works, collections of liturgies, etc.), are noted in the text and in the notes.

Articles

HURLBUT, S. A., 'A Liturgical Centenary', *The Living Church*, 20 Sept. 1942, 10–11.

JONES, R. K., 'The Catholic Apostolic Church: a Study in Diffused Commitment', in *A Sociological Yearbook of Religion in Britain*, 5 (London: SCM, 1972), 137–60.

STEVENSON, K. W., 'The Catholic Apostolic Church—its History and its Eucharist', *Studia Liturgica*, 13 (1979), 21–45.

—— 'The Liturgical Year in the Catholic Apostolic Church', *Studia Liturgica*, 16 (1982), 128–34.

TRIPP, D. H., 'The Liturgy of the Catholic Apostolic Church', *Scottish Jour. Theol.*, 22 (1969), 437–54.

PRIMARY SOURCES

Catholic Apostolic Works (including works by Irving): classified

Note: Many of the works classifed below cover a wider area than is immediately indicated. In general, they have been placed in the section to which they have the greatest relevance for the present work.

General works

ANDERSON, W. (angel-evangelist), *Truths of our Days* (London: Hodgson, 1865).

ARMSTRONG, N. (apostle), *Homilies on the Epistles and Gospels* (London: Bosworth, 1870).

—— *Sermons on Various Subjects*, ser. I/II (London: Bosworth, 1854/79).

—— and DRUMMOND, H. (apostles), *Tracts for the Church* (London: Bosworth, 1858).

BÖHM, C. J. T. (apostle's coadjutor), *Lights and Shadows in the Present Condition of the Church* (London: Bosworth, 1860).

CAIRD, W. T. (apostle's coadjutor), and LUTZ, J. E. G. (angel-evangelist), *God's Purpose with Mankind and the Earth* (Sidney: Cook, 1873).

CARDALE, J. B. (pillar of apostles), *A Manual or Summary of Special Objects of Faith and Hope* (London: Barclay, 1843).

——*The Character of our Present Testimony and Work* (London: Strangeways, 1865).

CARLYLE, T. (apostle), *Collected Works* (London: Bosworth, 1878).

COPINGER, H. B. (underdeacon), *A Bibliography of Works relating to the Catholic Apostolic Church* (privately published, n.d.).

DAVENPORT, J. S. (angel-evangelist), *Answers to Enquiries in regard to the Catholic Apostolic Church* (n.p. 1858).

DAVSON, W. M. (priest), *Sermons and Homilies on the Third Stage of the Lord's Work* (privately published, 1966).

DOW, W. A. M. (apostle), *Discourses on Practical Subjects*, ser. I/II (Edinburgh: Grant, 1847/50).

——*Sermons and Homilies* (Edinburgh: Grant, 1856).

DRUMMOND, H. (apostle), *Abstract Principles of Revealed Religion* (Murray, 1845).

——*Elements of the Christian Religion* (London: Hatchard, 1845).

GROSER, T. (angel), *Sermons*, ser. I/II (London: Bosworth 1871/4).

Homilies Preached at Albury, various authors (n.p.: Norton, 1888).

HUGHES, R. (archangel), *Apostles' Doctrine and Fellowship* (London: Boswell, 1871).

NORTON, R. (priest), *The True Position and Hope of the Catholic Apostolic Church* (London: Boswell, 1866).

THIERSCH, H. W. J. (apostle's pastor), *The Parables of Christ* (London: Boswell, 1869).

——*Summary of Christian Doctrine* (Glasgow: Hobbs, 1888).

THONGER, J. (archangel), *The Catechism with Aids to Parents* (London: Chiswick Press, 1908).

See also: *The Great Testimony* (n.p. 1838).
The Lesser Testimonies (n.p. 1836).
Book of Regulations (London: Strangeways, 1878).
Articles in *The Morning Watch* (London: Nisbet, 1829–33).
Letters in the Northumberland Collection: Alnwick Castle.

Angels, Saints, and the Departed

COPINGER, W. A. (angel), *The Holy Angels* (Glasgow: Hobbs, 1909).

488   *Classified Bibliography*

DE CAUX, W. (angel), *The Communion of Saints* (London: Central Church, 1926).
HAMILTON, R. M. (angel), *Right Views concerning the Faithful Departed* (London: Goodwin, 1900).
HUME, H. S. (angel), *Sermon on All Saints* (London: Central Church, 1900).
PROBY, W. H. B. (angel), *The State of the Departed* (Glasgow: Hobbs, 1904).
RAWSON, T. E. (angel), *Harvest and the Holy Angels* (n.p. 1927).
RUTTER, C. J. (layman ?), *Cremation versus Christian Burial: a Word of Warning* (Glasgow: Hobbs, 1901).
SYMES, L. W. (apostle's coadjutor), *The Recent Decree of the Immaculate Conception* (London: Bosworth, 1855).
WILLIAMS, J. (angel), *Lecture on the Cherubim and Seraphim* (Armagh: Mutual Improvement Society, 1879).
WILLIS, A. M. (priest), *St Michael and All Angels* (West Croydon Church, 1915).

Baptism

BOASE, C. W. (apostle's angel-evangelist), *Baptism* (Dundee: Matthew, 1866).
BÖHM, C. J. T. (apostle's coadjutor), *The Baptism of Infants* (London: Pitman, 1900).
—— *Holy Baptism* (Glasgow: Hobbs, 1902).
CARLYLE, T. (apostle), *On the Sacrament of Baptism* (London: Bosworth, 1850).
DAVENPORT, J. B. (angel-evangelist), *Christian Baptism* (Glasgow: Hobbs, 1901).
DOW, W. (apostle), *God's Ordinances are Evermore Realities* (London: Glaisher, 1924) (from *Discourses*, 1847/50).
FRANCIS, J. G. (angel-evangelist), *Discourses on Baptismal Regeneration* (n.p.: Golbourn, 1850).
GROSER, T. (angel), *Explanatory Note on Infant Baptism* (Wells: Backhouse, 1834).
HEATH, C. B. (elder), *Baptism* (London: Southwark Church, 1947).
IRVING, E. (angel), *Homilies on the Sacraments*, i. *On Baptism* (n.p.: Panton, 1828).
JARVIE, A. (angel-evangelist), *Conversations on Baptism*, Parts I/II (Glasgow: Hobbs, 1884/5).

LAW, G. (angel-evangelist), *On Baptism and the Subjects Thereof* (Glasgow: Ogle, 1858).

MATTHEW, J. M. (elder), *An Euchiridion on the Holy Baptism* (Glasgow: Hobbs, 1902).

MOORE, W. J. B. (elder), *On the Sacrament of Christian Baptism* (London: Pitman, 1894).

—— *Baptism Didache, or Scriptural Studies on Baptism* (London: Bemrose, 1907).

PHILLIPS, G. C. (prophet), *What is Christian Baptism* (Chelmsford: Durrant, 1882).

PROBY, W. H. B. (angel), *Considerations in Favour of Infant Baptism* (Glasgow: Hobbs, 1911).

REID, W. (priest-evangelist), *Dialogues on Baptism* (Murray, 1863).

—— *Dialogue on Baptismal Regeneration* (n.p. 1874).

SITWELL, F. (apostle), *The Covenant of Baptism* (n.p., repr. 1940).

TARBET, W. (angel), *Letter on Christian Baptism* (Liverpool: Smith, 1828).

—— *Discourses on Infant Baptism* (Liverpool: Marples, 1850).

Christology: the Incarnation, etc.

ACKERY, J. W. (angel), *The Word was Made Flesh* (London: Bosworth, 1882).

ANDREWS, S. J. (angel), *Outline of the Life of Christ* (Waterbury: Pearl, 1908).

ANDREWS, W. W. (apostle's angel-evangelist), 'The Types of Christ in the Old Testament', *The Christian Mirror* (1868).

—— 'Christ in the book of Genesis', *American Church Review* (1872).

—— *The Present and Abiding Humanity of Our Lord* (n.p. 1887).

—— *The Two Advents of Christ* (n.p. 1890).

BURNE, H. T. (angel), *Scripture Doctrine of the Person and Humanity of our Divine Redeemer* (London: Douglas, 1833).

CARDALE, J. B. (pillar of apostles), *The Doctrine of the Incarnation* (London: Strangeways, 1875).

CARLYLE, T. (apostle), *The Word Made Flesh* (Edinburgh: Lindsay, 1829).

—— *Extracts from Divines on the Humanity of Christ* (Edinburgh: Lindsay, 1830).

CARLYLE, T. (apostle), *The Doctrine held by the Church in Scotland concerning the Human Nature of Our Lord* (Edinburgh: Lindsay, 1830).

DALTON, H. (apostle), *The Incarnation* (Glasgow: Mackenzie, 1867).

DICKSON, D. S. (apostle's pastor), *God Manifest in Flesh* (n.p. 1887).

DOW, W. (apostle), *First Principles of the Doctrine of Christ* (Edinburgh: Grant, 1856).

DRUMMOND, H. (apostle), *A Candid Examination of the Controversy between Messrs. Irving, A. Thompson, and J. Haldane respecting Christ's Human Nature* (London: Nisbet, 1829).

——*Elementary Treatise on the Human Nature of Our Lord* (London: Nisbet, 1832).

FREER, G. A. M. (angel), *The Word Made Flesh* (London: Bosworth, 1865).

HEATH, C. B. (elder), *Some Lessons of the Lord's Resurrection* (London: Southwark Church, 1940).

——*A Narrative of the Resurrection* (London: Southwark Church, 1945).

——*An Outline of the Life of Christ* (London: Southwark Church, 1946).

HEATH, H. (angel), *The Incarnation, the Atonement, Redemption and Salvation* (n.p. 1927).

HEATH, J. S. (elder), *Who was Made Man* (London: Southwark Church, 1950).

IRVING, E. (angel), *The Orthodox and Catholic Doctrine of our Lord's Human Nature* (London: Baldwin, 1830).

——*Christ's Holiness in the Flesh* (Edinburgh: Lindsay, 1831).

McCLELLAND, G. (angel-evangelist), *The Human Nature of Christ* (Edinburgh: Laurie, 1864).

PITCAIRN, W. F. (angel), *The Passion and Resurrection of the Lord* (Edinburgh: Laurie, 1867).

PRIDDLE, D. (elder), *The Transfiguration* (London: Central Church, 1931).

SHAW, J. (priest-evangelist), *The Incarnation* (Bristol: 1909).

TAIT, W. (apostle's angel-evangelist), *Sermons Expository and Practical, with Appendices on the Incarnation, Atonement, and Ritual* (London: Hamilton Adams, 1877).

TARBET, W. (angel), *Word of Instruction concerning 'The Man Jesus Christ'* (London: Douglas, 1834).

TRIMEN, R. (angel-evangelist), *The Human Nature of our Lord* (London: Wright, 1832).

WELLS, C. A. E. (apostle's angel-evangelist), *The Mystery of the Incarnation* (London: Clowes, 1903).

Ecclesiology: the Church, Ministry, Christian Unity, etc.

ANDREWS, S. J. (angel), *The Church and its Organic Ministries* (Glasgow: Hobbs, 1889).

—— *Church Unity* (n.p. 1896).

—— *Christian Unity—a Dialogue* (n.p. 1898).

ANDREWS, W. W. (apostle's angel-evangelist), *The True Constitution of the Church and its Restoration* (New York: Moffet, 1854).

—— *The True Marks of the Church* (Hartford, Conn.: Case, 1867).

ARMSTRONG, N. (apostle), *The Church as it ought to be* (n.p. 1832).

BISHOP, W. (priest), *The Unity of the Church of Christ* (Wellington, NZ: Edwards, 1881).

CARDALE, J. B. (apostle), *The Mystery of the Candlestick* (letter, n.p. 1833).

—— *Notes of a Ministry on the Office of Coadjutor* (London: Strangeways, 1865).

—— *The Church in This Dispensation an Election* (London: Strangeways, 1868).

—— *The Fourfold Ministry* (London: Strangeways, 1871).

CAPADOSE, I. (apostle's coadjutor), 'On the Office of Angel in the Church of Christ' (MS, 1889).

CARLYLE, T. (apostle), *Apostles, Given, Lost, Restored* (London: Goodall, 1853).

CARRE, C. M. (angel), *The First and Last Days of the Church of Christ* (London: Goodall, 1851).

—— *The See of Rome, its Claims to Supremacy Examined* (London: Bosworth, 1852).

CORRADO, N. M. (priest), *Refutation of the Popish Doctrine of Christ's Gift of the Keys to St. Peter* (London: Partridge, 1849).

DALTON, H. (apostle), *Church and State* (Leeds: Harrison, 1846).

—— *What is the Church?* (London: Boswell, 1863).

492 Classified Bibliography

DALTON, H. (apostle), *The Fourfold ministry, a Permanent Gift unto the Church* (London: Boswell, 1866).

—— *The Office of Bishop under Apostles and the Office of Bishop without Apostles* (London: Bosworth, 1866).

DAVENPORT, J. S. (angel-evangelist), *The Permanence of the Apostolic Office* (New York: Wiley, 1853).

—— *The True Apostolic Succession* (New York: Moffet, 1858).

—— *Christian Unity and its Recovery* (New York: Appleton, 1866).

—— *Christ's Fourfold Ministry and the Special Ministry of Apostles* (Hartford, Conn.: Brown, 1889).

DRUMMOND, H. (apostle), *Remarks on the Churches of Rome and England* (London: Hatchard, 1841).

—— *Remarks on the Ministry of Instruction in the Church* (London: Bosworth, 1854).

—— *Discourse on the True Definition of the Church* (London: Bosworth, 1858).

DUKE, R. (elder), *Apostleship in its Relationship to the Christian Ministry* (Glasgow: Hobbs, 1908).

—— *Apostleship and Episcopacy Typified by Moses and Aaron* (Glasgow: Hobbs, 1909).

FLEWKER, W. (apostle's coadjutor), *On the Papal Supremacy* (n.p.: Rivington, 1850).

—— *The Restoration of the Gentile Apostleship* (London: Bosworth, 1874).

FRANCIS, J. G. (angel-evangelist), *A Discourse on Priesthood* (London: Goodall, 1851).

GROSER, T. (angel), *The Call of St. Paul to the Apostleship* (London: Bosworth, 1854).

—— *The Four Ministries of the Church* (London: Boswell, 1857).

—— *The Function and Credentials of Apostles* (London: Bosworth, 1872).

HEATH, C. E. L. (prophet), *The Four Colours* (London: Paddington Church, 1928).

HODGES, J. (angel), *The Original Constitution of the Church and its Restoration* (London: Bosworth, 1864).

HOLLICK, S. M. (angel), *The Church and the Nations* (n.p. 1938).

HUME, H. S. (angel), *On the Unity of Christendom* (London: Central Church, 1906).

—— *Observations on the Lambeth Conference* (London: Central Church, 1908).

—— *On the Office of Underdeacon* (London: Central Church, 1926).

LEAL, E. C. (angel-evangelist), *Note addressed to those who believe that the Apostolic Ministry never ceased, but is continued in Bishops* (n.p.: Ford, 1885).

LESLIE, J. (apostle's coadjutor), 'The Deaconship' (MS, 1860).

—— *Homily on Coadjutors* (London: Strangeways, 1870).

MACKENZIE, N. W. (priest), *The Schisms in the Church* (Calcutta: People's Press, 1878).

NORTON, R. (priest), *Reasons for Believing that the Lord has restored to the Church Apostles and Prophets* (London: Bosworth, 1852).

—— *The Restoration of Apostles and Prophets in the Catholic Church* (London: Bosworth, 1861).

OWEN, H. J. (angel), *Christ, not Peter, the Rock of the Church* (London: Nisbet, 1828).

PLACE, W. H. (pillar of evangelists), 'Church and State' (lithographed MS, 1846).

—— *Notes of a Ministry to the Deacons of the Churches* (London: Barclay, 1854).

STEVENSON, C. (angel-evangelist), 'Lectures on Unity', *Nottingham Journal* (1850).

—— 'On the Present Position and Future Prospects of the Church', *Nottingham Journal* (1850).

STEWART, H. (archangel), 'The Ministry of Archangels' (MS, Glasgow, 1907).

TARBET, W. (angel), *Some of the Divisions of Christendom* (Liverpool: Marples, 1851).

—— *On Catholicism* (London: Goodall, 1851).

—— *The Signs of Apostleship* (London: Goodall, 1852).

—— *An Abiding Priesthood* (London: Bosworth, 1855) (later published as *Shadows of the Law: the Realities of the Body of Christ*).

—— *An Holy Priesthood and Spiritual Sacrifices* (London: Bosworth, 1870).

—— *Priesthood* (n.p.: Walters, 1870).

TATHAM, F. (evangelist), *The Rationale of Christian Priesthood* (London: Bosworth, 1867).

THIERSCH, H. W. J. (apostle's pastor), *The Order of the Deaconship in the Christian Church: its Place and Duties* (London: Bosworth, 1875).

WHALLEY, A. C. (angel), 'On the Right Constitution of the Church', *Bath Gazette* (1869).

WOODHOUSE, F. V. (apostle), *The Substance of a Ministry on the Office of Apostle in the Gentile Church* (London: Bosworth, 1882).

Eschatology and the Prophetic Scriptures

ALBRECHT, L. (archangel), *The Church at the Time of the End* (n.p. 1930).

ARMSTRONG, N. (apostle), *The Second Appearing of Christ* (n.p.: Hardwick, 1831).

BAYFORD, J. (prophet), *Messiah's Kingdom and the Second Advent* (Glasgow: Ogle, 1820).

—— 'The Scheme and Structure of the Apocalypse', *Jewish Expositor* (1827).

BÖHM, C. J. T. (apostle's coadjutor), *The Signs of the Times and the Coming of the Lord* (London: Boswell, 1861).

—— *The Signs of the Times in which We Live* (London: Whibley, 1876).

BROWN, F. W. (priest), *Scriptural testimony of the Lord's Second Coming* (Swindon, 1882).

BURSTOW, A. J. (angel), *Nine Sermons on the Book of Revelation* (Wellington, NZ: Tolan, 1936).

BURWELL, A. H. (angel), *A Voice of Warnings and Instructions concerning the Signs of the Times and the Coming of the Son of Man* (Kingston, Ont., 1835).

CAMPBELL, G. (elder), *Things which must Shortly Come to Pass* (Edinburgh: Laurie, 1857).

—— *The Fulfilment of the Apocalypse: the First and Final Acts* (London: Stock, 1857).

CARLYLE, T. (apostle), *The First Resurrection and the Second Death*, Parts I/II (Ediburgh: Lindsay, 1830).

—— *On the Epistles to the Seven Churches* (London: Goodall, 1854).

CHINNERY, SIR N. (apostle's angel), *The Advent of Christ in His Millennial Glory* (Cheltenham: 1829).

DALTON, H. (apostle), *Four Lectures on the First and Second Advents* (London: Cleaver, 1846).

DANCE, E. (priest), *The Resurrection of the Dead* (n.p. 1939).

DAVENPORT, J. S. (angel-evangelist), *The Dispensation of the Parousia* (Hartford, Conn.: Brown, 1876).

—— *The Parousia: the Second Advent* (New York: Pott, 1888).

—— 'The Second Advent of Christ as related to the Purposes of God', *The Church Eclectic* (1889).

—— *The Historic Period of the Second Coming* (London: Pitman, 1890).

—— *The Last and Great Antichrist* (Hartford, Conn.: Case, 1895).

—— *What is meant by the Second Advent* (Hartford, Conn., 1898).

DAVIS, F. J. (angel), *Preparation for the Bridegroom* (London: Bosworth, 1877).

—— *'Behold the Bridegroom Cometh'* (London: Bosworth, 1877).

DRUMMOND, H. (apostle), *Dialogues on Prophecy* (3 vols.) (London: Nisbet, 1828/9).

—— *The Second Coming of the Lord Jesus Christ* (London: Seeley, 1829).

—— *Introduction to the Study of the Apocalypse* (London: Seeley, 1830).

—— *On the Numbers in Daniel* (n.p. 1835).

—— *Tracts for the Last Days* (London: Painter, 1844).

—— *The Second Advent of the Lord Jesus Christ* (Edinburgh: Jack, 1857).

—— *Discourses on the True Definition of the Church* (London: Boswell, 1958).

DUBOIS, H. O. (angel), *The Doctrine of the First Resurrection* (Philadelphia: 1888).

DUKE, R. (elder), *The Resurrection of the Body* (Glasgow: Hobbs, 1904).

DUNWORTH, W. (priest-evangelist), 'The Second Coming of Christ', *The Liverpool Daily Courier* (1866).

EASTON, J. M. (evangelist), *The Hope of Translation* (n.p.: Thiel, 1921).

EVILLE, J. (angel), *A Cry from the Desert 'Behold the Bridegroom Cometh'*, Part I/II (n.p.: Panton, 1828).

FRANCIS, J. G. (angel-evangelist), *Discourse on the Hope of the Promise* (London: Boswell, 1865).

—— *Certain Prophecies Yet Unfulfilled* (London: Bickers, 1873).

GEORGE, D. (evangelist), *The Scriptural Doctrine of the Second Advent* (Edinburgh: Smith, 1833).

HEATH, C. B. (elder), *The Return of the Lord* (London: Central Church, 1935).

HEATH, E. (apostle's coadjutor), *Resurrection and Change* (London: Chiswick Press, 1898).

—— *The Reign of Christ* (Guildford: Biddles, 1919).

HEATH, J. S. (elder), *The Life to Come* (Glasgow Church, 1944).

—— *'There shall be no more death'* (London: Southwark Church, 1948).

HENDERSON, A. (prophet), *Analytical Arrangement of the Book of Revelation* (1893; rev. edn. Glasgow: Hobbs, 1900).

HOLLICK, S. M. (angel), *The Coming Antichrist (and other sermons)* (Manchester: 1934).

IRVING, E. (angel), *For Missionaries after the Apostolic School* (London: Hamilton, 1825).

—— *Babylon and Infidelity Foredoomed of God* (n.p.: Chalmers, 1828).

—— *Preliminary Discourse to Ben Ezra* (London: Seeley, 1927).

—— *The Last Days: A Discourse on the Evil Character of these our Times* (London: Seeley, 1828).

—— *The Signs of the Times* (n.p.: Panton, 1829).

—— *Daniel's Vision of the Four Beasts and the Son of Man Opened* (London: Nisbet, 1829).

—— *Exposition of the Book of Revelation in a Series of Lectures*, i–iv (London: Baldwin, 1831).

MEJANEL, P. (angel-evangelist), *Miniature Sketch of the True Millennium*, Parts I–III (Edinburgh: Whyte, 1831).

MOORE, W. J. B. (elder), *The Church's Forgotten Hope* (Glasgow: Hobbs, 1902).

MORRIS, G. (angel-prophet), *The Second Coming: Two Discourses* (London: Bosworth, 1867).

NORTON, R. (priest), *The Nearness of the Second Coming of Christ* (London: Boswell, 1852).

ORME, J. (pastor), *The Resurrection of the Body* (Newcastle: 1949).

—— *'Watchman, What of the Night?'* (Newcastle: 1949).

PECK, J. A. M. (archdeacon), *The Times of the Restitution of All Things* (Chippenham: Noyes, 1835).

PHILLIPS, G. C. (prophet), *The War in Heaven between Christ and Antichrist* (Chelmsford: Dutton, 1878).

PITCAIRN, W. F. (angel), *Warnings and Exhortations* (Edinburgh: Wilson, 1858).

POPKIN, T. F. (prophet), *The Harvest in the End of the Age* (London: Central Church, 1904).

PROBY, W. H. B. (angel), *Notes on the Revelation of St. John* (London: Nisbet, 1910).

SADLER, R. (deacon), *The Apocalypse of St. John done into Modern English* (n.p. 1891).

SITWELL, F. (apostle), *The Purpose of God in Creation and Redemption* (Edinburgh: Laurie, 1865).

STEVENSON, C. (angel-evangelist), *The Future Revelation of Antichrist* (Newcastle: 1875).

SYMES, J. (angel), *Address on the Instant Coming of the Lord* (London: Paul, 1866).

SYMES, L. R. (apostle's coadjutor), *La Restauration de la Perfectionnement de l'Eglise aux Derniers Jours* (Paris: Didot, 1858).

TAPLIN, E. (pillar of prophets), *The Epistles to the Seven Churches* (n.p. 1848).

—— *The Construction of the Book of Revelation* (n.p. 1848).

—— *The Seven Epistles, Seals, Trumpets and Vials, and the Interpretation of the First of Them* (n.p. 1848).

—— *The Signs of the Coming of the Lord*, Parts I–X (n.p. 1851/2).

—— *The Chronology of the Scriptures* (London: Goodall, 1854).

—— *Translation: not an Instantaneous but a Progressive Work* (n.p. 1858).

TARBET, W. (angel), *The Mystery of the Woman and of the Beast which Carrieth Her* (London: Goodall, 1851).

—— *On Babylon* (London: Goodall, 1851).

—— *Signs of the Last Days* (Liverpool: Woollard, 1853).

—— *The Time of the End and other Teachings* (London: Pitman, 1900).

THIERSCH, L. (angel), *Immortality* (Glasgow: Hobbs, 1900).

THONGER, C. W. (angel), *Resurrection and Change* (n.p. 1941).

TUDOR, J. (apostle), *On the Structure of the Apocalypse* (n.p.: Panton, 1828).

—— *On the Interpretation of the Apocalypse* (n.p.: Panton, 1828).

—— 'On the Apocalypse', *Church of England Quarterly* (1849).

TUDOR, J. (apostle), *A Brief Interpretation of the Book of Revelation* (London: Painter, 1855).

—— *Six Lectures on the Apocalypse* (London: Bosworth, 1861).

WOOD, H. M. (angel-evangelist), *The Coming of our Lord Jesus Christ as a Thief in the Night* (Ontario: Izard, 1898).

WOODHOUSE, F. N. (apostle), *The Instant Coming of the Lord and the First Resurrection* (Edinburgh Church, 1870).

ZANGGER, T. (priest), *On Preparation for the Coming of the Lord* (Zurich: 1939).

History

AARSBO, J. (layman), *Komme dit Rige*, i–v (Copenhagen: 1930–6).

ALBRECHT, L. (archangel), *The Work by Apostles at the end of the Dispensation* (n.p. 1931; trans. from the German of 1924).

ANDREWS, W. W. (angel-evangelist), *The Work of the Catholic Apostolic Church in America* (New York: Moffet, 1856).

—— 'The History and Claims of the Body of Christians known as the Catholic Apostolic Church', *Bibliotheca Sacra* (1866).

BOASE, C. W. (apostle's angel-evangelist), *The Elijah Ministry* (with 'Supplementary Narrative') (Edinburgh: Grant, 1868).

BOASE, G. C. (angel), *The Restoration of Apostles and the True Position of those who acknowledge them in relation to the Rest of the Church* (Dundee: Shaw, 1867).

CARDALE, J. B. (pillar of apostles), 'On the Extraordinary Manifestations at Port Glasgow', *The Morning Watch* (1830).

—— *A Letter on certain statements contained in some late articles in 'The Old Church Porch' entitled 'Irvingism'* (London: Goodall, 1855).

CARLYLE, T. (apostle), *A Short History of the Apostolic Work* (London: Barclay, 1851).

CAUX, W. DE (angel), *Early Days of the Lord's Work in France* (n.p. 1899).

COPINGER, H. B. (underdeacon) (ed.), 'Annals: The Lord's Work in the Nineteenth and Twentieth Centuries' (MS, undated).

DOWGLASSE, T. (angel-evangelist), *A Chronicle of Certain Events which have taken place in the Church of Christ, principally in England between the Years 1826 and 1852* (London: Goodall, 1852).

DRUMMOND, H. (apostle), *Narrative of Circumstances which led to the Setting up of the Church at Albury* (n.p. 1834).
—— *A Brief Account of the Commencement of the Lord's Work* (n.p.: Whittingham, 1851).
HAMILTON, R. M. (angel), *A Short History of the Remarkable Spiritual Occurrence in 1827–8 among Peasants in Bavaria, and the Sequel in 1842, 1870* (London: Goodwin, 1893).
HEWETT, L. A. (deaconess), *The Story of the Lord's Work* (Glasgow: Hobbs, 1899).
MICKWITZ, K. VON (layman), *Ein Zeitbild in wichtigen Zeugnissen* (Berlin: Hoffman, 1902).
NORTON, R. (priest), *Memoirs of James and George Macdonald of Port Glasgow* (Dundee: Shaw, 1840).
RAWSON, T. E. (angel), *Teaching on the Removal of the Last Apostle and the Last Coadjutor* (London: Southwark Church, 1929).
—— *The Covering of the Altar* (London: Southwark Church, 1941).
ROSSTEUSCHER, E. A. (angel), 'The Rebuilding of the Church of Christ' (MSS, trans. 1850 and 1928, from the German of 1871).
SCHOLLER, L. W. (layman), *A Chapter of History from South Germany* (London: Longmans, Green, 1894).
SCHWARTZ, C. C. (archangel), 'The Chronicle of the Setting up of the Church in Berlin' (MS, trans. 1951).
THIERSCH, H. W. J. (apostle's pastor), *History of the Christian Church* (London: Bosworth, 1852).
TRIMEN, E. (angel-evangelist), *The Rise and Progress of the Lord's Work* (n.p. 1904).
VALENTIN, A. (priest-evangelist), *The Present Time of Silence* (trans. from the German, n.p. 1938).
WOODHOUSE, F. W. (apostle), *A Narrative of Events affecting the Position and Prospects of the whole Christian Church* (London: Barclay, 1847).
—— *On the possible call of New Apostles and the special hope of the Firstfruits, with particular reference to Herr H. Geyer and his New Apostolic Church* (n.p. 1863).
—— *The Census and the Catholic Apostolic Church* (London: Bosworth, 1854).
Note: 'Apostles' Reports' (1853).
Various unpublished manuscript histories exist, both in my

hands and in others'. A number of these have been consulted during the preparation of this book.

Irving

ANDREWS, W. W. (angel-evangelist), 'Edward Irving', *The New Englander* (1863).
—— 'Edward Irving: a Review of Mrs. Oliphant's life', *The New Englander* (1864).
—— *Martin Luther and Edward Irving compared* (London: Bosworth, 1884).
DAVENPORT, J. S. (angel-evangelist), *Edward Irving and the Catholic Apostolic Church* (New York: Moffet, 1863).
TARBET, W. (angel), *Edward Irving and the Catholic Apostolic Church* (London: Bosworth, 1856).

Liturgy, including Eucharistic Theology

BOASE, G. C. (angel), *Three Discourses on Symbols used in Worship* (Dundee: 1855).
BÖHM, C. J. T. (apostle's coadjutor), *The Lord's Supper* (Glasgow: Hobbs, 1902).
—— *Sacrifice and Priesthood* (Glasgow: Hobbs, 1902).
(Both works taken separately from 'Lights and Shadows . . .'; see above, under 'General' heading.)
BURNE, SIR O. T. (deacon), 'The Holy Eucharist', unpublished notes (1890).
CAIRD, W. R. (apostle's coadjutor), *On Worship in Spirit and in Truth* (London: Bosworth, 1877).
CARDALE, J. B. (pillar of apostles), *A Discourse on the Doctrine of the Eucharist as revealed by St. Paul* (London: Bosworth, 1856).
—— *A Discourse on the Real Presence* (London: Bosworth, 1867).
—— *Readings upon the Liturgy and other Divine Offices of the Church*, i–ii (London: Barclay/Bosworth, 1848–78).
CARLYLE, T. (apostle), *Concerning the Right Order of Worship* (n.p.: Crerar and Smith, 1850; from the preface to the German edn. of *The Liturgy*).
—— *On Symbols used in Worship* (London: Goodall, 1853).
DALTON, H. (apostle), *An Exposition of the Sacrament of the Lord's Supper*, Parts I–III (Edinburgh: Simpson, 1832).
DAVENPORT, J. S. (angel-evangelist), 'Sacramental Christianity and the Incarnation', *The Family Churchman* (1891).

DRUMMOND, H. (apostle), *On the Lord's Supper* (n.p. 1830).
—— *Rationale of the Offices and Liturgies of the Church* (n.p. 1843).
HEATH, C. B. (elder), *The Development of the Liturgy and the Origin of its Prayers*, i–ii (London: Southwark Church, 1950).
HEATH, R. M. (underdeacon), 'Vestments as Ordered by Apostles' (MS, 1942).
—— *The Full Services of Morning and Evening Prayer and their Relation to the Worship of the Tabernacle and the Temple* (n.p. 1946).
HUGHES, R. (archangel), *The Liturgy of the Holy Eucharist* (London: Bosworth, 1865).
—— *Eucharistic and Daily Sacrifice* (London: Bosworth, 1867).
MOORE, W. J. B. (elder), *A Tabular View of the Holy Eucharist* (London: Pitman, 1891).
OWEN, H. J. (angel), *A Discourse on the Sacrament of the Lord's Supper* (London: Tilling, 1830).
RAWSON, T. E. (angel), *The Restoration of the Holy Eucharist Ninety Years Ago* (n.p. 1923).
STUART, C. E. W. (angel's coadjutor), *Teachings on the Liturgy* (London: Central Church, 1907).
VALENTIN, A. (evangelist), *Sur le sacrement de l'eucharistie et son enlèvement solennel* (n.p. 1938).
WILLIS, A. M. (priest-evangelist), *Notes on the Liturgy*, i–v (Shrewsbury: Wilding/Glasgow: Hobbs, 1893–1915).
—— *Notes on Morning and Evening Prayer* (Glasgow: Hobbs, 1900).
—— *Chart of Morning and Evening Prayer* (London: Pitman, 1915).

See also: *The Liturgy and Other Divine Offices of the Church* (var. publishers, 1843–80; Scottish version, 1849).
General Rubrics (London: Strangeways, 1878).
Recording of extracts from the Eucharist (Zurich, 1951).

Man: Constitution and Characteristics

CAPADOSE, A. E. (pastor), *Body, Soul, and Spirit* (London: Central Church, 1942).
DALTON, H. (apostle), *Body, Soul, and Spirit* (London: Cleaver, 1847).

HOLLICK, S. M. (angel), *The Dedication of our Faculties to God* (n.p. 1946).

KER, D. (angel), *Man's Body, Soul, and Spirit* (Edinburgh: Simpson, 1864).

WILLIS, A. M. (priest-evangelist), *The Fourfold Ministry and the Constitution of Man*, from his *Notes on the Liturgy* (Glasgow: Hobbs, 1902).

ZANGGER, T. (priest), *Man's Destiny: Body, Soul, and Spirit* (London: Bedford, 1938).

Pneumatology and Prophesying

BROWNLIE, W. R. (priest-evangelist), and A. JARVIE (angel-evangelist), *The Gifts of the Spirit and the Ministries of the Lord* (London: Bosworth, 1869).

BURNE, H. T. (angel), *Scripture Doctrine concerning Baptism with the Holy Ghost as distinguished from His ordinary Influences* (London: Douglas, 1833).

BURWELL, A. H. (angel), *The Doctrine of the Holy Spirit* (Toronto: Coates, 1835).

CARDALE, J. B. (pillar of apostles), *A Short Discourse on Prophesying and the Ministry of the Prophet in the Christian Church* (London: Strangeways, 1868).

DALTON, H. (apostle), *The Baptism of the Holy Ghost* (n.p. 1833).

DAVENPORT, A. S. (angel-evangelist), 'The Work of the Holy Ghost in the Christian Church', *The Church Eclectic* (1899).

FLEGG, R. G. (prophet), *The Nature, Character, and Place of Prophecy in the Christian Church* (London: Goodwin Norton, 1888).

HEATH, C. B. (elder), *Symbols of the Holy Ghost* (London: Southwark Church, 1943).

—— *The Endowment of the Holy Ghost* (London: Southwark Church, 1947).

HEATH, J. B. (archangel), *The Procession of the Holy Ghost* (London: Bishopgate Church, 1903).

IRVING, E. (angel), *The Nature and Use of the Gift of Tongues* (Greenock: Tusk, 1829).

—— *The Day of Pentecost, or Baptism with the Holy Ghost* (London: Baldwin, 1831).

—— 'Facts connected with Manifestations of Spiritual Gifts', *Fraser's Magazine* (1832).

Sacraments: Confession, Sealing, Unction

ACKERY, J. W. (angel), *Teaching on Anointing of the Sick* (n.p. 1890).

ANDREWS, W. W. (apostle's angel-evangelist), *Sealing with the Holy Ghost* (n.p. 1890).

CAPADOSE, A. E. (pastor), *The Rite for the Anointing of the Sick* (London: Central Church, 1928).

HAMILTON, R. M. (angel), *The Divine Healing of the Sick* (London: Islington Church, 1891).

HEATH, C. B. (elder), *The Forgiveness of Sins*, i–iii (London: Southwark Church, 1942).

HUGHES, R. (archangel), *Confession and Absolution* (London: Bosworth, 1866).

HUME, H. S. (angel), *Absolution and Forgiveness* (n.p. 1903).

MORRIS, G. (angel-prophet), *Our Lord's Permanent healing Office in His Church* (London: Eliot Stock, 1887).

PARKER, T. H. (priest), *Supernatural healing* (Newcastle: 1929).

——*Letter to Distant Members on Holy Anointing* (Newcastle: 1941).

PATTIE, R. B. (angel), *Sermon on the Anointing of the Sick* (Glasgow: 1908).

SMITH, F. (angel), *The Ministry of Healing* (Brighton: 1925).

TARBET, W. (angel), *On Confession* (London: Goodall, 1851).

WRIGHT, W. W. (pillar of evangelists), *The Holy Sealing* (Walsall: 1892).

Scripture

ARMSTRONG, N. (apostle), *The Psalms and the Reading of the Scriptures* (Salem Chapel, 1832).

BAKER, E. (angel), *The Christ of the Psalms* (London: Bickers, 1872).

BREWSTER, R. (angel), *The Bible the Rule of Faith; the Church the Pillar of the Truth* (n.p. 1860).

——*The Bible and the Church* (Liverpool: Marples, 1860).

COPINGER, W. A. (angel-evangelist), *The Bible and its Transmission* (n.p.: Sotheran, 1897).

EASTON, J. M. (evangelist), *Ministry on the Book of Psalms* (n.p.: Taugye, 1923).

504   *Classified Bibliography*

FAESCH, L. (apostle's prophet), *On the Reading of the Holy Scripture in the Christian Church* (London: Pitman, 1890).

GROSER, T. (angel), *The Growth and Intent of Holy Scripture* (London: Bosworth, 1865).

HOLLICK, S. M. (angel), *The Value of the Holy Scriptures*, i–iii (n.p. 1945).

IRVING, E. (angel), *Introductory essay to Horne's Commentary on the Psalms* (London: Bosworth, 1827).

LANCE, W. (elder), *The Grounds of Biblical Belief* (London: Pitman, 1904).

MAUNDER, G. W. (elder), *The Historical Basis of Holy Scripture* (Bristol: 1909).

MONROE, W. (deacon), *The Graphic Harmony of the Gospels* (London: Bagster, n.d.).

PROBY, W. H. B. (angel), *The Ten Canticles of the Old Testament Canon* (n.p.: Rivington, 1874).

—— *On Certain Questions concerning the Book of Job* (n.p.: Rivington, 1886).

—— 'Midrash Tehillim: The Most Ancient Jewish Commentary on the Book of Psalms' (MS, 1881).

SITWELL, F. (apostle), *Bishop Colenso and the Inspiration of Scripture* (n.p. 1862).

TAIT, W. (apostle's angel-evangelist), *The Bible and the Church* (London: Hamilton Adams, 1883).

Sects and Societies

DAVENPORT, J. B. (angel-evangelist), *The Deadly Error of Christian Science* (Philadelphia: Library Publishing Co., 1901).

—— *The Spiritual Danger of Occultism and Sorcery* (Glasgow: Hobbs, 1902).

FOWKES, T. (elder), *Sectarianism* (London: Bosworth, 1874).

G——, A. (layman), *A Letter on Spiritualism* (Glasgow: Hobbs, 1902).

HEATH, H. (angel), *Freemasonry* (n.p. 1919).

HOLLICK, S. M. (angel), *The Substance of Addresses on Spiritualism and Hypnotism* (n.p.: Thiel, 1920).

HUME, H. S. (angel), *The Temperance Movement and the Salvation Army* (London: Strangeways, 1882).

IRVING, E. (angel), 'Sermon for the London Missionary Society', *The Pulpit* (1824).
—— 'Sermon on S.P.C.K.', *The Pulpit* (1825).
PARKER, T. H. (priest), *Sermon on Freemasonry* (n.p.: Bowes, 1927).
—— *Sermons on Spiritualism* (n.p.: Bowes, 1930).
—— *Sermon on Socialism* (n.p.: Bowes, 1931).
SITWELL, F. (apostle), *What is Mesmerism? and what its Concomitants —Clairvoyance and Necromancy* (London: Bosworth and Harrison, 1862; originally published 1853).
TARBET, W. (angel), *Spiritualism—a Sign and Prelude of the Coming Judgements* (London: Boswell, 1862).
WADDY, S. H. (deacon), *Sermon on the Evil of Socialism* (London: Islington, 1907).

Tithes and Offerings

ARSDALE, O. M. VAN (angel), and MERCER, J., *The Payment of Tithes* (Philadelphia: 1901).
BOASE, C. W. (apostle's angel-evangelist), *Tithes and Offerings* (Dundee: Matthew, 1864).
—— *Tithes and Offerings—a Treatise* (London: Clark, 1865).
BOASE, G. C. (angel), *Two Sermons on the Tithe* (Dundee: 1859).
BÖHM, C. J. T. (apostle's coadjutor), *Tithes* (Glasgow: Hobbs, 1898).
BREWSTER, R. (angel), *The Earth is the Lord's* (London: Bosworth, 1860).
CAPADOSE, A. E. (pastor), *Tithes and Offerings on the Lord's day* (London: Central Church, 1927).
CARDALE, J. B. (apostle), *Discourse on the Obligation of Tithe* (London: Bosworth, 1858).
DAVENPORT, J. B. (angel-evangelist), *The Payment of Tithes: Or the Lord's Portion a Tenth* (Glasgow: Hobbs, 1908).
GEERE, H. G. (deacon), *Tithe: How and Where to be Rendered* (London: Southwark Church, 1945).
HOLLICK, S. M. (angel), *Address on Tithes and Offerings* (n.p. 1933).
PEARCE, MRS M. (laywoman), *Memoranda in Reply to Objections to Payment of tithes* (n.p. 1880).

PECK, K. (deacon), *The Universal Obligation of Tithes* (London: Eliot Stock, 1901).

PITCAIRN, W. F. (angel), *Pastoral Letter on Tithes and Offerings* (Edinburgh: 1853).

RAWSON, T. E. (angel), *The Lord's Tithe* (1935).

—— *Tithes and Offerings* (1938).

SAFFERY, J. J. (deacon), 'Tithes and Offerings' (lithograph, 1870).

WADDY, S. H. (deacon), *On tithe* (n.p. 1907).

WEAVER, SIR L. W. W. (deacon), *Of the Love of Money and of Offerings* (London: Central Church, 1920).

Typology and the Tabernacle

BREWSTER, R. (angel), *The Tabernacle and the Church*, Parts I–III (London: Bosworth, 1859).

CAPADOSE, I. (apostle's coadjutor), *The Laver* (n.p.: Crerar and Smith, 1905).

CARLYLE, T. (apostle), *On the Office of Prayer as Typified in the Golden Altar* (London: Moyes, 1836).

—— *The Mosaic Tabernacle* (New York: Moffet, 1857).

CAUX, W. DE [?] (angel), *The Brazen Altar* (London: Central Church, 1926).

HEWETT, MISS L. A. (deaconess), *Papers on the Tabernacle* (Glasgow: Hobbs, 1881).

HEWETT, MISS M. (laywoman), *Millfield Cottage, or Conversation on the Church and the Tabernacle* (London: Pitman, 1877).

MOORE, W. J. B. (elder), *The Cherubim of Glory* (n.p. 1917).

PERCY, LADY E. C. (laywoman), *Notes of Lectures on the Tabernacle in Israel* (London, 1874).

PITCAIRN, W. F. (angel), *General Description and Explanation of a Drawing of the Tabernacle* (Edinburgh: Simpson, 1865).

PROBY, W. H. B. (angel), *Discourses on Old Testament Types* (Glasgow: Hobbs, 1904).

WILLIAMS, J. (angel-evangelist), *Lecture on the Cherubim and Seraphim* (Armagh: Mutual Improvement Society, 1879).

—— 'The Tabernacle built by Moses', *Ulster Gazette* (1882).

Women, Marriage, and Family Life

ANDREWS, W. W. (apostle's angel-evangelist), *Woman: Her True Place and Standing* (var. edns., 1872–1900).

CARDALE, J. B. (pillar of apostles), *Unlawfulness of Marriage with a Deceased Wife's Sister* (London: Bosworth, 1859).
—— *Directions on the Subject of Women Prophesying in Church* (n.p. 1866).
DAVENPORT, J. B. (angel-evangelist), *The Law of Christian Marriage* (New York, 1907).
DRUMMOND, H. (apostle), *A Plea for the Rights and Liberties of Women* (London: Bosworth, 1851).
—— *The Law of Marriage: Preface* (1857) (Preface to translation from the German of a work by E. L. von Gerlach).
GRAHAM, J. (deacon), *The Coming Kingdom and Woman's Place* (London: Central Church, 1908).
HEATH, H. (angel), *Marriage* (Hackney Church, 1904).
HOLLICK, S. M. (angel), *The Vocation of Women* (Manchester: 1943).
HUME, H. S. (angel), *The Law of God relating to Marriage* (London: Bosworth, 1885).
—— *Three Sermons on Marriage* (London: Pitman, 1907).
—— *Marriage* (n.p. 1910).
—— *On Women Suffrage* (n.p. 1911).
JENNINGS, S. (angel-evangelist), *Marriage: Its Institution and Purpose* (London: Stock, 1900).
LICKFOLD, J. M. (deacon), *On Women being Covered in Church* (n.p. 1942).
PEARL, S. T. (angel), *A Sermon on Christian Marriage* (Chicago: Edgewater, 1918).
RAWSON, T. E. (angel), *Women not Permitted to Teach in Church* (n.p. 1916).
RINTOUL, S. R. (angel), *Teaching upon Christian Marriage* (Waterbury, USA, n.d.).
THIERSCH, H. W. J. (apostle's pastor), *Christian Family Life* (London: Bosworth, 1856).

Note also: Various authors: *Ministries on the Subject of Woman, a type or figure of the Church, the Bride of Christ* (n.p., reissued 1974).

Miscellaneous

ANON.: *Upon the use of Holy Water and the Reservation of the Holy Sacrament* (London: Central Church, n.d. (between 1920 and 1924)).

BURNE, N. H. K. (angel), *Hymns with Tunes for Children and Young Persons* (n.p.: Crerar and Smith, 1890).

DRUMMOND, H. (apostle), *Principles of Ecclesiastical Buildings and Ornaments* (London: Bosworth, 1851).

FOWKES, T. (elder), *The Greek and Latin Churches in Russia and Turkey: an Historical retrospect* (New York: Whittaker, 1854).

IRVING, E. (angel), *Discourse and Charges at the Ordination of the Rev. H. B. McLean at the Scotch Church, London Wall* (London: Nisbet, 1827).

LICKFOLD, J. M. (deacon), *The Catholic Apostolic Church, Gordon Square, London: Notes on Architectural Features, Furniture, etc.* (London: Bedford, 1935).

THIERSCH, H. (layman), *Unsere russischen Bruder* (Berlin: Meier, 1932).

WILLIS, A. M. (priest-evangelist), *The Spirit of Church Architecture* (Shrewsbury: Wilding, 1915).

Note also: *Hymns for use in the Churches* (London: Pitman, 1900).

Works by Catholic Apostolic 'Defectors'

BAXTER, R. (formerly prophet), *Narrative of Facts Characterizing the Supernatural Manifestations in Members of Mr. Irving's Congregation and Other Individuals, in England and Scotland, and Formerly in the Writer Himself* (London: Nisbet, 1833).

—— *Irvingism in its Rise, Progress, and Present State* (London: Nisbet, 1836).

GRANT, W. (formerly priest), *Apostolic Lordship and the Interior Life: a Narrative of Five Years' Communion with Catholic Apostolic Angels* (n.p. 1873).

HARRISON, J. (formerly priest), *The Catholic Apostolic Church: Its Pretentions and Claims* (London: Stevenson, 1872).

PRIOR, H. M. (formerly priest), *My Experience of the Catholic Apostolic Church* (Stratford: Wilson and Whitworth, 1880).

Works by Non-Members of the Catholic Apostolic Church

ANON.: *The Trial of Edward Irving, a cento of Criticism* (n.p., n.d., c.1833).

BROWN, W. *The Tabernacle and its Priests and Services. Described and Considered in relation to Christ and the Church* (Edinburgh: Oliphant & Co., 1871).

CONNOR, W. H., *The Gospel of the Future* (London: Griffith Farren, 1891).

—— *The Second Advent and Prayer* (London: Skeffington, 1901).

—— *A Catechism of the Second Advent* (London: Knott, 1922).

—— *A Litany of the Second Advent* (n.p. 1922).

CUNNINGHAME, J., *A Dissertation on the Seals and the Trumpets of the Apocalypse* (London: 1813).

FABER, G. S., *Dissertation on the Prophecies, That Have Been Fulfilled, Are Now Being Fulfilled, Relative to the Great Period of 1260 Years* (London: 1804).

—— *Remarks on the Effusion of the Fifth Apocalyptic Vial* (London: 1815).

—— *A Sacred Calendar of Prophecy*, i–iii (London: 1828).

—— *The Many Mansions in the house of the Father Scripturally Discussed and Practically Considered* (London: 1854).

FRERE, J. H., *A Dissertation on the Seals and trumpets of the Apocalypse* (London: 1813).

—— *A Combined View of the Prophecies of Daniel, Esdras, and St. John, Shewing that All the Prophetic Writings are Formed upon One Plan. Accompanied by an explanatory Chart. Also a Minute Explanation of the Prophecies of Daniel; Together with Critical remarks upon the Interpretations of Preceding Commentators, and More Particularly upon the Systems of Mr. Faber and Mr. Cunninghame* (London: Hatchard, 1815).

LACUNZA, M. (J. J. Ben-Ezra), *The Coming of the Messiah in Glory and Majesty*, trans. by E. Irving from the Spanish (London: Seeley and Son, 1827).

NOEL, B., *Remarks on the Revival of Miraculous powers in the Church* (London: 1831).

MASSINGHAM, J. D., *Tithes* (London: Macintosh, 1870).

STEWART, J. H., *Importance of Special Prayer for the General Outpouring of the Holy Spirit* (London: Religious Tract Society, 1826).

TREGELLES, S. P., *The Hope of Christ's Coming* (London: Bagster, 1864).

Journals, etc.

Note: Considerable information of historical interest can be gleaned by consulting appropriate contemporary issues of the following:

The American Church Review
Bibliotheca Sacra
Blackwood's Magazine
The Christian Mirror
The Church Eclectic
The Church of England Quarterly
The Ecclesiologist
The English Review
The Evangelical Magazine
The Family Churchman
Fraser's Magazine
The Liverpool Daily Courier
The New Englander
The Old Church Porch
The Preacher
The Pulpit
The Saturday Review
The Times
The Ulster Gazette

Index

apostles, apostolic ministry, etc. 8, 60,
78–9, 113–15, 116, 118, 121–6,
166, 168–70, 172–3, 175, 178, 195,
198, 200–1, 220, 239, 266, 281,
348–51, 380, 391, 407, 419, 464,
474
  Chapel, Albury 90, 91, 266
  determinations 175 n.
  journeys 29, 72, 75–7, 465
  restoration of 57–8, 67, 118, 119–20,
122–3, 125, 137, 368, 371, 462, 475
  visitations 138–9
Apostolic College 65–6, 67, 76–7, 81,
85, 87–8, 90, 131, 169, 271, 456,
465
apostolic roots 57–60, 67
apostolic succession 113, 402, 449
archangels 138–9
Archbishops of Canterbury and York 73
Arian heresy 308, 361
Aristotle, Aristotelian 256, 286
Ark of the Covenant 116, 169, 238
Armageddon 296, 329, 331, 336, 358,
426
Arminius, Arminianism 298
Armstrong, N., apostle 14, 65–6, 68,
71, 88, 90
Ascension 103, 122, 223, 234, 240–1,
322, 372, 386, 396, 398
  Day 283, 417
Atonement 194, 453
Augustine, St 182, 275, 295, 307, 345,
362, 402, 467
automatic handwriting 192

Babylon 50, 107, 203, 344, 362, 365–6,
368–70, 390, 400, 402, 425, 445,
455
badgers 117
Baker, E. 29 n.
baptism, the baptized 85, 97–8, 103,
104–5, 130, 191, 196–7, 216, 239,
260–1, 268–9, 277, 282, 310, 348–
50, 366, 374, 387, 391, 393, 420,
425, 461, 472
  of Christ 100–1, 222
  of fire 58, 387
  of the Spirit 44, 197, 387
Barnabas, St 124–6, 134
  Epistle of 367
Barsabbas 123
Basil, St 308
Baxter, R. 22, 431, 458

Bayford, J. 37
Baylee, J. 438
beast(s) 294, 312, 313–15, 326, 341,
365, 368, 371–2, 377, 387, 425, 430
Beckett, Revd G. 37
Benedictus 226, 230
Ben-Ezra, J. J., *see* Lacunza, M.
Bengel, J. A. 120
Bennett, Revd. W. E. J. 25, 64
Bersier, E. 290
Bickersteth, E. 438
Bingham, J. 111, 276
Birks, T. R. 438
bishops 391
  see also angel; episcopate
Bishopsgate Church, congregation 68
black 266
blue 116, 166, 170
boards (of the Tabernacle) 151
Boase, C. W. 15, 21, 36 n., 62
body 153–5, 159–60, 168, 203, 224
Body of Christ 103, 109
  see also Church, nature of
book:
  of the gospels 238
  sealed 303, 356
  open 303, 357
Book of Common Order 289
Book of Life 378
Böhm, C. J. T. 19, 275
Bonar, H. 438
border 175
Born, K. 21
Borthwick, T. 37
Branden, R. 273
Bransby, J. H. 36 n.
brass 116–17, 158
brazen:
  altar 116–18, 152, 158, 226–7, 238,
262, 357
  laver 116, 238, 262
bread 220, 267–8, 470
Brethren, *see* Plymouth Brethren
Bride 82, 104, 111, 113, 122, 124–5,
203, 342, 343, 347, 355, 386,
390–1, 398, 424, 444
Bridegroom 82, 113, 122, 133, 195,
203, 347, 355, 362, 424, 440
  coming of the, *see* Second Advent
Brightman, F. E. 275
Brothers, R. 298–9
Bryan, Revd W. 37
buildings 263–5, 273–4, 284–5

404, 409–11, 433, 451–3, 457, 466, 471
  see also pneumatology
Holy Place 116–18, 138, 159, 225, 227, 238, 356, 376, 386
Holy Thursday 234
Holy Week 283
homily, homilist 235, 238, 282
Hooker, R. 137
Hooper, Revd J. 37
hope 99
horn(s) 117, 313–14, 365–6
  church 114
Hughes, R. 16, 275
human nature 117
  see also man
humanity of Christ 54–6, 101, 202, 253, 258, 277, 342, 462, 468
  see also Christology
Hume, H. S. 17
Huns 357
hypnosis, hypnotism 193–4, 206–7, 468

icons 469
idolatry, idolaters 157, 312, 335, 357
Ignatius, St 135 n.
Ignatius Loyola 364
imagination 160, 162–5, 173, 204
immortality of the soul 203, 453
impanation 258
imposition of hands 216
  see also laying on of apostles' hands
Incarnation, the 13, 54–7, 101, 103, 117, 191, 194, 216–18, 240, 372, 385–7, 394–5, 401, 424, 453
incense 216, 220, 228–30, 238, 242, 263, 267, 269, 282
  anthem 235–6
Index, the 323
infidelity of the Church, *see* apostasy
infidels 129, 304
  see also Islam
Innokenti of Cherson, Bishop 120
integral knowledge 205
intellect, intellectual powers, etc. 155–6, 160, 163
  see also reasoning
intercession(s) 116, 134, 218–20, 222, 226, 228–32, 245, 247, 267, 272, 281–2, 285, 288, 350–1, 357, 406, 419, 463, 467
  see also Great Intercession
interpretation 137–8, 200–1, 301, 307

invocation of the Holy Spirit, *see* epiclesis
Irenaeus, St 180, 295, 308, 369–70
Irving, Revd E. 1, 5, 6, 35–7, 38, 44, 45, 46–63, 65, 77, 120, 190, 285, 289, 299, 302, 304, 324–31, 335, 338–42, 423, 430–2, 435–6, 446, 451, 458, 461–2
  trial of 54, 451
  Preliminary Discourse to the Work of Ben Ezra 26 n., 40, 325–8, 330–2
Isaac 359, 385
Isaiah, *Book of Isaiah* 378, 399, 405
Isidore of Pelusa, St 276
Islam 302, 312, 357, 427–8, 474
  see also infidels; Mohammed

Jacob 180, 359, 385, 408
Jacobite rebellion 445
Jehovah's Witnesses 444
Jerome, St 119, 182, 306, 317, 371
Jerusalem 375–6, 378, 380, 385, 388, 391, 402, 421–2, 425–6
  Bishopric 375–6, 380
  heavenly, New, spiritual 89, 107, 125, 319–21, 324, 358, 376–7, 385–6, 388, 402, 426, 429
jewels 71, 263, 266
Jewish:
  apocalyptic 293–4
  apostleship 123–4
Jews, Jewish dispensation, etc. 38, 39, 104–5, 107, 116, 118, 124, 154, 258, 283, 299, 318–19, 330–2, 336–7, 339, 342, 359–60, 365, 368, 370–1, 374–6, 380–1, 384–90, 394–6, 399–400, 402–3, 407, 421–2, 425–7, 430, 432–3, 437, 454, 474
  Society 34
Job 318
John, St 134, 149, 269, 312, 321, 357, 365, 371, 378
John Chrysostom, St 274–6, 280, 324, 420
John the Baptist, St 237, 387, 411
Jones, W. 6
Joseph, St 149
Joshua 126, 390
Judas, St 134
judgement, the Judgement 13, 108–9, 295, 300, 306, 309, 311, 319–20, 322–3, 330–1, 342, 347–8, 357,